Managed C++ and .NET Development

Development

STEPHEN R. G. FRASER

apress™

Managed C++ and .NET Development
Copyright © 2003 by Stephen R. G. Fraser

ISBN (pbk): 1-59059-033-3
Printed and bound in the United States of America 12345678910

Technical Reviewers: Siva Challa, Douglas Milnes

Editorial Directors: Dan Appleman, Gary Cornell, Simon Hayes, Martin Streicher, Karen Watterson, John Zukowski

Assistant Publisher: Grace Wong

Project Managers: Tracy Brown Collins, Sofia Marchant

Copy Editor: Nicole LeClerc

Production Editor: Janet Vail

Compositor: Impressions Book and Journal Services, Inc.

Indexer: Rebecca Plunkett

Cover Designer: Kurt Krames

Artist: Cara Brunk

Production Manager: Kari Brooks

Manufacturing Manager: Tom Debolski

Distributed to the book trade in the United States by Springer-Verlag New York, Inc., 175 Fifth Avenue, New York, NY, 10010 and outside the United States by Springer-Verlag GmbH & Co. KG, Tiergartenstr. 17, 69112 Heidelberg, Germany.

In the United States: phone 1-800-SPRINGER, email orders@springer-ny.com, or visit http://www.springer-ny.com. Outside the United States: fax +49 6221 345229, email orders@springer.de, or visit http://www.springer.de.

For information on translations, please contact Apress directly at 2560 Ninth Street, Suite 219, Berkeley, CA 94710. Phone 510-549-5930, fax 510-549-5939, email info@apress.com, or visit http://www.apress.com.

The source code for this book is available to readers at http://www.apress.com in the Downloads section.

To my wife, Sarah, and my daughter, Shaina,
a continual reminder of what is truly important in life.

Contents at a Glance

Contents

Chapter 16 Multithreaded Programming 813

Chapter 17 Assembly Programming 857

Index 919

Foreword

C++ IS INCREDIBLY RESILIENT. First conceived to be merely a "better C," it evolved into a language that continues to amaze even its creators. It endures shifts in programming paradigms and changes in underlying platforms.

Support for object-oriented programming was the first improvement over C. Then exceptions and templates came along. Later, template metaprogramming was "discovered." Managed C++ is another enhancement of the language, which supports a rich runtime, with features such as garbage collection, a unified type system, networking and multithreading support, versioning, and others.

Though designed as a general-purpose programming language under .NET, Managed C++'s main strength is its scrupulous support of the "unmanaged" C++, easing the transition from unmanaged to managed code. Managed C++ allows you to maximally leverage your existing C++ code and start using "managed" features of the languages gradually. This is somewhat similar to how a C programmer would switch to C++: by continuing to use the C subset of C++, taking advantage of C++ as his or her knowledge of it matures.

Managed C++ is opportunistic, just like C++ is. Having to support the existing C++ code base explains many of the compromises the designers of Managed C++ had to make. One of them is the use of double underscores (__) in the new keywords, such as __gc, __value, and others. Although gc and value would have clearly been "prettier," introducing such keywords would break millions of lines of existing code where gc and value are used as identifiers.

Most .NET programming books focus on C# or Visual Basic .NET, and that's pretty much it. This makes Stephen's choice of Managed C++ as a general-purpose .NET programming language unusual and refreshing. As the examples in the book demonstrate, Managed C++ is in no way inferior to other, more "traditional" .NET languages. Plus, you will learn to do things that are simply not available in any other language.

This is a book for working programmers. It is not about the technicalities of the language and the intricacies of its syntax. Instead, it goes straight to the point and shows you how to use the language to "get the job done." Thanks to Stephen's easygoing style, you will find his explanation of Managed C++ very readable, and you will be able to digest it quickly and move on to what he calls "fun topics."

Stephen covers a lot of material in his book. No doubt, he has valuable experience in the field and he is successful at sharing it.

Artur Laksberg
Managed C++ Compiler Development Team
Microsoft Corporation

About the Author

Stephen R. G. Fraser has over 15 years of IT experience working for a number of consulting companies, ranging from the large consulting firms of EDS and Andersen Consulting (Accenture) to a number of smaller e-business companies. His IT experience covers all aspects of application and Web development and management, ranging from initial concept all the way through to deployment.

About the Technical Reviewers

Siva Challa is a software design engineer in the Visual C++ compiler development team at Microsoft. He was involved in the design and implementation of Managed Extensions for C++ from the very early stages. Siva is the primary author of the book *Essential Guide to Managed Extensions for C++*. He holds a master's degree in artificial intelligence from the University of Hyderabad and a doctorate in computer science from Virginia Polytechnic Institute and State University. Siva likes sports and loves to spend his spare time with his beautiful wife, Madhavi, and their adorable daughter, Ramya.

Douglas Milnes has been running his own consultancy and application development business since 1984. He has consulted for small businesses and major corporations such as IBM and Oracle and is a lead consultant with both DeeSoft and Boost Data (http://www.boost.net/Douglas). He lives in the heart of the United Kingdom's "Silicon Valley" near Reading, Berkshire, England. He has two children: Rebecca, 16, and Daniel, 13. Douglas can be contacted by e-mail at Douglas@Boost.net.

Introduction

.NET IS THE FUTURE. If you think otherwise, either you're in deep denial or you simply haven't been paying attention. Some people may not like it, but Microsoft Corporation is one of the most powerful entities in the computer world, and if Microsoft says something is the future, then there is a very high probability that it will be. Guess what, unless you've been locked away in a cell someplace without Internet access, you already know that Microsoft has said that .NET is the future. So, my original statement, ".NET is the future," can't be anything other than true (*quod erat demonstrandum*, or QED).

If you realized this, you probably sat down and started playing with C#. You didn't want to be left behind. As you continued playing, you thought, "This is nice, but why do I have to learn a completely new language just to get the benefits of .NET?" Then it hit you like a ton of bricks: You finally realized that you don't have to learn a new language.

You suddenly remember reading someplace that .NET is language independent. Hey, that means you can program it using any language. Well, not quite *any* language. The language, of course, has to be implemented for .NET.

You're in luck. Microsoft has implemented C++ for .NET. Microsoft calls the implementation *Managed Extensions for C++* or, more commonly, *Managed C++*.

What Is This Book About?

This book is about writing .NET applications. It's designed to start you with a clean slate, wiping away any need for developing COM, DCOM, COM+, or ActiveX components. Instead, it shows you how to code in the world of .NET, free of all that unneeded baggage.

More important, this is a book about writing .NET applications using C++. You'll cover a lot of ground in a short period of time. In the end, you'll be proficient at developing .NET applications, be they Console applications, Windows applications, Web applications, or Web services.

While you're learning the ins and outs of .NET application development, you'll also be learning the syntax of C++, both old and new to .NET. You also will gain a good understanding of the .NET architecture.

Who Should Read This Book?

If you're new to the Visual C++ language, plain and simple, this book is for you. The software world is changing, and learning a new language is hard enough without getting unnecessarily bogged down with a complex set of old technologies before you learn about the new ones.

If you're an experienced Visual C++ programmer, this book is also for you. Microsoft is changing your world. This book will show you these changes. You'll find many books on the market that try to teach you how to force your old world into this new one. This book isn't one of those. Instead, you'll learn the right way to develop .NET code, as the only focus here is the new world: .NET development.

This book is for Visual C++ programmers who don't care about COM, DCOM, COM+, or ActiveX components, either because they already know them or because they never had any reason to learn to code them. You'll use a pure .NET development environment. The only time you'll use components is when you access them—a necessary evil, as there are thousands of them out there that may never be converted to .NET.

This book is also for the (gasp!) non-Microsoft C++ developer who wants to dive into the .NET world without getting bogged down with all the things that he or she disliked about pre-.NET Windows development.

What Does This Book Cover?

This book addresses the topic of Managed C++ in two fashions.

The first six chapters cover the basics and background information that make up the Managed C++ and .NET worlds. I recommend that you read these chapters first, as they provide information that you'll need to understand the remainder of the book. I also recommend that you read the chapters in sequential order because they build on one another.

The remaining chapters of the book are stand-alone and cover specific topics. Here, you can pick and choose the chapters that interest you the most (hopefully every chapter) and read them in any order.

Chapter 1: Overview of the .NET Framework

In this chapter you address the basics of the .NET architecture. You're bombarded with many new .NET terms such as "assemblies," "common language runtime (CLR)," "Common Language Specification (CLS)," "common type system (CTS)," "just-in-time (JIT) compilation," "Microsoft intermediate language (MSIL or IL)," and "manifests." This chapter tries to soften the blow of your first foray into the .NET world.

Chapter 2: Managed C++ Basics

This chapter should be a refresher course on the basics of C++, but be careful when you read it because there have been a few changes, some of them subtle. This chapter covers the core syntax of C++. Old-time C++ programmers should pay attention to this new feature: built-in value and reference types.

Chapter 3: Object-Oriented Managed C++

Now with the basics covered, you delve into object-oriented development (OOD). This chapter covers topics that old-time C++ programmers will take for granted, such as inheritance, encapsulation, polymorphism, classes, methods, and operator overloading. But be careful with this chapter, as .NET makes some significant changes—in particular, properties, constructors, and destructors.

Chapter 4: Advanced Managed C++

In this chapter I start to discuss things that should make even seasoned C++ programmers sit up and take notice, because most of the topics I cover are new to C++. This chapter's topics include multifile programming, exception handling, and delegates.

Chapter 5: The .NET Framework Class Library

In this chapter, you start to work with .NET as you make your first strides into the .NET Framework class library. This chapter is just an overview and takes a cursory look at many of the Framework's base classes. I focus on helping you learn how to find the classes that you need. In later chapters, I go into some of these base classes in much more detail.

Chapter 6: Visual Studio .NET Development

Visual Studio isn't new to most of you. On the other hand, Visual Studio .NET will be. You'll find that software development is much easier with Visual Studio .NET, and this tutorial-style chapter shows you all the new tools and time-savers.

Chapter 7: Collections

Working with collections should be nearly second nature to the average software developer. Because collections are so commonplace, most programmers expect powerful and feature-rich ways of handling them, and .NET doesn't disappoint. This chapter covers the six common collections provided by .NET and then touches on a few less common ones.

Chapter 8: Input, Output, and Serialization

Many programs that you'll write in your career will involve moving, copying, deleting, renaming, reading, and/or writing files. More recently, with object-oriented programming, many of the file's I/O activity in a program involves serialization. With this in mind, you'll explore the `System::IO` and `System::Runtime::Serialization` namespaces.

Chapter 9: Basic Windows Forms Applications

Almost all Windows developers, sometime in their career, will create a Windows application. This chapter shows you how to do it ".NET style." You'll explore how Visual Studio .NET simplifies your development experience. You'll also cover the basic controls found in the `System::Windows::Forms` namespace in some detail.

Chapter 10: Advanced Windows Forms Applications

Having a handle on the basics is all well and good, but as a .NET developer I'm sure you will want to add more elaborate controls to your Windows applications. This chapter takes what you learned in Chapter 9 and expands on it by exploring some of the more advanced controls available to you in the `System::Windows::Forms` namespace.

Chapter 11: Graphics Using GDI+

If you're like me, you like a little pizzazz in the form of graphics to spice up a boring Windows application. This chapter shows you how .NET has made adding images and graphics a whole lot easier with the `System::Drawing` namespace.

Chapter 12: ADO.NET and Database Development

What is software development without databases? In most cases, the answer would be "Not much." Microsoft is well aware of this and has gone to great lengths to make database programming easier. Their solution is ADO.NET. In this chapter, you'll explore the many features of ADO.NET that you can find in the `System::Data` namespace.

Chapter 13: XML

XML is the new world order when it comes to data storage. Microsoft has embraced XML in a big way. This chapter shows the many ways that you can now access XML data in the .NET environment.

Chapter 14: Web Applications

Managed C++ was not meant for Web application development, and there are no tools available to help in the process, but it is possible. This chapter shows you how to develop Web applications using Managed C++. You'll briefly cover HTML and ASP.NET. You'll then learn about the `System::Web` namespace in some detail.

Chapter 15: Web Services

The concept of Web services is not unique. In this chapter you'll explore Web services within the .NET Framework. You'll examine how to design and create them by walking through the process yourself, creating a simple Web service and three different clients (console, Windows application, and Web application) to interact with the service.

Chapter 16: Multithreaded Programming

Being able to run multiple threads at the same time allows for better CPU usage and is a powerful feature. This chapter explores how the .NET Framework makes working with multiple threads concurrently a snap as you cover the .NET Framework's built-in multithreading capabilities.

Chapter 17: Assembly Programming

In traditional C++, application and library developers had few choices regarding what went into .exes and .dlls. With .NET assemblies this has changed, and you now have plenty of choices. This chapter explores those choices by looking at how you can augment your assemblies with resources, localization, attributes, and reflection.

What You Need to Use This Book

The first thing you should probably do is download the code for this book from the Downloads section of the Apress Web site (http://www.apress.com) or from http://www.contentmgr.com. (Contentmgr.com is my personal CMS site, which I developed in my other Apress book, *Real World ASP.NET: Building a Content Management System*. On this site, you can post error notices, fixes, other examples, and so on.) Most of the code in the book is listed in its entirety, but some of the larger programs (in particular, the Windows Forms applications) list only relevant code.

In addition to the source code, you should have a copy of Visual Studio .NET 2003 final beta or later. As long as you have the .NET Framework version 1.1 and its associated C++ compiler, however, you should be able to build nearly everything in the book (though with a lot more effort).

 CAUTION   *This book contains material that isn't supported in Visual Studio .NET 2002 and the .NET Framework 1.0.*

How to Reach Me

I would like to hear from you. Feel free to e-mail me at Stephen.Fraser@apress.com. I will respond to every e-mail that I can. Questions, comments, and suggestions are all welcome.

Oh, by the way, thank you for buying my book. Now, let's get started!

CHAPTER 1

Overview of the .NET Framework

FIRST OFF, LET'S GET ONE THING straight. This book is about developing code within the confines of the Microsoft .NET Framework. Therefore, it only makes sense that you start by getting acquainted with the underlying architecture with which you will be developing your code: the .NET Framework.

I cover a lot of material in this chapter, most at the 30,000-foot level. The main goal of this chapter isn't to make you a .NET Framework expert. This chapter is designed to provide you with a level playing field from which to start your Managed C++ code development while exploring this book.

I start with a brief description of what the .NET Framework is and why we programmers need it. Then, I briefly examine the assembly, which is the central building block for all .NET Framework application distribution and execution. Next, I move on to the core of .NET Framework: the common language runtime (CLR), the common type system (CTS), and the Common Language Specification (CLS). Finally, I discuss, at a very high level, the software components available to .NET Framework developers.

What Is .NET?

To put it in the simplest of terms, .NET is Microsoft's initiative to deliver software as a service. Another way of looking at it is that the impact of .NET will be the following:

- *For programmers:* A paradigm shift in the approach to software development and deployment.

- *For architectures:* Internet processing power to be distributed more on the peripheral clients and less on the Web servers, enabling much better use of the Internet.

- *For the future of the Internet:* Ultimately, the Internet will become more an operating system and less just a means of connecting computers together.

These things are mostly about the future. What does .NET mean to programmers here and now? The first major change that you will see with .NET is that the medium for software delivery will change from full-functionality CD-ROM installations to much smaller, as-needed-functionality Internet downloads.

.NET provides the functionality to place small elements of your application programs on a Web server. These elements can then be downloaded on an as-needed basis, when that application is executing. Basically, applications run as described in these steps:

1. A user attempts to start an application using the .NET runtime.

2. The runtime checks to see if an up-to-date version of the application is in the system's cache. If it is, the runtime executes it from the cache; otherwise, the runtime downloads the updated version and then executes it.

3. While the application is running, it may require other elements. When one such element is required, the runtime checks the cache to see if it exists. Then, the runtime makes one further check to ensure the element is up-to-date. If there is no version in the cache, or it is not up-to-date, then the element is downloaded.

As you can see, this is considerably different from how it is done now, whereby everything is placed on a CD-ROM and installed at one time. I'm sure you can see that the .NET method ensures that the "latest and greatest" are always being executed.

Does this mean that the only way of distributing software is via the Internet? No, there is nothing stopping you from distributing the old way or even combining the two methods, where you install everything up front and then use the Internet to keep everything up-to-date.

As you can imagine, developers now have to start designing their software in a much more modular fashion. Developers also have to be conscious of what modules will likely go together so that those modules can be downloaded concurrently to mitigate the amount of time a user has to wait between running different functionalities of the application. This will also allow for more efficient usage of the Internet.

Another major aspect of .NET that developers will become quickly aware of is that applications are no longer restricted only to the computer on which they are running. It is now possible to execute code from Web services on computers anywhere around the world. True, with some complex DCOM, COM+, CORBA, and so on coding, you could, before .NET, escape the sandbox of the application host computer. But now with .NET, the code to access the resources of the Internet is effortless. Equally as easy, it is possible to make your resources available to the Internet. With .NET, a computer does not have to be an island.

NOTE   *Wherever you read the word "Internet," you can assume "intranet" applies as well.*

What Is the .NET Framework?

The .NET Framework comprises all the pieces needed to develop, deploy, and execute Web services, Web applications, and Windows applications. I discuss each of these in more detail later in the chapter. You can think of the .NET Framework as a three-level hierarchy consisting of the following:

- Application development technologies

- .NET Framework class library

- Common language runtime (CLR)

This hierarchy is illustrated in Figure 1-1.

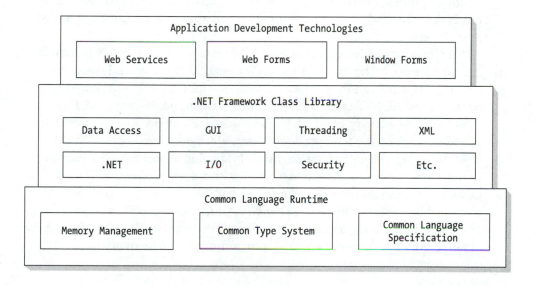

Figure 1-1. The .NET Framework hierarchy

Each of the layers in Figure 1-1 is dependant on the layer beneath it. The CLR lies just above the operating system and insulates the programmer from its intricacies. The .NET Framework is what actually loads, verifies, and executes Web services, Web Form applications, and Windows applications.

The .NET Framework class library is a large number of classes broken up by namespaces containing all the predeveloped functionality of .NET. They contain classes to handle things such as file I/O, database access, security, threading, garbage collection, and so on. As a Managed C++ developer, you will spend many hours perusing and using these classes.

The application development technologies provide a higher layer of abstraction than the class library. Managed C++ developers will use these technologies to build their Web applications, Web services, and Windows applications. Most of the functionality a developer needs can be found at this level of abstraction, but in those cases where more control is needed, the developer can dive down into the class library level.

.NET Programming Advantages

The .NET Framework was designed and developed from day one to be Internet aware and Internet enabled. It uses technologies such as HTML, SOAP, and XML as its underlying methods of communication. As a developer, you have the option of probing as deeply as you wish into each of these technologies, but with the .NET Framework you have the luxury, if you want, of staying completely ignorant of them.

You have probably heard that .NET is language neutral. This key feature of .NET is handled by the CLR. It is currently possible to develop code using C++, C#, J#, JScript .NET, and Visual Basic .NET. In the future, many other languages will be supported. All .NET-compatible languages have full access to the .NET Framework class library. I cover .NET multilanguage support briefly in this chapter.

Another thing you have probably heard whispers about is that .NET can be platform independent. This means that it is possible to port the .NET Framework to non-Windows platforms and then run it without recompiling .NET applications and services. The reason for this is that .NET-compatible code is compiled into something called *assemblies,* which contain code, along with several other things, in an intermediate language. I cover assemblies briefly in this chapter and then delve into the art of programming with them in Chapter 17.

NOTE   *It is true that the .NET Framework can be ported, but as of now this has not happened. Microsoft states that it has plans to do so, but no details have been disclosed as of this writing.*

If you've been coding and deploying Windows code in C++ for any length of time, I'm sure you've become painfully aware that it's anything but simple. Now, if you've gone beyond this to build distributed applications, the complexity has multiplied many times over. A key design goal of the .NET Framework is to dramatically simplify software development and deployment. Some of the most obvious ways that the .NET Framework does this are as follows:

- It shelters you from the complexities of the raw Windows application programming interface (API).

- It provides a consistent, self-documenting object model.

- Managed code provides garbage collection. You no longer have to worry about memory loss due to your forgetting to delete allocated pointers. In fact, if you use managed code, you don't even have to deallocate pointers because the .NET Framework will do it for you.

NOTE   *Managed code is made up of only managed objects, and unmanaged code is made up of unmanaged objects. This book only discusses managed code.*

- The intricacies of COM and COM+ have been removed. To be more accurate, COM and COM+ are not part of the .NET Framework. You can continue to use these technologies, but .NET supports them by placing COM and COM+ components in a class library derived wrapper. You no longer have to worry about things such as the VARIANT, IUnknown, IDL, and so on.

- Deployment components no longer use the registry or special directories. As an added bonus, there is no more DLL Hell.

- Deployment is frequently as simple as an xcopy.

A Closer Look at the .NET Framework

Okay, you have looked at .NET and the .NET Framework in general terms. Now, let's break it into the elements that are relevant to a Managed C++ programmer and then look at each element in some detail. There are five major elements that a Managed C++ developer should have at least a basic knowledge of before attempting to code:

- Assemblies

- CLR

- Common type system (CTS)

- Common Language Specification (CLS)

- .NET Framework class library

Each element impacts the Managed C++ programmer differently. Assemblies are a new form of binary distribution. The CLR is a new way of executing. The CTS is a new way of defining data-storage types. CLS is a specification of language-neutral support. The .NET Framework class library is a whole new set of development objects to learn. I discuss each of these elements in more detail in the following sections.

Assemblies

You need a basic understanding of assemblies before you can learn about any other element of the .NET Framework. I cover some basic information about assemblies in this chapter and then discuss working with them in detail in Chapter 17.

Assemblies are the core building blocks for all .NET Framework application distribution and execution. They are generated after compiling Managed C++ code. Like pre-.NET application deliverables, they end with either .exe or .dll, but that is as far as the similarities go.

Basic Structure

Assemblies are a self-describing collection of functionalities stored in an intermediate language and/or resources needed to execute some portion of an application. Assemblies are made up of four sections: the assembly metadata, type metadata, Microsoft intermediate language (MSIL) code, and resources (see Figure 1-2). All of the sections but the assembly metadata are optional, though an assembly made up of just this section won't do anything.

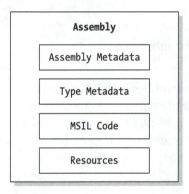

Figure 1-2. The basic assembly structure

Assemblies can be either private or shared. *Private assemblies* reside in the same directory as the application itself or in one of its child directories. *Shared assemblies*, on the other hand, are stored in the global assembly cache (GAC). The GAC is really nothing more than a directory structure that stores all the assemblies that are globally available to the computer (see Figure 1-3). A neat feature of the GAC is that more than one version of the same assembly can reside in it.

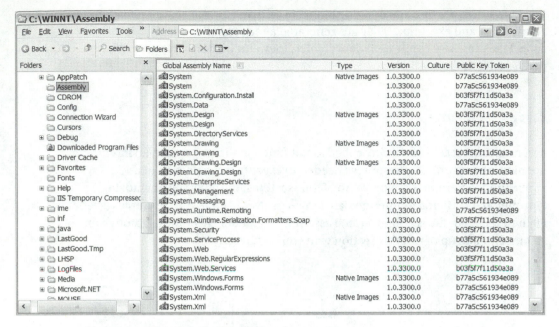

Figure 1-3. The global assembly cache

A key feature of all assemblies is that they are self-describing. In other words, all information needed to understand how to use the assembly can be found within the assembly itself. An assembly does this by including metadata directly within itself. There are two different metadata sections in an assembly: the assembly metadata and the type metadata.

Metadata

The *assembly metadata* is also known as the *assembly manifest*. As its name suggests, the assembly metadata describes the assembly. Here is a list of the assembly metadata's contents:

- The name of the assembly.

- The version number.

- The culture used by the assembly (i.e., language, currency, number formatting, and so on).

- Strong name information. This is a uniquely identifiable name that can be used for shared assemblies.

- A list of all files that make up the assembly.

- A list of all reference assemblies.

- Reference information for all exported classes, methods, properties, and so on found in the assembly.

The *type metadata*, on the other hand, describes the types within the assembly. The type metadata generated depends on the type being created. For example, if the type were a method, then the metadata generated would contain things such as the name, return types, number of arguments and their types, and access level. A property, on the other hand, would reference the get and set methods; these methods in turn would contain names, return types, and so on.

A nice feature of metadata is that it can be used by many of the tools available to the Managed C++ developer. For example, Visual Studio .NET's IntelliSense statement completion functionality (see Figure 1-4) is actually driven using the reference assembly's metadata and not some secondary description file. Because it comes directly from an assembly, IntelliSense will also work for assemblies you have written yourself without any additional effort on your part.

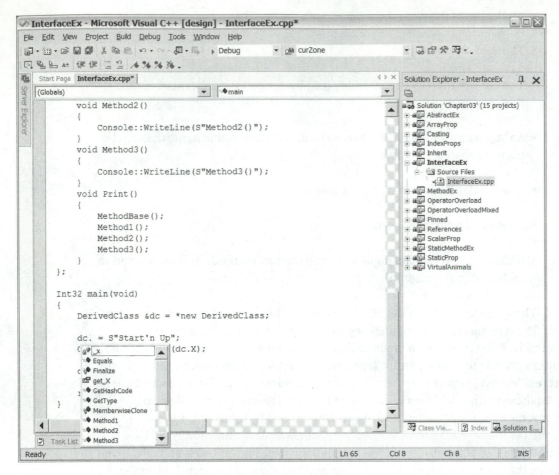

Figure 1-4. Visual Studio .NET's IntelliSense using metadata

Versioning

Application assemblies are very version-aware when they're referencing strong-named assemblies (usually out of the GAC). Every assembly has a version number. Also, every referencing assembly stores the version number of any assembly that it references. It's not until the referenced assembly is strong named that the referencing assembly automatically checks when executing, via the CLR, that the versions match before it continues to execute. You should note there's nothing stopping you from coding your referencing assembly to do this check manually. I cover assembly versioning in detail in Chapter 17.

Microsoft Intermediate Language

A major change that you are going to have to get used to as a Managed C++ programmer is that Managed C++ code gets compiled to Microsoft intermediate
language (MSIL) and not machine code. MSIL is a CPU-independent set of
instructions similar to an assembly language. For example, it contains arithmetic
and logical operators and flow control. But, unlike the average assembly language, it also contains higher-level instructions to load, store, initialize, and call
class objects.

Just for some grins and giggles, here is an example of some MSIL generated
from a simple Managed C++ program. See if you can figure out what it does.

```
IL_0000:   ldarg.0
IL_0001:   ldarg.1
IL_0002:   add
IL_0003:   stloc.0
IL_0004:   ldstr       "{0} + {1} = {2}"
IL_0009:   ldarga.s    val1
IL_000b:   call        instance string [mscorlib]System.Int32::ToString()
IL_0010:   ldarga.s    val2
IL_0012:   call        instance string [mscorlib]System.Int32::ToString()
IL_0017:   ldloca.s    total
IL_0019:   call        instance string [mscorlib]System.Int32::ToString()
IL_001e:   call        void [mscorlib]System.Console::WriteLine(string,
                                                    object,
                                                    object,
                                                    object)
IL_0023:   ret
```

For those of you who are curious, the preceding code adds two numbers
together and then writes the result out to the console.

MSIL is easily converted to native code. In fact, when the MSIL code is
loaded by the CLR, it gets rapidly compiled to native code.

NOTE *The MSIL in an assembly is compiled prior to execution. It is* not *interpreted at runtime.*

One key characteristic of MSIL is that it is an object-orientation-based language with the restriction of single class inheritance, though multiple inheritance of interfaces is allowed. All types, both value and reference, used within the MSIL must conform to the CTS. Any exposed types must follow the CLS. I cover both CTS and CLS later in this chapter. Error handling should be done using exceptions.

MSIL is the key to .NET's capability to be language neutral. All code, no matter what the programming language, gets compiled into the same MSIL. Because all languages ultimately compile to the same MSIL, it is now possible to have things such as encapsulation, inheritance, polymorphism, exception handling, debugging, and so on be language neutral.

MSIL will also be one of the keys to .NET's capability to be platform independent. With MSIL, you can have "write once, run anywhere" ability, just as you do with Java. All that is required for an assembly to run on a non-Windows platform is for the ported CLR to compile MSIL into non-Windows-specific code.

With the combination of MSIL and metadata, .NET is capable of providing a high level of security. For example, strong names found in metadata can ensure that only trusted assemblies are run. If you add to this code verification of MSIL, then the CLR can ensure that only managed code running with valid commands gets executed.

Resources

In .NET, resources (i.e., string tables, images, cursors, and so on) can be stored in two places: in external .resources files or directly within an assembly. Accessing the resources in either location is extremely easy, as the .NET Framework class library provides three straightforward classes for access within the `System::Resources` namespace. I cover these classes in detail in Chapter 17, but if you want to get a head start and look them up yourself, here they are:

- ResourceManager: Use to access resources from within an assembly

- ResourceWriter: Use to write resources to an external .resources file

- ResourceReader: Use to read resources from an external .resources file

In addition to these classes, the .NET Framework provides the utility resgen.exe, which creates a .resources file from a text file containing key/value pairs.

The resgen.exe utility is very useful if you wish to make your Windows applications support multiple (human) languages. It's easy to do this. Simply create multiple .resources files, one for each language. From these, build satellite assemblies for each language. Then the application will automatically access the correct language resource based on the current culture specified on the computer. You'll learn how to do this in Chapter 17.

Common Language Runtime

Runtimes are hardly a new concept when it comes to code execution. Visual Basic has msvbvm60.dll, and Java, of course, has the Java Virtual Machine (JVM). The common language runtime (CLR) is .NET's runtime system.

Do we need another runtime? What makes this one that much better than all the rest? It is simply the fact that the CLR is designed to be the runtime for all languages and (possibly) all platforms. Or, in other words, you no longer need a myriad of different runtimes to handle each programming language and platform. Instead, all you need is the CLR.

It's a pretty big claim. Does it hold water?

There are two common roles for runtimes: to execute code and/or to add common functionality used by most applications. The CLR performs both of these roles for the .NET Framework. But these roles are only the tip of the iceberg. The CLR also performs several other services, such as code verification, access security, garbage collection, and exception handling, and it also handles multilanguage support and compiles MSIL into the native language of the platform (see Figure 1-5).

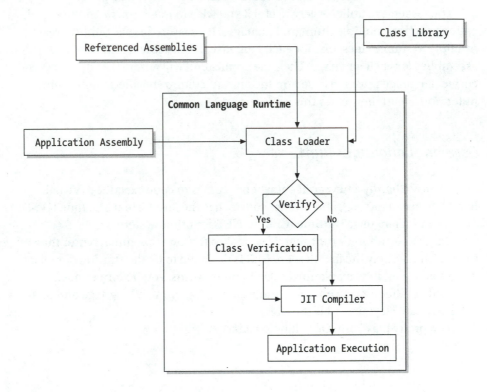

Figure 1-5. The CLR start-up process flow

Starting up an application in .NET is conceptually very simple. The CLR loads the application assembly, any referenced developer assemblies, and any referenced class library assemblies. Then, the application is optionally verified for type safety and valid access security. Next, the loaded MSIL, with the help of information found in the metadata from the assemblies, is compiled into native code. Finally, the application is executed.

The CLR was designed to provide

- *Simple, fast development:* This is possible through a large, consistent, reusable framework.

- *Simplified programming infrastructure:* Much of the plumbing (memory management, local and remote process communication, and so on) is handled automatically or hidden unless access is needed.

- *Scalability:* Areas that allow for scalability (memory management, process communication, component management, and so on) are contained, already optimized, within the framework.

- *Simple, safe deployment:* A simple xcopy is usually all that is required for deployment.

Managed Code

Basically, *managed code* is code targeted for the .NET Framework's CLR. Managed code must supply the metadata needed by the CLR to handle things such as memory management, code access security, and multilanguage integration. Essentially, if the code is compiled into MSIL within assemblies, then you can be confident that you are creating managed code.

Conversely, *unmanaged code* is any code not targeted for the CLR. It is possible for the .NET Framework to access C DLLs, COM, and COM+ services, even though all of these are unmanaged.

All of the compilers that come with the .NET Framework default to generating managed code except C++. To create managed code in C++, you need to add the command-line switch /CLR when compiling. When you use Visual Studio .NET, simply select one of the managed C++ project templates, as these will set the switch for you.

Managed Data

Managed data is data that is allocated by an application and then deallocated by the CLR's garbage collector. Like managed code, all .NET languages except C++ default to managed data, even if you use C++'s /CLR switch. To create managed data in C++, you must use the keyword __gc in your source code.

Common Language Runtime Services

Along with loading and executing an assembly, the CLR provides several other services. Code verification and code access verification are optional services available before the assembly is loaded. Garbage collection, on the other hand, is always active while the assembly is being executed.

Code Verification

The *code verification* service is executed prior to actually running the application. Its goal is to walk through the code, ensuring that it is safe to run. For example, it checks for things such as invalid pointer references and array indexes. The goal of code verification is to ensure that the code does not crash, and that if an error happens to occur, it is handled by the CLR by throwing an exception. This gives the application more control over how to recover or exit gracefully.

Code Access Verification

Code access verification also walks through the code and checks that all code has the permission to execute. The goal of this service is to try to stop malicious attacks on the user's computer.

A simplified way of looking at how this service works is that the CLR contains a list of actions that it can grant permission to execute, and the assembly contains a list of all the permissions it requires to run. If the CLR can grant all the permissions, then the assembly runs without problems. If, on the other hand, the CLR can't grant all the permissions, then it runs what it can but generates an exception whenever it tries to do something that it doesn't have permission to do.

Garbage Collection

Garbage collection is the mechanism that allows a computer to detect and remove managed objects from the heap that are no longer being accessed by an application. The .NET Framework's garbage collector has the added bonus of compacting the memory after it removes the unused portion, thus keeping the fingerprints of the applications as small as possible. This bonus also has a downside. Managed objects in .NET do not have a fixed location, but you can overcome this with the __pin keyword. I cover __pin in Chapter 3. Also, pointer arithmetic is gone except in unsafe sections of the code.

Garbage collection presents a big change to average C++ programmers, as it means an end to most of those annoying memory leaks that plague them while developing. It also has an added bonus: Programmers no longer have to figure out where to call the `delete` command to the classes that they've created using the `new` command.

Garbage collection is not the default for C++. Because this is the case, there are a few things (covered in Chapter 3) that Managed C++ programmers need to learn before they can use garbage collection—in particular, the keyword __gc. Also, programmers have no control of when a managed object that is no longer referenced gets deleted.

Attributes

Attributes are a way for developers to provide additional information about the classes, methods, or data types to the assemblies they are creating. This additional information is stored within the assembly's metadata.

There are several predefined attributes that the compiler can use to help during the compile process. For example, the `System::Obsolete` attribute causes the compiler to generate a warning when it encounters an obsolete method in a class library assembly.

You will see in Chapter 17 how to work with attributes and how it is possible to add your own custom attributes to the assembly metadata.

All attributes, developer code–created and compiler-generated, can be extracted using reflection.

Reflection

An interesting service provided by the CLR is *reflection*. This is the ability to programmatically examine the metadata within an assembly, including the one executing the reflection code. This service allows access to the metadata information, such as details about classes, methods, properties, and so on, contained within the assembly.

Most likely, you will use reflection to get attribute information out of the assembly metadata. For more advanced Managed C++ developers, reflection provides the ability to extract type information within a class so that they can use it to generate types dynamically.

Reflection is accomplished using the myriad classes in the `System::Reflection` namespace. Chapter 17 covers reflection.

Multiple Language Support

.NET had the ambitious goal of creating a completely language-neutral environment for developing software. Some of the features the .NET Framework and Visual Studio .NET developers had in mind when it came to being language-neutral were as follows:

- Common data types should be shared by all languages.

- Object pointers and/or references from any language should be able to be passed as an argument to a method.

- Calling methods from classes created in other languages should be possible.

- Classes should be able to contain instances of other classes created in a different language.

- Inheriting from classes created in another language should be possible.

- The development environment for all languages should be the same.

- Debugging all languages should be possible using the same environment.

- Debugging should be able to navigate between languages.

Believe it or not, every one of those features is now supported by the .NET Framework within the Visual Studio .NET development environment.

The idea is to pick the best language for the job. Each language has its strong and weak points when it comes to software development. With language-neutral development, you can select the language that best suits the type of development needed.

Will developers accept this concept? In this age of computer-language holy wars, it seems a little doubtful. Plus, allowing the use of multiple languages during the development of a project does add complexity. Having said that, though,

I've worked on a large project that used, alphabetically, C, C++, COBOL, HTML, Macro (Assembler), and SQL, plus an assortment of batch scripting languages. To make things worse, each of these languages had different tools for development, and debugging was a nightmare. I don't even want to talk about passing data between modules created in different languages. What I would have given for .NET back then.

How does the .NET Framework create a language-neutral environment? The key is a combination of MSIL and metadata. Basically, the MSIL code tells the CLR what to do (which commands to execute), and the metadata tells it how to do it (which interfaces and calling conventions to use). For a language to be .NET Framework compliant, it obviously needs to be compiled into MSIL code and metadata, and placed in an assembly (see Figure 1-6).

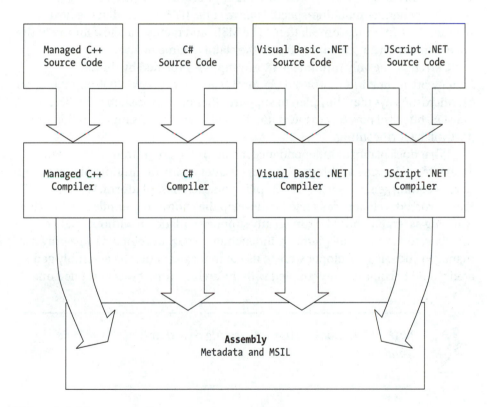

Figure 1-6. Many compilers, one output

Because all languages have this requirement, Microsoft was able to tweak each language they developed so that it created code to conform to their MSIL and metadata language-neutral requirements. These tweaks mostly enabled the languages to support true objects and exception handling, as these are the main characteristics of MSIL. Also, all languages were changed to conform to the common type system (CTS). I cover the CTS later in this chapter.

Multiple Platform Support

By its architecture, the .NET Framework is conducive to multiple platform support. The CLR enables platform independence by providing a runtime layer that sits between the operating system and the application. The just-in-time (JIT) compiler generates machine-specific native code. JIT is covered in the next section, "Just-in-Time Compilation." The MSIL and metadata allow for the "write once, run anywhere" capability that is the claim to fame of Java.

Currently, the only multiple platform support provided by the .NET Framework is for Windows-based platforms such as Windows 2000 and Windows XP. Microsoft says that they plan to support other platforms such as UNIX and Mac OS, but as of now Microsoft is not disclosing any details on when this support will be forthcoming.

What does platform independence mean to C++ programmers? It means a new way of looking at things. C++ programmers think of multiple platform support as coding generically and recompiling on each new platform. With the .NET Framework, developers only need to develop the code and compile it once. The resulting assembly could be run on any supported platform without change.

True, to develop true platform-independent code, developers must only use managed code. If a developer were to use unmanaged code, the assembly generated would become closely coupled with the architecture it was compiled on.

 NOTE   *This book focuses on creating code that is platform independent.*

Just-in-Time Compilation

Even though .NET applications are stored in an intermediate language, .NET applications are not interpreted. Instead, they are compiled into a native executable. It is the job of the JIT compiler, a key component of the CLR, to convert MSIL code into machine code with the help of metadata found in the executable assembly.

The JIT compiling process is, in concept, very easy. When an application is started, the JIT compiler is called to convert the MSIL code and metadata into machine code. To avoid the potentially slow start-up time caused by compiling the entire application, the JIT compiler only compiles the portions of code that it calls, when they are called (hence the name "just-in-time compiler"). After the code is compiled, it is placed in cached memory and then run. The compiled code remains in the cached memory for as long as the application is executing. This way, the portion of code can be grabbed from cached memory, instead of having to go through the compile process each time it is called. There is a bonus in compiling this way. If the code is not called, it does not get compiled.

Microsoft claims that managed code should run faster than unmanaged code. How can Microsoft make this claim? The JIT compiler is amazingly fast, but there still is the overhead of having to compile the application each time it is run. This leads one to believe that managed code would be slower.

The key to Microsoft's claim is that JIT compilers generate code specific to the processor type of the machine they are running on. On the other hand, traditional compilers generate code targeting a general range of processor types. For example, the Visual Studio 6.0 C++ compiler generates generic Pentium machine code. A JIT compiler, knowing that it is run on, let's say, a quad processor Pentium IV, would generate code specific to that processor. The execution time between these two sets of machine code will in many cases be quite different and always in the favor of the JIT compiler–generated code. This increase in speed in the managed code should offset the JIT compiling overhead and, in many cases, make the overall execution faster than the unmanaged code.

Common Type System

The common type system (CTS) defines how all types are declared, used, and managed within the .NET Framework and, more specifically, the CLR. It is also a key component for the CLR's multiple language support. The CTS was designed to perform the following functions:

- Provide an object-oriented data model that can support the data types of all .NET Framework–compatible programming languages

- Provide a set of constraints that the data types of a .NET-compatible language must adhere to so that it can interact with other .NET-compatible programming languages

- Provide a framework for .NET-compatible interlanguage integration and data type safety

There are two categories of data types defined by the CTS: the value type and the reference type. *Value types,* such as int, float, or char, are stored as the representation of the data type itself. *Reference types,* such as pointers, classes, or arrays, on the other hand, are stored as references to the location of the data type.

As you can see in Figure 1-7, all data types fall into one of these two categories.

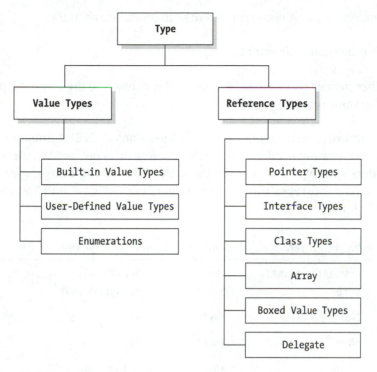

Figure 1-7. CTS hierarchy

Let's briefly walk through the hierarchy of all CTS types:

- *Arrays:* A single or multidimensional indexed grouping of types

- *Boxed value types:* A temporary reference to a value type so that it can be placed on the heap

- *Built-in value types:* Primitive value types that represent integers, real numbers, Booleans, and characters

- *Class types:* A user-defined grouping of types and methods

- *Delegates:* A type that holds a reference to a method

- *Enumerations:* A list of named integer constants

- *Interface types:* A class type where all methods are abstract

- *Pointer types:* A reference to a type

- *User-defined value types:* User-defined expansion to the standard, primitive value types

A point worth mentioning is that the CLS defines all .NET-compatible language data types, but a .NET-compatible language does not need to support all CLS-defined data types. You can see this in practice by comparing the built-in value and reference types supported by Visual Basic .NET, C#, and Managed C++ (see Table 1-1).

Table 1-1. Built-in Value and Reference Types and Their Language Keywords

BASE CLASS	VISUAL BASIC .NET	C#	MANAGED C++
System::Byte	Byte	byte	unsigned char
System::Sbyte	Not supported	sbyte	char
System::Int16	Short	short	short
System::Int32	Integer	int	int or long
System::Int64	Long	long	__int64
System::UInt16	Not supported	ushort	unsigned short
System::UInt32	Not supported	uint	unsigned int or unsigned long
System::UInt64	Not supported	ulong	unsigned __int64
System::Single	Single	float	float
System::Double	Double	double	double
System::Object	Object	object	Object*
System::Char	Char	char	__wchar_t
System::String	String	string	String*
System::Decimal	Decimal	decimal	Decimal
System::IntPtr	IntPtr	IntPtr	IntPtr
System::UIntPtr	UIntPtr	UIntPtr	UIntPtr
System::Boolean	Boolean	bool	bool

CAUTION   *You should take care when using* UInt64, *as unpre-dictable results are possible on Intel 32-bit platforms because they are not thread safe and do not load the registers automatically.*

Common Language Specification

As shown in Table 1-1, not all of the CTS data types are supported by every .NET-compatible language. How then does the .NET Framework maintain that these languages are in fact compatible? This is where the Common Language Specification (CLS) comes in. The CLS is a minimum subset of the CTS that all languages must support to be .NET compatible (see Figure 1-8).

To ensure interlanguage operability, it is only the CLS subset that can be exposed by assemblies. Because you can be assured that all languages' building assemblies are using this subset, you can thus also be assured that all languages will be able to interface with it.

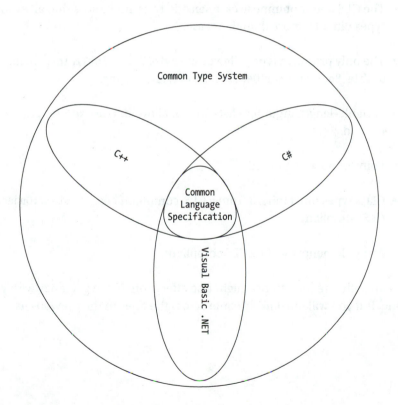

Figure 1-8. CLS intersection diagram

NOTE   *When you develop your .NET code, it is completely accept-able to use the entire CTS. It is only exposed types that need to adhere to the CLS for interlanguage operability.*

There is no imposed restriction on using the CLS. If you know that your assemblies will only be used by one language, then it is perfectly acceptable to use all the types available to that language, even those that are exposed. Just be aware that if there comes a time when you want to use your assemblies with another language, they may not work because they do not adhere to the CLS.

If you want to view the CLS, you can find it in the .NET documentation. Just search for "What is the Common Language Specification?" The key points that you should be aware of as a C++ programmer are as follows:

- Global methods and variables are not allowed.

- The CLS does not impose case sensitivity, so make sure that all exposed types differ by more than their case.

- The only primitive types allowed are `Byte`, `Int16`, `Int32`, `Int64`, `Single`, `Double`, `Boolean`, `Char`, `Decimal`, `IntPtr`, and `String`.

- Variable-length argument lists are not allowed. Use fixed-length arrays instead.

- Pointers are not allowed.

- Class types must inherit from a CLS-compliant class. `System::Object` is CLS compliant.

- Array elements must be CLS compliant.

Some other requirements might also affect you, if you get fancy with your coding. But you will most likely come across the ones in the previous list.

.NET Application Development Realms

.NET application development falls into one of four realms: Web applications, Web services, Windows applications, and console applications. Using languages such as C#, Visual Basic .NET, and Visual Studio .NET provides a simple, powerful, and consistent environment to develop all four. Unfortunately, for C++, only three are fully supported: console applications, Windows applications, and Web services.

Although Web applications aren't supported by Visual Studio .NET, this doesn't mean that you can't develop them. It just means you have to do more—in some cases, a lot more—legwork to get things done. But hey, you're a C++ programmer. You're used to this.

Console Applications

Console applications are basically extinct as a final software delivery. But as a developer tool, there is nothing like them. If you need to figure out how to do something, write out a console application. There is nothing simpler and nothing with less overhead. This book is full of console applications for just those reasons.

The key elements of all console applications are the `main()` function and the `System::Console::WriteLine()` method. In fact, that is almost all you need to write a console application.

Windows Applications

Windows applications may be the biggest change for C++ programmers. Managed C++ does not support MFC. Wow, don't panic—believe it or not, the .NET Framework has a better solution. It's called Windows Forms and I'm sure you'll think, as I do, that it's a godsend. With Windows Forms, you get the ease of Visual Basic along with the power of C++ when you develop Web applications. I cover Windows applications in Chapters 9 and 10.

When you create Windows Forms, you will use the massive `System::Windows::Forms` namespace. Though this namespace is large, it is consistent and well laid out. It will not take you long to get good at using it.

Just to add some variety to your Windows applications, .NET also provides a new and improved Graphical Device Interface (GDI) called, conveniently, GDI+. With GDI+, you can play with fonts, change colors and, of course, draw pictures. GDI+ is almost worth learning just for one class, `System::Drawing::Image`, which allows an application to load almost any commonly supported graphic file formats, including GIF, JPEG, and BMP, into memory, where they can be manipulated and drawn to the screen. To implement GDI+ in the .NET Framework, you need to explore the `System::Drawing` namespace. I cover GDI+ in Chapter 11.

Web Applications

ASP.NET is a large part of developing Web applications. But unlike traditional Web application development, .NET has changed things. Web applications no longer are run using interpreted scripts. Now they use full-blown compiled applications. These applications are usually written using C# and Visual Studio .NET, but Managed C++ will work as well.

When a user calls on a Web site, he will no longer be looking for .html or .asp files; instead, he will be looking for an .aspx file, a fully compiled Web application. I go into the details of Web applications in Chapter 14, but here are some of the high points.

With Web applications, you will, along with Managed C++, get exposed to ASP.NET, HTML, and ADO.NET. This book will not make you an expert on any of these technologies, but there are other great Apress books that will help you along with that goal. The .NET Framework supports Web applications predominately by using the `System::Web` namespace and its children. The most important class with Web applications is the `System:Web:UI::Page` class, which you will need to have intimate knowledge of when you code in Managed C++.

Web Services

You might want to think of a Web service as programmable functionality that you execute over the Internet. Talk about remote programming! Using a simple HTTP request, you can execute some functionality on some computer on the opposite side of the world. Okay, there are still some kinks, such as the possible bandwidth problems, but they will be overcome with the current technology advancement rate—that much I am certain of. Chapter 15 covers Web services.

Web services are based on the technology XML and, more specifically, the XML-derived Simple Object Access Protocol, better known as SOAP. SOAP was designed to exchange information in a decentralized and distributed environment using HTTP. For more technical details about SOAP, peruse the World Wide Web Consortium's Web pages on SOAP (`http://www.w3.org/TR/SOAP`).

When you code Web services, you will be working primarily with the `System::Web::Services` namespace. You also get to look at attributes again.

Web services are a key part of Microsoft's plans for .NET because, as you may recall, .NET is about delivering software as a service.

.NET Framework Class Library

Everything you've learned so far is all fine and dandy, but the thing that is really most important, and where Managed C++ programmers will spend many a day, is the massive .NET Framework class library. There are literally hundreds of classes and structures contained within a hierarchy of namespaces. Managed C++ programmers will use many of these classes and structures on a regular basis.

With such a large number of elements in the class library, you would think that a programmer would quickly get lost. Fortunately, this is not true. The .NET Framework class library is, in fact, well organized, easy to use, and virtually self-documenting. Namespaces, class names, properties, methods, and variable names usually make perfect sense. The only real exceptions to this that I have found are class library wrapped native classes. I am sure there are other exceptions, but by and large most namespaces and classes are understandable just by their names. This, obviously, differs considerably from the Win32 API, where obscure names are more the norm.

With the .NET Framework class library, you can have complete control of the computer, because the class library functionality ranges from a very high level, such as the Calendar class, which displays a single month of a calendar on a Web page, down to a very low level, such as the PowerModeChangedEventHandler, which notifies the application when the computer is about to be suspended, resumed, or changed from AC to battery or vice versa.

There are two hierarchies of namespaces in the .NET Framework class library: the platform-neutral System namespace and the Microsoft-specific (and aptly named) Microsoft namespace. Table 1-2 shows a brief subset of the namespaces that the average Managed C++ programmer will run into.

Table 1-2. Common .NET Framework Class Library Namespaces

NAMESPACE	DESCRIPTION
Microsoft::win32	Contains classes to handle events raised by the operating system and to manipulate the system registry
System	Contains classes that handle primitive types, mathematics, program invocation, and supervision of applications
System::Collections	Contains classes that define collections of objects, such as lists, queues, arrays, hashtables, and dictionaries
System::Data	Contains classes that handle database access

(continued)

Table 1-2. Common .NET Framework Class Library Namespaces (continued)

NAMESPACE	DESCRIPTION
System::Data::OleDb	Contains classes that handle access to OLE DB databases
System::Data::SqlClient	Contains classes that handle access to Microsoft SQL Server databases
System::Diagnostics	Contains classes that allow you to debug your application and trace application execution
System::DirectoryServices	Contains classes to access Active Directory
System::Drawing	Contains classes to handle the GDI+ graphics functionality
System::Drawing::Drawing2D	Contains classes that handle advanced two-dimensional and vector graphics functionality
System::Drawing:Imaging	Contains classes to handle advanced GDI+ imaging functionality
System::Drawing::Printing	Contains classes to handle custom printing
System::Globalization	Contains classes that define culture-related information, such as language, currency, and numbers
System::IO	Contains classes to handle reading and writing of data streams and files
System::Net	Contains classes to handle many of the protocols and services found on networks
System::Reflection	Contains classes that examine loaded types, methods, and fields, and also dynamically create and invoke types
System::Resources	Contains classes to create, store, and manage various culture-specific resources
System::Runtime::InteropServices	Contains classes to access COM objects and native APIs
System::Runtime::Remoting	Contains classes to create and configure distributed applications

(continued)

Table 1-2. Common .NET Framework Class Library Namespaces (continued)

NAMESPACE	DESCRIPTION
`System::Security`	Contains classes to handle the CLR security system
`System::Threading`	Contains classes to handle multithreaded programming
`System::Web`	Contains classes to handle browser/server communication
`System::Web::Mail`	Contains classes to create and send an e-mail using the SMTP mail service built into Microsoft Windows 2000
`System::Web::Security`	Contains classes to handle ASP.NET security in Web applications
`System::Web::Services`	Contains classes to build and use Web services
`System::Web::UI`	Contains classes to create controls and pages in Web applications
`System::Windows::Forms`	Contains classes to create Windows-based applications
`System::XML`	Contains classes to handle XML

Summary

This chapter created a level playing field on which to start your exploration of Managed C++. The chapter began with the big picture, examining what exactly .NET is, and it descended from there. It explored the .NET Framework generically and finally broke it down piece by piece, examining such things as assemblies, the common language runtime (CLR), the common type system (CTS), and the Common Language Specification (CLS). The chapter ended with a look at the myriad classes available to the Managed C++ developer.

The journey has begun. In the next chapter, you'll look at the basics of Managed C++. Let's continue.

Managed C++ Basics

YOU HAVE A LITTLE WORK TO do before you can have some fun. This chapter covers many basic but important aspects of Managed C++ programming.

You will start with variables and data types. Then you will move on to comments, literals, expressions, and operations. Next, you will explore looping and flow control. Finally, you will end with functions. You will focus on Managed C++ and its infrequently used capability to be strictly a procedure language. The next chapter will look at Managed C++ as an object-oriented language, its true claim to fame.

 CAUTION   *Even though you may know C++ very well, don't skip this chapter—several things vary between traditional C++ and Managed C++. True, some of the changes may not be significant, but recognizing and understanding these changes now may make your life easier in the future.*

The Obligatory "Hello, World!" Program

It seems like all the programming books I read always start with a "Hello, World!" program. Who am I to do things differently? Here is the "Hello, World!" program, Managed C++ style:

```
// Obligatory Hello World!

#using <mscorlib.dll>
using namespace System;

Int32 main(void)
{
    Console::WriteLine(S"Hello Managed World");
    return 0;
}
```

You can create the Hello.cpp program by typing it in with any text editor. You can use Edit or Notepad, as both come with all versions of Windows. To compile it into an assembly called Hello.exe, simply execute the following line from the command prompt:

```
cl Hello.cpp /CLR
```

 NOTE *You need the command prompt to be configured for the .NET development environment. Unless you have configured your default command prompt for this environment, I recommend that you use the command prompt provided by Visual Studio .NET.*

Even though this is an assembly, you run it like you would any other executable. If you run it from the command line, you should get something like Figure 2-1.

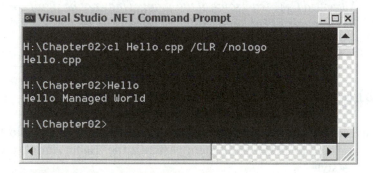

Figure 2-1. Executing Hello.exe from the command line

All Managed C++ programs will contain this line:

```
#using <mscorlib.dll>
```

#using is a preprocessor directive specific to Managed C++. When compiled, it generates metadata that is used by the common language runtime (CLR) to identify which assemblies to load. Those of you existing C++ programmers can think of this directive as being similar to the #include directive, except that instead of including an .h file, you are now including a compiled .dll assembly file. In the case of Hello.cpp, you are only using mscorlib.dll, which is an assembly that contains most of the core elements of the .NET Framework.

I don't cover namespaces until later in this chapter, but for now think of them as a way of assembling a bunch of functions and variables into a group. When you want to access this group, you use the `using` statement. Basically, the next line

```
using namespace System;
```

says you are going to use the stuff in this `System` namespace or grouping.

Every Managed C++ program must start with a `main()` function and every program can have only one `main()` function. When the `main()` function finishes executing, so does the program. In the case of Hello.cpp, `main()` also happens to be the only function. The first line of the `main()` function is this:

```
Int32 main(void)
```

There are other variations of `main()`, including the `WinMain()` function used to start Windows programs. I cover those other variations later in this chapter. In the preceding variation of `main()`, you are receiving no parameters, which is signified by the `(void)` placed after the `main`, and you are expecting the function to return a 32-bit integer number value, `Int32`, after it is completed.

A *function* is a block of code referenced by name, in this case main. It starts with an open curly bracket ({) and ends with a closed curly bracket (}). Within a function is the set of statements that it will execute. The `main()` function of Hello.cpp contains two statements:

```
System::Console::WriteLine(S"Hello Managed World");
return 0;
```

If more than one statement were present, as shown in the preceding code, the statements would be executed sequentially from beginning to end, unless a statement specifically altered the flow, either by looping back or by conditionally bypassing some of the code. You will see how this is done later in this chapter.

In Managed C++, displaying text strings, which are enclosed in quotation marks ("") and prefixed with an *S*, to a console window is handled using the static `WriteLine()` method of the class `Console` in the namespace `System`. Don't panic if that didn't mean much to you—it will shortly. You will learn about classes and static methods in Chapter 3. You will also examine text strings and namespaces in Chapter 3. For now, all you need to know about displaying your own text is to replace "Hello Managed World" with whatever you want to replace it with.

The final line

```
return 0;
```

simply tells the function `main()` that it is done and that it should return with a value of 0 back to the operating system.

Statements

Managed C++'s most basic element is the statement. A *statement* is a coding construct that performs a single Managed C++ action. You will learn about different types of statements as you progress through this book, but the main thing to remember about all statements is that they end with a semicolon (;). If you forget the semicolon, your compiler will throw up all over you. Here are some statements:

```
using namespace System;
System::Console::WriteLine(S"Hello Managed World");
Boolean IsOpen;
y = GetYCoord();
```

Not much to look at, are they?

Managed C++ provides a construct for compound statements. To create a compound statement, you simply enclose several simple statements within curly brackets:

```
{
    x = x + y;
    PrintAnswer(x);
}
```

These statements execute as a group and can be placed anywhere a simple statement can be placed. You will see them in the "Flow Control Constructs" and "Looping Constructs" sections later in this chapter.

Variables and Managed C++ Data Types

One of the key differences between traditional C++ and Managed C++, believe it or not, falls at this low level of the language. If you have worked with C++, then it may come as a little surprise that the data types int, long, float, and so on are no more. They have been replaced with .NET built-in value types. To simplify things for traditional C++ programmers, Managed C++ allows the use of the old data types, but they are, in fact, just aliases.

Alas, I'm getting ahead of myself. I'll start at the beginning, and that would be how to create or, more accurately, declare variables.

Declaring Variables

To use a variable in Managed C++, you must first declare it. The minimum declaration of a variable consists of a data type and a variable name:

```
Int32 counter;
Double yCoord;
```

Variable declarations can go almost anywhere in the code body of a Managed C++ program. One of the few criteria for declarations is that they have to occur before the variable is used. It once was required that all declarations occur as the first statements of a function due to C++'s original C background. You will still see this in practice today, as some programmers feel it makes the code cleaner to read. Personally, I prefer to place the variable closer to where it is first used—that way, I don't have to scroll to the top of every function to see how I declared something. How you code it is up to you. Following the standards of your company is always a good rule of thumb or, if you are coding on your own, stay consistent. You will find that it will save you time down the line.

There is an assortment of more complex declarations. For example, you can string together several comma-delimited variable names at the same time:

```
Int32 x, y, z;
```

A special data type called a *pointer,* which I'll explain later, requires an asterisk (*) in front of the variable name or after the data type:

```
String* name;
String *name;
```

You might think of these as saying "String pointer called name" or "name points to a String." They are equivalent. There is a complication with string pointers, as shown here:

```
Int32* isPointer, isNOTaPointer;
```

The preceding line actually declares a pointer to an Int32 and a variable of type Int32. This is probably not what you are expecting. If you want two pointers to Int32, you need to declare it like this:

```
Int32 *aPointer, *anotherPointer;
```

You have two possible ways to initialize the variable within the declaration statement. The first is by using a standard assignment:

```
Int32 counter = 0;
Double yCoord = 300.5;
```

The second is by using what is known as *functional notation,* as it resembles the calling of a function passing the initialization value as a parameter. In Managed C++, you should probably call this *constructor initialization,* as you are actually calling the data type's constructor to create these variables:

```
Int32 counter(0);
Double yCoord(300.5);
```

Again, use caution when initializing a variable within the declaration statement using standard assignment. This code may not do what you expect:

```
Int32 x, y, z = 200;
```

Only z is initialized to 200; all the other variables take on the default value of the data type. Enter the following to code this so that all variables are initialized to 200:

```
Int32 x = 200, y = 200, z = 200;
```

It is always a good thing to initialize your variables before you use them. If you don't initialize a variable, its contents can be almost anything when it is used. To help remind you of this, the compiler displays a warning about uninitialized variables while it is compiling.

Variable Name Restrictions

For those of you with a C++ background, there are really no big changes here. Variable names consist of upper- and lowercase letters, digits from 0 to 9, and the underscore character (_). The variable name must start with a letter or an underscore character. Also, variable names cannot be the same as C++ reserved keywords, including all variable names starting with two underscores, which C++ has also reserved. Table 2-1 contains a list of all C++ reserved keywords.

Table 2-1. C++ Reserved Keywords

KEYWORDS

asm	auto	bool	_Bool	break
case	catch	char	class	_Complex
const	const_cast	continue	default	delete
do	double	dynamic_cast	else	enum
explicit	export	extern	false	float
for	friend	goto	if	_Imaginary
inline	int	long	mutable	namespace
new	operator	private	protected	public
register	reinterpret_cast	restrict	return	short
signed	sizeof	static	static_cast	struct
switch	template	this	throw	true
try	typedef	typeid	typename	_typeof
union	unsigned	using	virtual	void
volatile	wchar_t	while		

Variables should probably be self-descriptive. However, there is nothing stopping you from writing a program that uses variable names starting with a0000 and continuing through z9999. If you do this, though, don't ask me to debug it for you.

There are also people who think that you should use Hungarian notation for variable names. This notation allows other programmers to read your code and know the data type by the prefix attached to its name. I find this notation cumbersome and don't use it myself unless, of course, company standards dictate its use.

Predefined Data Types

All data types, even the simplest ones, are truly objects in Managed C++. This differs from traditional C++, where primitive types such as int, float, and double were strictly stored values of data types themselves.

As a Managed C++ programmer, you have the luxury of programming simple data types just like you would in traditional C++, knowing that you can *box* them, making them objects if needed. I cover boxing later in this chapter.

Predefined data types fall into two different types: built-in value types and reference types. *Built-in value types* are the data types that default to just storing their values for efficiency but can be boxed to become full objects. *Reference types,* on the other hand, are always objects.

Built-in Value Types

All the standard C++ data types are available to the Managed C++ programmer. Or at least so it appears. In reality, the standard data types are just an alias for the .NET Framework's built-in value types. There is basically only one major difference between Managed C++'s built-in types and their traditional C++ aliases: Managed C++ value types default to being garbage collected when defined as pointers, whereas traditional C++ data types don't. Because this is the case, pointers that you allocate using int need to be deleted. Those you create with Int32 don't need to be deleted, as they are automatically garbage collected.

 NOTE *Throughout this book, I refer to the built-in value types only by their .NET names. I personally feel the .NET names are more descriptive, but feel free to use the standard C++ aliases if you are more comfortable with them.*

There are five distinct groups of built-in value types:

1. Integer

2. Floating point

3. Decimal

4. Boolean

5. Character

Programmers with a C++ background should readily recognize four of these groups. Decimal, most probably, is new to all. Let's go over all of them so that there are no surprises.

Integer Types

Eight different integer types are provided to Managed C++ programmers. These can all be broken down into unsigned and signed numbers. (In other words, can negative numbers be represented or just positive numbers?) Table 2-2 shows the integer types.

Table 2-2. Integer Point Built-in Value Types

C++ ALIAS	CLASS LIBRARY	DESCRIPTION	RANGE
unsigned char	System::Byte	8-bit unsigned integer	0 to 255
char	System::SByte	8-bit signed integer	−128 to 127
short	System::Int16	16-bit signed integer	−32,768 to 32,767
unsigned short	System::UInt16	16-bit unsigned integer	0 to 65,535
int or long	System::Int32	32-bit signed integer	−2,147,483,648 to 2,147,483,647
unsigned int or long	System::UInt32	32-bit unsigned integer	0 to 4,294,967,295
__int64	System::Int64	64-bit signed integer	−9,223,372,036,854,775,808 to 9,223,372,036,854,775,807
unsigned __int64	System::UInt64	64-bit unsigned integer	0 to 18,446,744,073,709,551,615

Byte and SByte are the smallest of the integer types, as they are only made up of 1 byte, hence their names. Their Managed C++ aliases are unsigned char and char, respectively. A Byte can range from 0 to 255, and an SByte can range from −128 to 127 inclusive. In traditional C++, char usually represents ASCII characters.

CAUTION   *The Managed C++ alias* char *is not the same as the .NET Framework class library* System::Char. *A* char *is an 8-bit unsigned integer that frequently represents an ASCII character, whereas a* System::Char *is a 16-bit Unicode character.*

The remainder of the integer types have fairly self-descriptive .NET Framework class library names, with their type and size merged into their name. Int16 are 16-bit integers, UInt16 are unsigned 16-bit integers, and so on. Personally, I think these names make more sense than short, int, and long. Plus, long and int are the same size (4 bytes), so you have to throw in __Int64.

Unlike traditional C++, Managed C++ integer types have predetermined bit sizes. This is probably done to enable future platform independence, which isn't possible with the definition of the integer types provided by traditional C++. With the traditional C++ definition of integer types, there's often confusion about how many bits make up a long. On some platforms it's 32 bits and on others it's 64 bits.

There is nothing complex about declaring integer type variables. Whenever you declare an integer type variable in Managed C++, it is immediately initialized to the value of zero. This differs from traditional C++ compilers, where the initialization is optional and up to the compiler. For traditional C++, it is possible that the value of a variable remains uninitialized and, thus, contains just about any numeric value.

To initialize integer types, you simply declare a variable and assign it a character: octal, decimal, or hexadecimal literal. You will examine literals later in this chapter.

Listing 2-1 is a simple piece of code showing integer types in action.

Listing 2-1. Integer Types in Action

```
#using <mscorlib.dll>
using namespace System;

Int32 main(void)
{
    Byte  w = 'F';              // Initialize using character literal
    Int16 x(123);              // Initializing using Functional Notation
    Int32 y = 456789;          // Decimal literal assigned
    Int64 z = 0x9876543210;    // Hex literal assigned
```

```
Console::WriteLine ( w );     // Write out a Byte
Console::WriteLine ( x );     // Write out a Int16
Console::WriteLine ( y );     // Write out a Int32
Console::WriteLine ( z );     // Write out a Int64
Console::WriteLine ( z.ToString("X") ); // Write out a Int64 in Hex

    return 0;
}
```

Figure 2-2 shows the results of this little program.

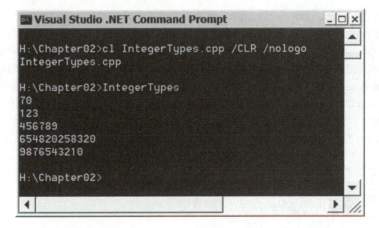

Figure 2-2. Results of IntegerTypes.exe

For those of you from traditional C++ backgrounds, the ToString() appended to the integer variables in the Console::WriteLine() method might be a little confusing. Remember, in Managed C++, integer types are objects and have several methods attached to them, and ToString() happens to be one of them. This is also part of the reason I use the .NET Framework class library name for my declaration instead of the alias, as it serves to remind me of this.

Floating-Point Types

Only two different floating-point types are provided by Managed C++. Table 2-3 describes the details of each.

Table 2-3. Floating-Point Built-in Value Types

C++ ALIAS	CLASS LIBRARY	DESCRIPTION	SIGNIFICANT DIGITS	RANGE
float	System::Single	32-bit single-precision floating point	7	significant digits $\pm 1.5 \times 10^{-45}$ to $\pm 3.4 \times 10^{38}$
double	System::Double	64-bit double-precision floating point	15	significant digits $\pm 5.0 \times 10^{-324}$ to $\pm 1.7 \times 10^{308}$

The .NET Framework class library System::Single is the smaller of the two floating-point types available to Managed C++. It is stored using 32 bits. Its alias for C++ programmers is the better-known float type. Singles can represent numbers from $\pm 1.5 \times 10^{-45}$ to $\pm 3.4 \times 10^{38}$, but only seven of the digits are significant.

The System::Double class library, which is the larger of the two, uses 64 bits of storage. Its alias is double. Doubles can represent numbers from $\pm 5.0 \times 10^{-324}$ to $\pm 1.7 \times 10^{308}$, but only 15 of the digits are significant.

Listing 2-2 is a simple piece of code showing floating-point types in action.

Listing 2-2. Floating-Point Types in Action

```
#using <mscorlib.dll>
using namespace System;

Int32 main(void)
{
    Single w = 123.456f;    // standard decimal notation
    Single x = 7890e3f;     // exponent notation
    Double y = 34525425432525764765.76476476547654; // too big will truncate
    Double z = 123456789012345e-300; // exponent will be reset

    Console::WriteLine ( w ); // Write out Single
    Console::WriteLine ( x ); // Write out Single with more zeros
    Console::WriteLine ( y ); // Write out Double truncated
    Console::WriteLine ( z ); // Write out Double shift back decimal
    return 0;
}
```

Figure 2-3 shows the results of this little program.

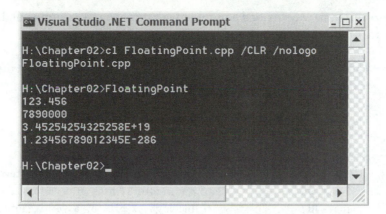

Figure 2-3. Results of FloatingPoint.exe

The .NET Framework class library `Double` is the default value used by most methods that deal with floating-point numbers. You might think `Single` would be a better choice, being small and thus faster. This is true, but other than for division, the speed of `Double` and `Single` operations do not differ much, and the accuracy gained by `Double` usually is more important than the slight difference in speed.

Decimal Type

Only one decimal type is supported by Managed C++. This type has no traditional C++ equivalent and thus has no alias. Table 2-4 describes the decimal type.

Table 2-4. Decimal Built-in Value Type

CLASS LIBRARY	DESCRIPTION	SIGNIFICANT DIGITS	RANGE
System::Decimal	128-bit high-precision decimal notation	28	$\pm 7.9 \times 10^{-28}$ to $\pm 7.9 \times 10^{28}$

This built-in type was designed specifically for financial calculations. Basically, it is a number with 28 significant digits. Within those 28 digits, you can place a decimal. In other words, you can place a very big number in a `System::Decimal` that will have a small fractional area, or you can make a very small number with a very big fractional part.

`System::Decimal`s are not a native C++ data type and, as such, they need a little magic to get them initialized if the number of significant digits you want to capture is larger than 15. The significance of 15 is that it is the number of significant digits provided by a `Double`, the closest data type available to initialize a `Decimal`.

Here are three ways to load a number with more than 15 significant digits (there are other ways, I'm sure):

1. The first method is to load the digits into a String and convert the String to Decimal.

2. The second method is to use the Decimal constructor:

```
public: Decimal(
    Int32 lo,                   // The low 32 bits of a 96-bit integer.
    Int32 mid,                  // The middle 32 bits of a 96-bit integer.
    Int32 hi,                   // The high 32 bits of a 96-bit integer.
    bool isNegative,            // false is positive
    unsigned char scale         // A power of 10 ranging from 0 to 28.
);
```

3. The third method is to add two Doubles together using the combined significant digits of both to make up the Decimal.

All three of these methods are shown in Listing 2-3. Also, for grins and giggles, I decided to use the Decimal method GetBits() to break the Decimal into its parts and then use the constructor to put it back together again.

Listing 2-3. Decimal Types in Action

```
#using <mscorlib.dll>
using namespace System;

Int32 main(void)
{
    Decimal w = System::Convert::ToDecimal(S"123456789012345678901.2345678");
    Console::WriteLine( w );

    Decimal x = 0.12345678901234567890123456778;       // will get truncated
    Decimal y = 0.00000000000000000789012345678;        // works fine

    Console::WriteLine ( x.ToString() );
    Console::WriteLine ( y.ToString() );

    // Decimal constructor
    Decimal z(0xeb1f0ad2, 0xab54a98c, 0, false, 0); // = 12345678901234567890
    Console::WriteLine ( z.ToString() );
```

```
// Create a 28 significant digit number
Decimal a = 123456789012345000000.00000000;
Decimal b = 678901.23456780;
Decimal c = -(a + b);

// Break it up into 4 parts
Int32 d[] = Decimal::GetBits(c);

// Reassemble using Decimal constructor
Decimal e(d[0], d[1], d[2],                       // digits
         ((d[3] & 0x80000000) == 0x80000000), // sign
         ((d[3] >> 16) & 0xff) );                // decimal location

Console::WriteLine ( c.ToString() );        // display pre broken Decimal
Console::WriteLine ( d[0].ToString() );     // display part 1
Console::WriteLine ( d[1].ToString() );     // display part 2
Console::WriteLine ( d[2].ToString() );     // display part 3
Console::WriteLine ( d[3].ToString("X") ); // display part 4 in hex
Console::WriteLine ( e.ToString() );         // display reassembled Decimal
return 0;
}
```

Figure 2-4 shows the results of this program.

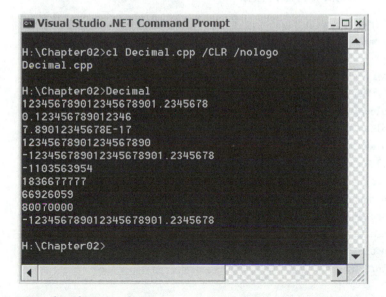

Figure 2-4. Results of Decimal.exe

Even though the Decimal type was designed for financial calculations, there's nothing stopping you from using it for other calculations where the number of significant digits is important and you'd rather have an exception than a rounding during calculation.

Boolean Type

Only one Boolean type is provided by Managed C++. Table 2-5 describes the details of it.

Table 2-5. Boolean Built-in Value Type

C++ ALIAS	CLASS LIBRARY	VALUES
bool	System::Boolean	true|not 0 or false|0

The System::Boolean built-in value type has the Managed C++ alias of bool. Booleans can only have a value of true or false.

Managed C++ is a little lenient when it comes to initializing Booleans, as it allows them to be assigned with the value of zero for false and any number other than zero for true. The compiler does give a warning if the value assigned is not one of the following: true, false, 1, or 0.

Listing 2-4 is a simple piece of code showing the Boolean type in action.

Listing 2-4. Boolean Type in Action

```
#using <mscorlib.dll>
using namespace System;

Int32 main(void)
{
    Boolean a = 18757;    // will give a warning but sets it to true
    Boolean b = 0;        // false
    Boolean c = true;     // obviously true
    Boolean d = false;    // obviously false

    Console::WriteLine ( a );
    Console::WriteLine ( b );
    Console::WriteLine ( c );
    Console::WriteLine ( d );
    return 0;
}
```

Figure 2-5 shows the results of this little program.

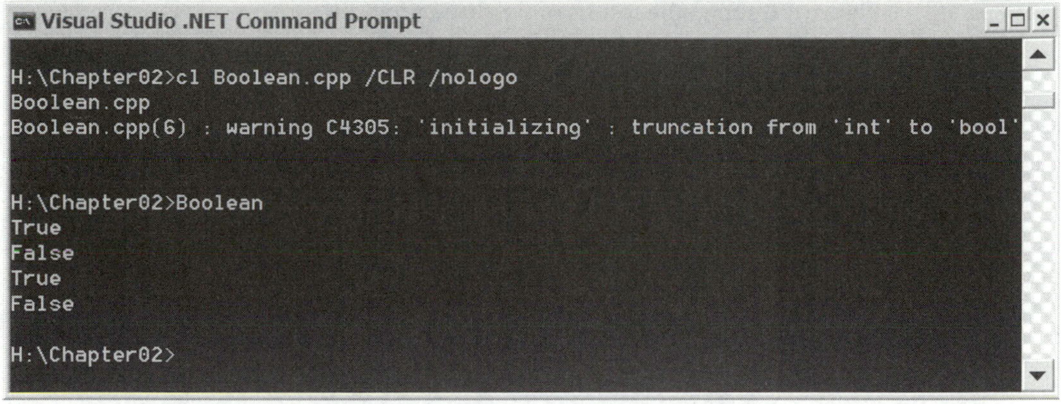

```
Visual Studio .NET Command Prompt                              _ □ ×

H:\Chapter02>cl Boolean.cpp /CLR /nologo
Boolean.cpp
Boolean.cpp(6) : warning C4305: 'initializing' : truncation from 'int' to 'bool'


H:\Chapter02>Boolean
True
False
True
False

H:\Chapter02>
```

Figure 2-5. Results of Boolean.exe

Character Type

Only one character type is provided by Managed C++. Table 2-6 describes the details of this character type.

Table 2-6. Character Built-in Value Type

C++ ALIAS	CLASS LIBRARY	VALUE
wchar_t	System::Char	A single 16-bit Unicode character

The .NET Framework class library System::Char is a 16-bit Unicode character, which has a Managed C++ alias of __wchar_t (or wchar_t, if the Zc:wchar_t flag is set on the compiler).

Listing 2-5 is a simple piece of code showing the Char type in action.

Listing 2-5. Char Type in Action

```
#using <mscorlib.dll>
using namespace System;

Int32 main(void)
{
    Char a = L'A';          // character literal 'A'
    Char b = L'\x0041';     // Unicode notation also an 'A'

    Console::WriteLine ( a.ToString() );
    Console::WriteLine ( b.ToString() );
    return 0;
}
```

Figure 2-6 shows the results of this little program.

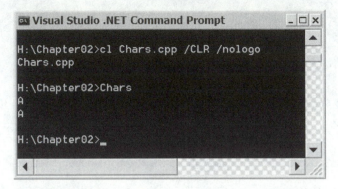

Figure 2-6. Results of Chars.exe

Not long ago, all Windows programs used ASCII, an 8-bit, English-only character set. Unfortunately, this was not very helpful for languages such as Chinese, which requires more than the 256-character limit imposed by ASCII. To try to solve this obvious problem, a new encoding protocol was developed called *Unicode*, within which many character sets could be defined. Unicode uses 16 bits to represent each character instead of ASCII's 8. ASCII is a subset of Unicode.

 CAUTION   *Traditional C++ programmers must be wary of the C++ alias* char, *as it is not the same as the .NET Framework's class library* Char. *A* char *is an 8-bit ASCII character, whereas a* Char *is a 16-bit Unicode character.*

Reference Types

As a Managed C++ programmer, you can think of reference types as pointers that you can't manipulate the address of and don't have to worry about deleting. In other languages such as C#, there are no such things as pointers, or so we're told. This isn't entirely true. The fact is, references are pointers. It's just that the syntax of the language (C# in this case) doesn't allow you to manipulate a reference as you can a pointer.

Managed C++ also restricts pointer manipulation for reference types. In other words, pointer arithmetic is illegal for references. This doesn't mean you can't do pointer arithmetic on regular nonreference pointers if you need to, though.

All Managed C++ developers will deal with two predefined reference types. One is the `Object` type, the root of all classes in the .NET Framework class library. The other is the `String` type.

Object Type

The `System::Object` is the root type of the entire .NET Framework class library hierarchy. In other words, every object found in the .NET Framework ultimately has, as a parent, the `Object` type.

Because all objects in the .NET Framework derive from `System::Object`, all objects inherit several general-purpose methods, such as

- `Object()`: A constructor that creates a new instance of an object

- `Equals()`: Compares two object instances to see if they are equal

- `GetHashCode()`: Returns a hash code for the object

- `GetType()`: Returns the data type of the object

- `ReferenceEquals()`: Checks if two instances of an object are the same

- `ToString()`: Returns a string representation of the object

A developer can replace a few of these methods. For example, replacing `ToString()` allows an object to represent itself in a user-readable fashion.

String Type

As a Managed C++ programmer, you will probably become very intimate with `System::String`. Many of your programs will involve character strings. The `String` type was built to handle them. Traditional C++ programmers should forget character arrays—you now have a powerful, predefined built-in data type to work with. Plus, it is completely garbage collected. In other words, no more memory leaks due to working with strings.

Being a reference type, strings are allocated to the heap and referenced using a pointer. `String` types are also immutable, meaning their value cannot be modified once they have been created. This combination allows for the optimized capability of multiple String objects representing the same character string to reference the same heap location. When a `String` object changes, a completely new character string is allocated to the heap and, if the original String object was not referenced by any other String object, it will be garbage collected.

Listing 2-6 is a little program showing the String type in action.

Listing 2-6. String Type in Action

```
#using <mscorlib.dll>
using namespace System;

Int32 main(void)
{
    // Create some strings
    String *s1 = S"This will ";
    String *s2 = S"be a ";
    String *s3 = S"String";
    Console::WriteLine(String::Concat(s1, s2, s3));

    // Create a copy, then concatenate new text
    String *s4 = s2;
    s4 = String::Concat(s4, S"new ");
    Console::WriteLine(String::Concat(s1, s4, s3));

    // Replace stuff in a concatenated string
    String *s5 = String::Concat(s1, s2, s3)->Replace(S"i", S"*");
    Console::WriteLine(s5);

    // Insert into a string
    String *s6 = s3->Insert(2, S"range St");
    Console::WriteLine(String::Concat(s1, s2, s6));

    // Remove text from strings
    s1 = s1->Remove(4, 5);  // remove from middle and overwriting
    s2 = s2->Remove(0, 3);  // remove from start and overwriting
    Console::WriteLine(String::Concat(s1, S"is ", s2, s3));

    return 0;
}
```

Figure 2-7 shows the results of this little program.

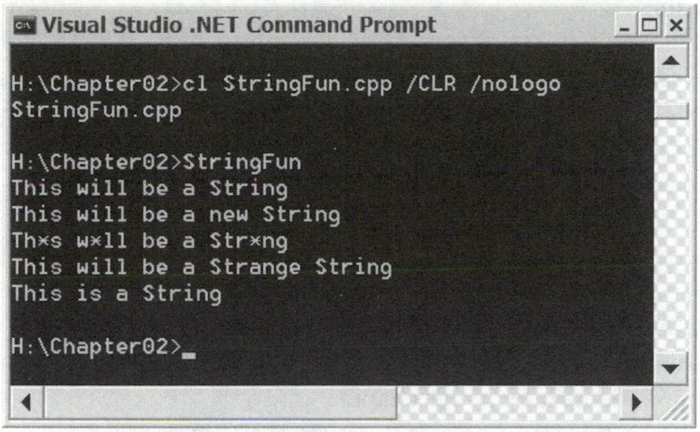

Figure 2-7. Results of StringFun.exe

User-Defined Data Types

With Managed C++, you can create your own data types. Like predefined data types, user-defined data types fall into two groups: value types or reference types. As I pointed out earlier, value types are placed directly on the stack, whereas reference types are placed on the heap and referenced via the stack.

Value Types

Only three kinds of user-defined value types can be created using Managed C++:

- __value enum

- __value struct

- __value class

The __value enum type is simply a named constant. The __value struct and __value class types are identical, except that the default access __value struct members are public, whereas __value class members are private.

__value enum

Enums are really nothing more than a programmer's tool for making source code more self-descriptive. Basically, enums allow the programmer to group common words together and use them instead of numeric literals. Personally, I think reading code that has descriptive enums as opposed to a bunch of numbers is much easier. So, I use enums. But hey, it's your code.

Like the built-in value types already discussed, enums default to being placed on the stack but will, in fact, become true objects when boxed. Unlike the built-in value types, which will on many occasions do the boxing for you, you must manually box the enum whenever it is to be accessed as an object. I cover boxing in more detail later in this chapter.

The following example creates an enum of all the primary colors. Then the function prints the string equivalent of the primary color enum using a `switch` statement. You will look at the `switch` statement later in this chapter.

The `System::Object` from which enums are derived provides a simpler way of doing this exact same thing. The `ToString()` method for enums prints out the enum name as a character string.

Listing 2-7 is a little program showing enums in action.

Listing 2-7. Enums in Action

```
#using <mscorlib.dll>
using namespace System;

__value enum PrimeColors { Red, Blue, Yellow };

Int32 main(void)
{
    PrimeColors color;

    color = PrimeColors::Blue;

    switch (color)  // Old way
    {
        case PrimeColors::Red :
            Console::WriteLine(S"Red");
            break;
        case PrimeColors::Blue :
            Console::WriteLine(S"Blue");
            break;
```

```
        case PrimeColors::Yellow :
            Console::WriteLine(S"Yellow");
            break;
    }

    Console::WriteLine(__box(color)->ToString()); // New way

    return 0;
}
```

Figure 2-8 shows the results of this program.

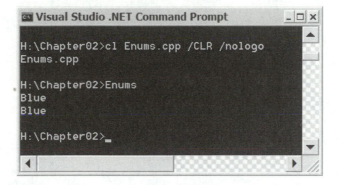

Figure 2-8. Results of Enums.exe

__value struct

The __value struct type is very similar to the class type, which I cover briefly later in this chapter and in detail in Chapter 3. Basically, a struct (without the __value) is a way of combining data types and methods into one unit and placing it onto the heap.

With Managed C++, programmers now have the ability to move a struct from the heap and place it on the stack. Using the keyword __value in front of the keyword struct does this. Being on the stack, a struct can be created and copied a little more efficiently than the class, which has to deal with heap memory management.

The __value struct is Managed C++'s way of providing programmers with a method of creating their own value types, thus allowing for expansion beyond the basic built-in value types.

All __value structs are derived from the .NET Framework class library's System::ValueType, which allows for the __value struct's ability to be placed on the stack. A __value struct can inherit from only interfaces, and no class or struct can inherit from a __value struct.

Listing 2-8 is a simple example of a __value struct called Coord3D. It is made up of three Doubles and a constructor, and it overrides the ToString() method. You will look at constructors and overriding in Chapter 3. The main() function creates the two copies of Coord3D on the stack, one using the default constructor and the other using the one user-defined constructor. Notice that to assign a __value struct to another, you simply use the equal sign (=).

Listing 2-8. Struct in Action

```
#using <mscorlib.dll>
using namespace System;

__value struct Coord3D
{
    Double x;
    Double y;
    Double z;

    Coord3D (Double x, Double y, Double z)
    {
        this->x = x;
        this->y = y;
        this->z = z;
    }

    String *ToString()
    {
        return String::Format(S"{0},{1},{2}", x.ToString(), y.ToString(),
                                            z.ToString());
    }
};

int main(void)
{
    Coord3D coordA;
    Coord3D coordB(1,2,3);

    coordA = coordB;   // Assign is simply an =
```

```
coordA.x += 5.5;   // Operations work just like usual
coordA.y *= 2.7;
coordA.z /= 1.3;

Console::WriteLine(coordB.ToString());
Console::WriteLine(coordA.x);
Console::WriteLine(coordA.y);
Console::WriteLine(coordA.z);

return 0;
}
```

Figure 2-9 shows the results of this program.

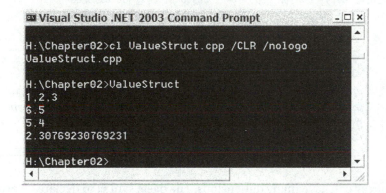

Figure 2-9. Results of ValueStruct.exe

Reference Types

User-defined reference types are basically data types a programmer develops that are accessed using their address, and where the actual data object is located on the heap. All reference types in Managed C++ can be defined so that they are garbage collected.

Managed C++ provides four kinds of user-defined reference types: arrays, classes, interfaces, and delegates.

Arrays

Arrays, like all other data types in Managed C++, are objects, unlike their traditional C++ counterparts, which are simply pointers into heap memory. In fact, the only resemblance between a Managed C++ and a traditional C++ array is its single-dimension syntax.

All Managed C++ arrays are garbage collected. Also, they can be made up of any data type that derives from System::Object. If you recall, that is every data type in the .NET Framework class library.

Managed C++ arrays have specific dimensions which, when violated, will generate an exception. All arrays are derived from a System::Array object, which provides them with many helpful methods and properties, in particular the Count property for single-dimension arrays and the GetLength() method for single- or multidimensional arrays. Both of these provide the dimensions of the array.

There are no stack base declarations of Managed C++ arrays using subscripts, like in traditional C++. All Managed C++ arrays are references and created on the heap. For example, the following code will generate an error:

```
Int32 errorArray[5];    // Oops stack based arrays not allowed
```

 NOTE   *It is still possible to create stack-based declarations of unmanaged C++ arrays, just as you would in traditional C++, as that syntax is still available to you. But then you lose all the benefits of Managed C++ development.*

An array can have many dimensions. The basic syntax to declare an array is as follows:

```
data-type array-name[,,,];
Int32 array4dim[3,4,5,6];
```

where the number of commas determines the number of dimensions or, basically, the number of commas plus one.

In the case of a single-dimensional array, no commas are placed between the square brackets:

```
data-type array-name[];
Int32 array1dim[];
```

To initialize an array, you need to use the new keyword because the array will be allocated to the heap. Follow the new keyword with the data type and then give the array dimensions within square brackets:

```
Int32 a[] = new Int32[5];
String d[,] = new String*[4,3];
```

Unlike traditional C++, subscripting is not a synonym for pointer arithmetic, and it is not commutative. Thus, the only way to access data from an array is by using subscripts with all dimensions starting at a value of zero.

Two very helpful static methods of the System::Array are Sort() and Reverse(), which provide quick ways to sort and reverse the order of the elements in an array. Reverse() is shown in the following example.

Listing 2-9 is a program showing Managed C++ arrays in action.

Listing 2-9. Managed C++ Arrays in Action

```
#using <mscorlib.dll>
using namespace System;

Int32 main(void)
{
    // Single dimension
    Int32 a[] = new Int32[5];
    String *b[] = new String*[5];

    // Initializing an array with incrementing numbers
    for (Int32 i = 0; i < a->Count; i++)
    {
        a[i] = i;
    }

    // Initializing an array with incrementing number strings
    for (Int32 i = 0; i < b->Count; i++)
    {
        b[i] = a[i].ToString();
    }

    // Write out the array
    for (Int32 i = 0; i < b->Count; i++)
    {
        Console::WriteLine(b[i]);
    }

    // Reverse the order of the array and write it out
    Console::WriteLine(S"");  // Separate to make easier to read
    Array::Reverse(b);        // reverse the array order
    for (Int32 i = 0; i < b->Count; i++)
```

```
        {
            Console::WriteLine(b[i]);
        }

    // Multi dimension
    Int32 c[,] = new Int32[4,3];

    // Initialize the array so that the 10s digit is the x column value
    // and the 1s digit is the y value
    for (Int32 x = 0; x < c->GetLength(0); x++)
    {
        for (Int32 y = 0; y < c->GetLength(1); y++)
        {
            c[x,y] = (x*10)+y;
        }
    }

    // Write out the 2 dimensional array
    Console::WriteLine(S"");   // Separate to make easier to read
    for (Int32 x = 0; x < d->GetLength(0); x++)
    {
        for (Int32 y = 0; y < d->GetLength(1); y++)
        {
            Console::Write(c[x,y]);
            Console::Write(S"\t");
        }
        Console::WriteLine();
    }

    return 0;
}
```

Figure 2-10 shows the results of this little program.

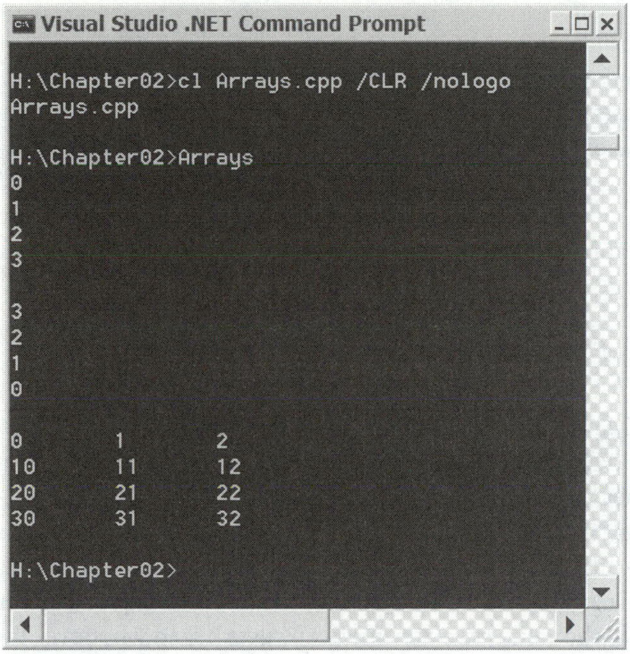

Figure 2-10. Results of Arrays.exe

Classes

A *class* is a fundamental building block of most Managed C++ programs. Classes are made up of data members, properties, and methods. Basically, classes are designed to provide the object-oriented nature of the Managed C++ programming language. In other words, they provide encapsulation, inheritance, and polymorphism.

Chapter 3 covers classes in great detail.

Interfaces

An *interface* is a collection of methods and properties, without actual definitions, placed into a single unit. In other words, an interface has no implementations for its own methods and properties. You might want to think of an interface as a binding contract of all the methods and properties that an inheriting class must provide.

Chapter 3 covers interfaces.

Delegates

A *delegate* is a reference type that acts as a "function pointer" that can be bound to either an instance or a static method within a Managed C++ class. Delegates can be used whenever a method needs to be called in a dynamic nature, and they are usually used as callback functions or for handling events within .NET Framework applications.

You will examine delegates in Chapter 4.

Boxing and Unboxing

Boxing is the Managed C++ technique for converting value types into reference types. And, conversely, *unboxing* is the technique for converting reference types into value types.

The default form of storage for the .NET Framework built-in value types is on the stack, as a simple value. In this form, a data type cannot access its methods, such as `ToString()`, as the value type needs to be in an object (reference) format. To remedy this, the value type automatically gets boxed whenever the `ToString()` method is called. For example, the following two lines are equivalent for all built-in value types:

```
__box(x)->ToString();
x.ToString();
```

This boxing is more apparent in user-defined value types, as this automatic conversion does not take place and the programmer has to do it manually. For user-defined value types, only the previous manually boxed version is allowed. The other one generates an error.

 CAUTION   *The created boxed object is a copy of the value type. Therefore, any modifications made to the boxed object will not be reflected in the contents of the value type.*

It is possible to create a boxed reference by placing the prefix __box in front of the data type:

```
__box Int32 *bx;
```

Unboxing a reference type back into its value type simply requires a type cast. Personally, I've never had a reason to do this. I cover type casting later in this chapter.

```
bx = __box(x);                          // Boxing
Int32 y  = static_cast<Int32>(*bx);   // Unboxing
```

Type Modifiers and Qualifiers

Three modifiers and one data type qualifier are provided to Managed C++ programmers. Basically, they provide a little information to help define the variables they precede.

auto

This modifier tells the compiler that it should create the variable when entering a block and destroy it when exiting the block. If this sounds like most variables to you, you would be right, as it is the default modifier for all variables. Placing the auto keyword in front of variables is optional. In fact, I have never seen it used myself, but if you like typing, here is how you would use it in a program:

```
auto Int32 normalInteger;
```

const

The const qualifier tells the compiler that the variable that it is associated with cannot change during execution. It also means that objects pointed to by a const pointer cannot be changed. Basically, constants are the opposite of variables. The syntax to create a const data type is simply this:

```
const Int32 integerConstant = 42;
```

Note that you need to initialize a const at the time of declaration.

CAUTION   *Managed C++ does not support* const *member methods on managed data types. For example,* Boolean GetFlag() const {} *is not allowed within a* __value struct *or* class *and thus by default an interface.*

extern

The extern modifier tells the compiler that the variable is defined elsewhere, usually in a different file, and will be added in when the final executable or library is linked together. It tells the compiler how to define a variable without actually allocating any storage for it. You will see this variable modifier usually when a global variable is used in more than one source file (I discuss this later in the chapter).

NOTE   *An error will occur during the linking of the application if an external variable is not defined in some other source file.*

Using the extern modifier looks like this:

```
extern Int32 externVariable;
```

static

The static modifier has four meanings based on where it is used.

When the static modifier is applied to a global variable, the variable's global nature is restricted to the source file in which it is declared. In other words, the variable is accessible to all functions, classes, and so on declared within the file, but an extern variable or class in another source file will not have access to it.

When the static modifier is applied to a variable within a function (I cover functions later in the chapter), then the variable will not go out of scope or be deleted when the function exits. This means that the next time the function is called, the static variable will retain the same value it had when the function was left the previous time.

When the static modifier is applied to a variable within a class (I discuss classes in Chapter 3), then only one copy of the variable is created, and it is shared by all instances of the class.

When the static modifier is applied to a method within a class, then the method is accessible without the need to instantiate the class.

Here are some basic examples of the static modifier in use:

```
static Int32 staticVariable;
static void staticFunction ( Int32 arg) { }
```

Type Conversions

Any time the data type on the left side of an assignment statement has a different data type than the evaluated result of the right side, a type conversion will take place. When the only data types used in the statement are built-in value types, then the conversion will happen automatically. Unfortunately, converting automatically may not always be a good thing, especially if the left side data type is smaller, as the resulting number may lose significant digits. For example, when assigning a UInt16 to a Byte, the following problem may occur:

```
UInt16 a = 43690;
Byte b = a;      //  b now equals 170 not 43690.
```

Here is what happened. UInt16 is a 16-bit number, so 43690 decimal represented as a 16-bit number is 1010 1010 1010 1010 in binary. Byte is an 8-bit number, so only the last 8 bits of the UInt16 can be placed into the Byte. Thus, the Byte now contains 1010 1010 in binary, which happens to only equal 170 decimal.

The Managed C++ compiler will notify you when this type of error may occur. Being warned, the compiler and, subsequently, the program it generates go merrily on their way.

If you don't want the warning, but you still want to do this type of conversion, then you can do something called an *explicit cast*. Basically, it's the programmer's way of saying "Yes, I know, but I don't care." To code an explicit cast, you use the following syntax:

```
static_cast<data-type-to-convert-to>(expression)
Byte b = static_cast<Byte>(a);
```

In Managed C++, when resolving an expression, all data types that make up the expression must be the same. If the expression is made up of more than one type, then type conversion occurs to make all the data types the same. Basically, if all the data types are integer types, then the data types get converted to an Int32 or Int64 data type. If a data type is float, then all get converted to a Single or Double.

All these types of conversions happen automatically. There are cases, though, where you may want all data types to be converted to a data type of your choosing. Here again, you use explicit casting, as shown here:

```
Double realA = 23.67;
Double realB = 877.12;
Int32 intTotal = static_cast<Int32>(realA) + static_cast<Int32>(realB);
```

Variable Scope

There are basically two different scopes: global and local. There are subtleties that might bend these scopes a bit, but they're something most programmers don't care about.

Global scope for a variable means that it is declared outside of all functions, classes, and structures that make up a program, even the main() functions. They are created when the program is started and exist for the entire lifetime of the program. All functions, classes, and structures can access global variables. The static modifier has the capability to restrict a global variable to only the source file in which it is declared.

Local variables are local to the block of code that they are declared in. This means that local variables exist within the opening and closing curly brackets within which they were declared. Most commonly, local variables are declared within a function call, but it is perfectly acceptable to declare them within flow control and looping constructs, which you will learn about later in this chapter. It is also valid to create a block of code only to reduce the scope of a variable.

The following code shows some global and local variable declarations:

```
Int32 globalVar;
Int32 main()
{
    Int32 localFunctionVar;
    { Int32 localToOwnBlock; }
}
```

Namespaces

Some programmers program in an isolated world where their code is the only code. Others use code from many sources. A problem with using code from many sources is that there is a very real possibility that the same names for classes, functions, and so on, can be used by more than one source.

To allow for the same names to be used by multiple sources, namespaces were created. *Namespaces* create a local scope declarative region for variables, functions, classes, and structures. In other words, namespaces allow programmers to group their code under a unique name.

Creating a namespace simply requires combining all of the code within a named region, such as

```
namespace MyNamespace
{
    // classes, structs, functions, namespace-global variables
}
```

It is possible to use the same namespace across multiple source code files. The compiler will combine them into one namespace.

To reference something out of a namespace requires the use of the :: operator. For example:

```
MyNamespace::NSfunc();
```

Typing the namespace repeatedly can get very tiring, so Managed C++ allows the programmer to bring a namespace into the local scope using

```
using namespace MyNamespace;
```

Now, with the namespace brought into local scope, the function NSfunc from the previous example can be accessed just like any other function of local scope:

```
NSfunc();
```

 CAUTION *Bringing multiple namespaces into the local scope could cause duplicate function, class, and* struct *names to occur.*

Literals

Other than Decimals, each of the preceding data types has literals that can be used for things such as initializing variables or as constants. In the preceding programs, I have shown many different literals. In this section, I go over them in more detail.

Numeric Literals

Numeric literals come in five flavors:

- Octal numbers

- Integer numbers

- Hexadecimal numbers

- Decimal numbers

- Exponential numbers

Octal numbers are hardly ever used anymore. They mainly are sticking around just for backward compatibility with some ancient programs. They are base-8 numbers and thus made up of the numbers 0 through 7. All octal numbers start with a 0. Some examples are as follows:

0123 (an integer value of 83)   01010 (an integer value of 520)

You need to be aware of octal numbers because if you mistakenly start an integer number with a 0, then the compiler will happily treat it as an octal number. For example, if you type in **0246**, the compiler will think its value is equivalent to the integer value 166.

Integer numbers are straightforward. They are simply whole numbers. Some examples are as follows:

1234   −1234   +1234

The symbols − and + are not actually part of the number but, in fact, are unary operators that convert the whole number into a negative or positive number. The + unary operator is assumed, so 1234 and +1234 mean the same thing.

Hexadecimal numbers are the most complex of the numeric constants. They are base-16 numbers and are made up of the numbers 0 through 9 and the letters A through F (or a through f, as case does not matter). The letters represent the numbers 10 through 15. A hexadecimal literal always starts with "0x". Some examples of hexadecimal numbers are as follows:

0x1234 (an integer value of 4660) 0xabcd (an integer value of 43981)

Decimal numbers are the same as integer numbers, except they also contain a decimal and a fractional portion. They are used to represent real numbers. Some examples are as follows:

1.0   3.1415   −1.23

Just like integer numbers, the minus symbol (−) is a unary operator and not part of the decimal number.

The last numeric literals are the exponential numbers. They are similar to decimal numbers except that along with the decimal—or more accurately, the *mantissa*—is the exponent, which tells the compiler how many times to multiply or divide the mantissa by 10. When the exponent is positive, the mantissa is multiplied by ten exponent times. If the exponent is negative, the mantissa is divided by ten exponent times. Some examples are as follows:

1.23e4 (a decimal value of 12300.0)   1.23e-4 (a decimal value of 0.000123)

An interesting feature that comes along with Managed C++ is that numeric literals are also objects. This means that they also have the `ToString()` method. Listing 2-10 shows a numeric literal object in action. Note that you need to surround the numeric literal with brackets.

Listing 2-10. Numeric Literals in Action

```
#using <mscorlib.dll>
using namespace System;

Int32 main(void)
{
    Console::WriteLine (  010 );  // An Octal 10 is a base-10 8
    Console::WriteLine ( -010 ); // Negative Octal 10 is a base-10 -8

    Console::WriteLine (  0x10 ); // A Hex 10 is a base-10 16
    Console::WriteLine ( -0x10 ); // Negative Hex 10 is a base-10 -16

    // This is kind of neat. Number literals are objects too!
    Console::WriteLine ( (1234567890).ToString() );
    Console::WriteLine ( (0xABCDEF).ToString("X") );

    return 0;
}
```

Figure 2-11 shows the results of this little program.

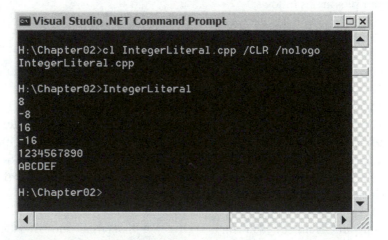

Figure 2-11. Results of IntegerLiteral.exe

Boolean Literals

There are only two boolean literals: the values `true` and `false`.

Like numeric literals, *boolean literals* are objects in Managed C++. Thus, they too provide the `ToString()` method. Listing 2-11 shows a boolean literal object in action.

Listing 2-11. Boolean Literals in Action

```
#using <mscorlib.dll>
using namespace System;

Int32 main(void)
{
    // This is kind of neat. Boolean literals are objects too!
    Console::WriteLine ( true.ToString () );
    Console::WriteLine ( false.ToString () );
    return 0;
}
```

Figure 2-12 shows the results of this little program.

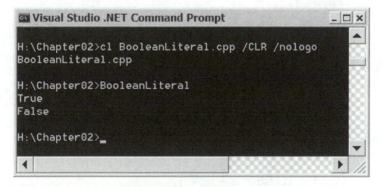

Figure 2-12. Results of BooleanLiteral.exe

Character Literals

Managed C++ provides two different types of character literals:

- Character

- Escape sequence

Character literals are the most basic form and are simply a printable letter, number, or symbol enclosed in single quotes. These literals can be placed in both Byte types (or any other integer type, for that matter) and Char types. Here are a few examples:

```
'A'      '0'      '+'
```

Escape sequences are a little more elaborate and come in a few flavors. Like the character literal form, escape sequences are placed within single quotes. The first character within the quotes is always a backslash (\). After the backslash will be a character such as the ones shown in Table 2-7, an octal number, or an *x* followed by a hexadecimal number. The octal or hexadecimal numbers are the numeric equivalent of the character you want the literal to represent.

Table 2-7. Special Escape Sequences

ESCAPE SEQUENCE	CHARACTER
\?	Question mark
\'	Single quote
\"	Double quote
\\	Backslash
\0	Null
\a	Bell or alert
\b	Backspace
\f	Form feed
\n	New line
\r	Carriage return
\t	Tab
\v	Vertical tab

All the character literal types can be prefixed with the letter *L* to tell the compiler to create a Unicode equivalent of the character literal. Remember that Unicode characters are 16 bits, so they will not fit in Byte types; instead, they should be placed in Char types.

Listing 2-12 is a program showing character literals in action.

Listing 2-12. Character Literals in Action

```cpp
#using <mscorlib.dll>
using namespace System;

Int32 main(void)
{
    Byte a = 'a';          // character 'a'
    Char b = L'b';         // Unicode 'b'

    Byte t = '\t';         // tab escape
    Char s = L'\\';        // Unicode backslash escape

    Byte d = '\45';        // octal escape
    Char e = L'\x0045';    // Unicode hexadecimal escape

    Console::WriteLine ( a ); // displays numeric equiv of 'A'
    Console::WriteLine ( b ); // displays the letter 'b'
    Console::WriteLine ( t ); // displays numeric equiv of tab
    Console::WriteLine ( s ); // displays backslash
    Console::WriteLine ( d ); // displays integer equiv of octal 45
    Console::WriteLine ( e ); // displays the letter 'e'
    return 0;
}
```

Figure 2-13 shows the results of this little program.

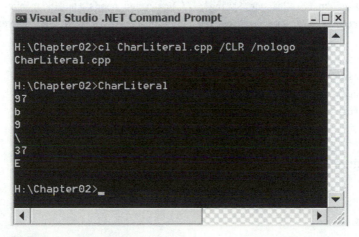

Figure 2-13. Results of CharLiteral.exe

String Literals

Managed *string literals* are simply character strings enclosed in double quotes and prefixed by the letter *S*.

You can also create literal strings without a prefix, creating an unmanaged string literal or, when you prefix with the letter *L*, creating an unmanaged Unicode string literal. Both of these will work with Managed C++ but suffer in performance, as they have to get converted at runtime to managed Strings before they can be used with the String type.

By the way, the escape sequences shown previously also work within Strings. You must be careful to avoid too many characters after the backslash being taken as the escape sequence. Realistic examples of this are difficult with the Latin alphabet, but this illustrates the point:

```
String *s1 = S"\x61";  // a
String *s2 = S"\x611"; // is NOT a1 but a Unicode hexadecimal escape of 611
```

Listing 2-13 is a program showing string literals in action.

Listing 2-13. String Literals in Action

```
#using <mscorlib.dll>
using namespace System;

Int32 main(void)
{
    String *a = S"Managed String"; // The preferred String Literal for Managed
C++
    String *b = L"Unicode String"; // Unmanaged needs runtime conversion
    String *c =  "Unmanaged String"; // Unmanaged need runtime conversion

    Console::WriteLine(a);
    Console::WriteLine(b);
    Console::WriteLine(c);
    return 0;
}
```

Figure 2-14 shows the results of this little program.

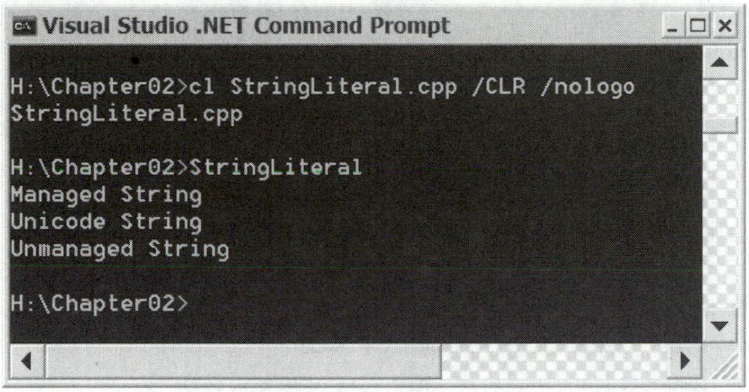

Figure 2-14. Results of StringLiteral.exe

Comments

Documenting programs is a very important practice all software developers should do, no matter what programming language they use. Unfortunately, documentation is often the first thing to suffer when a project is crunched for time.

If you are the only developer for a program, you might think that because you wrote the program, you should have no problem remembering how the program works. From experience, leaving a piece of code and coming back to it a year or more later is nearly equivalent to reading someone else's code, unless of course it is documented.

Managed C++, like traditional C++, provides two comment styles: the single-line comment and the multiline comment.

The single-line comment begins with a double slash (//). Anything after the double slash is a comment. Depending on where you place the double slash, you can use a single-line comment to comment an entire line or just part of a line. By the way, you probably noticed the comments in the previous example code, but here are a couple more examples:

```
// This entire line is a comment.
Int32 x = 0;    // This comment uses part of the line.
```

The multiline comment starts with /* and ends with */. You can place multiline comments anywhere in the code, even on different lines. You must use care with this kind of comment, as embedding a multiline comment within a multiline comment will cause errors. Here are some multiline comments:

```
/*****************************************************
 * Common comment box. You will see these frequently *
 * within programs.                                  *
 *****************************************************/

Int32 x = 0;  /*  This is a comment on a single line */
Int32 y = 0;  /*  This is a comment that stretched for
                  More than one line */
/* Embedded comments like this /* do not work
   as you  might expect */ this portion would
   not be commented and will in this case cause errors */
```

Because of the embedded comment problem, many programmers, myself
included, prefer to use the double slash comment.

Operators

Managed C++ and traditional C++ are identical when it comes to operators. If you
have programmed before in C++, then you should find nothing new in this section,
but it might serve as a bit of a refresher. For anyone else reading this book, this section is essential because it shows all the basic operations available to a Managed
C++ programmer.

Arithmetic Operators

Arithmetic operators are used to perform arithmetic operations on integer, floating-
point, and decimal data types. Seven arithmetic operations are available, as shown
in Table 2-8.

Table 2-8. Arithmetic Operators

OPERATOR	ACTION
-	Subtraction or unary minus
+	Addition
*	Multiplication
/	Division
%	Modulus
--	Decrement
++	Increment

The -, +, *, and / operators perform exactly as expected. The % operator evaluates to the remainder of a division operation. The -- and ++ operators decrease and increase the operand by one, respectively. You can place the -- and ++ operators before the operand, and in this way, the increment or decrement happens before any other operations take place in the expression. You can also place them after the operand, and in this case, the increment or decrement happens after all operations in the expression.

When an expression contains more than one arithmetic operator, the arithmetic operators will get evaluated according to the precedence shown in Table 2-9. If two operators of the same precedence occur in the expression, then they are evaluated from left to right.

Table 2-9. Arithmetic Precedence

PRECEDENCE	OPERATORS
Highest	-- ++ - (unary minus)
	* / %
Lowest	- +

Comparisons and Logical Operators

Comparison operators are used to compare two expressions and then generate a Boolean value (true/false) based on the result of the comparison. There are six comparison operators, as shown in Table 2-10.

Table 2-10. Comparison Operators

OPERATOR	MEANING
>	Greater than
>=	Greater than or equal to
<	Less than
<=	Less than or equal to
==	Equal to
!=	Not equal to

Logical operators are similar to comparison operators except that they compare Boolean values instead of expressions. The three logical operators are shown in Table 2-11.

Table 2-11. Logical Operators

OPERATOR	MEANING
!	NOT: If the operand was true, then false is evaluated or vice versa.
&&	AND: If both operands are true, then evaluate to true; otherwise, evaluate to false.
||	OR: If either or both operands are true, then evaluate to true; otherwise, evaluate to false.

Often, you will find both a comparison and a logical operator in the same comparison statement. For grins and giggles, figure out what this means:

```
a < b && c >= d || !e
```

 CAUTION   *Be very careful when using the assignment operator = and the equal to operator ==. When you mistakenly use = for the comparison operator, the left value gets overwritten by the right and, if the left value is nonzero, then the comparison will have a true result. This is unlikely to be what you want.*

When a statement contains more than one comparison or logical operator, then they will get evaluated according to the precedence shown in Table 2-12. If two operators of the same precedence occur in the expression, then they are evaluated from left to right.

Table 2-12. Comparison and Logical Operator Precedence

PRECEDENCE	OPERATORS
Highest	!
	> >= < <=
	== !=
	&&
Lowest	||

Bitwise Operators

The *bitwise operators* are used to manipulate the bits of an integer type value. There are six bitwise operators, as shown in Table 2-13.

Table 2-13. Bitwise Operators

OPERATOR	ACTION
&	Bitwise AND
|	Bitwise OR
^	Bitwise XOR
~	Ones complement
>>	Right shift
<<	Left shift

The bitwise AND operator compares the bit pattern of its two operands. If both the bits at the same offset in the bit pattern are 1s, then the resulting bit pattern will become a 1; otherwise, it will become a 0. For example:

```
0101 & 0011 becomes 0001
```

The bitwise OR operator compares the bit pattern of its two operands. If either or both the bits at the same offset in the bit pattern are 1s, then the resulting bit pattern will become a 1; otherwise, it will become a 0. For example:

```
0101 & 0011 becomes 0111
```

The bitwise XOR operator compares the bit pattern of its two operands. If either, but not both, of the bits at the same offset in the bit pattern is a 1, then the resulting bit pattern will become a 1; otherwise, it will become a 0. For example:

```
0101 & 0011 becomes 0110
```

The ones complement operator simply flips the bits. If it was a 1, then it becomes a 0 and vice versa:

```
0101 becomes 1010
```

The shift operators shift all the bits of the operand per the number of bits specified right (>>) or left (<<). For example:

```
Right shift -  00101100 >> 2 becomes 00001011
Left shift  -  00101100 << 2 becomes 10110000
```

 TIP   *Right-shifting by 1 bit is equivalent to dividing by 2, and left-shifting by 1 bit is equivalent to multiplying by 2. Both shifts are far faster than either dividing or multiplying on a computer. So, if you need a little more speed in your application, and you are working with integer types and dividing or multiplying by factors of 2, you might want to consider shifting instead.*

When a statement contains more than one bitwise operator, then the bitwise operators will get evaluated according to the precedence shown in Table 2-14. If two operators of the same precedence occur in the expression, then they are evaluated from left to right.

Table 2-14. Bitwise Operator Precedence

PRECEDENCE	OPERATORS
Highest	~
	>> <<
	&
	^
Lowest	|

Conditional Operator

The *conditional operator* is the only ternary operator available to Managed C++ programmers. A *ternary* operator uses three expressions.

The conditional operator takes the first expression and sees if it is true (nonzero) or false (zero). If it is true, then the second expression is executed. If it is false, then the third expression is executed. A conditional operator looks like this:

```
expression1 ? expression2 : expression3;
a < b ? S"a is less than b" : S"a is greater than or equal to b";
```

Comma Operator

The *comma operator* causes a sequence of expressions to act as a single expression, with the last expression ultimately becoming what the total expression evaluates to. You can place a series of comma-delimited expressions anywhere you can place a normal expression.

You will probably see the comma operator most frequently used in the initialization and increment sections of a for loop, but there is nothing stopping a programmer from using it elsewhere. I discuss for loops later in this chapter.

The following example, though completely contrived, shows the comma operator in action. First, b is incremented, then a is assigned the value of multiplying postincremented a and b, and finally c is assigned the value of a modulus b:

```
Int32 a = 2;
Int32 b = 3;
Int32 c = (b++, a = b++ * a++, a % b);
```

The values of the variables after this code snippet finishes are

```
a = 9
b = 5
c = 4
```

Assignment Operators

There are a total of 11 *assignment operators* available to Managed C++, as shown in Table 2-15.

Table 2-15. Assignment Operators

OPERATOR	ACTION
=	Assign
+=	Add then assign
-=	Subtract then assign
*=	Multiply then assign
/=	Divide then assign
%=	Modulus then assign
>>=	Shift right then assign
<<=	Shift left then assign
&=	AND then assign
^=	XOR then assign
|=	OR then assign

The operator to assign one value to another is simply the equal sign (=). What basically happens is the expression on the right side of the equal sign is calculated and then assigned to the value on the left side of the equal sign.

You have seen assignment used several times already in this chapter, but here are a few more examples:

```
String *str = S"This is a managed string.";
Int32 num1 = 0x1234;
Int32 num2 = 4321;
num1 = num2;
```

Assigning a common value to several different variables can be accomplished by stringing together several assignments. For example, to assign 42 to the variables a, b, and c, you would write:

```
a = b = c = 42;
```

It is a common practice to take a value, do some operation it, and then place the results back into the original operator. For example:

```
a = a + 5;
b = b * 2;
```

So common is this that Managed C++ provides a set of special assignments to handle it:

```
a += 5;
b *= 2;
```

Address of and Indirection Operators

Two operators are available to Managed C++ programmers for handling pointers, as shown in Table 2-16.

Table 2-16. Address of and Indirection Operators

OPERATOR	ACTION
&	Address of
*	Indirection

The *address of operator* returns the address of the object after it. For example, if x were located at address 1024, then to place the address (1024) in variable y, you would write this:

```
y = &x;    // place the address of x into y
```

The *indirection operator,* on the other hand, gets its value from the address stored within itself. For example, if y contains the address 1024, then to place the value of 50 at the address 1024, you would write:

```
*y = 50;  // place the value of 50 at the address y points to
```

Listing 2-14 is a program that shows the address of and indirection operators in action.

Listing 2-14. Address of and Indirection Operators in Action

```
#using <mscorlib.dll>
using namespace System;

Int32 main(void)
{
    Int32 x;     // create a variable
    Int32 *y;    // create a pointer to an Int32

    y = &x;      // place the address of x in the pointer y
    *y = 50;     // place 50 at the address y points to
    Console::WriteLine(x);  // print out x. This should contain 50.

    return 0;
}
```

Figure 2-15 shows the results of this little program.

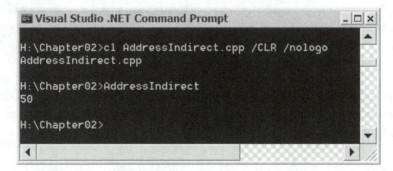

Figure 2-15. Results of AddressIndirect.exe

Operator Precedence

I have shown operator precedence for each operator in its own section, but what if operators from different sections occur in the same statement? Table 2-17 shows the precedence of all the operators.

Table 2-17. Operator Precedence

PRECEDENCE	OPERATORS
Highest	() [] ::
	! ~ ++ -- - * &
	* / %
	+ -
	<< >>
	< <= > >=
	== !=
	&
	^
	&&
	?:
Lowest	= += -= *= /= %= >>= <<= &= ^= |=

Flow Control Constructs

Normally in a Managed C++ program, statements are executed sequentially from beginning to end. There will be times when a program is going to execute a portion of code only if certain conditions are true. To handle conditional execution of code, Managed C++ provides two flow control constructs: if and switch.

if Statement

The if statement enables the conditional execution of code based on the evaluated value of some condition. An if statement in its simplest form is as follows:

```
if ( condition )
{
    statements;
}
```

The condition can be any expression, but to make more sense it should eval-uate to a Boolean value of either `true` or `false`. It is perfectly valid to evaluate to a zero (`false`) or nonzero (`true`) condition, as well.

Obviously, it is possible to execute a block of code when a condition is not true, as shown here:

```
if ( ! condition )
{
    statements;
}
```

What if you want a block of code to execute when a condition is `true` and some other block of code to execute when the condition is `false`? You could write two `if` statements, one for the `true` condition and one for the `false` condition, or you could use the `if-else` statement, which looks like this:

```
if ( condition )
{
    statements;
}
else  // ! condition (the comment is optional)
{
    statements;
}
```

There is one more construct for `if` statements. What if you want different blocks of code to be executed based on mutually exclusive conditions? You could write a stream of `if` conditions, one for each condition, but then each condition would have to be checked, which is a waste of time. Instead, you should use the `if-else if-else` or nested `if` construct, which exits the `if` construct once it matches a condition. The nested `if` construct looks like this:

```
if ( condition1 )  // first mutually exclusive condition
{
    statements;
}
else if ( condition2 )  // second mutually exclusive condition
{
    statements;
}
else  // optional catch the rest condition
{
    statements;
}
```

This example will display a different string depending on the value of the animal variable:

```
enum Creature {Dog, Cat, Eagle};
Creature animal;

// assign a value to animal
animal = Cat;

if ( animal == Dog )
{
    Console::WriteLine (S"The animal is a dog");
}
else if ( animal == Cat )
{
    Console::WriteLine (S"The animal is a cat");
}
else  // animal is not a dog or cat
{
    Console::WriteLine (S"Maybe the animal is a bird");
}
```

switch Statement

The switch statement is a multiple-choice flow-control construct. It functions in a very similar manner to the nested if construct, except that it only works for integer value types or expressions that evaluate to integers. Basically, the switch statement works like this: The switch expression is checked against each case constant. If a case constant matches the expression, then its associated statements are executed. If no case constant matches the expression, then the default statements are executed. Then the switch statement is exited.

A switch statement looks like this:

```
switch ( expression )
{
    case constant1:
        statements1;
        break;
    case constant2:
        statements2;
        break;
```

```
    default:
        statements3;
}
```

You can write the preceding nested `if` statement as a `switch` statement, like this:

```
switch ( animal )
{
    case Dog:
        Console::WriteLine (S"The animal is a dog");
        break;
    case Cat:
        Console::WriteLine (S"The animal is a cat");
        break;
    default:
        Console::WriteLine (S"Maybe the animal is a bird");
}
```

The first thing you may notice is that each `case` ends with a break statement. This break statement tells the `switch` that it is finished. If you fail to place a break statement at the end of a `case`, then the following case will also be executed. This may sound like a mistake, but there are times when this falling through to the next `case` is exactly what you will want. For example, this case statement executes the same code for lower- and uppercase characters:

```
switch ( keypressed )
{
    case 'A':
    case 'a':
        Console::WriteLine (S"Pressed the A key");
        break;
    case 'B':
    case 'b':
        Console::WriteLine (S"Pressed the B key");
        break;
    default:
        Console::WriteLine (S"Pressed some other key");
}
```

CAUTION *A missing* break *statement is a very common and diffi-cult error to debug, because often the error caused by it does not occur until later in the program.*

Looping Constructs

So far, you have seen that Managed C++ programs are statements that are exe-cuted sequentially from beginning to end, except when flow control dictates otherwise. Obviously, there are scenarios in which you would like to be able to repeat a single statement or a block of statements a certain number of times or until a certain condition occurs. Managed C++ provides three looping constructs for this: while, do-while, and for.

while Loop

The while loop is the simplest looping construct provided by Managed C++. It simply repeats a statement or a block of statements while the condition is true (some people prefer to say until the condition is false). The basic format of a while loop is as follows:

```
while ( condition )
{
    statements;
}
```

The condition is checked at the start of every iteration of the loop, including the first. Thus, if the condition evaluates at the start to false, then the statements never get executed. The while loop condition expression is exactly the same as an if statement condition.

In its simplest form, the while loop repeats a statement or a block of state-ments forever:

```
while ( true )
{
    statements;
}
```

I cover how to break out of this type of loop a little later.

More commonly, you will want the while loop condition to be evaluated. Here is an example of how to display all the numbers from 1 to 6 inclusive:

```
Int32 i = 0;
while ( i < 6)
{
    i++;
    Console::WriteLine(i);
}
```

do-while Loop

There are scenarios in which you will want or need the loop to always execute at least once. You could do this in one of two ways:

- Duplicate the statement or block of statements before the while loop.

- Use the do-while loop.

Obviously, the do-while loop is the better of the two solutions.

Like the while loop, the do-while loop loops through a statement or a block of statements until a condition becomes false. Where the do-while differs is that it always executes the body of the loop at least once. The basic format of a do-while loop is as follows:

```
do {
    statements;
} while ( condition );
```

As you can see, the condition is checked at the end of every iteration of the loop. Therefore, the body is guaranteed to execute at least once. The condition is just like the while statement and the if statement.

Like the while statement, the most basic form of the do-while loop loops forever, but because this format has no benefit over the while statement, it is seldom used. Here is the same example previously used for the while statement. It displays the numbers 1 to 6 inclusive.

```
Int32 i = 0;
do {
    i++;
    Console::WriteLine(i);
} while ( i  < 6 );
```

 CAUTION *Do not forget the semicolon (;) after the closing bracket of the condition. If you do, the compiler will generate a few angry messages and not compile successfully.*

for Loop

The for loop is the most complex construct for handling looping and can be used for almost any kind of loop. In its simplest form, the for loop, like the other two loop constructs, simply repeats a statement or a block of statements forever:

```
for ( ; ; )
{
    statements;
}
```

Normally, you will want control of how your program will loop, and that's what the for loop excels at. With the for loop, you can not only check to see if a condition is met like you do in the while loop, but you can also initialize and increment variables on which to base the condition. The basic format for a for loop is this:

```
for (initialization; condition; increment)
{
    statements;
}
```

When the code starts executing a for loop (only the first time), the initialization is executed. The initialization is an expression that initializes variables that will be used in the loop. It is also possible to actually declare and initialize variables that will only exist while they are within the loop construct.

The condition is checked at every iteration through the loop, even the first. This makes it similar to the while loop. In fact, if you don't include the initialization and increment, the for loop acts in an identical fashion to the while loop. You can use almost any type of condition statement, so long as it evaluates to false or zero when you want to exit the loop.

The increment executes at the end of each iteration of the for loop and just before the condition is checked. Usually the code increments (or decrements) the variables that were initialized in the initialization, but this is not a requirement.

Let's look at a simple for loop in action. This for loop creates a counter i, which will iterate so long as it remains less than ten or, in other words, because you start iterating at zero, this for loop will repeat six times.

```
for (Int32 i = 0; i < 6; i++)
{
    Console::WriteLine ( i );
}
```

The output of this for loop is as follows:

```
0
1
2
3
4
5
6
```

One thing to note is that the initialization variable is accessible within the for loop, so it is possible to alter it while the loop is executing. For example, this for loop, though identical to the previous example, will only iterate three times:

```
for (Int32 i = 0; i < 6; i++)
{
    i++;
    Console::WriteLine ( i );
}
```

The output of this for loop is as follows:

```
1
3
5
```

for loops are not restricted to integer type. It is possible to use floating-point or even more advanced constructs. Though this might not mean much to some of you, for loops are a handy way of iterating through link lists. (I know it is a little advanced at this point in the book, but I am throwing it in here to show how powerful the for loop can be.) For those of you who want to know what this does, it loops through the elements of a link list to the maximum of ten link list elements:

```
for (Int32 i=0, list *cur=headptr; i<10 && cur->next != 0; i++, cur=cur->next)
{
    statements;
}
```

Skipping Loop Iterations

Even though you have set up a loop to iterate through multiple iterations of a block of code, there may be times that some of the iteration doesn't need to be executed. In Managed C++, you do this with a continue statement.

You will almost always find the continue statement in some type of condition statement. When the continue statement is executed, the program jumps immediately to the next iteration. In the case of the while and do-while loops, the condition is checked and the loop continues or exits depending on the result of the condition. If continue is used in a for loop, the increment executes first, and then the condition executes.

Here is a simple and quite contrived example that will print out all the prime numbers under 30:

```
for (Int32 i = 1; i < 30; i++)
{
    if ( i % 2 == 0 && i / 2 > 1)
        continue;
    else if ( i % 3 == 0 && i / 3 > 1)
        continue;
    else if ( i % 5 == 0 && i / 5 > 1)
        continue;
    else if ( i % 7 == 0 && i / 7 > 1)
        continue;
    Console::WriteLine(i);
}
```

Breaking Out of a Loop

Sometimes you need to leave a loop early, maybe because there is an error condition and there is no point in continuing or, in the case of the loops that will loop indefinitely, you simply need a way to exit the loop. In Managed C++, you do this with a break statement. The break statement in a loop works the same way as the switch statement you saw earlier.

There is not much to the break statement. When it is executed, the loop is terminated and the flow of the program continues after the loop.

Though this is not really a very good example, the following sample shows how you could implement do-while type flow in a for loop. This loop breaks when it gets to 10:

```
for ( Int32 i = 0; ; i++ )
{
    Console::WriteLine(i);

    if (i >= 10)
        break;
}
```

Functions

At the core of all Managed C++ programs is the *function*. It is the source of all activity within a program. Functions also enable programmers to break their programs into manageable chunks. You have already been using a function called main(). Now let's see how you can go about creating a few of your own.

The general format of a function looks like this:

```
return-type function-name ( parameter-list )
{
    statements-of-the-function;
}
```

The return-type of the function is the value type, a pointer or a reference that is returned by the function when it finishes. The return type can be any value type, reference, or pointer, even ones that are user defined. If no return type is specified for the function, then Managed C++ defaults the return value to int. If the function does not return a value, then the return value should be set to the keyword void.

The function-name is obviously the name of the function. The rules of naming a function are the same as those for naming a variable.

The parameter-list is a comma-separated list of variable declarations that define the variable, which will be passed to the function when it starts executing. Parameter variables can be any value types, references, or pointers, even ones that are user defined.

Passing Arguments to a Function

You have two different ways of passing arguments to a function: by value and by reference. Syntactically, there is little difference between the two. In fact, the only difference is that passing by reference has an additional ampersand (&) placed before the value name:

```
Int32 example ( Int32 ByValue, Int32 &ByReference )
{
}
```

The big difference is in how the actual values are passed. When passing by value, a copy of the variable is passed to the function. Because the argument is a copy, the function can't change the original passed argument value. For example, this function takes the value of parameter a and adds 5 to it:

```
Int32 example ( Int32 a )
{
    a = a + 5;
    return a;
}
```

When the function is called

```
Int32 a = 5;
Int32 b = example(a);
```

the value of a will still be 5, whereas the value of b will be 10.

What if you want to actually update the value of the parameter passed so that it reflects any changes made to it within the function? You have two ways to handle this. The first is to pass a pointer by value. Because you are passing an address to the value, and not the actual value, any changes that you make to the value within the function will be reflected outside the function. The problem of passing by pointer is that now the syntax of the function is more complicated because you have to worry about pointers.

```
Int32 example ( Int32 *a )
{
    *a = *a + 5;
    return *a;
}
```

When the function is called

```
Int32 a = 5;
Int32 b = example(&a);
```

the value of a and b will both be 10.

The second approach is to pass the arguments by reference. When passing arguments by reference, the argument value is not copied; instead, the function is accessing an alias of the argument or, in other words, the function is accessing the argument directly.

```
Int32 example ( Int32 &a )
{
    a = a + 5;
    return a;
}
```

When the function is called

```
Int32 a = 5;
Int32 b = example(a);
```

the value of a and b will both be 10.

There is a pro and a con to using references. The pro is that it is faster to pass arguments by reference, as there is no copy step involved. The con is that, unlike using pointers, other than &, there is no difference between passing by value or reference. This can make for the very real possibility of changes happening to argument variables within a function without the programmer knowing about them.

The speed benefit is something some programmers don't want to give up, but they still want to feel secure that calling a function will not change argument values. To solve this problem, it is possible to pass const reference values. When these are implemented, the compiler makes sure that nothing within the function will cause the value of the argument to change:

```
Int32 example ( const Int32 &a )
{
//    a = a + 5;      // This line will cause a compiler error because
                      // we are trying to change the const a

    return a + 5;
}
```

When the function is called

```
Int32 a = 5;
Int32 b = example(a);
```

the value of a will still be 5, and the value of b will be 10.

Returning Values from a Function

Returning a value from a function is a two-step process. First, specify the type of value the function will return, and second, using the return statement, pass a return value of that type:

```
Double example()
{
    Double a = 8.05;
    // do some stuff
    return a;
}
```

Returning Pointers

You need to take care when you return a pointer from a function.

 CAUTION   *Never return a pointer to a variable of local scope to a function, because it will not be a valid pointer upon exiting the function.*

Never do this:

```
Int32* ERRORexample()
{
    Int32 a = 8;
    // do some stuff;
    return &a;      // This variable will disappear when the function ends so
}                   // pointer will be invalid
```

Instead, you should return the pointer a that was passed to the function or the pointer b that was created by the new operator in the function:

```
Int32* Okexample( Int32* a)
{
    Int32 *b= new Int32(8);  // Initialize to 8
    // do some stuff;
    if (*a > *b)
        return a;
    else
        return b;
}
```

In traditional C++, the variable b in the preceding example would be a classic location for a memory leak, as the developer would have to remember to call the delete statement on the returned value b. This is not the case in Managed C++, because pointers to Int32 value types are garbage collected automatically when no longer used, thus delete need not be called.

Returning References

You also need to take care when you return a reference from a function.

 CAUTION   *Never return a reference to a variable of local scope to a function, because it will not be a valid reference upon exiting the function.*

Never do this:

```
Int32& ERRORexample()
{
    Int32 a = 8;
    // do some stuff;
    return a;      // This variable will disappear when the function ends so
}                  // reference will be invalid
```

Instead, you should return a reference that was passed to the function, or a pointer or reference to a variable that was created by the new operator within the function:

```
Int32& OKexample( Int32& a) // Passing a reference
{
    Int32 &b= *new Int32(8);   // Creating a reference
    // do some stuff;
    if (a > b)
        return a;
    else
        return b;
}
```

Something worth noting in this function is the creation of a reference using the new operator. Again, with traditional C++ you would have to delete the reference. Fortunately, because Int32 references such as pointers get garbage collected in Managed C++, there is no need for the delete statement and no memory leak occurs.

Returning Managed Arrays

Another thing that you will probably return from a function is an array. In traditional C++, this would be handled by returning a pointer to the array. Unfortunately, this does not work for managed arrays, as managed arrays are not pointers. It is true that they are reference types, but there is no syntax for accessing arrays using the address of (&) operator. As this is the case, a new syntax for return arrays has been added for Managed C++:

```
Int32 MethodName() []
{
}
```

For example:

```
Int32 retArray() []
{
    Int32 array[] = new Int32[5];

    for (Int32 i = 0; i < array.Length; i++)
    {
        array[i] = i;
    }

    return array;
}
```

To assign the return value to an array is simple enough:

```
Int32 i[];
i = retArray();
```

Or you can do it in one statement, like this:

```
Int32 i[] = retArray();
```

Prototypes

You can't use a function until after it has been defined. Okay, there is nothing stopping you from placing function declarations in every *.cpp file where it is used, but then you would have a lot of redundant code.

The correct approach is to create prototypes of your functions and place them within an include (.h) file. (I cover include files in Chapter 4.) This way, the compiler will have the definition it needs and the function implementation will be in only one place. A prototype is simply a function without its body followed by a semicolon:

```
Int32 example ( const Int32 &a );
```

Function Overloading

In the dark ages of C, it was a common practice to have many functions with very similar names doing the same functionality for different data types. For example, you would see functions such as `PrintInt(int x)` to print an integer, `PrintChar(char c)` to print a character, `PrintString(char *s)` to print an array of characters, and so on. Having many names doing the same thing became quite a pain. Then along came C++, and now Managed C++, with an elegant solution to this annoyance: function overloading.

Function overloading is simply Managed C++'s capability to have two or more methods with exactly the same name but with a different number or type of parameter. Usually, the overloaded functions provide the same functionality but use different data types. Sometimes the overloaded functions provide a more customized functionality due to having more parameters to more accurately solve the problem. But, in truth, the two overloaded functions could do completely different things. This, however, would probably be an unwise design decision, as most developers would expect similar functionality from functions using the same name.

When a function overloaded call takes place, the version of the method to run is determined at compile time by matching the calling function's signature with those of the overloaded function. A function signature is simply a combination of the function name, number of parameters, and types of parameters. For function overloading, the return type is not significant when it comes to determining the correct method. In fact, it is not possible to overload functions by changing only the return type. When you do this, the compiler will give a bunch of errors, but only the one indicating that a function is duplicated is relevant.

There is nothing special about coding overloaded functions. For example, here is one function overloaded three times for the super-secret `Test` function:

```
Int32 Test () { /* do stuff */ }
Int32 Test (Int32 x) { /* do stuff */ }
Int32 Test (Int32 x, Int32 y, Double z) { /* do stuff */ }
```

Calling an overloaded function is nothing special either. Simply call the function you want with the correct parameters. For example, here is some code to call the third super-secret `Test` function:

```
Test (0, 1, 2.0);
```

The only thing that a Managed C++ programmer needs to concern herself with that a traditional C++ programmer doesn't is that built-in value types and their corresponding runtime __value types produce the same signature. Thus, these two functions are the same and will produce an error:

```
Int32 Test (Int32 x) { /* do stuff */ }
int Test (int x) { /* do stuff */ }  // Error Duplicate definition of Test
```

Passing Arguments to the main() Function

So far in every example in this book, the main() function has had no arguments. If you have worked with C++ before, you know that it is possible to retrieve the parameters passed to a program from the command line via the main() function's arguments. (If you haven't, well, now you know too.)

Basically, the main() function counts all the parameters passed to it, including the program that is being run, and places the count in the first argument, traditionally called argc. Next, it takes all the parameters and places them in a char or SByte array, each parameter being a separate element of the array. Finally, it passes a pointer to this array as the second argument, usually called argv.

In Managed C++, the main() function actually compiles to native code and not MSIL code, so the argv argument is not garbage collected. Fortunately, the cleanup of argv is handled automatically (so I guess you could say that it is sort of garbage collected). Unfortunately, because it is not garbage collected, it adds a minor wrinkle in its declaration. SByte by default uses garbage collection when defined as a pointer; therefore you need to add the __nogc keyword after SByte to let the compiler know that you do not want a garbage collected pointer definition. I cover __nogc in much more detail in Chapter 3. (By the way, if you were to use char, you would not have this problem, because all the class library aliases do not default to garbage collection.)

Listing 2-15 is a little program that reads in all the parameters passed to it and then writes them out.

Listing 2-15. Parsing a Command Line

```
#using <mscorlib.dll>
using namespace System;

Int32 main ( Int32 argc, SByte __nogc *argv[] )
{
    Console::WriteLine ( argc.ToString() );
    for (int i = 0; i < argc; i++)
    {
        Console::WriteLine ( new String(argv[i]) );
    }
    return 0;
}
```

Figure 2-16 shows the results of this little program when passed the parameter "This is a test this is only a test".

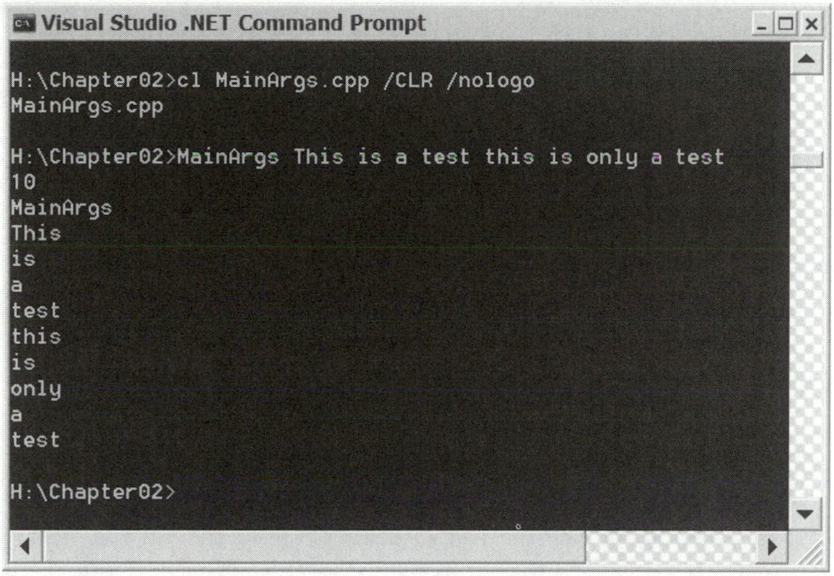

Figure 2-16. Results of MainArgs.exe

Summary

You have covered a lot of ground in this chapter. You started with variables and Managed C++'s built-in value types. Next, you learned about literals and operators. Then you examined two basic Managed C++ constructs: flow control and looping. You finished by exploring functions.

For the traditional C++ programmer, much of this chapter was not new. The areas that you should pay close attention to are .NET Framework class library built-in data types, `String` types, `__value` types, arrays, all the literals (in particular, string literals), and returning pointers and references from functions.

In the next chapter, you will continue to expand on your knowledge of the basics. This time you will focus on the object-oriented aspects of Managed C++.

CHAPTER 3

Object-Oriented Managed C++

IN THE PREVIOUS CHAPTER, I covered in detail the basics of Managed C++, focusing on programming strictly in a procedural style. This chapter explores the real strength of Managed C++: as an object-oriented language.

You will start by reviewing object-oriented programming (OOP) in general. You will then explore Managed C++'s OOP capabilities, focusing primarily on managed classes, which are the cornerstones of Managed C++ OOP. You will do this by breaking classes down into their parts and examining each part in detail. You will then revisit __value structs and __value classes. Finally, you will learn about managed interfaces.

 CAUTION   *Don't skip this chapter, even if you know C++ very well, as several things are different between traditional C++ and Managed C++. True, some of the changes may not be significant, but recognizing and understanding these changes now may make your life easier in the future.*

OOP is more a way of thinking than a programming technique. For those making the transition from procedural programming, you must understand that OOP programming will involve a paradigm shift for you. But, once you realize this and make the shift, you will wonder why you programmed any other way.

OOP is just an abstraction taken from everyday life and applied to software development. The world is made up of objects. In front of you is a book. It is an object. You are sitting on a chair or a couch, or you might be lying on a bed—all objects. I could go on but I'm sure you get the point. Almost every aspect of our lives revolves around interacting with, fixing, and improving objects. It should be second nature to do the same thing with software development.

Object-Oriented Concepts

All objects support three specific concepts: encapsulation, inheritance, and poly-morphism. Think about the objects around you—no, scratch that, and think about yourself. You are an object: You are made up of arms, legs, a torso, and a head, but how they work does not matter to you—this is encapsulation. You are a mammal, human, and male or female—this is inheritance. When greeted, you respond with "Good day," "Bonjour," "Guten Tag," or "Buon giorno"—this is poly-morphism.

As you shall see shortly, you can apply the object paradigm to software devel-opment as well. Managed C++ does it by using software objects called classes and structs. But before I get into software objects, let's examine the concepts of an object more generically.

Encapsulation

All objects are made up of a combination of different things or objects. Many of these things are not of any concern to the other objects that interact with them. Going back to you as an example of an object, you are made up of things such as blood, muscles, and bone, but most objects that interact with you don't care about that level of things. Most objects that interact with you only really care that you have hands, a mouth, ears, and other features at this level of abstraction.

Encapsulation basically means hiding the parts of an object that do things internal to that object from other objects that interact with it. As you saw in the previous example, the internal workings of hands, a mouth, and ears are irrele-vant to other objects that interact with you.

Encapsulation simplifies the model that other objects have to interact with. It allows other objects to only have to worry about using the right interface and passing the correct input to get the required response. For example, a car is a very complex object. But to me, a car is simple: A steering wheel, an accelerator, and a brake represent the interface, and turning the steering wheel, stepping on the accelerator, and stepping on the brake represent input.

Encapsulation also allows an object to be fixed, updated, or replaced with-out having to change the other objects interacting with it. When I trade in my Mustang LX for a Mustang GT, I still only have to worry about turning the steering wheel, stepping on the accelerator, and stepping on the brake.

The most important thing about encapsulation is that because portions of the object are protected from external access, it is possible to maintain the inter-nal integrity of the object. This is because it is possible to allow only indirect access, or no access at all, to private features of the object.

Inheritance

Inheritance is hardly a new concept. We all inherit many traits (good and bad) from both of our parents. We also inherit many traits from being a mammal, such as being born, being nursed, having four limbs, and so on. Being human, we inherit the traits of thumbs, upright stature, capacity for language, and so forth. I'm sure you get the idea. Other objects also inherit from other more generic objects.

You can think of inheritance as a tree of objects starting with the most generic traits and expanding to the most specific. Basically, each level of the tree expands upon the definition of the previous level, until finally the object is fully defined.

Inheritance allows for the reuse of previously defined objects. For example, when you say that a Mustang is a car, you know that it has four wheels and an engine. If you say a mustang is a horse, you know that it has four legs and eats grass. In both of these scenarios, the base object definition came for free—you didn't have to define it again.

Notice, though, that a Mustang is always a car (or a horse), but a car need not be a Mustang. The link of inheritance is one way, toward the root.

Polymorphism

The hardest concept to grasp is polymorphism; not that it's difficult, it's just taken so much for granted that it's almost completely overlooked. Basically, *polymorphism* is simply the ability for more than one object to respond to the same stimuli in completely different ways.

For example, if a teacher were to ask a classroom full of students to draw a picture of their favorite food, then most of the students would draw completely different things. With the same stimuli to the same type of objects, in this case students, you are getting different responses.

You might have noted from the previous example that some students may select the same food to draw. There is a good chance the reason for this comes from some form of inherited link of the students in question. Polymorphism is closely related to inheritance, and common responses can often be attributed to something that both objects inherit or have in common.

A key thing about polymorphism is that you know that you will get a response of a certain type, but the object responding, and not the object requesting, determines what the actual response will be.

Applying Objects to Software Development

Okay, you know what objects and their concepts are and how to apply them to software development. With procedural programming, there is no concept of an object, just a continual stream of logic and data. Let me back up a bit on that. It could be argued that even in procedural programming objects exist, as variables, literals, and constants could be considered objects (albeit simple ones). In procedural programming, breaking up the logic into smaller, more manageable pieces is done by way of functions. To group common data elements together, the structure or class is used depending on language.

Before you jump on me, I would like to note that there were (obviously) other object-oriented languages before C++, but this book only covers Managed C++'s history.

It wasn't until C++ that computer data and its associated logic was packaged together into the struct and a new construct known as the class. With the combination of data and logic associated with this data into a single construct, object-oriented concepts could be applied to programming.

Here in a nutshell is how objected-oriented concepts are applied to Managed C++ development. Classes and structures are programming constructs that implement within the C++ language the three key object-oriented concepts: encapsulation, inheritance, and polymorphism.

Encapsulation, or the hiding of complexity, is accomplished by not allowing access to all data and functionality found in a class. Instead, only a simpler and more restricted interface is provided to access the class.

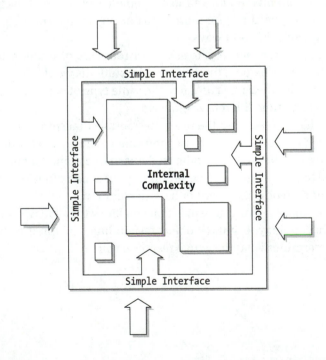

Inheritance is the ability to reuse functionality and data of one class within another class, without having to worry about the complexity of the first. The class has the ability to derive itself from another class.

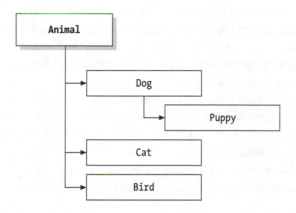

Polymorphism is the ability for different classes to respond to the same request in different ways. Classes provide something called the *virtual method, or function,* which allows any class derived from the same parent class to respond differently to the same request.

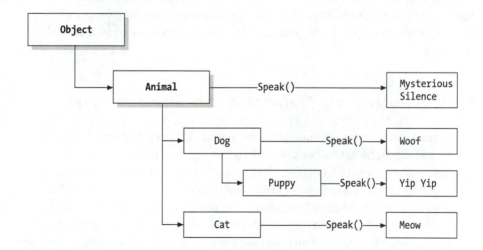

I expand on each of these concepts as the chapter progresses.

Now that you understand OOP conceptually, let's see how it is actually done with Managed C++.

Managed Class and Struct Basics

First off, there is nothing forcing you to program in an objected-oriented fashion with classes or structs, and using classes and structs does not mean you are doing OOP. For example, it is possible to break the code based on function areas instead of objects. It may appear to be OOP, but what you really are doing is just using a class as a namespace. Plus, you gain none of the benefits of OOP.

It is the organization of code and data into unique objects that distinguishes procedural coding from object-oriented coding.

For those totally new to object programming, you need to understand that each time you implement a class definition a new instance of it will be created. In other words, no matter how many instances you want, they will all be created from the same class definition.

But before you look at objects and OOP, you will look at the class and the struct and what makes up a class and a struct in general terms.

Declaring Managed Classes and Structs

Managed classes and structs are basically an extension of traditional C++ classes and structs. Like traditional C++ classes and structs, managed classes and structs are made up of variables and methods. Unlike traditional classes and structs, managed classes and structs are created and destroyed in a completely different manner. Also, managed classes and structs have an additional construct called the property.

Private, Public, and Protected Member Access Modifiers

There really is no real difference between a class and struct except for the default access to its members. Classes default to private access to their members, whereas structs default to public. Notice that I used the term "default." It is possible to change the access level of either the class or the struct. So, truthfully, the usage of a class or a struct is just a matter of taste. Most people who code C++ use the keyword class when they create objects, and they use structs to simply group data together, without any methods or with simply a constructor method.

The way you declare managed classes is very similar to the way you declare traditional classes. Let's take a look at a class declaration. With what you covered in the last chapter, much of a class definition should make sense. First, there is the declaration of the class itself and then the declaration of the class's variables, properties, and methods.

The following example is the Square class, which is made up of a constructor, a method to calculate the square's area, and a dimension variable:

```
__gc class Square
{
    // constructor
    Square ( Int32 d)
    {
        Dims = d;
    }

    // method
    Int32 Area()
    {
        return Dims * Dims;
    }

    // variable
    Int32 Dims;
};
```

The first thing to note about this class is that because the access to classes defaults to private, the constructor, the method, and the variable are not accessible outside the class. This is probably not what you want. To make the class's members accessible outside of the class, you need to add the access modifier public: to the definition:

```
__gc class Square
{
public:
    // public constructor
    Square ( Int32 d)
    {
        Dims = d;
    }

    // public method
    Int32 Area()
    {
        return Dims * Dims;
    }
```

```
    // public variable
    Int32 Dims;
};
```

With this addition, all the class's members are accessible. What if you want some members private and some public? For example, what if you want the variable Dims only accessible through the constructor? To do this, you add the private: access modifier:

```
__gc class Square
{
public:
    Square ( Int32 d)
    {
        Dims = d;
    }

    Int32 Area()
    {
        return Dims * Dims;
    }
private:
    Int32 Dims;
};
```

Besides public and private, Managed C++ provides one additional member access modifier: protected. Protected access is sort of a combination of public and private; where a protected class member has public access when it's inherited but private access (i.e., can't be accessed) by methods that are members of a class that don't share inheritance.

Here is a quick recap of the access modifiers for members.

If the member has public access, it is

- Accessible by external functions and methods

- Accessible to inheriting

If the member has private access, it is

- Not accessible by external functions and methods

- Not accessible to inheriting

If the member has protected access, it is

- Not accessible by external functions and methods

- Accessible to inheriting

If you are visually oriented like me, maybe Figure 3-1 will help clear up member access modifiers.

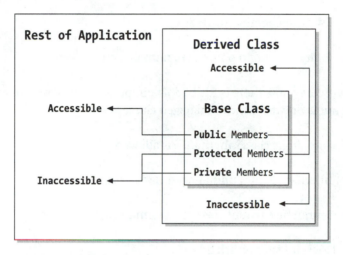

Figure 3-1. Summary of the three member access modifiers

The __gc and __nogc Keywords

If you have come from the traditional C++ world, you may have noticed the new keyword __gc in front of the class's definition. This is one of the biggest and most important changes between traditional C++ and Managed C++. The use of the __gc keyword tells the compiler, which in turn tells the common language runtime (CLR), that this class will be managed or garbage collected (hence the g and c). Managed C++ does not, even though the name suggests it, default to garbage-collected classes. Instead, it is up to the developer to decide if he wants the class to be managed or garbage collected and, if so, he must manually place the __gc in front of the class.

For this minor inconvenience, you get several benefits:

- Garbage collection

- Inheritance from any .NET Framework base class that is not sealed or, if no base class is specified, automatic inheritance from the System::Object class

- Ability for the class to be used within .NET Framework collections and arrays

- Inheritance from any number of managed interfaces

- Ability to contain properties

- Ability to contain pointers to unmanaged classes

With the good, there is the bad. Traditional C++ programmers might find these items drawbacks with managed classes:

- Only single class inheritance is allowed.

- Inheritance from unmanaged classes is not allowed.

- Cannot be a parent class of an unmanaged type.

- Does not support friends.

- Cannot contain an overridden new or delete operator.

- Must use public inheritance.

- Cannot be used with the sizeof or offsetof operator.

- Pointer arithmetic with class pointers is not allowed.

On the other hand, these drawbacks may not be as bad as you might think. Managed classes allow multiple interface inheritance. The .NET Framework is quite extensive, so inheritance of unmanaged classes may not be needed as frequently as you might expect. Overriding new and delete seems to defeat the purpose of managed classes. Because pointer arithmetic is not allowed, sizeof and offsetof are kind of useless, anyway, and pointer arithmetic is a very big contributor to memory leaks and programs aborting due to illegal memory access.

Even though it is the default for classes and structs, the __nogc keyword explicitly marks a class or struct as unmanaged and, thus, not subject to any of the restrictions or benefits of being managed.

The __gc and __nogc Keywords and Arrays

The keywords __gc and __nogc can be applied to arrays whose element type is a Managed C++ built-in value type or its corresponding runtime __value type. When __gc is applied to the runtime __value type, the value type will be placed in a managed array on the heap.

For example, you can define a managed array of int runtime __value types as follows:

```
int ManagedArray __gc[] = new int __gc[100];
```

Now, because it is a managed array, you get all the benefits of being derived from System::Array. A much simpler and clearer way to generate the same managed code is this:

```
Int32 ManagedArray[] = new Int32[100];
```

Note that without the __gc keyword, the compiler will error out because runtime __value types such as int are not managed types. Thus, the following will cause the compiler to generate an error:

```
int ErroArray[] = new int __gc[100];      // Oops int is not a __gc
```

When __nogc is applied to a Managed C++ built-in value type, the value will create a stack-based array:

```
Int32 UnmanagedArray __nogc[100];
```

By the way, the following code has the same effect and is easier to read:

```
int UnmanagedArray[100];
```

Inheriting Classes

Even though writing a stand-alone class can provide quite a lot of functionality to an object, it is in the object-oriented nature of classes and their capability to inherit from other classes that their real strength lies.

As I mentioned earlier, managed classes have the ability to inherit from a single class and multiple interfaces. You will focus on class inheritance now, and later in this chapter you will look at interface inheritance.

Inheriting from a class allows an inheriting class (usually known as the *child*) to get access to all the public and protected members of the inherited class (usually known as the *parent* or *base class*). You can think of inheritance in one of two ways: It allows the functionality of the base class to expand without the need to duplicate any of the code, or it allows the child class to fix or augment some feature of its parent class without having to know or understand how the parent functions (this is encapsulation, by the way). But really, they both mean the same thing.

A restriction imposed by Managed C++ on classes is that a class can only use public inheritance. For example:

```
__gc class childClass : public baseClass {}
```

is allowed, but the following will generate compile time errors:

```
__gc class childClass : protected baseClass {}
__gc class childClass : private baseClass {}
```

This means that with the public access to a base class, the child can access any public or protected member of the base class as if it were one of its own members. Private members of the base class, on the other hand, are not accessible by the child class, and trying to access them will generate a compilation error.

Unmanaged (__nogc) classes can have public, protected, or private access to their base class. Notice there is no "__gc" in front of these classes:

```
class childClass : public baseClass {}
class childClass : protected baseClass {}
class childClass : private baseClass {}
```

Basically, for private class access, all base class members are inherited as private and thus are not accessible. Protected class access allows access to public and protected base class members but changes the public access to protected. Personally, I've never used private or protected base class access, as I've simply never had a use for it, but it's available if you ever need it.

Listing 3-1 shows the Cube class inheriting from a Square class. Notice that because both the member access and the class access of the Square class are public, the Cube class has complete access to the Square class and can use all the Square class's members as if they were its own.

Listing 3-1. Inheritance in Action

```
#using <mscorlib.dll>
using namespace System;

__gc class Square
{
public:
    Int32 Area()
    {
        return Dims * Dims;
    }

    Int32 Dims;
};

__gc class Cube : public Square
{
public:
    Int32 Volume()
    {
        return Area() * Dims;
    }
};

int main(void)
{
    Cube *cube = new Cube();
    cube->Dims = 3;
```

```
Console::WriteLine(cube->Dims);
Console::WriteLine(cube->Area());
Console::WriteLine(cube->Volume());

return 0;
}
```

Figure 3-2 shows the results of this little program.

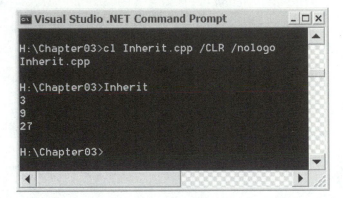

Figure 3-2. Results of Inherit.exe

Sealed Classes

A *sealed class* or struct is one that cannot be inherited from. All value type classes are always sealed. Indirectly, this means that all boxed values are also sealed.

The sealed class enables a developer to stop all other developers from inheriting from her class. I have never had an opportunity to seal any of my classes. I have come across it a few times. Almost every time, I was forced to create my own similar class because I needed additional functionality that the sealed class lacked. Personally, I feel the sealed class goes against object-oriented development, as it stops one of the key OOP cornerstones: inheritance. But the tool is available for those who wish to use it.

The code to seal a class is simply this:

```
__sealed __gc class sealEx
{
};
```

NOTE *From here on, I'll use only "class" as opposed to "class and struct." You can assume anything you can do with a class you can also do with a* struct, *except that the default access of the* struct *is public whereas the default access of the class is private.*

Using the Class

Unlike procedural code, the declaration of a class is simply that: a declaration. The class's methods do nothing on their own and only have meaning within the confines of an object. An object is an instantiated class. A neat thing about when a class is instantiated is that automatically all the classes it is derived from also get instantiated.

The code to instantiate or create an object from the class in the previous section is simply this:

```
Square *sqr = new Square();  // a pointer
```

or this:

```
Square &sqr = *new Square();  // a reference
```

Notice that you can create either a pointer or a reference to the Square object. For those of you coming from a traditional C++ background, working with pointers and their more complex syntax will not be an issue. I personally have found working with references a little easier, as you will see later when I cover references to objects.

Pointer to an Object

If you recall from the previous chapter, Managed C++ data types can fall into one of two types: value types and reference types. Managed classes are reference types. What this means is that the class, when created using the new operator, allocates itself on the heap, and then a reference or pointer is placed on the stack indicating the address of the allocated object.

This is only half the story, though. It is the CLR that places the class on the heap. The CLR will maintain this class on the heap so long as a pointer or reference is using it. When all references to the class go out of scope or, in other words, no variables are accessing it, the CLR will delete it automatically.

NOTE   *If the class accesses certain unmanaged resources that hold resources, the CLR will hold the class for an indefinite (not necessarily infinite) period of time. Using COM-based ADO is a classic example of this. Code in a destructor will sometimes, but not always, be able to resolve this issue. Because you are not dealing with unmanaged resources in this book, this should not be an issue.*

Once you have created a class using the following:

```
Square *sqr = new Square();  // a pointer
```

you now have access to its variables, properties, and methods. The code to access an object pointer is simply the name of the object you created followed by the -> operator. For example:

```
Sqr->Dims = 5;
Int32 area = Sqr->Area();
```

You might be wondering why pointer arithmetic is not allowed on managed class pointers. They seem harmless enough. Well, the problem comes from the fact that the location of the class can move. The garbage collection process not only deletes unused heap space, it also compresses it. Thus, it is possible that a class can be relocated during the compression process.

Pinning Pointers

If you are a seasoned traditional C++ programmer, you probably saw an immediate problem with allowing a pointer's address to change. Passing a pointer to a managed class's data, as a parameter to an unmanaged function call, may fail. Because the pointer is passed by value, if the class moves, the value of the parameter will no longer be valid.

To solve this problem, Managed C++ has added the __pin keyword, which stops the CLR from changing its location during the compression phase of garbage collection. The pointer remains pinned so long as the pinned pointer stays in scope or until the pointer gets assigned the value of 0. Listing 3-2 shows the __pin keyword in action.

Listing 3-2. __pin in Action

```
#using <mscorlib.dll>
using namespace System;

__gc class Test
{
public:
    Int32 i;
    Test()
    {
        i = 0;
    }
};

void incr (int * i)    // unmanaged function
{
    (*i)++;
}

Int32 main ()
{
    Test __pin *ptrTest = new Test;  // ptrTest is a pinned pointer
    incr( &ptrTest->i);           // pointer to managed data passed as actual
                        // parameter of unmanaged function call
    Console::WriteLine ( ptrTest->i.ToString() );
}
```

Figure 3-3 shows the results of this little program.

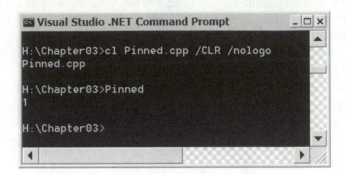

Figure 3-3. Results of Pinned.exe

References to an Object

I assume that up until now you've been using the member access operator or dot (.) operator on faith that I would explain it later. There really isn't anything special about the dot operator, as it's only used for accessing individual member variables, properties, or methods out of a class. Its syntax is simply this:

```
class-name . member-data-or-method
Int32 intval;
String *s = intval.ToString();
```

You have seen both the -> and . operators used when accessing class members. What is the difference? Basically, the -> operator is used to access data or methods from a pointer, whereas the . operator is used to access the actual object.

You should be scratching your head right now in confusion. Aren't all managed classes reference-type-only? The answer to this question is yes, but remember that Int32s are value type objects and not reference types, so when you access value type objects, you are accessing the actual object, and thus you must use the . operator.

You might be wondering what all this has to do with references to an object. Well, when you access the actual object, you are actually referencing the object.

References to objects are similar to pointers to objects in that they both store the address of the object in the stack. But there's one major difference between them: Pointers can change what they point to, but a reference can't be changed once initialized.

Why would you use a reference to an object when a pointer to an object is so much more powerful? The reason is simple: References are safer to work with. You know that once a reference to an object is created, it will always point to that object. The reference will cause a compile-time error if you try to change its value.

Whether or not you create your own references to objects is really just a matter of taste. I like using references to objects because they seem to make things clearer for me. I know that if I am using a pointer to an object, then the object that the pointer is pointing to may change, whereas with a reference to an object I know that the same object will always be referenced. I use references in this book when I know the address will not change, but whether you use them or not is totally up to you and your company standards. Listing 3-3 presents both a pointer to an object and a reference to an object in one example.

Listing 3-3. Pointers and References in Action

```
#using <mscorlib.dll>
using namespace System;

__gc class Square
{
public:
    Square(Int32 v)
    {
        Dims = v;
    }

    Int32 Area()
    {
        return Dims * Dims;
    }

    Int32 Dims;
};
```

```
int main(void)
{
    Square *sqr1 = new Square( 2 );          // Pointer
    Square &sqr2 = *new Square( 3 );         // Reference

    Console::WriteLine( sqr1->Dims);         // Pointer
    Console::WriteLine( sqr1->Area() );

    Console::WriteLine( sqr2.Dims );         // Reference
    Console::WriteLine( sqr2.Area() );

    return 0;
}
```

Figure 3-4 shows the results of this little program.

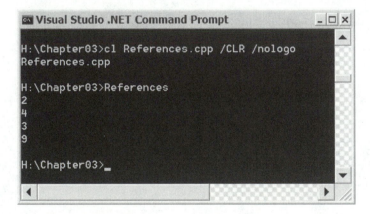

Figure 3-4. Results of References.exe

Member Variables

This fancy name is simply C++'s way of reminding programmers that classes and structs are objects. Member variables are simply variables defined within the definition of a class or a struct.

The syntax of defining member variables is identical to that of ordinary variables except for one important thing: You cannot initialize a variable in its definition. I explain how to initialize variables later in this chapter when I cover constructors. The definition of a variable is simply a data type and a variable name, or a comma-delimited list of variable names:

```
__gc class varExample
{
    Int32 x;
    String *str1, *str2;
};
```

In Managed C++, member variables can be either managed data types or a pointer to an unmanaged data type.

Member variables can be public, protected, or private. With Managed C++ and managed classes, public member variables should be handled with care, especially if invalid values in these variables will cause problems in the program's execution. A better solution is to make them private (or protected, so that inherited access can still access them directly), and then make public properties to them for external methods to access. Properties can, if coded correctly, perform validation on the data entered into the variable. Otherwise, they work just like normal member variables. I cover properties later in this chapter.

Static Member Variables

Static member variables are variables that provide class-wide storage. In other words, the same variable is shared by all instances of a class. To define a static member variable in a managed class, simply define it as static and assign a value to it in that class definition like this:

```
__gc class staticVar
{
    static Int32 staticVar = 3;
};
```

You might be wondering how initializing the variable within the class can work, as it would appear that the value would be reset for each instance of the class. Fortunately, this is not the case; as only the first time that the class is instantiated does the variable get created and initialized.

Member Methods

Just like member variables, member methods are Managed C++'s way of reminding programmers that they are working with objects. A *member method* is simply a function declared within a class or struct. Everything you learned about functions in the previous chapter is applicable to member methods. You might consider revisiting Chapter 2's section on functions if you are uncertain how they are defined or how they work.

Like all members of a class, member methods can be public, protected, or private. Public methods are accessible outside of the class and are the workhorse of interclass communication. It is via methods that classes pass messages, requesting and being requested to perform some type of functionality. Protected member methods are the same as private member methods except that inherited classes have access to them. Private classes encapsulate the functionality provided by the class, as they are not accessible from outside the class except via some public member method that uses it.

Just as a quick recap, Listing 3-4 is a public member method that calls a protected member method that calls a private member method.

Listing 3-4. Member Methods in Action

```
#using <mscorlib.dll>
using namespace System;

__gc class MethodEx
{
public:
    void printPublic(Int32 num)
    {
        for (Int32 i = 0; i < num; i++)
        {
            Console::WriteLine( S"Public" );
        }
        printProtected(num/2);
    }
protected:
    void printProtected(Int32 num)
    {
        for (Int32 i = 0; i < num; i++)
        {
            Console::WriteLine( S"Protected" );
```

```
        }
        printPrivate(num/2);
    }
private:
    void printPrivate(Int32 num)
    {
        for (Int32 i = 0; i < num; i++)
        {
            Console::WriteLine( S"Private" );
        }
    }
};


Int32 main()
{
    MethodEx &ex = *new MethodEx();  // reference to MethodEx

    ex.printPublic(4);
    // ex.printProtected(4);   // Error cannot access
    // ex.printPrivate(4);     // Error cannot access
}
```

Figure 3-5 shows the results of this little program.

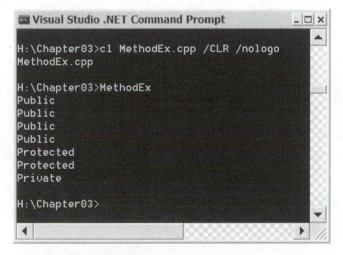

Figure 3-5. Results of MethodEx.exe

Static Member Methods

Static member methods are methods that have class scope. In other words, they exist without your having to create an instance of the class. Because they are not associated with any particular instance of a class, they can use only static member variables, which also are not associated with a particular instance. For the same reason, a static member method cannot be a virtual member method, as virtual member methods are also associated with class instances.

Coding static member methods is no different than coding normal member methods, except that the function declaration is prefixed with the static keyword.

Listing 3-5 uses a static member method to print out a static member variable.

Listing 3-5. Static Member Methods and Variables in Action

```
#using <mscorlib.dll>
using namespace System;

__gc class StaticTest
{
private:
    static Int32 x = 42;
public:
    static Int32 get_x()
    {
        return x;
    }
};

Int32 main()
{
    Console::WriteLine ( StaticTest::get_x() );
    return 0;
}
```

Figure 3-6 shows the results of this little program.

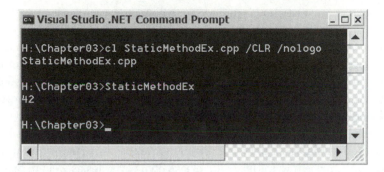

Figure 3-6. Results of StaticMethodEx.exe

You might have noticed that to access the static member method, you use the class name and the :: operator instead of the . or -> operator. The reason is you've not created an object, so you're effectively accessing the namespace tree.

Managed Class Constructors

The *class constructor* is a special class function that is different in many ways from the member method. In Managed C++, a constructor is called whenever a new instance of a class is created. Instances of managed classes are created using the operator __gc new. When you create an instance of a managed class, you can omit the __gc keyword from the new operator. Memory for the instance is allocated on the heap that is maintained by the CLR.

The purpose of the constructor is to initialize the member variables in the new instance of the class. The managed class constructor process differs from the unmanaged class constructor process in that, for managed class constructors, all member variables are initialized to zero before the actual constructor is called. Thus, even if the constructor does nothing, all member variables would still have been initialized to zero or the data type's equivalent. For example, the DateTime data type initializes to 1/1/0001 12:00:00am, which is this data type's equivalent of zero.

A managed class constructor method always has the same name as the class itself. A managed class constructor method does not return a value and must not be defined with the void return type. A constructor method can take any number of parameters. Note that a constructor method needs to have public accessibility to be accessible by the new operator.

If no constructor method is defined for a class, then a default constructor method is generated. This constructor method does nothing of its own, except it calls the constructor method of its parent and sets all member variables to a zero value. If you define a constructor method, then a default constructor method will not be generated. Thus, if you create a constructor method with parameters and you expect the class to be able to be created without parameters, then you must manually create your own default zero-parameter constructor method.

A special construct of a constructor method is the *initializer list*. It's basically a list of variables that need to be initialized before the constructor method itself is called. You can use it to initialize the class's own variables as well; in fact, it's more efficient to do it this way, but it's also much harder to read in this format. The most common uses for an initializer list are to initialize references (because they can't be initialized using assignments) and to initialize abstract classes. You'll examine abstract classes later in this chapter. The syntax for an initializer list involves simply placing a colon (:) and a comma-delimited list of functional notation variable declarations between the constructor method's declaration and the constructor method's implementation:

```
Constructor (Int32 x, Int32 y, Int32 z) : var1(x, y), var2(z) { }
```

This example shows the constructors for a managed class called DotNet:

```
__gc class DotNet
{
public:
    DotNet () {}      // default constructor
    DotNet (Int32 val) : value1(val), value2(2) {}
    DotNet (Int32 val1, Int32 val2)
    {
        value1 = val1;
        value2 = val2;
    }
private:
    Int32 value1, value2;
};
```

CAUTION   *Those of you who are experienced C++ programmers should be aware that user-defined copy constructors are not allowed for managed classes in Managed C++.*

Static Class Constructors

In traditional C++, the syntax for initializing static member variables was rather cumbersome. It forced you to define it in the class and then initialize it outside the class before the main() function was called. You saw that with managed classes you could directly assign a value to a static member variable—but what happens if you need something more elaborate than a simple assignment? Managed C++ has provided a new construct for managed classes called the *static class constructor.*

The static class constructor's purpose is to initialize static member variables normally with something more complex than a simple assignment, but not necessarily. Any managed class can have a static class constructor, though it only really makes sense if the class has static member variables, as the static class constructor is not allowed to initialize any nonstatic member variables.

When the static class constructor is invoked it is undefined, but it is guaranteed to happen before any instances of the class are created or any references are made to any static members of the class.

If you recall, it is possible to initialize static member variables directly in the definition of the class. If you use the static class constructor, then these default values are overwritten by the value specified by the static class constructor.

The static class constructor syntax is identical to the default constructor syntax, except that the static keyword is placed in front. This means that a static class constructor cannot take any parameters.

In the following example, the managed class Test is made up of two static member variables initialized to 32 and a static class constructor that overwrites the first constant with the value of 42:

```
__gc class Test
{
public:
    static Test()
    {
        value1 = 42;
    }
    static Int32 value1 = 32;
    static Int32 value2 = 32;
};
```

By the way, you can have both static and nonstatic (standard, I guess) constructor methods in the same class.

Destructors

All objects allocated on the heap need to be deallocated. The process for unmanaged objects is manual. Basically, when a program is finished with the object, then the `delete` operator must be called for the object:

```
delete classname;
```

For managed objects, on the other hand, the process for the programmer is a lot easier. When the object is no longer needed, simply do nothing. It is the job of the CLR to detect when an object is no longer being accessed and then garbage collect it.

The destructor method has the same syntax as the default constructor method except that a tilde (~) is placed before the destructor method's name:

```
__gc class Test
{
    ~Test() {}    // destructor
}
```

Things may have become easier for the programmer, but behind the scenes things have become slightly more complex. In fact, the compiler is actually doing a little magic behind the scenes.

The first thing I must point out is that other languages do not support the `delete` operator. So, if you plan on using a managed class in other languages, you can't rely on the `delete` operator being called. In fact, the garbage collector doesn't use the `delete` operator either. Don't panic—this is really not an issue.

What the garbage collector and, subsequently, all .NET-compatible languages, use to delete classes is a protected virtual member method called `Finalize`. You don't have to worry about creating a `Finalize` member method for your class—in fact, you can't. It's up to the compiler to create one for you from the destructor you coded into your class. The following is a sample of what the compiler actually creates when you add a destructor to your managed class.

Original code by the programmer:

```
__gc class Test
{
public:
    ~Test()
```

```
    {
        Console::WriteLine(S" Test Destructor ");
    }
};
```

Generated code:

```
__gc class Test
{
public:
    Test::Finalize()
    {
        Console::WriteLine(S" Test Destructor ");
    }

    virtual ~Test()
    {
        System::GC::SuppressFinalize(this);
        Test::Finalize();
    }
};
```

You may have noticed the System::GC::SuppressFinalize method call within the newly generated destructor. This method is placed here so that the garbage collector does not call the Finalize member method again if the delete operator was called manually.

As a Managed C++ programmer, you can't call the Finalize method directly, but you still have the option of calling the delete statement for the object. This will call the destructor and, as you can see in the preceding code, the garbage collector, because the method SuppressFinalize() forgets about the object.

Because the destruction of the class is handled by the CLR, when the destructor occurs can't be determined. If you're doing things such as cleaning up resources (files, for example) in the destructor, then you should be calling delete manually. If you're planning on using this object in C#, you can't do this, so you should place the cleanup functionality in a member method called, by convention, Dispose().

Note that the Dispose() method doesn't call the destructor; the garbage collector still does that. This can cause a problem. Resources can be deallocated twice. This is usually not a good thing and it quite often results in exceptions being thrown. To fix this, you have to make sure that you code your program in such a way that this doesn't happen. Fortunately, a simple Boolean variable will suffice:

```
__gc class DisposedClass
{
    Boolean isDisposed;

    DisposedClass()
    {
        isDisposed = false;
    }

    ~DisposedClass()
    {
        if (!isDisposed)
        {
            // clean up resources
        }
    }

    void Dispose()
    {
        // clean up resources
        isDisposed = true;
    }
};
```

Virtual Methods

Virtual methods are the cornerstone of class polymorphism, as they allow the different classes derived from a common base class to respond to the same method call and generate a different response. Polymorphism occurs when a virtual method is called through a base class pointer or reference. This is because when the call is made it is the type of the actual object pointed to that determines which copy of the virtual method is called.

Technically, when you declare a virtual method, you are telling the compiler that you want dynamic or runtime binding to be done on any method with an identical signature in a derived class. To make a method virtual, you simply need to place the keyword virtual in front of the method declaration.

Any method that you declare as virtual will automatically be virtual for any directly or indirectly derived class. It is not necessary to include the keyword virtual in the derived class method, but by including it you will make it clear to other developers that the method is, in fact, virtual.

The method signature of the base class must be the same as the derived class. This means that the name of the method and the number of parameters and their types must be identical. The return type of the method need not be identical, but it must at least be derived from the same type as that of the base method's return type.

Listing 3-6 is the standard virtual animal example. First, you declare a base class Animal with a virtual method of Speak(). You then create specific animal-type classes derived from Animal and override the virtual method Speak(). In the main() function, you create an array of Animals and assign specific type animals to it. Finally, you loop through the Animal array. Because the Speak() method is virtual, the actual object type assigned to the Animal array determines which Speak() to execute.

Listing 3-6. Virtual Methods in Action

```
#using <mscorlib.dll>
using namespace System;

__gc class Animal
{
public:
    virtual void Speak ()
    {
        Console::WriteLine(S"Mysterious Silence");
    }
};

__gc class Dog : public Animal
{
public:
    virtual void Speak ()
    {
        Console::WriteLine(S"Woof");
    }
};

__gc class Puppy : public Dog
{
public:
    virtual void Speak ()  // Note the keyword virtual is not needed but I
    {                      // include it so I will remember that it is virtual
                           // the next time it's inherited.
        Console::WriteLine(S"Yip Yip");
    }
```

```cpp
};

__gc class Cat : public Animal
{
public:
    virtual void Speak ()
    {
        Console::WriteLine(S"Meow");
    }
};

Int32 main(void)
{
    Animal *a[] = new Animal*[4];      // Array of __gc class pointers
    a[0] = new Cat();
    a[1] = new Dog();
    a[2] = new Puppy();
    a[3] = new Animal();

    for (Int32 i = 0; i < a->Count; i++)
    {
        a[i]->Speak();
    }

    return 0;
}
```

Figure 3-7 shows the results of this little program.

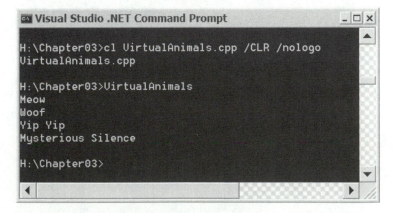

Figure 3-7. Results of VirtualAnimals.exe

Pure Virtual Method

When you look at the previous example, you may notice that the base class virtual method Speak() really has a nonsense implementation and shouldn't even be included in the class. A better way to implement this example and ensure that the virtual method is always overridden is to force the inheriting classes to override the virtual method and, if it doesn't, generate an error. You can do this with a *pure virtual method.*

The big difference between a pure virtual method and a virtual method is that a class that contains pure virtual methods cannot be instantiated. In other words, a class that has pure virtual methods must be inherited to be used. You will look at this in more detail later in the chapter when you examine abstract classes.

A pure virtual method is simply a definition of a method without any implementation. When you use it, the compiler checks to make sure that the pure virtual method is overwritten. If it is not, then the compiler generates an error.

A pure virtual method has the same syntax as a regular virtual method, except that instead of a method implementation, a = 0; is appended:

```
virtual void PureVirtualFunction() = 0;
```

Sealed Virtual Method

There is essentially no difference between a Managed C++ and a traditional C++ virtual method. What has changed is with Managed C++ there is an additional keyword that can seal a virtual method or, in other words, stop a virtual method from being used as a virtual method in all subsequent derived classes.

Sealing a method only works for virtual methods, for obvious reasons. To seal a virtual method, you simply place __sealed in front of it:

```
__sealed virtual void Speak();
```

If you were to apply the __sealed keyword to the VirtualAnimal example—for example, on the Dog's virtual method Speak()—then the Puppy class's virtual method Speak() will error out, as it is illegal to override a sealed virtual method.

Method Overriding

Method overriding is defining a method in a derived class that has an identical signature to the base class. How the derived class actually works depends on whether the method is virtual or not. If the method is virtual, it runs as I described previously.

On the other hand, if the method is not virtual, then it works completely differently. First off, no dynamic binding occurs, just standard static or compile-time binding. What this means is that whatever type the method is called with is executed. For example, in the VirtualAnimal example, if the Speak() method were not virtual, then the Animal class's Speak() method would be called every time in the for loop. This displays "Mysterious Silence" for a time as opposed to the assorted messages generated by the virtual version of the example. The reason this happens is because the array pointer is of type Animal.

Basically, overriding a nonvirtual method simply has the effect of hiding the base class's copy of the method.

Method Overloading

There is nothing special about coding overloaded methods, as they are handled in exactly the same way as function overloading, which I covered in the previous chapter. The only real difference is that they are now methods inside a class and not functions out on their own. For example, here is the same super-secret method (this time) overloaded three times in a Secret class:

```
__gc class Secret
{
    Int32 Test () { /* do stuff */ }
    Int32 Test (Int32 x) { /* do stuff */ }
    Int32 Test (Int32 x, Int32 y, Double z) { /* do stuff */ }
};
```

Calling an overloaded method is nothing special either. Simply call the method you want with the correct parameters. For example, here is some code to call the second super-secret Test method from a pointer object called secret and the third method from a referenced object:

```
secret->Test (0, 1, 2.0);   // if the class is a pointer
secret.Test(5);             // if the class is a reference
```

For those of you coming from a traditional C++ or Visual Basic background, you might have used default arguments. Unfortunately, with Managed C++, managed (__gc) classes and structs do not support default arguments in member methods. In fact, they generate an error.

A suggested solution to this change in syntax is to use overloaded methods. That is, define a method with fewer parameters and then initialize the variable in the method body. For example, here are four methods that when combined together are equivalent to one method with three defaulted arguments:

```
__gc class NoDefaultArgs
{
    // Invalid method with default values
    // Int32 DefArgs ( Int32 x = 1, Int32 y = 2, Int32 z = 3) { /* do stuff */ }

    // Equivalent combination of overloaded methods
    Int32 DefArgs ()
    {
        x = 1;
        y = 2;
        z = 3;
        /* do stuff */
    }
    Int32 DefArgs ( Int32 x )
    {
        y = 2;
        z = 3;
        /* do stuff */
    }
    Int32 DefArgs ( Int32 x, Int32 y )
    {
        z = 3;
        /* do stuff */
    }
    Int32 DefArgs ( Int32 x, Int32 y, Int32 z )
    {
        /* do stuff */
    }
}
```

I'm sure there is a good reason why Microsoft eliminated default arguments, but personally I hope they put them back in, as using overloads can get quite cumbersome.

Managed Operator Overloading

Operator overloading is one important feature that most traditional C++ programmers learn to work with early in their careers. It is one of C++'s claims to fame and is the ability to use standard operators and give them meaning in a class—for example, adding two strings together to get a new concatenated string.

Managed C++'s managed classes support operator overloading as well, but in a completely different way than traditional C++. First, managed classes do not support the operator keyword. In fact, using the operator keyword in managed classes causes an error. Instead, they are defined as ordinary static methods with specific names. Managed C++ then maps these specially named methods into infix operators for the defining class. Table 3-1 contains a list of all operator names and equivalent infix operators.

Table 3-1. Operators Supported by CLS That Can Be Implemented by Managed C++

MANAGED OPERATOR NAME	INFIX OPERATOR SYMBOL
op_Implicit	N/A
op_Explicit	N/A
op_Addition	+ (binary)
op_Subtraction	- (binary)
op_Multiply	* (binary)
op_Division	/
op_Modulus	%
op_ExclusiveOr	^
op_BitwiseAnd	& (binary)
op_BitwiseOr	|
op_LogicalAnd	&&
op_LogicalOr	||
op_Assign	=
op_LeftShift	<<
op_RightShift	>>
op_SignedRightShift	N/A
op_UnsignedRightShift	N/A

(continued)

Table 3-1. Operators Supported by CLS That Can Be Implemented by Managed C++ (continued)

MANAGED OPERATOR NAME	INFIX OPERATOR SYMBOL
op_Equality	==
op_GreaterThan	>
op_LessThan	<
op_Inequality	!=
op_GreaterThanOrEqual	>=
op_LessThanOrEqual	<=
op_MultiplicationAssignment	*=
op_SubtractionAssignment	-=
op_ExclusiveOrAssignment	^=
op_LeftShiftAssignment	<<=
op_RightShiftAssignment	>>=
op_ModulusAssignment	%=
op_AdditionAssignment	+=
op_BitwiseAndAssignment	&=
op_BitwiseOrAssignment	|=
op_Comma	,
op_DivisionAssignment	/=
op_Decrement	--
op_Increment	++
op_UnaryNegation	- (unary)
op_UnaryPlus	+ (unary)
op_Negation	!
op_OnesComplement	~

Listing 3-7 is an example of the op_Inequality and op_Equality operators and the != and == infix operators. Notice how you can use either the static method call or the infix operator when you do the equality check.

Listing 3-7. Operator Overload in Action

```
#using <mscorlib.dll>
using namespace System;

__gc class M
{
    Int32 i;
public:
    M(Int32 x) { i = x; }
    static bool op_Inequality(M &m1, M &m2)  // maps to operator !=
    {
        Console::WriteLine(S"In op_Inequality");
        return m1.i != m2.i;
    }

    static bool op_Equality(M &m1, M &m2)  // maps to operator ==
    {
        Console::WriteLine(S"In op_Equality");
        return m1.i == m2.i;
    }
};

Int32 main(void)
{
    M *m1 = new M(5);
    M *m2 = new M(5);
    M *m3 = new M(10);

    if ( M::op_Inequality(*m2, *m3) )
        Console::WriteLine(S"Don't Equal");
    else
        Console::WriteLine(S"Equal");

    if ( *m1 != *m2 )    // infix operator !=
        Console::WriteLine(S"Don't Equal");
    else
        Console::WriteLine(S"Equal");

    if ( M::op_Equality(*m2, *m3) )
        Console::WriteLine(S"Equal");
    else
        Console::WriteLine(S"Don't Equal");
```

```
    if ( *m1 == *m2 )    // infix operator ==
        Console::WriteLine(S"Equal");
    else
        Console::WriteLine(S"Don't Equal");

    return 0;
}
```

Figure 3-8 shows the results of this little program.

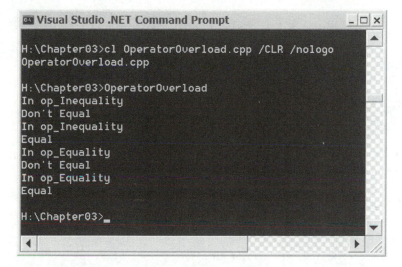

Figure 3-8. Results of OperatorOverload.exe

 CAUTION *Be careful when you use an infix operator with managed class pointers. When you compare* m1 == m2 *you are comparing if the pointers are equal, which is not what you want. Make sure you are comparing the actual value of the classes* *m1 == *m2.

One other thing to be aware of is that at least one of the managed operands must be of the same type as the defining class. Listing 3-8 compares whether the __value struct N is greater than an Int32.

Listing 3-8. Operator Overload for Mixed Data Types in Action

```
#using <mscorlib.dll>
using namespace System;

__value struct N
{
    Int32 i;
public:
    N(Int32 x) { i = x; }
    static bool op_GreaterThan(N n, Int32 v)  // maps to operator >
    {
        return n.i > v;
    }
    static bool op_GreaterThan(Int32 v, N n)  // maps to operator >
    {
        return v > n.i;
    }
};

Int32 main(void)
{
    N n(5);

    if ( n > 6 )
        Console::WriteLine(S"Greater than");
    else
        Console::WriteLine(S"Less than or Equal");

    if ( 6 > n )
        Console::WriteLine(S"Greater than");
    else
        Console::WriteLine(S"Less than or Equal");

     return 0;

}
```

Figure 3-9 shows the results of this little program.

Figure 3-9. Results of OperatorOverloadMixed.exe

Member Properties

The purpose of properties is to enrich encapsulation for classes and `structs`. Properties are successful in doing this, and as an added benefit, they provide an improved and simplified interface to a member variable.

A problem with traditional C++ classes is that there is no simple and standardized way of maintaining member variables. Frequently, programmers will simplify the syntax of interfacing with their class and allow public access to member variables even at the risk of having invalid data placed into them. Seeing the risk of exposing some of the more volatile variables, a programmer then might decide to write getter and setter methods. These methods would protect the member variables, but would then complicate the necessary syntax for their access.

Properties solve this problem by providing direct member variable–like access to member variables, but with the security and flexibility of getter and setter methods. To the programmer accessing the class, properties act like member variables. Member properties resemble simple scalar variables, static variables, arrays, and indexes. To the developer of the class, properties are simply getter and setter methods with specific rules and syntax. The complexity of these methods is totally up to the class creator.

Scalar Properties

The most common implementation of a property is getter and setter methods accessing a single member variable. Properties can be write-only, read-only, or both.

To create a writable property, you need to use Managed C++'s new __property keyword. Then, simply use the following syntax:

```
__property void set_<property name> ( <property type> value) { }
```

For example:

```
__property void set_Name (String *name) { }
```

You now have full access to the parameter to do as you please. The most common thing you will do is validate the parameter and then assign it to a private member variable.

The only real catch you might encounter is that the property name cannot be the same as a member variable. A conversion I use, which is by no means a standard, is to prefix member variable storage for properties with an underscore (_) and lowercase the first letter in the property name:

```
<property type> _<property name>;  // with first letter of name lowercase
```

For example:

```
String* _name;
```

A programmer who is actually writing to the property will access it using the property name (without the set_ prefix), as if it were a simple variable of the property type:

```
<property name> = statement;
```

For example:

```
Name = S"Stephen";
```

To create a readable property, you need to use the __property keyword again, but this time using this syntax:

```
__property <property type> get_<property name> () { }
```

For example:

```
__property String* get_Name () {}
```

You are now free to put any calculation you want within the method, but it must return the type specified. For this type of property, the most common body of the method is a simple return of the member variable storage of the property.

A programmer accessing the property will do as he would any other member variable, but he will use the property name without the get_ prefix.

To create a property that is both readable and writable, simply create both a readable and writable property. The only thing you need to be aware of is that the property name and property type must be the same for both the get_ and set_ methods.

Listing 3-9 shows a readable property, a writable property, and a property that is both readable and writable.

Listing 3-9. Scalar Properties in Action

```cpp
#using <mscorlib.dll>
using namespace System;

__value struct ScalarProp
{
    // Write only property
    __property void set_Name(String *name)
    {
        _name = name;
    }

    // Ready only property
    __property String *get_Description()
    {
        return String::Concat(_name, S" ", _desc);
    }

    // Read/write validated parameter
    __property void set_Number(Int32 num)
    {
        if (num < 1)
            num = 1;
        else if (num > 10)
            num = 10;

        _num = num;
    }
    __property Int32 get_Number()
    {
```

```
            return _num;
        }

        ScalarProp()
        {
            _name = S"Blank Name";
            _desc = S"Scalar Property";
        }
private:
        String *_name;
        String *_desc;
        Int32    _num;
};


Int32 main(void)
{
    ScalarProp sp;

    sp.Name = S"The Struct";

    Console::WriteLine(sp.Description);

    sp.Number = 20;     // Will be changed to 10
    Console::WriteLine(sp.Number);

    sp.Number = -5;     // Will be changed to 1
    Console::WriteLine(sp.Number);

    sp.Number = 6;      // Will not change
    Console::WriteLine(sp.Number);

    return 0;
}
```

Figure 3-10 shows the results of this program.

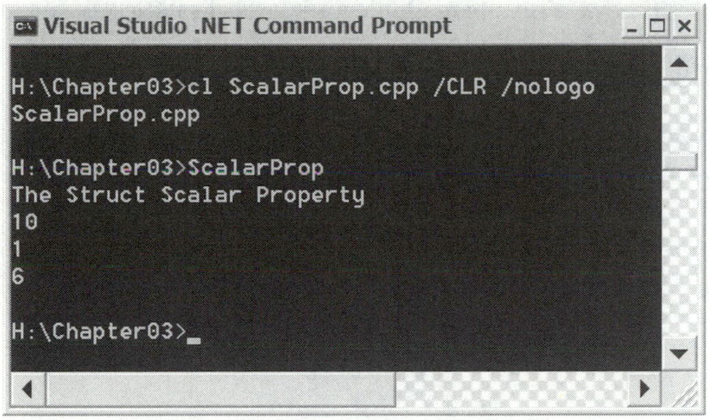

Figure 3-10. Results of ScalarProp.exe

Static Properties

As I mentioned previously, classes also contain static member variables. Likewise, Managed C++ provides property syntax to support *static properties,* or properties that have class-wide storage.

Static properties are nearly identical to scalar properties except that they contain the keyword `static` in their definition and they can only use static variables for storage. To create a readable and writable static property, simply use this syntax:

```
__property static void set_<property name> ( <property type> value) { }
__property static <property type> get_<property name> () { }
```

For example:

```
__property static void set_Name (String *name) { }
__property static String* get_Name () {}
```

A programmer accesses a static property in the same way she would a static member variable, by using class name and the :: operator:

```
<class>::<property name>
```

For example:

```
StaticProp::Name = S"Static Property";
Console::WriteLine(StaticProp::Name);
```

Listing 3-10 shows a simple readable and writable static `Name` property.

Listing 3-10. Static Properties in Action

```
#using <mscorlib.dll>
using namespace System;

__gc class StaticProp
{
    static String* _name;

public:
    __property static void set_Name (String* name)
    {
        _name = name;
    }
    __property static String* get_Name ()
    {
        return _name;
    }
};

Int32 main(void)
{
    StaticProp::Name = S"Static Property";

    Console::WriteLine(StaticProp::Name);
    return 0;
}
```

Figure 3-11 shows the results of this little program.

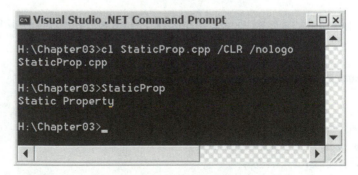

Figure 3-11. Results of StaticProp.exe

Array Properties

Managed C++ provides simple array syntax for properties. This is a big improvement over traditional C++, where getter and setter methods simply don't perform that elegantly.

The syntax for array properties is virtually the same as that for the scalar property except for the addition of the open and close square brackets:

```
__property <property type> get_<property name> () []  { }
__property void set_<property name> ( <property type> value [] )  { }
```

For example:

```
__property Int32 get_NumArray() []  { }
__property void set_NumArray ( Int32 NumArray[] )  { }
```

Notice the weird syntax (for traditional C++) of placing the square brackets between the ending brace of the parameter list and the opening curly bracket of the method body. Remember that managed arrays cannot be manipulated using pointer arithmetic. Therefore, the type returned from an array property has to be an array type.

By the way, if you look back in the previous chapter, the get_ method syntax has a strong resemblance to that of the returning of an array from a function.

Once the get_ and set_ methods have been created, it is a simple matter to access an array property using normal array syntax. Listing 3-11 shows how to add an assignable, readable, and writable array property to a class.

Listing 3-11. Array Properties in Action

```
#using <mscorlib.dll>
using namespace System;

__gc class ArrayProp
{
    Int32 _numArray[];
public:
    __property Int32 get_NumArray() []
    {
        return _numArray;
    }

    __property void set_NumArray ( Int32 NumArray[] )
    {
```

```
            _numArray = NumArray;
        }

};

Int32 main()
{
    ArrayProp &array = *new ArrayProp;

    array.NumArray = new Int32[5];

    for ( int i = 0 ; i < array.NumArray->Count ; ++i )
        array.NumArray[i] = i;

    for ( int i = 0 ; i < array.NumArray->Count ; ++i )
        Console::WriteLine(array.NumArray[i].ToString());

    return 0;
}
```

Figure 3-12 shows the results of this little program.

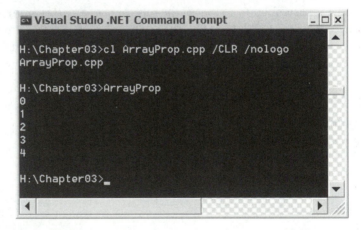

Figure 3-12. Results of ArrayProp.exe

You might have noticed that the property array storage is an unallocated private member variable. Obviously, it is possible to allocate the member variable storage in the constructor.

Indexed Properties

At first glance, *indexed properties* may appear to provide the same thing as array properties. Basically, they allow you to look up a property based on an index. The syntax to allow you to do this is much more complex than that of the array property:

```
__property <ProType> get_<ProName>(<IndxType> v1,..., <IndxType> vn) {}
__property void set_<ProName>(<IndxType> v1,..., <IndxType> vn, <ProType> p) {}
```

or

```
__property Student &get_ReportCard(String *n) {}
__property void set_ReportCard(String *n, Student &s) {}
```

So why would a programmer go through all of the problems of using indexed properties? It boils down to one thing: The index doesn't have to be numeric. In other words, when you use indexed properties, you get the ability to work with an array index of any type.

In the preceding sample, the index is of type String. So, when a programmer wants to access an indexed property, he would access it like this:

```
<ProName>[v1,..., vn]
```

or

```
<ProName>[v1]...[vn]
```

in the preceding example:

```
ReportCard[<string name>];   // where <string name> is a value index
```

If the index properties are a little hazy still, Listing 3-12 is a more complex example to show them in action. You start by defining a Student class with two read-only properties. You then create a Course class, which, using a nested class, stores a linked list of students and their grades for the course. You use an indexed property ReportCard to extract the grades from the linked list using the student's name.

Listing 3-12. Indexed Properties in Action

```cpp
#using <mscorlib.dll>
using namespace System;

__gc class Student
{
   String *_name;
   Int32   _grade;

public:
   Student(String * s, Int32 g)
   {
      _name = s;
      _grade = g;
   }
   __property String *get_Name()
   {
      return _name;
   }
   __property Int32 get_Grade()
   {
      return _grade;
   }
};

__gc class Course
{
   __gc struct StuList
   {
      Student *stu;
      StuList *next;
   };
   StuList *pStu;
   static StuList *ReportCards = 0;

public:
   __property Student &get_ReportCard(String *n)
   {
      for(pStu = ReportCards; pStu && (pStu->stu->Name != n); pStu = pStu->next)
         ;
      if (pStu != 0)
         return *pStu->stu;
```

```
        else
            return *new Student(0,0);   // empty student
    }


    __property void set_ReportCard(String *n, Student &s)
    {
        for(pStu = ReportCards; pStu && (pStu->stu->Name != n); pStu = pStu->next)
            ;
        if (pStu == 0)
        {
            StuList *stuList = new StuList;
            stuList->stu = &s;
            stuList->next = ReportCards;
            ReportCards = stuList;
        }
    }
};


Int32 main()
{
    Course  &EnglishLit = *new Course;
    Student &Stephen    = *new Student(S"Stephen", 95);
    Student &Sarah      = *new Student(S"Sarah", 98);

    EnglishLit.ReportCard[ S"Stephen" ] = Stephen;   // index String lit
    EnglishLit.ReportCard[ Sarah.Name ] = Sarah;      // index String*

    Console::WriteLine(EnglishLit.ReportCard[ Stephen.Name ].Grade);
    Console::WriteLine(EnglishLit.ReportCard[ S"Sarah" ].Grade);

    return 0;
}
```

Figure 3-13 shows the results of this little program.

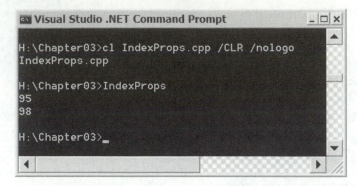

Figure 3-13. Results of IndexProps.exe

Nested Classes

As their name suggests, *nested classes* are classes defined inside another class. You might think of them as member classes.

Like all members of a class, a nested class's accessibility is determined by whether it is located within the public, protected, or private area of its class. Unlike member types, a nested class, though limited to the scope of the enclosing class, has its own members, and these members adhere to the accessibility of the nested class. For example, if the nested class has public accessibility, but the accessibility of the nested class's member variable is private, then the member variable is private as far as the surrounding class is concerned, even though the nested class is accessible to external functions and methods.

In Listing 3-13 you can see a surrounding class with a nested class. The nested class has three members: a public, a protected, and a private member variable. The surrounding class has three member variable references to the nested class: public, protected, and private. The surrounding class also has an initializer list constructor for the member variables and a method to access all the nested class instances within the surrounding class. The listing shows an inheriting class to the surrounding class with a method showing how to access the nested class instances of its parent class. Finally, the listing shows a main() function that shows how to reference the member variable found within the nested class within the surrounding class. The class has no output. Its purpose is to show you a method of accessing nested classes' public members.

Listing 3-13. Indexed Properties in Action

```
#using <mscorlib.dll>
using namespace System;


__gc class SurroundClass
```

```
{
protected:
    __gc class NestedClass          // Declaration of the nested class
    {
    public:
        Int32 publicMember;
    protected:
        Int32 protectedMember;
    private:
        Int32 privateMember;
    };

    NestedClass &protectedNC;    // protected variable reference to NestedClass

private:
    NestedClass &privateNC;       // private variable reference to NestedClass

public:
    NestedClass &publicNC;        // public variable reference to NestedClass

    // Constructor for SurroundClass
    // Notice the initializer list declaration of the reference member variable
    SurroundClass() : publicNC(*new NestedClass),
                      protectedNC(*new NestedClass),
                      privateNC(*new NestedClass)
    {}

    // A member showing how to access NestedClass within SurroundClass
    // Notice only public member variables of the nested class are accessed
    // The private and protected are hidden
    void method()
    {
        Int32 x;

        NestedClass &nc1 = *new NestedClass();  // Declared another reference
                                                // NestedClass
        x = nc1.publicMember;           // Accessing new NestedClass variable

        x = publicNC.publicMember;    // Accessing public NestedClass variable
        x = protectedNC.publicMember;// Accessing protected NestedClass variable
        x = privateNC.publicMember;  // Accessing private NestedClass variable
    }
};
```

```
// An inherited class showing how to access NestedClass within a member method
// Notice only public and protected NestedClass are accessed
// The private is hidden
__gc class inheritSurroundClass : public SurroundClass
{
public:
    void method()
    {
        Int32 x;

        NestedClass &nc1 = *new NestedClass(); // can access because NestedClass
                                               // declaration protected
        x = nc1.publicMember;

        x = publicNC.publicMember;
        x = protectedNC.publicMember;
    }
};

// The main function shows how to access NestedClass from outside SurroundClass
// inheritance tree
// Notice only the public NestedClass reference is accessible
Int32 main()
{
    SurroundClass &sc = *new SurroundClass();
    Int32 x = sc.publicNC.publicMember;
    return 0;
}
```

There is a lot of code in Listing 3-13. Figure 3-14 should clear up any confusion.

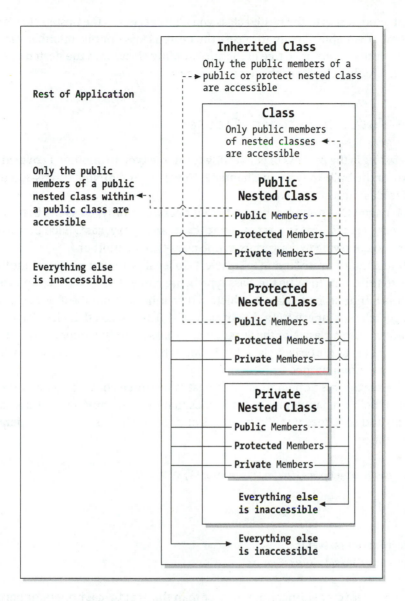

Figure 3-14. Accessing nested class members

Only public members are accessible outside of a nested class. For the surrounding class to access the public variable, the nested class can be public, protected, or private. For an inheriting class of the surrounding class, only public or protected access to the nested class will allow access to the nested class's public member variable. Finally, to access the nested class's public member variable outside of the inheritance tree of the surrounding class, both the nested class and the surrounding class must have public access.

Type Casting Between Classes

Type casting is the process of converting from one type to another. I covered type casting of the built-in types in Chapter 2. Now I expand on that discussion to include class and struct types.

Managed C++ provides three different operators for type casting between classes or structs: static_cast, dynamic_cast, and __try_cast. Each performs the process of trying to convert from one class type to another.

Notice that I wrote "trying to" convert. To legally convert a class to another, it needs to inherit from or be the class type being converted to. For example, let's say class B inherits from class A, which in turn inherits from the Object class (all managed classes inherit from the Object class). This means that class B can safely be converted to a class A or the Object class. Class A, on the other hand, can safely convert to the Object class, but it would be an invalid conversion to class B, as class A is not inherited from class B.

The static_cast operator is the fastest of the three conversion operators, but it is also the most dangerous, as it assumes that the programmer knows what she is doing and so it does no validity checks of its own. The syntax for the operator is simply this:

```
static_cast<target_type>(object_to_convert);
```

or

```
static_cast<Int32>(var);
static_cast<ClassA*>(ClassBvar);
```

The dynamic_cast operator is slower than the static_cast operator because it verifies that the type casting is valid. If the conversion is allowed, then the dynamic_cast operator completes the conversion. On the other hand, if it's not a valid conversion, then the dynamic_cast operator returns a null pointer. The syntax of the dynamic_cast operator is identical to the static_cast operator except that static is replaced with dynamic in the following statement:

```
dynamic_cast<ClassA*>(ClassBvar);
```

A nifty little trick to check if a class is of a certain type can be done using the dynamic_cast operator. If you come from the C# world, this is equivalent to the is operator:

```
if ( dynamic_cast<ClassA*>(ClassB) != 0)
{
    // ClassB is of type ClassA
}
```

The last conversion operator is the __try_cast. This operator is similar to the dynamic_cast operator except that instead of returning a null pointer, it throws an exception of type System::InvalidCastException. I cover exceptions in Chapter 4.

The __try_cast operator is really, as far as I'm concerned, a testing tool, so you should use it only during the development phase. My reasoning is that the __try_cast exception should only occur when there's a mistake in the code and, thus, after the testing phase the __try_cast should always succeed. You should convert all references to __try_cast to static_casts before you release the software to production.

Listing 3-14 doesn't produce any output. I've provided comments on what the result of each statement is. If you want to prove to yourself that I'm right, you can run the code through a debugger and watch the results as you execute each statement.

Listing 3-14. Type Casting in Action

```
#using <mscorlib.dll>
using namespace System;

__gc class A {};
__gc class B : public A {};
__gc class C {};

Int32 main(void)
{
    Object *v1 = new A();
    Object *v2 = new B();
    Object *v3 = new C();
```

```
    A *a1 = new A();

    A *a2 = new B();

    A *a3 = dynamic_cast<A*>(v1);   // cast from Object(actual A) to A

    A *a4 = dynamic_cast<A*>(v2);   // cast from Object(actual B) to A

    A *a5 = static_cast<A*>(v3);    // a5 has invalid value of type C class


    B *b1 = new B();

    B *b2 = dynamic_cast<B*>(v2);   // cast from Object(actual B) to B

    B *b3 = dynamic_cast<B*>(v3);   // Fails b3 = null. Mismatch classes

    B *b4 = dynamic_cast<B*>(a2);   // cast from A(actual B) to B


    C *c1 = new C();

    C *c2 = dynamic_cast<C*>(v1);   // Fails c2 = null. Mismatch classes

    C *c3 = static_cast<C*>(v2);    // c3 has invalid value of type B class

    C *c4 = __try_cast<C*>(v3);     // cast from Object(actual C) to C


    B *e1 = __try_cast<B*>(c1);     // aborts with exception


    return 0;
}
```

Abstract Classes

An *abstract class* is basically an incomplete definition of a class, and it contains at least one pure virtual member method. It is a binding agreement between the class that derives from the abstract class and the class that calls the methods of that derived class.

In every other way, an abstract class is the same as a normal class. It can have variables, methods, properties, constructors, and destructors. The only thing it can't do is instantiate an object from itself. Thus, it can't be used as a parameter or return type. However, pointers and references to abstract classes can be used as a parameter or return type.

You might be wondering why you would need a constructor if you can't create an abstract class. The constructor of an abstract class serves the same purpose it does in a normal class: to initialize the member variables. There's one catch, though. The only place you can put an abstract class constructor is in the derived class's initializer list. Because the constructor only needs to be accessed by the deriving class, it's safest to declare the constructor as protected.

Any class that derives from an abstract class must implement the pure virtual function or it will become an abstract class itself.

Any class that has pure virtual methods is abstract. In fact, even though Managed C++ has added the keyword __abstract to declare a class as abstract, the keyword is optional and not really needed. What it does is simply make the class notation explicit. It also makes your code more readable, as now you can see that a class is abstract from its initial declaration and you do not have to search the class for pure virtual methods.

Because an abstract class has to be inherited, obviously a __sealed class is not allowed, but it is legal to __seal a virtual method, if the abstract class implements it.

To show abstract classes in action, Listing 3-15 shows an abstract class defined with a constructor and two methods, one of which is a pure virtual method. Another class inherits this class and seals Method1, but because it does not implement Method2, it too is abstract. Finally, this second abstract class is called by a third class, which implements the pure virtual function. Because the class now has all classes implemented, it can be instantiated. The example also shows how to pass an abstract class pointer as a parameter.

Listing 3-15. Abstract Classes in Action

```
#using <mscorlib.dll>
using namespace System;

__abstract __gc class AbstractExClass
{
protected:
    Int32 AbstractVar;
    AbstractExClass(Int32 val): AbstractVar(val) {}
public:
    virtual void Method1() = 0;   // unimplemented method
    virtual void Method2() = 0;   // unimplemented method
    void Method3()
    {
        Console::WriteLine(AbstractVar.ToString());
    }
};


__abstract __gc class MidAbstractExClass : public AbstractExClass
{
public:
    __sealed void Method1()
    {
        Console::WriteLine((AbstractVar * 3).ToString());
    }
```

```
protected:
    MidAbstractExClass(Int32 val) : AbstractExClass(val) {}
};

__gc class DerivedExClass : public MidAbstractExClass
{
public:
    DerivedExClass(Int32 val) : MidAbstractExClass(val) {}
    void Method2()
    {
        Console::WriteLine((AbstractVar * 2).ToString());
    }
};

void testMethod(AbstractExClass &aec)
{
    aec.Method1();
    aec.Method2();
    aec.Method3();
}

Int32 main(void)
{
    AbstractExClass &Ab1 = *new DerivedExClass(5);
    Ab1.Method1();
    Ab1.Method2();
    Ab1.Method3();

    AbstractExClass &Ab2 = *new DerivedExClass(6);
    testMethod(Ab2);

    DerivedExClass *dc = new DerivedExClass(7);
    testMethod(*dc);

    return 0;
}
```

Figure 3-15 shows the results of this little program.

Object-Oriented Managed C++

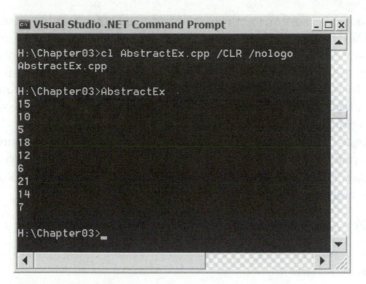

Figure 3-15. Results of AbstractEx.exe

Interfaces

An *interface* is similar to an abstract class in that it is a binding agreement between the class that derives from the abstract class and the class that calls the methods of that derived class. The key difference is that an interface only contains public, pure virtual methods. As the name suggests, it defines an interface to a class. But defining is all it does, as it does not contain variables or implementations for any methods.

Though classes can only inherit one class, they are able to inherit as many interfaces as needed to define the interface to the class. It is up to the class to implement all interfaces.

Like an abstract class, you can't instantiate an object from an interface. Thus, it can't be used as a parameter or return type. However, just like an abstract class, pointers and references to abstract classes can be used as a parameter or return type.

Traditionally, C++ programmers have defined an interface as a class that contains only pure virtual methods. With Managed C++, it has been formalized with the keyword __interface. Basically, to create an interface, replace the keyword class in the definition and then place in the body of the interface a set of public, pure virtual methods.

Because only public access is allowed within an interface, the default logically for interface access is public. This means there is no need to include the public access modifier, as you would if it were a class.

Obviously, because an interface is only made up of pure virtual methods, the
__sealed keyword has no relevance to interfaces and will generate an error.

One additional note about interfaces: Even though they cannot contain
method variables, is it is perfectly legal to define properties within an interface.
The definition of the properties cannot have an implementation—like other
methods in the interface, the properties need to be implemented in the interface's inheriting class.

Listing 3-16 shows how to create a couple of interfaces, one with pure virtual
methods only and another with a combination of methods and property definitions. It then shows how to do multiple inheritances in a managed class (one
base class and two interfaces).

Listing 3-16. Interfaces in Action

```
#using <mscorlib.dll>
using namespace System;


__gc __interface Interface1
{
public:
    virtual void Method1() = 0;
    virtual void Method2() = 0;
};


__gc __interface Interface2
{
    virtual void Method3() = 0;
    __property String* get_X();
    __property void   set_X(String*);
};


__gc class Base
{
public:
    void MethodBase()
    {
        Console::WriteLine(S"MethodBase()");
    }
};


__gc class DerivedClass : public Base, public Interface1, public Interface2
{
    String* _x;
public:
```

```
        __property String* get_X()
        {
            return _x;
        }
        __property void   set_X(String* x)
        {
            _x = x;
        }


        void Method1()
        {
            Console::WriteLine(S"Method1()");
        }
        void Method2()
        {
            Console::WriteLine(S"Method2()");
        }
        void Method3()
        {
            Console::WriteLine(S"Method3()");
        }
        void Print()
        {
            MethodBase();
            Method1();
            Method2();
            Method3();
        }
};

Int32 main(void)
{
    DerivedClass &dc = *new DerivedClass;

    dc.X = S"Start'n Up";
    Console::WriteLine(dc.X);

    dc.Print();

    return 0;
}
```

Figure 3-16 shows the results of this little program.

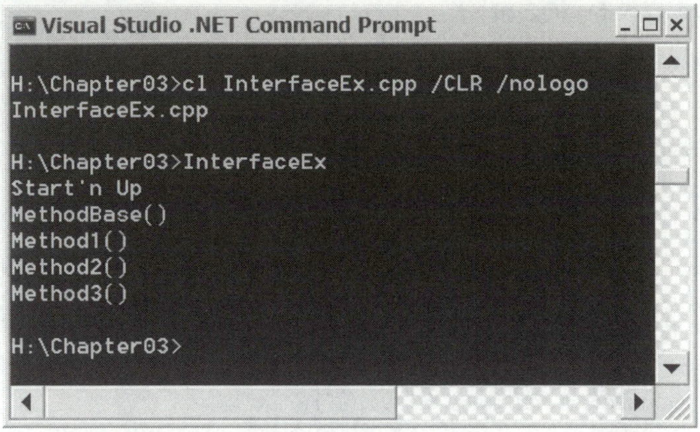

```
Visual Studio .NET Command Prompt                    _ □ ×

H:\Chapter03>cl InterfaceEx.cpp /CLR /nologo
InterfaceEx.cpp

H:\Chapter03>InterfaceEx
Start'n Up
MethodBase()
Method1()
Method2()
Method3()

H:\Chapter03>
```

Figure 3-16. Results of InterfaceEx.exe

Summary

This chapter covered the basics of objected-oriented development using Managed C++. You started with a quick refresher on what objects are and their fundamental concepts. From there, you saw how these concepts fit into the world of Managed C++. You looked at classes in general, and then you broke down a class into its parts: member variables, member methods, and member properties. You finished the chapter by looking at abstract classes and interfaces.

Unlike the basics, Managed C++ has implemented many changes to traditional C++. Though none of the changes are complex—in fact, many simplify things—this chapter should be read carefully by experienced C++ programmers.

You will continue to examine Managed C++ in the next chapter, but now that you have covered the basics, you can move onto a few more complex and, dare I say, fun topics.

CHAPTER 4

Advanced Managed C++

You HAVE COVERED THE BASICS of Managed C++ and moved on to explore its object-oriented nature. Now it is time to start looking at some of the more advanced features of Managed C++. Unlike the previous chapters, this one does not have a common thread from start to finish; instead, it consists of an assortment of more advanced topics that didn't fit into the previous two chapters.

This chapter covers the following topics:

- Working with preprocessor directives

- Using multifile libraries and building an assembly from them

- Referencing the custom-built assemblies in your applications

- Handling errors in Managed C++ using exceptions

- Working with delegates

- Using delegates in events

Preprocessor Directives

Before any actual compiling occurs on a piece of program source code in Managed C++, it must first go through the preprocessor, just like in traditional C++. The purpose of the preprocessor is to prepare the program source code for compiling using a number of instructions called *preprocessor directives*.

These preprocessor directives provide the ability to do things such as include or exclude code based on conditions, define constants, and so on. All of the directives are prefixed with the # symbol (variously called pound, number sign, and hash), which makes them stand out from the rest of the program source code. Table 4-1 shows a complete set of all preprocessor directives for Managed C++.

Table 4-1. Managed C++ Preprocessor Directives

DIRECTIVE	DESCRIPTION
#define #undef	Defines or undefines a meaningful name to a constant or macro in your program.
#if #ifdef #ifndef #elif #else #endif	Allows for conditional compilation of program source code.
#error	Intended to allow you to generate a diagnostic error when something goes wrong in the preprocessor stage.
#include	Provides header file insertion.
#line	Redefines the compiler's internally stored line number and filename with the provided line number and filename.
#pragma	Provides machine/operating system–specific features while retaining compatibility with C++. Most likely, the only #pragma directives that you will encounter in managed C++ are once, which causes an include file to be only included once, and managed and unmanaged, which allow for function-level control of compiling functions as managed or unmanaged.
#using	Imports .NET assembly metadata into program source code using Managed C++.

The four directives that you'll most likely deal with using Managed C++ are the defining, conditional, include, and using directives. Other than the #using directive, there's no difference between Managed C++ and traditional C++ when it comes to the available processor directives, though the #import and many #pragma directives don't make sense and won't be used with Managed C++. This is appropriate, as Managed C++ wasn't designed to change how C++ works; instead, it's supposed to extend C++ to work with .NET.

By convention, preprocessor directives are placed near the top of the source code. In actuality, other than a select few exceptions (the #using preprocessor directive comes to mind as it needs global scope) you can place a preprocessor directive on its own line almost anywhere in the code—basically where it makes sense. The #define declarative, for instance, just needs to be placed before it is used.

Defining Directives

The #define directive is used to execute a macro substitution of one piece of text for another. Here are the three basic syntaxes for implementing #define:

```
#define identifier
#define identifier token-string
#define identifier(parameter1,..., parameterN) token-string
```

The first syntax defines the existence of a symbol. The second syntax allows for the substitution of text identified by the identifier with the following token-string. The third syntax provides the same functionality as the second, plus the passed parameters are placed within the token-string. Listing 4-1 shows the source code before it has been passed through the preprocessor.

Listing 4-1. Original #defined Code

```
#define DISAPPEARS
#define ONE 1
#define TWO 2
#define POW2(x) (x)*(x)

Int32 main ()
{
    Console::Write(S"The following symbol disappears->" DISAPPEARS);
    Console::WriteLine(S"<-");

    Int32 x = TWO;
    Int32 y = POW2(x + ONE);

    Console::WriteLine(y);

    return 0;
}
```

Listing 4-2 shows the source code after it has passed through the preprocessor. Notice that all identifiers have been substituted with their token-string, or lack of token-string in the case of the DISAPPEARS identifier.

Listing 4-2. Processed #defined Code

```
Int32 main ()
{
    Console::Write(S"The following symbol disappears->" );
    Console::WriteLine(S"<-");
```

```
Int32 x = 2;
Int32 y = (x + 1)*(x + 1);

Console::WriteLine(y.ToString());

return 0;
}
```

The #undef directive's purpose is to remove a previously defined symbol. Unlike #define, there is only one syntax:

```
#undef identifier
```

The #undef directive undefines symbols that have been previously defined using the #define directive or the /D compile time switch. If the symbol was never defined, then the #undef directive will be ignored by the preprocessor. If you forget to #undef a symbol before you #define it again, the compiler will generate a warning but will let you continue. It is probably a good idea whenever you see this warning to #undef the variable just before you #define it again to get rid of the warning, but there is nothing saying you have to.

Another approach that you can use to get rid of the warning for an already assigned symbol is to use the #pragma push_macro() and #pragma pop_macro() directives in conjunction with the #undef and #define directives. With this approach, the value of the symbol is stored so that it can be reassigned later after the application no longer needs the new symbol definition. Here is a simple example:

```
#define MY_SYMBOL S"Original"

#pragma push_macro("MY_SYMBOL")
#undef MY_SYMBOL
#define MY_SYMBOL S"New Value"
    Console::WriteLine(MY_SYMBOL);

#pragma pop_macro("MY_SYMBOL")
    Console::WriteLine(MY_SYMBOL);
```

Conditional Directives

Conditional directives provide the ability to selectively compile various pieces of a program. They work in a similar manner to the "if" flow control construct covered in Chapter 2. The big difference is that instead of not executing a particular section of code, now it will not be compiled.

The basic syntax for conditional directives is as follows:

```
#if constant-expression
// code
#elif constant-expression
// code
#else
// code
#endif
```

Something like the "if" flow control construct, the first #if or #elif constant-expression that evaluates to nonzero or true will have its body of code compiled. If none of the constant-expressions evaluates to true, then the #else body of code is compiled.

Only one of the blocks of code will be compiled, depending on the result of the constant-expressions. The constant-expressions can be any combination of symbols, integer constants, character constants, and preprocessor operators (see Table 4-2).

Table 4-2. Preprocessor Operators

OPERATOR	DESCRIPTION
+	Addition
-	Subtraction
*	Multiplication
/	Division
%	Modulus
&	Bitwise AND
|	Bitwise OR
^	Bitwise XOR
&&	Logical AND
||	Logical OR
<<	Left shift
>>	Right shift
==	Equality

(continued)

Table 4-2. Preprocessor Operators (continued)

OPERATOR	DESCRIPTION
!=	Inequality
<	Less than
>	Greater than
<=	Less than or equal to
>=	Greater than or equal to
defined	Symbol is defined
!defined	Symbol is not defined

Though usually quite simple, an expression can become quite complex, as the following example suggests:

```
#define ONE      1
#define TWO      2
#define THREE    3

#if ((ONE & THREE) && (TWO <= 2)) || defined FOUR
    Console::WriteLine(S"IF");
#else
    Console::WriteLine(S"ELSE");
#endif
```

The #if directive has two special preprocessor operators called defined and !defined. The first evaluates to true on the existence of the identified symbol. The second, obviously, evaluates to true if the identified symbol does not exist. To simplify the syntax, and because the defined and !defined operators are the most commonly used preprocessor operators with the #if directive, special versions of the directive were created: #ifdef and #ifndef.

These two directives are equivalent:

```
#if defined symbol
#ifdef symbol
```

and so are these two:

```
#if !defined symbol
#ifndef symbol
```

Include Directive

The #include directive causes the compiler to insert a piece of code into another piece of code. The most common usage of the #include directive is to place header files containing type definitions at the top of a piece of source file to ensure that the types are defined before they are used.

There are two different #include directive syntaxes for including a file in a source. The first uses angle brackets (<>) to enclose the file's path and the second uses double quotes (""):

```
#include <file-path-spec>
#include "file-path-spec"
#include <windows.h>
#include "myclassdef.h"
#include "c:/myincludes/myclassdef.h"
```

Each directive syntax causes the replacement of that directive by the entire contents of its specified file. The difference when processing the two syntaxes is the order that files are searched for when a path is not specified. If the file's path is specified, then no search is done and the file is expected to be at the location specified by the path. One major drawback is that the path cannot be a network path (per the Universal Naming Convention [UNC]). In a corporate, multideveloper site, this inability could be quite a nuisance or possibly even crippling. Table 4-3 summarizes the differences between the angle bracket and double quote syntax search methods when no path is specified.

Table 4-3. #include Syntax Search Differences

SYNTAX FORM	SEARCH METHOD
#include <...>	Check for files along the path specified by the /I compiler option and then along paths specified by the INCLUDE environment variable.
#include "..."	Check for files in the same directory of the file that contains the #include statement, then along the path specified by the /I compiler option, and, finally, along paths specified by the INCLUDE environment variable.

 CAUTION *Though the C++ compiler supports the* INCLUDE *environment variable, Visual Studio .NET does not.*

Using Directive

I covered the #using directive in passing in Chapter 2. Conceptually, there isn't much to it, as all it does is import metadata from within a .NET assembly and place it within the Managed C++ source file. This functionality is very similar to the #include directive discussed in the previous section.

The syntax of the #using directive purposely resembles that of the #include directive. This makes sense, as the #using directive's function resembles that of the #include directive. The only difference in the syntax between #using and #include is that you replace "include" with "using":

```
#using <assembly-path-spec>
#using "assembly-path-spec"
#using <mscorlib.dll>
#using "myassembly.dll"
#using <DEBUG/myassembly.dll>
```

There is no difference between using quotes and angle brackets as there is with the #include directive. Because this is the case, you will almost always see angle brackets used with #using directives. With either the double quote method or the angle bracket method, the compiler searches for the assembly using the following path:

- The path specified by the #using directive

- The current directory

- The .NET Framework system directory

- Directories added with the /AI compiler option

- Directories in the LIBPATH environment variable

 CAUTION   *The* #using *directive is only used to help the compiler and the Visual Studio .NET IDE find the assembly. It does not tell the CLR where to find it. To run the application, you must still place the assembly in a location where the CLR knows to find it.*

It should be noted that the keyword using and the preprocessor directive #using are different. The using keyword enables coding without the need of explicit qualifications. Basically, the using keyword says, "Whenever a class or variable does not exist in the current scope, check the scope of the namespace specified by the using statement and, if it is there, use it just like it is part of the current scope."

Multifile Libraries

So far, in every example, you have used only one file as the source of an application. For small example or demonstration programs this might be okay, but for more complex applications, using multiple source files to break up an application to make it more readable is a much better approach.

Breaking up the source code of an application into its possible many parts can be done in any number of different ways. One of the most common approaches is to break off the source into groups of common functionality, better known as *libraries*. Libraries are a powerful means of breaking up an application because they are more conducive to code reuse, and only at the cost of some minor up-front design work.

The first thing that you will confront when building multifile libraries is that all types need to be declared before they are used in Managed C++. This is not a problem in a single file, as all you have to do is place the declaration of the type before it is used. The only time you might have problems with this is in the case of recursive types that call themselves before they are declared. To solve this, you have prototyping.

With multifile libraries, you run into the problem of how to access a type that is declared in a different file. You could create a whole bunch of prototypes and copy the class definition that you need in every file that uses them, but then you are going to be living in maintenance hell for the lifetime of the library. A better solution is to use header files to hold all these definitions and then #include them at the start of any source file that uses these definitions.

Basically, almost all Managed C++ libraries (and applications, for that matter) should be broken up into two types of files: header files and source files. A *header file* is made up of the code needed to describe the types that are used, and a *source file* is made up of all the code that implements these types.

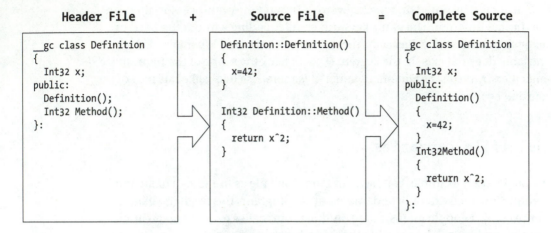

```
      Header File              +        Source File          =      Complete Source

 __gc class Definition                Definition::Definition()          __gc class Definition
 {                                    {                                 {
    Int32 x;                             x=42;                             Int32 x;
 public:                              }                                 public:
    Definition();                                                         Definition()
    Int32 Method();                   Int32 Definition::Method()           {
 }:                                   {                                       x=42;
                                         return x^2;                       }
                                      }                                  Int32Method()
                                                                         {
                                                                            return x^2;
                                                                         }
                                                                       }:
```

With this split, it is a simple thing to place all needed definitions of types by a source file at its top. You discovered earlier that it is a simple matter to place all the declarations in a header file and then insert the contents of the header into the main source code using the #include directive. Coding this way also ensures that all types will be declared before they are used, just as they need to be, by Managed C++.

Okay, you know that you can split source code into two parts, and you know how to actually include the definition part of the source. Let's examine the two parts in more detail.

Header Files

Header files look very similar to all the examples that you have seen in this book so far. Instead of ending in .cpp, they usually end in .h, but that is not mandatory and they can end with anything. The only real difference between what you have seen in the previous chapter's header file is that they only contained the definition portion of functions, member properties, and member methods. Basically, header files are made up of function prototypes and class definitions. In fact, it is legal to place the implementation of a class within a header file.

Here is an example of a header file:

```
//square.h


__gc class Square
{
        Int32 Dims;

public:
        Square ( Int32 d);
        Int32 Area();
};
```

Notice, the only difference between this file and what you have seen previously is that there is no main() function, and the constructor, Square(), and the member method, Area(), are only declared and have no implementation. You could, in fact, have implemented both the constructor and the member method and the header file still would have been valid because classes in Managed C++ are just definitions. What you can't include in header files are function implementations, for example, the main() function. What you can include are only function prototypes.

Source Files

You have seen source files previously in this book. They are Managed C++ files that end with .cpp. With traditional C++ source files, the definition is not found in the source file, unlike all the examples you have seen thus far. Instead, they contain only the implementation of the definitions specified in the header file.

The syntax for implementing member methods in a separate source file from their definitions is similar to that of the function, which was covered in Chapter 2, except that the member method is prefixed with the name of the class it is implementing and the scope resolution (::) operator.

The following example shows the source file for the square.h header file listed previously. Its structure is very typical of all Managed C++ source files. It starts off with the standard #using declarative found in all Managed C++ source files, which is then followed by the using namespace System; statement. Next comes the include statement for the header file, which this source file will be defining, and then, finally, the actual implementations of all the unimplemented member methods.

```
// square.cpp

#using <mscorlib.dll>
using namespace System;

#include "square.h"

Square::Square ( Int32 d)
{
    Dims = d;
}

Int32 Square::Area()
{
    return Dims * Dims;
}
```

Namespaces

Adding a namespace to a library is optional but highly recommended. Remember that all identifiers have to be unique in Managed C++, at least within their own scope. When you develop code on your own, keeping identifiers unique should not be a problem. With careful coordination and a detailed naming convention, a small group of programmers can keep all their identifiers unique. However, with the addition of third-party source code, unique identifiers become increasingly harder to maintain. That is, unless namespaces are used.

Namespaces basically create a local-scope declarative region for types. In other words, namespaces allow a programmer to group code under a unique name. Thus, with the use of a namespace, it is possible for the programmer to create all types with any names she wants and be secure in the knowledge that the types will be unique within the application if they are placed within a uniquely identified namespace.

NOTE *Chapter 2 covers namespaces.*

The basic syntax of a namespace is simply this:

```
namespace name
{
    // all types to be defined within the namespace
}
```

Thus, if you want a namespace called Test to provide local scope to the Square class defined previously, you would simply code it like this:

```
namespace Test
{
    public __gc class Square
    {
        Int32 Dims;

    public:
        Square ( Int32 d);
        Int32 Area();
    };
}
```

Those of you with a traditional C++ background may have noticed the additional keyword public placed in front of the class declaration. Managed C++ handles namespaces differently from traditional C++. Types within a namespace have private access. Thus, to make the class accessible outside the namespace, it has to be declared public. In traditional C++, all types are public within a namespace.

Personally, I don't like the new syntax, as it is inconsistent with C++. It should be public: (be careful, this is invalid syntactically), as it is in classes and structures. This syntax resembles C# and Java instead.

 CAUTION   *If you fail to make any of the classes within the namespace public, then the namespace will not be accessible and will generate an error when you attempt to use the* using *statement for the namespace.*

The syntax to implement a member method within a namespace does not change much. Simply add the namespace's name in front of the class name, delimited by the scope resolution (::) operator.

```
#using <mscorlib.dll>
using namespace System;

#include "square.h"

Test::Square::Square ( Int32 d)
{
    Dims = d;
}

Int32 Test::Square::Area()
{
    return Dims * Dims;
}
```

Building Assemblies from Multifile Libraries

I don't cover assemblies until Chapter 17, so let's not get bogged down with the details of what an assembly really is until then. For now, think of an assembly as a specially formatted .dll or .exe file that is executed by the CLR.

A key feature that you need to know about assemblies is that they're self-describing. What does that mean to a Managed C++ programmer? Simply put, you don't need header files to use the types placed within an assembly. Or, in other words, all those header files you meticulously created when you built your library are no longer needed once you finish creating your assembly. This is a major change from traditional C++.

NOTE *Header files are not needed with assemblies!*

Building Multifile Library Assemblies Using the Traditional Method

You will look at how to actually access an assembly later in this chapter. But the fact that headers are not needed can play a big role in how you code your libraries. The traditional C++ way of creating a library, either static or dynamic, is to create a set of header files to describe all the functionality found within the library. Then, in separate source files, implement all the functionality defined by these header files. All of the source code, along with all the associated header files, is run through the compiler to generate object files. Then all the object files are linked together to create a library file.

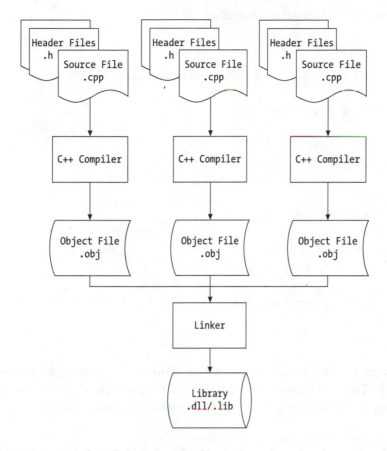

The main reason for all these header files is that when the class is implemented, all the classes, structures, variables, and so on are defined and thus are accessible.

This exact process can be used to generate library assemblies as well. The only difference in the process would be that the Managed C++ flags are turned on for the compiler and linker. Because this method of creating libraries is so commonplace, I will show you how it's done here so that when you see it—and you will see it—you will understand what is happening. Later in the chapter, I will show you a better solution for building library assemblies.

The following example, which consists of Listings 4-3 through 4-6, shows how to create an assembly using the traditional C++ method.

Listing 4-3 shows the header definition to the Card.h file. This file defines an enum of playing card Suits and a Card class within the namespace of Cards. Notice that the keyword public is placed in front of both the enum and the class, as both need to be publicly accessible.

Listing 4-3. Card.h: Traditional Method

```
namespace Cards
{
    public __value enum Suits { Heart, Diamond, Spade, Club };

    public __gc class Card
    {
        Int32 _type;
        Suits _suit;

    public:
        Card(Int32 type, Suits suit);

        __property Int32 get_Type();
        __property Suits get_Suit();

        virtual String *ToString();
    };
}
```

Listing 4-4 shows the implementation of the class's constructor and member methods. The only thing of note in this file is that you override the virtual method ToString(); as you can see, there is nothing special to doing this.

Listing 4-4. Card.cpp: Traditional Method

```
#using <mscorlib.dll>
using namespace System;

#include "card.h"

Cards::Card::Card(Int32 type, Suits suit)
{
    _type = type;
    _suit = suit;
}

Int32 Cards::Card::get_Type()
{
    return _type;
}
```

```
Cards::Suits Cards::Card::get_Suit()
{
    return _suit;
}


String *Cards::Card::ToString()
{
    String *t;

    if (_type > 1 && _type < 11)
        t = _type.ToString();
    else if (_type == 1)
        t = S"A";
    else if (_type == 11)
        t = S"J";
    else if (_type == 12)
        t = S"Q";
    else
        t = S"K";

    switch (_suit)
    {
        case Heart:
            return String::Concat(t, S"H");
        case Diamond:
            return String::Concat(t, S"D");
        case Spade:
            return String::Concat(t, S"S");
        default:
            return String::Concat(t, S"C");

    }
}
```

Listing 4-5 defines a second class named Deck. Notice that you use the Card class within the class, yet you never declare it within the header file. The trick to handling this is to remember that header files are basically pasted wholesale into the source file during compilation. Because this is the case, you simply place the include file of Card.h before Deck.h in the Deck.cpp source file, as you will see in Listing 4-6. Thus, the Card class is pasted in first and, therefore, defined as needed before the Deck class.

Listing 4-5. Deck.h: Traditional Method

```
namespace Cards
{
    public __gc class Deck
    {
        Card  *deck[];
        Int32 curCard;

    public:
        Deck(void);

        Card *Deal();
        void Shuffle();
    };
}
```

Listing 4-6 shows the final source file to the minilibrary. Notice, as I stated previously, that Card.h is included before Deck.h. If you're observant, you might also notice that the Random class is used. You can find this class within the .NET Framework class library.

Listing 4-6. Deck.cpp: Traditional Method

```
#using <mscorlib.dll>
using namespace System;

#include "card.h"
#include "deck.h"

Cards::Deck::Deck(void)
{
    deck = new Card*[52];

    for (Int32 i = 0; i < 13; i++)
    {
        deck[i]    = new Card(i+1, Suits::Heart);
        deck[i+13] = new Card(i+1, Suits::Club);
        deck[i+26] = new Card(i+1, Suits::Diamond);
        deck[i+39] = new Card(i+1, Suits::Spade);
    }
    curCard = 0;
}
```

```
Cards::Card *Cards::Deck::Deal()
{
    if (curCard < deck->Count)
        return deck[curCard++];
    else
        return 0;
}

void Cards::Deck::Shuffle()
{
    Random *r = new Random();
    Card *tmp;
    Int32 j;

    for( int i = 0; i < deck->Count; i++ )
    {
        j       = r->Next(deck->Count);
        tmp     = deck[j];
        deck[j] = deck[i];
        deck[i] = tmp;
    }

    curCard = 0;
}
```

The command you need to execute to build a library assembly from the command line is a little more complex than what you have seen so far, but it is hardly rocket science. The syntax is simply as follows (without the ellipsis):

```
cl source1.cpp source2.cpp...sourceN.cpp /CLR /LD /o OutputName.dll
```

The first change to the command line is that it takes a list of source file names. The next change is the /LD argument, which tells the linker to create a .dll and then, finally, the /o argument, which indicates the name of the .dll file to create.

To compile the previous example, you would use

```
cl card.cpp deck.cpp /CLR /LD /o cards.dll
```

Building Multifile Library Assemblies Using the New Assembly Method

Personally, maintaining header files is a big pain. And I am happy to see them disappear because of .NET's new assemblies. I always seem to forget one or more and have to search for their names. They have to be stored off on a disk some-place. Splitting source code in half increases the risk of something going missing or getting out of sync during the development process.

Because the splitting of header and source files is not needed, it is possible to take a new approach to coding a library. After playing around a bit, I came up with this simplified method. First code all classes, both definition and implementation, using only class (.h) files. Then, using a single linker (.cpp) file, include all the .h files. The only tricky part to this method is making sure that you place the .h files in the right order so that everything is defined before it is used, but this same problem must also be dealt within the traditional method.

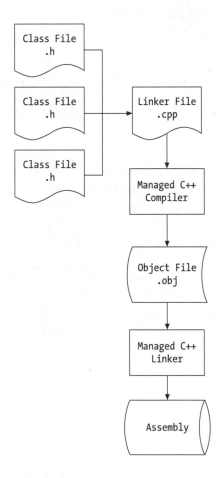

With this method, you need to maintain half the number of files and, because definition and source are defined together, they cannot get out of sync. The combination makes maintaining the library far easier. Add to this the fact that it is easier to read and documentation is only required in one place and, I think, this method is better. The only drawback I see is that it is different for someone who has been coding C++ for a while, so it may take a while to catch on.

Listings 4-7 through 4-9 show the same library you built previously, except that it uses my new approach. As you can see, Listing 4-7 is a combination of the traditional method's Card.h and Card.cpp files. Basically, instead of defining the methods in a separate file, I just place the definitions directly within the class definition.

Listing 4-7. Cards.h: Assembly Method

```
namespace Cards
{
    public __value enum Suits { Heart, Diamond, Spade, Club };

    public __gc class Card
    {
        Int32 _type;
        Suits _suit;

    public:
        Card(Int32 type, Suits suit)
        {
            _type = type;
            _suit = suit;
        }

        __property Int32 get_Type()
        {
            return _type;
        }

        __property Suits get_Suit()
        {
            return _suit;
        }

        virtual String *ToString()
        {
            String *t;
```

```
            if (_type > 1 && _type < 11)
                t = _type.ToString();
            else if (_type == 1)
                t = S"A";
            else if (_type == 11)
                t = S"J";
            else if (_type == 12)
                t = S"Q";
            else
                t = S"K";

            switch (_suit)
            {
                case Heart:
                    return String::Concat(t, S"H");
                case Diamond:
                    return String::Concat(t, S"D");
                case Spade:
                    return String::Concat(t, S"S");
                default:
                    return String::Concat(t, S"C");
            }
        }
    };
}
```

Similarly, Listing 4-8 is a combination of the traditional Deck.h and Deck.cpp. Notice that as in the traditional method, you are accessing other classes within this class without having defined them within the file. Obviously, the linker file needs to make sure that it places all class definitions in the right order so that they will be defined before they are used.

Listing 4-8. Deck.h: Assembly Method

```
namespace Cards
{
    public __gc class Deck
    {
        Card  *deck[];
        Int32 curCard;
```

```cpp
public:
    Deck(void)
    {
        deck = new Card*[52];

        for (Int32 i = 0; i < 13; i++)
        {
            deck[i]     = new Card(i+1, Suits::Heart);
            deck[i+13] = new Card(i+1, Suits::Club);
            deck[i+26] = new Card(i+1, Suits::Diamond);
            deck[i+39] = new Card(i+1, Suits::Spade);
        }
        curCard = 0;
    }


    Card *Deal()
    {
        if (curCard < deck->Count)
            return deck[curCard++];
        else
            return 0;
    }


    void Shuffle()
    {
        Random *r = new Random();
        Card *tmp;
        Int32 j;

        for( int i = 0; i < deck->Count; i++ )
        {
            j         = r->Next(deck->Count);
            tmp       = deck[j];
            deck[j] = deck[i];
            deck[i] = tmp;
        }

        curCard = 0;
    }
};
}
```

The linker file is the only unusual file, as it contains nothing but include statements. It is needed because the Managed C++ compiler only compiles .cpp files; therefore, to have the compiler do anything, you need to have this file (see Listing 4-9). A convenient side effect of this file is that it is easy to add or remove classes from the library, and you have documented in a single place all the classes that make up the library.

Listing 4-9. Cards.cpp: Assembly Method

```
#using <mscorlib.dll>
using namespace System;

#include "card.h"
#include "deck.h"
```

Another thing that you should notice about the linker file is that it is a great location to place testing code during development.

An added bonus to this method of building an assembly library is that the command to run from the command line is simpler:

```
cl cards.cpp /CLR /LD
```

Assembly Referencing

Once you place all of your library logic in an assembly, you are going to want to access it. With Managed C++, getting access to or referencing an assembly is remarkably easy: one file copy (even this step can be eliminated) and one line of code. In fact, the command to compile the application doesn't even change.

After you have done these two things, you can access the library classes as if they were coded directly within your application. If you are using Visual Studio .NET, then you will even have full access to the type definitions within the assembly using IntelliSense.

You'll learn more about configuring access to library assemblies in Chapter 17, but the simplest method is just to place the assembly in the same directory where the final .exe file is going to be placed. Moving or copying the assembly can be done by using the simple copy.exe command or by just dragging and dropping using Windows Explorer. That's it. There's no registering, unregistering, GUIDs, or variants.

You've already covered the line that needs to be added to the source code: #using. Simply add a #using statement at the top of the source code, and voila! The library is available as if it were coded right there in your code. You don't even need any header files—the assembly fully describes itself to the compiler so that it doesn't need any headers.

Listing 4-10 shows an application called PlayCards that references the Cards.dll assembly that you created (in two ways) earlier. Notice that you have access to the namespace and classes, just like you would if you had coded them in the application. You can make references and pointers to the classes. In fact, you can even inherit from them. Basically, you can use them just as you do any other class in the application.

Listing 4-10. PlayCards.cpp: Reference a User Assembly

```cpp
#using <mscorlib.dll>
#using <cards.dll>

using namespace System;
using namespace Cards;

Int32 main(void)
{
    Deck &deck = *new Deck;

    deck.Shuffle();

    Card *card;
    Int32 cnt = 0;
    while ((card = deck.Deal()) != 0)
    {
        Console::Write(card->ToString());
        Console::Write("\t");
        cnt++;

        if (cnt > 4)
        {
            Console::WriteLine("");
            cnt = 0;
        }
    }
    Console::WriteLine("");

    return 0;
}
```

To build this application from the command line, simply copy Cards.dll to the same directory as the source of PlayCards.cpp and then execute the same command from the command line as you always have:

```
cl PlayCards.cpp /CLR
```

Figure 4-1 shows a sample output of this random program.

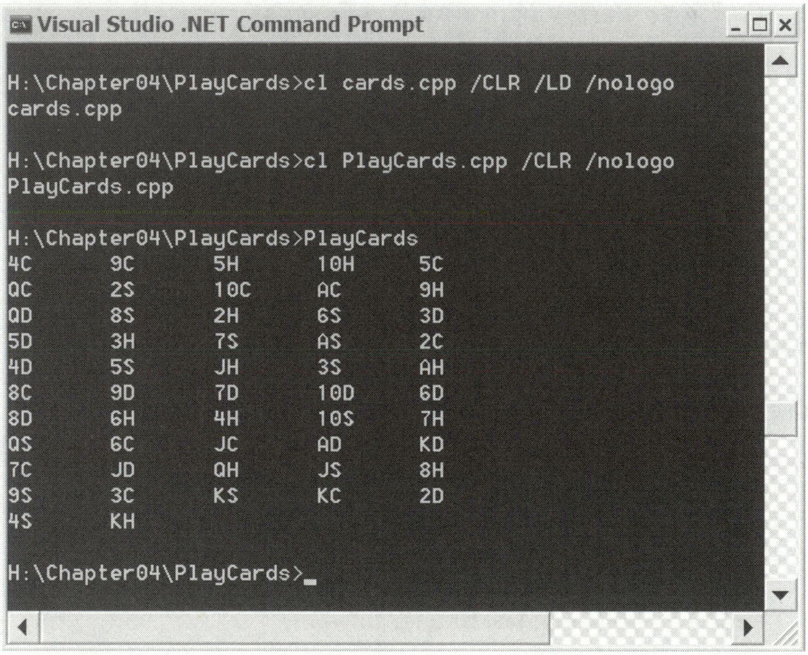

Figure 4-1. Example results of PlayCards.exe

Exceptions

Error handling should be nothing new to software developers. All programmers have written code that verifies that the processes in their code work properly and, if they don't, does something special to correct them. Wouldn't it be nice if nothing could go wrong with your programs and you could write code without having to worry about whether something might go wrong?

Well, you can use exceptions to do that—sort of. Along with the exception's normal role of handling all unforeseen problems, it can actually allow you to code in a manner as if nothing will go wrong and then capture all the possible errors at the end. This separation of error handling from the main code logic can make the program much easier to work with. It eliminates multiple layers of `if` statements with the sole purpose of trapping errors that might occur but most probably won't.

With Managed C++, exceptions have been taken one step further than with traditional C++. Exceptions can now be thrown across language boundaries. That means that if, for example, you code a managed class in Managed C++, and the class is used in some C# code, any exceptions thrown in the managed C++ class can be caught by the C# code. A major benefit of this is there is no need for checking the HResult for errors any longer (if implemented using exceptions). You just have to code as if things worked correctly, because if they didn't, the error would be caught by the exception handler. I won't go into multilanguage programming in this book, but rest assured it does work.

Basics of Exception Handling

Coding for exceptions is very easy. Basically, you break your code up into three parts: the code for successful execution, the errors, and the code to clean up afterward. In Managed C++, these three parts are known as the try block, the catch block, and the __finally block. You will look at the try and catch blocks now and examine the __finally block at the end of this section.

The process for handling exceptions is a little tricky for new developers because the linear flow of the code is broken. Basically, whenever an error occurs, the program throws an exception. At this point, normal execution flow of the program ends and the program goes in search of a handler for the exception that it threw. You'll see how the program searches for exceptions later in the section "Catching Multiple Exceptions." If it doesn't find an exception, the program terminates. Before Managed C++, this termination would have left programs without cleaning up after themselves, but if you code with managed classes you don't have to worry about this.

Exceptions also have to be thrown within a try block or they will immediately terminate without searching for a handler. The try block is simply a block of code enclosed in curly brackets and prefixed with the keyword try:

```
try
{
    // code body where exception can be thrown
}
```

After the try block are one or more catch blocks. Each catch block handles a different type of error. A catch block looks similar to a function with one parameter, except that the function name is always catch, there is no return type, and the parameter is the exception type to trap.

```
catch (<exception-type> e1)
{
    // code to handle exception
}
// repeat for all specific exception types
catch (<exception-type> eN)
{
    // generic code to handle exception
}
```

Listing 4-11 shows a simple example of an exception. I noted in Chapter 3 that the __try_cast operator throws a System::InvalidCastException when it is unable to convert from one try to another. This coding example shows how to capture this exception so that it can be handled more elegantly than the abrupt termination that would normally happen.

Listing 4-11. CatchException.exe: Simple Exception Handling Example

```
#using <mscorlib.dll>
using namespace System;

__gc class X {};
__gc class Y {};

Int32 main(void)
{
    X *x = new X;

    try
    {
        Y *y = __try_cast<Y*>(x);
        Console::WriteLine(S"No Exception");  // Should not execute
    }
    catch (InvalidCastException *e)
    {
        Console::WriteLine(S"Invalid Cast Exception");
        Console::WriteLine(e->StackTrace);
    }

    return 0;
}
```

Figure 4-2 shows the results of this little program.

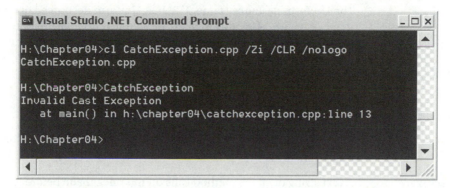

Figure 4-2. Results of CatchException.exe

.NET Framework Base Class: Exception Classes

The .NET Framework has an extensive set of exceptions that it may throw. You'll encounter two different types of exceptions while using .NET:

- ApplicationException

- SystemException

System::ApplicationException is the base class of those exceptions that are user-defined or, in other words, the ones that you have defined yourself.

System::SystemException, on the other hand, handles exceptions created within the CLR, for example, exceptions caused by stream I/O, databases, security, threading, XML, and so on. You can be sure that if the program has aborted due to a system problem you can catch it using the generic System::SystemException.

Both of these exceptions derive from the System::Exception class, which is the root of all .NET exceptions. The System::Exception class provides many useful properties (see Table 4-4) to help resolve any exceptions that might occur.

Table 4-4. Key System::Exception Member Properties

PROPERTY	DESCRIPTION
Helplink	The Uniform Resource Name (URN) or Uniform Resource Locator (URL), if appropriate, to a help file providing more information about the exception.
InnerException	This property gives access to the exception that caused this exception, if any.
Message	A textual description of the error.
Source	The name of the object, assembly, or application that caused the exception.
StackTrace	A text string of all the method calls on the stack made before triggering the exception.
TargetSite	The name of the method that triggered the exception.

SystemException

You can't begin to explore all the exceptions that the .NET Framework class library provides to developers. Even the following illustration, which shows some of the more common exceptions, only shows the tip of the iceberg.

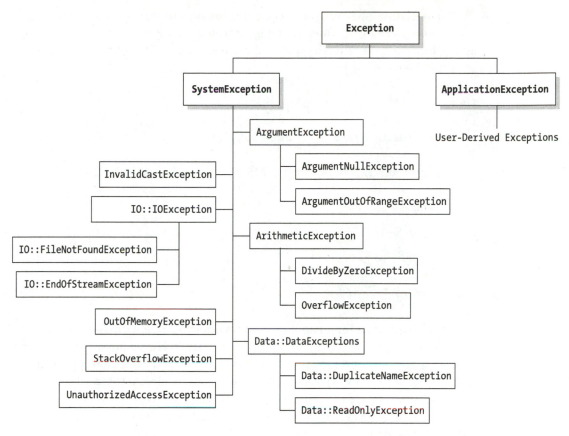

The .NET Framework provides developers with a huge set of classes. Basically, if something could go wrong, the .NET Framework class library provides an exception for it. As you can see from the preceding illustration, the names of the exceptions are pretty self-explanatory, and if you add to them the properties mentioned previously, you have a great tool for finding where your application threw its exception and why.

The best resource to find out about exceptions is the documentation provided by the .NET Framework. You should start your search by looking up `System.Exception`. From there you should quickly be able to navigate to the exception in question.

There is nothing special about catching exceptions thrown by the system. As long as you place the methods that might throw an exception within a try block, all you have to do is catch the system-thrown exception. Here is about as simple as exception handling comes:

```
try
{
    // Methods that throw OutOfMemoryException
}
catch (OutOfMemoryException *oome) // If a method throws an exception
{                                  // Execution will continue here
    // Process exception
}
```

ApplicationException

Truthfully, there is nothing stopping you from throwing exceptions derived from the class System::SystemException or System::Exception. It is even possible to derive an exception from one of the exceptions derived from System::SystemException. The .NET Framework only really added the System::ApplicationException class for readability purposes. In fact, neither System::SystemException nor System::ApplicationException adds any additional functionality to System::Exception.

There is nothing difficult about creating an application exception class. It is just a standard Managed C++ class, but instead of inheriting from System::Object or some other class, you inherit from System::ApplicationException.

```
__gc class MyException : public ApplicationException
{
};
```

Within the custom exception, you can implement anything you want but, in practice, you probably only want to implement things that will help resolve the cause of the exception.

If you are an experienced traditional C++ developer, you know that you could derive your exception from any data type. For example, you could create your exception simply from the System::Object class or even a built-in type such as Int32. This still works in Managed C++ as well, but if you do this you lose the ability to have your exceptions caught by other languages besides Managed C++.

NOTE *All exceptions you create for your applications should be inherited from* System::ApplicationException.

Throwing ApplicationExceptions

Obviously, if you can create your own exceptions, you must be able to throw them too. Technically, you can throw an exception at any time you want, but in practice, it is best only to throw an exception when something in your program fails unexpectedly and normal process flow can no longer continue. The reason for this is that the processing of an exception has a lot of overhead, which can slow the program down when executing. Often, it is better to use if statements to process errors.

Syntactically, the throwing of an exception is very easy. Simply throw a new instance of an exception class. In other words, add code with the following syntax:

```
throw new <Exception-Class>(<constructor-parameters>);
```

or, for example:

```
throw new ApplicationException("Error Message");
```

If you create your own derived exception, just replace ApplicationException with it and pass any parameters to its constructor—if the construct has any parameters, that is.

The actual throw statement does not have to be physically in the try block. It can be located in any method that gets executed within the try block or any nested method that is called within a try block.

Listing 4-12 shows how to create a custom exception from the .NET Framework's System::ApplicationException. Notice that because you're using the System namespace, you don't have to prefix the exceptions with System::. This program simply loops through the for loop three times, throwing an exception on the second iteration.

Note that the try block is within the for loop. This is because even though you can resolve an exception and allow code to continue processing, the only place you are allowed to start or resume a try block is from its beginning. So, if the for loop was found within the try block, there would be no way of resuming the loop, even if you used the dreaded goto statement to try to jump into the middle of the try block.

Listing 4-12. ThrowDerived.exe: Throwing an Exception

```cpp
#using <mscorlib.dll>
using namespace System;

__gc class MyException : public ApplicationException
{
public:
    MyException( String *err ) : ApplicationException(err) {}
};

Int32 main(void)
{
    for (Int32 i = 0; i < 3; i++)
    {
        Console::WriteLine(S"Start Loop");
        try
        {
            if (i == 0)
            {
                Console::WriteLine(S"\tCounter equal to 0");
            }
            else if (i == 1)
            {
                throw new MyException(S"\t**Exception** Counter equal to 1");
            }
            else
            {
                Console::WriteLine(S"\tCounter greater than 1");
            }
        }
        catch (MyException *e)
        {
            Console::WriteLine(e->Message);
        }
        Console::WriteLine(S"End Loop");
    }
    return 0;
}
```

Figure 4-3 shows the results of this little program.

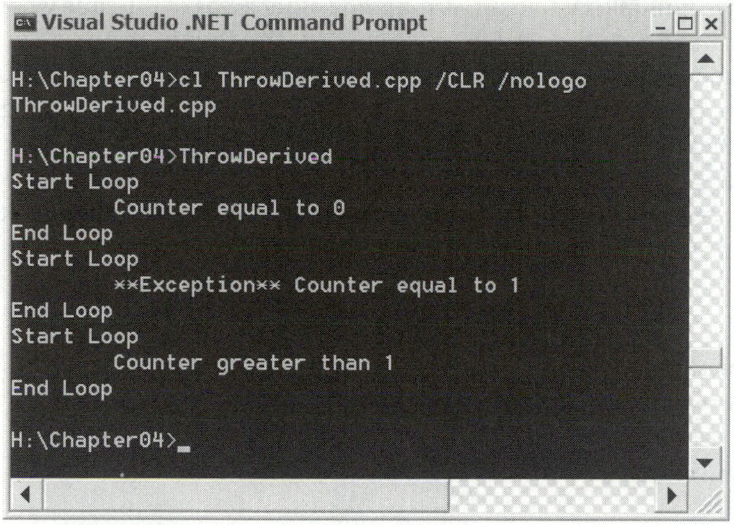

```
Visual Studio .NET Command Prompt                    _ □ ×

H:\Chapter04>cl ThrowDerived.cpp /CLR /nologo
ThrowDerived.cpp

H:\Chapter04>ThrowDerived
Start Loop
        Counter equal to 0
End Loop
Start Loop
        **Exception** Counter equal to 1
End Loop
Start Loop
        Counter greater than 1
End Loop

H:\Chapter04>_
```

Figure 4-3. Results of ThrowDerived.exe

As you can see, there is nothing spectacular about throwing an exception of your own. It is handled exactly the same way as a system exception, except now you are catching an exception class you created instead of one created by the .NET Framework.

Rethrowing Exceptions and Nested Try Blocks

Sometimes it is possible that your program may catch an exception that it cannot completely resolve. In these cases, the program might want to rethrow the exception so that another catch block can resolve the exception.

To rethrow an exception, simply add this statement within the catch block:

```
throw;
```

Once you rethrow the exception, that exact same exception continues to make its way up the stack looking for another catch block that matches the exception. Rethrowing an exception only works with nested try blocks. It will not be caught in a catch block at the same level as it was originally caught and thrown but instead will be caught in a catch block at a higher level.

There is no limit on nesting try blocks. In fact, it is a common practice to have one try block that surrounds the entire program within the main() function and to have multiple try blocks surrounding other areas of the code where an exception has a higher probability of occurring. This format allows the program to catch and resolve exceptions close to where the exception occurred, but it still allows the program to catch other unexpected exceptions before the program ends, so that the program may shut down more gracefully.

Listing 4-13 is a contrived example showing an exception being rethrown within nested try blocks. Of course, nesting try blocks immediately together like this doesn't make much sense.

Listing 4-13. RethrowException.exe: Rethrowing an Exception

```
#using <mscorlib.dll>
using namespace System;

Int32 main(void)
{
    try
    {
        try
        {
            throw new ApplicationException(S"\t***Boom***");
            Console::WriteLine(S"Imbedded Try End");
        }
        catch (ApplicationException *ie)
        {
            Console::WriteLine(S"Caught Exception ");
            Console::WriteLine(ie->Message);
            throw;
        }
        Console::WriteLine(S"Outer Try End");
    }
    catch (ApplicationException *oe)
    {
        Console::WriteLine(S"Recaught Exception ");
        Console::WriteLine(oe->Message);
    }

    return 0;
}
```

Figure 4-4 shows the results of this little program.

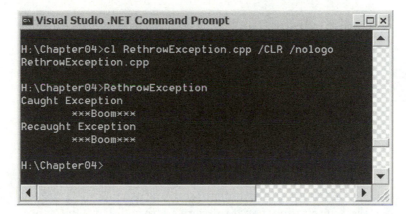

Figure 4-4. Results of RethrowException.exe

Catching Multiple Exceptions

So far, you have only dealt with a single catch block associated with a try block. In reality, you can have as many catch blocks associated with a try block as there are possible exception classes that can be thrown by the try block. (Actually, you can have more, but catching exceptions that are not thrown by the try block is a waste of time and code.)

Using multiple catch blocks can be a little trickier in Managed C++ than in traditional C++ because all exceptions are derived from a single class. As this is the case, the order in which the catch blocks are placed after the try block is important. For catch blocks to work properly in Managed C++, the most-derived class must appear first and the least-derived class or the base class, System::Exception, must appear last.

For example, System::IO::FileNotFoundException must be caught before System:IO::IOException is caught, which in turn must be caught before System::SystemException is caught, which ultimately must be caught before System::Exception. You can find the order of system exception inheritance in the documentation provided by the .NET Framework.

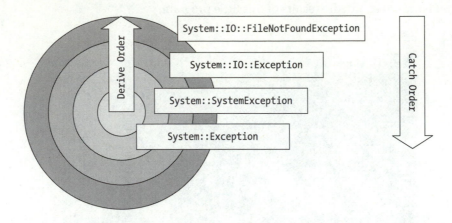

Listing 4-14 shows the correct order of catching exceptions of derived exception class, but this time they are all derived from the System::ApplicationException class. You might want to change the order of the catch blocks to see what happens.

Listing 4-14. MultiException.exe: Catching Multiple Exceptions

```
#using <mscorlib.dll>
using namespace System;

__gc class LevelOneException : public ApplicationException
{
public:
    LevelOneException( String *err ) : ApplicationException(err) {}
};

__gc class LevelTwoException : public LevelOneException
{
public:
    LevelTwoException( String *err ) : LevelOneException(err) {}
};
```

```
Int32 main(void)
{
    for (Int32 i = 0; i < 4; i++)
    {
        Console::WriteLine(S"Start Loop");
        try
        {
            if (i == 1)
                throw new ApplicationException(S"\tBase Exception Thrown");
            else if (i == 2)
                throw new LevelOneException(S"\tLevel 1 Exception Thrown");
            else if (i == 3)
                throw new LevelTwoException(S"\tLevel 2 Exception Thrown");

            Console::WriteLine(S"\tNo Exception");
        }
        catch (LevelTwoException *e2)
        {
            Console::WriteLine(e2->Message);
            Console::WriteLine(S"\tLevel 2 Exception Caught");
        }
        catch (LevelOneException *e1)
        {
            Console::WriteLine(e1->Message);
            Console::WriteLine(S"\tLevel 1 Exception Caught");
        }
        catch (ApplicationException *e)
        {
            Console::WriteLine(e->Message);
            Console::WriteLine(S"\tBase Exception Caught");
        }
        Console::WriteLine(S"End Loop");
    }
    return 0;
}
```

Figure 4-5 shows the results of this little program.

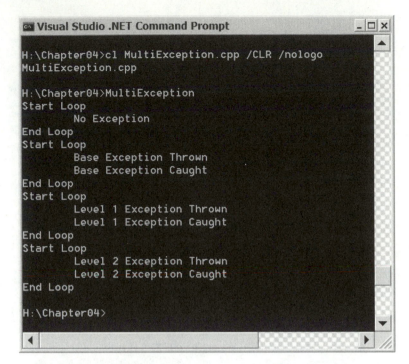

Figure 4-5. Results of MultiException.exe

Catching All Previously Uncaught Exceptions

If you want to correctly code Managed C++ code, which is used in a multilanguage environment, then the easiest way of catching all exceptions is simply to add the catching of System::Exception to the end of your catch block, because all .NET exceptions—of both system and application origin—are derived from this class.

There is also another way of catching all uncaught exceptions, even those not derived from System::Exception. It is simply a catch block without an exception call. In the class's place is an ellipsis:

```
catch (...)
{
}
```

This form of catch block doesn't provide much in the way of information to help determine what caused the exception, as it doesn't have as a parameter any type of exception to derive from. Thus, there's no way to print out the stack or messages associated with the exception that's generated. All you actually know is that an exception occurred.

In Managed C++, this form of catch block should probably only be used as a last resort or during testing, because if this catch block is executed, your code will not work properly in the .NET portable managed multilanguage environment anyway. Of course, if your code is not destined for such an environment, then you may need to use this form of catch block.

The usual reason that this type of exception occurs in Managed C++ is that the developer forgot to derive his exception class from System::ApplicationException. Listing 4-15 shows exactly this occurring.

Listing 4-15. CatchAll.exe: Catching All Exceptions

```cpp
#using <mscorlib.dll>
using namespace System;

__gc class MyDerivedException : public ApplicationException
{
public:
    MyDerivedException( String *err ) : ApplicationException(err) {}
};


__gc class MyException    // Not derived from Exception class
{
};


Int32 main(void)
{
    for (Int32 i = 0; i < 4; i++)
    {
        Console::WriteLine(S"Start Loop");
        try
        {
            if (i == 1)
                throw new ApplicationException(S"\tBase Exception");
            else if (i == 2)
                throw new MyDerivedException(S"\tMy Derived Exception");
            else if (i == 3)
                throw new MyException();

            Console::WriteLine(S"\tNo Exception");
        }
        catch (Exception *e)
        {
            Console::WriteLine(e->Message);
```

```
        }
        catch (...)
        {
            Console::WriteLine(S"\tMy Exception");
        }
        Console::WriteLine(S"End Loop");
    }
    return 0;
}
```

Figure 4-6 shows the results of this little program.

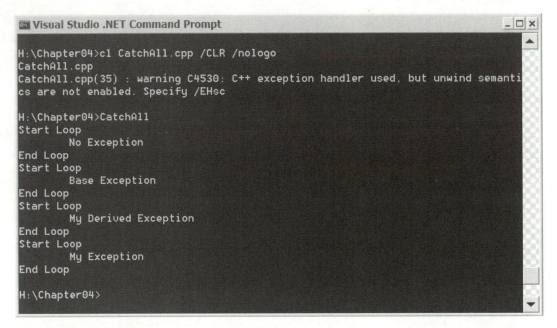

Figure 4-6. Results of CatchAll.exe

Executing Code Regardless of an Exception

There are times when code needs to be run at the completion of a try block, whether the try block completed cleanly or threw an exception. For example, you may want to close a file stream or database that has been open in the try block. Up until now, if you threw an exception, there was no way to ensure that such code was always run unless you put the close statement at the end of each of the try and catch blocks.

With Managed C++, it is now possible to remove this redundant coding by adding a __finally block after the last catch block. The syntax for a __finally block is this:

```
__finally
{
    // Code to always be executed
}
```

All code within the __finally block will always be executed after the completion of the try block or after the completion of the caught catch block.

As you can see in Listing 4-16, the __finally block is run both at the successful completion of the try block and after the System::ApplicationException catch block is executed.

Listing 4-16. Finally.exe: The Finally Block

```
#using <mscorlib.dll>
using namespace System;

Int32 main(void)
{
    for (Int32 i = 0; i < 3; i++)
    {
        Console::WriteLine(S"Start Loop");
        try
        {
            if (i == 0)
            {
                Console::WriteLine(S"\tCounter equal to 0");
            }
            else if (i == 1)
            {
                throw new ApplicationException(S"\t*Exception* Counter = to 1");
            }
            else
            {
                Console::WriteLine(S"\tCounter greater than 1");
            }
        }
        catch (ApplicationException *e)
        {
            Console::WriteLine(e->Message);
```

```
        }
        __finally
        {
            Console::WriteLine(S"\tDone every time");
        }
        Console::WriteLine(S"End Loop");
    }
    return 0;
}
```

Figure 4-7 shows the results of this little program.

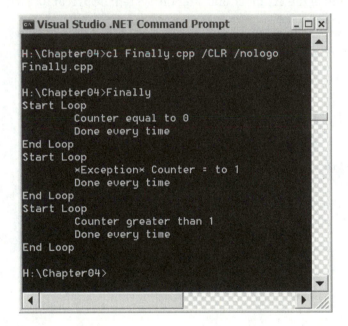

```
Visual Studio .NET Command Prompt                    _ □ ×

H:\Chapter04>cl Finally.cpp /CLR /nologo
Finally.cpp

H:\Chapter04>Finally
Start Loop
        Counter equal to 0
        Done every time
End Loop
Start Loop
        *Exception* Counter = to 1
        Done every time
End Loop
Start Loop
        Counter greater than 1
        Done every time
End Loop

H:\Chapter04>
```

Figure 4-7. Results of Finally.exe

Delegates and Events

Delegates and events are completely new concepts to the traditional C++ developer. Truth be told, both provide the same functionality, basically allowing functions to be manipulated as pointers. Because a pointer can be assigned to more than one value in its lifetime, it is possible to have functions executed based on whichever function address was last placed in the pointer.

For those of you with a C++ background, you might notice that this object-oriented approach is very similar to function pointers. Where they differ is that delegates and events are a class and not a pointer, and delegates and events only invoke member methods of managed (__gc) classes.

You might be wondering, If they all do basically the same thing, why introduce the new concepts? Remember that a key aspect of .NET is language independence. Unfortunately, function pointers are strictly a C++ language feature and are not easily implemented in other languages, especially languages where there are no pointers. Also, function pointers are far from easy to implement. Delegates and events were designed to overcome these problems.

Delegates

A *delegate* is a class that accepts and then invokes one or more methods that share the same signature from other classes that have methods with this same signature.

The .NET Framework supports two forms of delegates:

- `System::Delegate`: A delegate that accepts and invokes only a single method.

- `System::MulticastDelegate`: A delegate that accepts and invokes a chain of methods. A `MulticastDelegate` can perform something known as *multicast chaining*, which you can think of as a set of delegates linked together and then later, when called, executed in sequence.

Managed C++ only supports multicast delegates, but this really isn't a problem because there's nothing stopping a multicast delegate from accepting and invoking only one method.

The creating and implementing of delegates is a three-part process with an optional fourth part if multicast chaining is being implemented:

1. Create the delegate.

2. Create the method to be delegated.

3. Place the method on the delegate.

4. Combine or remove delegates from the multicast chain.

Creating a Delegate

The code involved in creating a delegate is extremely easy. In fact, it is just
a method prototype prefixed with the keyword __delegate. By convention, a delegate is suffixed with "delegate" but this is not essential. For example:

```
__delegate void SayDelegate(String *name);
```

What happens in the background during the compilation process is a lot
more complex. This statement actually gets converted to a class with a constructor to accept delegated methods and three member methods to invoke these
methods. Figure 4-8 shows the effects of the resulting compilation by running the
program ILDASM on Listing 4-17 shown later.

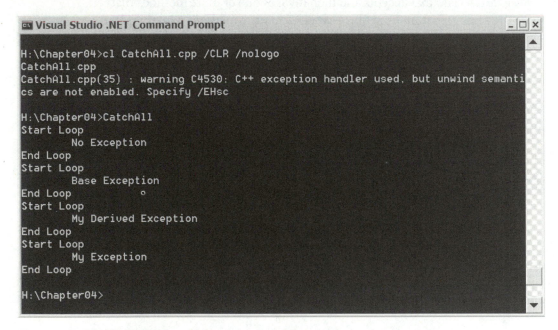

Figure 4-8. ILDASM snapshot of the generated delegate class

Creating a Method to Be Delegated

There is absolutely nothing special about creating a member method for delegating. The only criteria are that it has the same signature as the delegate and that it
is a public member method of a managed (__gc) class. The method can be either
a static member method:

```
__gc class Talkative
{
public:
    static void SayHello(String *name)
    {
        Console::Write(S"Hello there ");
        Console::WriteLine(name);
    }
}
```

or a nonstatic member method:

```
__gc class Talkative
{
public:
    void SayStuff(String *name)
    {
        Console::Write(S"Nice weather we are having. Right, ");
        Console::Write(name);
        Console::WriteLine(S"?");
    }
}
```

Placing a Method on the Delegate

This is the least obvious part of the delegating process. The reason is that you need to implement the autogenerated constructor of the delegate class. If you were not aware that a delegate was a class, then the syntax would appear quite confusing. But, because you are, it should be quite obvious that all you are doing is creating a new instance of the delegate class for each method that you want to delegate.

There is only one constructor for a delegate, and it takes two parameters:

```
delegate-name (address-of-object, address-of-method);
```

The delegate-name is the same as what you specified when you created the delegate. The address-of-object has two possible values. For static member methods, the value should be set to 0. For nonstatic member methods, the value should be the address of a previously created object within which the member method can be found. The address-of-method should contain the fully referenced address of the method. For example, here are delegations of a static and a non-static member method:

```
// Static member functions
SayDelegate *hello = new SayDelegate(0, &Talkative::SayHello);

// Non-static member functions
Talkative *computer = new Talkative();
SayDelegate *stuff = new SayDelegate(computer, &Talkative::SayStuff);
```

Combining and Removing Delegates from a Multicast Chain

These are the trickiest parts of the delegating process, which doesn't say much. The reason they're tricky is that they require the use of two static member methods of the Delegate class, aptly named Combine and Remove. Also, they require typecasting.

The syntax for both combining and removing is exactly the same, except for, of course, the name of the method being called:

```
// Multicast delegate combine
SayDelegate *wind = dynamic_cast<SayDelegate*>(Delegate::Combine(hello, stuff));
// Multicast delegate remove
SayDelegate *gruff = dynamic_cast<SayDelegate*>(Delegate::Remove(wind, stuff));
```

Basically, the Combine method takes the two delegates, chains them together, and then places them on a new delegate. Because the Combine method generates a generic Delegate instance, it needs to be typecast to that specific delegate class required.

The Remove method does the opposite of the Combine method. It removes the specified delegate from the delegate multicast chain and then places the new chain on a new delegate. The Remove method also generates a generic Delegate instance, so it too needs to typecast to the delegate class required.

Invoking a Delegate

Doing this is quite simple but not obvious if you were not aware that a delegate is a class. All you have to do is call the autogenerated member method Invoke with the parameter list that you specified when you created the delegate:

```
hello->Invoke(S"Mr Fraser");
wind->Invoke(S"Stephen");
```

There is no difference in the syntax, whether you invoke one method or a whole chain of methods. The Invoke method simply starts at the top of the chain and executes methods until it reaches the end. If there is only one method, then it only executes one.

Listing 4-17 is a complete example of creating, implementing, and invoking delegates. It uses the same methods found in the function point example, but this time they are member methods of a managed (__gc) class. The example simply creates three delegates, combines two, and then invokes a single delegate and a chained delegate. Then it removes one of the delegates from the chain and invokes a single delegate and a chained delegate, but this time the chain contains only one delegate.

Listing 4-17. Delegates.exe: Programming Delegates

```
#using <mscorlib.dll>
using namespace System;

__delegate void SayDelegate(String *name);

__gc class Talkative
{
public:
    static void SayHello(String *name)
    {
        Console::Write(S"Hello there ");
        Console::WriteLine(name);
    }

    void SayStuff(String *name)
    {
        Console::Write(S"Nice weather we are having. Right, ");
        Console::Write(name);
        Console::WriteLine(S"?");
    }

    void SayBye(String *name)
    {
        Console::Write(S"Good-bye ");
        Console::WriteLine(name);
    }
};
```

```
Int32 main(void)
{
    SayDelegate *hello, *stuff, *bye;

    // Static member functions
    hello = new SayDelegate(0, &Talkative::SayHello);

    Talkative *computer = new Talkative();

    // Non-static member functions
    stuff = new SayDelegate(computer, &Talkative::SayStuff);
    bye   = new SayDelegate(computer, &Talkative::SayBye);

    // Multicast delegate combine
    SayDelegate *winded =
            dynamic_cast<SayDelegate*>(Delegate::Combine(hello, stuff));

    winded->Invoke(S"Mr Fraser");
    bye->Invoke(S"Stephen");

    Console::WriteLine(S"----------------");

    // Multicast delegate remove
    SayDelegate *gruff =
            dynamic_cast<SayDelegate*>(Delegate::Remove(winded, stuff));

    gruff->Invoke(S"Mr Fraser");
    bye->Invoke(S"Stephen");

    return 0;
}
```

Figure 4-9 shows the results of this little program.

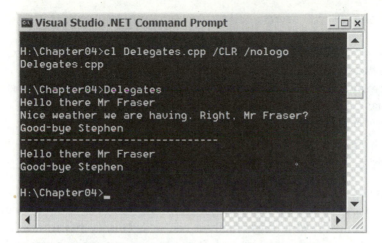

Figure 4-9. Results of Delegates.exe

Events

An *event* is a specific implementation of delegates. You'll see it used quite extensively when I start discussing Windows Forms in Chapter 9 and 10. For now, you'll explore what events are and how they work without worrying about the .NET Framework event model.

In simple terms, events allow one class to trigger the execution of methods found in other classes without knowing anything about these classes or even from which classes it is invoking the method. This allows a class to execute methods and not have to worry about how, or even if, they are implemented. Because events are implemented using multicast delegates, it is possible for a single class to call a chain of methods from multiple classes.

There are always at least two classes involved with events. The first is the source of the event. This class generates an event and then waits for some other class, which has delegated a method to handle the event, to process it. If there are no delegated methods to process the event, then the event is lost. The second and subsequent classes, as was hinted at previously, receive the event by delegating methods to handle the event. I guess, truthfully, only one class is needed to handle an event, as the class that created the event could also delegate a method to process the event. But why would you want to do this, when a direct call to the method could be used, avoiding the event altogether, and it would also be much more efficient?

Building Event Source Class

Before you create an event source class, you need to define a delegate class on which the event will process. The delegate syntax is exactly the same as was covered previously. In fact, there is no difference between a standard delegate and one that handles events. To differentiate between these two types of delegates, by convention delegates that handle events have a suffix of "Handler":

```
__delegate void SayHandler(String *name);
```

Once you have the delegate defined, you can then create an event source class. There are basically two pieces that you will find in all event source classes: the event and an event trigger method. Like delegates, events are easy to code but do a little magic in the background. To create an event, include within a managed (__gc) class in a public scope area a delegate class declaration prefixed by the keyword __event:

```
__gc class EventSource
{
public:
    __event SayHandler* OnSay;
//...
};
```

Simple enough, but when the compiler encounters this, it gets converted into three member methods:

- `add_<delegate-name>`: A public member method that calls the `Delegate::Combine` method to add delegated receiver class methods. To simplify the syntax, you use the overloaded `+=` operator instead of calling `add_<delegate-name>` directly.

- `remove_<delegate-name>`: A public member method that calls the `Delegate::Remove` method to remove delegated receiver class methods. To simplify the syntax, you use the overloaded `-=` operator instead of calling `remove_<delegate-name>` directly.

- `raise_<delegate-name>`: A protected member method that calls the `Delegate::Invoke` method to call all delegated receiver class methods. This method is protected so that client classes cannot call it. It can only be called through a managed internal process.

Figure 4-10 is an ILDASM snapshot that shows the methods that were created by the __event keyword within the event source class of Listing 4-18, which is shown later.

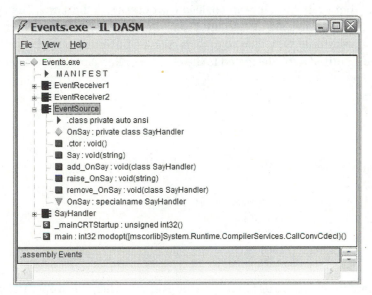

Figure 4-10. ILDASM snapshot of the generated event member methods

Finally, now that you have an event, you need a way to trigger it. The triggering event can be almost anything. In Web forms, the triggering event will be handled by things such as mouse clicks and keypresses. In this case, you will simply call the delegate directly:

```
__gc class EventSource
{
public:
    __event SayHandler* OnSay;

    void Say(String *name)
    {
        OnSay(name);
    }
};
```

Building Event Receiver Class(es)

One or more classes can process an event. The process for delegating a member class to an event is identical for each class. Other than the simplified syntax, you will find that event handling and delegate processing is the same. First, you create the member method to delegate. Then you combine it on the event handler.

The first thing you will need to do is create a public managed (__gc) class member method to be delegated to the event handler. Nothing is new here:

```
__gc class EventReceiver
{
public:
//...
    void SayBye(String *name)
    {
        Console::Write(S"Good-bye ");
        Console::WriteLine(name);
    }
};
```

Then, to combine this method on the event handler, the event receiver class must know which event source class it will be associated with. The easiest way to do this is to pass it through the constructor. To avoid a null pointer error, check to make sure that the pointer was passed. I could have made more thorough validations, such as verifying the type of class, but this is enough to get the idea across.

Now that you have the event source class and a member method to place, it is simply a matter of creating a new instance of a delegate of the event's delegate type and combining it. Or, in this case, using the operator += to combine the new delegate to the event within the source event class:

```
__gc class EventReceiver
{
    EventSource *source;
public:
    EventReceiver(EventSource *src)
    {
        if (src == 0)
            throw new ArgumentNullException(S"Must pass an Event Source");
        source = src;
        source->OnSay += new SayHandler(this, &EventReceiver::SayBye);
    }
//...
};
```

What if you have a delegated method that you no longer want to be handled by the event? You would remove it just as you would a standard delegate. The only difference is that you can now use the `-=` operator. With its simplified syntax, you don't have to worry about typecasting:

```
source->OnSay -= new SayHandler(this, &EventReceiver::SayStuff);
```

Implementing the Event

You now have both a source and a receiver class. All that you need to do is create instances of each and then call the event trigger method.

```
Int32 main(void)
{
    EventSource *source     = new EventSource();
    EventReceiver *receiver = new EventReceiver(source);

    source->Say(S"Mr Fraser");

    return 0;
}
```

Listing 4-18 shows all of the code needed to handle an event. This time, the event source class has two event receiver classes. The event is triggered twice. The first time, all delegates are combined and executed. The second time, one of the delegates is removed. You might notice that the member methods are very familiar.

Listing 4-18. Events.exe: Programming Events

```
#using <mscorlib.dll>
using namespace System;

__delegate void SayHandler(String *name);

__gc class EventSource
{
public:
    __event SayHandler* OnSay;

    void Say(String *name)
    {
        OnSay(name);
    }
```

```
    };

    __gc class EventReceiver1
    {
        EventSource *source;
    public:
        EventReceiver1(EventSource *src)
        {
            if (src == 0)
                throw new ArgumentNullException(S"Must pass an Event Source");
            source = src;
            source->OnSay += new SayHandler(this, &EventReceiver1::SayHello);
            source->OnSay += new SayHandler(this, &EventReceiver1::SayStuff);
        }

        void RemoveStuff()
        {
            source->OnSay -= new SayHandler(this, &EventReceiver1::SayStuff);
        }

        void SayHello(String *name)
        {
            Console::Write(S"Hello there ");
            Console::WriteLine(name);
        }

        void SayStuff(String *name)
        {
            Console::Write(S"Nice weather we are having. Right, ");
            Console::Write(name);
            Console::WriteLine(S"?");
        }
    };

    __gc class EventReceiver2
    {
        EventSource *source;
```

```
public:
    EventReceiver2(EventSource *src)
    {
        if (src == 0)
            throw new ArgumentNullException(S"Must pass an Event Source");
        source = src;
        source->OnSay += new SayHandler(this, &EventReceiver2::SayBye);
    }

    void SayBye(String *name)
    {
        Console::Write(S"Good-bye ");
        Console::WriteLine(name);
    }
};

Int32 main(void)
{
    EventSource *source = new EventSource();

    EventReceiver1 *receiver1 = new EventReceiver1(source);
    EventReceiver2 *receiver2 = new EventReceiver2(source);

    source->Say(S"Mr Fraser");

    Console::WriteLine(S"----------------");

    receiver1->RemoveStuff();

    source->Say(S"Stephen");

    return 0;
}
```

Figure 4-11 shows the results of this little program.

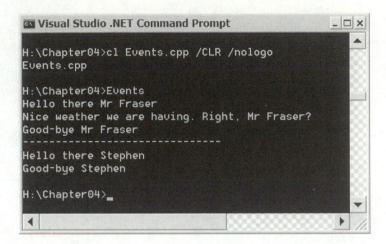

Figure 4-11. Results of Events.exe

Summary

In this chapter, you looked at some more advanced C++ language topics. You started with the preprocessor directives, and then you moved on to multifile software development. In the process, you examined a new way of coding assembly libraries. Next, you covered exceptions and, finally, you ended with function pointers, delegates, and events.

This chapter covered a lot of new ground for the traditional C++ developer, though much of it had a very familiar flavor to it. You will be using much of this chapter later in the book, so a good understanding of these topics is essential.

Okay, you have finally covered Managed C++ as a language. In the next chapter, you will make your first real foray into the world of .NET software development by looking at the .NET Framework class library.

CHAPTER 5

The .NET Framework Class Library

To put it bluntly, the .NET Framework class library is just plain huge. I see in the future several books devoted solely to describing all the interfaces, structures, enumerations, classes, methods, variables, and so on that are contained within this library. One chapter like this one could never do it justice. The goal instead for this chapter is to focus on giving you a head start in learning how to navigate through this massive library.

Even though the library is big, it is well organized and (gasp!) well documented. Once you understand the basics of how the library is organized, it will be easy for you to locate what you are looking for. It should also be quite simple to figure out if what you are looking for is not included in the library.

You will just briefly touch upon the contents of the class library here. In the following chapters, you will delve deeper into many specific areas in the library.

Library Organizational Structure

The first thing you need to know about the .NET Framework class library is that it is an object-oriented tree derived from a single root: `System::Object`. The next important characteristic is that the .NET Framework class library strictly follows the rules specified by the Common Language Specification (CLS), as covered in Chapter 1. The key rules that you should be aware of are as follows:

- Global methods and variables are not allowed.

- There is no imposed case sensitivity, so all exposed types differ by more than their case.

- The only primitive types allowed are `Byte`, `Int16`, `Int32`, `Int64`, `Single`, `Double`, `Boolean`, `Char`, `Decimal`, `IntPtr`, and `String`.

- Variable length argument lists are not allowed. Fixed-length arrays are used instead.

- Pointers are not allowed.

- Class types must inherit from a CLS-compliant class.

- Only single class inheritance is allowed, though multiple inheritance of interfaces is permitted.

The final and most important aspect of the .NET Framework class library is that the current version is broken up into nearly 100 namespaces. Unlike many other libraries, the component identifiers used for the namespaces are self-describing, and thus have the benefit of making it easy to understand what functionality resides within a namespace.

You should be aware that even though namespaces in the .NET Framework class library appear to be broken up into a hierarchy, there is, in fact, no actual "class inheritance hierarchy" that corresponds directly to this "namespace hierarchy." Instead, the namespaces are simply a way of organizing classes into common functionality groups. For example, there is a "namespace hierarchy" of `System::Collections::Specialized`, but many of the classes found in the `System::Collections::Specialized` namespace don't inherit from `System::Collections`.

The .NET Framework class library is physically made up of multiple assembly .dlls. An assembly does not necessarily correspond directly to a namespace, as some of the namespaces spread across multiple assemblies. Also, an assembly may contain multiple namespaces. This does complicate things, but the .NET Framework class library has placed the most commonly used classes into one assembly: mscorlib.dll. Then, it spread out the less common classes into assemblies made up of common functionality.

Unfortunately, I know of no way of easily figuring out which assembly contains which classes. I've tried to help you in this regard by pointing out the necessary assemblies to include for each namespace. The only other way I know of to figure out which assembly is needed is to look for the C1190 error when compiling (I guess "linking" is more accurate). This error tells you which assembly is missing.

Library Namespaces

It's unlikely that you'll use every namespace in the .NET Framework class library. (That's not to say you won't—it's just unlikely.) Instead, you'll probably work with the subset of namespaces that follow.

I will start with the root namespace `System` and then progress alphabetically through the most common namespaces. This chapter will not provide you everything you need to implement the classes within a namespace. Instead, it will give you an understanding of what functionality resides within it. If you want a deeper understanding of all the details of the classes within a namespace, and I do not cover the namespace in the subsequent chapters, then I suggest you peruse the documentation provided with the .NET Framework, as it is remarkably well done.

NOTE *Originally, I was going to include the Microsoft root name-space in this chapter, but when I examined it, I found that it went against the platform-independent direction of this book. The classes found in the Microsoft root namespace are very Microsoft Windows–specific.*

System

The System namespace is the root of the .NET Framework class library name-space hierarchy. The namespace is defined within the mscorlib.dll assembly.

Unlike the other namespaces of the .NET Framework class library, which focus on a particular area of functionality, the System namespace is more a mish-mash of core data types and basic functionality that is needed by the rest of the namespace hierarchy.

The most important class within the System namespace would probably be the Object class because it is the root of all other classes found within the class library. When you create managed (__gc) classes of your own, the Object class is inherited by default if you do not specify a parent class. Remember, because managed (__gc) classes can only inherit from other managed (__gc) classes, ulti-mately your class will inherit the Object class.

Some of the other common functional areas covered by the System name-space are as follows:

- Primitive types, such as Byte, Int32, Double, and String

- Arrays

- Data type conversion

- Attributes

- Delegates

- Enums

- Events

- Exceptions

- Garbage collection

- Math

- Operating system information

- Random numbers

As you can see, you have already covered most of these areas in prior chapters.

Normally, a developer would allow garbage collection to be handled automatically by the CLR because it's a well-tuned process. For some applications, there might be occasions when garbage collection simply doesn't run often enough or at the times wanted by the developer. For these cases, the .NET Framework class library provides the System::GC class. This class doesn't allow the programmer the ability to change the garbage collection process, but it changes the triggering process and helps determine what memory is garbage.

The Math class is an important class that I haven't yet covered. It's made up of a set of static data type overloaded member methods such as Abs(), Exp(), Max(), and Sin(). These methods are easy to use. For example, to find the square root of a number, simply code the following:

```
double val = 16, root;
root = System::Math::Sqrt( val );
```

Another class that can come in handy is System::OperatingSystem. This class provides information such as the version and platform identifier. The System::Version class is used to hold the four-part version (Build, Major, Minor, and Revision) used by the .NET Framework.

Being a games program developer at heart, one of the first classes I went in search of was the random number generator. System::Random provides random numbers in both integer and floating-point formats.

```
System::Random &rand = *new System::Random();
Int32  Int32RandomNumber  = rand.Next(1, 10);   // between 1 and 10 inclusive
Double DoubleRandomNumber = rand.NextDouble(); // between 0.0 and 1.0
```

System::Collections

There are, in fact, two sets of collections available to the .NET Framework programmer: System::Collections and System::Collections::Specialized. As the namespaces suggest, the first set contains generic collection types and the second contains collection types with a more specific purpose. You will find the more common and frequently used System::Collections in the mscorlib.dll assembly, whereas the less frequently used System::Collections::Specialized is in the system.dll assembly.

Because collections are an integral part of most .NET software development, Chapter 7 goes into many of these collections in much greater detail.

Table 5-1 shows you at a quick glance what collection types are found in the System::Collections namespace.

Table 5-1. Collection Types Found Within System::Collections

COLLECTION	DESCRIPTION
ArrayList	An array that grows dynamically
BitArray	An array of bit values (either 1 or 0)
Hashtable	A collection of key/value pairs organized based on a hash code of the key
Queue	A collection of first-in-first-out objects
SortedList	A collection of key/value pairs sorted by key and accessible by either key or index value
Stack	A collection of first-in-last-out objects

Table 5-2 lists all the collection types that you will find in System::Collection::Specialized. As you can see, you will probably use these collections less often, but the .NET Framework class library is nice enough to provide them if you ever end up needing to use one of them.

Table 5-2. Collection Types Found Within System::Collections::Specialized

COLLECTION	DESCRIPTION
BitVector32	A small collection that will represent Boolean or small integers within 32 bits of memory
HybridDictionary	A collection that switches from a list dictionary, when small, to a hash table, when larger
ListDictionary	A singular link list recommended for lists of ten objects or less
NameValueCollection	A collection of string key/value pairs organized on the string key and accessible by either string key or index
StringCollection	A collection of strings
StringDictionary	A hash table with the key strongly typed to be a string

System::Data

The System::Data namespace is the root for all ADO.NET classes found in the .NET Framework class library. ADO.NET is a new data access technology written for the .NET Framework and meant to replace the use of ADO where it is important to remain entirely within .NET. Accessing a database is a very common practice in software development, so you might think that it would be included in the mscorlib.dll default assembly, but you would be wrong. You need to reference two different assemblies. The first is the System.Data.dll assembly, which makes sense now that you know that it's a separate assembly. The second is the System.Xml.dll assembly. I'll go into detail about why this assembly is needed later in Chapter 12. A simple reason is that ADO.NET uses a lot of XML and exposes member methods that use XML. To include these assemblies, if you don't remember, simply add these lines to the top of your source:

```
#using <System.data.dll>
#using <System.Xml.dll>
```

The System::Data namespace comprises most of the classes that make up the ADO.NET architecture. The classes that represent the specific databases to which ADO.NET will connect are missing. These classes are known in ADO.NET-speak as *data providers*. Currently, ADO.NET supports multiple data providers. The data providers found in the System::Data namespace are

- `System::Data::SqlClient`: For Microsoft SQL Server database access

- `System::Data::Odbc`: For ODBC database access

- `System::Data::OleDb`: For OLE DB database access

- `System::Data::OracleClient`: For Oracle database access

Many classes are contained within the `System::Data` namespace. Depending on your database needs, you may require the use of many of these classes. Most likely, though, you'll only have to rely on a few. Table 5-3 provides a list of the more common classes that you may encounter. But don't despair immediately if the specific database access functionality you require isn't in this table. Chances are that there's a class within this namespace that does what you need because `System::Data` is quite thorough.

Table 5-3. Common System::Data Namespace Classes

CLASS NAME	DESCRIPTION
`Constraint`	A constraint enforced on a data column—for example, a foreign key constraint or a unique key constraint.
`DataColumn`	A strong typed column in a data table.
`DataRelation`	A relationship between two data tables within the data set.
`DataRelationCollection`	A collection of all the data relations for a data set.
`DataRow`	A row of data in a data table.
`DataSet`	An in-memory cache of all retrieved data from the data provider.
`DataTable`	An in-memory cache of a single data table within the data set.
`DataTableCollection`	A collection of all data tables within the data set.
`DataView`	A customized view of a data table used for sorting, filtering, searching, editing, and navigation. This view can be bound to higher-level constructs such as GUI tables and lists.

You will look at the `System::Data` and its two data provider namespaces when you learn about ADO.NET in great detail in Chapter 12.

System::Diagnostics

Executing a program in the CLR environment has its advantages, one of those being readily available diagnostic information. True, it is possible to code your traditional C++ to capture diagnostic information but, with .NET, you get it virtually free with the classes within the System::Diagnostics namespace. The only catch is that because this namespace is not used that frequently, you need to implement the system.dll assembly:

```
#using <System.dll>
```

The diagnostic functionality available ranges from simply allowing viewing of event log files and performance counters to allowing direct interaction with system processes. An added bonus is that this namespace provides classes to handle debugging and tracing.

Two main classes handle event logs in the System::Diagnostics namespace. EventLog provides the ability to create, read, write, and delete event logs or event sources across a network. EntryWrittenEventHandler provides asynchronous interaction with event logs. Numerous supporting classes provide more detailed control over the event logs.

It is possible to monitor system performance using the class PerformanceCounter. It is also possible to set up your own custom performance counters using the class PerformanceCounterCategory. You can only write to local counters, but the restriction is eased when it comes to reading counters. Of course, you need to have the right to access the remote machine from where you want to read the counter.

The System::Diagnostics namespace provides an amazing amount of power when it comes to processes. For example, the Process class has the ability to start, monitor, and stop processes on your local machine. In fact, the Process class can also monitor processes on remote machines. Added to this are the ProcessThread and ProcessModule classes, which allow you to monitor the process threads and modules. It is also possible to control how a process runs by having control over things such as arguments and environment variables, and input, output, and error streams using the ProcessStartInfo class.

Almost every programmer uses debug and/or trace statements within his code. So common is the practice that the .NET Framework class library includes the Debug and Trace classes to ease your coding life. Syntactically, the Debug and Trace classes are nearly identical. The difference between them lies in the time of compilation and the current development environment being used. Trace statements are executed no matter what the environment (unless you code otherwise), whereas debug statements are only included and executed while within the Debug environment.

Table 5-4 provides you with a quick lookup table of the classes you might find useful within the System::Diagnostics namespace.

Table 5-4. Common System::Diagnostics Namespace Classes

CLASS NAME	DESCRIPTION
Debug	Methods and properties to help debug a program
Debugger	Provides communication to a debugger
DefaultTraceListener	The default output method for Trace
EntryWrittenEventHandler	Handler to provide asynchronous interaction with event logs
EventLog	Provides interaction with event logs
PerformanceCounter	Provides access to system performance counters
PerformanceCounterCategory	Creates and provides access to custom performance counters
Process	Provides access to local and remote processes and the ability to start and stop local processes
ProcessModule	Provides access to process modules
ProcessStartInfo	Provides control over the environment for which a process starts
ProcessThread	Provides access to process threads
Trace	Provides methods and properties to help trace a program

System::DirectoryServices

System::DirectoryServices is a small namespace providing easy access to Active Directory. Not the most commonly used namespace, it has been placed in its own assembly, System.Directoryservices.dll. To add the namespace, you require the following code at the top of your source:

```
#using <System.Directoryservices.dll>
```

It is assumed that you have prior knowledge of Active Directory before you use the class but, in a nutshell, here is how to use the class. First, you use the class DirectoryEntry constructor to get access to a node or object within Active Directory.

Then, with the `DirectoryEntry` node and some help classes, you are now capable of activities such as creating, deleting, renaming, setting passwords, moving a child node, and enumerating children.

You can use the classes in this namespace with any of the Active Directory service providers. The current providers are

- Internet Information Services (IIS)

- Lightweight Directory Access Protocol (LDAP)

- Novell NetWare Directory Service (NDS)

- Windows NT

Another class that you might find of some use in `System::DirectoryServices` is the `DirectorySearcher` class. This class allows you to perform a query against an Active Directory hierarchy. Unfortunately, as of now only LDAP supports `DirectorySearcher`.

System::Drawing

Computer software without some form of graphics is nearly a thing of the past, especially in the PC world. The .NET Framework relies on a technology named GDI+ to handle graphics. GDI+ is easy to use. It is designed to handle the myriad of graphic adapters and printers in a device-independent fashion, thus saving you from having to worry about coding for each graphic device on your own. Of course, this is not a new concept as Windows has had a Graphical Device Interface (GDI) since its earliest versions. Those of you from the GDI world should see a considerable simplification of how you now have to code graphics. But you will also find a huge increase in added functionality.

`System::Drawing` provides the core graphic classes of GDI+, whereas the following four other child namespaces provide more specialized graphics capabilities:

- `System::Drawing::Drawing2D`: Adds advanced two-dimensional (2D) and vector graphics

- `System::Drawing::Imaging`: Adds advanced GDI+ imaging

- `System::Drawing::Printing`: Adds print-related services

- `System::Drawing::Text`: Adds advanced GDI+ typography

Every `System.Drawing` namespace requires that you add the System.Draw.dll assembly to the top of your source:

```
#using <System.Drawing.dll>
```

I'll go into GDI+ software development in detail in Chapter 11, but for those of you who can't wait that long, here's a brief summary of the functionality.

The core of all GDI+ classes can be found in the `System::Drawing` namespace. This large namespace contains classes to handle things ranging from a point on the graphics device all the way up to loading and displaying a complete image in many graphic file formats, including BMP, GIF, and JPEG.

The key to all graphics development is the aptly named `Graphics` class. This class basically encapsulates the graphics device—for example, the display adaptor or printer. With it you can draw a point, line, polygon, or even a complete image. When you use the `Graphics` class with other `System::Drawing` classes, such as `Brush`, `Color`, `Font`, and `Pen`, you have the means to create amazing and creative images on your display device.

Though you can do almost any 2D work you want with `System::Drawing`, the .NET Framework class library provides you with another set of classes found within the `System::Drawing::Drawing2D` that allows for more fine-tuned 2D work. The basic principle is similar to the "connect-the-dots" pictures that you did as a kid. The image you want to draw is laid out in 2D space by drawing straight and curved lines from one point to another. Images can be left open or closed. They can also be filled. Filling and line drawing can be done using a brush and/or using a color gradient.

The `System::Drawing` namespace can handle most imaging functionality. With the `System::Drawing::Imaging` namespace, you can add new image formats that GDI+ does not support. You can also define a graphic metafile that describes a sequence of graphics operations that can be recorded and then played back.

GDI+ can display (or, more accurately, print) to a printer. To do so is very similar to displaying to a monitor. The difference is that a printer has many different controls that you will not find on a monitor—for example, a paper source or page feed. All these differences were encapsulated and placed into the `System::Drawing::Printing` namespace.

Nearly all the functionality to handle text is located within the `System::Drawing` namespace. The only thing left out and placed in the `System::Drawing::Text namespace` is the ability to allow users to create and use collections of fonts.

System::Globalization

The `System::Globalization` namespace contains classes that define culture-related information, such as language, currency, numbers, and calendar. Because globalization is a key aspect of .NET, the namespace was included within the mscorlib.dll assembly.

You will cover globalization when you learn about assembly programming in Chapter 17. The `CultureInfo` class contains information about a specific culture, such as the associated language, the country or region where the culture is located, and even the culture's calendar. Within the `CultureInfo` class, you will also find reference to the date, time, and number formats the culture uses. Table 5-5 shows some of the more common classes within the `System::Globalization` namespace.

Table 5-5. Common System::Globalization Namespace Classes

CLASS NAME	DESCRIPTION
Calendar	Specifies how to divide time into pieces (for example, weeks, months, and years)
CultureInfo	Contains specific information about a culture
DateTimeFormatInfo	Specifies how dates and times are formatted
NumberFormatInfo	Specifies how numbers are formatted
RegionInfo	Contains information about the country and region
SortKey	Maps a string to its sort key
TextInfo	Specifies the properties and behaviors of the writing system

System::IO

If you are not using a database to retrieve and store data, then you are most probably using file and/or stream input and output (I/O). Of course, it is completely possible that you are using a database and file and stream I/O within the same application. As you can guess by the `System::IO` namespace's name, it handles the .NET Framework library class's file and stream I/O. To access `System::IO`, you need to reference the mscorlib.dll assembly:

```
#using <mscorlib.dll>
```

Typically when you deal with the `System::IO` namespace's classes, you are working with files and directories on your local machine and network, or streams of data probably via the Internet. These, however, are not the only uses of the classes found within the System::IO namespace. For example, it is possible to read data from and write data to computer memory, usually either a string buffer or a specific memory location.

You will be going into the .NET Framework class library's I/O capabilities in some detail in Chapter 8. For now, Table 5-6 shows some of the more common classes that you might come across in the System::IO namespace.

Table 5-6. Common System::IO Namespace Classes

CLASS NAME	DESCRIPTION
BinaryReader	Reads in .NET primitive types from a binary stream.
BinaryWriter	Writes out .NET primitive types to a binary stream.
Directory	A collection of static methods for creating, moving, and enumerating directories.
DirectoryInfo	A collection of instance methods for creating, moving, and enumerating directories.
File	A collection of static methods for creating, copying, deleting, moving, and opening files. It also can be used in the creation of a FileStream.
FileInfo	A collection of instance methods for creating, copying, deleting, moving, and opening files. It also can be used in the creation of a FileStream.
FileNotFoundException	An exception that is thrown when a file on a disk is not found.
FileStream	Provides support for both synchronous and asynchronous read and write operations to a stream.
FileSystemWatcher	Monitors and then raises events for file system changes.
IOException	An exception that is thrown when an I/O exception occurs.
MemoryStream	Provides support for reading and writing a stream of bytes to memory.
Path	Provides support for operations on a String that contains a file or directory.
StreamReader	Reads a UTF-8 encoded byte stream from a TextReader.

(continued)

Table 5-6. Common System::IO Namespace Classes (continued)

CLASS NAME	DESCRIPTION
StreamWriter	Writes a UTF-8 encoded byte stream to a TextWriter.
StringReader	Reads a String using a TextReader.
StringWriter	Writes a String using a TextWriter.
TextReader	An abstract reader class that can represent a sequence of characters.
TextWriter	An abstract writer class that can represent a sequence of characters.

System::Net

This namespace will be hidden from most Web developers using .NET, as they will most likely use ASP.NET's higher-level extraction of Internet communication. For those of you who are more intimate with the networks, the .NET Framework class library has provided the System::Net and System::Net::Sockets namespaces. To access both the System::Net and System::Net::Sockets namespaces, you need to reference the system.dll assembly near the top of your code:

```
#using <system.dll>
```

The System::Net namespace provides a simple programming interface for many of today's network protocols. It enables you to do things such as manage cookies, make DSN lookups, and communicate with HTTP and FTP servers.

If that is not intimate enough for you, then the System::Net::Sockets namespace provides you with the ability to program at the sockets level.

For those of you who want to program your network at this lower level, Table 5-7 shows some of the more commonly used System::Net and System::Net::Sockets classes.

Table 5-7. Common System::Net and System::Net::Sockets Namespace Classes

CLASS NAME	DESCRIPTION
Authorization	Contains an authentication message specifying whether a client is authorized to access the server
Cookie	A set of properties and methods to handle cookies
Dsn	Provides domain name resolution functionality
GlobalProxySelection	A global default proxy instance for HTTP requests
HttpVersion	Specifies the HTTP version supported by the HttpWebRequest and HttpWebResponse
HttpWebRequest	Provides an HTTP implementation of WebRequest
HttpWebResponse	Provides an HTTP implementation of WebResponse
IPAddress	Contains an Internet protocol address
NetworkCredential	Provides credentials for password-based authentication schemes
ServicePoint	Provides connection management for Internet connections
SocketPermission	Controls the rights to create or connect to a socket
Sockets::Socket	Provides a Berkeley socket interface
Sockets::TcpClient	Provides a client for a TCP network service
Sockets::TcpListener	Listens for TCP client connections on a TCP network service
Sockets::UdpClient	Provides a UDP network service
WebClient	Provides methods for sending and receiving data over a network
WebPermission	Controls the rights to HTTP resources

System::Reflection

Most of the time when you develop code, it will involve static loading of assemblies and the data types found within. You will know that, to execute properly, application X requires class Y's method Z. This is pretty standard and most programmers do it without thinking.

This is the normal way of developing with the .NET Framework class library as well. There are times, though, that a developer may not know which class, method, or other data type is needed for successful execution until the time that the application is running. What is needed is dynamic instance creation of data types. With the .NET Framework class library, this is handled by the classes within the System::Reflection namespace found within the mscorlib.dll assembly:

```
#using <mscorlib.dll>
```

The System::Reflection namespace provides a class that encapsulates assemblies, modules, and types. With this encapsulation, you can now examine loaded classes, structures, methods, and so forth. You can also create dynamically an instance of a type and then invoke one of its methods, or access its properties or member variables.

You will explore System::Reflection in more detail when you examine assembly programming in Chapter 17. Table 5-8 shows some of the more common classes that you might use within the System::Reflection namespace.

Table 5-8. Common System::Reflection Namespace Classes

CLASS NAME	DESCRIPTION
Assembly	Defines an assembly
AssemblyName	Provides access to all the parts of an assembly's name
AssemblyNameProxy	A remotable version of AssemblyName
Binder	Selects a method, property, etc., and converts its actual argument list to a generic formal argument list
ConstructorInfo	Provides access to the constructor's attributes and metadata
EventInfo	Provides access to the event's attributes and metadata
FieldInfo	Provides access to the field's attributes and metadata
MemberInfo	Provides access to the member's attributes and metadata
MethodInfo	Provides access to the method's attributes and metadata
Module	Defines a module
ParameterInfo	Provides access to the parameter's attributes and metadata
Pointer	Provides a wrapper class for a pointer
PropertyInfo	Provides access to the property's attributes and metadata
TypeDelegator	Provides a wrapper for an object, and then delegates all methods to that object

System::Resources

The .NET Framework can handle resources in several different ways: in an assembly, in a satellite assembly, or as external resource files and streams. The handling of resources within the .NET Framework class library for any of these three ways lies in the classes of the System::Resources namespace. Handling resources is a very common task, so it was placed within the mscorlib.dll assembly:

```
#using <mscorlib.dll>
```

Resources can be fixed for an application divided by culture. You will examine resources programming when you cover assembly programming in Chapter 17. You will be dealing mostly with three classes within the System::Resources namespace, as shown in Table 5-9.

Table 5-9. Common System::Resources Namespace Classes

CLASS NAME	DESCRIPTION
ResourceManager	Provides the ability to access culture-specific resources from an assembly or satellite assembly. It can also read from a specified resource file or stream.
ResourceReader	Provides the ability to read from a specified resource file or stream.
ResourceWriter	Provides the ability to write to a specified resource file or stream.

System::Threading

Multithread programming can be a very powerful feature, as it allows for more optimal CPU usage and better response time. Very seldom is a computer at 100 percent usage, and running more than one thread concurrently can help you get more out of your CPU.

The .NET Framework has built-in multithreading. In fact, an important feature of .NET, garbage collection, is handled using multithreading. The .NET Framework exposes its multithreading capabilities with the classes found in the System::Threading namespace. Multithreading, being an important and frequently used feature of the .NET Framework, is found in the mscorlib.dll assembly:

```
#using <mscorlib.dll>
```

The System::Threading namespace provides a class to manage groups of threads, a thread scheduler, a class to synchronize mutually exclusive threads, and an assortment of other functionalities to handle multithreading. I will cover multithreading in Chapter 16. For now, Table 5-10 lists all the common classes in the System::Threading namespace that you might use.

Table 5-10. Common System::Threading Namespace Classes

CLASS NAME	DESCRIPTION
Interlocked	Provides atomic operations for a shared variable across multiple threads
Monitor	Provides a lock for critical sections of a thread, allowing for synchronized access
Mutex	Provides synchronized access to shared resources across mutually exclusive threads
ReaderWriterLock	Provides a lock that allows a single writer for many readers
Thread	Creates and controls threads
ThreadPool	Provides a pool of efficient worker threads that are managed by the system
Timer	Provides the ability for threads to execute at discrete intervals

System::Web

The System::Web namespace and the hierarchy of namespaces below it make up a major portion of the .NET Framework class library. This makes sense, as .NET came into being because of the Internet and the World Wide Web.

The System::Web hierarchy is too massive to cover fully here, so I'll leave it to the .NET Framework documentation to provide any detailed explanations you need of any particular class. The .NET Framework breaks Web development into two pieces: Web applications and Web services, which you'll examine in Chapters 14 and 15, respectively. These chapters really just scratch the surface of the functionality available to you as a .NET Web developer.

Table 5-11 will help you to navigate through the myriad of classes provided by the System::Web namespace hierarchy by providing you with a list of some of the more common namespaces (you read that right, *namespaces*) that you might use.

Table 5-11. Common System::Web Hierarchy Namespaces

NAMESPACE	DESCRIPTION
System::Web	Contains classes to handle browser-server communications. This namespace contains HttpRequest and HttpResponse to handle the HTTP dialog between the browser and the Web server.
System::Web::Caching	Contains the cache class used to provide caching of frequently used data on the Web server.
System::Web::Configuration	Contains classes to help set up the ASP.NET configuration.
System::Web::Hosting	Provides the ability to host managed applications that reside outside of the Microsoft Internet Information Services (IIS).
System::Web::Mail	Contains classes to create and send e-mail using either the SMTP mail service built into Microsoft Windows 2000 or an arbitrary SMTP server.
System::Web::Security	Contains classes to handle ASP.NET security in Web applications.
System::Web::Services	Contains classes to create and implement Web services using ASP.NET and XML Web service clients.
System::Web::SessionState	Contains classes to store the data specific to a client within a Web application, giving to the user the appearance of a persistent connection.
System::Web::UI	Contains classes and interfaces to create server controls and pages for Web applications.
System::Web::UI::HtmlControls	Contains classes to create HTML server controls on Web Form pages of Web applications.
System::Web::UI::WebControls	Contains classes to create Web server controls on Web pages of Web applications.

System::Windows::Forms

Visual Basic has been using forms for many versions, and Windows Forms is modeled on Visual Basic's form technology, but with a much finer grain of control. Normally you will create Windows Forms using a drag-and-drop tool but you also have full access to all aspects of the Win form within your code.

As of the current release, Windows Forms and Windows-based GUI applications are pretty much synonymous. On the other hand, if the .NET Framework starts to get ported to other platforms, as it can be, then a Windows Form will be more equivalent to a GUI application.

First off, all the classes that make up the .NET Windows Forms environment are actually found within the System::Windows::Forms namespace. This namespace is large, containing around 400 different types (classes, structures, enumerations, and delegates). You probably will not use every type within the namespace, but there is a good chance that you may use a large number of them, especially if your Windows Form has any complexity involved.

You will cover Windows Forms in detail in Chapters 9 and 10, but you will also see them used many times in subsequent chapters. For those of you who want a head start, Table 5-12 shows a good number of common classes that you will become quite familiar with if you plan to build Windows Forms.

Table 5-12. Common System::Windows::Forms Namespace Classes

CLASS NAME	DESCRIPTION
Application	Provides static methods and properties for managing an application
Button	Represents a Windows Forms Button control
CheckBox	Represents a Windows Forms CheckBox control
CheckListBox	Represents a Windows Forms CheckListBox control
Clipboard	Provides methods to place data in and retrieve data from the system clipboard
ComboBox	Represents a Windows Forms ComboBox control
Control	Represents the base class of all controls in the Windows Forms environment
Cursor	Represents a Windows Forms cursor
Form	Represents a window or dialog box, which makes up part of the application's user interface
Label	Represents a Windows Forms Label control

(continued)

Table 5-12. Common System::Windows::Forms Namespace Classes (continued)

CLASS NAME	DESCRIPTION
LinkLabel	Represents a Windows Forms label control that can display a hyperlink
ListBox	Represents a Windows Forms ListBox control
Menu	Represents the base functionality of all Windows Forms menus
PictureBox	Represents a Windows Forms PictureBox control
RadioButton	Represents a Windows Forms RadioButton control
RichTextBox	Represents a Windows Forms RichTextBox control
ScrollBar	Represents a Windows Forms ScrollBar control
StatusBar	Represents a Windows Forms StatusBar control
TextBox	Represents a Windows Forms TextBox control
ToolBar	Represents a Windows Forms ToolBar
TreeView	Represents a hierarchical display list of TreeNodes

System::Xml

XML is a key component of the .NET Framework. Much of the underlying technological architecture of .NET revolves around XML. No matter what type of application you plan on developing, be it for the Web or a local machine, there is a good chance that somewhere in your application XML is being used. You just might not be aware of it. Because of this, there are a lot of specialized XML classes available to a .NET developer.

To provide XML support to your .NET applications requires the addition of the System.Xml.dll assembly to the top of your source code:

```
#using <System.Xml.dll>
```

The .NET Framework provides a developer two different methods of processing XML data: a fast, noncaching, forward-only stream, and a random access in-memory Document Object Model (DOM) tree. You will cover both methods in Chapter 13. You will also see a little bit of XML in Chapter 15.

Table 5-13 shows all of the .NET Framework class library's XML-related classes that fall within the System::Xml namespace hierarchy.

Table 5-13. Common System::Xml Namespace Classes

CLASS NAME	DESCRIPTION
System::Xml	All the core classes needed to create, read, write, and update XML
System::Xml::Schema	Provides XML Schema support
System::Xml::Serialization	Provides the ability to serialize .NET managed objects to and from XML
System::Xml::Xpath	Provides support for the XPath and evaluation engine
System::Xml::Xsl	Provides support for Extensible Stylesheet Transformations (XSLT)

Summary

In this chapter, you took a high-level look at the core library provided to .NET developers: the .NET Framework class library. You started by learning the basic structure of the .NET Framework class library. You then moved on to examine many of the namespaces, at a high level, that make up the class library. You will see many of these namespaces in later chapters. You should now have an appreciation of how large the library is and a good idea of how to navigate through it.

In the next chapter, you will start to have some real fun. You will take a look at the powerful tool, Visual Studio .NET, provided to Managed C++ developers to build .NET Framework Windows applications, Web applications, and Web services.

CHAPTER 6

Visual Studio .NET Development

I THINK YOU'VE HAD ENOUGH theory for now. Let's have a little fun and look at the Visual Studio .NET development environment, which is at your disposal for developing your Managed C++ code.

In Visual Studio .NET, Microsoft has tried to keep the development environment the same across all development languages. For the most part, if you learn how to use the Visual Studio .NET IDE in one language, you can use it in the same way for any other language. The one exception to this is Web Forms, which the GUI drag-and-drop tools do not support in the Managed C++ development environment. Chapter 14 goes into this issue in more depth.

The Visual Studio .NET development environment is packed with helpful tools to aid you in the development of your .NET code. You will look at many of these tools as you rebuild the PlayCards.exe application you saw in Chapter 4. You will name the application you build in this chapter DeckPlayer.exe, so that you can differentiate between the two applications.

The Visual Studio .NET Desktop

Okay, first you'll need to start up Visual Studio .NET (see Figure 6-1). If you chose to install Visual Basic .NET or C#, you'll notice that they use Visual Studio .NET as well. This ability for your code to be language neutral, as discussed in Chapter 1, is a core feature of the .NET Framework. It only makes sense that the environment for developing your code is language neutral as well.

Figure 6-1. The Visual Studio .NET splash screen

Once you get beyond the splash screen, you are placed directly into the Visual Studio .NET development environment. At first glance, those of you who have worked in any of the more recent Microsoft development environments might be in for a bit of culture shock. A lot has changed, but you can return your environment to the way you like it. Mostly what Microsoft has done is provide you with more control over how your desktop looks. They've also made better use of space by providing nearly everything as a border-tab window.

A border-tab window allows you to tuck the window away in the border for safekeeping when you aren't using it, as shown in Figure 6-2. You can also tack it up to the border and leave it fully expanded or pull it away from the border and make it a stand-alone window. With a border-tab window, you can make your desktop look exactly how you want it and not how the package designer thinks you want it.

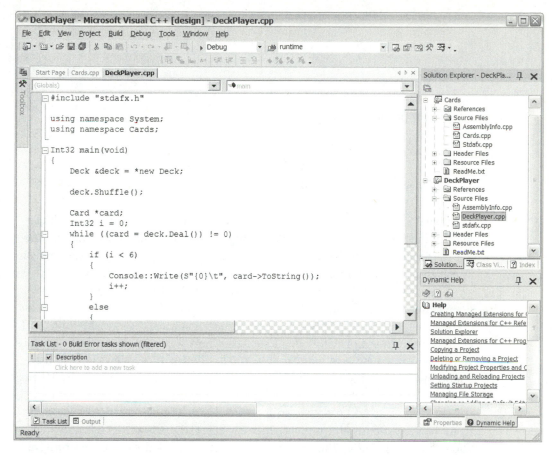

Figure 6-2. A fully tabbed development window

I personally like to tuck away the views when I'm not using them, which gives me a larger area to display code. But with higher and higher resolution monitors coming out every other day, I think my tucking days are quickly coming to an end.

Managed C++ developers will probably be more concerned with the following ten views while developing their code. All but the first and last are border-tab windows.

1. Menu and standard toolbars

2. Class View

3. Index window

4. Solution Explorer

5. Server Explorer

6. Task List

7. Toolbox

8. Properties window

9. Output window

10. Main development tab window

Visual Studio .NET provides many other development views. You won't use most of these views as a Managed C++ programmer. On the other hand, be sure to experiment with the Visual Studio .NET IDE—you might find a hidden treasure or two that I don't cover in this chapter that will make your coding life easier.

There's also another set of views that you'll work with when you're elbow deep in debugging. If you've worked with a symbolic GUI debugger before, none of the views will come as any great surprise. For instance, the Visual Studio .NET debug environment provides an autovariable view, a breakpoint view, a call stack view, an output view, and many others. You'll examine these views later in this chapter when you blow up DeckPlayer.exe and then try to figure out why it's not working.

By the way, to add a view to your environment, you need to select the view from the View menu. Alternatively, in many cases, there is a hot key equivalent you can use to bring up the view. To remove a view, click the close view button, which looks like a standard window close button (i.e., an *X*).

Menu and Toolbars

What's a Windows application without a main menu and toolbars? You can lay these elements out as you like, just as you can with border-tab windows. In fact, you can pull out a toolbar, make it its own view, and place it anywhere on the desktop. It seems the main menu is about the only thing that you can't change the position of. Not that I can think of a reason to change its position, but I'm sure somebody will be upset and ask Microsoft for the menu to be moveable as well.

As you spend more time with Visual Studio .NET, you will notice that the menu and toolbars change as you perform different functions. This is a cool feature and something that most Microsoft products have included for quite some time. Figure 6-3 shows the default starting menu and toolbars after you open up a project.

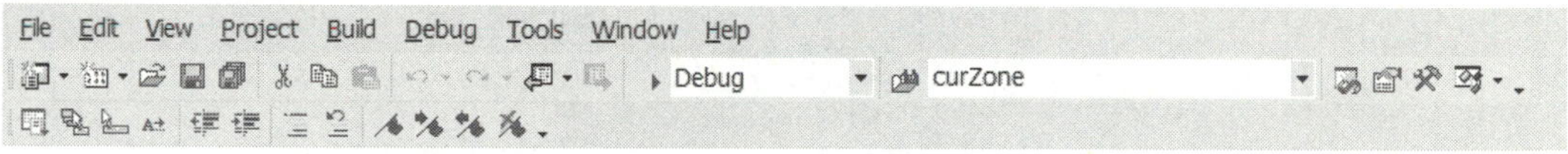

Figure 6-3. Default project menu and toolbars

Because this isn't a book about Visual Studio .NET, I won't go into detail about the menu and toolbars. Truthfully, I think most programmers work with menus and toolbars without needing much guidance.

Class View

The Class Wizard is gone. To some, this might be a huge step backward, as the wizard did provide a lot of functionality. If you're planning on continuing to code MFC, I can see the removal of this tool as a problem, but for those of you moving to Windows Forms, it isn't a great loss.

The reason it isn't a great loss is that developing Windows Forms is much different than developing MFC Windows. With Windows Forms, all you need to do is drag user interface controls to the form you want to build and then update its properties and events—very simple and clean. You don't need a wizard to handle that.

What you might use instead of the wizard is the Class View (see Figure 6-4). This tool allows you to drill down through the entire application and examine every class, property, and variable. It also allows you to add more classes, properties, and variables of your own with easy-to-use wizards. Personally, I find it easier just to type the code in directly, but that might be just me.

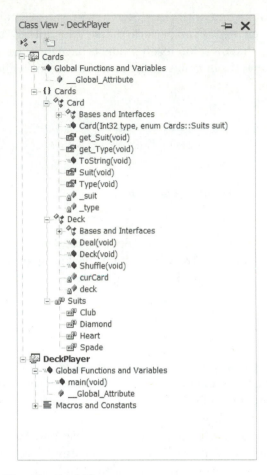

Figure 6-4. Class View for DeckPlayer

Index Window

Most likely you will spend many an hour working with the Index window because, if nothing else, the .NET Framework is well documented and this tool provides you access to the documentation. Visually, there is not much to the Index window, as you can see in Figure 6-5. It just contains a search string for the index and a drop-down box to filter your search through the index to the areas in the documentation that are most applicable.

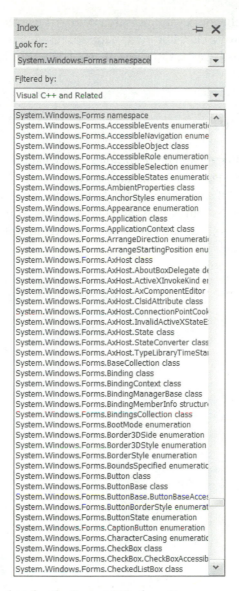

Figure 6-5. Index window for the System.Windows.Forms namespace

It is possible to search the contents of the .NET Framework documentation using the Search window, but I find that the Index window is quicker and, in many cases, provides more relevant documentation than the Search window. With the Index window, though, you have to sort of know what you are looking for. (This is the main reason why I provide Chapter 5, which covers the .NET Framework class library.)

A drawback of the Index window is that it doesn't use Managed C++ syntax for the .NET Framework class library, as namespaces aren't delimited by two colons (::), but instead use the C# syntax of being delimited by a period (.). This really isn't a big deal.

Solution Explorer

As your projects get larger and more complex, you will find Solution Explorer extremely handy (see Figure 6-6). Not only does it provide you with the ability to maintain the names of all the files that make up your solution, but it also allows you to organize the files into projects and folders. When you add versioning with Microsoft Visual SourceSafe, you have a powerful environment in which to maintain your source code.

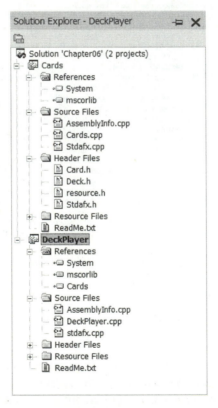

Figure 6-6. Solution Explorer for the DeckPlayer project

Solution Explorer is the heart of all your development with Visual Studio .NET. You will add, delete, and maintain all your files using it. You can initiate activities such as debugging sessions or building and running executables. It will also be the location where you set up the autocopying of assemblies from local build directories to the global assembly cache (GAC) or application root directories.

Something that you should note is that even though it appears that you have created multiple folders and placed files in them, in reality, the code files all stay within one directory. The only exception to this is that subprojects reside within their own directory structure.

Server Explorer

This new feature of Visual Studio .NET provides you with considerable control over your system. No longer do you need to exit the development environment to examine your event logs, message queues, and performance counters. In addition, Server Explorer provides for full service and database maintainability.

Server Explorer allows you to examine your local server, and with the proper privileges, you can also work with remote servers. In Figure 6-7, the data connection DOTNET.CONTENTMGR.dbo is a remote database that I access over the Internet. There, I store my data for my content management system, which I developed in my previous Apress book, *Real-World ASP.NET: Building a Content Management System.*

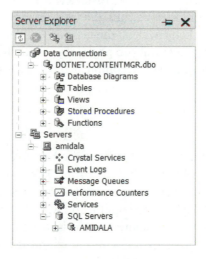

Figure 6-7. Server Explorer for local and remote servers

With all this functionality available from Server Explorer, you will most likely (at least at first) use it mainly as a tool to design, create, and maintain your databases. You will be pleasantly surprised by the amount of control you have over your database construction. Chapter 12 covers Server Explorer's database functionality.

Task List

The Task List (see Figure 6-8) is a handy view that adds a couple of features to your development environment. The most important feature, obviously, is its error-detection capability—errors from an unsuccessful compile are listed here. The Task List provides a description of the error, the file that the error occurred in and, finally, the line number where the error was detected. Double-clicking the Task List on the error task brings your cursor to the line of code in error.

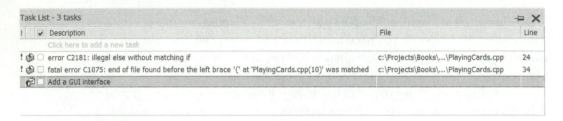

Figure 6-8. Task List with an error and a to-do

The second feature of the Task List is the lesser-used to-do list. If you are new to the programming world, you will be amazed at how quickly you start to forget things that need to be done. This view provides you a way of jotting down to-do tasks as you think of them. And, because the tasks are now part of the project, you will not forget them. You check off the tasks as you complete them. To-do tasks remain with the project until you physically delete them, which provides you with a history of the tasks you accomplished while developing the code.

Toolbox

You will become intimately familiar with the Toolbox view (see Figure 6-9), especially when you start developing Windows Forms. The Toolbox contains an assortment of controls and components that you can drag and drop to your main development window. This view, in conjunction with the main development window and Properties window, allows you to visually build your Windows application's GUI front ends. You will explore this drag-and-drop aspect of the Toolbox view in more detail in Chapters 9 and 10.

Figure 6-9. The Toolbox view for Windows Forms development

In the Visual Basic .NET and C# development environments, the Toolbox view is also used in Web Forms development, but unfortunately this drag-and-drop functionally is not supported in Managed C++.

Another neat feature of the Toolbox is its General tab, which can store things like code so that you can use them again at a later time. I'll show you how to use the Toolbox's General tab a little later in this chapter.

Properties Window

Like the Toolbox view, the Properties window (see Figure 6-10) is a something that you will use when developing your Windows Forms. It is your primary method of updating the look and feel of the controls that you placed on your main development window. It also provides you with a way to quickly add event handlers to the events generated by your controls. You will examine this window in detail in Chapters 9 and 10.

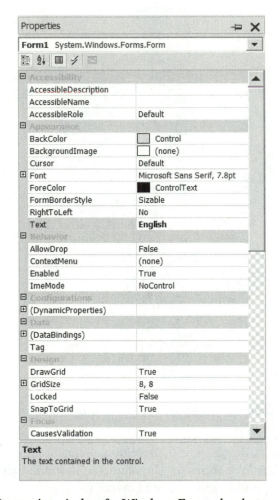

Figure 6-10. The Properties window for Windows Forms development

Output Window

The Output window is read-only, but it's still valuable because it is here that the Visual Studio .NET environment dumps all its output. Most important, at least during development, this view displays the results of the compilation process (see Figure 6-11).

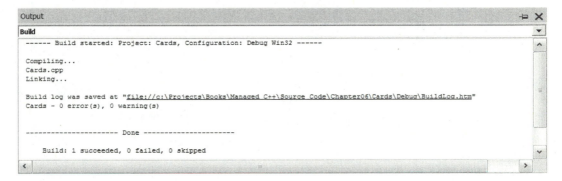

```
Output                                                                    ⟿ ✕
Build                                                                        ▼
  ------ Build started: Project: Cards, Configuration: Debug Win32 ------      ∧

  Compiling...
  Cards.cpp
  Linking...

  Build log was saved at "file://c:\Projects\Books\Managed C++\Source Code\Chapter06\Cards\Debug\BuildLog.htm"
  Cards - 0 error(s), 0 warning(s)


  --------------------- Done ---------------------

     Build: 1 succeeded, 0 failed, 0 skipped                                   ∨
◄                                      ▥                                   ►
```

Figure 6-11. Output of a successful build

Main Development Tab Window

The majority of Visual Studio .NET's desktop is the main development tab window (see Figure 6-12). Those of you who have used Microsoft products for a while might recognize this as a multiple document interface (MDI) viewer using a tab control. With this viewer, you can code your program, create resources, edit your database, create XML documents, view Help files, read online news, and much more.

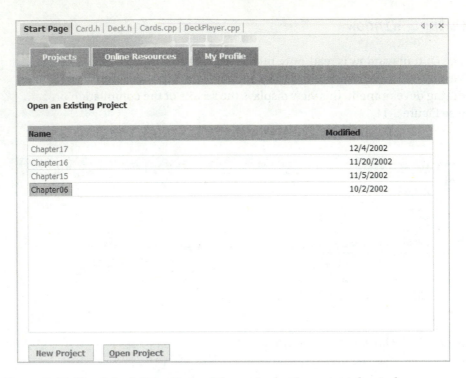

Figure 6-12. The default Start Page of the main development tab window

For those of you who don't know what a MDI viewer is, basically it's a window that presents documents to a user for viewing and, most likely, editing. The viewer is smart enough to know how to display a document based on the document's type. It also allows the document to be displayed in multiple formats. For example, an HTML file can be displayed as WYSIWYG or simply as a text document. As shown in Figure 6-12, the main development tab window has tabs for the HTML Start Page, Card.h, Deck.h, Cards.cpp, and DeckPlayer.cpp documents.

 NOTE *Unlike the other views mentioned in this section, you access the Start Page view from the Help menu, not the View menu.*

The main purpose of the main development tab window is for software development, but Microsoft also uses the window to communicate with the developer community by providing a standard HTML Start Page for all their users. On this page, you will find the latest news from Microsoft on Visual Studio .NET and the .NET Framework in general. The Start Page provides links to an online user community where you can get help from your peers. For those of you creating ASP.NET pages, Microsoft provides a list of Web hosts that can host your newest Web creations.

The Start Page also supplies a unique link called My Profile. The My Profile link provides you with a quick way of configuring your desktop. It comes in handy if you use multiple languages to develop your code. By using a single drop-down list, you can reconfigure your desktop for that language. Figure 6-13 shows My Profile configured for a Visual C++ developer. By simply selecting a different profile, you can configure the desktop for a Visual Basic .NET developer or a Visual C# developer, or you could even create your own custom configuration.

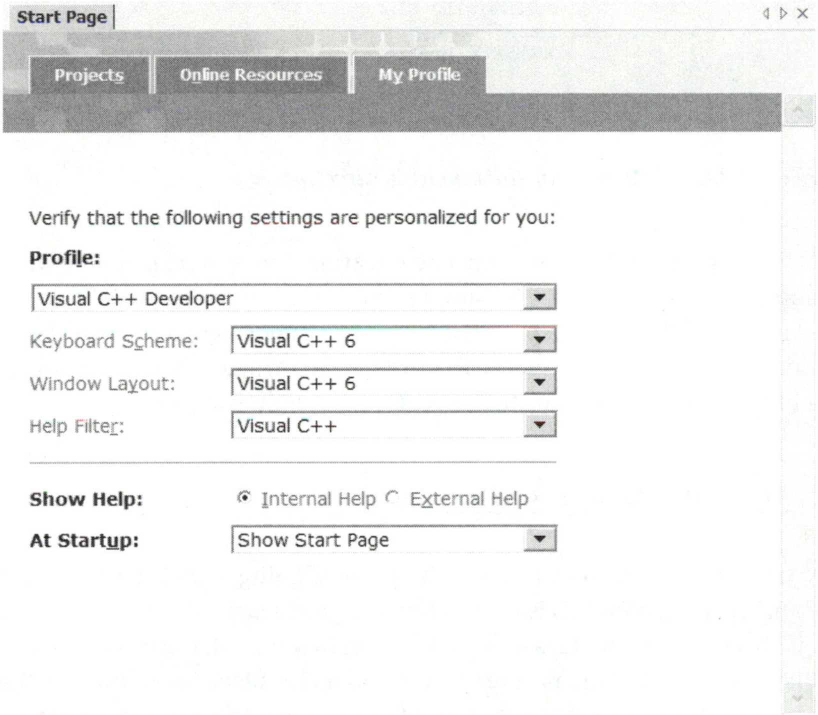

Figure 6-13. Visual C++ developer profile

Dynamic Help

Another view that many developers might find helpful is the Dynamic Help window (see Figure 6-14). This view provides help in a dynamic way by updating itself as you perform tasks in the Visual Studio .NET environment. For example, as you edit a document and set your cursor over the preprocessor directive `#include`, the Dynamic Help window will present you with information about using the directive and possibly provide examples.

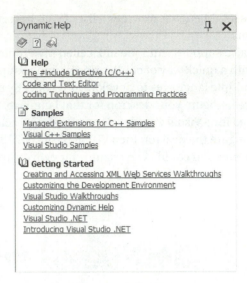

Figure 6-14. Dynamic help for the #include directive

At first, I thought dynamic help a neat feature, but as time passed I found it distracting, so I stopped using it. Now, I keep all my border tabs closed so Dynamic Help will not be displayed anyway. But that is my preference. As mentioned previously, you can configure your desktop however you want, and how I like my screen has no bearing on how you might like yours.

Creating an Empty Solution

Enough exploring, let's play! The first thing you're going to do is create an empty solution. The reason for this is to simplify things. At least, I think it simplifies things. This solution provides a single location to house all the projects it consists of. This makes it easier to find everything, and it also places everything within a single directory structure. A solution differs from a project in that a solution contains projects, whereas a project contains the elements needed to create an assembly. In the case of Managed C++, you can create an application, a library, or a Web service assembly.

This step is not mandatory, though. It is possible to create separate projects for each part of your product. A drawback of this approach is that you have to exit one project to enter another. For example, if you want to make a change in a library but you are currently working in the main application, you have to exit the main application project and enter the library project. With a solution, both projects are part of a single solution, so you don't need to exit any projects.

There are two ways of creating a new empty solution. The first is to simply click the New Project button on the Start Page. The other is to select File ➢ New ➢ Blank Solution from the main menu. Once you have executed either method, you are presented with the New Project dialog box shown in Figure 6-15.

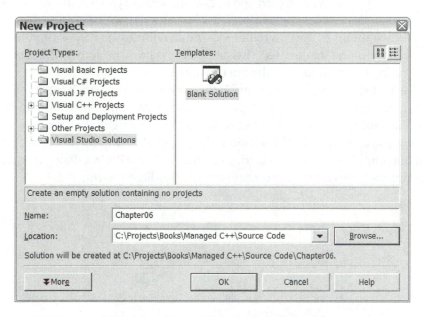

Figure 6-15. Managed C++ class library New Project dialog box

To finish creating the empty solution, simply follow these steps:

1. Make sure the Blank Solution icon is selected in the Templates window.

2. Enter the name of the solution in the Name text box. To make things easy to find, I named the solution **Chapter06**, but I'm sure you can come up with something better.

3. Enter the location where you want the solution to be placed in the Location text box. Note that the solution name will be automatically added as a subdirectory of the location specified. I placed the solution location on my system at **C:\Projects\Books\Managed C++\Source Code**, but you can place it just about anywhere you want on your system.

Creating a Managed C++ Class Library

Now that you have an empty solution, you'll put a project in it so you can start developing some code. The first project you're going to create is a class library called Cards to hold generic card and deck classes. Later you will use this library in your main DeckPlayer application.

The first thing you have to remember is that libraries are .NET assemblies. So are applications, for that matter. This being the case, you can create the assembly library using the method described in Chapter 3.

The first step in creating a library is the same no matter which method you use to create your library: You add a new project to the empty solution. You can do this in a number of ways, the easiest being to simply right-click the empty solution you created earlier in Solution Explorer and then select Add New Project from the drop-down menu. This brings up the Add New Project dialog box, which you saw when you created the empty solution (see Figure 6-16).

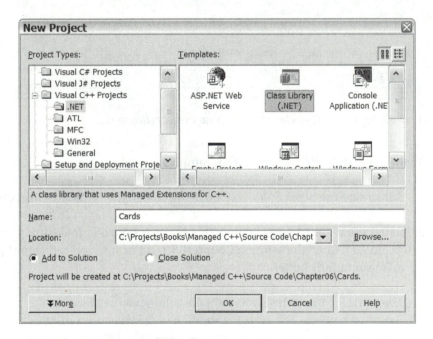

Figure 6-16. The New Project dialog box

This time, to finish creating the empty solution, simply follow these steps:

1. Make sure that the Class Library (.NET) icon is selected in the Templates window.

2. Enter **Cards** as the name of the solution.

3. You don't need to change the location, as it should default to **C:\Projects\Books\Managed C++\Source Code\Chapter06**. This is the exact location I want to put the library.

CAUTION   *If you used the Start Page to create a new project instead of the method described previously, make sure that the Add to Solution radio button is also selected.*

Unlike traditional class libraries, the class file automatically generated by the New Project dialog box will be used as a class linker and not a stand-alone class. If you recall from Chapter 3, the class linker does not need a header file, so you can just remove the header file that was autogenerated, as all it does is clutter up Solution Explorer. You will find Cards.h in the Header Files folder. To delete it, simply right-click Cards.h and then select Remove from the drop-down menu (see Figure 6-17).

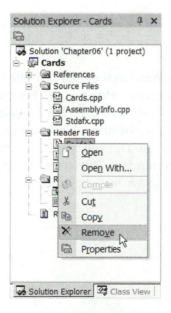

Figure 6-17. Removing Cards.h from Solution Explorer

NOTE *Removing a file from Solution Explorer* does not *physically delete the file from the solution's disk directory structure.*

Updating the Library Linker File

Because you have done all your design work beforehand (like you are supposed to), you know that the class library is made up of two classes: Card and Deck. This being the case, you can update Cards.cpp as shown in Listing 6-1.

Listing 6-1. Cards.cpp: The Class Library Linker File

```
// Cards.cpp the Class Linker file.

#include "stdafx.h"

using namespace System;

#include "card.h"
#include "deck.h"
```

For grins and giggles, add the following two to-do tasks to the Cards project:

- Create Card Class

- Create Deck Class

Okay, the tasks are obvious, but they demonstrate the process of adding tasks. First, click the "Click here to add new task" bar on the Task List view. Then type in the to-do task that needs to be completed. Optionally, you can add a priority to the task by left-clicking the first column (the one with the exclamation mark [!] header) of the Task List. This will bring up a small drop-down list from which you can select a low, normal, or high priority. Figure 6-18 shows what the Task List looks like after these two tasks have been added.

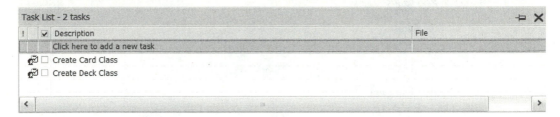

Figure 6-18. Two normal-priority to-do tasks

Adding a Managed C++ Class Using Wizards

You have several approaches for adding classes to a class library assembly. Two of the methods that work best with the new method of building class library assemblies described in Chapter 3 are using a class-building wizard and adding the class manually.

The traditional method for creating a class is to generate both header and source files using a class-building wizard. In the new method of building class library assemblies, as you have seen, there is no need for the source (.cpp) file. Fortunately, Visual Studio .NET's class-building wizard has an option that also eliminates the need for the source (.cpp) file. The process is quite simple.

1. Right-click the project to which you want to add the class.

2. Select Add ➤ Add Class from the drop-down menu. This brings up the Add Class dialog box (see Figure 6-19).

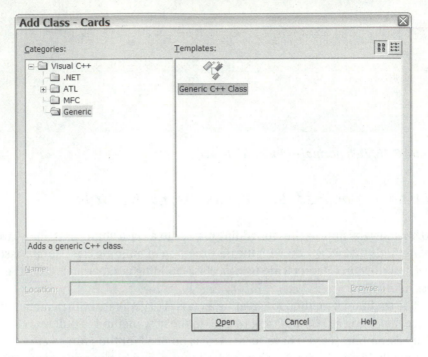

Figure 6-19. The Add Class dialog box

3. Navigate the Categories tree and open the Generic folder.

4. Select the Generic C++ Class icon from the Templates window.

5. Click Open. This brings up the Generic C++ Class Wizard dialog box (see Figure 6-20).

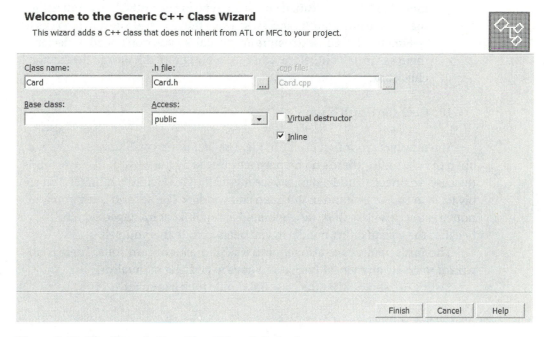

Welcome to the Generic C++ Class Wizard

This wizard adds a C++ class that does not inherit from ATL or MFC to your project.

Class name:	.h file:	.cpp file:
Card	Card.h	Card.cpp

Base class:

Access:
public

☐ Virtual destructor

☑ Inline

[Finish] [Cancel] [Help]

Figure 6-20. The Generic C++ Class Wizard dialog box

6. Enter **Card** in the Class name text box.

7. Add **C** in front of the .h file text box. The reason you do this is that Microsoft has a default naming convention that places a *C* before a class. As this is the case, the .h file text box automatically strips this *C*. Because I don't follow this standard, I need to add the *C* back onto the .h file. By the way, the .cpp file also works the same way, but you're not going to create a .cpp file.

8. Put a check mark in the Inline box. This is important because if you don't check this option, the source (.cpp) file will be generated.

9. Leave the remaining controls as they are. Because you're inheriting from the default System::Object class, you don't need to fill in the Base class input field, but you can, if you want, type in **System::Object**. You want the class to have public access, so leave the Access drop-down box as it is. Finally, all .NET destructors are virtual, so you don't need to declare them as virtual. Therefore, you can safely ignore the Virtual destructor check box.

10. Click the Finish button.

You now have your first class (.h) file. The first thing you'll notice when you open the class file is there's no namespace created by the wizard. Because this is the case, you need to add a namespace manually. This is hardly difficult. You simply have to code it by hand in the main edit window. The second thing you'll notice is the new class that was generated isn't public or managed. Again, because the wizard didn't handle it, you need to code this yourself.

The Cards namespace also requires a public enum of card suits. There is no wizard to create an enum, either, so you have to add this manually.

Listing 6-2 shows what the class file should look like so far.

Listing 6-2. Initial Card.h File

```
#pragma once

namespace Cards
{
    public __value enum Suits { Heart, Diamond, Spade, Club };

    public __gc class Card
    {
    public:

        Card(void)
        {
        }

        ~Card(void)
        {
        }
    };
}
```

Adding a Member Variable by Wizard

Now that you have the basic shell of the Card class completed, you need to add the member variables _type and _suit. The steps for creating these by wizard are virtually the same. The only differences are the variable type and the variable name. Here are the steps to create a member variable by wizard:

1. Open the Class View by selecting its tab from the View menu or by pressing Ctrl-Shift-C. I'm sure there are other ways to access the Class View as well.

2. Right-click the class to which you want to add the member variable—in this case, Card.

3. Select Add ➢ Add Variable from the drop-down menu. The Add Member Variable Wizard appears, as shown in Figure 6-21.

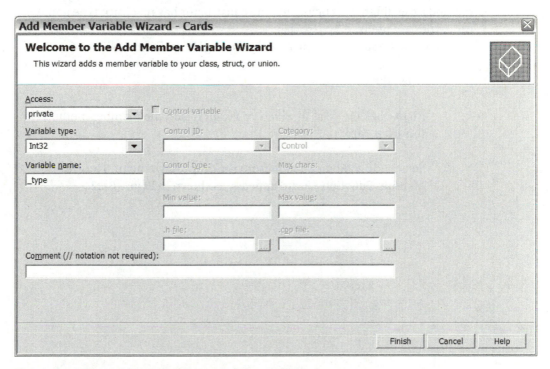

Figure 6-21. The Add Member Variable Wizard dialog box

4. Select private from the Access drop-down list.

5. Enter a variable type of **Int32** for _type or **Suits** for _suit.

6. Enter the appropriate variable name, either **_type** or **_suit**.

7. Click the Finish button.

After you have completed these steps for both variables, you should have two private member variables for the Card class.

Adding a Constructor, a Member Method, and Two Properties by Wizard

To finish off the Card class, you need to add a constructor, two properties, and a virtual function. The process for adding each of them is nearly the same. This makes sense, as they are, from a syntactical perspective, just different types of methods, the differences being that the constructor has no return type and the properties are prefixed by __property.

Here are the steps to create a method using Visual Studio .NET's wizards:

1. Open the Class View.

2. Right-click the class to which you want to add the member method—in this case, Card.

3. Select Add ➤ Add Function from the drop-down menu. The Add Member Function Wizard appears, as shown in Figure 6-22.

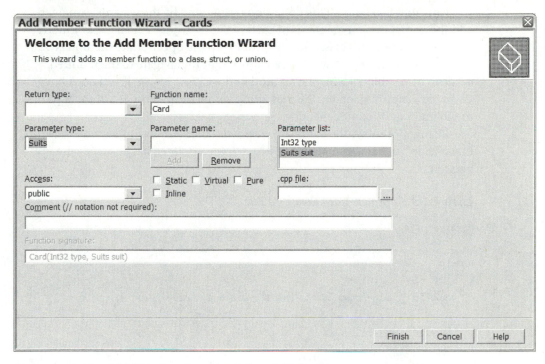

Figure 6-22. The Add Member Function Wizard dialog box

4. Enter the return type of the member method. Remember, if the return type is a pointer, place the asterisk (*) after the return type. In the case of a constructor, leave this text box empty. For a property, you can only enter the return type. You get an error if you prefix the return type with __property in the return type edit box. Currently, you are going to have to add __property manually in the property declaration at the same time as you enter its implementation.

5. Enter the appropriate function name: Card, get_Type, get_Suit, or ToString.

6. For each parameter, enter its type and name, and then click the Add button.

7. Click the Finish button.

Now that you have all the definitions generated by the wizards, you need to add the actual implementations of each of the methods. Because there aren't many methods in this class, simply scrolling to the appropriate method is quite easy. On larger classes, it will probably be easier to navigate to the required method by double-clicking the method in the Class View or, if you don't have the Class View handy, selecting the method from the drop-down list at the top right of the main development window.

Listing 6-3 shows the complete class with all methods implemented. Notice that the default constructor and destructor were deleted because they are not needed.

Listing 6-3. Complete Card Class (.h) File

```
#pragma once

namespace Cards
{
    public __value enum Suits { Heart, Diamond, Spade, Club };

    public __gc class Card
    {
    private:
        Int32 _type;
        Suits _suit;

    public:
        Card(Int32 type, Suits suit)
        {
            _type = type;
            _suit = suit;
        }

        __property Int32 get_Type()
        {
            return _type;
        }

        __property Suits get_Suit()
        {
            return _suit;
        }
```

```
virtual String* ToString()
{
    String *t;

    if (_type > 1 && _type < 11)
        t = _type.ToString();
    else if (_type == 1)
        t = S"A";
    else if (_type == 11)
        t = S"J";
    else if (_type == 12)
        t = S"Q";
    else
        t = S"K";

    switch (_suit)
    {
        case Heart:
            return String::Concat(t, S"H");
        case Diamond:
            return String::Concat(t, S"D");
        case Spade:
            return String::Concat(t, S"S");
        default:
            return String::Concat(t, S"C");
    }
}
};
}
```

As you can see, even if you prefer to use wizards, you still need to perform several steps manually. It's almost easier to code the class without the help of the wizards. In fact, let's do that now.

Adding a Managed C++ Class Manually

As you now know, there's no need for a source (.cpp) file when you create a class library assembly. Thus, to add a new class to the library, you simply have to add a class (.h) file. The first step in the manual process still requires the use of a wizard (actually, it's more of a glorified dialog box) to create the class (.h) file and add it to Solution Explorer. To add the class (.h) file, follow these steps:

1. Right-click the Header Files folder in Solution Explorer. If you don't have Solution Explorer open, press Ctrl-Alt-L to make it the current active task window.

2. Select Add ➤ Add New Item from the drop-down menu. The Add New Item dialog box appears, as shown in Figure 6-23.

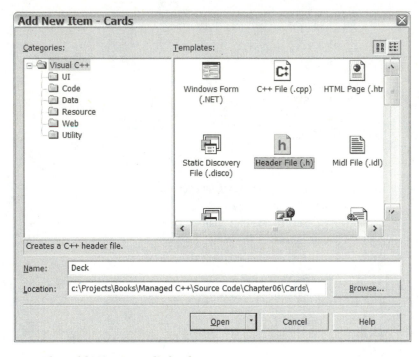

Figure 6-23. The Add New Item dialog box

3. Navigate the Categories tree and open up the Visual C++ folder.

4. Select the Header File (.h) icon from the Templates window.

5. Enter the name of the class in the Name text box—in this case, **Deck**.

6. Verify the location where the class (.h) file will be placed. If the location is incorrect, change it.

7. Click Open. This creates an empty class (.h) file for you to start entering your code into.

8. Enter the code shown in Listing 6-4.

Listing 6-4. Complete Deck Class (.h) File

```
#pragma once

namespace Cards
{
    public __gc class Deck
    {
        Card   *deck[];
        Int32 curCard;

    public:
        Deck(void)
        {
            deck = new Card*[52];

            for (Int32 i = 0; i < 13; i++)
            {
                deck[i]    = new Card(i+1, Suits::Heart);
                deck[i+13] = new Card(i+1, Suits::Club);
                deck[i+26] = new Card(i+1, Suits::Diamond);
                deck[i+39] = new Card(i+1, Suits::Spade);
            }
            curCard = 0;
        }

        Card *Deal()
        {
            if (curCard < deck->Count)
                return deck[curCard++];
            else
                return 0;
        }

        void Shuffle()
        {
            Random *r = new Random();
            Card *tmp;
            Int32 j;

            for( int i = 0; i < deck->Count; i++ )
            {
                j       = r->Next(deck->Count);
```

```
            tmp      = deck[j];
            deck[j] = deck[i];
            deck[i] = tmp;
        }

        curCard = 0;
    }
};
}
```

Saving Templates in the Toolbox

Something that you'll notice as you code more and more classes is that they usually start with a common template (see Listing 6-5). If you're like me and you like to take every shortcut available, then you can save this template in the Toolbox so you don't have to type it again.

Listing 6-5. Class Template

```
#pragma once

namespace XXX
{
    public __gc class YYY
    public:
        YYY(void)
        {
        }
    };
}
```

Along with the drag-and-drop GUI design functionality, the Toolbox view provides a General tab for you to store things that you might want to use later. For example, you might want to save the class template shown in Listing 6-5. To move code to the Toolbox, simply select the code you want to move in the main development edit window and then drag it to the General tab in the Toolbox (see Figure 6-24). Once there, you can rename it by right-clicking the pasted item and selecting Rename from the drop-down menu. To copy the code out of the Toolbox, simply drag the entry you made in the Toolbox under the General tab to the main development edit window. You can also place the saved item on the edit window's current cursor location by double-clicking the item.

Figure 6-24. The Toolbox view's General tab

The Toolbox also stores all items that you have placed on the Clipboard for the current session in the Clipboard Ring tab. Be careful, though—these items disappear when you exit Visual Studio .NET. To make sure that the entry remains for your next session, you must copy it out of the Clipboard Ring tab and paste it into the General tab. You can do this by simply dragging and dropping the entry between the tabs.

Autoupdating the Class View

A neat feature of Visual Studio .NET is that when you edit your code in the main development window, the Class View and the drop-down method list at the top right of the edit window are updated as well. Figure 6-25 shows the Class View after the code for the Deck class has been entered.

Figure 6-25. Autoupdated Class View

Compiling a Project

Now that you have completed the code for the Cards class library, it is a simple matter to compile it into an assembly. Remember that all .NET libraries and applications compile into assemblies. Because you selected the Managed C++ Class Library project type previously, the project automatically configures the compile options to include /CLR. Therefore, to build the assembly, you simply have to select Build ➤ Build Solution from the main menu or press Ctrl-Shift-B.

Figure 6-26 shows the output of a successful compile. If you don't get this output, then make corrections to the errors that appear in your Task List and compile again.

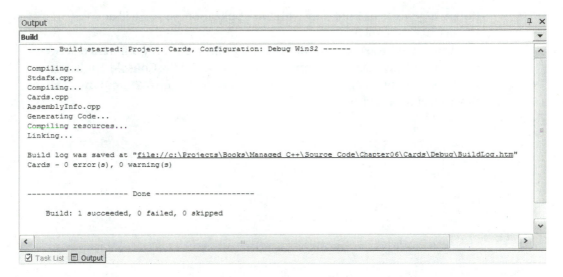

Figure 6-26. Successful build of the Cards class library

After you have compiled your assembly successfully, you should have a file called Cards.dll in the directory Chapter06\cards\Debug. This file is your new library assembly.

NOTE *If you are in release configuration instead of the default debug configuration, then you will find the assembly in the directory Chapter06\cards\Release.*

Creating a Managed C++ Application

I guess I could have made the example easy and just put all the application code in Cards.cpp, but I decided to add a little real-world programming and separate the library from the application. This being the case, you will start by creating another project to place the application in. You have two options:

1. Create the project as its own solution.

2. Include the project in the Chapter06 solution you already created.

It might make more sense to separate the application if the library you just created is going to be shared by multiple applications. But, in this case, the library is going to be used only with this application, so you will add the project to the Chapter06 solution.

You have already seen how to create a project. The only difference between a library and an application project is that you select the Console Application (.NET) icon in the Templates window, as shown in Figure 6-27, and the name of the project is DeckPlayer.

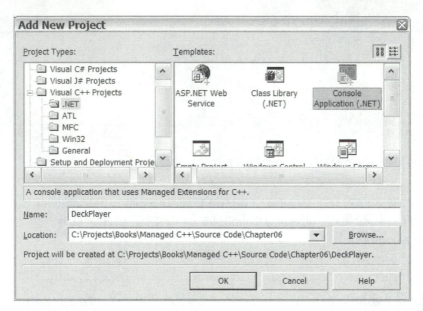

Figure 6-27. Add New Project dialog box with the Console Application (.NET) icon selected

Now all you have to do is replace the autogenerated code with the code in Listing 6-6 in the autogenerated DeckPlayer.cpp file (you have already seen this in Chapter 3). Then you are ready to test your application.

Listing 6-6. Complete DeckPlayer.cpp File

```
#include "stdafx.h"

using namespace System;
using namespace Cards;

Int32 main(void)
{
    Deck &deck = *new Deck;

    deck.Shuffle();
```

```
    Card *card;
    Int32 i = 0;
    while ((card = deck.Deal()) != 0)
    {
        if (i < 6)
        {
            Console::Write(S"{0}\t", card->ToString());
            i++;
        }
        else
        {
            Console::WriteLine(S"{0}\n", card->ToString());
            i = 0;
        }
    }
    Console::WriteLine(S"\n");

    return 0;
}
```

If you recall, in Chapter 3, you used the line #using <Cards.dll> to reference the class library assembly. This command makes the assembly available to the application and provides declarations so that no header file is needed for the library. You may have noticed now that #using <Cards.dll> is no longer at the top of the source. In fact, you do not see any #using statements. The reason is that Visual Studio .NET provides a folder called References that contains all referenced assemblies so you no longer need to include the statement in the source. (You can still include it if you want, but it is not needed.)

Go ahead and compile DeckPlayer exactly as you compiled the Cards assembly. The easiest way to do so is to press Ctrl-Shift-B. Once the compiler is finished, you should have another "build succeeded" message in the Output window.

Before you run the new program, you have to let Visual Studio .NET know which project contains the starting point for the application. In other words, you have to let Visual Studio .NET know which project contains the main() function. To do this, right-click the DeckPlayer project folder in Solution Explorer and then select the Set as Startup Project menu item. Now run the new program by selecting Debug ➢ Start Without Debugging from the main menu or by pressing Ctrl-F5. If everything goes as it should, you see output similar to that shown in Figure 6-28. Of course, the order of the cards will be completely different; otherwise, it wouldn't be much of a shuffle routine.

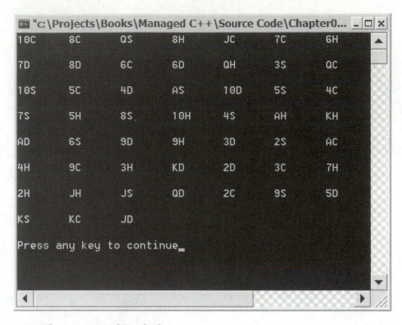

Figure 6-28. The output of DeckPlayer.exe

Let's see what you built. If you've worked with Visual Studio in the past, you would expect that DeckPlayer.exe would be in the Debug directory within the DeckPlayer project directory that you created when you first built the project (unless you're in the release configuration, in which case it should be in the Release directory). Look all you want, it isn't there. Visual Studio .NET placed it in the Debug directory off of the Solution directory. This is one of the bonuses of creating a solution and then placing projects within it. Why is it a bonus? It saves you from having to worry about assembly referencing because all assemblies in the solution are placed in the same directory. Remember, all assemblies for an application must be in the same directory or in the GAC.

Okay, let's simulate the application-development scenario where the class library assemblies and the executable assembly are in different solutions. (This scenario will probably be more the norm when you start developing your own applications.)

So how do you get DeckPlayer.exe back in the Debug directory where you expect it to be? The reason that the program is in the solution's Debug directory can be found in the DeckPlayer Property Pages (see Figure 6-29) and the Cards Property Pages. You can find these pages by right-clicking the DeckPlayer or Cards project folder and selecting the Properties menu item. Do you notice that the Configuration Properties ➤ General ➤ Output Directory text box contains the macro $(SolutionDir)$(ConfigurationName)? Well, that's the culprit. This macro tells the compiler to place DeckPlayer.exe and Cards.dll in the solution's Debug directory.

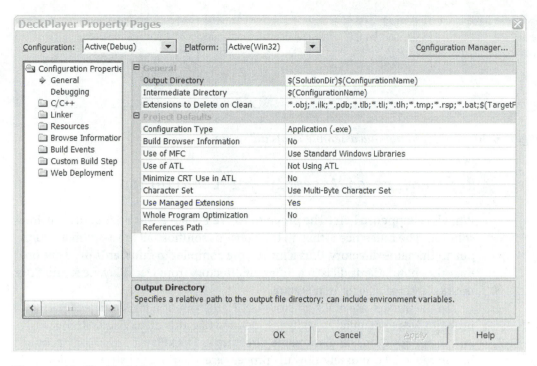

Figure 6-29. The DeckPlayer Property Pages dialog box

To place the DeckPlayer and Cards project assemblies back into their own Debug directories, you need to do the following for both projects:

1. Open the appropriate Property Pages by selecting Properties from the menu item presented after you right-click the Project folder within Solution Explorer.

2. Change the Configuration drop-down box to All Configurations.

3. Delete the $(SolutionDir) macro from the Configuration Properties ➢ General ➢ Output Directory text box.

Once you have done this for both projects, you have in effect created two projects that reside in the same directory structure.

Now let's build DeckPlayer. Oops . . . I got the error shown in Figure 6-30.

Figure 6-30. The "could not find assembly 'cards.dll'" error

Referencing an Assembly for Compilation

What has happened here? The program worked when it was built in the previous solution. The difference is that, in the previous solution, all the assemblies compile to the same directory, thus allowing the compiler to find Cards.dll. Now, on the other hand, Cards.dll is in a different directory from DeckPlayer.exe and thus not readily available for referencing.

In the first release of Visual Studio .NET, the solution for Managed C++ to this problem was to manually specify the location of Cards.dll to Visual Studio .NET and then copy Cards.dll to the same directory as DeckPlayer.exe so that it could be referenced. Fortunately, now the process is a lot easier because it is handled by a Visual Studio .NET menu option, as follows:

1. Highlight the DeckPlayer project within Solution Explorer.

2. Select Project ➤ Add Reference from the main menu. The Add Reference dialog box appears, as shown in Figure 6-31.

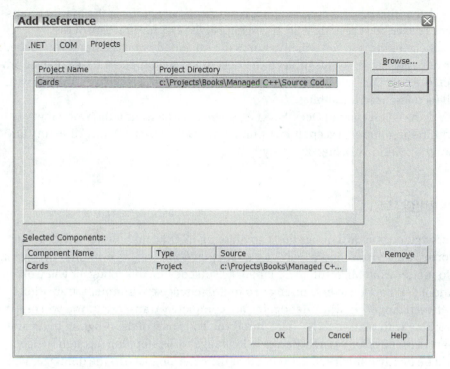

Figure 6-31. The Add Reference dialog box

Alternatively, you could follow these steps:

1. Right-click the Reference folder within the DeckPlayer project.

2. Select the Add References menu item. The Add Reference dialog box appears, as shown in Figure 6-31.

3. Select the Projects tab.

4. Select the Cards project. If there is more than one assembly you need to reference, select multiple projects.

5. Click the Select button.

6. Click the OK button.

What this process does in effect is automatically perform the manual steps that I described previously. So, if you look in the Debug directory of the DeckPlayer project, you will find Cards.dll. An added bonus is that if you make any changes to the Cards project, the next time you compile the DeckPlayer project, the new Cards.dll will be copied over, thus keeping DeckPlayer in sync with all its referenced assemblies.

Now when you run DeckPlayer.exe, it works exactly as it did when it was within the solution, except it is running from DeckPlayer's Debug directory and not the solution's Debug directory.

Debugging

So, what do you do if things don't go quite right? Obviously, you need to debug. Fortunately, Visual Studio .NET has a very powerful, language-neutral debugger. No matter what Microsoft .NET language you code in, the debugger will work. And if you happen to be working in a multilanguage environment, transitions between languages while debugging are completely transparent. You will only be working with Managed C++ here, but if you code part of the program in C# and part in Managed C++, any change in language while stepping through the code will be nearly unnoticeable, except that the code language in the debugger will change.

The Visual Studio .NET debugger has all the standard features of a modern debugger, including

- Unconditional breakpoints

- Conditional breakpoints

- Single-line stepping

- Stepping into methods

- Stepping over methods

- Stepping out of methods

- Auto variable display

- Local variable display

- Variable watching

- Immediate commands

- Call stack

- Threads

- Registers

- Modules

- Memory

You will probably use most of these features at one time or another while debugging code. Of course, a well-placed debug statement also comes in handy sometimes. This book is about Managed C++, and not debugging, so you'll just take a quick look at some of the debugger's features.

Setting Breakpoints

Two types of breakpoints, unconditional and conditional, are available to you while you're debugging. *Unconditional* breakpoints stop the program whenever the break line is about to be executed. *Conditional* breakpoints, on the other hand, examine some type of condition first and, if the condition meets certain criteria, stop execution at the line where the break is specified.

Unconditional breakpoints are simple to set. All you need to do is click the border to the left of the line you want to break on. A longer but equivalent method is to select the line to break on, right-click, and then select Insert Breakpoint from the drop-down menu.

Conditional breakpoints are a little more complex to set. To create a new conditional breakpoint, you need to right-click the line where you want the break to occur and then select New Breakpoint. This will bring up the dialog box shown in Figure 6-32. If the line currently has an unconditional breakpoint, you can change it to a conditional by right-clicking the breakpoint and selecting Breakpoint Properties from the drop-down menu.

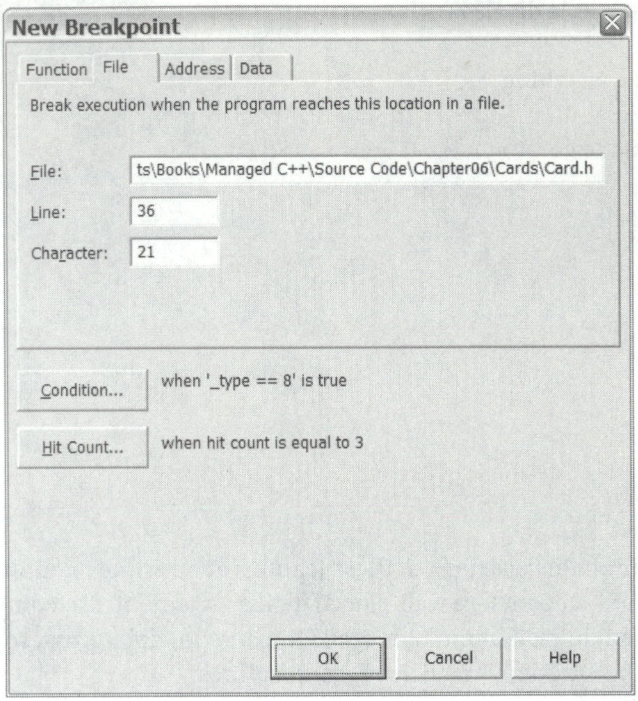

Figure 6-32. New Breakpoint dialog box

From within the dialog box, you can set a condition to break on by clicking the Condition button. You can use almost any condition that would be valid in an if statement at the location of a break. In Figure 6-32, the condition being set is _type == 8. You can also set the program to break based on the number of times the breakpoint has been executed by clicking the Hit Count button. In Figure 6-32, the program will break the third time the breakpoint is executed. As you can see, you can get pretty accurate in specifying when to break execution. In Figure 6-32, you are breaking when the third card with a value of 8 is dealt.

After you set a breakpoint—either conditional or unconditional—the debugger responds by placing a red dot in the left border next to the line on which you want the break to occur (see Figure 6-33).

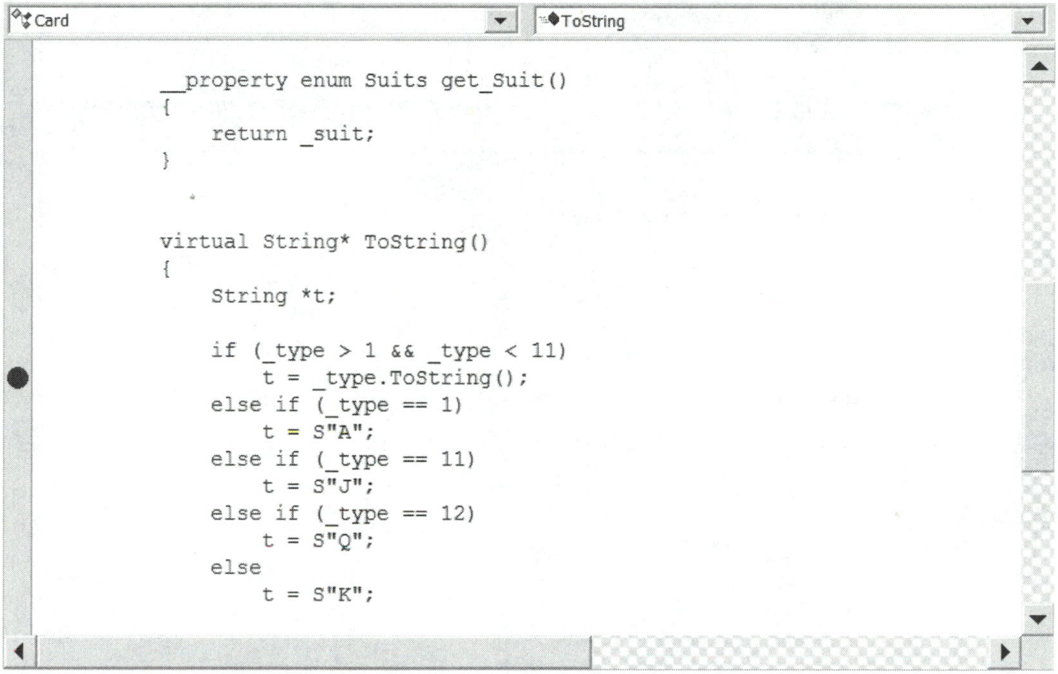

```
┌─────────────────────────────────────────────┬──────────────────────────┐
│ ⬦⬩ Card                                    ▼ │ ⬩◆ ToString            ▼ │
├─────────────────────────────────────────────┴──────────────────────────┤
│              __property enum Suits get_Suit()                        ▲  │
│              {                                                          │
│                  return _suit;                                          │
│              }                                                          │
│                                                                         │
│                                                                         │
│              virtual String* ToString()                                 │
│              {                                                          │
│                  String *t;                                             │
│                                                                         │
│                  if (_type > 1 && _type < 11)                           │
│  ⬤                   t = _type.ToString();                              │
│                  else if (_type == 1)                                   │
│                      t = S"A";                                          │
│                  else if (_type == 11)                                  │
│                      t = S"J";                                          │
│                  else if (_type == 12)                                  │
│                      t = S"Q";                                          │
│                  else                                                ▼  │
│                      t = S"K";                                          │
│  ◄ ▐▐▐▐▐▐▐▐▐▐▐▐▐▐▐▐▐▐▐▐▐                                          ►    │
└─────────────────────────────────────────────────────────────────────────┘
```

Figure 6-33. The breakpoint's red dot (in black and white)

Navigating

Now that you have a breakpoint, it is possible to run the application and have it stop at the location specified. The quick way to run a program in debug mode is to press F5. A more long-winded way of starting the debugger is to select Debug ➤ Start from the main menu.

Once the debugger starts, you will see Visual Studio .NET change into a desktop more suited to debugging. The views change to enable monitoring of the variable and the stack location. The toolbar changes to enable code navigation. And, as you can see in Figure 6-34, an arrow is placed over the red dot. This arrow specifies the next line that will be executed if you were to continue the program.

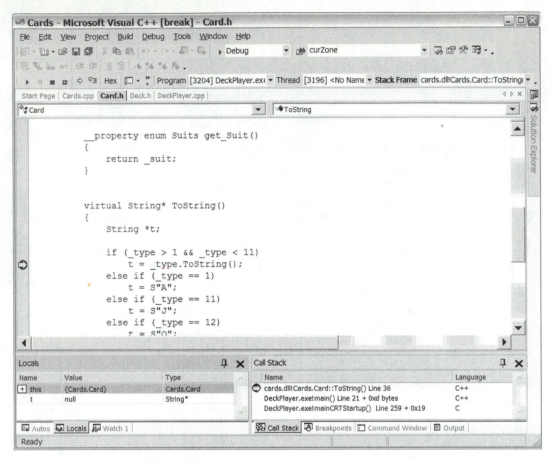

Figure 6-34. The debugger transformation

Visual Studio .NET has a lot of flexibility when it comes to navigating around the source code. The following options are available to you:

- Step through the program line by line (F10 and F11). When you arrive at a method, you have the option to step into (F10) or over (F11) this method.

- Execute to the location of the cursor (right-click at cursor location and select Run To Cursor from the drop-down menu).

- Run until you exit the current method (Shift-F11).

- Run until the next breakpoint or the end of the program (F5).

Two other, less frequently used navigational tools are Solution Explorer and the Call Stack window. Solution Explorer allows you to select a different source code module to navigate to. Once in the new module, you have the option of setting a breakpoint or executing to your current cursor location. The Call Stack window (see Figure 6-35) allows you to quickly navigate to the call stack. This can come in handy if you want to figure out which methods were called to get to your breakpoint. You can also use it to quickly navigate out of a deeply nested breakpoint by navigating to the cursor at a method higher up the stack. This is equivalent to pressing Shift-F11 a few times.

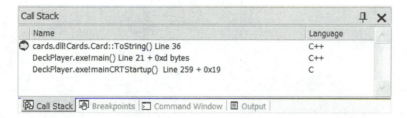

Figure 6-35. The Call Stack window

Examining Variables

It's all fine and dandy that you can navigate around the code, but if you can't see what values the variables contain, then the debugger is pretty useless. Visual Studio .NET provides several ways of examining the contents of the variable in the program you're debugging.

A unique feature of Visual Studio .NET's debug environment is that passing the cursor over a variable and leaving it there for a second will cause the value of the variable to be displayed (see Figure 6-36). The value can be retrieved through the more conventional methods that I describe next, but this feature comes in handy.

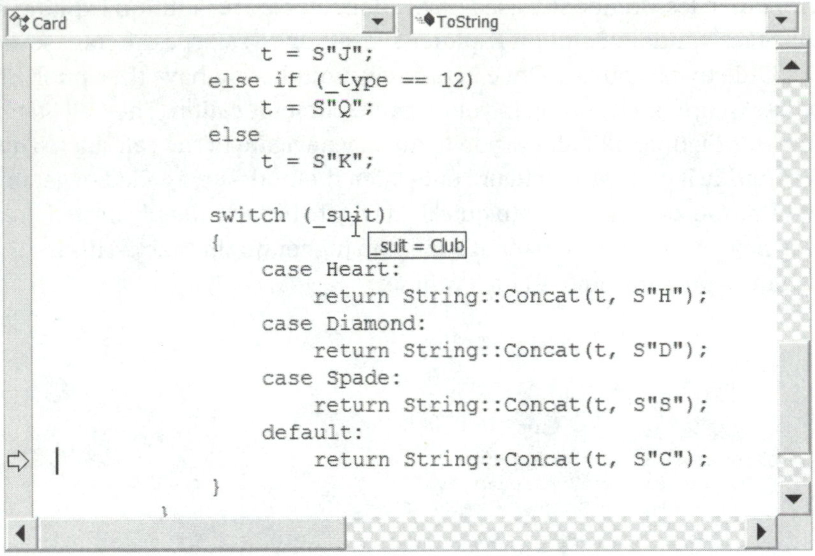

Figure 6-36. Pop-up variable values in the debug window

The Autos window is convenient if you only care about the variables being used by the current line being executed or the previous one. Frequently when you debug a program, you set a breakpoint on a line where you want to monitor the value of a variable. This being the case, the Autos window provides a shortcut in retrieving this information, as the only variables that are contained in this view are those on the line being executed and the line immediately before (see Figure 6-37).

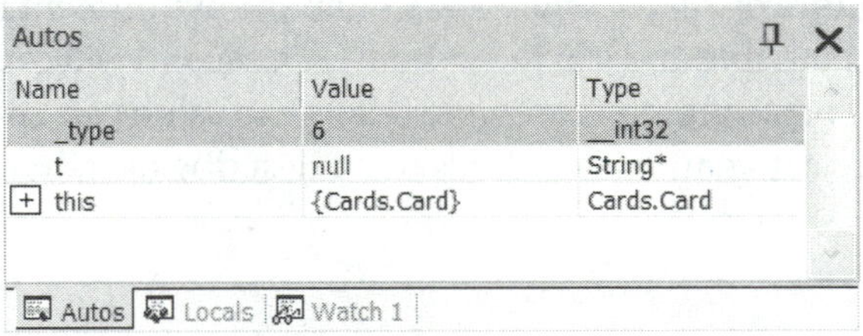

Figure 6-37. The Autos window during debugging

The Locals window displays all the variables with local scope to the current line of code being executed (see Figure 6-38). For programs with few variables, the Locals window can resemble the Autos window. For more complex programs with many variables with local scope, this view can become quite packed with variables, making it potentially difficult to find the exact variable you want.

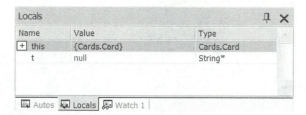

Figure 6-38. The Locals window during debugging

Sometimes there is one variable that you want to pay careful attention to. This is a job for the Watch window (see Figure 6-39). Usually, I use this view to monitor a variable that has an unexpected value when the program ends. By using a watch on the variable, I can see exactly when the unexpected value is set in the variable. Because you are selecting a specific variable to watch, it requires an extra step on your part to place the variable in the view. All you have to do is simply select the variable in the main debug window and then drag it to the Watch window.

Figure 6-39. The Watch window during debugging

Summary

In this chapter, you looked at the Visual Studio .NET development environment. You started off by exploring the most common customizable views available to developers. You then walked through building a class library assembly and an application assembly that references the class library assembly. You finished off by examining the debugging facilities provided by the development environment.

This chapter covered a lot of familiar ground for traditional Visual C++ programmers. Visual Studio .NET has not changed drastically from the previous version, but it has changed enough that developers might get slightly lost—at least for a short time.

In the next chapter, you'll begin exploring the .NET development and, in particular, the collection functionality provided by the .NET Framework class library. From here on, most of the material will be new for all programmers making their initial foray into the world of Managed C++.

CHAPTER 7

Collections

ANYONE WHO HAS BEEN around the coding world for any length of time has more than likely written her own collection routine—probably a simply linked list. Newer programmers may not have written one of their own, but instead, in the case of C++ programmers, used the Standard Template Library (STL) version of a link list. Either way, most programmers have found a need to work with collections. The .NET Framework uses collections as well. Because collections are so common, the .NET Framework class library provides a large number of different types.

The .NET Framework class library divides its generic collections into two different namespaces. The more common collections are in the System::Collections namespace. Those collections that are specialized or less common are in the System::Collections::Specialized namespace. Something to be aware of is that the two namespaces seem to imply that the specialized collections are inherited from the common, but in fact there is no such relationship. The namespaces are just groupings of different types of collections.

This chapter will focus on the generic collection set shown in Table 7-1. However, the .NET Framework class library has many other specific collections scattered throughout the many namespaces—for example, System::Text::RegularExpressions::Group, System::Web::UI::WebControls::DataKeyCollection, System::Security::PermissionSet, and even System::Array.

Table 7-1. .NET Collection Classes

COLLECTION	DESCRIPTION
ArrayList	An array that grows dynamically
BitArray	An array of bit values (either 1 or 0)
BitVector32	A small collection that will represent Boolean or small integers within 32 bits of memory
CollectionBase	An abstract base class for deriving strongly typed collections
DictionaryBase	An abstract base class for deriving strongly typed collections of key/value pairs
Hashtable	A collection of key/value pairs organized based on a hash code of the key
HybridDictionary	A collection that switches from a ListDictionary when small, to a Hashtable when large
ListDictionary	A singular link list recommended for lists of ten objects or less
NameValueCollection	A collection string of key/value pairs organized on the string key and accessible by either string key or index
Queue	A collection of first-in-first-out objects
SortedList	A collection of key/value pairs sorted by key and accessible by either key or index value
Stack	A collection of first-in-last-out objects
StringCollection	A collection of strings
StringDictionary	A Hashtable with the key strong typed to be a string

To make things easier for the developer, the .NET Framework class library provides a number of interfaces (see Table 7-2) that help provide some commonality between the collections. Learning collections is simplified because many of the collections share these interfaces, and once you learn an interface in one collection, it requires little effort to learn it in a second one.

Table 7-2. .NET Collection Interfaces

INTERFACE	DESCRIPTION
ICollection	Defines methods to determine the size of and enable thread safety for the collection
IComparer	Exposes a method to compare objects of the collection
IDictionary	Defines methods to allow access to key/value pairs within the collection
IDictionaryEnumerator	Exposes methods to access keys and values while enumerating a collection
IEnumerable	Exposes a method to retrieve an object that implements the IEnumerator interface
IEnumerator	Exposes a method to enumerate through a collection
IHashCodeProvider	Exposes a method to provide a custom hash algorithm
IList	Defines methods to add, insert, delete, and access objects using an index

IEnumerable, IEnumerator, and ForEach

Even though each of the collections in Table 7-1 is implemented differently internally, all except BitVector32 implement the IEnumerable interface. This interface exposes one member method, GetEnumerator(). This method returns a pointer to an object that implements the IEnumerator interface. And the IEnumerator interface exposes member methods that allow all collections to be handled the exact same way if there is a need.

The IEnumerator interface is fairly simple. You call the method MoveNext() to advance the enumerator to the next item in the collection, and then you grab the item out of the Current property. You know you have reached the end of the collection when MoveNext() returns false. If you want to move back the enumerator to the start of the collection, call the Reset() method.

In the languages C# and Visual Basic .NET, you don't really have to worry about the IEnumerable or IEnumerator interfaces because you would normally just use the foreach or for each statement, depending on the language. Because Managed C++ doesn't have a foreach statement, I thought I would try to implement one.

The following code hides all the details of the IEnumerable and IEnumerator interfaces within the ForEach class:

```
__gc class ForEach
{
    IEnumerator *enumerator;
    IEnumerable *collection;

public:
    Boolean foreach (Object **out, IEnumerable *collection)
    {
        if (this->collection != collection)
        {
            this->collection = collection;
            this->enumerator = collection->GetEnumerator();
        }

        Boolean end = this->enumerator->MoveNext();

        if (end)
            *out = this->enumerator->Current;
        else
            this->enumerator->Reset();

        return end;
    }
};
```

The two member variables are used to keep track of which collection is currently being enumerated and which object was the last one enumerated.

The foreach() method takes a pointer to a pointer Object and any collection class as parameters. To be more accurate, the second parameter takes any class that implements the IEnumerable interface.

The first thing that the foreach() method does is check to see if the same collection is being enumerated. If it is the first time the class is being enumerated, then the enumerator is retrieved along with the pointer to the collection. The code from here on is just standard enumerator code. This means it just calls the MoveNext() method and then extracts the object from the collection using the Current property. You end the foreach() method by resetting the enumerator when the last object has been retrieved so that the foreach() method can be run again on the same collection, if it happens to be called again before any other collection.

As you can see, to implement the foreach() method for a collection class, you can be completely ignorant of the IEnumerable or IEnumerator interface:

```
Int32 ints[] = { 1, 2, 3, 5, 7, 11 };

ForEach &loop = *new ForEach();
Object *val;

while ( loop.foreach(&val, /*in*/ dynamic_cast<Array*>(ints)) )
{
    Console::WriteLine(val);
}
```

All you need is a collection, an instance of the ForEach class and, finally, an Object pointer to place the value for each of the iterations. Because you need to loop the foreach() method, you need to place it within a while loop.

Notice the dynamic_cast<Array*>(ints). This syntax is needed because the Array class has the IEnumerable interface while the Int32[] array doesn't. Fortunately, Int32[], as well as any other type of managed array, can be dynamically typecast to the Array class.

There is a catch to the ForEach class. If you want to iterate a foreach within a foreach, you need to create another instance of the ForEach class. If you don't, the inner foreach will overwrite the internal variable of the class and the enumerator will lose its place.

Listing 7-1 shows how to implement a foreach statement using Managed C++. Notice that it doesn't matter what type of collection class you are using. The example uses both an Array and an ArrayList, but it could have used a Stack, Queue, Hashtable, and so on.

Listing 7-1. A Managed C++ foreach Statement

```
#using <mscorlib.dll>

using namespace System;
using namespace System::Collections;

__gc class ForEach
{
    IEnumerator *enumerator;
    IEnumerable *collection;

public:
    ForEach()
```

```
        {
            enumerator = 0;
            collection = 0;
        }

        Boolean foreach (Object **out, IEnumerable *collection)
        {
            if (this->collection != collection)
            {
                this->collection = collection;
                enumerator = collection->GetEnumerator();
            }

            Boolean end = enumerator->MoveNext();

            if (end)
                *out = enumerator->Current;
            else
                enumerator->Reset();

            return end;
        }
};

void SimpleForEach()
{
    Int32 ints[] = { 1, 2, 3, 5, 7, 11 };
    ForEach &loop = *new ForEach();
    Object *val;

    Console::WriteLine(S"Simple foreach");
    while ( loop.foreach( &val, /*in*/ dynamic_cast<Array*>(ints)) )
    {
        Console::Write(S"{0} ", val);
    }

    Console::WriteLine(S"\n");
}
```

```
void ImbeddedForEach()
{
    Int32 ints[] = { 1, 2, 3, 4, 5};
    ArrayList *nums = new ArrayList(5);
    for (Int32 i = 0; i < 5; i++)
    {
        nums->Add(__box((Char)(i+65)));
    }

    ForEach &loopOuter = *new ForEach();
    ForEach &loopInner = *new ForEach();
    Object *val1, *val2;

    Console::WriteLine(S"Imbedded foreach");

    Console::WriteLine(S"Outer foreach");
    while ( loopOuter.foreach( &val1, /*in*/ nums) )
    {
        Console::WriteLine(val1);
        Console::Write(S"\tInner foreach\n\t");
        while ( loopInner.foreach( &val2, /*in*/ (Array*)ints ))
        {
            Console::Write(S"{0} ", val2);
        }
        Console::WriteLine();
    }
}

Int32 main(void)
{
    SimpleForEach();
    ImbeddedForEach();

    return 0;
}
```

Figure 7-1 shows the results of the ForEach.exe program.

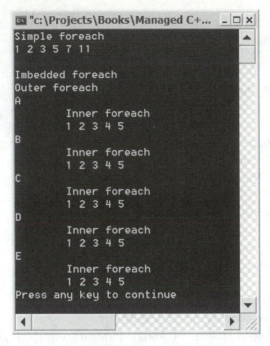

Figure 7-1. Results of ForEach.exe

If you find the ForEach class helpful, you might consider extracting it into its own header file and including it at the top of source files that use it. You could also add it to a custom utility library assembly and then reference the assembly with the #using command.

Standard Collections

Now that you've looked at the major similarities among the .NET Framework class library collections, you'll take a look at how they differ. You'll start with the standard, or more common, collections of the class library. There's nothing new about these collection types, as they've been around for quite a long time. What's different is how the .NET Framework class library implements them and what interfaces the library provides.

ArrayList

If you've never coded an array, then you probably haven't been coding very long. Arrays, with their simple syntax, are the easiest of all collections to work with, especially when you know exactly how much data you're working with. Unfortunately, they quickly lose their usefulness when the number of data elements is unknown.

The `ArrayList` is a solution to the shortcomings of the simple array. You get the simple syntax of an array without having to worry about the number of data elements. Well, that's not quite accurate: You actually get a slightly more complex array syntax, but only after the array is already loaded. Loading the `ArrayList` requires member method calls—simple ones, but method calls just the same. Once the `ArrayList` is loaded, though, you can treat it almost exactly as you would a simple array.

There is nothing difficult about creating an `ArrayList`; it is simply a standard class. It does have three different constructors. The default takes no parameters. This constructor creates an `ArrayList` with a starting `Capacity` of 16:

```
ArrayList *alist = new ArrayList();
```

That doesn't mean that the `ArrayList` is restricted to 16; it just means that the first internal array contains space for 16 elements. If the number of elements, also known as the `Count`, exceeds the `Capacity`, then the `Capacity` is doubled or, in other words, the internal array of the `ArrayList` doubles and the original array are copied to the new, expanded array.

 CAUTION *When the size of the* `ArrayList` *exceeds its capacity, the capacity is doubled. This could cause the* `ArrayList` *to be larger than is useful. For example, if your capacity is 20,000 and you add a 20,001st element, then the capacity becomes 40,000, which might not be what you want.*

The second constructor allows you to set the initial `Capacity`. This allows you to optimize the loading of the `ArrayList`, as no doubling of the `Capacity` need occur if you can restrict the size of the `ArrayList` to less than the `Capacity`.

```
ArrayList *alist = new ArrayList(300);
```

The last constructor allows you to create an ArrayList from another specified collection. This constructor copies the elements from the originating collection and then sets the Capacity and Count to the number of elements copied.

```
ArrayList *org = new ArrayList();
//...populate orgArrayList *alist = new ArrayList(org);
```

It is possible to get the Count or Capacity.

```
Int32 count = alist->Count;
Int32 capacity = alist->Capacity;
```

It is also possible to change the Capacity of an ArrayList at runtime by changing the Capacity property. If you change the Capacity to 0, the Capacity changes to the default Capacity of 16. Here is how you would code the setting of the capacity to 123:

```
alist->Capacity = 123;
```

 CAUTION *Setting the* Capacity *to a value less than the* Count *of the* ArrayList *will result in an* ArgumentOutOfRangeException *being thrown.*

Loading an ArrayList requires the use of member methods. All of the member methods are quite simple to use and self-explanatory. You can append or insert one or a range of elements to an ArrayList. You can also remove a specific element either by index or by specific content, or you can remove a range of elements by index.

```
alist->Add(S"One");

String* morenums1[] = {S"Three", S"Six"};
alist->AddRange(dynamic_cast<Array*>(morenums1));

alist->Insert(1, S"Two");
```

```
String* morenums2[] = {S"Four", S"Five"};
alist->AddRange(dynamic_cast<Array*>(morenums2));

alist->Remove(S"Six");
alist->RemoveAt(1);
alist->RemoveRange(0,4); // Index, Count
```

Once the ArrayList is loaded, it is possible to access the ArrayList in nearly the same way as a simple array. The only difference is that you access an array called Item found in the ArrayList instead of accessing the array directly.

```
alist->Item[1] = S"Three";

for (Int32 i = 0; i < alist->Count; i++)
{
    Console::Write(S"{0} ", alist->Item[i]);
}
```

 CAUTION *Trying to access an* ArrayList *element that does not exist via the* Item *array will throw an* ArgumentOutOfRangeException.

 NOTE *The* Item *array's index starts at 0, just like any other array in C++.*

The preceding code is the same as the following code, if you prefer using member methods. Why you would use this syntax escapes me, but it is available.

```
alist->set_Item(1, S"Three");

for (Int32 i = 0; i < alist->Count; i++)
{
    Console::Write(S"{0} ", alist->get_Item(i));
}
```

The ArrayList provides a few useful methods that might make your coding life a little easier. For example, it is possible to reverse the order of all the elements of the ArrayList with Reverse().

```
alist->Reverse();
```

Another useful method is the Sort() method, which allows you to sort the ListArray.

```
Alist->Sort();
```

It is also possible to do a binary search of a sorted ArrayList to search for a specific element. With this method, the elements index is returned. If the element is not found, search method returns a negative number that indicates the index of the next largest object in the ArrayList.

```
Int32 indx = alist->BinarySearch(S"Four");
```

Similar to the binary search, you can do a linear search to check if the ArrayList contains an element. If the search finds the element, it returns true. If not, it returns false.

```
Boolean fnd = alist->Contains(S"One");
```

Listing 7-2 shows the ArrayList in action and demonstrates many of the functionalities described previously.

Listing 7-2. Working with ArrayLists

```
 #using <mscorlib.dll>

using namespace System;
using namespace System::Collections;

Int32 main(void)
{
    ArrayList *alist = new ArrayList();
    alist->Add(S"One");
    alist->Add(S"-");
    alist->Item[1] = S"Three";
```

```
alist->Insert(1, S"Two");

String* morenums[] = {S"Four", S"Five"};

alist->AddRange(dynamic_cast<Array*>(morenums));

alist->Reverse();

Console::WriteLine(S"*** The ArrayList ***");
for (Int32 i = 0; i < alist->Count; i++)
{
    Console::Write(S"{0} ", alist->Item[i]);
}

Console::WriteLine(S"\n\nCapacity is: {0}", alist->Capacity.ToString());

alist->Capacity = 10;
Console::WriteLine(S"New capacity is: {0}", alist->Capacity.ToString());

Console::WriteLine(S"Count is: {0}", alist->Count.ToString());

Alist->Sort();

Int32 indx = alist->BinarySearch(S"Four");
Console::WriteLine(S"Four found at index: {0}", indx.ToString());

Boolean fnd = alist->Contains(S"One");
Console::WriteLine(S"ArrayList contains a 'One': {0}", fnd.ToString());

Console::WriteLine(S"");
return 0;
}
```

Figure 7-2 shows the results of the ArrayList.exe program.

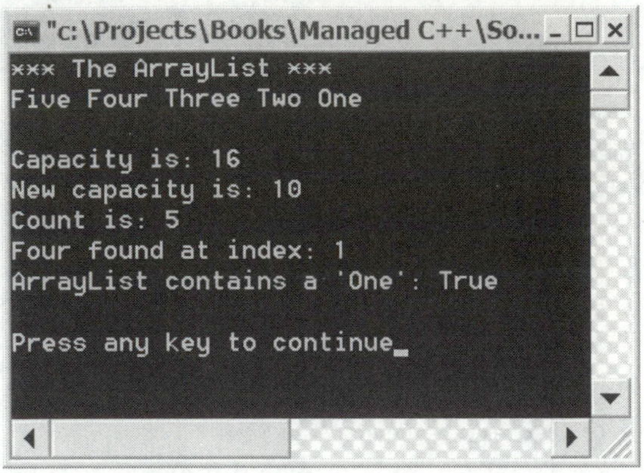

Figure 7-2. Results of ArrayList.exe

BitArray

This is a neat little collection that stores an array containing only true and false values. Unlike the ArrayList, the length of the BitArray is fixed at creation. It can, on the other hand, be set to any length (memory permitting, of course).

There are several constructors for creating a BitArray. You can divide them into three different types. The first type simply sets a predetermined array length of Booleans to either true or false.

```
BitArray *barray1 = new BitArray( 8 );     // Sets to false
BitArray *barray2 = new BitArray( 32, false );
BitArray *barray3 = new BitArray( 256, true );
```

The second type takes an array of Booleans, Bytes, or Int32s and moves their bit values into the BitArray, where, in the case of Bytes and Int32s, bits of 1 are true and bits of 0 are false.

```
Boolean bools[] = { true, false, true, true, false };
BitArray *barray1 = new BitArray( bools );

Byte bytes[] = { 0x55, 0xAA };
BitArray *barray2 = new BitArray( bytes );

Int32 ints[] = { 0x55555555, 0xAAAAAAAA };
BitArray *barray3 = new BitArray( ints );
```

The last constructor type takes one BitArray and copies it to another BitArray.

```
BitArray *barray1 = new BitArray( 8 );
BitArray *barray2 = new BitArray(barray1);
```

A convenient feature of `BitArrays` is that they can be treated as arrays of Booleans. The array is manipulated in the same way as an `ArrayList`—that is, using the `Item` property—but this time the array items are only `Booleans`.

```
barray1->Item[1] = false;
barray1->Item[4] = true;

Console::WriteLine(S"Item[0]={0}", __box(barray1->Item[0]));
Console::WriteLine(S"Item[7]={0}", __box(barray1->Item[7]));
```

Notice that you need to __box() the `Items[]` because they return a `bool` value and not `System::Boolean`, which `WriteLine()` needs.

The functionality associated with `BitArrays` is obviously related to bit manipulation or, more specifically, AND, OR, XOR, and NOT. The basic idea around these bit manipulation methods is to take the original `BitArray`, and then take another and apply a bitwise operation on the two `BitArrays`.

```
BitArray *barray1 = new BitArray( 8 );
//...Manipulate bits for barray1
BitArray *barray2 = new BitArray( 8 );
//...Manipulate bits for barray2

barray2->And(barray1);
barray2->Or(barray1);
barray2->Xor(barray1);
```

The NOT method is a little different in that it only works on its own `BitArray`.

```
barray1->Not();
```

One last method that could come in handy is `SetAll()`. This method returns all the values in the `BitArray` back to either `true` or `false` depending on the value passed to it.

```
barray2->SetAll(true);
barray2->SetAll(false);
```

Listing 7-3 shows the `BitArray` in action and demonstrates many of the functionalities described previously.

Listing 7-3. Working with BitArrays

```
#using <mscorlib.dll>

using namespace System;
using namespace System::Collections;

#include "ForEach.h"

 void Print( BitArray *barray, String *desc)
{
    ForEach &loop = *new ForEach();
    Object *val;

    Console::WriteLine(desc);

    Int32 i = 0;
    while ( loop.foreach( &val, /*in*/ barray ))
    {
        Console::Write(S"{0} ", val);
        i++;
        if (i > 7)
        {
            Console::WriteLine(S"");
            i = 0;
        }
    }
    Console::WriteLine(S"");
}

Int32 main(void)
{
    BitArray *barray1 = new BitArray( 8, true );
    Print(barray1, S"BitArray( 8, true );");

    barray1->Item[1] = false;
    barray1->Item[4] = false;
    barray1->Not();
    Print(barray1, S"Modified bit 1&4 then Not");

    BitArray *barray2 = new BitArray( 8, true );
    barray2->And(barray1);
    Print(barray2, S"And with BitArray( 8, true )");
```

```
    barray2->SetAll(true);
    barray2->Or(barray1);
    Print(barray2, S"Or with BitArray( 8, true )");

    barray2->SetAll(true);
    barray2->Xor(barray1);
    Print(barray2, S"Xor with BitArray( 8, true )");

    Console::WriteLine(S"");

    Byte bytes[] = { 0x55, 0xAA };
    BitArray *barray3 = new BitArray( bytes );
    Print(barray3, S"BitArray(0x55, 0xAA);");

    Console::WriteLine(S"Item[0]={0}", __box(barray3->Item[0]));
    Console::WriteLine(S"Item[8]={0}", __box(barray3->Item[8]));

    Console::WriteLine(S"");
    return 0;
}
```

Figure 7-3 shows the results of the BitArray.exe program.

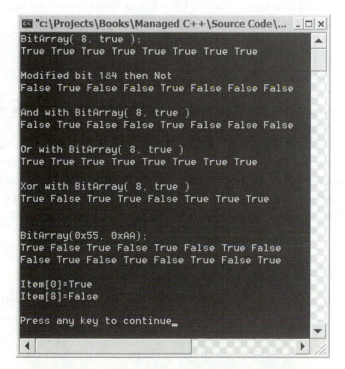

Figure 7-3. Results of BitArray.exe

Hashtable and SortedList

The Hashtable is a powerful method for storing data. The Hashtable works by storing its values in memory and then uses its key to later look up these values. What makes the Hashtable so powerful is that it doesn't search through all the keys to find a match; instead, it takes the key and analyzes it to figure out the index to the key's value. It then retrieves the value using this index.

The SortedList is a combination of a Hashtable and an Array. Depending on how you access the SortedList, it will respond like a Hashtable or an Array. For example, if you access the SortedList using the Item indexed property, it works like a Hashtable. On the other hand, if you use the GetByIndex() method, the SortedList works like an Array.

A SortedList can do everything that a Hashtable can do and more. To access the values out of a Hashtable, you use the key. With a SortedList, on the other hand, you can use the key or access the data in a sorted manner directly using an index. The cost of this added functionality is that the SortedList is slower to work with.

The reason the SortedList is slower is that both the keys and the values must be accessible in a sorted manner. This means that when data is added to or removed from the SortedList, the values may be inserted into or removed from the internal value array. This requires memory manipulation. For the Hashtable, the values do not require this manipulation.

Both the Hashtable and SortedList have numerous constructors, but in most cases, you will probably simply use the default constructor.

```
Hashtable *hashtable  = new Hashtable();
SortedList *sortedlist = new SortedList();
```

On the other hand, all the other constructors provide parameters to help with the efficiency of the collection.

A major factor both the Hashtable and SortedList have in common is Capacity. If many entries are to be made into these collection types, then creating them with a sufficiently large capacity allows the entries to be inserted more efficiently than if you let them perform automatic rehashing as needed to grow the collections.

```
Hashtable *hashtable  = new Hashtable(300);
SortedList *sortedlist = new SortedList(300);
```

A Hashtable constructor provides another parameter to further refine the collections' efficiency: the load factor. The *load factor* is the ratio of the number of filled buckets to the total number of buckets available. A bucket is full when it points to or contains a data element. The load factor is a value between 0.1 and

1.0. A smaller load factor means faster lookup at the cost of increased memory consumption. Conversely, a larger load factor uses memory more efficiently at the cost of longer expected time per lookup. The default load factor of 1.0 generally provides the best balance between speed and size.

```
Hashtable *hashtable  = new Hashtable(300, 0.75);
```

You use the Add() method to load these collections. Neither the Hashtable nor the SortedList have an insert method. If you think about it, an insert really doesn't make sense, because the Hashtable analyzes the key and doesn't care where the values are located, and the SortedList is sorted whenever the Add() method is invoked.

```
hashtable->Add(__box(0), S"zero");
sortedlist->Add(S"A", S"two");
```

NOTE   *For you database programmers, as you can see in the preceding example, null is a valid key.*

Unloading individual elements in the Hashtable and SortedList requires the use of the Remove() method and the specific key. The SortedList also allows elements of the collection to be removed by index value using the RemoveAt() method. It is also possible to remove all the elements of the collections using the Clear() method.

```
hashtable->Remove( __box(0) );
hashtable->Clear();
sortedlist->Remove( S"A" );
sortedlist->RemoveAt( 2 );
sortedlist->Clear();
```

Now that you can put key/value pairs into a Hashtable and a SortedList, you need to be able to get them out. Both of these collection types provide a plethora of methods to do just that. One of the easiest methods is to use the Item indexed property. Be careful: This is not an array property like you have seen in the previous collection types. An indexed property, if you recall from Chapter 3, takes an Object instead of an integer value type between the square brackets, which you normally associate with an array. In this case, the object you would use is the key of the value you wish to retrieve.

```
Console::WriteLine(S"key="A" value={1}", hash->Item[S"A"]);
Console::WriteLine(S"key="A" value={1}", sort->Item[S"A"]);
```

If you don't know the keys or you simply want all the data and, in the case of a Hashtable, don't care about the order, then you can enumerate through the collections. It's possible to enumerate by key, by value, or by both key and value at the same time. To get the enumerator, you need to use the Keys property, the Values property, or the GetEnumerator() method.

```
IDictionaryEnumerator *enum1 = hash->GetEnumerator();
IDictionaryEnumerator *enum2 = sort->GetEnumerator();
IEnumerator *keys1 = hash->Keys->GetEnumerator();
IEnumerator *keys2 = sort->Keys->GetEnumerator();
IEnumerator *vals1 = hash->Values->GetEnumerator();
IEnumerator *vals2 = sort->Values->GetEnumerator();
```

Enumerating by both key and value at the same time is a little different from what you have seen so far. You need to use the IDictionaryEnumerator interface instead of IEnumerator. Also, to retrieve the key and value from the collection, you use the Key and Value properties and not the Current property (see Listing 7-4 for an example).

The code to enumerate keys and values on their own, though, is no different than any other collection.

If you are not sure, but you want a quick way to see if a Hashtable or SortedList contains a key or a value, you would use the ContainsKey() (or Contains()) method and the ContainsValue() method. Simply use the key or value you are searching for as a parameter. The methods will return true or false.

```
Boolean b1 = hash->Contains(S"A");
Boolean b2 = sort->Contains(S"A");
Boolean b3 = hash->ContainsKey(S"Z");
Boolean b4 = sort->ContainsKey(S"Z");
Boolean b5 = hash->ContainsValue(S"cat");
Boolean b6 = sort->ContainsValue(S"cat");
```

Three methods specific to SortedList are based on indexes to values. Because a Hashtable doesn't have an index to its values, these methods wouldn't make sense, so they aren't included. You can get a value by index or you can get the index of a key or a value.

```
Console::WriteLine(S"Index {0} contains: {1}", __box(i), sort->GetByIndex(i));
Console::WriteLine(S"Index key 'B': {0}", __box(sort->IndexOfKey(S"B")));
Console::WriteLine(S"Index val 'cat': {0}", __box(sort->IndexOfValue(S"cat")));
```

Listing 7-4 shows the `Hashtable` and `SortedList` in action and demonstrates the functionality described previously.

Listing 7-4. Working with Hashtables and SortedLists

```
 #using <mscorlib.dll>

using namespace System;
using namespace System::Collections;

Int32 main(void)
{
    Hashtable *hash  = new Hashtable();
    SortedList *sort = new SortedList();

    String *keys[]  = { S"B", S"A", S"C", S"D" };
    String *skeys[] = { S"A", S"B", S"C", S"D" };
    String *values[] = { S"moose", S"zebra", S"frog", S"horse" };

    for (Int32 i = 0; i < keys->Count; i++)
    {
        hash->Add(keys[i], values[i]);
        sort->Add(keys[i], values[i]);
    }

    Console::WriteLine(S"Hashtable\tSortedList");

    Console::WriteLine(S"By indexed property");
    for (Int32 i = 0; i < hash->Count; i++)
    {
        Console::WriteLine(S"{0} {1}\t\t{2} {3}", skeys[i],
            hash->Item[skeys[i]], skeys[i], sort->Item[skeys[i]]);
    }

    Console::WriteLine(S"\nBy index");
    for (Int32 i = 0; i < sort->Count; i++)
    {
        Console::WriteLine(S"N/A\t\t{0} {1}", __box(i), sort->GetByIndex(i));
    }

    Console::WriteLine(S"\nBy enumerator");
    IDictionaryEnumerator *enum1 = hash->GetEnumerator();
    IDictionaryEnumerator *enum2 = sort->GetEnumerator();
    while ( enum1->MoveNext() && enum2->MoveNext())
```

```
{
    Console::Write(S"{0} {1}\t\t", enum1->Key, enum1->Value);
    Console::WriteLine(S"{0} {1}", enum2->Key, enum2->Value);
}


Console::WriteLine(S"\nEnumerate Keys");
IEnumerator *keys1 = hash->Keys->GetEnumerator();
IEnumerator *keys2 = sort->Keys->GetEnumerator();
while ( keys1->MoveNext() && keys2->MoveNext())
{
    Console::Write(S"{0}\t\t", keys1->Current);
    Console::WriteLine(S"{0}", keys2->Current);
}


Console::WriteLine(S"\nEnumerate Values");
IEnumerator *vals1 = hash->Values->GetEnumerator();
IEnumerator *vals2 = sort->Values->GetEnumerator();
while ( vals1->MoveNext() && vals2->MoveNext())
{
    Console::Write(S"{0}\t\t", vals1->Current);
    Console::WriteLine(S"{0}", vals2->Current);
}


Console::WriteLine(S"\nContains a Key 'A' and 'Z'");
Console::WriteLine(S"{0}\t\t{1}", __box(hash->Contains(S"A")),
                                  __box(sort->Contains(S"A")));
Console::WriteLine(S"{0}\t\t{1}", __box(hash->ContainsKey(S"Z")),
                                  __box(sort->ContainsKey(S"Z")));


Console::WriteLine(S"\nContains a Value 'frog' and 'cow'");
Console::WriteLine(S"{0}\t\t{1}", __box(hash->ContainsValue(S"frog")),
                                  __box(sort->ContainsValue(S"frog")));
Console::WriteLine(S"{0}\t\t{1}", __box(hash->ContainsValue(S"cow")),
                                  __box(sort->ContainsValue(S"cow")));


Console::WriteLine(S"\n\t\t'B' key index: {0}",
    __box(sort->IndexOfKey(S"B")));


Console::WriteLine(S"\t\t'frog' value index: {0}",
    __box(sort->IndexOfValue(S"frog")));


return 0;
}
```

Figure 7-4 shows the results of the HashSortList.exe program.

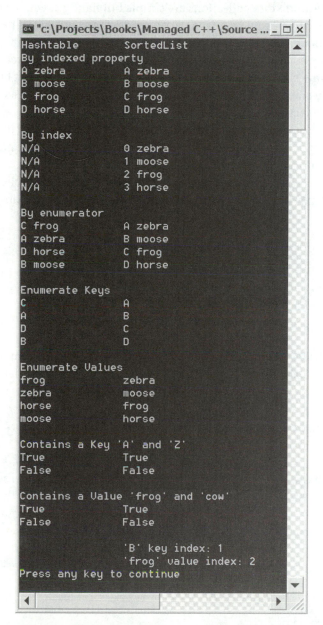

Figure 7-4. Results of HashSortList.exe

Queue and Stack

The Queue and Stack collections are simple but handy. If you have ever been to an amusement park and waited to get on a ride, then you should be very familiar with a queue. Basically, the order you go in is the order you come out. A Queue is often known as a *first-in-first-out* (FIFO) collection. The best real-world example that I know of a stack is a plate dispenser at an all-you-can-eat buffet. Here, the last plate placed in is the first one out. A Stack is often known as a *last-in-first-out* (LIFO) collection.

The Queue and Stack collections don't provide a vast array of methods, as many of the other collections do. They do both contain the standard Count property, and the GetEnumerator() and Contains() methods.

Even the constructors of a Queue and a Stack are quite simple. You can create them from another collection, specifying their initial size or taking the default size.

```
Queue *que1 = new Queue();
Stack *stk1 = new Stack();
Queue *que2 = new Queue(8);
Stack *stk2 = new Stack(8);
Queue *que3 = new Queue(stk1);
Stack *stk3 = new Stack(que1);
```

Both the Queue and Stack have one more method in common: the Peek() method. This method allows the program to see the next element that is going to come off the Queue or Stack but does not actually remove it.

```
Console::WriteLine( que->Peek() );
Console::WriteLine( stk->Peek() );
```

Both the Queue and Stack collections have the same process of placing elements on and off. However, they use different method names that more closely resemble the type of collection they are. To place an element onto a Queue, you use the Enqueue() method, and to take an element off the Queue, you use the Dequeue() method. (I know, neither of these method names are actually English words, but hey, we're programmers, not authors. Wait a minute—I am!)

```
que->Enqueue(S"First");
que->Dequeue();
```

To place an element onto a Stack, you use the Push() method, and to take it off, you use the Pop() method.

```
stk->Push(S"First");
stk->Pop();
```

There are occasions when you want to Dequeue or Pop all elements of the
Queue or Stack. You can do this with the single method Clear().

Listing 7-5 shows the Queue and Stack in action and demonstrates the functionality described previously.

Listing 7-5. Working with Queues and Stacks

```
#using <mscorlib.dll>

using namespace System;
using namespace System::Collections;

Int32 main(void)
{
    Queue *que = new Queue();
    Stack *stk = new Stack();

    String *entry[] = { S"First", S"Second", S"Third", S"Fourth" };

    Console::WriteLine(S"Queue\t\tStack");

    Console::WriteLine(S"** ON **");
    for (Int32 i = 0; i < entry->Count; i++)
    {
        que->Enqueue(entry[i]);
        stk->Push(entry[i]);

        Console::WriteLine(S"{0}\t\t{1}", entry[i], entry[i]);
    }

    Console::WriteLine(S"\n** OFF **");
    while ((que->Count > 0) && (stk->Count > 0))
    {
        Console::WriteLine(S"{0}\t\t{1}", que->Dequeue(), stk->Pop());
    }

    que->Clear();
    stk->Clear();

    Console::WriteLine(S"\n");
    return 0;
}
```

Figure 7-5 shows the results of the QueueStack.exe program.

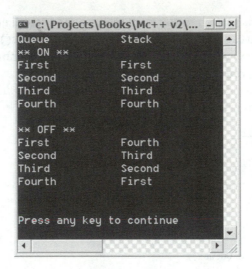

Figure 7-5. Results of QueueStack.exe

Specialized Collections

Now that you have covered all of the standard collections, you'll take a look at a few of the more commonly used specialized collections provided by the .NET Framework class library. Unlike the standard set of collections that I discussed previously, these specialized collections require the referencing of the system.dll assembly and use the System::Collections::Specialized namespace.

```
#using <system.dll>
using System::Collections::Specialized;
```

ListDictionary

If you require quick access to a short list of elements, a ListDictionary might just be what you need. It has very little overhead. It is just a singular link list, which makes it very fast if you plan on restricting the number of data elements to ten or less. When you plan on having more than ten elements, it is probably better to use a Hashtable.

In fact, the .NET Framework class library provides a specialized collection called the HybridDictionary that starts off as a ListDictionary when the number of entries is small and automatically changes to a Hashtable when the number of elements increases.

The ListDictionary has few methods, all of which you learned about earlier in this chapter. A feature that the ListDictionary shares with the Hashtable (and the SortedList), which you haven't covered already, is the capability to add key/value pairs using the Item indexed property. As you might expect, when the key passes, the value gets changed because the indexed property already exists.

NOTE   *What you might not expect is that if the key is unique, then the key/value pair is added.*

CAUTION   Add() *works when adding a unique key only. Duplicate keys passed to the* Add() *method throw an* ArgumentException *instead of replacing the value.*

Listing 7-6 shows the ListDictionary in action and demonstrates the functionality described previously.

Listing 7-6. Working with ListDictionary

```
#using <mscorlib.dll>
#using <system.dll>

using namespace System;
using System::Collections::Specialized;

Int32 main(void)
{
    ListDictionary *ldict = new ListDictionary();

    ldict->Add(S"A", S"First");
    ldict->Add(S"B", S"Second");
    ldict->Add(S"C", S"Third");

    ldict->Item[S"D"] = S"Fourth";
```

```
try {
    ldict->Add(S"C", S"Third Replaced");
}
catch (ArgumentException *e)
{
    Console::WriteLine(S"ldict->Add(S\"C\", S\"Third Replaced\");");
    Console::WriteLine(S"Throws exception: {0}", e->Message);
}
ldict->Item[S"B"] = S"Second Replaced";

Console::WriteLine(S"\nEnumerate");
IEnumerator *keys = ldict->Keys->GetEnumerator();
IEnumerator *vals = ldict->Values->GetEnumerator();
while ( keys->MoveNext() && vals->MoveNext())
{
    Console::WriteLine(S"{0}\t\t{1}", keys->Current, vals->Current);
}

Console::WriteLine(S"\n");
return 0;
}
```

Figure 7-6 shows the results of the ListDict.exe program.

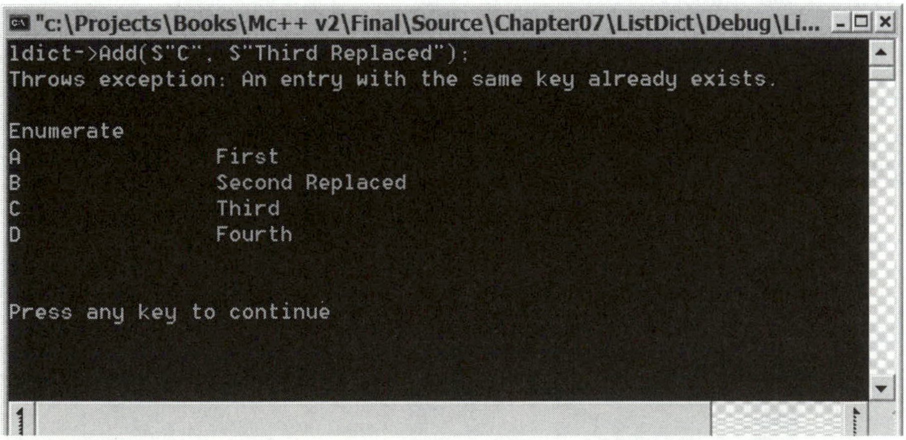

Figure 7-6. Results of ListDict.exe

StringCollection

When you plan on maintaining many strings, it might be more advantageous to use a StringCollection than of any of the other collection types, as a StringCollection is optimized to handle strings. A StringCollection resembles a simplified ArrayList in many ways, except that it lacks a few of its methods and uses the StringEnumerator instead of the IEnumerator.

Listing 7-7 shows the StringCollection in action. As you can see, it has many of the same methods of an ArrayList and is strongly typed to strings.

Listing 7-7. Working with StringCollection

```
#using <mscorlib.dll>
#using <system.dll>

using namespace System;
using System::Collections::Specialized;

Int32 main(void)
{
    StringCollection &strcol = *new StringCollection();

    strcol.Add(S"The first String");

    String *tmpstr[] = {S"Third", S"Fourth" };
    strcol.AddRange(tmpstr);

    strcol.Insert(1, S"Second");

    strcol.Item[0] = S"First";

    StringEnumerator *strenum = strcol.GetEnumerator();
    while ( strenum->MoveNext())
    {
        Console::WriteLine(strenum->Current);
    }

    Console::WriteLine(S"");
    return 0;
}
```

Figure 7-7 shows the results of the StringColl.exe program.

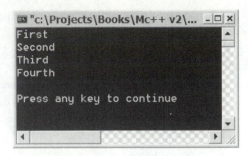

Figure 7-7. Results of StringColl.exe

StringDictionary

The StringDictionary sounds impressive, don't you think? It's really just a Hashtable strongly typed and optimized for strings. There's nothing new here, other than pretty well all methods expect the String type instead of the Object type.

Listing 7-8 shows the StringDictionary in action. This example shows one of the many ways of displaying the StringDictionary in alphabetical order, as a StringDictionary does not sort its entries. If you recall, a Hashtable works by simply analyzing the key to find its value, and no sorting occurs. In the example, you get a copy of all the keys and place them into an ArrayList. Then, you use the ArrayList's built-in Sort() method.

Listing 7-8. Working with StringDictionary

```
#using <mscorlib.dll>
#using <system.dll>

using namespace System;
using System::Collections::Specialized;

Int32 main(void)
{
    StringDictionary &strdict = *new StringDictionary();

    strdict.Add(S"Dog", S"Four leg, hydrant loving, barking, mammal");
    strdict.Add(S"Frog", S"Green, jumping, croaking, amphibian");

    strdict.Item[S"Crocodile"] = S"Ugly, boot origin, snapping, reptile";
```

```
ArrayList *alist = new ArrayList();
alist->AddRange(strdict.Keys);
alist->Sort();

for (Int32 i = 0; i < alist->Count; i++)
{
    Console::WriteLine(S"{0,10}:\t{1}", alist->Item[i],
        strdict.Item[dynamic_cast<String*>(alist->Item[i])]);
}

Console::WriteLine(S"");
return 0;
}
```

Figure 7-8 shows the results of the StringDict.exe program.

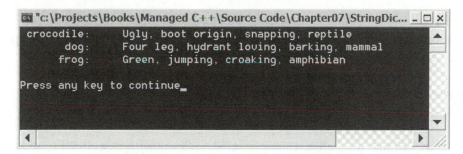

Figure 7-8. Results of StringDict.exe

NameValueCollection

Let's finish off the chapter with one final collection type: NameValueCollection. This collection is similar in many ways to the StringDictionary. It uses a Hashtable internally and is optimized for handling string. Where it differs is in its ability to have multiple values for a single key.

You can add a key/value pair to a NameValueCollection using the Add() or Set() method or the indexed property Item. However, only the Add() method allows multiple values to be assigned to a single key:

```
nvCol.Set(S"Flower", S"Rose");
nvCol.Add(S"Animal", S"Dog");
nvCol.Item[S"Fruit"] = S"Plum";
```

You can update the value of a key using either the Item property or the Set()
method, but in both cases only a single value can be assigned to a key.

 CAUTION *The indexed property* Item *and the* Set() *method will
overwrite a key with multiple values with a single value. In other
words, you will lose all values assigned to the key and they will be
replaced with the new single value.*

To get all the keys in the collection, you use the AllKeys property. This property returns an array, which has been cached for better performance and which is
automatically refreshed when the collection changes.

```
String *keys[] = nvCol.AllKeys;
```

There are two different ways of getting the values using a key: either as an
array of strings using the GetValues() method or as a comma-delimited list using
the Get() method.

```
String *vals[] = nvCol.GetValues(S"Flower");
String *vals = nvCol.Get(S"Flower");
```

It is also possible to manipulate the collection using indexes. To get a key at
a specific index, use the GetKey() method.

```
String *key = nvCol.GetKey(1);
```

To get the values at a specific index, you use the Item property, but this time as
an array property. Using Item this way returns a comma-delimited list of values.

```
String *vals = nvCol.Item[3];
```

You remove a specific key and all its values from the collection by passing the
index of the key you want to remove into the Remove() method.

Listing 7-9 shows the NameValueCollection in action.

Listing 7-9. Working with NameValueCollection

```
#using <mscorlib.dll>
#using <system.dll>
```

```
using namespace System;
using namespace System::Collections::Specialized;

Int32 main(void)
{
    NameValueCollection &nvCol = *new NameValueCollection();

    nvCol.Add(0, S"void");

    nvCol.Set(S"Flower", S"Rose");

    nvCol.Add(S"Animal", S"Dog");
    nvCol.Add(S"Animal", S"Cat");
    nvCol.Add(S"Animal", S"Cow");

    nvCol.Add(S"Fruit", S"Apple");
    nvCol.Add(S"Fruit", S"Pear");
    nvCol.Add(S"Fruit", S"Peach");

    String *keys[] = nvCol.AllKeys;

    Console::WriteLine(S"Key\t\tValues");
    for (Int32 i = 0; i < keys->Count; i++)
    {
        String *vals[] = nvCol.GetValues(keys[i]);

        Console::WriteLine(S"{0}:\t\t{1}", keys[i], vals[0]);
        for (Int32 j = 1; j < vals.Count; j++)
        {
            Console::WriteLine(S"\t\t{0}", vals[j]);
        }
    }
    Console::WriteLine(S"--- Index Lookups ---");
    Console::WriteLine(S"Key @[1]:\t{0}", nvCol.GetKey(1));
    Console::WriteLine(S"Values @[3]:\t{0}", nvCol.Item[3]);

    nvCol.Remove(0);

    nvCol.Item[S"Fruit"] = S"Plum";

    nvCol.Set(S"Animal", S"Deer");
    nvCol.Add(S"Animal", S"Ape");
```

```
    keys = nvCol.AllKeys;

    Console::WriteLine(S"----- Updated ----");
    for (Int32 i = 0; i < keys->Count; i++)
    {
        Console::WriteLine(S"{0}:\t\t{1}", keys[i], nvCol.Get(keys[i]));
    }
    return 0;
}
```

Figure 7-9 shows the results of the NameValue.exe program.

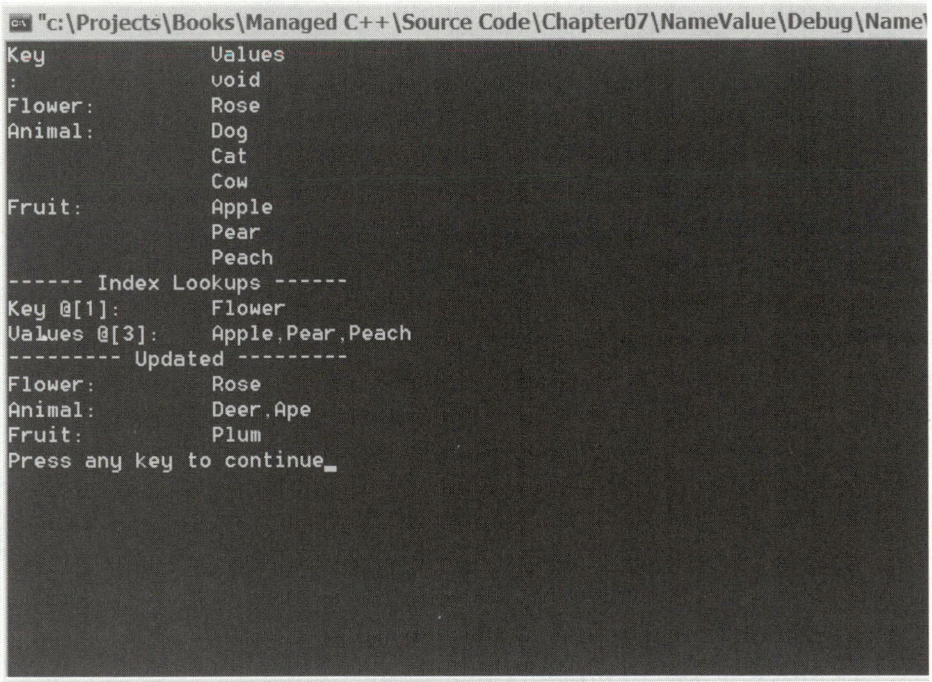

Figure 7-9. Results of NameValue.exe

Summary

In this chapter you took a somewhat detailed look at some of the collections made available by the .NET Framework class library. You started by looking at the IEnumerable interface, which is common to most collections. Next, you covered all the common collections. You finished off by examining a few of the more specialized collections provided by the .NET Framework class library.

In the next chapter, you're going to look at how the .NET Framework addresses the important areas of file I/O.

CHAPTER 8

Input, Output, and Serialization

MOST PROGRAMS ARE OF LITTLE use if there is no way of retrieving input from some source and outputting it to the same or another source. There are several options available for handling input/output (I/O). In this chapter, you will examine file and directory I/O, I/O manipulation and, finally, serialization or the saving of class for later retrieval.

There are other I/O mechanisms. For example, this book covers, in later chapters, databases, XML, and GUI interfaces. Before you cover these more complex I/O systems, you'll start with simple files. Files are the core of most I/O-related activities in a program.

The first thing you need to look at is the file system. Anybody who plays (oops, I mean *works*) on a computer sees the file system as an uncomplicated means of placing files wherever he wants them. Usually, the file system is taken for granted. Truthfully, the file system is anything but simple and, without the .NET Framework class library, a developer would see just how complicated it really is.

Once you have the file system under your belt, you will end this chapter with serialization. *Serialization* is the process of storing a class off to the file system for later retrieval. You will see how unbelievably easy this is to do with the .NET Framework class library.

File System Input and Output

When you think of the file system, you need to consider its two parts: files and directories. The .NET Framework class library tries to treat files and directories in a very similar way. But, obviously, there are things that you can do with one that you can't do with the other. Because of this, the .NET Framework class library has split the functionality of files and directories into two. Well, that is not actually correct, the functionality was split into four: two classes for files and two for directories.

The reason files and directories were split into two classes each is because of the two different ways programmers tend to work with them, either one time quick-and-dirty or over the lifetime of a method, a class, or even an application. Quick-and-dirty operations on a file or directory really don't need the overhead of creating an instance of a class to handle the operation. Instead, the use of static methods seems more appropriate. On the other hand, if the file or directory is going to be around for a while, it makes sense to create a class instance to hold the file or directory. This makes even more sense when you add the wrinkle that when you use static methods, system security has to be checked every time, but with instantiated classes, security only needs to be checked once on the creation of the class object.

The two classes that make up file access are File and FileInfo. The File class contains static methods to access files, whereas you need to create an instance of a FileInfo class to access files. They have much of the same functionality, so selecting one over the other based on functionality does not normally make sense. Instead, you should choose one class over the other based on the number of times the file will be accessed. If it will be accessed one time only, then File makes sense. If you need repeated access to the file, you should probably use the FileInfo class.

Managing the File System

As someone who has coded before, you know that you can open, read, and write to files. The .NET Framework class library takes files and the file system in general a step further. It treats files and directories like the objects they are. It provides not only the standard I/O features you have come to expect in a framework, but also ways of dealing with files and directories as a whole. For example, it is possible to copy, move, get information about, and delete complete file and directory objects. With these functions, you now have a way of providing for the maintenance of the file system as a whole and not just the files that make up the system.

FileSystemInfo

You will look at files and directories separately, but you could almost cover them as one, because they have numerous methods and properties in common. In fact, both DirectoryInfo and FileInfo are derived from the same abstract class, FileSystemInfo.

The FileSystemInfo class provides the numerous properties and methods that the DirectoryInfo and FileInfo classes have in common (see Table 8-1).

Table 8-1. Commonly Used FileSystemInfo Class Members

PROPERTY/METHOD	DESCRIPTION
Attributes	Gets or sets attributes associated with the current file system object.
CreationTime	Gets or sets creation date and time of current file system object.
Exists	Determines if the file system object exists.
Extension	Gets the string extension associated with the current file system object.
FullName	Gets full name of the current file system object. This will include the file or directories path.
LastAccessTime	Gets or sets last access date and time of current file system object.
LastWriteTime	Gets or sets last date and time current file system object was updated.
Name	Gets the name of the file or the last directory of current file system object.
Delete()	Deletes the current file system object.

As you can see, other than the Delete() method, each of the FileSystemInfo class members in Table 8-1 provides information about the file or directory of the current instance. Some even provide you with update abilities.

Directory and DirectoryInfo

The Directory and DirectoryInfo classes provide you with a means of maintaining the directory structure under which your program has control. If you've ever worked directly with the directory structure without the aid of some form of framework, then you'll quickly come to appreciate the ease with which you can maintain the directory system using the .NET Framework class library. To prove that it's simple to work with directories in the .NET Framework class library, let's examine a few of the more common methods and properties.

Whether you are using the static methods provided by Directory or the properties and member method of DirectoryInfo will determine if you need to call a constructor. Obviously, calling static member methods does not require you to instantiate a class, and thus there is no need for a constructor.

The constructor for the DirectoryInfo class simply takes the full path to the directory you wish to manipulate as a parameter, though the directory doesn't need to exist if you're creating it. As you continue, you'll see that the `Directory` static member calls have this same full path as the member's first parameter.

```
DirectoryInfo *dir = new DirectoryInfo(S"C:\\WinNT\\Temp");
```

To examine the details of a directory using the `DirectoryInfo` class, you need to implement the inherited properties of the `FileSystemInfo` class. On the other hand, if you are implementing the `Directory` class, the static member methods are a bit different.

```
// DirectoryInfo implementation:
String         *Name       = dir->FullName;
DateTime        Created    = dir->CreationTime;
DateTime        Accessed   = dir->LastAccessTime;
DateTime        Updated    = dir->LastWriteTime;
FileAttributes Attributes = dir->Attributes;


// Directory implementation
// No equivalent for dir->FullName
DateTime Created  = Directory::GetCreationTime(S"C:\\WinNT\\Temp");
DateTime Accessed = Directory::GetLastAccessTime(S"C:\\WinNT\\Temp");
DateTime Updated  = Directory::GetLastWriteTime(S"C:\\WinNT\\Temp");
// No equivalent for dir->Attributes
```

Commonly, you are going to want to list all the files and directories that are contained within the current directory. Both `Directory` and `DirectoryInfo` provide methods to get all the files and subdirectories separately in two method calls or together in one method call. Notice, though, that the `DirectoryInfo` implementation returns an `Object`, whereas the `Directory` implementation returns complete directory strings.

```
// DirectoryInfo implementation:
DirectoryInfo  *subDirs[]    = dir->GetDirectories();
FileInfo        *files[]     = dir->GetFiles();
FileSystemInfo *dirsFiles[] = dir->GetFileSystemInfos();


// Directory implementation
String *subDirs[]    = Directory::GetDirectories(S"C:\\WinNT\\Temp");
String *files[]      = Directory::GetFiles(S"C:\\WinNT\\Temp");
String *dirsFiles[] = Directory::GetFileSystemEntries(S"C:\\WinNT\\Temp");
```

Three useful methods that `Directory` has that `DirectoryInfo` doesn't are as follows:

```
String *currentDirectory = Directory::GetCurrentDirectory();
Directory::SetCurrentDirectory(currentDirectory);
String *logicalDrives[] = Directory::GetLogicalDrives();
```

These methods get and set the current working directory and get all current logical drives on the system.

A handy auxiliary class that you can use to manipulate the complete directory strings is the Path class. This class contains several static methods to combine, extract, and manipulate path strings. Table 8-2 shows some of the more useful static methods.

Table 8-2. Commonly Used Path Class Members

METHOD	DESCRIPTION
ChangeExtension()	Changes the extension of the path string.
GetDirectoryName()	Extracts the directory name out of the path string. Notice that for a directory, this method extracts the parent path.
GetExtension()	Gets the extension from the filename contained in the path string.
GetFileName()	Gets the filename or the directory name.
GetFileNameWithoutExtension()	Gets the extension from the filename contained in the path string.
GetFullPath()	Gets the absolute path of the path string.

To extract the filename out of a complete directory string, you would use the following GetFileName() method of the Path class:

```
String *files[] = Directory::GetFileSystemEntries(path);
for (Int32 i = 0; i < files->Count; i++)
{
    Console::WriteLine(Path::GetFileName(files[i]));
}
```

The activities that you will probably do most with directories are checking if the directory exists, creating a directory, moving or renaming an existing directory, and deleting a directory.

```
// DirectoryInfo implementation:
if (dir->Exists) {}
```

```
dir->Create();  // Notice it creates the directory specified by constructor
dir->CreateSubdirectory(S"SubDir");
dir->MoveTo(S"C:\\WinNT\\TempXXX"); // move or rename the current directory tree
dir->Delete();  // will fail if directory is not empty
dir->Delete(true);  // deletes the entire directory tree (security permitting)

// Directory implementation
if (Directory::Exists(S"C:\\WinNT\\Temp")) {}
Directory::CreateDirectory(S"C:\\WinNT\\TempXXX");
Directory::Move(S"C:\\WinNT\\Temp", S"C:\\WinNT\\TempXXX");
Directory::Delete(S"C:\\WinNT\\TempXXX");
Directory::Delete(S"C:\\WinNT\\TempXXX", true);
```

Listing 8-1 shows the DirectoryInfo class in action and demonstrates many of the functionalities described previously.

Listing 8-1. Working with DirectoryInfo

```
#using <mscorlib.dll>

using namespace System;
using namespace System::IO;
using namespace System::Text;

Int32 main( Int32 argc, SByte __nogc *argv[] )
{
    if (argc <= 1)
    {
        Console::WriteLine(S"Usage: DirInfo <Directory>");
        return -1;
    }

    StringBuilder *tmppath = new StringBuilder();
    for (Int32 i = 1; i < argc; i++)
    {
        tmppath->Append(argv[i]);
        tmppath->Append(S" ");
    }

    String *path = tmppath->ToString()->Trim();
    DirectoryInfo *dir = new DirectoryInfo(path);
    if (!dir->Exists)
    {
        Console::WriteLine(S"Directory Not Found");
```

```
        return -1;
    }


    Console::WriteLine(S"Name:        {0}", dir->FullName);
    Console::WriteLine(S"Created:     {0} {1}",
                        dir->CreationTime.ToShortDateString(),
                        dir->CreationTime.ToLongTimeString());
    Console::WriteLine(S"Accessed:    {0} {1}",
                        dir->LastAccessTime.ToShortDateString(),
                        dir->LastAccessTime.ToLongTimeString());
    Console::WriteLine(S"Updated:     {0} {1}",
                        dir->LastWriteTime.ToShortDateString(),
                        dir->LastWriteTime.ToLongTimeString());
    Console::WriteLine(S"Attributes: {0}",
                        __box(dir->Attributes)->ToString());
    Console::WriteLine(S"Sub-Directories:");

    DirectoryInfo *subDirs[] = dir->GetDirectories();
    if (subDirs->Count == 0)
        Console::WriteLine(S"\tNone.");
    else
    {
        for (Int32 i = 0; i < subDirs->Count; i++)
        {
            Console::WriteLine(S"\t{0}", subDirs[i]->Name);
        }
    }


    Console::WriteLine(S"Files:");
    FileInfo *files[] = dir->GetFiles();
    if (files->Count == 0)
        Console::WriteLine(S"\tNone.");
    else
    {
        for (Int32 i = 0; i < files->Count; i++)
        {
            Console::WriteLine(S"\t{0}", files[i]->Name);
        }
    }

    return 0;
}
```

Figure 8-1 shows the results of the DirInfo.exe program.

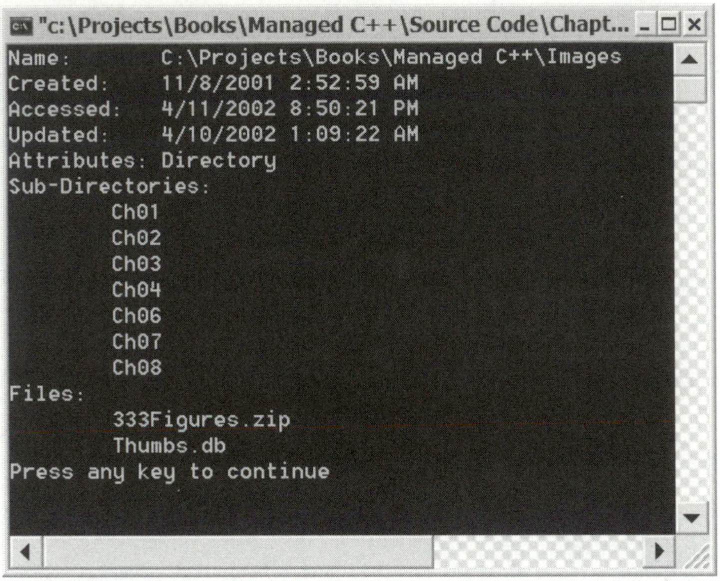

```
"c:\Projects\Books\Managed C++\Source Code\Chapt...
Name:        C:\Projects\Books\Managed C++\Images
Created:     11/8/2001 2:52:59 AM
Accessed:    4/11/2002 8:50:21 PM
Updated:     4/10/2002 1:09:22 AM
Attributes: Directory
Sub-Directories:
        Ch01
        Ch02
        Ch03
        Ch04
        Ch06
        Ch07
        Ch08
Files:
        333Figures.zip
        Thumbs.db
Press any key to continue
```

Figure 8-1. Results of DirInfo.exe

File and FileInfo

Once you understand how to manage directories, it's not a big leap to manage files. Most of the properties and methods you use to manage files are identical to those you use to manage directories. The big difference, obviously, is that the class names have changed to File and FileInfo. In addition, there are a few additional file-specific methods added and a couple of directory-specific methods removed. There are also several methods to open up files in different ways. You will cover those a little later in the chapter.

Just like directories, having a constructor depends on whether you are using the static methods of File or the instance member methods of FileInfo.

```
FileInfo *fileinfo = new FileInfo(S"C:\\WinNT\\Temp\\file.dat");
```

NOTE *You could also have coded the previous line as*
`FileInfo *fileinfo = new FileInfo(S"file.dat");`
so long as the current directory is C:\WinNT\Temp. You can get and set the current directory with the Directory *class's* `GetCurrentDirectory()` *and* `SetCurrentDirectory()` *methods.*

Examining the details of a file while implementing the FileInfo class requires the use of the inherited properties of the `FileSystemInfo` class. You will see very little difference between the file methods and the directory methods. The `File` class's static methods are also the same as the directory equivalent, but this time there is a static method to retrieve attributes (see Table 8-3). There is an additional property to get the length of the file out of a `FileInfo` class but, oddly enough, there is no static method in the `File` class.

```
// FileInfo implementation:
String          *Name      = fileinfo->FullName;
DateTime        Created    = fileinfo->CreationTime;
DateTime        Accessed   = fileinfo->LastAccessTime;
DateTime        Updated    = fileinfo->LastWriteTime;
FileAttributes Attributes = fileinfo->Attributes;
Int64           Length     = fileinfo->Length; // physical, uncompressed, and
                                               //   unclustered size


// File implementation
// No equivalent for file->FullName
DateTime        Created    = File::GetCreationTime(S"C:\\WinNT\\Temp\\file.dat");
DateTime        Accessed   = File::GetLastAccessTime(S"file.dat");
DateTime        Updated    = File::GetLastWriteTime(S"file.dat");
FileAttributes Attributes = File::GetAttributes(S"file.dat");
// No equivalent for file->Length;
```

Table 8-3. Common File Attributes

ATTRIBUTE	DESCRIPTION
Archive	This attribute marks a file for archive or backup.
Directory	The file is a directory.
Encrypted	For a file, it means it is encrypted. For a directory, it means that all newly created files in the directory will be encrypted.
Hidden	The file is hidden from normal directory display.
Normal	The file is normal and has no other attributes set. (Note: This attribute is only valid if it is the only attribute set.)
ReadOnly	The file is read-only.
System	The file is part of the operating system.

Other than open files, which I cover next, the most likely activities you will do with files are check if a file exists, copy or move an existing file, or simply delete a file. You will find that the methods closely resemble those of the directory.

```
// FileInfo implementation:
if (fileinfo->Exists) {}
fileinfo->CopyTo(S"C:\\WinNT\\Temp\\file.dat");
fileinfo->CopyTo(S"file.dat", true);  // overwrite existing
fileinfo->MoveTo(S"C:\\WinNT\\Temp\\file.dat"); // target file can't exist
fileinfo->Delete(); // delete the file

// File implementation
if (File::Exists(S"C:\\WinNT\\Temp\\file.dat")) {}
File::Copy(S"C:\\WinNT\\Temp\\file1.dat", S"C:\\WinNT\\Temp\\file2.dat");
File::Copy(S"file1.dat", S"file2.dat", true);  //overwrite existing
File::Move(S"C:\\WinNT\\Temp\\file1.dat", S"file2.dat");
File::Delete(S"file1.dat");
```

 CAUTION *Even though the documentation sort of suggests other-wise, the destination of the* Move() *and* MoveTo() *methods cannot be a directory. The destination must be a nonexistent filename or a complete path including the filename.*

Listing 8-2 shows the `FileInfo` class in action and demonstrates many of the functionalities described previously.

Listing 8-2. Working with FileInfo

```
#using <mscorlib.dll>

using namespace System;
using namespace System::IO;
using namespace System::Text;

Int32 main( Int32 argc, SByte __nogc *argv[] )
{
    if (argc <= 1)
    {
        Console::WriteLine(S"Usage: FileInfo <File>");
        return -1;
    }

    StringBuilder *tmpfile = new StringBuilder();
    for (Int32 i = 1; i < argc; i++)
    {
        tmpfile->Append(argv[i]);
        tmpfile->Append(S" ");
    }

    String *strfile = tmpfile->ToString()->Trim();
    FileInfo *file = new FileInfo(strfile);
    if (!file->Exists)
    {
        Console::WriteLine(S"File Not Found");
        return -1;
    }

    Console::WriteLine(S"Name:     {0}", file->FullName);
    Console::WriteLine(S"Created:  {0} {1}",
                    file->CreationTime.ToShortDateString(),
                    file->CreationTime.ToLongTimeString());
    Console::WriteLine(S"Accessed: {0} {1}",
                    file->LastAccessTime.ToShortDateString(),
                    file->LastAccessTime.ToLongTimeString());
    Console::WriteLine(S"Updated:  {0} {1}",
                    file->LastWriteTime.ToShortDateString(),
```

```
                                      file->LastWriteTime.ToLongTimeString());
            Console::WriteLine(S"Length:      {0}",
                                      __box(file->Length)->ToString());
            Console::WriteLine(S"Attributes: {0}",
                                      __box(file->Attributes)->ToString());

            return 0;
    }
```

Figure 8-2 shows the results of the FileInfo.exe program.

Figure 8-2. Results of FileInfo.exe

Opening Files

There is no shortage of ways that you can open a file using the .NET Framework class library. There are 14 methods combined in the File and FileInfo class (see Table 8-4). Many of these methods have numerous parameter combinations. Both File and FileInfo use the same 7 method names and each of the methods with the same name do the same thing. Though the methods have the same name, the parameters passed differ, or at least the first parameter differs.

There always seems to be one exception. The File::Create() has an overloaded method that has a buffer size parameter that the FileInfo class's Create() method lacks.

Table 8-4. Opening a File Using the File and FileInfo Classes

METHOD	DESCRIPTION
Open()	Creates a FileStream to a file providing a plethora of read/write and share privilege options
Create()	Creates a FileStream providing full read and write privileges to a file
OpenRead()	Creates a read-only FileStream to an existing file
OpenWrite()	Creates a write-only unshared FileStream to a file
AppendText()	Creates a StreamWriter that appends text to the end of an existing file
CreateText()	Creates a StreamWriter that writes a new text file
OpenText()	Creates a StreamReader that reads from an existing file

You will cover FileStream, StreamWriter, and StreamReader later in this chapter.

Of these 14 (7×2) methods, only 2 actually take any parameters (other than the name of the file you wish to open for the static methods). Basically, the .NET Framework class library provides 2 equivalent file open methods and 12 shortcuts.

The Open Methods

There are only two root open methods in the .NET Framework class library: File::Open() and FileInfo::Open(). These methods are virtually the same, except the File::Open() method has one additional parameter: the path to the file you want to open. The FileInfo::Open() method gets this information from its constructor.

The Open() method is made up of three overloaded methods. Each overload provides progressively more information about how you want the file opened. The first overload takes as a parameter the file mode with which you wish to open the file (see Table 8-5). Because the other two parameters are not specified, the file will open by default with read/write access and as unshared.

```
FileInfo &fileinfo = *new FileInfo(S"file.dat");
FileStream *fs = fileinfo.Open(FileMode::Truncate);
// or
FileStream *fs = File::Open(S"file.dat", FileMode::CreateNew);
```

Table 8-5. FileMode Enumeration Values

FILEMODE	DESCRIPTION
Append	Opens a file if it exists and sets the next write point to the end of the file. If the file does not exist, it creates a new one. You can only use `FileMode::Append` with a file access of write-only, as any attempt to read throws an `ArgumentException`.
Create	Creates a new file. If the file already exists, it will be overwritten.
CreateNew	Creates a new file. If the file already exists, an `IOException` is thrown.
Open	Opens an existing file. If the file does not exist, a `FileNotFoundException` is thrown.
OpenOrCreate	Opens an existing file. If the file does not exist, it creates a new file.
Truncate	Opens an existing file and truncates it to a length of 0 bytes. If the file does not exist, a `FileNotFoundException` is thrown.

The second overload takes the additional parameter of the file access you require the file to have (see Table 8-6). The file will also be opened by default as unshared.

```
FileInfo *fileinfo = new FileInfo(S"file.dat");
FileStream *fs = fileinfo->Open(FileMode::Truncate, FileAccess::ReadWrite);
// or
FileStream *fs = File::Open(S"file.dat", FileMode::Append, FileAccess::Write);
```

Table 8-6. FileAccess Enumeration Values

FILEACCESS	DESCRIPTION
Read	Allows data only to be read from the file
ReadWrite	Allows data to be read from and written to the file
Write	Allows data only to be written to the file

The final overload has one more parameter. It specifies how the file is shared with others trying to access it concurrently (see Table 8-7).

```
FileInfo *fileinfo = new FileInfo(S"file.dat");
FileStream *fs = fileinfo->Open(FileMode::Truncate, FileAccess::ReadWrite,
                                FileShare::Read);
// or
FileStream *fs = File::Open(S"file.dat", FileMode::Append, FileAccess::Write,
                                        FileShare::None);
```

Table 8-7. FileShare Enumeration Values

FILESHARE	DESCRIPTION
None	Specifies exclusive access to the current file. Subsequent openings of the file by a process, including the current one, will fail until the file closes.
Read	Specifies that subsequent openings of the file by a process, including the current one, will succeed only if it is for a `FileMode` of Read.
ReadWrite	Specifies that subsequent openings of the file by a process, including the current one, will succeed for either reading or writing.
Write	Specifies that subsequent openings of the file by a process, including the current one, will succeed only if it is for a `FileMode` of Write.

All those parameters make the file open process very configurable, but also a little tedious. This is especially true if you just want to open the file in a very generic and standard way. The .NET Framework class library provides you with a way to simplify file opening if the way you want to open a file happens to fall in one of six standard open configurations.

```
FileInfo &fileinfo = *new FileInfo(S"file.dat");
FileStream   *CreateFile     = fileinfo.Create();
FileStream   *OpenReadFile   = fileinfo.OpenRead();
FileStream   *OpenWriteFile  = fileinfo.OpenWrite();
StreamWriter *AppendTextFile = fileinfo.AppendText();
StreamWriter *CreateTextFile = fileinfo.CreateText();
StreamReader *OpenTextFile   = fileinfo.OpenText();
// or
```

```
FileStream    *CreateFile    = File::Create(S"file.dat");
FileStream    *OpenReadFile  = File::OpenRead(S"file.dat");
FileStream    *OpenWriteFile = File::OpenWrite(S"file.dat");
StreamWriter *AppendTextFile = File::AppendText(S"file.dat");
StreamWriter *CreateTextFile = File::CreateText(S"file.dat");
StreamReader *OpenTextFile   = File::OpenText(S"file.dat");
```

Notice that none of the preceding file opening methods takes any parameters, except the file path in the case of the static method of the File class. Personally, I think the names of the methods make them pretty self-explanatory.

I/O Manipulation

Okay, you now have a file open and it is time to actually do something with it. Oops, did I say "file"? Files are only one thing that you can do I/O manipulation with. You can also do I/O manipulation in and out of memory using the MemoryStream and BufferedStream classes and in and out of network sockets using NetworkStream. You will look at the MemoryStream class a little later to see how it differs from a FileStream.

There are several different means to accomplish I/O manipulation. You will examine the three most common: using Streams, using TextReaders and TextWriters, and using BinaryReaders and BinaryWriters. Figure 8-3 shows the class hierarchy for manipulating files.

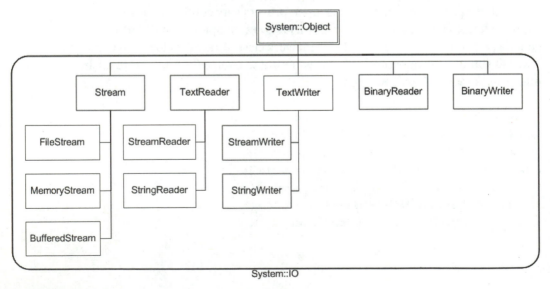

Figure 8-3. The class hierarchy for I/O manipulation

Using Streams

In the computer world, streams are a method of transferring blocks of data to and from one source to another in either a synchronous or asynchronous manner. The .NET Framework class library sends this data as a stream of bytes. A stream can also transfer these blocks of data starting from any location in one source to any location in another source.

What does this mean to you? Basically, you can read data, write data, and adjust the current location where you access the data. Not much to it, is there?

All stream-based I/O in the .NET Framework class library derives from the abstract base class Stream. The Stream class contains several virtual methods, which the inheriting class must define (see Table 8-8). Basically, these virtual methods define core Stream functionality and thus ensure that the inheriting class satisfies the definition of a stream as stated previously.

Table 8-8. The Virtual Methods and Properties of the Stream Class

MEMBER	DESCRIPTION
CanRead	A Boolean value specifying whether reading is supported.
CanSeek	A Boolean value specifying whether seeking is supported.
CanWrite	A Boolean value specifying whether writing is supported.
Close()	A method that closes the file and releases resources associated with the stream.
Flush()	This method moves the data from the source buffer to its destination source and then clears the buffer. If the stream does not support a buffer, this method does nothing.
Length	The length of the stream in bytes.
Position	If seeking is supported, then this property can be used to get or set the position in the stream.
Read()	Reads a specified number of bytes from the stream and then advances the position after the last read byte.
ReadByte()	Reads a single byte from the stream and then advances the position after the byte.
Seek()	If seeking is supported, then this method can be used to set the position in the stream.
SetLength()	Sets the length of the stream in bytes.

(continued)

Table 8-8. The Virtual Methods and Properties of the Stream Class (continued)

MEMBER	DESCRIPTION
Write()	Writes a specified number of bytes to the stream and then advances the position after the last written byte.
WriteByte()	Writes one byte to the stream and then advances the position after the byte.

You will see some of these properties and methods implemented in the following stream implementations.

FileStreams

One of the most common implementations of a Stream is the FileStream class. This class provides implementations for the abstract Stream class so that it can perform file-based streaming. Or, in other words, it allows you to read from and write to a file.

You have already seen several ways to open a FileStream. It is also possible to open a FileStream directly without using File or FileInfo. To do this, you use one of the FileStream's many constructors. The most common parameters passed to the constructor are identical to those passed to the static File::Open() method.

```
FileStream *fs = new FileStream(S"file.dat", FileMode::CreateNew);
FileStream *fs = new FileStream(S"file.dat", FileMode::Append,
                                FileAccess::Write);
FileStream *fs = new FileStream(S"file.dat", FileMode::Create,
                                FileAccess::Write, FileShare::None);
```

Once you finally have the FileStream open, you can start to read and/or write Bytes of data from or to it. As you saw from the virtual methods defined by the Stream class in Table 8-8, there are two ways of reading and writing to a stream. You can do it either by individual Bytes or by arrays of Bytes.

```
Byte data[] = { 'A', 'p', 'p', 'l', 'e' };
fso->Write(data, 0, 4);
fso->WriteByte(data[4]);

Byte ba[] = new Byte[5];
ba[0] = fsi->ReadByte();
fsi->Read(ba, 1, 4);
```

Simply placing the location in the `Position` property sets the location of the next place to read from or write to the file.

```
fsi->Position = 0;
```

You can also set the location of the next read or write by the `Seek()` method. This method allows you to use offsets from the beginning of the file (same as the `Position` property), the current location, or the end of the file.

```
fsi->Seek(0, SeekOrigin::Begin);
```

If you desire further access but want the data available in the file (for another operation or just for safety), flush the file buffer.

```
fso->Flush();
```

You should always close your files after you are done with them.

```
fso->Close();
```

Listing 8-3 shows the `FileStream` class in action and demonstrates many of the functionalities described previously.

Listing 8-3. Working with a FileStream

```
#using <mscorlib.dll>

using namespace System;
using namespace System::IO;

Int32 main(void)
{
    FileStream *fso = new FileStream(S"file.dat", FileMode::Create,
                                FileAccess::Write, FileShare::None);

    Byte data[] = { 'T', 'h', 'i', 's', ' ', 'i', 's', ' ', 'a',
                    ' ', 't', 'e', 's', 't', '!', '\r', '\n', 'T',
                    'h', 'i', 's', ' ', 'i', 's', ' ', 'o', 'n',
                    'l', 'y', ' ', 'a', ' ', 't', 'e', 's', 't', '.','\r', '\n'
                  };
```

```
    for (Int32 i = 0; i < data.Count-5; i += 5)
    {
        fso->Write(data, i, 5);
    }

    for (Int32 i = data.Count-4; i < data.Count; i++)
    {
        fso->WriteByte(data[i]);
    }

    fso->Close();

    FileInfo *fi = new FileInfo(S"file.dat");
    FileStream *fsi = fi->OpenRead();

    Int32 b;
    while ((b = fsi->ReadByte()) != -1)
    {
        Console::Write((Char)b);
    }

    fsi->Position = 0;

    Byte ba[] = new Byte[17];
    fsi->Read(ba, 0, 17);
    for (Int32 i = 0; i < ba.Count; i++)
    {
        Console::Write((Char)ba[i]);
    }

    Console::WriteLine();

    fsi->Close();

    // fi->Delete();  // If you want to get rid of it

    return 0;
}
```

Figure 8-4 shows the file output generated by the FileStream.exe program.

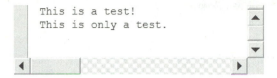

Figure 8-4. File output of FileStream.exe

MemoryStreams

Programming with a MemoryStream is not much different from working with a FileStream. Obviously, what's happening behind the scenes, on the other hand, is completely different. You're no longer dealing with files; instead, you're dealing with computer memory.

There are only a few differences from a coding perspective when you deal with a MemoryStream. Obviously, the constructor is different.

```
MemoryStream *fs = new MemoryStream();
```

A MemoryStream has an additional property and a couple of unique methods (see Table 8-9).

Table 8-9. Additional MemoryStream Property and Methods

MEMBER	DESCRIPTION
Capacity	This property gets or sets the number of bytes allocated to the stream.
GetBuffer()	Returns an unsigned array of bytes that the stream created.
WriteTo()	Writes the contents of the MemoryStream to another stream. This comes in handy if you want to write the stream out to a FileStream.

Listing 8-4 shows the MemoryStream class in action and demonstrates many of the functionalities described previously.

Listing 8-4. Working with a MemoryStream

```
Int32 main(void)
{
    Byte data[] = { 'T', 'h', 'i', 's', ' ', 'i', 's', ' ', 'a',
                    ' ', 't', 'e', 's', 't', '!', '\r', '\n', 'T',
                    'h', 'i', 's', ' ', 'i', 's', ' ', 'o', 'n',
                    'l', 'y', ' ', 'a', ' ', 't', 'e', 's', 't', '.','\r', '\n' };
```

```
MemoryStream *ms = new MemoryStream();
ms->Capacity = 40;

for (Int32 i = 0; i < data.Count-5; i += 5)
{
    ms->Write(data, i, 5);
}

for (Int32 i = data.Count-4; i < data.Count; i++)
{
    ms->WriteByte(data[i]);
}

Byte ba[] = ms->GetBuffer();
for (Int32 i = 0; i < ba.Count; i++)
{
    Console::Write((Char)ba[i]);
}
Console::WriteLine(S"");

FileStream *fs = File::OpenWrite(S"file.dat");
ms->WriteTo(fs);

fs->Close();
ms->Close();

return 0;
}
```

Figure 8-5 shows a display of the buffer contained within the MemoryStream. Figure 8-6 shows the results displayed to the console. Figure 8-7 shows the resulting file output generated by the MemoryStream.exe program. Notice that Figures 8-5 through 8-7 all have the same results, as expected.

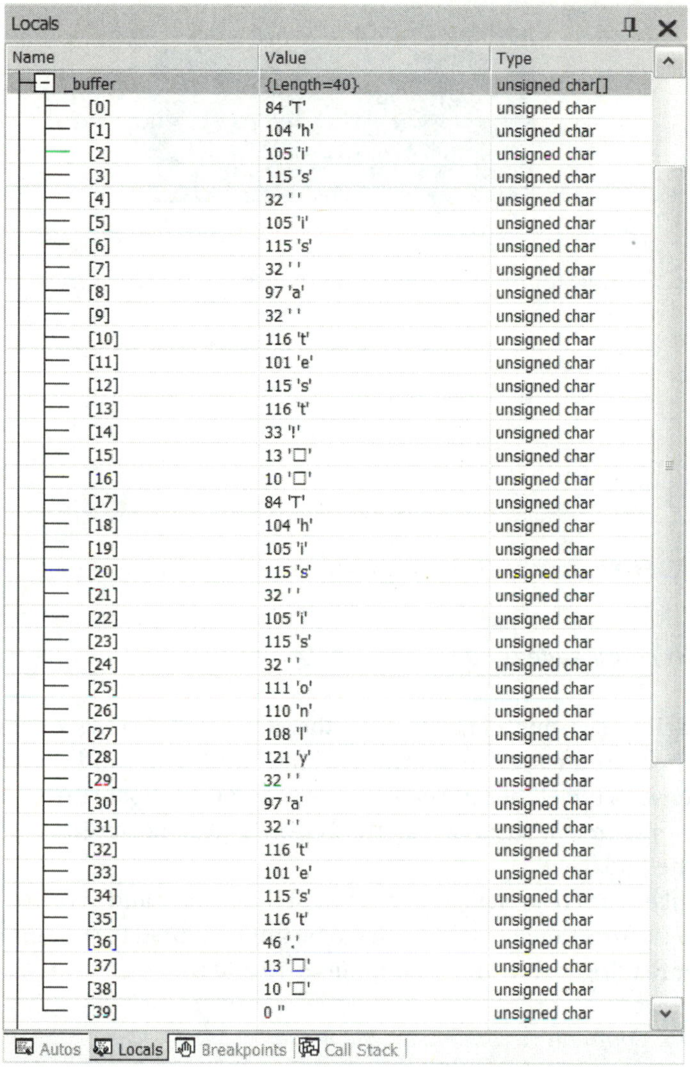

Locals			
Name	Value	Type	
− _buffer	{Length=40}	unsigned char[]	
[0]	84 'T'	unsigned char	
[1]	104 'h'	unsigned char	
[2]	105 'i'	unsigned char	
[3]	115 's'	unsigned char	
[4]	32 ' '	unsigned char	
[5]	105 'i'	unsigned char	
[6]	115 's'	unsigned char	
[7]	32 ' '	unsigned char	
[8]	97 'a'	unsigned char	
[9]	32 ' '	unsigned char	
[10]	116 't'	unsigned char	
[11]	101 'e'	unsigned char	
[12]	115 's'	unsigned char	
[13]	116 't'	unsigned char	
[14]	33 '!'	unsigned char	
[15]	13 '□'	unsigned char	
[16]	10 '□'	unsigned char	
[17]	84 'T'	unsigned char	
[18]	104 'h'	unsigned char	
[19]	105 'i'	unsigned char	
[20]	115 's'	unsigned char	
[21]	32 ' '	unsigned char	
[22]	105 'i'	unsigned char	
[23]	115 's'	unsigned char	
[24]	32 ' '	unsigned char	
[25]	111 'o'	unsigned char	
[26]	110 'n'	unsigned char	
[27]	108 'l'	unsigned char	
[28]	121 'y'	unsigned char	
[29]	32 ' '	unsigned char	
[30]	97 'a'	unsigned char	
[31]	32 ' '	unsigned char	
[32]	116 't'	unsigned char	
[33]	101 'e'	unsigned char	
[34]	115 's'	unsigned char	
[35]	116 't'	unsigned char	
[36]	46 '.'	unsigned char	
[37]	13 '□'	unsigned char	
[38]	10 '□'	unsigned char	
[39]	0 ''	unsigned char	

Autos Locals Breakpoints Call Stack

Figure 8-5. Display of the buffer of the MemoryStream created by MemoryStream.exe

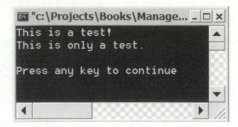

Figure 8-6. Console results of MemoryStream.exe

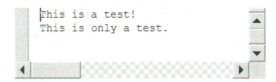

Figure 8-7. File output of MemoryStream.exe

Using StreamReaders and StreamWriters

A drawback when using a `FileStream` is that it isn't very `String`- or character-friendly. Because what you often want to store are `Strings` and characters, it only makes sense that methods be made to optimize and simplify the process of writing these to a stream. This is where the `StreamReader` and `StreamWriter` classes become helpful.

Just like the `Stream` class, the abstract `StreamReader` and `StreamWriter` classes define all the functionality that needs to be implemented to support `String` and character reading and writing (see Tables 8-10 and 8-11).

Table 8-10. Common StreamReader Members

METHOD	DESCRIPTION
Close()	Closes the file and releases any resources
Peek()	Reads the next character without advancing the stream pointer
Read()	Reads data from the input stream
ReadBlock()	Reads a specified number of characters from the stream to a specified starting location in an input buffer
ReadLine()	Reads a line of data from the input stream and returns it as a `String`
ReadToEnd()	Reads the rest of the data from the current file location to the end and returns it as a single `String`

Table 8-11. Common StreamWriter Members

METHOD	DESCRIPTION
Close()	Closes the file and releases any resources
Flush()	Forces the writing of the current buffer and then clears it
Write()	Writes the specified String to the output stream
WriteLine()	Writes the specified String to the output stream, then writes the NewLine String

There are many ways to create a StreamReader and a StreamWriter. You can start from the File or FileInfo class and create one directly from its methods. It is also possible to build one from a FileStream, again using the File or FileInfo class or with the FileStream constructor.

```
StreamReader *sr1 = File::OpenText(S"file.dat");
StreamWriter *sw1 = fileinfo->CreateText(S"file.dat");

StreamReader *sr2 = new StreamReader(File::Open(S"file.dat",
                        FileMode::Open, FileAccess::Read, FileShare::None));
StreamWriter *sw2 = new StreamWriter(new FileStream(S"file.dat",
                        FileMode::Create, FileAccess::Write, FileShare::None));
```

Writing to the StreamWriter, after you have created it, is no different than writing to the console. You should be very familiar with the Write() and WriteLine() methods. Reading is a little trickier, as you can read one character, an array of characters, or the rest of the characters in the stream. In most cases, you will most likely be using the StreamReader methods ReadLine() and ReadToEnd(). The first reads a single line of text while the second reads all the text remaining on the stream. Both return their results as a String.

```
String *in1 = sr->ReadLine();
String *in2 = sr->ReadToEnd();
```

Listing 8-5 shows the StreamWriter and StreamReader classes in action and demonstrates many of the functionalities described previously. It also resembles the previous examples but, as you can see, the code is much simpler.

Listing 8-5. Working with a StreamWriter and a StreamReader

```
Int32 main(void)
{
    String *data[] = { S"This is ", S"a test!", S"This is only a test." };

    StreamWriter *sw = new StreamWriter(new FileStream(S"file.dat",
                        FileMode::Create, FileAccess::Write, FileShare::None));

    for (Int32 i = 0; i < data.Count-1; i++)
    {
        sw->Write(data[i]);
    }
    sw->WriteLine(S"");
    sw->WriteLine(data[2]);

    sw->Close();

    StreamReader *sr = File::OpenText(S"file.dat");

    String *in = sr->ReadLine();
    Console::WriteLine(in);
    Console::WriteLine(sr->ReadToEnd());

    sw->Close();

    return 0;
}
```

Figure 8-8 shows the results of StreamRW.exe displayed to the console. Figure 8-9 shows the resulting file output generated by the StreamRW.exe program. Notice that Figures 8-8 and 8-9 have the same results, as expected.

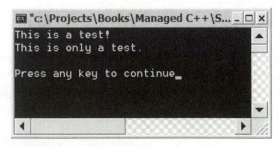

Figure 8-8. Console results of StreamRW.exe

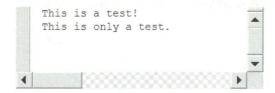

Figure 8-9. File output of StreamRW.exe

Using BinaryReader and BinaryWriter

You have looked at I/O for Bytes and Strings. What if you want to store all the other data types, such as Booleans, integers, and floating points? This is where the BinaryReader and BinaryWriter come into play. These classes were designed specifically to handle all the .NET Framework's built-in data types (including Byte and String).

To create a BinaryReader or BinaryWriter class, you need to use its constructor and pass it a Stream. This means, by the way, that BinaryReaders and BinaryWriters can take as a parameter a FileStream, MemoryStream, NetworkStream, and so on.

```
FileStream *fs = File::OpenRead(fname);
BinaryReader *br = new BinaryReader(fs);

MemoryStream *ms = new MemoryStream();
BinaryWriter *br = new BinaryWriter(ms);
```

The process of writing with the BinaryWriter is very simple. After you create your BinaryWriter, you only need to use two more methods, Write() and Close(). The Write() method takes care of all the hard work by being made up of numerous overloaded versions of itself (one for each supported data type).

The BinaryReader class is a little harder to work with. This time, you need to work with many different read methods (one for each supported type). They all have the same syntax: Readxxx(), where xxx is the data type. Examples of read methods are ReadInt32(), ReadBoolean(), and ReadSingle().

A drawback of the BinaryReader is that you need to know the data type you are reading in before you actually do the read, so that you can make the correct call.

Listing 8-6 shows the BinaryWriter and BinaryReader classes in action and demonstrates many of the functionalities described previously. You might want to notice the special coding you need to be do to handle DateTime classes.

Listing 8-6. Working with a BinaryWriter and a BinaryReader

```
__gc class Player
{
    String *Name;
    Int32   Strength;
    Boolean IsMale;

public:
    Player() {}

    Player (String *Name, Int32 Str, Boolean IsMale)
    {
        this->Name     = Name;
        this->Strength = Str;
        this->IsMale   = IsMale;
    }

    void Print()
    {
        Console::WriteLine(S"Name: {0} ({1})", Name, (IsMale ? S"M" : S"F"));
        Console::WriteLine(S"Str:  {0}", __box(Strength));
        Console::WriteLine(S"Date: {0}", CreateDate.ToString());
    }

    void Save(String *fname)
    {
        FileStream *fs = File::OpenWrite(fname);
        BinaryWriter *bw = new BinaryWriter(fs);

        bw->Write(Name);
        bw->Write(Strength);
        bw->Write(IsMale);

        // Due to multiculture this is a safe way of storing DateTimes
        bw->Write(CreateDate.Ticks);

        bw->Close();
        fs->Close();
    }
```

```
    void Load(String *fname)
    {
        FileStream *fs = File::OpenRead(fname);
        BinaryReader *br = new BinaryReader(fs);

        Name     = br->ReadString();
        Strength = br->ReadInt32();
        IsMale   = br->ReadBoolean();

        // Due to multicultures this is a safe way of retrieving DateTimes
        CreateDate = DateTime( br->ReadInt64() );

        br->Close();
        fs->Close();
    }
};


Int32 main(void)
{
    Player *Joe = new Player(S"Joe", 10, true);
    Joe->Save(S"Player.dat");

    Console::WriteLine(S"Original Joe");
    Joe->Print();

    Player *JoeClone = new Player();
    JoeClone->Load(S"Player.dat");

    Console::WriteLine(S"\nCloned Joe");
    JoeClone->Print();

    return 0;
}
```

Figure 8-10 shows the results of BinaryRW.exe displayed to the console. Figure 8-11 shows the resulting file output generated by the BinaryRW.exe program. Notice that Figure 8-11 is pretty unreadable unless you know the format in which it was stored. The fact that Figure 8-10 and Figure 8-11 represent the same data is not obvious.

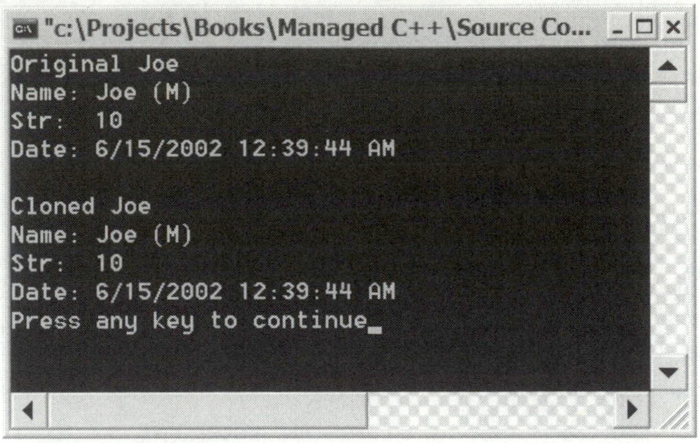

Figure 8-10. Console results of BinaryRW.exe

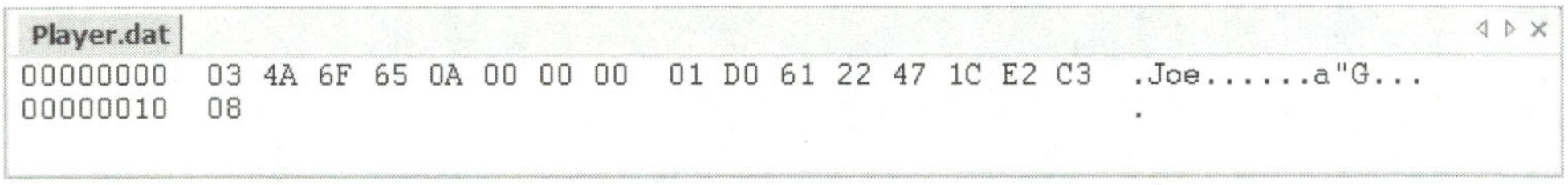

Figure 8-11. File output of BinaryRW.exe

Serialization of Managed Classes

The BinaryReader and BinaryWriter classes are okay when it comes to storing small classes to disk and retrieving them later, as you saw in the last section. But classes can become quite complicated. What happens when your class has numerous member variables and/or linked objects? How do you figure out which data type belongs with which class? In what order were they saved? It can become quite a mess very quickly. Wouldn't it be nice if you didn't have to worry about the details and could just say, "Here's the file I want the class saved to. Now, save it." I'm sure you know where I'm going with this; this is the job of serialization.

Serialization is the process of storing the class off (most probably to disk, but not necessarily) for later retrieval. *Deserialization* is the process of restoring a class from disk (or wherever you saved it). Sounds tough, but the .NET Framework class library actually makes it quite simple to do.

Setting Up Classes for Serialization

The process of setting a class up for serialization is probably one of the easiest things that you can do in Managed C++. You simply place the [Serializable] attribute in front of the managed class you want to serialize. Yep, that is it!

```
[Serializable]
__gc class ClassName
{
//...
};
```

The reason this is possible is because all the class's information is stored in its metadata. This metadata is so detailed that all the information regarding serializing and deserializing the class is available at runtime for the CLR to process the serialization or deserialization request.

Listing 8-7 shows the entire process of setting up the Player class for serialization. To make things interesting, I split PlayerAttr off into its own class. As you will see, even the serialization of a linked object like this only requires placing the [Serializable] attribute in front of it.

Listing 8-7. Making a Class Ready for Serialization

```
[Serializable]
__gc class PlayerAttr
{
    Int32    Strength;
    Int32    Dexterity;
    Int32    Constitution;
    Int32    Intelligence;
    Int32    Wisdom;
    Int32    Charisma;

public:
    PlayerAttr(Int32 Str, Int32 Dex, Int32 Con, Int32 Int, Int32 Wis, Int32 Cha)
    {
        this->Strength     = Str;
        this->Dexterity    = Dex;
        this->Constitution = Con;
        this->Intelligence = Int;
        this->Wisdom       = Wis;
        this->Charisma     = Cha;
    }

    void Print()
    {
        Console::WriteLine(S"Str: {0}, Dex: {1}, Con {2}",
            __box(Strength), __box(Dexterity), __box(Constitution));
        Console::WriteLine(S"Int: {0}, Wis: {1}, Cha {2}",
            __box(Intelligence), __box(Wisdom), __box(Charisma));
```

```
    }
};

[Serializable]
__gc class Player
{
    String *Name;
    String *Race;
    String *Class;
    PlayerAttr *pattr;

public:
    Player (String *Name, String *Race, String *Class,
        Int32 Str, Int32 Dex, Int32 Con, Int32 Int, Int32 Wis, Int32 Cha)
    {
        this->Name  = Name;
        this->Race  = Race;
        this->Class = Class;
        this->pattr = new PlayerAttr(Str, Dex, Con, Int, Wis, Cha);
    }

    void Print()
    {
        Console::WriteLine(S"Name:  {0}", Name);
        Console::WriteLine(S"Race:  {0}", Race);
        Console::WriteLine(S"Class: {0}", Class);
        pattr->Print();
    }
};
```

If you can't tell, I play Dungeons and Dragons (D&D). These classes are a very simplified player character. Of course, you would probably want to use enums and check minimums and maximums and so forth, but I didn't want to get too complicated.

BinaryFormatter vs. SoapFormatter

Before you actually serialize a class, you have to make a choice. In what format do you want to store the serialized data? Right now, the .NET Framework class library supplies you with two choices. You can store the serialized class data in a binary format or in an XML format or, more specifically, in a Simple Object Access Protocol (SOAP) format.

The choice is up to you. Binary is more compact, faster, and works well with the CLR. SOAP, on the other hand, is a self-describing text file that can be used with a system that doesn't support the CLR. Which formatter type you should use depends on how you plan to use the serialized data.

It is also possible to create your own formatter. This book does not cover how to do this, because this book is about .NET, and the main reason that you might want to create your own formatter is if you are interfacing with a non-CLR (non-.NET) system that has its own serialization format. You should check the .NET Framework documentation for details on how to do this.

Serialization Using BinaryFormatter

As I hinted at previously, the process of serializing a class is remarkably easy. First off, all the code to handle serialization is found in the mscorlib.dll assembly. This means you don't have to worry about loading any special assemblies. The hardest thing about serialization is that you have to remember that the `BinaryFormatter` is located in the namespace `System::Runtime::Serialization::Formatters::Binary`. You have the option of using the fully qualified version of the formatter every time, but I prefer to add a using statement and save my fingers for typing more important code.

```
using namespace System::Runtime::Serialization::Formatters::Binary;
```

The simplest constructor for the `BinaryFormatter` is just the standard default, which takes no parameters.

```
BinaryFormatter *bf = new BinaryFormatter();
```

To actually serialize a class, you need to call the `BinaryFormatter`'s `Serialize()` method. This method takes a `Stream` and a class pointer. Make sure you open the `Stream` for writing. You also need to truncate the `Stream` or create a new copy each time. And don't forget to close the `Stream` when you're done.

```
BinaryFormatter *bf = new BinaryFormatter();

FileStream *plStream = File::Create(S"Player.dat");
bf->Serialize(plStream, Joe);
plStream->Close();
```

The process of deserializing is only slightly more complicated. This time, you need to use the `deserialize()` method. This method only takes one parameter, a pointer to a `Stream` open for reading. Again, don't forget to close the `Stream` after you're finished with it. The tricky part of deserialization is that the deserialize() method returns a generic Object class. Therefore, you need to typecast it to the class of the original serialized class.

```
plStream = File::OpenRead(S"Player.dat");
Player *JoeClone = dynamic_cast<Player*>(bf->Deserialize(plStream));
plStream->Close();
```

Listing 8-8 shows the entire process of serializing and deserializing the Player class.

Listing 8-8. Serializing and Deserializing the Player Class

```
#using <mscorlib.dll>

using namespace System;
using namespace System::IO;
using namespace System::Runtime::Serialization::Formatters::Binary;

Int32 main(void)
{
    Player *Joe = new Player(S"Joe", S"Human", S"Thief", 10, 18, 9, 13, 10, 11);

    Console::WriteLine(S"Original Joe");
    Joe->Print();

    FileStream *plStream = File::Create(S"Player.dat");

    BinaryFormatter *bf = new BinaryFormatter();
    bf->Serialize(plStream, Joe);
    plStream->Close();

    plStream = File::OpenRead(S"Player.dat");

    Player *JoeClone = dynamic_cast<Player*>(bf->Deserialize(plStream));
    plStream->Close();

    Console::WriteLine(S"\nCloned Joe");
    JoeClone->Print();

    return 0;
}
```

Figure 8-12 shows the results of BinFormSerial.exe displayed to the console. Figure 8-13 shows the resulting binary-formatted serialization output file generated.

Figure 8-12. Console results of BinFormSerial.exe

```
Player.dat                                                                    ↓ ▷ ✕
00000000  00 01 00 00 00 FF FF FF  FF 01 00 00 00 00 00 00    ................
00000010  00 0C 02 00 00 00 44 42  69 6E 46 6F 72 6D 53 65    ......DBinFormSe
00000020  72 69 61 6C 2C 20 56 65  72 73 69 6F 6E 3D 30 2E    rial, Version=0.
00000030  30 2E 30 2E 30 2C 20 43  75 6C 74 75 72 65 3D 6E    0.0.0, Culture=n
00000040  65 75 74 72 61 6C 2C 20  50 75 62 6C 69 63 4B 65    eutral, PublicKe
00000050  79 54 6F 6B 65 6E 3D 6E  75 6C 6C 05 01 00 00 00    yToken=null.....
00000060  06 50 6C 61 79 65 72 04  00 00 00 04 4E 61 6D 65    .Player.....Name
00000070  04 52 61 63 65 05 43 6C  61 73 73 05 70 61 74 74    .Race.Class.patt
00000080  72 01 01 01 04 0A 50 6C  61 79 65 72 41 74 74 72    r.....PlayerAttr
00000090  02 00 00 00 02 00 00 00  06 03 00 00 00 03 4A 6F    ..............Jo
000000a0  65 06 04 00 00 00 05 48  75 6D 61 6E 06 05 00 00    e......Human....
000000b0  00 05 54 68 69 65 66 09  06 00 00 00 05 06 00 00    ..Thief.........
000000c0  00 0A 50 6C 61 79 65 72  41 74 74 72 06 00 00 00    ..PlayerAttr....
000000d0  08 53 74 72 65 6E 67 74  68 09 44 65 78 74 65 72    .Strength.Dexter
000000e0  69 74 79 0C 43 6F 6E 73  74 69 74 75 74 69 6F 6E    ity.Constitution
000000f0  0C 49 6E 74 65 6C 6C 69  67 65 6E 63 65 06 57 69    .Intelligence.Wi
00000100  73 64 6F 6D 08 43 68 61  72 69 73 6D 61 00 00 00    sdom.Charisma...
00000110  00 00 00 08 08 08 08 08  08 02 00 00 00 0A 00 00    ................
00000120  00 12 00 00 00 09 00 00  00 0D 00 00 00 0A 00 00    ................
00000130  00 0B 00 00 00 0B                                   ......
```

Figure 8-13. Binary-formatted file output of the serialization of the Player class

Serialization Using SoapFormatter

There is very little difference in the code required to serialize using the SoapFormatter when compared with the BinaryFormatter. One obvious difference is that you use the SoapFormatter object instead of a BinaryFormatter object. There is also one other major difference, but you have to be paying attention to notice it, at least until you finally try to compile the serializing application. The SoapFormatter is not part of the mscorlib.dll assembly. To use the SoapFormatter, you need to reference the .NET assembly system.runtime.serialization.formatters.soap.dll. You will also find the SoapFormatter class in the namespace System::Runtime::Serialization::Formatters::Soap, which also differs from the BinaryFormatter.

```
#using <system.runtime.serialization.formatters.soap.dll>
using namespace System::Runtime::Serialization::Formatters::Soap;
```

The biggest difference is one that doesn't occur in the code. Instead, it's the serialized file generated. BinaryFormatted serialization files are in an unreadable binary format, whereas SoapFormatted serialization files are in a readable XML text format.

Listing 8-9 shows the entire process of serializing and deserializing the Player class using the SoapFormatter. Notice that the only differences between SOAP and binary are the #using and using statements and the use of SoapFormatter instead of BinaryFormatter.

Listing 8-9. Serializing and Deserializing the Player Class Using SoapFormatter

```
#using <mscorlib.dll>
#using <system.runtime.serialization.formatters.soap.dll>

using namespace System;
using namespace System::IO;
using namespace System::Runtime::Serialization::Formatters::Soap;

Int32 main(void)
{
    Player *Joe = new Player(S"Joe", S"Human", S"Thief", 10, 18, 9, 13, 10, 11);

    Console::WriteLine(S"Original Joe");
    Joe->Print();

    FileStream *plStream = File::Create(S"Player.xml");

    SoapFormatter *sf = new SoapFormatter();
    sf->Serialize(plStream, Joe);
    plStream->Close();
```

```
    plStream = File::OpenRead(S"Player.xml");

    Player *JoeClone = dynamic_cast<Player*>(sf->Deserialize(plStream));
    plStream->Close();

    Console::WriteLine(S"\nCloned Joe");
    JoeClone->Print();

    return 0;
}
```

Figure 8-14 shows the resulting SOAP-formatted serialization output file generated by SoapFormSerial.exe.

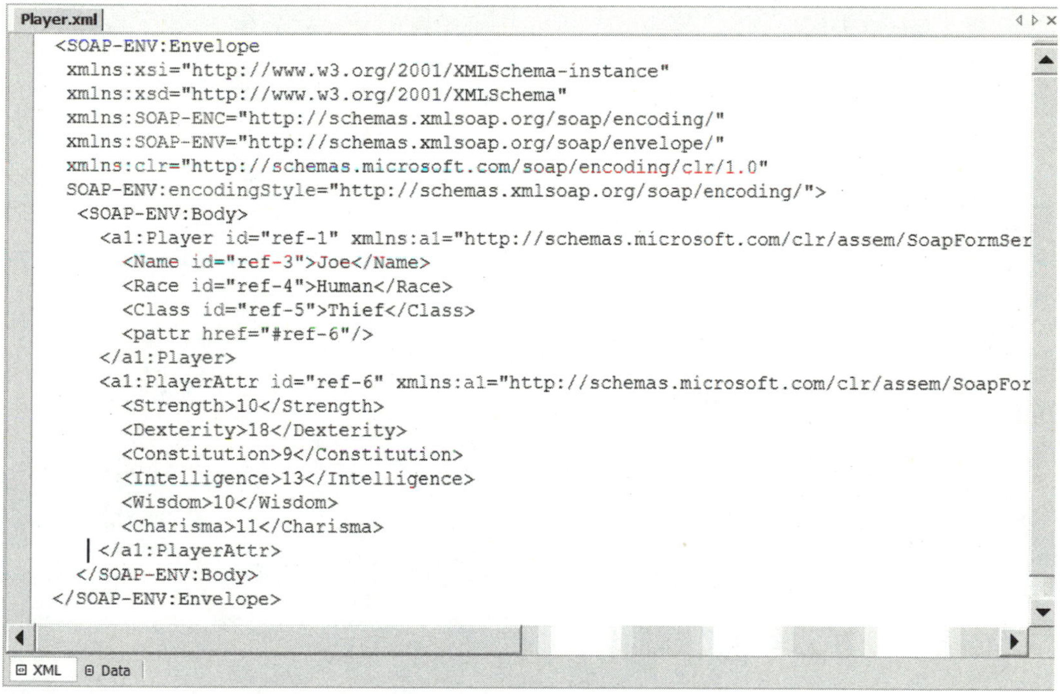


```
<SOAP-ENV:Envelope
 xmlns:xsi="http://www.w3.org/2001/XMLSchema-instance"
 xmlns:xsd="http://www.w3.org/2001/XMLSchema"
 xmlns:SOAP-ENC="http://schemas.xmlsoap.org/soap/encoding/"
 xmlns:SOAP-ENV="http://schemas.xmlsoap.org/soap/envelope/"
 xmlns:clr="http://schemas.microsoft.com/soap/encoding/clr/1.0"
 SOAP-ENV:encodingStyle="http://schemas.xmlsoap.org/soap/encoding/">
  <SOAP-ENV:Body>
    <a1:Player id="ref-1" xmlns:a1="http://schemas.microsoft.com/clr/assem/SoapFormSer
      <Name id="ref-3">Joe</Name>
      <Race id="ref-4">Human</Race>
      <Class id="ref-5">Thief</Class>
      <pattr href="#ref-6"/>
    </a1:Player>
    <a1:PlayerAttr id="ref-6" xmlns:a1="http://schemas.microsoft.com/clr/assem/SoapFor
      <Strength>10</Strength>
      <Dexterity>18</Dexterity>
      <Constitution>9</Constitution>
      <Intelligence>13</Intelligence>
      <Wisdom>10</Wisdom>
      <Charisma>11</Charisma>
    </a1:PlayerAttr>
  </SOAP-ENV:Body>
</SOAP-ENV:Envelope>
```

Figure 8-14. SOAP-formatted file output of the serialization of the Player class

Summary

In this chapter you covered a major component of software development: I/O. You started by looking at how the .NET Framework class library provides an object-style approach to the Windows file system, covering files and directories. You then moved on to look at how to open files for I/O manipulation. Next, you learned how to perform many different methods of reading, writing, and seeking to not only files, but also memory streams. You finished by looking at a specialized I/O system known as serialization.

Though none of the concepts in this chapter should be new to anyone who has worked with file I/O before, how it is done with the .NET Framework class library is new. And, as you should suspect, I/O manipulation can be accomplished in many different ways.

In the next chapter, you will move away from the humdrum of the console and start playing with one of Windows' claims to fame: the graphical user interface (GUI).

CHAPTER 9

Basic Windows Forms Applications

CONSOLE APPLICATIONS ARE fine for quick utilities and testing functionality, but Windows applications really shine when they present a graphical user interface (GUI) to the world. With the release of Visual Studio .NET 2003, Microsoft has ushered in the era of "easy-to-build" Managed C++ windows applications. It is effortless to drag and drop your complete user interface using the built-in design tool provided by Visual Studio .NET. Adding event handling to these GUI components is a breeze as well—all it requires is a double-click at design time on the component.

The available GUI options in the .NET Framework are quite staggering, and no one chapter can do them justice. As this is the case, I have broken up the topic into two parts. In this chapter I cover the more basic areas of .NET Framework Windows GUI development, better known as *Windows Forms* (or *Win Forms*). On completing this chapter, you should have a firm background on how to develop (albeit bland) Win Forms on your own. You will have to wait for the next chapter to learn more of the bells and whistles.

In this chapter you will learn how to use the design tool, but that is not the only focus of the chapter. You will also learn how to build your Win Forms without the design tool. The reason I cover both approaches is that I feel the intimate knowledge of the Win Form components that you gain by manual development will allow you to build better interfaces. Once you know both methods, you can combine the two to create the optimal interface to your Windows application.

Win Forms Are Not MFC

The first thing you need to know about Win Forms is that they are not an upgrade, enhancement, new version, or anything else of the Microsoft Foundation Classes (MFC). They are a brand-new, truly object-oriented Windows GUI implementation. A few classes have the same names and support the same functionalities, but that is where the similarities end.

Win Forms have a much stronger resemblance to Visual Basic's (pre-.NET) forms. In fact, Microsoft has taken the Visual Basic GUI development model of forms, controls, and properties and created a language-neutral equivalent for the .NET Framework.

When you create Windows applications with the .NET Framework, you will be working with Win Forms. It is possible to still use MFC within Visual Studio .NET, but then you are not developing .NET Framework code. However, once you have worked with Win Forms for a while, you will see that it is a much easier to code, cleaner, more object-oriented, and more complete implementation of the Windows GUI.

"Hello, World!" Win Form Style

Okay, you did the obligatory "Hello, World!" for a console application, so now you'll do it again for a Win Form application. The first thing you need to do is create a project using the Windows Forms Application (.NET) template, exactly like you did for the console application (see Figure 9-1).

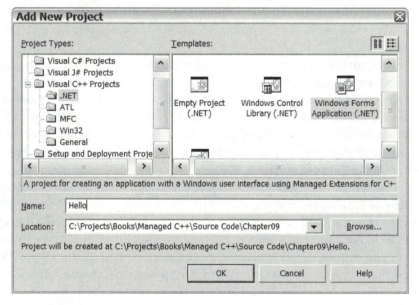

Figure 9-1. Creating a Win Form "Hello, World!" application project

Once the project template is finished being built, you have a complete Windows application. Okay, on to the next chapter . . . Just kidding!

The process of building the "Hello, World!" application involves the following steps:

1. Expand the GUI Toolbox view.

2. Click the required GUI component in the Toolbox view.

3. Drag the component to the design form.

4. Change the component's properties in the Properties view.

5. Double-click the component to create the event handler for the component. This will bring up the IDE editor.

6. Enter the code in the IDE editor to handle the event for the component.

This is very easy and very straightforward. If this level of simplicity gives you the willies, as it did me, be comforted by the fact that you can go in and code everything by hand if you want. After a while, you will come to realize that you do not have to code much in the way of the GUI interface manually.

So what code is provided? Listing 9-1 shows Form1.cpp. It doesn't look like there's much going on, but looks can be deceiving.

Listing 9-1. The Default Form1.cpp

```
#include "stdafx.h"
#include "Form1.h"
#include <windows.h>

using namespace Hello;

int APIENTRY _tWinMain(HINSTANCE hInstance,
                       HINSTANCE hPrevInstance,
                       LPTSTR    lpCmdLine,
                       int       nCmdShow)
{
    System::Threading::Thread::CurrentThread->ApartmentState =
        System::Threading::ApartmentState::STA;
    Application::Run(new Form1());
    return 0;
}
```

The first thing you notice is that the wizard includes the <windows.h> header file. The only reason I see for this is for using Windows typedef data types. Notice the header file is even included after the Form1.h file, which, as you'll see, contains the definition of the form. Being included after Form1.h means none of its defined types are even referenced within Form1.h.

Start up the Windows application using a standard WinMain. Do you notice the heavy use of Windows data types? This could also be coded as

```
int __stdcall WinMain(long hInst, long hPrevInst, long lpCmdLine, int nCmdShow)
{
}
```

Then #include <windows.h> could have been removed, but it doesn't hurt as it is.

The next thing the code does is initialize the current thread's apartment state. If you don't know what an *apartment state* is, don't worry about it—it's a process threading thing for COM, and this book avoids COM because it isn't managed code. In fact, the .NET Framework doesn't use apartment threads, but just to be safe, the apartment state is set to a *single-threaded apartment* (STA) in case a COM object is wrapped and used later in the application.

Finally, the program uses the Application class to start up Form1. The Application class is a fairly powerful class containing several static methods and properties to manage an application. The most common tasks you will use it for are starting and stopping your applications and processing Windows messages. You may also find it useful for getting information about an application via its properties.

You know what? There wasn't much there, was there? Okay, maybe all the magic is in the Form1.h file (see Listing 9-2). To access the source code of Form1.h, you need to right-click Form1.h within Solution Explorer and select the View Code menu item. You can also right-click within the form designer window.

Listing 9-2. The Default Form1.h

```
#pragma once

namespace Hello
{
    using namespace System;
    using namespace System::ComponentModel;
    using namespace System::Collections;
    using namespace System::Windows::Forms;
    using namespace System::Data;
    using namespace System::Drawing;

    public __gc class Form1 : public System::Windows::Forms::Form
    {
    public:
        Form1(void)
        {
            InitializeComponent();
        }
```

```
    protected:
        void Dispose(Boolean disposing)
        {
            if (disposing && components)
            {
                components->Dispose();
            }
            __super::Dispose(disposing);
        }

    private:
        System::ComponentModel::Container * components;

        void InitializeComponent(void)
        {
            this->Size = System::Drawing::Size(300,300);
            this->Text = S"Form1";
        }
    };
}
```

Believe it or not, this is complete Win Forms code. You want to know something else? If you code this by hand, all you need is this:

```
#pragma once

namespace Hello
{
    using namespace System;
    using namespace System::Windows::Forms;

    public __gc class Form1 : public Form
    {
    public:
        Form1(void)
        {
            this->Size = Drawing::Size(300,300);
            this->Text = S"Form1";
        }
    };
}
```

All the rest of the code is for the design tool. Now this is simple! All the code does is specify the form's size and title. The rest is handled within the .NET Framework.

Okay, now for grins and giggles, change the title of the form to **Hello World**. To do this, just change the form's Text property. You can do this in a couple of ways. First, you can just type **Hello World** in the source code replacing the string Text property value **Form1**. Second, you can change the Text text box within the Properties view. Notice that if you change the property in one place, the other automatically gets updated as well.

As a thought, I guess the developers of the .NET Framework could have made things easier by calling this the Title property, but as you will soon see, the Text property is found in all Win Forms controls and is used for the default text-based property of the control.

When you finally finish staring in disbelief, go ahead and try compiling and running hello.exe. (Pressing Ctrl-F5 is the fastest way of doing this.) Rather unexciting, as you can see in Figure 9-2, but hey, what do you expect from two lines of relevant code?

Figure 9-2. The "Hello World" form

Customizing the Form

A form by itself is not the most exciting thing, but before you move on and give it some functionality, let's look at what you'll be getting in the default form. Then let's see what else you can customize.

So what do you get for free with a form? Among many things, you get the following:

- Sized

- Minimized

- Maximized

- Moved

- Closed

It displays an icon, provides a control box, and does a lot of stuff in the background such as change the cursor when appropriate and take Windows messages and convert them into .NET events.

The Form is also very customizable. By manipulating a few of the Form's properties you can get a completely different look from the default, along with some additional functionality that was disabled in the default form configuration. Some of the more common properties are as follows:

- AutoScroll is a Boolean that specifies if the form should automatically display scroll bars if sizing the window obscures a displayable area. The default value is true.

- ClientSize is a System::Drawing::Size that specifies the size of the client area. The *client area* is the size of the window within the border and caption bar. You use this control to adjust the size of the window to your liking or to get the dimensions of it for GDI+ drawing. You will examine GDI+ in Chapter 11.

- Cursor is a Cursor control that you use to specify the cursor to display when over the Win Form. The default is conveniently named Cursors::Default.

- FormBorder is a FormBorderStyle enum that specifies the style of the border. You use this control to change the look of the form. Common styles are FixedDialog, FixedToolWindow, and SizableToolWindow, but the style you will see most often is the default Sizable.

- Icon is a System::Drawing::Icon that you use to specify the icon associated with the form.

- MaximizeBox is a Boolean that specifies if the maximize button should be displayed on the caption bar. The default is true.

- Menu is a MainMenu control you use as the menu displayed on the form. The default is null, which signifies that there is no menu.

- MinimizeBox is a Boolean that specifies if the minimize button should be displayed on the caption bar. The default is true.

- Size is a System::Drawing::Size that specifies the size of the form. The size of the window includes the borders and caption bar. You use this control to set the size of the Win Form.

- WindowState is a FormWindowState enum that allows you to find out or specify if the Win Form is displayed as Normal, Minimized, or Maximized. The default window state is FormWindowState::Normal.

There's nothing special about working with Form class properties. You can either change them using the Properties view as shown in Figure 9-3 or directly in code as Listing 9-3 points out. The choice is yours. Frequently you'll start off by making general changes using the Properties window and then go into the code's InitializeComponent() method (which you can find in the Form1.h file for all the examples in the book) to fine-tune the changes. It doesn't really matter if you make the changes in the code or in the Properties window, as any changes you make in one will immediately be reflected in the other.

 CAUTION *Be careful when you make changes within the InitializeComponent() method. The changes have to be made in exactly the same manner as the code generator or you may cause Visual Studio .NET's GUI design tool to stop functioning.*

To customize a form (or any other control, for that matter), you just assign the appropriate types and values you want to the properties and let the form handle the rest. The example in Figure 9-3 and Listing 9-3 shows a hodgepodge of different form customizations just to see what the form will look like when it's done. The biggest change happened when I changed FormBorderStyle.

Figure 9-3. Customizing Form1 using the Properties view

 TIP *Properties that differ from the default appear in boldface within the Properties view.*

Listing 9-3. Customizing Form1.h

```cpp
#pragma once

namespace CustomHello
{
    using namespace System;
    using namespace System::ComponentModel;
    using namespace System::Collections;
    using namespace System::Windows::Forms;
    using namespace System::Data;
    using namespace System::Drawing;

    public __gc class Form1 : public System::Windows::Forms::Form
    {
    public:
        Form1(void)
        {
            InitializeComponent();
        }
    protected:
        void Dispose(Boolean disposing)
        {
            if (disposing && components)
            {
                components->Dispose();
            }
            __super::Dispose(disposing);
        }
    private:
        System::ComponentModel::Container * components;

        void InitializeComponent(void)
        {
            this->AutoScaleBaseSize = System::Drawing::Size(6, 15);
            this->BackColor = System::Drawing::Color::Black;
            this->ClientSize = System::Drawing::Size(692, 272);
            this->Cursor = System::Windows::Forms::Cursors::UpArrow;
            this->FormBorderStyle =
                    System::Windows::Forms::FormBorderStyle::SizableToolWindow;
            this->Name = S"Form1";
            this->SizeGripStyle = System::Windows::Forms::SizeGripStyle::Show;
```

```
            this->Text = S"Custom Form";
            this->TopMost = true;


        }
    };
}
```

Running CustomHello.exe results in the display in Figure 9-4. Notice that this form is quite a bit different from the default form generated by the previous example Hello.exe. For example, this form has no control box and no minimize or maximize buttons, and in the bottom right there is a form-sizing grip and an up-arrow cursor.

Figure 9-4. A very customized form

NOTE   *For the rest of the chapter I will not list the .cpp file or repeat the constructor or dispose methods (unless something changes within them), as they are the same for every example.*

Handling Win Form Delegates and Events

Remember back in Chapter 4 when I discussed delegates and events and you thought to yourself, "That would be a great way to handle an event-driven GUI application!" You know what? You were right. This is exactly how the Win Form handles its user- and system-generated events.

Win Forms uses the .NET Framework's event model to handle all the events that take place within the form. What this requires is a delegate, an event source class, and an event receiver class. (You might want to revisit Chapter 4 if this means nothing to you.) Fortunately, all the delegates and event source classes you need to worry about are already part of the .NET Framework class library. You need to define the event receiver class.

For the following example, you'll use the MouseDown event that's defined in the event source class System::Windows::Forms::Control.

```
__event MouseEventHandler *MouseDown;
```

This event uses the MouseEventHandler delegate, which is defined in the System::Windows::Forms namespace.

```
public __gc __delegate void MouseEventHandler (
    System::Object* sender,
    System::Windows::Forms::MouseEventArgs* e
);
```

For those of you who are curious, the class MouseEventArgs provides five properties that you can use to figure out information about the MouseDown event:

- Button: An enum specifying which mouse button was pressed down.

- Clicks: The number of times the mouse was pressed and released.

- Delta: The number of detents the mouse wheel was rotated. A *detent* is one notch of the mouse wheel.

- X: The horizontal location of the mouse where it was clicked.

- Y: The vertical location of the mouse where it was clicked.

The first step in creating an event receiver class is to create the event handler that will handle the event generated by the event source class. So, in the case of MouseDown, you need to create a method with the same signature as MouseEventHandler. Notice also that you make the handler private. You don't want any outside method calling this event by accident, as it's only intended to be called within the event receiver class.

```
private:
    void Mouse_Clicked(System::Object * sender,
                        System::Windows::Forms::MouseEventArgs * e)
    {
    }
```

Once you have the handler, all you need to do is delegate it onto the MouseDown event. As you may recall from Chapter 4, Managed C++ uses multicast delegates; therefore you can chain as many handler methods as you need to complete the MouseDown event.

```
MouseDown += new MouseEventHandler(this, Mouse_Clicked);
```

If at a later time you no longer want this handler to handle the MouseDown event, all you need to do is remove the delegated method.

```
MouseDown -= new MouseEventHandler(this, Mouse_Clicked);
```

After describing all this, I'll now tell you that you can create and delegate event handlers automatically using the design tool and you don't have to worry about syntax or coding errors for the declarations. All you have to code is the functionality that handles the event. To add event handlers to a control or (in this case) a form, follow these steps:

1. In the Properties window, click the icon that looks like a lightning bolt. This will change the view from properties to events (see Figure 9-5).

Figure 9-5. Properties view of event handlers

2. Double-click the event you want to add to the control or form. This will create all the appropriate code in the form using the default name.

or

Enter the name of the new method in the text box next to the event handler you are creating.

or

If you have already written the method, select the method from the drop-down list next to the event that you want it to handle.

Listing 9-4 is a fun little program that jumps your Win Form around the screen depending on where your mouse pointer is and which mouse button you press within the client area of the form. As you can see, event handling is hardly challenging. Most of the logic of this program is just to determine where to place the form on a MouseDown event.

Listing 9-4. Mouse Jump: Press a Mouse Button and See the Form Jump

```
namespace MouseJump
{
    using namespace System;
    using namespace System::ComponentModel;
    using namespace System::Collections;
    using namespace System::Windows::Forms;
    using namespace System::Data;
    using namespace System::Drawing;

    public __gc class Form1 : public System::Windows::Forms::Form
    {
    public:
        Form1(void)
        //...
    protected:
        void Dispose(Boolean disposing)
        //...
    private:
        System::ComponentModel::Container * components;

        void InitializeComponent(void)
        {
            this->ClientSize = System::Drawing::Size(450, 300);
            this->Name = S"Form1";
            this->Text = S"Mouse Jump";
            this->MouseDown +=
                    new System::Windows::Forms::MouseEventHandler(this,
                                        Form1_MouseDown);
        }
    private:
        System::Void Form1_MouseDown(System::Object * sender,
                                    System::Windows::Forms::MouseEventArgs * e)
        {
            // Get mouse x and y coordinates
            Int32 x = e->X;
            Int32 y = e->Y;
```

```
// Get Forms upper left location
Point loc = DesktopLocation;

// Handle left button mouse click
if (e->Button == MouseButtons::Left)
{
    Text = String::Format(S"Mouse Jump - Left Button at {0},{1}",
        __box(x), __box(y));
    DesktopLocation = Drawing::Point(loc.X + x, loc.Y +y);
}
// Handle right button mouse click
else if (e->Button == MouseButtons::Right)
{
    Text = String::Format(S"Mouse Jump - Right Button at {0},{1}",
        __box(x), __box(y));
    DesktopLocation = Point((loc.X+1) - (ClientSize.Width - x),
                           (loc.Y+1) - (ClientSize.Height - y));
}
// Handle middle button mouse click
else
{
    Text = String::Format(S"Mouse Jump - Middle Button at {0},{1}",
        __box(x), __box(y));
    DesktopLocation = Point((loc.X+1) - ((ClientSize.Width/2) - x),
                           (loc.Y+1) - ((ClientSize.Height/2) - y));
}
        }
    };
}
```

The MouseJump.exe application shown in Figure 9-6 is hardly exciting, because you can't see the jumping of the form in a still image. You might want to notice that the coordinates at which the mouse was last clicked are displayed in the title bar.

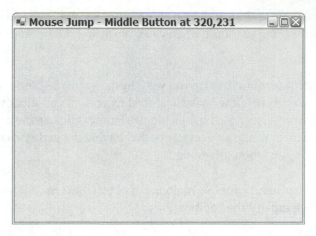

Figure 9-6. The form after a mouse jump

Adding Controls

Okay, now that you have covered the basics of a form and how to handle events from a form, you'll go ahead and make the form do something constructive. To do this, you need to add what the .NET Framework class library calls *controls*.

Controls provide you the ability to build an interface by breaking it down into smaller components. Each control provides a specific type of input and/or output functionality to your Win Form. For example, there are controls to place a label on the screen, display and input text data, select a data item from a list, and display and (if you want) update a tree of data. There is even a control to display a calendar.

All controls inherit from the `Component` and `Control` classes, with each class providing a number of standard methods and properties. Each control will have a few methods and properties of its own that make it unique. Also, all controls have events, for which you can create handlers. You can find all controls provided by the .NET Framework class library within the `System::Windows::Forms` namespace.

You can add controls to a Win Form in one of two ways, just like almost any other process when it comes to Win Forms. You can use Visual Studio .NET GUI tool to drop and drag the controls to the Win Form, or you can code the controls by hand using Visual Studio .NET's IDE editor.

Let's look at how to drag and drop controls onto a Win Form, as this is essentially what you're going to mimic when you code by hand. The steps are as follows:

1. Resize the form to the size you want by dragging the borders of the form in the design window. Make it a little bigger than you think you'll need. Don't worry—you can change the size later to enclose the controls better. I've learned from past experience that having the extra real estate makes things easier when designing.

2. Bring the cursor over the Toolbox tab (if you don't have it tacked open). This will expand the Toolbox.

3. Click, hold, and then drag the control you want from the Toolbox to the form. (If you don't have the Toolbox tacked open, you may need to drag the control to an open location on the form and release it there. This will cause the Toolbox to close so that you can click again and drag the control to the desired location on the form.)

4. Alter the properties of the controls as you wish by changing them within the Properties view. I recommend changing the `Name` property at a minimum, but there is nothing stopping you from using the default generated name for the control.

5. Add event handlers as desired. You might consider holding off on this step until you have the entire Win Form laid out.

6. Repeat steps 1 through 5 for all other required controls.

What these steps do behind the scenes is add a definition of the control to the class and then create an instance of it. Each property that is changed adds a line of code that updates one of the control's properties. Each event handler added adds a delegation statement and then creates an event handler.

As a developer, you can rely solely on the drag-and-drop functionality of Visual Studio .NET or you can do as I do and use the tool to build the basic design but then fine-tune it within the code itself. You could also be a glutton for punishment and do it all by hand. But why bother? The tool is there, so why not use it?

Okay, now that you know how to add a control to the Win Form, you'll take a look at an assortment of the more common controls provided by the .NET Framework class library, starting with one of the easiest: `Label`.

The Label Control

The name of this control is a little misleading. It gives you the impression that it is just good for displaying static text in the form. Nothing could be further from the truth. The Label control is also great for displaying dynamic text to the form. Heck, the Label control can even trigger an event when clicked.

In general, though, you'll normally use a Label control to statically label something else. The usual process of creating a label is simply to create the Label control and then set its properties so that the Label control looks the way you want it to. Here are some of the more common properties used by the Label control:

- BackColor is a System::Drawing::Color that represents the background color of the label and defaults to the DefaultBackColor property.

- Font is a System::Drawing::Font that represents the font used by the label and defaults to the DefaultFont property.

- ForeColor is a System::Drawing::Color that represents the foreground color (or the actual color of the text) of the label and defaults to the DefaultForeColor property.

- Image is a System::Drawing::Image that represents the image displayed within the label. The default is null, which signifies that no image is to be displayed.

- ImageAlign is a ContentAlignment enum that represents the alignment of the image within the label. I like to visualize the different alignments by picturing a tic-tac-toe game in my head, with each box a possible alignment. The default alignment is the center box of the tic-tac-toe game or ContentAlignment::MiddleCenter.

- Text is a String containing the actual text to be displayed.

- TextAlign is a ContentAlignment enum that represents the alignment of the image within the label. The default is based on the culture of the computer. Because my computer has a culture of en-us, the default alignment is the top-left corner or ContentAlignment::TopLeft.

- UseMnemonic is a Boolean that represents if the ampersand (&) character should be interpreted as an access-key prefix character. The default is true.

Now that you have seen the more common properties, for grins and giggles you'll implement a Label control using some of its less common properties (see Listing 9-5).

Listing 9-5. The MightyLabel, an Implementation of the Uncommon Properties

```
namespace MightyLabel
{
    using namespace System;
    using namespace System::ComponentModel;
    using namespace System::Collections;
    using namespace System::Windows::Forms;
    using namespace System::Data;
    using namespace System::Drawing;

    public __gc class Form1 : public System::Windows::Forms::Form
    {
        Boolean labelSwitch;

    public:
        Form1(void)
        {
            labelSwitch = true;
            InitializeComponent();
        }

    protected:
        void Dispose(Boolean disposing)
        //...
    private: System::Windows::Forms::Label *  MightyLabel;

    private:
        System::ComponentModel::Container * components;

        void InitializeComponent(void)
        {
            this->MightyLabel = new System::Windows::Forms::Label();
            this->SuspendLayout();
            //
            // MightyLabel
            //
            this->MightyLabel->BorderStyle =
                    System::Windows::Forms::BorderStyle::FixedSingle;
```

```
        this->MightyLabel->Cursor = System::Windows::Forms::Cursors::Hand;
        this->MightyLabel->Location = System::Drawing::Point(60, 90);
        this->MightyLabel->Name = S"MightyLabel";
        this->MightyLabel->Size = System::Drawing::Size(180, 40);
        this->MightyLabel->TabIndex = 0;
        this->MightyLabel->Text =
            S"This is the mighty label! It will change when you click it";
        this->MightyLabel->TextAlign =
            System::Drawing::ContentAlignment::MiddleCenter;
        this->MightyLabel->Click +=
            new System::EventHandler(this, MightyLabel_Click);
        //
        // Form1
        //
        this->AutoScaleBaseSize = System::Drawing::Size(6, 15);
        this->ClientSize = System::Drawing::Size(300, 300);
        this->Controls->Add(this->MightyLabel);
        this->Name = S"Form1";
        this->Text = S"The Mighty Label";
        this->ResumeLayout(false);
    }
private:
    System::Void MightyLabel_Click(System::Object *  sender,
                                    System::EventArgs *  e)
    {
        if (labelSwitch)
            MightyLabel->Text = S"Ouchie!!!  That hurt.";
        else
            MightyLabel->Text = S"Ooo!!!  That tickled.";
        labelSwitch = !labelSwitch;
    }
};
}
```

As you can see, dragging and dropping can save you a lot of time when you're designing a form, even in such a simple case. But even this simple program shows that a programmer is still needed. A designer can drag and drop the label to where it's needed, and he or she can even change the control's properties, but a programmer is still needed to give the controls life or, in other words, to handle events.

Notice that a Form class is like any other Managed C++ class in that you can add your own member variables, methods, and properties. In this example, I added a Boolean member variable called labelSwitch to hold the current state of the label. I initialize it in the constructor just like I would in any other class and then use it within the Click event handler. Basically, as long as you don't code within the areas that the generated code says not to, you're safe to use the Form class as you see fit.

Figure 9-7 shows what MightyLabel.exe looks like when you execute it. Be sure to click the label a couple of times.

Figure 9-7. The MightyLabel example

The Button Controls

Buttons are one of the most commonly used controls for getting user input found in any Win Forms application, basically because the average user finds buttons easy to use and understand. And yet they are quite versatile for the software developer.

The .NET Framework class library provides three different types of buttons: Button, CheckBox, and RadioButton. All three inherit from the abstract ButtonBase class, which provides common functionality across all three. Here are some of the common properties provided by ButtonBase:

- FlatStyle is a FlatStyle enum that represents the appearance of the button. The default is FlatStyle::Standard, but other options are Flat and Popup.

- Image is a System::Drawing::Image that represents the image displayed on the button. The default is null, meaning no image is to be displayed.

- IsDefault is a protected Boolean that specifies if the button is the default for the form. In other words, it indicates if the button's Click event gets triggered when the Enter key is pressed. The default is false.

- Text is a String that represents the text that will be displayed on the button.

Remember, you also get all the properties of Control and Component. Thus, you have a plethora of properties and methods to work with.

Button

The Button control does not give much functionality beyond what is defined by abstract ButtonBase class. You might think of the Button control as the lowest level implementation of the abstract base class.

Most people think of Button as a static control that you place on the Win Form at design time. As the following example in Listing 9-6 points out (over and over again), this is not the case. Yes, you can statically place a Button control, but you can also dynamically place it on the Win Form.

Listing 9-6. The Code for "Way Too Many Buttons!"

```
namespace TooManyButtons
{
    using namespace System;
    using namespace System::ComponentModel;
    using namespace System::Collections;
    using namespace System::Windows::Forms;
    using namespace System::Data;
    using namespace System::Drawing;

    public __gc class Form1 : public System::Windows::Forms::Form
    {
    public:
        Form1(void)
        //...
    protected:
        void Dispose(Boolean disposing)
        //...
    private:
        System::Windows::Forms::Button *  TooMany;
        System::ComponentModel::Container * components;
```

```
        void InitializeComponent(void)
        {
            this->TooMany = new System::Windows::Forms::Button();
            this->SuspendLayout();
            //
            // TooMany
            //
            this->TooMany->Location = System::Drawing::Point(24, 16);
            this->TooMany->Name = S"TooMany";
            this->TooMany->TabIndex = 0;
            this->TooMany->Text = S"Click Me!";
            this->TooMany->Size = System::Drawing::Size(72, 24);
            this->TooMany->Click +=
                    new System::EventHandler(this, TooMany_Click);
            //
            // Form1
            //
            this->AutoScaleBaseSize = System::Drawing::Size(6, 15);
            this->ClientSize = System::Drawing::Size(292, 270);
            this->Controls->Add(this->TooMany);
            this->Name = S"Form1";
            this->Text = S"Too Many Buttons";
            this->ResumeLayout(false);
        }
    private:
        System::Void TooMany_Click(System::Object * sender,
                                    System::EventArgs * e)
        {
            // Grab the location of the button that was clicked
            Point p = dynamic_cast<Button*>(sender)->Location;

            // Create a dynamic button
            Button *Many = new Button();
            Many->Location = Drawing::Point(p.X + 36, p.Y + 26);
            Many->Size = Drawing::Size(72, 24);
            Many->Text = S"Click Me!";
            Many->Click += new System::EventHandler(this, TooMany_Click);

            // Add dynamic button to Form
            Controls->Add(Many);
        }
    };
}
```

There really isn't much difference between adding a `Label` control and a `Button` statically, as you can see in the `InitializeComponent()` method. The fun code in Listing 9-6 is in the `TooMany_Click()` event handler method. The first thing this method does is grab the location of the button that was clicked and place it into a `Point` struct so that you can manipulate it. You'll examine `System::Drawing::Point` in Chapter 10. You could have grabbed the whole button but you only need its location. Next, you build a button. There's nothing tricky here, except the button is declared within the event handler. Those of you from a traditional C++ background are probably jumping up and down screaming *"Memory leak!"* Sorry to disappoint you, but this is Managed C++ and the memory will be collected when it's no longer referenced, so this code is perfectly legal. And finally, the last step in placing the button dynamically on the Win Form is adding it.

Figure 9-8 shows what TooManyButtons.exe looks like when you execute it. Be sure to click a few of the newly created buttons.

Figure 9-8. Way too many buttons

CheckBox

The `CheckBox` control is also an extension of the `ButtonBase` class. It's similar to a normal `Button` control in many ways. The two major differences are that it looks different on the Win Form and that it retains its check state when clicked. Well, the first difference isn't always true—there's a property to make a `CheckBox` look like a `Button`.

The `CheckBox` control, if configured to do so, can have three states: checked, unchecked, and indeterminate. I'm sure you understand checked and unchecked states, but what is this *indeterminate* state? Visually, in this state, the check boxes are shaded. Most likely you saw this type of check box when you installed Visual Studio .NET on your machine. Remember when you set which parts to install and some of the check marks were gray? When you selected the gray box, you found that some of the subparts were not checked. Basically, the indeterminate state of the parent was because not all child boxes were checked.

In addition to supporting the properties provided by `ButtonBase`, the `CheckBox` control also supports some properties unique to itself:

- `Appearance` is an `Appearance` enum that specifies whether the check box looks like a button or a standard check box. The default, `Appearance::Normal`, is a standard check box.

- `CheckAlign` is a `ContentAlignment` enum that represents the alignment of the check box within the `CheckBox` control. The default alignment is centered and to the left: `ContentAlignment::MiddleLeft`.

- `Checked` is a `Boolean` that represents whether the check box is checked or not. This property returns `true` if the check box is in an indeterminate state as well. The default is `false`.

- `CheckState` is a `CheckState` enum that represents the current state of the check box, either `Checked`, `Unchecked`, or `Indeterminate`. The default is `CheckState::Unchecked`.

- `ThreeState` is a `Boolean` that specifies if the check box can have an indeterminate state. The default is `false`.

In following example (see Listing 9-7) you'll have a little fun with the `CheckBox` control, in particular the `Visibility` property. Enter the following code and have some fun.

Listing 9-7. The Code for "You Can't Check Me!"

```
namespace CheckMe
{
    using namespace System;
    using namespace System::ComponentModel;
    using namespace System::Collections;
    using namespace System::Windows::Forms;
    using namespace System::Data;
    using namespace System::Drawing;
```

```
public __gc class Form1 : public System::Windows::Forms::Form
{
public:
    Form1(void)
    //...
protected:
    void Dispose(Boolean disposing)
    //...
private: System::Windows::Forms::CheckBox *  TopCheck;
private: System::Windows::Forms::CheckBox *  checkBox1;
private: System::Windows::Forms::CheckBox *  checkBox2;
private: System::Windows::Forms::CheckBox *  BottomCheck;
private: System::ComponentModel::Container * components;

    void InitializeComponent(void)
    {
        this->TopCheck = new System::Windows::Forms::CheckBox();
        this->checkBox1 = new System::Windows::Forms::CheckBox();
        this->checkBox2 = new System::Windows::Forms::CheckBox();
        this->BottomCheck = new System::Windows::Forms::CheckBox();
        this->SuspendLayout();
        //
        // TopCheck
        //
        this->TopCheck->Location = System::Drawing::Point(50, 50);
        this->TopCheck->Name = S"TopCheck";
        this->TopCheck->Size = System::Drawing::Size(160, 25);
        this->TopCheck->TabIndex = 2;
        this->TopCheck->TabStop = false;
        this->TopCheck->Text = S"You Can\'t Check Me!";
        this->TopCheck->Enter +=
                new System::EventHandler(this, TopCheck_Entered);
        this->TopCheck->MouseEnter +=
                new System::EventHandler(this, TopCheck_Entered);
        //
        // checkBox1
        //
        this->checkBox1->Checked = true;
        this->checkBox1->CheckState =
                System::Windows::Forms::CheckState::Indeterminate;
        this->checkBox1->Location = System::Drawing::Point(50, 100);
        this->checkBox1->Name = S"checkBox1";
        this->checkBox1->Size = System::Drawing::Size(160, 25);
```

```
                    this->checkBox1->TabIndex = 0;
                    this->checkBox1->Text = S"Check Me! Check Me!";
                    this->checkBox1->ThreeState = true;
                    //
                    // checkBox2
                    //
                    this->checkBox2->Location = System::Drawing::Point(50, 150);
                    this->checkBox2->Name = S"checkBox2";
                    this->checkBox2->Size = System::Drawing::Size(160, 25);
                    this->checkBox2->TabIndex = 1;
                    this->checkBox2->Text = S"Don\'t Forget ME!";
                    //
                    // BottomCheck
                    //
                    this->BottomCheck->Enabled = false;
                    this->BottomCheck->Location = System::Drawing::Point(50, 200);
                    this->BottomCheck->Name = S"BottomCheck";
                    this->BottomCheck->Size = System::Drawing::Size(160, 25);
                    this->BottomCheck->TabIndex = 0;
                    this->BottomCheck->TabStop = false;
                    this->BottomCheck->Text = S"You Can\'t Check Me!";
                    this->BottomCheck->Visible = false;
                    this->BottomCheck->Enter +=
                            new System::EventHandler(this, BottomCheck_Entered);
                    this->BottomCheck->MouseEnter +=
                            new System::EventHandler(this, BottomCheck_Entered);
                    //
                    // Form1
                    //
                    this->AutoScaleBaseSize = System::Drawing::Size(6, 15);
                    this->ClientSize = System::Drawing::Size(300, 300);
                    this->Controls->Add(this->BottomCheck);
                    this->Controls->Add(this->checkBox2);
                    this->Controls->Add(this->checkBox1);
                    this->Controls->Add(this->TopCheck);
                    this->Name = S"Form1";
                    this->Text = S"Can\'t Check Me";
                    this->ResumeLayout(false);
            }
        private:
            System::Void TopCheck_Entered(System::Object *  sender,
                                          System::EventArgs *  e)

                {
```

```
            // Hide Top checkbox and display bottom
            TopCheck->Enabled = false;
            TopCheck->Visible = false;
            BottomCheck->Enabled = true;
            BottomCheck->Visible = true;
        }
    private:
        System::Void BottomCheck_Entered(System::Object *  sender,
                                    System::EventArgs *  e)
        {
            // Hide Bottom checkbox and display top
            BottomCheck->Enabled = false;
            BottomCheck->Visible = false;
            TopCheck->Enabled = true;
            TopCheck->Visible = true;
        }
    };
}
```

You may have noticed that I threw in the indeterminate state in the first/second/first...(whichever) check box, just so you can see what it looks like.

An important thing to take from this example is that it shows you can delegate the same event handler to more than one event. To do this in the Visual Studio .NET Properties view requires that you use the drop-down list to select the event handler that you want to redelegate.

The example also shows how to enable/disable and show/hide both in the Properties view and at runtime.

Figure 9-9 shows what CheckMe.exe looks like when you execute it. Who says programmers don't have a sense of humor!

Figure 9-9. You can't check me!

RadioButton

From a coding perspective, there isn't much to say about the RadioButton control other than you code it in exactly the same way you code a CheckBox control. The only differences between the RadioButton and CheckBox controls are that with the RadioButton you lose the CheckState property and its associated CheckStateChanged event.

The RadioButton control works a little differently than the CheckBox control. Only one RadioButton can be checked at a time within a given container, which at this point is the Win Form. (You will see that you can have multiple containers placed on a Win Form later in this chapter in the section "The GroupBox Control.") If you have ever played with a car radio, you should understand exactly how a RadioButton works.

Listing 9-8 shows a neat little trick that the C# GUI design tool can't do—it shows how to create an array of radio buttons. Having unique names for what amounts to a single entity with multiple values seems a little silly in most cases, and at worst the code goes on forever. I think developing a set of radio buttons, as shown in Listing 9-8, makes good sense.

Listing 9-8. The Code for an Array of Radio Buttons

```
namespace ArrayOfRadios
{
    using namespace System;
    using namespace System::Collections;
    using namespace System::Windows::Forms;
    using namespace System::Drawing;


    public __gc class Form1 : public System::Windows::Forms::Form
    {
        RadioButton *radios[];
        Label        *label;

    public:
        Form1(void)
        {
        String *rbText[] = {S"Can", S"You", S"Click", S"More", S"Than", S"One"};
        radios = new RadioButton*[6];
        label  = new Label();

        for (Int32 i = 0; i < radios->Count; i++)
        {
            Int32 j = 50*i;
```

```
        radios[i] = new RadioButton();
        radios[i]->BackColor = Color::FromArgb(255, j+5, j+5, j+5);
        radios[i]->ForeColor = Color::FromArgb(255, 250-j, 250-j, 250-j);
        radios[i]->Location = Drawing::Point(90, 5+(40*i));
        radios[i]->TabIndex = i;
        radios[i]->TabStop = true;
        radios[i]->Text = rbText[i];
        radios[i]->CheckedChanged +=
            new EventHandler(this,radioCheckedChanged);
    }
    Controls->AddRange(radios);

    label->Location = Drawing::Point(90, 5+(40*radios->Count));
    Controls->Add(label);

    Text = S"An Array Of Radios";
}


private:
    void radioCheckedChanged(Object *sender, EventArgs *e)
    {
        RadioButton *rb = dynamic_cast<RadioButton*>(sender);

        if (rb->Checked == true)
            label->Text = rb->Text;
    }
};
}
```

The code in Listing 9-8 is pretty straightforward. (This example doesn't include the design tool–specific code as it was written by hand.) First, you create an array of RadioButton controls and then you populate the array. I also threw in a Label control to show how to extract the currently checked RadioButton control.

You should notice a couple of things going on in this listing. First, only one event handler method is needed, as the sender parameter will tell you which RadioButton sent the event. Second, you need to check for a true Checked value because the CheckedChanged event is also triggered on the unchecking event, which also always occurs when a different RadioButton is checked. And the final thing you might want to notice is that you can use the AddRange() method instead of the Add() method to add controls to the form because there is a ready-made array using this method, as the array of RadioButtons is also an array of controls.

I also play with colors a bit, but you look at colors in detail in Chapter 11, so I will hold off the explanation until then.

Figure 9-10 shows what ArrayOfRadios.exe looks like when you execute it.

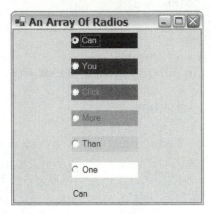

Figure 9-10. An array of radio buttons

The GroupBox Control

The GroupBox control does basically what its name suggests: It groups controls into a box. Not only does the GroupBox group controls visually, but it also binds the controls so that they act as a group.

The GroupBox control is predominately used for RadioButton controls, but that isn't a requirement. The requirement is that everything it groups is a control. Grouping random control types is usually done just for cosmetic reasons. Grouping RadioButton controls, on the other hand, provides the RadioButton control with additional functionality. Instead of being able to select only a single RadioButton on the form, you now can select a unique RadioButton for each GroupBox.

The following example (see Listing 9-9) shows how it is now possible to select more than one RadioButton—in this case, one of the RadioButton controls attached to the form and one from each of the GroupBoxes. Notice I use three arrays of RadioButtons. If you were to create a unique RadioButton each time instead of the array, as is the case for the generated GUI-designed code, you would then be declaring and implementing 12 different RadioButtons. I think this is a good example of how knowing how to code Win Forms by hand improves the code.

Listing 9-9. The Code for Grouping RadioButtons

```
namespace GroupingRadios
{
    using namespace System;
    using namespace System::ComponentModel;
    using namespace System::Collections;
    using namespace System::Windows::Forms;
    using namespace System::Data;
    using namespace System::Drawing;

    public __gc class Form1 : public System::Windows::Forms::Form
    {
    public:
        Form1(void)
        {
            InitializeComponent();
            BuildRadios();
        }

    protected:
        void Dispose(Boolean disposing)
        //...
    private:
        System::Windows::Forms::GroupBox * groupBox1;
        System::Windows::Forms::GroupBox * groupBox2;

        System::ComponentModel::Container * components;

        System::Windows::Forms::RadioButton * radio1[];
        System::Windows::Forms::RadioButton * radio2[];
        System::Windows::Forms::RadioButton * radio3[];

        void InitializeComponent(void)
        {
            this->groupBox1 = new System::Windows::Forms::GroupBox();
            this->groupBox2 = new System::Windows::Forms::GroupBox();
            this->SuspendLayout();
            //
            // groupBox1
            //
            this->groupBox1->Location = System::Drawing::Point(150, 15);
            this->groupBox1->Name = S"groupBox1";
```

```
            this->groupBox1->Size = System::Drawing::Size(150, 130);
            this->groupBox1->TabIndex = 0;
            this->groupBox1->TabStop = false;
            this->groupBox1->Text = S"You";
            //
            // groupBox2
            //
            this->groupBox2->Location = System::Drawing::Point(150, 160);
            this->groupBox2->Name = S"groupBox2";
            this->groupBox2->Size = System::Drawing::Size(150, 130);
            this->groupBox2->TabIndex = 1;
            this->groupBox2->TabStop = false;
            this->groupBox2->Text = S"Use";
            //
            // Form1
            //
            this->AutoScaleBaseSize = System::Drawing::Size(6, 15);
            this->ClientSize = System::Drawing::Size(352, 330);
            this->Controls->Add(this->groupBox2);
            this->Controls->Add(this->groupBox1);
            this->Name = S"Form1";
            this->Text = S"Using Group Boxes";
            this->ResumeLayout(false);
        }


        void BuildRadios()
        {
            this->SuspendLayout();
            // Text for RadioButton places on Form directly
            String *rbText1[]=
                    {S"Can", S"You", S"Click", S"More", S"Than", S"One"};
            // Build a RadioButton for each rbText1
            radio1 = new RadioButton*[6];
            for (Int32 i = 0; i < radio1->Count; i++)
            {
                radio1[i] = new RadioButton();
                radio1[i]->Location = Drawing::Point(20, 20+(40*i));
                radio1[i]->Text = rbText1[i];
            }
            // Add RadioButtons to Form
            Controls->AddRange(radio1);
```

```
// Text for RadioButton places in first GroupBox
String *rbText2[] = {S"Can", S"If", S"You"};
// Build a RadioButton for each rbText2
radio2 = new RadioButton*[3];
for (Int32 i = 0; i < radio2->Count; i++)
{
    radio2[i] = new RadioButton();
    radio2[i]->Location = Drawing::Point(40, 30+(35*i));
    radio2[i]->Text = rbText2[i];
}
// Add RadioButtons to GroupBox
groupBox1->Controls->AddRange(radio2);

// Text for RadioButton places in second GroupBox
String *rbText3[] = {S"Different", S"Group", S"Boxes"};
// Build a RadioButton for each rbText3
radio3 = new RadioButton*[3];
for (Int32 i = 0; i < radio3->Count; i++)
{
    radio3[i] = new RadioButton();
    radio3[i]->Location = Drawing::Point(40, 30+(35*i));
    radio3[i]->Text = rbText3[i];
}
// Add RadioButtons to GroupBox2
groupBox2->Controls->AddRange(radio3);
this->ResumeLayout(false);
        }
    };
}
```

Only a couple of things are new here. First, notice now that you add the GroupBox to the form and then add the RadioButtons to the GroupBox, as opposed to adding the RadioButtons to the form. You can also add the RadioButtons to the GroupBox and then add the GroupBox to the form. Which of the previous methods you choose is not important, so long as the controls are defined and instantiated before being added.

The second new thing is the location where you put the RadioButtons. The location is relative to the GroupBox and not the form. Notice that the exact same code is used to specify the location of the RadioButtons for both GroupBoxes.

As you can see, you can combine the autogenerated GUI tool code and the hand-coded code together, but you have to be careful. You can't add your code within the InitializeComponent() method, because the GUI design tool will overwrite it any time you change the form using the design tool. Because this is the case, I had to create the `BuildRadios()` method to add my hand-designed code instead of embedding it directly within the `InitializeComponent()` method.

Figure 9-11 shows what GroupingRadios.exe looks like when you execute it. Try to click the radio buttons. Now you are able to select three different ones.

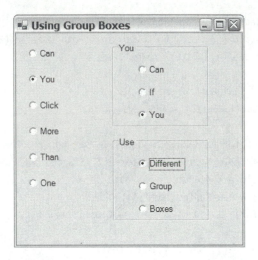

Figure 9-11. Groups of radio buttons

The Panel Control

The `Panel` control is similar in many ways to the `GroupBox` control. It also groups controls visually into a box and binds them so that they act as a group. It differs in that you can enable it to support scrolling, thus letting the `Panel` control contain more controls than its area would normally allow.

A feature that both the `Panel` and `GroupBox` controls share is that when you disable the `Panel`, all the controls within the `Panel` are also disabled. You do this by setting the `Enable` property to `false`. Another feature I particularly like is that you can make the `Panel` invisible by setting the `Visible` property to `false`. Using this feature, you can make the form less cluttered by hiding `Panel`s that are not currently relevant.

Listing 9-10 shows how it is now possible to enable, disable, and make `Panel`s reappear. It also highlights how to enable autoscrolling within a `Panel`.

Listing 9-10. The Code for Disabling and Hiding Panels

```
namespace Panels
{
    using namespace System;
```

```cpp
using namespace System::ComponentModel;
using namespace System::Collections;
using namespace System::Windows::Forms;
using namespace System::Data;
using namespace System::Drawing;

public __gc class Form1 : public System::Windows::Forms::Form
{
public:
    Form1(void)
    //...
protected:
    void Dispose(Boolean disposing)
    //...
private: System::Windows::Forms::Panel *  Leftpanel;
private: System::Windows::Forms::Panel *  Rightpanel;
private: System::Windows::Forms::Button *  bnDisable;
private: System::Windows::Forms::Button *  bnHide;
private: System::Windows::Forms::Button *  button1;
private: System::Windows::Forms::Button *  button2;
private: System::ComponentModel::Container * components;

    void InitializeComponent(void)
    {
        this->Leftpanel = new System::Windows::Forms::Panel();
        this->Rightpanel = new System::Windows::Forms::Panel();
        this->bnDisable = new System::Windows::Forms::Button();
        this->bnHide = new System::Windows::Forms::Button();
        this->button1 = new System::Windows::Forms::Button();
        this->button2 = new System::Windows::Forms::Button();
        this->Leftpanel->SuspendLayout();
        this->Rightpanel->SuspendLayout();
        this->SuspendLayout();
        //
        // Leftpanel
        //
        this->Leftpanel->BorderStyle =
                System::Windows::Forms::BorderStyle::FixedSingle;
        this->Leftpanel->Controls->Add(this->bnHide);
        this->Leftpanel->Controls->Add(this->bnDisable);
        this->Leftpanel->Location = System::Drawing::Point(32, 24);
        this->Leftpanel->Name = S"Leftpanel";
        this->Leftpanel->Size = System::Drawing::Size(145, 110);
```

```
this->Leftpanel->TabIndex = 0;
//
// Rightpanel
//
this->Rightpanel->AutoScroll = true;
this->Rightpanel->BorderStyle =
      System::Windows::Forms::BorderStyle::Fixed3D;
this->Rightpanel->Controls->Add(this->button2);
this->Rightpanel->Controls->Add(this->button1);
this->Rightpanel->Location = System::Drawing::Point(192, 24);
this->Rightpanel->Name = S"Rightpanel";
this->Rightpanel->Size = System::Drawing::Size(145, 70);
this->Rightpanel->TabIndex = 1;
//
// bnDisable
//
this->bnDisable->Location = System::Drawing::Point(20, 8);
this->bnDisable->Name = S"bnDisable";
this->bnDisable->Size = System::Drawing::Size(100, 24);
this->bnDisable->TabIndex = 0;
this->bnDisable->Text = S"Disable Panel";
this->bnDisable->Click +=
      new System::EventHandler(this, bnDisable_Click);
//
// bnHide
//
this->bnHide->Location = System::Drawing::Point(20, 72);
this->bnHide->Name = S"bnHide";
this->bnHide->Size = System::Drawing::Size(100, 24);
this->bnHide->TabIndex = 1;
this->bnHide->Text = S"Hide Panel";
this->bnHide->Click += new System::EventHandler(this, bnHide_Click);
//
// button1
//
this->button1->Location = System::Drawing::Point(24, 8);
this->button1->Name = S"button1";
this->button1->TabIndex = 0;
this->button1->Text = S"button1";
//
// button2
//
```

```
        this->button2->Location = System::Drawing::Point(24, 72);
        this->button2->Name = S"button2";
        this->button2->TabIndex = 1;
        this->button2->Text = S"button2";
        //
        // Form1
        //
        this->AutoScaleBaseSize = System::Drawing::Size(6, 15);
        this->ClientSize = System::Drawing::Size(370, 160);
        this->Controls->Add(this->Rightpanel);
        this->Controls->Add(this->Leftpanel);
        this->Name = S"Form1";
        this->Text = S"A hidden fourth button";
        this->Leftpanel->ResumeLayout(false);
        this->Rightpanel->ResumeLayout(false);
        this->ResumeLayout(false);
    }
private:
    System::Void bnDisable_Click(System::Object * sender,
                                  System::EventArgs * e)
    {
        Rightpanel->Enabled = !Rightpanel->Enabled;
    }
private:
    System::Void bnHide_Click(System::Object * sender,
                               System::EventArgs * e)
    {
        Rightpanel->Visible = !Rightpanel->Visible;
    }
};
}
```

What's interesting in this form is the ability to use a button to disable and hide Panels. Another neat feature is that you can use the Enable and Visible properties as toggles:

```
Rightpanel->Enabled = !Rightpanel->Enabled;
Rightpanel->Visible = !Rightpanel->Visible;
```

To get RightPanel to scroll, you have to set its client size smaller than the visual area needed to view all controls. Basically, because a control is going to be obscured, the Panel automatically creates the appropriate scroll bar (either vertical or horizontal) so that the control can be exposed.

Figure 9-12 shows what Panels.exe looks like when you execute it and click the Disable Panel button. I guess I could have also clicked the Hide Panel button, but then the `RightPanel` would have disappeared and you wouldn't be able to tell that it was disabled.

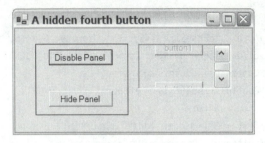

Figure 9-12. Disabling and hiding panels

The Text Controls

There is obviously a need to enter text into most Win Forms applications. To handle this, the .NET Framework provides two highly configurable text controls: `TextBox` and `RichTextBox`. Both text controls are very powerful. In fact, the simpler of the two, the `TextBox` control, has so much functionality that you will probably use it most, if not all, of the time. A few possible exceptions are when you require font styles such as boldface, italic, or underline within the text being entered.

As is the common theme in the .NET Framework class library, the text controls derive from a common abstract base class, `TextBoxBase`. This class provides a common set of functionality that you can use for both text controls and it's also a great starting point for those programmers who need to write a text control to meet specific needs.

The abstract `TextBoxBase` class is composed of numerous properties and methods that can handle text input from the user. Being that `TextBoxBase` is an abstract class, you can't instantiate from it; instead, you need to use one of its child classes. Here are some common `TextBoxBase`-specific properties:

- `AcceptsTab` is a `Boolean` that represents, in a multiline text control, whether the Tab key will be used as a control character or as a means to move to the next control. The default is `false`.

- `CanUndo` is a `Boolean` that represents whether the control can undo the previous operation that occurred. The default is `false`.

- MaxLength is an Int32 that represents the maximum number of characters allowed to be entered into the control. The default is 0, which means the allowable number of characters enterable is only restricted by the memory of the computer.

- Modified is a Boolean that represents whether the content of the control has been modified since the control was created or the contents were set. The default is false.

- Multiline is a Boolean that represents whether the control is made up of more than one line. The default is false.

- ReadOnly is a Boolean that represents whether the control is read-only. The default is false.

- SelectedText is a String containing selected text from the control. The default is a zero-length String (not null).

- SelectionLength is an Int32 that represents the length of the selected text. If the SelectionLength property is set to a value larger than the length of text within the control, it's automatically set to the number of characters in the control minus the SelectionStart property.

- SelectionStart is an Int32 that represents the starting location of the selected text within the control. If the SelectionStart property is set to a value larger than the number of characters within the control, it's automatically set to the value after the last character in the control.

- Text is a String that represents the text of the control.

- WordWrap is a Boolean that represents, in a multiline text control, whether a word wraps automatically to the beginning of a line when necessary. If the value is false, the control will scroll horizontally when text is entered beyond the width of the control. The default is true.

Here are some common TextBoxBase-specific methods:

- AppendText() adds text to the end of the current text of the control.

- Clear() sets the text in the control to be empty.

- ClearUndo() removes the last undo operation from the undo buffer.

- Copy() takes the selected text and places it on the Clipboard. The control is unaffected.

- Cut() removes the selected text from the control and places it on the Clipboard.

- Paste() copies the text in the Clipboard to the current location of the cursor in the control.

- Select() selects text within the control using a start location and a length.

- SelectAll() selects all the text within the control.

- Undo() restores the contents in the text control back to the previous state before the last operation.

TextBox

As stated earlier, you can configure the TextBox control in many ways ranging from long to short, normal to password hidden, and single to multilined. If you enable this control, you have a built-in undo buffer. You can cut and paste to it. The functionality this control has is simply amazing.

Along with the properties provided by TextBoxBase, the TextBox control adds a few properties of its own:

- AcceptReturn is a Boolean that represents, in a multiline control, whether pressing the Enter key creates a new line of text or passes control to the default button of the form. If this property is set to false, then Ctrl-Enter must be pressed to create a new line of text. The default is true.

- CharacterCasing is a CharacterCasing enum that notifies the control as characters are entered into the control that it should convert the character to uppercase, lowercase, or leave the character as typed. The default is CharacterCasing::Normal or leave the characters as they are typed.

- PasswordChar is a Char that represents the character to be used to replace all the characters typed in, thus hiding the password from view. The default is the value 0, meaning do not use PasswordChar.

- TextAlign is a HorizontalAlignment enum that represents whether the text should be right justified, left justified, or centered when entered. The default is HorizontalAlignment::Left or left justified.

The following example (see Listing 9-11) demonstrates some features of the TextBox control. First it creates a text box to handle input. When you press Enter or click the Submit button, the text gets inserted into the front of the read-only, multiline text box. This multiline text box can be made editable if you enter **Editable** in the bottom password text box.

Notice a few things about this example. Pressing the Tab key creates a tab character in the multiline text box (when editable, obviously), but jumps to the next control when any other control has the focus. Also, pressing the Enter key creates a new line of text in the multiline text box when it has the focus, but causes the AcceptButton to be triggered if any other control has focus.

Listing 9-11. Some TextBox Code

```
namespace TextEntry
{
    using namespace System;
    using namespace System::ComponentModel;
    using namespace System::Collections;
    using namespace System::Windows::Forms;
    using namespace System::Data;
    using namespace System::Drawing;

    public __gc class Form1 : public System::Windows::Forms::Form
    {
    public:
        Form1(void)
        //...
    protected:
        void Dispose(Boolean disposing)
        //...
    private: System::Windows::Forms::TextBox *  Entry;
    private: System::Windows::Forms::TextBox *  Result;
    private: System::Windows::Forms::Button *  bnSubmit;
    private: System::Windows::Forms::TextBox *  Password;
    private: System::ComponentModel::Container * components;

        void InitializeComponent(void)
        {
            this->Entry = new System::Windows::Forms::TextBox();
            this->Result = new System::Windows::Forms::TextBox();
            this->Password = new System::Windows::Forms::TextBox();
            this->bnSubmit = new System::Windows::Forms::Button();
            this->SuspendLayout();
            //
```

```
// Entry
//
this->Entry->Location = System::Drawing::Point(25, 25);
this->Entry->Name = S"Entry";
this->Entry->Size = System::Drawing::Size(260, 22);
this->Entry->TabIndex = 0;
//
// Result
//
this->Result->AcceptsReturn = true;
this->Result->AcceptsTab = true;
this->Result->Location = System::Drawing::Point(25, 65);
this->Result->Multiline = true;
this->Result->Name = S"Result";
this->Result->ReadOnly = true;
this->Result->ScrollBars =
        System::Windows::Forms::ScrollBars::Vertical;
this->Result->Size = System::Drawing::Size(330, 240);
this->Result->TabIndex = 1;
//
// Password
//
this->Password->Location = System::Drawing::Point(25, 320);
this->Password->Name = S"Password";
this->Password->PasswordChar = '*';
this->Password->Size = System::Drawing::Size(330, 22);
this->Password->TabIndex = 2;
this->Password->Text =
        S"You cannot cut or copy but you can paste text";
this->Password->TextChanged +=
        new System::EventHandler(this, Password_TextChanged);
//
// bnSubmit
//
this->bnSubmit->Location = System::Drawing::Point(290, 25);
this->bnSubmit->Name = S"bnSubmit";
this->bnSubmit->Size = System::Drawing::Size(60, 25);
this->bnSubmit->TabIndex = 3;
this->bnSubmit->Text = S"Submit";
this->bnSubmit->Click +=
        new System::EventHandler(this, bnSubmit_Click);
```

```
                //
                // Form1
                //
                this->AcceptButton = this->bnSubmit;
                this->AutoScaleBaseSize = System::Drawing::Size(6, 15);
                this->ClientSize = System::Drawing::Size(370, 360);
                this->Controls->Add(this->bnSubmit);
                this->Controls->Add(this->Password);
                this->Controls->Add(this->Result);
                this->Controls->Add(this->Entry);
                this->Name = S"Form1";
                this->Text = S"Simple Text Entry";
                this->ResumeLayout(false);
            }
        private:
            System::Void Password_TextChanged(System::Object *  sender,
                                              System::EventArgs *  e)
            {
                // if the Password TextBox Text equals "Editable" then make
                // the multiline TextBox editable
                if (Password->Text->Equals(S"Editable"))
                    Result->ReadOnly = false;
                else
                    Result->ReadOnly = true;
            }
        private:
            System::Void bnSubmit_Click(System::Object *  sender,
                                        System::EventArgs *  e)
            {
                // Grab a StringBuilder from the Text of the Multiline Textbox
                Result->Text = String::Concat(Entry->Text, S"\r\n", Result->Text);
                Entry->Clear();
            }
        };
}
```

There is nothing special about the code in Listing 9-11. In fact, I created it entirely using the GUI design tool, except (obviously) the event handler code.

Figure 9-13 shows what TextEntry.exe looks like when you execute it.

Figure 9-13. Assorted text boxes

RichTextBox

Plain and simple, the RichTextBox control is overkill, for most cases, when you need text input. This control provides advanced formatting features, such as boldface, italics, underline, color, and different fonts. It is also possible to format paragraphs. You can assign text directly to the control using the Text property, or you can load it from a Rich Text Format (RTF) or plain text file using the LoadFile() method.

The RichTextBox control is a little tricky to use, as most of the added functionality over the TextBox control requires the handling of events or other controls, such as buttons, to implement. For example, implementing boldfacing of text within a RichTextBox requires implementing the SelectionFont property, which needs to be referenced somehow. In the following example I do this by pressing the F1 key, but you could do it any number of other ways.

The RichTextBox control provides a number of additional properties to handle the formatting features it provides. Here are some of the more common properties:

- BulletIndent is an Int32 that represents the number of pixels inserted as the indentation after a bullet. The default is zero.

- CanRedo is a Boolean that represents whether undone operations can be reapplied.

- `RedoActionName` is a `String` that represents the name of the next redo action to be applied. If the return `String` is empty (a zero-length `String`, not a `null`), then there are no more actions that can be redone.

- `RightMargin` is an `Int32` that represents the number of pixels from the left side of the control where the nonvisible right margin is placed.

- `Rtf` is a `String` that represents the RTF-formatted data in the control. The content of the `Rtf` property differs from that of the `Text` property in that the `Rtf` property is in Rich Text Format, whereas the `Text` property is in just plain text.

- `Scrollbars` is a `RichTextScrollbars` enum that represents which (if any) scroll bars will be visible within the control. The default is `RichTextScrollbars::Both`, which will display both vertical and horizontal scroll bars if needed. I prefer to use `ForceVertical` instead because it stops the control from having to readjust itself when the content extends beyond the vertical height of the control. It now simply enables the already visible vertical scroll bar.

- `SelectedRtf` is a `String` containing selected RTF-formatted text from the control. The default is a zero-length `String` (not null).

- `SelectionBullet` is a `Boolean` that represents whether the bullet style should be applied to the current selected text or insertion point. The default is `false`.

- `SelectionColor` is a `System::Drawing::Color` that represents the color of the selected text. If more than one color falls within the selected text, then `Color::Empty` is returned.

- `SelectionFont` is a `System::Drawing::Font` that represents the font of the selected text. If more than one font falls within the selected text, then `null` is returned.

- `SelectionHangingIndent` is an `Int32` that represents the distance in pixels between the left edge of the first line of text in the selected paragraph and the left edge of subsequent lines in the same paragraph.

- `SelectionIndent` is an `Int32` that represents the distance in pixels between the left edge of the control window and the left edge of the current selected text or text added after the insertion point.

- SelectionRightIndent is an `Int32` that represents the distance in pixels between the right edge of the text and the right edge of the control.

- SelectionTabs is an array of `Int32` that represents a set of absolute tab locations in pixels.

- ShowSelectionMargin is a Boolean that represents whether the selection margin on the left side of the control is expanded for easier access. Clicking the margin highlights the entire row. The default is `false`.

- UndoActionName is a `String` that represents the name of the next undo action to be applied. If the return `String` is empty (a zero-length `String`, not a `null`), then there are no more actions that can be undone.

The `RichTextBox` control provides a number of additional methods as well:

- Find() searches for the specified text within the control.

- LoadFile() loads a text or RTF-formatted file into the control.

- Redo() will redo the last undo operation done on the control.

- SaveFile() saves a text or RTF-formatted file to specified path/file location.

- Undo() will undo the last operation done on the control.

The following example (see Listing 9-12) is an extremely simple and limited use of the functionality of the `RichTextBox`. It lacks many of the features that are available, but it is a good starting point and gives you some ideas about how to implement your own RTF editor, if you are so inclined.

In the example, pressing the F9 key loads a couple of pages from a novel I am writing. You can save the file back by pressing F10. To test out the special features of this `RichTextBox`, select some text with the mouse and then press one of the remaining function keys (F1–F8).

Listing 9-12. Implementing a Simple RTF Editor

```
namespace RichText
{
    using namespace System;
    using namespace System::ComponentModel;
    using namespace System::Collections;
```

```
using namespace System::Windows::Forms;
using namespace System::Data;
using namespace System::Drawing;


public __gc class Form1 : public System::Windows::Forms::Form
{
public:
    Form1(void)
    //...
protected:
    void Dispose(Boolean disposing)
    //...
private: System::Windows::Forms::RichTextBox *  rtBox;
private: System::Windows::Forms::Label *labels[];


private: System::ComponentModel::Container * components;


    void InitializeComponent(void)
    {
        this->rtBox = new System::Windows::Forms::RichTextBox();
        this->SuspendLayout();
        //
        // rtBox
        //
        this->rtBox->Anchor = (System::Windows::Forms::AnchorStyles)
            (((System::Windows::Forms::AnchorStyles::Top |
                System::Windows::Forms::AnchorStyles::Bottom) |
                System::Windows::Forms::AnchorStyles::Left) |
                System::Windows::Forms::AnchorStyles::Right);
        this->rtBox->Location = System::Drawing::Point(0, 32);
        this->rtBox->Name = S"rtBox";
        this->rtBox->RightMargin = 900;
        this->rtBox->ScrollBars =
                System::Windows::Forms::RichTextBoxScrollBars::ForcedVertical;
        this->rtBox->ShowSelectionMargin = true;
        this->rtBox->Size = System::Drawing::Size(950, 488);
        this->rtBox->TabIndex = 0;
        this->rtBox->Text = S"";
        this->rtBox->KeyDown +=
            new System::Windows::Forms::KeyEventHandler(this, rtBox_KeyDown);
        //
        // Form1
        //
```

```
            this->AutoScaleBaseSize = System::Drawing::Size(6, 15);
            this->ClientSize = System::Drawing::Size(950, 520);
            this->Controls->Add(this->rtBox);
            this->Name = S"Form1";
            this->Text = S"(Very Simple Rich Text Editor)";
            this->ResumeLayout(false);

        }


    private:
        void BuildLabels()
        {
            String *rtLabel[] = {S"F1-Bold", S"F2-Italics", S"F3-Underline",
                                 S"F4-Normal", S"F5-Red", S"F6-Blue",
                                 S"F7-Green", S"F8-Black", S"F9-Load",
                                 S"F10-Save"};
            labels = new Label*[10];
            // Build the labels
            for (Int32 i = 0; i < labels->Count; i++)
            {
                labels[i] = new Label();
                labels[i]->BackColor = SystemColors::ControlDark;
                labels[i]->BorderStyle = BorderStyle::FixedSingle;
                labels[i]->Location = Drawing::Point(5+(95*i), 8);
                labels[i]->Size = Drawing::Size(85, 16);
                labels[i]->Text = rtLabel[i];
                labels[i]->TextAlign = ContentAlignment::MiddleCenter;
            }
            // Place labels on the Form
            Controls->AddRange(labels);
        }
    private:
        System::Void rtBox_KeyDown(System::Object *  sender,
                                   System::Windows::Forms::KeyEventArgs *  e)
        {
            try
            {
                if (rtBox->SelectionLength > 0)
                {
                    // Change selected text style
                    FontStyle fs;
                    switch (e->KeyCode)
                    {
```

```
        case Keys::F1:
            fs = FontStyle::Bold;
            break;
        case Keys::F2:
            fs = FontStyle::Italic;
            break;
        case Keys::F3:
            fs = FontStyle::Underline;
            break;
        case Keys::F4:
            fs = FontStyle::Regular;
            break;
    // Change selected text color
        case Keys::F5:
            rtBox->SelectionColor = Color::Red;
            break;
        case Keys::F6:
            rtBox->SelectionColor = Color::Blue;
            break;
        case Keys::F7:
            rtBox->SelectionColor = Color::Green;
            break;
        case Keys::F8:
            rtBox->SelectionColor = Color::Black;
            break;
    }
    // Do the actual change of the selected text style
    if (e->KeyCode >= Keys::F1 && e->KeyCode <= Keys::F4)
    {
        rtBox->SelectionFont = new Drawing::Font(
            rtBox->SelectionFont->FontFamily,
            rtBox->SelectionFont->Size,
            fs
        );
    }
}
// Load hard coded Chapter01.rtf file
else if (e->KeyCode == Keys::F9)
{
    rtBox->LoadFile(S"Chapter01.rtf");
}
// Save hard coded Chapter01.rtf file
else if (e->KeyCode == Keys::F10)
```

```
            {
                    rtBox->SaveFile(S"Chapter01.rtf",
                                    RichTextBoxStreamType::RichText);
            }
        }
        // Capture any blowups
        catch (Exception *e)
        {
            MessageBox::Show(String::Format(S"Error: {0}", e->Message));
        }
    }
};
}
```

As you can see, implementing the functionality of the RichTextBox is done externally to the control itself. You need some way of updating the properties. I took the easy way out by capturing simple function keystroke events and updating the selected RichTextBox text as appropriate. You will probably want to use a combination of keystrokes, button clicks, and so on to make the editing process as easy as possible.

Another interesting bit of code in this example is the use of the Anchor property:

```
this->rtBox->Anchor = (System::Windows::Forms::AnchorStyles)
                      (((System::Windows::Forms::AnchorStyles::Top |
                         System::Windows::Forms::AnchorStyles::Bottom) |
                         System::Windows::Forms::AnchorStyles::Left) |
                         System::Windows::Forms::AnchorStyles::Right);
```

This property allows you to have a control anchor itself to any or all (as shown in the previous code) sides of the parent window. Thus, when the parent resizes so does the control.

Be careful when you run this program, as it is dependant on where it is executed. To make things easier, I hard-coded the program to load and save to the current working directory. When you run this program within Visual Studio .NET, the current working directory is located where your source code is. Thus, the Chapter01.rtf file is located in the same directory as the source code. If you run this program on its own out of Windows Explorer, for example, then it will not find the .rtf file. In this scenario, you need to copy the file to the same directory as the executable. Obviously, if you wanted to make the program more robust, you would allow a user to specify where the .rtf file is, so this dependency would not be an issue.

Figure 9-14 shows what RichText.exe looks like when you execute it.

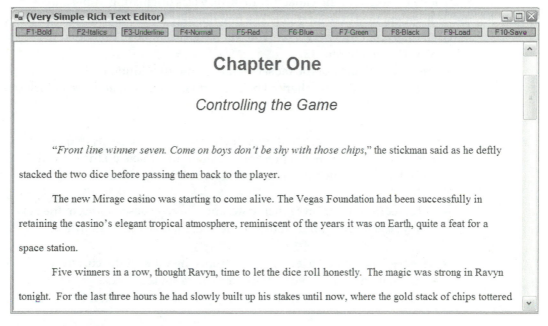

Figure 9-14. The simple RTF editor in action

The Selection Controls

The three common selection controls, ListBox, ComboBox, and CheckedListBox, are the last of the more basic controls provided by the .NET Framework class library that you will cover in this chapter. Each of the controls represents a selectable scrolling list of items.

When you create a selection control, you provide it with a collection of values for it to display. Each value within the collection has a unique index. The control keeps track of these indices for you, along with their associated values. All you have to do is handle selection events sent by the selection controls or query the control for which a value or values have been selected, either by value or index.

Selection controls are helpful when you want to select from a list of items of a "reasonable" size. "Reasonable," though, is a very relative term and it depends on what the user is selecting and where the data is coming from (fetching 300 rows from a local hard disk is different than fetching them from a mainframe in another country). For example, a list of 50 items may seem excessive in a selection control if there is no rhyme or reason to it, but it is just right when you are looking for a state in America.

All of the selection controls inherit from the abstract class `ListControl`. This provides a common set of properties and methods from which to build upon. Selection controls have the capability to display lists originating from sources that implement the `IList` interface. The functionality is provided by the `ListControl`'s property, `DataSource`. You will see an example of this when you cover ADO.NET in Chapter 12.

Here is a list of some of the most common properties found in the `ListControl` class and thus inherited by the `ListBox`, `ComboBox`, and `CheckListBox` controls:

- `DataSource` is an `Object` that implements the `IList` interface, frequently an `Array` or `DataSet`, which represents the items that make up the control. The default is `null`, which means no `DataSource` is being used.

- `SelectedIndex` is an `Int32` that represents the zero-based index of the currently selected item. If no index is selected, then –1 will be returned.

- `SelectedValue` is an `Object` that represents the value of the currently selected item as specified by the control data source's `ValueMember`. If the `ValueMember` is not specified, then the `ToString()` value is returned.

- `ValueMember` is a `String` that represents the property of the control's data source to use as the value. The default is an empty `String` (and not `null`), meaning that it uses the `ToString()` value.

The `ListBox` is truly just a selection list, whereas the `ComboBox` is a combination of a `ListBox` and a `TextBox`. The `CheckListBox`, on the other hand, is a combination of a `ListBox` and a `CheckBox`. In fact, the `CheckListBox` inherits directly from `ListBox` and thus only indirectly from `ListControl`.

ListBox

The `ListBox` control is a simple scrollable list of items from which a user can select one or more items, depending on the `SelectionMode` of the `ListBox`. Four modes are available:

- `SelectionMode::None`: No items can be selected.

- `SelectionMode::One`: Only one item can be selected at a time.

- `SelectionMode::MultiSimple`: More than one item can be selected.

- `SelectionMode::MultiExtended`: More than one item can be selected. The method of selecting the multiple items uses the Shift and Ctrl keys to allow for swifter selection of items.

The `ListBox` control provides a number of additional properties from the `ListControl` to configure the control and organize, find, and select the data within:

- `Items` is a `ListBox::ObjectCollection` that represents the collection of items within the control. The `ObjectCollection` allows you to do things such as add and remove items from the `ListBox`. Note that this method of providing items to the `ListBox` is not the same as using a `DataSource`. If you use a `DataSource`, you cannot manipulate the items in the `ListBox` using the `ObjectCollection`.

- `MultiColumn` is a `Boolean` that represents whether the control can be broken into multiple columns. The default is `false`.

- `SelectedIndices` is a `ListBox::SelectedIndexCollection` that represents the collection of zero-based indices of currently selected items within the control.

- `SelectedItems` is a `ListBox::SelectedObjectCollection` that represents the collection of currently selected items within the control.

- `Sorted` is a `Boolean` that represents whether the control is automatically sorted. The default is `false`.

- `Text` is a `String` that represents the value of the currently selected item. If you set the value of the `Text` property, then the `ListBox` searches itself for an item that matches the `Text` property and selects that item.

The `ListBox` control also provides a number of additional methods:

- `ClearSelected()` deselects all selected items in the control.

- `FindString()` finds the first item that starts with a given `String`.

- `FindStringExact()` finds the first item that exactly matches a given `String`.

- `GetSelected()` determines if a given item is currently selected.

- `SetSelected()` selects the items at the given index.

- `Sort()` sorts the items in the control.

Listing 9-13 shows how to transfer selected items between two different lists. The ListBox on the left is sorted and is a MultiExtended list, whereas the one on the right is not sorted and is a MultiSimple list.

Listing 9-13. Transferring Items Between ListBoxes

```
namespace ListTransfers
{
    using namespace System;
    using namespace System::ComponentModel;
    using namespace System::Collections;
    using namespace System::Windows::Forms;
    using namespace System::Data;
    using namespace System::Drawing;

    public __gc class Form1 : public System::Windows::Forms::Form
    {
    public:
        Form1(void)
        //...
    protected:
        void Dispose(Boolean disposing)
        //...
    private: System::Windows::Forms::Label *  lOrg;
    private: System::Windows::Forms::Label *  lDest;
    private: System::Windows::Forms::Button *  bnL2R;
    private: System::Windows::Forms::Button *  bnR2L;
    private: System::Windows::Forms::ListBox *  LBOrg;
    private: System::Windows::Forms::ListBox *  LBDest;
    private: System::ComponentModel::Container * components;

        void InitializeComponent(void)
        {
            this->lOrg = new System::Windows::Forms::Label();
            this->lDest = new System::Windows::Forms::Label();
            this->bnL2R = new System::Windows::Forms::Button();
            this->bnR2L = new System::Windows::Forms::Button();
            this->LBOrg = new System::Windows::Forms::ListBox();
            this->LBDest = new System::Windows::Forms::ListBox();
            this->SuspendLayout();
            //
            // lOrg
            //
```

```
this->lOrg->Location = System::Drawing::Point(24, 16);
this->lOrg->Name = S"lOrg";
this->lOrg->Size = System::Drawing::Size(136, 23);
this->lOrg->TabIndex = 0;
this->lOrg->Text = S"Sorted Multiextended";
//
// lDest
//
this->lDest->Location = System::Drawing::Point(256, 16);
this->lDest->Name = S"lDest";
this->lDest->Size = System::Drawing::Size(136, 23);
this->lDest->TabIndex = 1;
this->lDest->Text = S"Unsorted Multisimple";
//
// bnL2R
//
this->bnL2R->Location = System::Drawing::Point(200, 88);
this->bnL2R->Name = S"bnL2R";
this->bnL2R->Size = System::Drawing::Size(40, 23);
this->bnL2R->TabIndex = 2;
this->bnL2R->Text = S"==>";
this->bnL2R->Click += new System::EventHandler(this, bnL2R_Click);
//
// bnR2L
//
this->bnR2L->Location = System::Drawing::Point(200, 120);
this->bnR2L->Name = S"bnR2L";
this->bnR2L->Size = System::Drawing::Size(40, 23);
this->bnR2L->TabIndex = 3;
this->bnR2L->Text = S"<==";
this->bnR2L->Click += new System::EventHandler(this, bnR2L_Click);
//
// LBOrg
//
this->LBOrg->ItemHeight = 16;
System::Object* __mcTemp__1[] = new System::Object*[10];
__mcTemp__1[0] = S"System";
__mcTemp__1[1] = S"System::Collections";
__mcTemp__1[2] = S"System::Data";
__mcTemp__1[3] = S"System::Drawing";
__mcTemp__1[4] = S"System::IO";
__mcTemp__1[5] = S"System::Net";
__mcTemp__1[6] = S"System::Threading";
```

```
            __mcTemp__1[7] = S"System::Web";
            __mcTemp__1[8] = S"System::Windows::Forms";
            __mcTemp__1[9] = S"System::Xml";
            this->LBOrg->Items->AddRange(__mcTemp__1);
            this->LBOrg->Location = System::Drawing::Point(24, 48);
            this->LBOrg->Name = S"LBOrg";
            this->LBOrg->SelectionMode =
                  System::Windows::Forms::SelectionMode::MultiExtended;
            this->LBOrg->Size = System::Drawing::Size(160, 164);
            this->LBOrg->Sorted = true;
            this->LBOrg->TabIndex = 0;
            this->LBOrg->DoubleClick +=
                  new System::EventHandler(this, LBOrg_DoubleClick);
            //
            // LBDest
            //
            this->LBDest->ItemHeight = 16;
            this->LBDest->Location = System::Drawing::Point(256, 48);
            this->LBDest->Name = S"LBDest";
            this->LBDest->SelectionMode =
                  System::Windows::Forms::SelectionMode::MultiSimple;
            this->LBDest->Size = System::Drawing::Size(160, 164);
            this->LBDest->TabIndex = 1;
            this->LBDest->DoubleClick +=
                  new System::EventHandler(this, LBDest_DoubleClick);
            //
            // Form1
            //
            this->AutoScaleBaseSize = System::Drawing::Size(6, 15);
            this->ClientSize = System::Drawing::Size(440, 231);
            this->Controls->Add(this->LBDest);
            this->Controls->Add(this->LBOrg);
            this->Controls->Add(this->bnR2L);
            this->Controls->Add(this->bnL2R);
            this->Controls->Add(this->lDest);
            this->Controls->Add(this->lOrg);
            this->Name = S"Form1";
            this->Text = S"List Box Transfers";
            this->ResumeLayout(false);
      }
  private:
      System::Void LBOrg_DoubleClick(System::Object *
                                        sender, System::EventArgs *  e)
```

```
        {
            // Add Selected item to other ListBox
            // Then remove item from original
            if (LBOrg->SelectedItem != 0)
            {
                LBDest->Items->Add(LBOrg->SelectedItem);
                LBOrg->Items->Remove(LBOrg->SelectedItem);
            }
        }
private:
    System::Void LBDest_DoubleClick(System::Object *  sender,
                                    System::EventArgs *  e)
        {
            // Add Selected item to other ListBox
            // Then remove item from original
            if (LBDest->SelectedItem != 0)
            {
                LBOrg->Items->Add(LBDest->SelectedItem);
                LBDest->Items->Remove(LBDest->SelectedItem);
            }
        }
private:
    System::Void bnL2R_Click(System::Object *  sender,
                             System::EventArgs *  e)
        {
            // Add all Selected items to other ListBox
            // Then remove the all items from original
            Object *tmp[] = new Object*[LBOrg->SelectedItems->Count];
            LBOrg->SelectedItems->CopyTo(tmp, 0);
            LBDest->Items->AddRange(tmp);
            for (Int32 i = 0; i < tmp->Count; i++)
                LBOrg->Items->Remove(tmp[i]);
        }
private:
    System::Void bnR2L_Click(System::Object *  sender,
                             System::EventArgs *  e)
        {
            // Add all Selected items to other ListBox
            // Then remove all the items from original
            Object *tmp[] = new Object*[LBDest->SelectedItems->Count];
            LBDest->SelectedItems->CopyTo(tmp, 0);
            LBOrg->Items->AddRange(tmp);
            for (Int32 i = 0; i < tmp->Count; i++)
```

```
                        LBDest->Items->Remove(tmp[i]);
        }
    };
}
```

The code is pretty straightforward. It creates two `ListBoxes` and configures them using their properties. Things you need to pay attention to in Listing 9-13 are that when handling the double-click event for a list, make sure that an item is actually selected by checking the `SelectedItem` for a non-zero (`null`) value before trying to work with the `SelectedItem`. The reason is double-clicking an area of the list that is not an item generates an event with no selection.

The second thing to watch out for is removing items from a list using the `SelectedItems` property. The `SelectedItems` property does not create a copy of the items selected; instead, it uses the original items. Thus, if you try to remove items from a list such as the following:

```
// This code DOES NOT work
for (Int32 i = 0; i < LBDest->SelectedItems->Count; i++)
{
    LBDest->Items->Remove(LBDest->SelectedItems->Item[i]);
}
```

not all the selected items get removed—in fact, only half do. What is happening is that `LBDest->SelectedItems->Count` decreases when you call `LBDest->Items->Remove()` because the `SelectedItems` enumeration is decreasing in size at the same time as the `ListBox` entries are. The solution I came up with was to create a copy of the `SelectedItems` and then use that instead of `SelectedItems` directly:

```
// This DOES work
Object *tmp[] = new Object*[LBDest->SelectedItems->Count];
LBDest->SelectedItems->CopyTo(tmp, 0);
for (Int32 i = 0; i < tmp->Count; i++)
    LBDest->Items->Remove(tmp[i]);
```

On a personal note, the preceding code was generated by Visual Studio .NET. I would have defined __mcTemp__1 like this:

```
    Object *__mcTemp__1[] = { S"System", S"System::Collections",
                              S"System::Data", S"System::Drawing",
                              S"System::IO", S"System::Net",
                              S"System::Threading", S"System::Web",
                              S"System::Windows::Forms", S"System::Xml" };
```

This way, I can add entries without having to change the array size each time. But hey, it's not my call.

Figure 9-15 shows what ListTransfers.exe looks like when you execute it.

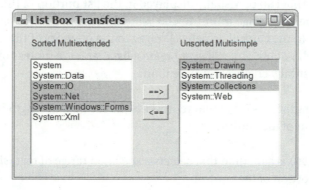

Figure 9-15. Transferring items between list boxes

ComboBox

The ComboBox control is a combination of a ListBox control with a TextBox control attached to the top. The ListBox control provides a quick click response, and the TextBox control allows the user to type in an answer.

There are three different DropDownStyles of ComboBox:

- ComboBoxStyle::Simple: The list is always expanded and the text field can be edited.

- ComboBoxStyle::DropDown: The list starts collapsed but can be expanded and the text field can be edited.

- ComboBoxStyle::DropDownList: The list starts collapsed but can be expanded and the text field only accepts strings that are part of the selection list. (This style of ComboBox does not allow responses that are not part of the list.)

Like all other controls, the ComboBox provides several properties and methods to support the functionality of the control. You will probably recognize that these members are half TextBox and half ListBox in nature. Some of the common members unique to the ComboBox are as follows:

- DroppedDown is a Boolean that represents whether the list portion of the control has been expanded.

- MaxDropDownItems is an Int32 that represents the maximum number of items that can be visually displayed in the list portion of the control. This number can range from 1 to 100. Note that this is not the same as the total items in the control, which is limited to the memory of the computer, though I doubt you will ever create a list that large (unless of course you accidentally create an infinite loop).

- MaxLength is an Int32 that represents the maximum length of the text box portion of the control.

- Select() is a method that selects a specified range of text within the text box portion of the control.

- SelectAll() is a method that selects all the text in the text box portion of the control.

- SelectionLength is an Int32 that represents the length of the selected text within the text box portion of the control.

- SelectionStart is an Int32 that represents the zero-based starting position of the selected text within the text box portion of the control.

Listing 9-14 shows that you can keep all three ComboBox style controls in sync. Selecting an item in one control will automatically update the other two. If you type an entry in the text box area, the other two controls are updated appropriately. You should notice that if you type in a value that is not on the selection list, then the DropDownList style control does not update.

Listing 9-14. Synchronizing ComboBoxes

```
namespace SyncCombos
{
    using namespace System;
    using namespace System::ComponentModel;
    using namespace System::Collections;
    using namespace System::Windows::Forms;
    using namespace System::Data;
    using namespace System::Drawing;
```

```cpp
public __gc class Form1 : public System::Windows::Forms::Form
{
public:
    Form1(void)
    {
        InitializeComponent();
        PopulateLists();
    }
protected:
    void Dispose(Boolean disposing)
    //...
private: System::Windows::Forms::ComboBox *  ddown;
private: System::Windows::Forms::ComboBox *  simple;
private: System::Windows::Forms::ComboBox *  ddlist;
private: System::ComponentModel::Container * components;

    void InitializeComponent(void)
    {
        this->ddown = new System::Windows::Forms::ComboBox();
        this->simple = new System::Windows::Forms::ComboBox();
        this->ddlist = new System::Windows::Forms::ComboBox();
        this->SuspendLayout();
        //
        // ddown
        //
        this->ddown->Location = System::Drawing::Point(16, 24);
        this->ddown->MaxDropDownItems = 3;
        this->ddown->MaxLength = 10;
        this->ddown->Name = S"ddown";
        this->ddown->Size = System::Drawing::Size(121, 24);
        this->ddown->TabIndex = 0;
        this->ddown->TextChanged +=
                new System::EventHandler(this, ddown_Change);
        this->ddown->SelectedIndexChanged +=
                new System::EventHandler(this, ddown_Change);
        //
        // simple
        //
        this->simple->DropDownStyle =
                System::Windows::Forms::ComboBoxStyle::Simple;
        this->simple->Location = System::Drawing::Point(184, 24);
        this->simple->Name = S"simple";
        this->simple->Size = System::Drawing::Size(121, 128);
```

```
                this->simple->Sorted = true;
                this->simple->TabIndex = 1;
                this->simple->TextChanged +=
                        new System::EventHandler(this, simple_Change);
                this->simple->SelectedIndexChanged +=
                        new System::EventHandler(this, simple_Change);
                //
                // ddlist
                //
                this->ddlist->DropDownStyle =
                        System::Windows::Forms::ComboBoxStyle::DropDownList;
                this->ddlist->Location = System::Drawing::Point(352, 24);
                this->ddlist->Name = S"ddlist";
                this->ddlist->Size = System::Drawing::Size(121, 24);
                this->ddlist->TabIndex = 2;
                this->ddlist->SelectedIndexChanged +=
                        new System::EventHandler(this, ddlist_Change);
                //
                // Form1
                //
                this->AutoScaleBaseSize = System::Drawing::Size(6, 15);
                this->ClientSize = System::Drawing::Size(496, 167);
                this->Controls->Add(this->ddlist);
                this->Controls->Add(this->simple);
                this->Controls->Add(this->ddown);
                this->Name = S"Form1";
                this->Text = S"Synchronized Combo boxing";
                this->ResumeLayout(false);
        }
    private:
        void PopulateLists()
        {
            // Item to be placed in all ComboBoxes
            Object *ddItems[] = { S"oranges", S"cherries", S"apples",
                                  S"lemons",  S"bananas",  S"grapes" };
            ddown->Items->AddRange(ddItems);
            simple->Items->AddRange(ddItems);
            ddlist->Items->AddRange(ddItems);
        }
    private:
        System::Void ddown_Change(System::Object *  sender,
                                  System::EventArgs *  e)
        {
```

```
        // Update simple and dropdownlist with dropdown text
        simple->Text = ddown->Text;
        ddlist->SelectedItem = ddown->Text;
    }
private:
    System::Void simple_Change(System::Object *  sender,
                               System::EventArgs *  e)
    {
        // Update dropdown and dropdownlist with simple text
        ddown->Text = simple->Text;
        ddlist->SelectedItem = simple->Text;
    }
private:
    System::Void ddlist_Change(System::Object *  sender,
                               System::EventArgs *  e)
    {
        // Update simple and dropdown with dropdownlist SelectedText
        ddown->SelectedItem = ddlist->SelectedItem;
        simple->SelectedItem = ddlist->SelectedItem;
    }
};
}
```

When you are working with Simple or DropDown ComboBoxes, all you usually need to worry about is what is currently in the Text property. This property tells you what the current value is in the ComboBox and by placing the value in it automatically changes the SelectedItem property. On the other hand, when you are working with the DropDownList, it is better to work with the SelectedItem property, because it is more efficient for the control as the editing overhead of the text field goes unused.

Figure 9-16 shows what SyncCombos.exe looks like when you execute it.

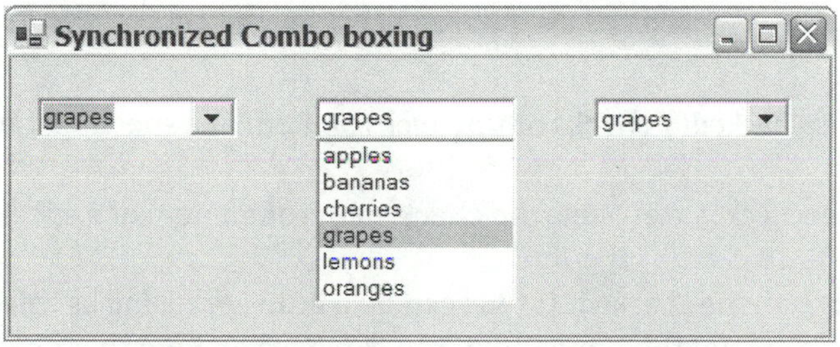

Figure 9-16. Synchronized combo boxes

CheckedListBox

The CheckedListBox control provides you a way to group related check boxes in a scrollable and selectable ListBox control. In other words, this control provides the functionality of an array of check boxes and at the same time the functionality of a ListBox, allowing the selection of a checkable item without actually checking the item off.

The CheckedListBox control directly inherits from the ListBox control, so in addition to the functionality provided by the ListBox, the CheckedListBox provides numerous other properties. Some of the more common are as follows:

- CheckedIndices is a CheckedListBox::CheckedIndexCollection that represents the collection of zero-based indices of currently checked or indeterminate state items within the control.

- CheckedItems is a CheckedListBox::CheckedItemCollection that represents the collection of currently checked or indeterminate state items within the control.

- CheckOnClick is a Boolean that represents whether the check box is toggled immediately on the selection of the check box item. The default is false.

- ThreeDCheckBoxes is a Boolean that represents if 3D or flat check boxes are used. The default is false or a flat appearance.

Along with the preceding properties, the CheckListBox control provides several methods. The following methods get access to the checked status of the CheckListBox's items:

- GetItemChecked() checks using a specified index whether an item is checked.

- GetItemCheckState() checks using a specified index what the check state of the item is.

- SetItemChecked() checks or unchecks an item at a specified index.

- SetItemCheckState() sets the check status of an item at a specified index.

Working with the CheckedListBox can be a little confusing as selected and checked items are not the same thing. You can have an item that does not check or uncheck when selected.

To get the selected item (you can only have one, unless you select SelectionMode::None), you use the properties prefixed by "Selected". Even though there are properties that suggest more than one item can be selected, these properties return a collection of one item. Basically, the difference between SelectedIndex and SelectedIndices, and SelectedItem and SelectedItems, is that the first returns a single item and the second returns a collection of one item.

To get the checked items from the control, you need to use the properties and methods that contain "Check(ed)" within their name. One thing you should note is that there are two common ways of getting all the checked items in the CheckedListBox. The first method is to use the properties CheckIndices and CheckItems:

```
for (Int32 i = 0; i < checkedlistbox->CheckedItems->Count; i++)
{
    //...do what you want with:
    //      checkedlistbox->CheckedItems->Item[i];
}
```

The second method is to use the methods GetItemChecked() and GetItemCheckState():

```
for (Int32 i = 0; i < checkedlistbox->Items->Count; i++)
{
    if (checkedlistbox->GetItemChecked(i))
    {
        //...do what you want with:
        //      checkedlistbox->Items[i];
    }
}
```

The main difference between the two is that the first method provides only a list of checked items, whereas the second requires an iteration through all the items and checks the check status of each.

The example in Listing 9-15 shows how closely the CheckListBox is to an array of Checkboxes and a ListBox. It does this by synchronizing input using these controls.

Listing 9-15. Splitting the CheckedListBox

```
namespace SplitCLB
{
    using namespace System;
    using namespace System::ComponentModel;
```

```
using namespace System::Collections;
using namespace System::Windows::Forms;
using namespace System::Data;
using namespace System::Drawing;

public __gc class Form1 : public System::Windows::Forms::Form
{
public:
    Form1(void)
    {
        InitializeComponent();

        Object *Items[] = { S"Appleman", S"Challa", S"Chand", S"Cornell",
                            S"Fraser", S"Gunnerson", S"Harris", S"Rammer",
                            S"Symmonds", S"Thomsen", S"Troelsen", S"Vaughn"
        };
        clBox->Items->AddRange(Items);
        lBox->Items->AddRange(Items);
        // Create a Check box for each entry in Items array.
        cBox = new CheckBox*[Items->Count];
        Int32 j = cBox->Count/2;
        for (Int32 i = 0; i < j; i++)
        {
            // Build Left Column
            cBox[i] = new CheckBox();
            cBox[i]->Location = Drawing::Point(50, 160+(30*i));
            cBox[i]->TabIndex = i+2;
            cBox[i]->Text = Items[i]->ToString();
            cBox[i]->CheckStateChanged +=
                new EventHandler(this, cBox_CheckStateChanged);
            // Build Right Column
            cBox[i+j] = new CheckBox();
            cBox[i+j]->Location = Drawing::Point(180, 160+(30*i));
            cBox[i+j]->TabIndex = i+j+2;
            cBox[i+j]->Text = Items[i+j]->ToString();
            cBox[i+j]->CheckStateChanged +=
                new EventHandler(this, cBox_CheckStateChanged);
        }
        // Add all CheckBoxes to Form
        Controls->AddRange(cBox);
    }
```

```
protected:
    void Dispose(Boolean disposing)
    //...
private: System::Windows::Forms::CheckedListBox *  clBox;
private: System::Windows::Forms::ListBox *  lBox;
private: System::ComponentModel::Container * components;
private: CheckBox *cBox[];

    void InitializeComponent(void)
    {
        this->clBox = new System::Windows::Forms::CheckedListBox();
        this->lBox = new System::Windows::Forms::ListBox();
        this->SuspendLayout();
        //
        // clBox
        //
        this->clBox->Location = System::Drawing::Point(16, 16);
        this->clBox->MultiColumn = true;
        this->clBox->Name = S"clBox";
        this->clBox->Size = System::Drawing::Size(304, 106);
        this->clBox->TabIndex = 0;
        this->clBox->ThreeDCheckBoxes = true;
        this->clBox->SelectedIndexChanged +=
                new System::EventHandler(this, clBox_SelectedIndexChanged);
        this->clBox->ItemCheck +=
    new System::Windows::Forms::ItemCheckEventHandler(this, clBox_ItemCheck);
        //
        // lBox
        //
        this->lBox->ItemHeight = 16;
        this->lBox->Location = System::Drawing::Point(360, 16);
        this->lBox->Name = S"lBox";
        this->lBox->Size = System::Drawing::Size(136, 196);
        this->lBox->TabIndex = 1;
        this->lBox->SelectedIndexChanged +=
                new System::EventHandler(this, lBox_SelectedIndexChanged);
        //
        // Form1
        //
        this->AutoScaleBaseSize = System::Drawing::Size(6, 15);
        this->ClientSize = System::Drawing::Size(528, 357);
        this->Controls->Add(this->lBox);
        this->Controls->Add(this->clBox);
```

```
                this->Name = S"Form1";
                this->Text = S"Splitting The Check List Box";
                this->ResumeLayout(false);
            }
    private:
        System::Void clBox_ItemCheck(System::Object *  sender,
                            System::Windows::Forms::ItemCheckEventArgs *  e)
        {
            //update state of CheckBox with same index as checked CheckedListBox
            cBox[e->Index]->CheckState = e->NewValue;
        }
    private:
        System::Void clBox_SelectedIndexChanged(System::Object *  sender,
                                                System::EventArgs *  e)
        {
            //update ListBox with same selected item in the CheckedListBox
            lBox->SelectedItem = clBox->SelectedItem->ToString();
        }
    private:
        System::Void lBox_SelectedIndexChanged(System::Object *  sender,
                                                System::EventArgs *  e)
        {
            //update CheckedListBox with same selected item in the ListBox
            clBox->SelectedItem = lBox->SelectedItem;
        }
    private:
        void cBox_CheckStateChanged(Object *sender, EventArgs *e)
        {
            //update state of CheckedListBox with same index as checked CheckBox
            CheckBox *cb = dynamic_cast<CheckBox*>(sender);
            clBox->SetItemCheckState(Array::IndexOf(cBox, cb), cb->CheckState);
        }
    };
}
```

The CheckedListBox provides an event to handle the checking of a box within the control. To handle this event, you need to create a method with the template:

```
ItemCheck(System::Object *sender, System::Windows::Forms::ItemCheckEventArgs *e)
```

Conveniently, the handler provides the parameter of type ItemCheckEventArgs, which among other things provides the index of the box being checked and the current and previous state of the box. I use this information to update the external array of check boxes.

```
cBox[e->Index]->CheckState = e->NewValue;
```

One other thing of note in the code is the trick I used to get the index of the CheckBox, which triggered the state change event out of the CheckBox array. The Array class has a neat little static method, Array::IndexOf(), which you pass as arguments to the array containing an entry and the entry itself, with the result being the index to that entry. I used this method by passing it the array of CheckBoxes along with the dynamically cast sender Object.

Figure 9-17 shows what SplitCLB.exe looks like when you execute it.

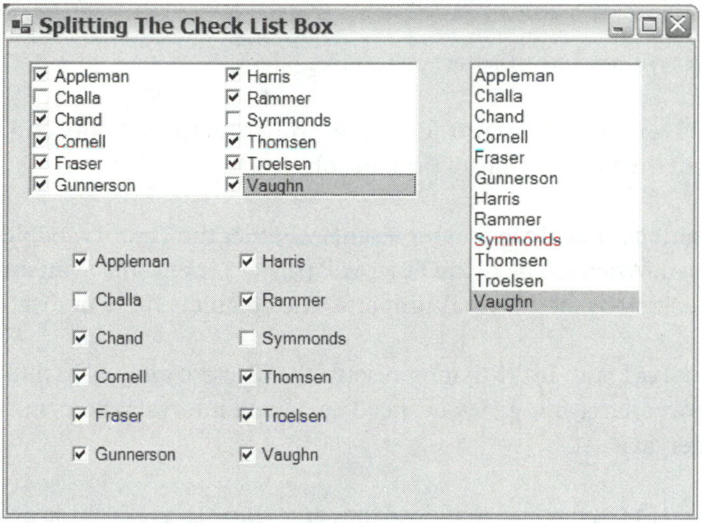

Figure 9-17. Splitting the checklist box

Timers

A few timers are sprinkled throughout the .NET Framework class library. One relevant to this chapter is found in the System::Windows::Forms namespace. Though not a GUI control, the Timer is an important component for scheduling events that occur at discrete user-defined intervals.

Notice I called Timer a "component" and not a "control," as it inherits from the Component class but not the Control class. This fact is apparent when you implement a Timer in Visual Studio .NET, because when you drag the component to the Win Form it does not get placed on the form. Instead, it gets placed in its own area at the bottom of the designer window. Even though it is placed there, you still work with the Timer the same way you do with a control. You use the Properties view to update the Timer's properties and events.

The Timer component is easy to use. Just instantiate it in your program:

```
Timer *timer = new Timer();
```

Create an event handler to accept Tick events:

```
void timer_Tick(Object *sender, System::EventArgs *e)
{
    //...Process the Tick event
}
```

And then delegate that event handler:

```
timer->Tick += new EventHandler(this, timer_Tick);
```

The Timer component provides a few properties to configure and methods to implement the functionality of the control:

- Enabled is a Boolean that represents whether the Timer is enabled or disabled. When enabled, the Timer will trigger Tick events at an interval specified by the Interval property. The default is false or disabled.

- Interval is an Int32 that represents the discrete interval in milliseconds between triggering Tick events. The default interval is zero, meaning no interval is set.

- Start() is a method that does the same thing as the Enabled property being set to true.

- Stop() is a method that does the same thing as the Enabled property being set to false.

The Timer is such a simple example (see Listing 9-16) that I decided to throw another less frequently used control, the ProgressBar, into the program. You have seen a progress bar whenever you install software (it's that bar that seems to take forever to slide across). The example is simply a repeating one-minute timer.

Listing 9-16. The One-Minute Timer

```
namespace MinuteTimer
{
    using namespace System;
    using namespace System::ComponentModel;
    using namespace System::Collections;
    using namespace System::Windows::Forms;
    using namespace System::Data;
    using namespace System::Drawing;

    public __gc class Form1 : public System::Windows::Forms::Form
    {
    public:
        Form1(void)
        {
            InitializeComponent();
            seconds = 0;
        }

    protected:
        void Dispose(Boolean disposing)
        //...
    private: System::Windows::Forms::Timer *  timer;
    private: System::Windows::Forms::Label *  lbsecs;
    private: System::Windows::Forms::ProgressBar *  progressBar;
    private: System::ComponentModel::IContainer *  components;

    Int32 seconds;

        void InitializeComponent(void)
        {
            this->components = new System::ComponentModel::Container();
            this->lbsecs = new System::Windows::Forms::Label();
            this->progressBar = new System::Windows::Forms::ProgressBar();
            this->timer = new System::Windows::Forms::Timer(this->components);
            this->SuspendLayout();
            //
            // lbsecs
            //
            this->lbsecs->Location = System::Drawing::Point(25, 25);
            this->lbsecs->Name = S"lbsecs";
            this->lbsecs->Size = System::Drawing::Size(50, 25);
```

```cpp
            this->lbsecs->TabIndex = 0;
            this->lbsecs->TextAlign =
                    System::Drawing::ContentAlignment::MiddleRight;
            //
            // progressBar
            //
            this->progressBar->Location = System::Drawing::Point(80, 25);
            this->progressBar->Maximum = 60;
            this->progressBar->Name = S"progressBar";
            this->progressBar->Size = System::Drawing::Size(300, 25);
            this->progressBar->TabIndex = 1;
            //
            // timer1
            //
            this->timer->Enabled = true;
            this->timer->Tick += new System::EventHandler(this, timer_Tick);
            //
            // Form1
            //
            this->AutoScaleBaseSize = System::Drawing::Size(6, 15);
            this->ClientSize = System::Drawing::Size(450, 80);
            this->Controls->Add(this->progressBar);
            this->Controls->Add(this->lbsecs);
            this->Name = S"Form1";
            this->Text = S"The One Minute Timer";
            this->ResumeLayout(false);
        }
    private:
        System::Void timer_Tick(System::Object * sender, System::EventArgs * e)
        {
            // Write current tick count (int 10th of second) to label
            seconds++;
            seconds %= 600;
            lbsecs->Text = String::Format(S"{0}.{1}", (seconds/10).ToString(),
                                            (seconds%10).ToString());
            // Update ProgressBar
            progressBar->Value = seconds/10;
        }
    };
}
```

The `ProgressBar` simply shows the amount complete of some activity. You specify the starting point (`Minimum`) and the end point (`Maximum`) for which you want to monitor the progress, and then you simply update the value of the `ProgressBar` between these two points. The default start and end values are 0 to 100, representing progress from 0 percent to 100 percent, which is the most common use for the `ProgressBar`. In this example, because I am representing seconds in a minute, it made more sense to go from 0 to 60. Updating the `ProgressBar` itself is very simple, as it will move over automatically when the value exceeds the specified step factor.

Figure 9-18 shows what MinuteTimer.exe looks like when you execute it.

Figure 9-18. The one-minute timer

Summary

You covered a lot in this chapter. You started with the lowly "Hello, World!" form and worked your way up to building fully functional Win Forms. Along the way, you explored a number (most, actually) of the more common simple GUI controls provided by the .NET Framework class library. You should now be able to build a simple Win Form with a high level of confidence.

In the next chapter, you will continue to look at the GUI interface provided by the .NET Framework class library, but this time you look at some of the more advanced Win Form topics such as views, menus, and dialog boxes.

CHAPTER 10

Advanced Windows Forms Applications

IN THE PREVIOUS CHAPTER you got all the basics squared away. It is now time to look at some of the more exciting controls and features provided by the .NET Framework. Even though this chapter covers more advanced Win Form applications, this does not mean they are more complex or difficult to develop. The main reason is that the .NET Framework uses encapsulation quite extensively in its classes and hides much of the complexities of Win Forms from you. On the other hand, you can still access these complexities if you really want to.

In this chapter I continue using the approach of covering both manual development and development using the GUI design tool. As I pointed out in the previous chapter, I feel the intimate knowledge of Win Form components, attained by building Win Forms manually, will allow you to build better GUI interfaces to your Windows application.

This chapter covers some of the more powerful GUI controls provided by the .NET Framework. It also looks at three other Win Form development areas: menus, dialog boxes, and the MDI interface.

In Chapter 9, I covered most of the more commonly used data entry controls. There is nothing stopping you from using these controls in a simple form every time you need data from the user. However, doing so is not always the best way to interact with or present information to the user.

Let's now start a whirlwind tour of some of the remaining controls provided by the .NET Framework class library.

Views

This section starts off with a couple of views provided by the .NET Framework: ListView and TreeView. If you have used Windows for any amount of time, then you have seen and used both of these views as they are used quite extensively. The reason is that these views provide, when used correctly, a better way of displaying data to the user.

A point that may not be apparent about views is that they are controls. This means that they are inheritable and derive from both component and control classes. Thus, they have all the benefits provided by both.

ListView

The ListView is a powerful (but slightly complicated) control that displays a list of items. You can see what a ListView control looks like by opening up Windows Explorer. The ListView is the right-hand panel if two panels are being displayed. The items can consist of a combination of a record (array) of text, a large icon, and/or a small icon. I cover working with icons later in the chapter in the "ToolBar" section.

You can display a ListView in one of four different View property modes:

- View::LargeIcon displays a large icon with text underneath in a grid layout.

- View::SmallIcon displays a small icon with text along the side in columns.

- View::List displays the root text associated with the item in a single column.

- View::Details displays the root text and subtext in multiple columns.

Providing the functionality of the ListView requires a number of properties, many of which you have seen before. Here are some of the common ones unique to the ListView:

- Activation is an ItemActivation enum that represents whether one or two clicks are required to activate an item. The default is two clicks or ItemActivation::Standard.

- AllowColumnReorder is a Boolean that represents whether the headings can be dragged to reorder the columns. The default is false.

- AutoArrange is a Boolean that represents whether the items are automatically arranged. The default is true.

- Columns is a ListView::ColumnHeaderCollection that represents a collection of column headers to be used if the View property mode is set to View::Details.

- FocusItem is a ListViewItem that represents the item that currently has focus. If no item has focus, null is returned.

- FullRowSelect is a Boolean that represents whether clicking an item selects all its subitems as well. The default is false.

- GridLines is a Boolean that represents whether grid lines are displayed. The default is false.

- HeaderStyle is a ColumnHeaderStyle enum that represents whether the header is displayed and if it is clickable. The default is displayed and clickable: ColumnHeaderStyle::Clickable.

- HoverSelection is a Boolean that represents whether the item is automatically selected when the cursor hovers over it for a few seconds. The default is false.

- LabelEdit is a Boolean that represents whether the label of an item can be edited. The default is false.

- LabelWrap is a Boolean that represents whether the label wraps when displayed. The default is true.

- LargeImageList is an ImageList of the large icons to be used if the View property is set to View::LargeIcon.

- SmallImageList is an ImageList of the small icons to be used if the View property is set to View::SmallIcon.

Along with these properties, the ListView provides a number of methods. These are some of the common methods unique to ListView:

- ArrangeIcons() arranges the icons in large and small icon views.

- EnsureVisible() ensures that an item is visible even if the ListView must scroll to make it visible.

- GetItemAt() gets an item at a specified *x* and *y* location.

Listing 10-1 shows a ListView of fruit, their price, and the month when they are available for harvest. (The data was derived using a high-tech research facility. Okay, you caught me—I made it up.) When an item is selected, its price is displayed in a label.

Listing 10-1. A ListView of Fruit

```cpp
namespace ListView1
{
    using namespace System;
    using namespace System::ComponentModel;
    using namespace System::Collections;
    using namespace System::Windows::Forms;
    using namespace System::Data;
    using namespace System::Drawing;

    public __gc class Form1 : public System::Windows::Forms::Form
    {
    public:
        Form1(void)
        {
            InitializeComponent();
            FillListView();
        }

    protected:
        void Dispose(Boolean disposing)
        //...
    private: System::Windows::Forms::ColumnHeader *  Fruit;
    private: System::Windows::Forms::ColumnHeader *  Price;
    private: System::Windows::Forms::ColumnHeader *  Available;
    private: System::Windows::Forms::ListView *  lView;
    private: System::Windows::Forms::Label *  label;
    private: System::ComponentModel::Container * components;

        void InitializeComponent(void)
        {
            this->lView = new System::Windows::Forms::ListView();
            this->Fruit = new System::Windows::Forms::ColumnHeader();
            this->Price = new System::Windows::Forms::ColumnHeader();
            this->Available = new System::Windows::Forms::ColumnHeader();
            this->label = new System::Windows::Forms::Label();
            this->SuspendLayout();
            //
            // lView
            //
            this->lView->Anchor = (System::Windows::Forms::AnchorStyles)
                ((System::Windows::Forms::AnchorStyles::Top |
```

```
          System::Windows::Forms::AnchorStyles::Left) |
          System::Windows::Forms::AnchorStyles::Right);
System::Windows::Forms::ColumnHeader* __mcTemp__1[] =
    new System::Windows::Forms::ColumnHeader*[3];
__mcTemp__1[0] = this->Fruit;
__mcTemp__1[1] = this->Price;
__mcTemp__1[2] = this->Available;
this->lView->Columns->AddRange(__mcTemp__1);
this->lView->FullRowSelect = true;
this->lView->GridLines = true;
this->lView->Location = System::Drawing::Point(0, 0);
this->lView->MultiSelect = false;
this->lView->Name = S"lView";
this->lView->Size = System::Drawing::Size(424, 248);
this->lView->TabIndex = 0;
this->lView->View = System::Windows::Forms::View::Details;
this->lView->SelectedIndexChanged +=
        new System::EventHandler(this, lView_SelectedIndexChanged);
//
// Fruit
//
this->Fruit->Text = S"Fruit";
//
// Price
//
this->Price->Text = S"Price";
//
// Available
//
this->Available->Text = S"Available";
this->Available->Width = 100;
//
// label
//
this->label->BorderStyle =
        System::Windows::Forms::BorderStyle::FixedSingle;
this->label->Location = System::Drawing::Point(170, 260);
this->label->Name = S"label";
this->label->Size = System::Drawing::Size(60, 24);
this->label->TabIndex = 1;
this->label->TextAlign =
        System::Drawing::ContentAlignment::MiddleCenter;
//
```

```
          // Form1
          //
          this->AutoScaleBaseSize = System::Drawing::Size(6, 15);
          this->ClientSize = System::Drawing::Size(400, 300);
          this->Controls->Add(this->label);
          this->Controls->Add(this->lView);
          this->Name = S"Form1";
          this->Text = S"The List View Control";
          this->ResumeLayout(false);

      }
  private:
      void FillListView()
      {
          String *itemRec1[]  = { S"Apple",  S"1.50", S"September" };
          lView->Items->Add(new ListViewItem(itemRec1));

          String *itemRec2[]  = { S"Orange", S"2.50", S"March" };
          lView->Items->Add(new ListViewItem(itemRec2));

          String *itemRec3[]  = { S"Grape",  S"1.95", S"November" };
          lView->Items->Add(new ListViewItem(itemRec3));
      }
  private:
      System::Void lView_SelectedIndexChanged(System::Object *  sender,
                                              System::EventArgs *  e)
      {
          if (lView->FocusedItem != 0)
              label->Text = lView->FocusedItem->SubItems->Item[1]->Text;
      }
  };
}
```

Working with the ListView is a little tricky because the GUI designer doesn't place things in the code where you expect them (or at least I don't think so). So I'll group the code together so that you can see what's happening more clearly.

First, like any control, you create the ListView and then configure it using its properties. The example ListView is anchored and uses full row selection, display gridlines, no multiple selections, and the detailed view.

```
private: System::Windows::Forms::ListView *  lView;
//...
this->lView = new System::Windows::Forms::ListView();
this->lView->Anchor = (System::Windows::Forms::AnchorStyles)
                      ((System::Windows::Forms::AnchorStyles::Top |
                        System::Windows::Forms::AnchorStyles::Left) |
                        System::Windows::Forms::AnchorStyles::Right);
this->lView->FullRowSelect = true;
this->lView->GridLines = true;
this->lView->MultiSelect = false;
this->lView->Size = System::Drawing::Size(424, 248);
this->lView->View = System::Windows::Forms::View::Details;
this->lView->SelectedIndexChanged +=
                   new System::EventHandler(this, lView_SelectedIndexChanged);
this->Controls->Add(this->lView);
```

Next, because the detailed view is used, you need to create headers for the
ListView's items. Notice that you add the headers to the ListView control's Column
property.

```
// Create and configure Header
this->Available = new System::Windows::Forms::ColumnHeader();
this->Available->Text = S"Available";
this->Available->Width = 100;
// Add header to ListView
System::Windows::Forms::ColumnHeader* __mcTemp__1[] =
    new System::Windows::Forms::ColumnHeader*[3];
        __mcTemp__1[0] = this->Fruit;
        __mcTemp__1[1] = this->Price;
        __mcTemp__1[2] = this->Available;
this->lView->Columns->AddRange(__mcTemp__1);
```

Finally, once the ListView is ready for the world to see, you add the list items
to the view. I showed this being done manually, but you could also use the
designer to add list items.

```
// Add an Apple to the listview
String *itemRec1[]  = { S"Apple",  S"1.50", S"September" };
lView->Items->Add(new ListViewItem(itemRec1));
```

Figure 10-1 shows what ListView.exe looks like when you execute it.

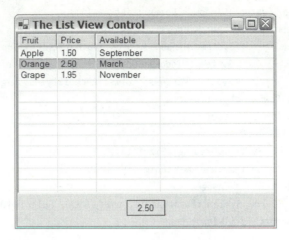

Figure 10-1. A ListView of fruit

TreeView

If you have worked with Visual Studio .NET, then you should be familiar with the TreeView control. It is used in numerous places—Solution Explorer, Server Explorer, and Class View, just to name a few. It is a control that displays a hierarchy of items in a tree format.

The TreeView, like the ListView just covered, can be a little complicated when you first try to develop code for it. Once you get the hang of it, though, you will realize that it is worth the effort of learning. The TreeView is a powerful tool that you will probably use several times in your coding career.

Configuring the TreeView control requires setting properties, just as with every other control. Here are the common properties you will likely use:

- CheckBoxes is a Boolean that represents whether check boxes are displayed next to each node in the tree. The default is false.

- ImageIndex is a zero-based Int32 index to the ImageList that represents the position of the default image used by all nodes of the tree. The default is 0. A value of –1 specifies that no image will be used.

- ImageList is a collection of bitmaps, icons, and metafiles that will be used to display the images on the tree control. If the Image list is null, which is the default, no images are displayed on the tree.

- Indent is an Int32 that represents the distance in pixels to indent for each tree hierarchy level. The default is 19.

- LabelEdit is a Boolean that represents whether the label is editable. The default is false.

- Nodes is a TreeNodeCollection that represents all the TreeNodes that make up the tree. You will always have to populate this property and there is no default.

- SelectedImageIndex is a zero-based Int32 index to the ImageList that represents the position of the default selected image used by the tree. The default is 0. A value of −1 specifies that no image will be used.

- SelectedNode is a TreeNode that represents the currently selected node. The default is null, which means no node has been selected.

- ShowLines is a Boolean that represents whether lines will be displayed between nodes. The default is true, which means that lines will be displayed.

- ShowPlusMinus is a Boolean that represents whether the expand (+) and contract (–) buttons are displayed for nodes that have child nodes. The default is true, which means that they will be displayed.

- ShowRootLines is a Boolean that represents whether lines will be displayed between nodes that are at the root of the tree. The default is true, which means that lines will be displayed.

The key to working with the TreeView, like any other control, is to know which event to handle (see Table 10-1). All the events of the TreeView have default handlers, but if you want the control to do anything other than expand and contract, you need to handle the events yourself.

Table 10-1. Common TreeView Events

EVENT	DESCRIPTION
AfterCheck	Occurs after a check box is checked
AfterCollapse	Occurs after a node is collapsed
AfterExpand	Occurs after a node is expanded
AfterLabelEdit	Occurs after a label is edited
AfterSelect	Occurs after a node is selected
BeforeCheck	Occurs before a check box is checked
BeforeCollapse	Occurs before a node is collapsed
BeforeExpand	Occurs before a node is expanded
BeforeLabelEdit	Occurs before a label is edited
BeforeSelect	Occurs before a node is selected

The basic building block of a tree hierarchy is the TreeNode. There is always at least one root node and from it sprouts (possibly many) subnodes. A subnode in turn is also a TreeNode, which can spout its own TreeNodes.

There are several constructors for the TreeNode, but you'll probably deal mostly with two of them, unless you create the tree at design time (then you won't have to deal with them at all). The first constructor takes as a parameter a String as the label for the TreeNode and the second constructor also takes a String label but also an array of child TreeNodes. The second constructor allows for a node to have one or more child nodes. To make a node with only one child, you need to assign to the second parameter an array of child TreeNodes containing only one node.

```
// Constructor for a node with no children
TreeNode *rtnA = new TreeNode(S"Root Node A");
// Constructor for a node with children
TreeNode *tnodes[] = { new TreeNode(S"Node A"), new TreeNode(S"Node B") };
TreeNode *rtnB = new TreeNode(S"Root Node A", tnodes);
```

The TreeNode has a number of properties to handle its functionality. Many of the properties are used in navigating the tree. Here are some of the more common TreeNode properties:

- Checked is a Boolean that represents whether the current node is checked. The default is false.

- FirstNode is the first TreeNode in the Nodes collection of the current node in the TreeView. If the current node has no child nodes, then the property returns a null value.

- FullPath is a String containing the entire path from the root to the current node delimited by backslashes (\). The path is all the nodes that need to be navigated to get to the current node.

- ImageIndex is a zero-based Int32 index to the TreeView::ImageList associated with the current node that represents the position of the unselected image for the node. The default is the same value as is specified in the TreeView::ImageIndex associated with the current node.

- Index is a zero-based Int32 index that represents the index of the current node within the TreeView's Nodes collection.

- LastNode is the last TreeNode in the Nodes collection of the current node in the TreeView. If the current node has no child nodes, then the property returns a null value.

- NextNode is the next sibling TreeNode in the Nodes collection of the current node in the TreeView. If the current node has no next sibling node, then the property returns a null value.

- Nodes is a TreeNodeCollection that represents all the children nodes that make up the current tree node.

- Parent is a TreeNode that represents the parent node of the current tree node.

- PrevNode is the previous sibling TreeNode in the Nodes collection of the current node in the TreeView. If the current node has no previous sibling node, then the property returns a null value.

- SelectedImageIndex is a zero-based Int32 index to the TreeView::ImageList associated with the current node that represents the position of the selected image for the node. The default is the same value as is specified in the TreeView::ImageIndex associated with the current node.

- Text is a String that represents the text label of the current tree node.

- TreeView is a TreeView that represents the TreeView that the current node in a member of.

Listing 10-2 shows how to build a tree hierarchy at runtime as opposed to prebuilding it statically. This example builds a new tree hierarchy every time it runs as it generates its node information randomly.

Listing 10-2. Random Tree Builder

```
namespace TreeView1
{
    using namespace System;
    using namespace System::ComponentModel;
    using namespace System::Collections;
    using namespace System::Windows::Forms;
    using namespace System::Data;
    using namespace System::Drawing;

    public __gc class Form1 : public System::Windows::Forms::Form
    {
    public:
        Form1(void)
        //...
    protected:
        void Dispose(Boolean disposing)
        //...
    private: System::Windows::Forms::TreeView *  tView;
    private: System::ComponentModel::Container * components;

        void InitializeComponent(void)
        {
            this->tView = new TreeView();
            this->SuspendLayout();
            //
            // tView
            //
            this->tView->Dock = System::Windows::Forms::DockStyle::Fill;
            this->tView->LabelEdit = true;
            this->tView->Name = S"tView";
            TreeNode* __mcTemp__1[] = new TreeNode*[2];
            TreeNode* __mcTemp__2[] = new TreeNode*[1];
```

```
        __mcTemp__2[0] = new TreeNode(S"<Holder>");
        __mcTemp__1[0] = new TreeNode(S"Root Node A", __mcTemp__2);
        TreeNode* __mcTemp__3[] = TreeNode*[1];
        __mcTemp__3[0] = new TreeNode(S"<Holder>");
        __mcTemp__1[1] = new TreeNode(S"Root Node B", __mcTemp__3);
        this->tView->Nodes->AddRange(__mcTemp__1);
        this->tView->Size = System::Drawing::Size(200, 450);
        this->tView->BeforeExpand +=
                new TreeViewCancelEventHandler(this, tView_BeforeExpand);
        //
        // Form1
        //
        this->AutoScaleBaseSize = System::Drawing::Size(6, 15);
        this->ClientSize = System::Drawing::Size(200, 450);
        this->Controls->Add(this->tView);
        this->Name = S"Form1";
        this->Text = S"The Tree View";
        this->ResumeLayout(false);
    }
private:
    System::Void tView_BeforeExpand(System::Object *  sender,
                System::Windows::Forms::TreeViewCancelEventArgs *  e)
    {
        // Already expanded before?
        if (e->Node->Nodes->Count > 1)
            return;   // Already expanded
        else if (e->Node->Nodes->Count == 1)
        {
            if (e->Node->Nodes->Item[0]->Text->Equals(S"<Holder>"))
                e->Node->Nodes->RemoveAt(0); // node ready for expanding
            else
                return; // Already expanded but only one subnode
        }
        // Randomly expand the Node
        Random *rand = new Random();
        Int32 rnd = rand->Next(1,5);
        for (Int32 i = 0; i < rnd; i++) // Random number of subnodes
        {
            TreeNode *stn =
                new TreeNode(String::Format(S"Sub Node {0}", __box(i+1)));
            e->Node->Nodes->Add(stn);
```

```
            if (rand->Next(2) == 1)   // Has sub subnodes
                stn->Nodes->Add(new TreeNode(S"<Holder>"));
        }
    }
};
}
```

The first steps, as with every other control, are to create the TreeView, configure it using properties, and then add it to the Form.

```
this->tView = new TreeView();
this->tView->Dock = System::Windows::Forms::DockStyle::Fill;
this->tView->LabelEdit = true;
this->tView->Size = System::Drawing::Size(200, 450);
this->tView->BeforeExpand +=
        new TreeViewCancelEventHandler(this, tView_BeforeExpand);
this->Controls->Add(this->tView);
```

Because in this example you're building a tree hierarchy on the fly, you need
to handle an event that occurs just before the tree node is expanded. The
BeforeExpand event meets the bill. The BeforeExpand event takes as a handler
TreeViewCancelEventHandler. You might note that the handler has the word
"Cancel" in it, which means that it's triggered before the expansion of the node
and it's possible to have the code cancel the expansion.

Now that you have a tree you need to add one or more root TreeNodes. You
also have to add a holder sub-TreeNode or the expansion box will not be generated. The following code was autogenerated and is hardly pretty:

```
TreeNode* __mcTemp__1[] = new TreeNode*[2];
TreeNode* __mcTemp__2[] = new TreeNode*[1];
__mcTemp__2[0] = new TreeNode(S"<Holder>");
__mcTemp__1[0] = new TreeNode(S"Root Node A", __mcTemp__2);
this->tView->Nodes->AddRange(__mcTemp__1);
```

If I were to code this by hand, the code would look more like this:

```
TreeNode *rtnA = new TreeNode(S"Root Node A");
tView->Nodes->Add(rtnA);
rtnA->Nodes->Add(new TreeNode(S"<Holder>"));
```

At this point, if you were to execute the program (assuming you created a stub for the BeforeExpand event handler) you would get a TreeView with a root TreeNode and a sub-TreeNode. The sub-TreeNode would have the label <Holder>.

The last thing you need to do is replace the holder TreeNode when the expansion box is clicked with its own, randomly generated TreeNode hierarchy. Before you replace the holder TreeNode, you need to make sure that this is the first time the node has been expanded. You do this by looking for the holder TreeNode in the first child (and it should be the only child) of the selected expanded TreeNode. You can find all child nodes in the Nodes property in the Node property. (Look at the code—this is easier to code than explain.)

```
if (e->Node->Nodes->Count > 1)
    return;   // Already expanded
else if (e->Node->Nodes->Count == 1)
{
    if (e->Node->Nodes->Item[0]->Text->Equals(S"<Holder>"))
        e->Node->Nodes->RemoveAt(0); // Holder node ready for expanding
    else
        return; // Already expanded but only one subnode
}
```

If the node has been expanded previously, just jump out of the handler and let the TreeView re-expand the node with its original tree. If this is the first time the node has been expanded, then remove the holder and randomly create a new sub-TreeNode. The code to create the sub-TreeNode is virtually the same as that of the root TreeNode, except now you add it to the selected to-be-expanded TreeNode.

```
Random *rand = new Random();
Int32 rnd = rand->Next(1,5);
for (Int32 i = 0; i < rnd; i++) // Random number of subnodes
{
    TreeNode *stn = new TreeNode(String::Format(S"Sub Node {0}", __box(i+1)));
    e->Node->Nodes->Add(stn);

    if (rand->Next(2) == 1)  // Has sub subnodes
        stn->Nodes->Add(new TreeNode(S"<Holder>"));
}
```

Figure 10-2 shows a sample of what TreeView.exe looks like when you execute it.

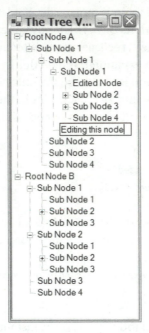

Figure 10-2. Randomly generated and editable TreeView

Container Controls

You saw two container controls, GroupBox and Panel, in the previous chapter. These controls simply group controls together. In this chapter you will look at two more powerful controls: TabControl and Splitter.

Container controls are controls whose primary purpose is to group other controls together. These controls by themselves don't provide much value to the user. Where they shine is that they provide a much better use of Win Form real estate (except the GroupBox control, which really only has the purpose of visually and physically grouping controls together). You saw the improved use of real estate with the Panel control, in that it allowed more controls to be placed in a smaller area of the screen by implementing scroll bars. In this section you'll see how the TabControl and Splitter controls improve on this paradigm.

TabControl

After the complexity of the previous two view controls, it's nice to cover a powerful but easy-to-implement control. You can think of the TabControl control as several forms or, more accurately, TabPages layered on top of each other. The actual TabPage displayed is determined by which TabPage's tab is selected. It's a neat tool to conserve desktop real estate and group common but stand-alone functionality together.

Several properties are associated with the TabControl control, but in most cases you will simply configure the control, assign the appropriate controls to each tab panel, and then forget about it. The internal default functionally of the TabControl is usually good enough that you will not have to interfere with how it works.

The following are some TabControl properties that you might actually work with:

- Alignment is a TagAlignment enum that represents which side (Top, Left, Right, or Bottom) of the control the tabs of the TabPages will be displayed. The default is Top.

- Appearance is a TabAppearance enum that represents the appearance of the control's tabs. Possible appearances are Buttons, FlatButtons, and Normal. The default is the standard tab appearance of Normal.

- HotTrack is a Boolean that represents whether the tab changes color when the mouse passes over it. The default is false, which means that the tab's color will not change when passed over.

- ImageList is a collection of bitmaps, icons, and metafiles that will be used to display the images on the tab control. If the Image list is null, which is the default, no images are displayed on the control.

- Multiline is a Boolean that represents whether the tabs can be displayed on multiple lines. The default is false, which forces all tabs to be placed on one line.

- SelectedTab is a TabPage that represents the currently selected tab. If no page is selected, null is returned.

- ShowToolTips is a Boolean that represents whether ToolTips are displayed when the mouse passes over the control's tabs. The default is false, meaning no ToolTips are displayed.

- TabCount is an Int32 that represents the number of tabs found on the control.

- TabPages is a TabPageCollection that represents all the TabPages that make up the control.

You work with a TabPage class in almost the exact same way you do a Form class, as it has many of the same properties. Really the only difference between a Form and a TabPage is that the TabPage provides a few properties to configure how the actual tab of the TabPage is displayed. Here are those properties:

- ImageIndex is a zero-based Int32 index to the TabControl::ImageList associated with the current TabPage that represents the position of the image for the tab.

- Text is a String that represents the text found on the tab.

- ToolTip is a String that represents the text found in the ToolTip for the tab.

Listing 10-3 is a simple two-page TabControl that displays each tab along the left side of the Form, and has HotTrack and ShowToolTips set on. The tab pages themselves have a different color background and each has a different label displayed within it. I could have used any control(s) I wanted within each tab page, but I didn't want to cloud the issue of building the TabControl.

Listing 10-3. A Simple TabControl

```
namespace TabControl1
{
    using namespace System;
    using namespace System::ComponentModel;
    using namespace System::Collections;
    using namespace System::Windows::Forms;
    using namespace System::Data;
    using namespace System::Drawing;

    public __gc class Form1 : public System::Windows::Forms::Form
    {
    public:
        Form1(void)
        //...
    protected:
        void Dispose(Boolean disposing)
        //...
    private: System::Windows::Forms::TabControl *  tabControl1;
    private: System::Windows::Forms::TabPage *   tabPage1;
    private: System::Windows::Forms::TabPage *   tabPage2;
    private: System::Windows::Forms::Label *   label1;
    private: System::Windows::Forms::Label *   label2;
    private: System::ComponentModel::Container * components;
```

```
void InitializeComponent(void)
{
    this->tabControl1 = new System::Windows::Forms::TabControl();
    this->tabPage1 = new System::Windows::Forms::TabPage();
    this->label1 = new System::Windows::Forms::Label();
    this->tabPage2 = new System::Windows::Forms::TabPage();
    this->label2 = new System::Windows::Forms::Label();
    this->tabControl1->SuspendLayout();
    this->tabPage1->SuspendLayout();
    this->tabPage2->SuspendLayout();
    this->SuspendLayout();
    //
    // tabControl1
    //
    this->tabControl1->Alignment =
            System::Windows::Forms::TabAlignment::Left;
    this->tabControl1->Controls->Add(this->tabPage1);
    this->tabControl1->Controls->Add(this->tabPage2);
    this->tabControl1->Dock = System::Windows::Forms::DockStyle::Fill;
    this->tabControl1->HotTrack = true;
    this->tabControl1->Location = System::Drawing::Point(0, 0);
    this->tabControl1->Multiline = true;
    this->tabControl1->Name = S"tabControl1";
    this->tabControl1->SelectedIndex = 0;
    this->tabControl1->ShowToolTips = true;
    this->tabControl1->Size = System::Drawing::Size(250, 150);
    this->tabControl1->TabIndex = 0;
    //
    // tabPage1
    //
    this->tabPage1->Controls->Add(this->label1);
    this->tabPage1->Location = System::Drawing::Point(25, 4);
    this->tabPage1->Name = S"tabPage1";
    this->tabPage1->Size = System::Drawing::Size(221, 142);
    this->tabPage1->TabIndex = 0;
    this->tabPage1->Text = S"Tab One";
    this->tabPage1->ToolTipText = S"This is tab one";
    //
    // label1
    //
    this->label1->Location = System::Drawing::Point(60, 60);
    this->label1->Name = S"label1";
    this->label1->TabIndex = 0;
```

```
                    this->label1->Text = S"This is tab one";
                    //
                    // tabPage2
                    //
                    this->tabPage2->Controls->Add(this->label2);
                    this->tabPage2->Location = System::Drawing::Point(25, 4);
                    this->tabPage2->Name = S"tabPage2";
                    this->tabPage2->Size = System::Drawing::Size(221, 142);
                    this->tabPage2->TabIndex = 1;
                    this->tabPage2->Text = S"Tab Two";
                    this->tabPage2->ToolTipText = S"This is tab two";
                    //
                    // label2
                    //
                    this->label2->Location = System::Drawing::Point(60, 60);
                    this->label2->Name = S"label2";
                    this->label2->TabIndex = 0;
                    this->label2->Text = S"This is tab two";
                    //
                    // Form1
                    //
                    this->AutoScaleBaseSize = System::Drawing::Size(6, 15);
                    this->ClientSize = System::Drawing::Size(250, 150);
                    this->Controls->Add(this->tabControl1);
                    this->Name = S"Form1";
                    this->Text = S"Simple Tab Control";
                    this->tabControl1->ResumeLayout(false);
                    this->tabPage1->ResumeLayout(false);
                    this->tabPage2->ResumeLayout(false);
                    this->ResumeLayout(false);
                }
            };
        }
```

The best part about TabControls is that you don't have to know anything about them because Visual Studio .NET's design GUI tool can handle everything for you. The only real issue about TabControls is that there is no TabPage control in the Toolbox view to drag to the TabControl. Instead, to add a TabPage, you need to add it to the TabPages collection property within the TabControl's Properties view.

I think the generated code is pretty self-explanatory. You add the TabPage to the TabControl, add the Label to a TabPage, and finally add the TabControl to the Form.

Figure 10-3 shows what TabControl.exe looks like when you execute it. Unfortunately, you can't see it action in this still image.

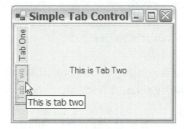

Figure 10-3. A simple TabControl

Splitter

The Splitter is a simple little control that takes two docked controls and allows you to resize them at runtime. You used it in Visual Studio .NET when you adjusted the size of Solution Explorer. It is that little area between the editing area and Solution Explorer that changes the cursor into what Windows calls a VSplit or HSplit cursor, depending on if you split vertically or horizontally.

The Splitter control is one of the few controls where I tell you to use only the design tool for building the control. The reason is that it is far easier to create the control using the tool than by hand. Also, there are no common events that you might likely use.

It is so much easier to build the Splitter with the design tool that I will walk you through the process with Visual Studio .NET. Then, I will just provide the code for those of you who want to try to puzzle your way through building the Splitter by hand.

In the example I use TextBox controls when it comes to what the Splitter splits. Though, this is not a restricting factor. You can use any control. Remember, things like the Panels, ListViews, TreeViews, and TabControls are all controls.

Here is an example of the steps required to add a Splitter, both vertically and horizontally, to your Win Form:

1. Drag and drop a TextBox control from the Toolbox view to the design form and make it multiline.

2. In the Properties view of the TextBox, set the Dock property to Left.

3. Size the TextBox control as desired.

4. Drag and drop a Splitter control from the Toolbox view to the right side of the design form. The Splitter will dock to the left by default, so you do not need to do anything further to the Splitter control.

5. Drag and drop a second TextBox control from the Toolbox view to the right side of the design form and make it multiline.

6. In the Properties view of the TextBox, set the Dock property to Top.

7. Size the TextBox control as desired.

8. Drag and drop a second Splitter control from the Toolbox view to the right and below the second TextBox.

9. In the Properties view of the Splitter, set the Dock property to Top. This will reorient the Splitter to be horizontal below the second TextBox.

10. Drag and drop a third TextBox control from the Toolbox view to the right and below the Splitter and make it multiline.

11. In the Properties view of this TextBox, set the Dock property to Full. This will cause the third TextBox to fill the remaining area of the form.

Listing 10-4 shows the code generated when you follow the preceding steps. More than likely, the locations and sizes of the controls will differ, but that is just because you will size the TextBoxes differently than I did.

Listing 10-4. The Splitter Control

```
namespace Splitter1
{
    using namespace System;
    using namespace System::ComponentModel;
    using namespace System::Collections;
    using namespace System::Windows::Forms;
    using namespace System::Data;
    using namespace System::Drawing;

    public __gc class Form1 : public System::Windows::Forms::Form
    {
    public:
        Form1(void)
        //...
    protected:
        void Dispose(Boolean disposing)
        //...
    private: System::Windows::Forms::TextBox *  textBox1;
```

```cpp
private: System::Windows::Forms::Splitter *  splitter1;
private: System::Windows::Forms::TextBox *  textBox2;
private: System::Windows::Forms::Splitter *  splitter2;
private: System::Windows::Forms::TextBox *  textBox3;
private: System::ComponentModel::Container * components;

    void InitializeComponent(void)
    {
        this->textBox1 = new System::Windows::Forms::TextBox();
        this->splitter1 = new System::Windows::Forms::Splitter();
        this->textBox2 = new System::Windows::Forms::TextBox();
        this->splitter2 = new System::Windows::Forms::Splitter();
        this->textBox3 = new System::Windows::Forms::TextBox();
        this->SuspendLayout();
        //
        // textBox1
        //
        this->textBox1->Dock = System::Windows::Forms::DockStyle::Left;
        this->textBox1->Location = System::Drawing::Point(0, 0);
        this->textBox1->Multiline = true;
        this->textBox1->Name = S"textBox1";
        this->textBox1->Size = System::Drawing::Size(120, 300);
        this->textBox1->TabIndex = 0;
        this->textBox1->Text = S"textBox1";
        //
        // splitter1
        //
        this->splitter1->Location = System::Drawing::Point(120, 0);
        this->splitter1->Name = S"splitter1";
        this->splitter1->Size = System::Drawing::Size(3, 300);
        this->splitter1->TabIndex = 1;
        this->splitter1->TabStop = false;
        //
        // textBox2
        //
        this->textBox2->Dock = System::Windows::Forms::DockStyle::Top;
        this->textBox2->Location = System::Drawing::Point(123, 0);
        this->textBox2->Multiline = true;
        this->textBox2->Name = S"textBox2";
        this->textBox2->Size = System::Drawing::Size(177, 144);
        this->textBox2->TabIndex = 2;
        this->textBox2->Text = S"textBox2";
        //
```

```
            // splitter2
            //
            this->splitter2->Dock = System::Windows::Forms::DockStyle::Top;
            this->splitter2->Location = System::Drawing::Point(123, 144);
            this->splitter2->Name = S"splitter2";
            this->splitter2->Size = System::Drawing::Size(177, 3);
            this->splitter2->TabIndex = 3;
            this->splitter2->TabStop = false;
            //
            // textBox3
            //
            this->textBox3->Dock = System::Windows::Forms::DockStyle::Fill;
            this->textBox3->Location = System::Drawing::Point(123, 147);
            this->textBox3->Multiline = true;
            this->textBox3->Name = S"textBox3";
            this->textBox3->Size = System::Drawing::Size(177, 153);
            this->textBox3->TabIndex = 4;
            this->textBox3->Text = S"textBox3";
            //
            // Form1
            //
            this->AutoScaleBaseSize = System::Drawing::Size(6, 15);
            this->ClientSize = System::Drawing::Size(300, 300);
            this->Controls->Add(this->textBox3);
            this->Controls->Add(this->splitter2);
            this->Controls->Add(this->textBox2);
            this->Controls->Add(this->splitter1);
            this->Controls->Add(this->textBox1);
            this->Name = S"Form1";
            this->Text = S"Splitters";
            this->ResumeLayout(false);
        }
    };
}
```

Keep these two things in mind when you work with Splitters:

- The order in which you add the controls is important.

- Docking the controls is the key to successfully getting Splitters to work.

CAUTION *I did say any control can be split using the Splitter. Although this is true, working with the Button control doesn't seem to work properly within the design tool.*

Figure 10-4 shows what Splitter.exe looks like when you execute it.

Figure 10-4. A simple Splitter control

ToolBar

Most Windows applications have a toolbar. In this section you'll learn how to implement one using the .NET Framework class library. Being that it's so common, you would expect a control and you would be right. The ToolBar control is so easy to implement that I thought I would include a discussion on adding an icon ImageList to a control as well.

Implementing a toolbar requires a control (ToolBar) and a component (ToolBarButton). The basic idea is to place all your ToolBarButtons on your ToolBar and then place the ToolBar on the Form.

The ToolBar control has a few overall toolbar configuration properties. These properties work in conjunction with those of the ToolBarButtons to get the final look and feel of the toolbar. Here are some of the more commonly used ToolBar properties:

- Appearance is a `ToolBarAppearance` enum that represents the appearance of the toolbar. The `ToolBar` supports the appearances `Flat` and `Normal`, which has a 3D look. The default is `Normal`.

- AutoSize is a `Boolean` that represents whether the `ToolBar` automatically adjusts itself based on the size of the button and `ToolBar`'s docking style. The default is `true`.

- Buttons is a `ToolBarButtonCollection` that represents a collection of all `ToolBarButtons` that make up the `ToolBar`.

- ButtonSize is a `Size` object that represents the size of the `ToolBar`'s buttons. The default is the larger of a width of 24 pixels and a height of 22 pixels, and the size large enough to accommodate the button's image or text.

- DropDownArrows is a `Boolean` that represents whether drop-down buttons display a down arrow. If it is `true`, the user must click the arrow to bring up the drop-down menu associated with the button. When it is `false`, clicking the button displays the menu. The default is `false`.

- ImageList is a collection of bitmaps, icons, and metafiles that will be used to display the images on the `ToolBar`. The default is `null` or no image list.

- ImageSize is a `Size` object that represents the size of all the `ToolBar`'s images within the `ImageList`.

- ShowToolTips is a `Boolean` that represents whether tool tips are displayed for all buttons when the mouse passes over them. The default is `false`.

- TextAlign is a `ToolBarTextAlign` that represents how the text is aligned on the button on the `ToolBar`. The text can be aligned either to the `Right` or `Underneath`. The default is `Underneath`.

The `ToolBarButton` properties focus on configuring the toolbar buttons themselves. As you can see by the properties that follow, the `ToolBarButton` accepts both text and icons. A text-only toolbar is rather boring (thus the addition a little later of image lists and icons), but mixing text and an icon sometimes looks okay—it really depends on how often you expect a user to see your application and how obvious you can make the functionality of your buttons with just a graphic. Here are some of the more common `ToolBarButton` properties:

- **DropDownMenu** is a **Menu** object that represents a menu associated with the drop-down button. The default is **null** or no menu.

- **Enabled** is a **Boolean** that represents whether the button is enabled. The default is **true**.

- **ImageIndex** is a zero-based **Int32** index to the **ToolBar::ImageList** associated with the current **ToolBarButton** that represents the position of the image for the button. The default is –1 or no image will appear on the button.

- **Parent** is a **ToolBar** object that represents the parent **ToolBar** for the current button.

- **Pushed** is a **Boolean** that represents whether a toggle-style button is in the pushed state. The default is **false**.

- **Style** is a **ToolBarButtonStyle** that represents the style of the button. The styles available are **DropDownButton**, **PushButton**, **Separator**, and **ToggleButton**. The default is **PushButton**.

- **Text** is a **String** that represents the text displayed on the button.

- **ToolTip** is a **String** that represents the **ToolTip** associated with the button.

- **Visible** is a **Boolean** that represents whether the button is visible. The default is **true**.

The code in Listing 10-5 builds a toolbar with two toolbar buttons: a happy face and a sad face. At the right of each is a text label, though most probably your toolbars will not have much text on them. When you click either of the buttons, the label in the body of the form is updated with the **ToolTip** of the button.

Listing 10-5. An Emotional Toolbar

```
namespace ToolBarEx
{
    using namespace System;
    using namespace System::ComponentModel;
    using namespace System::Collections;
    using namespace System::Windows::Forms;
    using namespace System::Data;
    using namespace System::Drawing;
```

```
public __gc class Form1 : public System::Windows::Forms::Form
{
public:
    Form1(void)
    //...
protected:
    void Dispose(Boolean disposing)
    //...
private: System::Windows::Forms::ToolBar *  toolBar;
private: System::Windows::Forms::ToolBarButton *  ttbHappy;
private: System::Windows::Forms::ToolBarButton *  ttbSad;
private: System::Windows::Forms::Label *  label;
private: System::Windows::Forms::ImageList *  imageList;
private: System::ComponentModel::IContainer *  components;

    void InitializeComponent(void)
    {
        this->components = new System::ComponentModel::Container();
        System::Resources::ResourceManager *  resources =
         new System::Resources::ResourceManager(__typeof(ToolBarEx::Form1));
        this->toolBar = new System::Windows::Forms::ToolBar();
        this->ttbHappy = new System::Windows::Forms::ToolBarButton();
        this->ttbSad = new System::Windows::Forms::ToolBarButton();
        this->imageList =
                new System::Windows::Forms::ImageList(this->components);
        this->label = new System::Windows::Forms::Label();
        this->SuspendLayout();
        //
        // toolBar
        //
        System::Windows::Forms::ToolBarButton* __mcTemp__1[] =
                new System::Windows::Forms::ToolBarButton*[2];
        __mcTemp__1[0] = this->ttbHappy;
        __mcTemp__1[1] = this->ttbSad;
        this->toolBar->Buttons->AddRange(__mcTemp__1);
        this->toolBar->DropDownArrows = true;
        this->toolBar->ImageList = this->imageList;
        this->toolBar->Location = System::Drawing::Point(0, 0);
        this->toolBar->Name = S"toolBar";
        this->toolBar->ShowToolTips = true;
        this->toolBar->Size = System::Drawing::Size(292, 44);
        this->toolBar->TabIndex = 0;
        this->toolBar->TextAlign =
```

```
            System::Windows::Forms::ToolBarTextAlign::Right;
    this->toolBar->ButtonClick +=
        new System::Windows::Forms::ToolBarButtonClickEventHandler(this,
            toolBar_ButtonClick);
    //
    // ttbHappy
    //
    this->ttbHappy->ImageIndex = 0;
    this->ttbHappy->Text = S"Happy";
    this->ttbHappy->ToolTipText = S"Happy Face";
    //
    // ttbSad
    //
    this->ttbSad->ImageIndex = 1;
    this->ttbSad->Text = S"Sad";
    this->ttbSad->ToolTipText = S"Sad Face";
    //
    // imageList
    //
    this->imageList->ImageSize = System::Drawing::Size(32, 32);
    this->imageList->ImageStream =
        (dynamic_cast<System::Windows::Forms::ImageListStreamer * >
        (resources->GetObject(S"imageList.ImageStream")));
    this->imageList->TransparentColor =
         System::Drawing::Color::Transparent;
    //
    // label
    //
    this->label->Location = System::Drawing::Point(88, 120);
    this->label->Name = S"label";
    this->label->TabIndex = 1;
    //
    // Form1
    //
    this->AutoScaleBaseSize = System::Drawing::Size(6, 15);
    this->ClientSize = System::Drawing::Size(292, 270);
    this->Controls->Add(this->label);
    this->Controls->Add(this->toolBar);
    this->Name = S"Form1";
    this->Text = S"An Emotional ToolBar";
    this->ResumeLayout(false);
}
```

```
private:
    System::Void toolBar_ButtonClick(System::Object * sender,
                    System::Windows::Forms::ToolBarButtonClickEventArgs * e)
    {
        label->Text = e->Button->ToolTipText;
    }
};
}
```

The process for creating a ToolBar within Visual Studio .NET is relatively straightforward, once you know how to do it. The steps are as follows:

1. Drag and drop the ToolBar from the Toolbox to the form within the design view.

2. Within the ToolBar's Properties dialog box, click the ellipses button next to the Buttons property. This will bring up a dialog box similar the one shown in Figure 10-5.

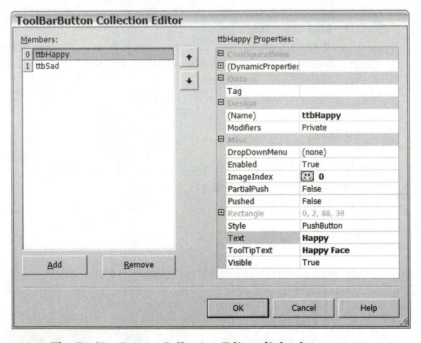

Figure 10-5. The ToolBarButton Collection Editor dialog box

3. Click the Add button and then update the ToolBarButton properties as appropriate.

4. Repeat step 3 for all the buttons.

5. Click the OK button.

I could have stuck to the text-only theme of the rest of the chapter, but text-only toolbars simply don't make sense. When is the last time you saw a text-only toolbar? Doesn't happen too often, does it?

The process of creating an `ImageList` is extremely easy with Visual Studio .NET, though behind the scenes a lot is taking place. The steps to create an `ImageList` are as follows:

1. Drag and drop an `ImageList` to the form you want to place images on.

2. Within the `ImageList` property, click the ellipses button next to the Images property. This will bring up a dialog box similar to the one shown in Figure 10-6.

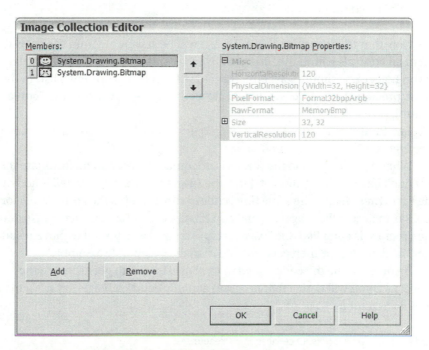

Figure 10-6. The Image Collection Editor dialog box

3. Click the Add button and then navigate to and open the image file within the present Open File dialog box.

4. Repeat step 3 for all desired images.

5. Click the OK button.

Once you have added the images to the ImageList, there are three ImageList properties that you may need to configure:

-   ColorDepth is a ColorDepth object that represents the color depth of the icon. The default is 4-bit color so most likely you will want to change this property.

-   ImageSize is a Size object that represents the size of the images contained in the list. The default is 16×16 but the maximum is 256×256. Note that all images in the list are the same size.

-   TransparentColor is a Color object that represents the transparent color. You probably will be able to ignore this property, as the default is Transparent.

Now that the ImageList is available, it will be selectable from the drop-down list of all controls within the form that use ImageLists. For a control to get access to the ImageList, simply select the ImageList from this drop-down list. In the case of the preceding example, you would select the ImageList within the ToolBar control.

The final step is to update the ImageIndex within the ToolBarButton property (see Figure 10-6) to the desired image.

What happens behind the scenes is not quite as easy, and it's fortunate that you don't have to worry about it. First, the ImageList that you created is added to the Form1.resx file. At the same time, code is also added to the Form1.h file for the ToolBar to access the ImageList and add images to the ToolBarButtons. Next, when the program is compiled, the ImageList is serialized and placed within a resource file. The resource file then gets embedded in the executable assembly.

If you examine the code added to the Form1.h file to get access to the ImageList, you will notice that program actually gets the ImageList from the executable assembly:

```
System::Resources::ResourceManager * resources =
    new System::Resources::ResourceManager(__typeof(ToolBarEx::Form1));
//...
this->imageList->ImageStream =
    (dynamic_cast<System::Windows::Forms::ImageListStreamer * >
    (resources->GetObject(S"imageList.ImageStream")));
```

You will examine resources and how the preceding code works in much more detail in Chapter 17.

Figure 10-7 shows what ToolBarEx.exe looks like when you execute it.

Figure 10-7. The emotional toolbar

StatusBar

The StatusBar is an easy-to-use control for displaying status information to the user. You will find the status bar at the bottom of many Windows applications. There are two approaches to the status bar provided by the .NET Framework class library. You can use that status bar as one long text area within which you can place your status information, or you can break the status bar into panels. Each of these panels can be updated independently.

In most cases when you work with the StatusBar, you will only have to deal with three properties. If you are working with the status bar as one long area to enter text into, then you only really have to worry about placing your status information into the Text property. If, on the other hand, you are breaking your status bar into panels, you need to work with Panels property, which you will place your collection of StatusBarPanels components and the ShowPanels property, which turns these panels on and off.

Creating a status bar as a single long text area is trivial. Either drag the StatusBar control to the design form or enter the following code:

```
private:
StatusBar *statusbar;
//...In constructor
statusBar = new StatusBar();
Controls->Add(statusBar);
```

```
//...Later when you want to update the status
StatusBar->Text = S"status info goes here";
```

Creating a status bar using panels is not much more difficult, but the StatusBarPanel does have a number of properties available for configuration. Some of the more common properties are as follows:

- Alignment is a HorizontalAlignment enum that represents how the text and/or icon are aligned (Left, Right, or Center) within the panel. The default is HorizonalAlignment::Left. It should be noted that there is no way of aligning the text and the icon separately, because the icon will always be positioned to the left of the text.

- AutoSize is a StatusBarPanelAutoSize enum that represents whether the panel is a fixed size (None), fits to the text and or icon content of the panel (Content), or adjusts to the slack space (Spring). The default is StatusBarPanelAutoSize::None, meaning that the panel is a fixed size.

- BorderStyle is a StatusBarPanelBorderStyle enum that represents the border style of the panel. The default is no border being displayed or StatusBarPanelBorderStyle::None. Other options are Raised and Sunken.

- Icon is an Icon that represents the icon to display on the panel.

- MinWidth is an Int32 that represents the minimum allowable width for the panel in pixels. The value must be greater than zero. This property is used in conjunction with the AutoSize property so that a panel will not autosize to one that is too small.

- Parent is a StatusBar that represents the parent of the panel.

- Text is a String that represents the text displayed on the panel.

- ToolTip is a String that represents the ToolTip associated with the panel.

- Width is an Int32 that represents the width of the panel in pixels. The value must be greater than zero. If AutoSize is enabled, then this property reflects the actual autosized width of the panel.

Listing 10-6 shows the creation of the status bar with panels. The status information displayed is the mouse *x, y* location and the last mouse button pressed while within the client area of the form.

Listing 10-6. Status Bar Display of x, y Coordinates

```
namespace StatusBar1
{
    using namespace System;
    using namespace System::ComponentModel;
    using namespace System::Collections;
    using namespace System::Windows::Forms;
    using namespace System::Data;
    using namespace System::Drawing;

    public __gc class Form1 : public System::Windows::Forms::Form
    {
    public:
        Form1(void)
        //...
    protected:
        void Dispose(Boolean disposing)
        //...
    private: System::Windows::Forms::StatusBar *  statusBar;
    private: System::Windows::Forms::StatusBarPanel *  statusButtons;
    private: System::Windows::Forms::StatusBarPanel *  statusXCoord;
    private: System::Windows::Forms::StatusBarPanel *  statusYCoord;
    private: System::ComponentModel::Container * components;

        void InitializeComponent(void)
        {
            this->statusBar = new System::Windows::Forms::StatusBar();
            this->statusButtons = new System::Windows::Forms::StatusBarPanel();
            this->statusXCoord = new System::Windows::Forms::StatusBarPanel();
            this->statusYCoord = new System::Windows::Forms::StatusBarPanel();
            (dynamic_cast<System::ComponentModel::ISupportInitialize * >
            (this->statusButtons))->BeginInit();
            (dynamic_cast<System::ComponentModel::ISupportInitialize * >
            (this->statusXCoord))->BeginInit();
            (dynamic_cast<System::ComponentModel::ISupportInitialize * >
            (this->statusYCoord))->BeginInit();
            this->SuspendLayout();
            //
            // statusBar
            //
            this->statusBar->Name = S"statusBar";
            System::Windows::Forms::StatusBarPanel* __mcTemp__1[] =
```

```
                      new System::Windows::Forms::StatusBarPanel*[3];
            __mcTemp__1[0] = this->statusButtons;
            __mcTemp__1[1] = this->statusXCoord;
            __mcTemp__1[2] = this->statusYCoord;
            this->statusBar->Panels->AddRange(__mcTemp__1);
            this->statusBar->ShowPanels = true;
            //
            // statusButtons
            //
            this->statusButtons->AutoSize =
                   System::Windows::Forms::StatusBarPanelAutoSize::Spring;
            //
            // statusXCoord
            //
            this->statusXCoord->Width = 50;
            //
            // statusYCoord
            //
            this->statusYCoord->Width = 50;
            //
            // Form1
            //
            this->AutoScaleBaseSize = System::Drawing::Size(6, 15);
            this->ClientSize = System::Drawing::Size(300, 322);
            this->Controls->Add(this->statusBar);
            this->Name = S"Form1";
            this->Text = S"Status Bar Mouse Tracking";
            this->MouseDown +=
      new System::Windows::Forms::MouseEventHandler(this, Form1_MouseDown);
            this->MouseMove +=
      new System::Windows::Forms::MouseEventHandler(this, Form1_MouseMove);
            (dynamic_cast<System::ComponentModel::ISupportInitialize * >
            (this->statusButtons))->EndInit();
            (dynamic_cast<System::ComponentModel::ISupportInitialize * >
            (this->statusXCoord))->EndInit();
            (dynamic_cast<System::ComponentModel::ISupportInitialize * >
            (this->statusYCoord))->EndInit();
            this->ResumeLayout(false);
        }
    private:
        System::Void Form1_MouseMove(System::Object *  sender,
                    System::Windows::Forms::MouseEventArgs *  e)
        {
```

```
                    // x,y coords in second and third status bar panels
                    statusXCoord->Text = String::Format("X={0}", __box(e->X));
                    statusYCoord->Text = String::Format("Y={0}", __box(e->Y));
               }
          private:
               System::Void Form1_MouseDown(System::Object *  sender,
                            System::Windows::Forms::MouseEventArgs *  e)
               {
                    // clicked mouse button in first status bar panel
                    if (e->Button == MouseButtons::Right)
                         statusButtons->Text = S"Right";
                    else if (e->Button == MouseButtons::Left)
                         statusButtons->Text = S"Left";
                    else
                         statusButtons->Text = S"Middle";
               }
          };
     }
```

The preceding code builds a three-panel status bar. The first panel expands to take up any unclaimed area on the status bar due to StatusBarPanelAutoSize::Spring. The other two panels are 50 pixels wide. All of the panels are added to the StatusBar, which in turn is added to the form. The only tricky part of this program is remembering to set the property ShowPanels to true.

Figure 10-8 shows what StatusBar.exe looks like when you execute it.

Figure 10-8. A three-panel status bar

Bells and Whistles Controls

You'll finish off looking at Win Form controls by exploring some fun controls that you may not use that often but that can occasionally come in handy.

PictureBox

The PictureBox is a handy little control for displaying an existing image file. What makes it really cool is that it has built-in support for bitmaps, metafiles, and icons and .jpg, .gif, and .png files. You implement all of them the same way:

1. Drag and drop the PictureBox to your Win Form.

2. Update the Image property in the PictureBox's Properties view with the location of your file using the provided Open dialog box.

Like all controls, PictureBox provides properties to manipulate itself. In most cases you will only have to worry about the following:

- BorderStyle is a BorderStyle enum that represents the border to surround your image. Three borders are available: Fixed3D, FixedSingle, and the default None.

- Image is an Image object that represents the image to be displayed. The Image object supports bitmaps, metafiles, and icons and .jpg, .gif, and .png files.

- Size is a Size object that represents the height and width of the control. If the SizeMode is set to StretchImage, then the images inside will stretch or shrink to fit this size.

- SizeMode is a PictureBoxSizeMode that represents how the image will be displayed. The four modes are AutoSize, which forces the control to be the same size as the image; CenterImage, which centers the image within the control (the image will be clipped if the control is too small); the default Normal, which aligns the picture with the upper-left corner; and StretchImage, which make the image the same size as the control.

The code in Listing 10-7 shows a picture of my daughter in a StretchImage mode PictureBox.

Listing 10-7. PictureBox of Shaina

```
namespace PictureBoxEx
{
    using namespace System;
    using namespace System::ComponentModel;
    using namespace System::Collections;
    using namespace System::Windows::Forms;
    using namespace System::Data;
    using namespace System::Drawing;

    public __gc class Form1 : public System::Windows::Forms::Form
    {
    public:
        Form1(void)
        //...
    protected:
        void Dispose(Boolean disposing)
        //...
    private: System::Windows::Forms::PictureBox *  pictureBox;
    private: System::ComponentModel::Container * components;

        void InitializeComponent(void)
        {
            System::Resources::ResourceManager *  resources =
          new System::Resources::ResourceManager(__typeof(PictureBoxEx::Form1));
            this->pictureBox = new System::Windows::Forms::PictureBox();
            this->SuspendLayout();
            //
            // pictureBox
            //
            this->pictureBox->Anchor = (System::Windows::Forms::AnchorStyles)
                (((System::Windows::Forms::AnchorStyles::Top |
                    System::Windows::Forms::AnchorStyles::Bottom) |
                    System::Windows::Forms::AnchorStyles::Left) |
                    System::Windows::Forms::AnchorStyles::Right);
            this->pictureBox->BorderStyle =
                    System::Windows::Forms::BorderStyle::Fixed3D;
            this->pictureBox->Image = (dynamic_cast<System::Drawing::Image * >
                                    (resources->GetObject(S"pictureBox.Image")));
            this->pictureBox->Location = System::Drawing::Point(16, 16);
            this->pictureBox->Name = S"pictureBox";
            this->pictureBox->Size = System::Drawing::Size(272, 274);
```

```
        this->pictureBox->SizeMode =
            System::Windows::Forms::PictureBoxSizeMode::StretchImage;
        //
        // Form1
        //
        this->AutoScaleBaseSize = System::Drawing::Size(6, 15);
        this->ClientSize = System::Drawing::Size(304, 314);
        this->Controls->Add(this->pictureBox);
        this->Name = S"Form1";
        this->Text = S"Shaina Shoshana";
        this->ResumeLayout(false);
    }
};
}
```

You might want to note in the preceding code that Visual Studio .NET creates a resource of the PictureBox's image and places it within the assembly in a similar fashion to the ImageList, instead of referencing the file. If you don't want the image placed in the assembly for some reason, then you'll have to code the updating of the Image property manually with code similar to this:

```
this->pictureBox->Image = new Drawing::Bitmap(S"ShainaFace.jpg");
```

Figure 10-9 shows what PictureEx.exe looks like when you execute it.

Figure 10-9. A PictureBox of Shaina

MonthCalendar

The `MonthCalendar` is a neat little control that provides the ability to display a month to the user and then allow the user to do things such as navigate from month to month and select a year, month, day, or range of days. Another feature of the `MonthCalendar` control is it allows the user to highlight specific dates on the control, either on an annual, monthly, or specific single-day basis.

Like all controls, you configure `MonthCalendar` using properties. Here are some of the most commonly used properties:

- `AnnuallyBoldedDates` is an array of `DateTime` objects that represents which dates to bold every year.

- `BoldedDates` is an array of `DateTime` objects that represents which specific dates to bold.

- `CalendarDimensions` is a `System::Drawing::Size` that represents the number of rows and columns of months to be displayed within the control. The maximum number of months that can be displayed is 12.

- `MaxDate` is a `DateTime` that represents the maximum date that can be shown in the control. The default is 12/31/9998.

- `MaxSelectionCount` is an `Int32` that represents the maximum number of dates that can be selected at one time. The default is seven.

- `MinDate` is a `DateTime` that represents the minimum date that can be shown in the control. The default is 01/01/1753.

- `MonthlyBoldedDates` is an array of `DateTime` objects that represents which dates to bold every month.

- `SelectionEnd` is a `DateTime` that represents the end date of the selected date range. The default is `SelectionEnd` (equaling `SelectionStart`).

- `SelectionRange` is a `SelectionRange` that represents the selected range of dates within the control.

- `SelectionStart` is a `DateTime` that represents the start date of the selected date range.

- `ShowToday` is a `Boolean` that represents whether the date specified in the `TodayDate` property is shown at the bottom of the control.

- ShowTodayCircle is a Boolean that represents whether the date specified in the TodayDate property is circled.

- ShowWeekNumbers is a Boolean that represents whether the week number is displayed for each week.

- TodayDate is a DateTime representing any date that you want to be set as today's date. The default is the current system date.

- TodayDateSet is a Boolean that represents whether the TodayDate property was explicitly set.

Something you might want to note about the MonthCalendar control is that you can't select dates at random intervals. You can only select individual days or a range of days sequentially.

Listing 10-8 presents the MonthCalendar in action. The code simply shows a two-by-two MonthCalendar control that that generates DateChanged events when clicked. It also has two additional labels to display the selected day or ranges of days.

Listing 10-8. The MonthCalendar Control

```
namespace MonthCalendar1
{
    using namespace System;
    using namespace System::ComponentModel;
    using namespace System::Collections;
    using namespace System::Windows::Forms;
    using namespace System::Data;
    using namespace System::Drawing;

    public __gc class Form1 : public System::Windows::Forms::Form
    {
    public:
        Form1(void)
        //...
    protected:
        void Dispose(Boolean disposing)
        //...
    private: System::Windows::Forms::MonthCalendar *  monthCal;
    private: System::Windows::Forms::Label *  Start;
    private: System::Windows::Forms::Label *  End;
    private: System::ComponentModel::Container * components;
```

```
void InitializeComponent(void)
{
    this->monthCal = new System::Windows::Forms::MonthCalendar();
    this->Start = new System::Windows::Forms::Label();
    this->End = new System::Windows::Forms::Label();
    this->SuspendLayout();
    //
    // monthCalendar1
    //
    System::DateTime __mcTemp__1[] = new System::DateTime[1];
    __mcTemp__1[0] = System::DateTime(2002, 10, 31, 0, 0, 0, 0);
    this->monthCal->AnnuallyBoldedDates = __mcTemp__1;
    this->monthCal->CalendarDimensions = System::Drawing::Size(2, 2);
    this->monthCal->Location = System::Drawing::Point(8, 8);
    this->monthCal->MaxSelectionCount = 365;
    System::DateTime __mcTemp__2[] = new System::DateTime[2];
    __mcTemp__2[0] = System::DateTime(2002, 10, 1, 0, 0, 0, 0);
    __mcTemp__2[1] = System::DateTime(2002, 10, 15, 0, 0, 0, 0);
    this->monthCal->MonthlyBoldedDates = __mcTemp__2;
    this->monthCal->Name = S"monthCal";
    this->monthCal->ShowWeekNumbers = true;
    this->monthCal->TabIndex = 0;
    this->monthCal->DateChanged +=
new System::Windows::Forms::DateRangeEventHandler(this, monthCal_DateChanged);
    //
    // Start
    //
    this->Start->BorderStyle =
            System::Windows::Forms::BorderStyle::FixedSingle;
    this->Start->Location = System::Drawing::Point(150, 375);
    this->Start->Name = S"Start";
    this->Start->TabIndex = 1;
    //
    // End
    //
    this->End->BorderStyle =
            System::Windows::Forms::BorderStyle::FixedSingle;
    this->End->Location = System::Drawing::Point(290, 375);
    this->End->Name = S"End";
    this->End->TabIndex = 2;
    //
    // Form1
    //
```

```
        this->AutoScaleBaseSize = System::Drawing::Size(6, 15);
        this->ClientSize = System::Drawing::Size(540, 410);
        this->Controls->Add(this->End);
        this->Controls->Add(this->Start);
        this->Controls->Add(this->monthCal);
        this->Name = S"Form1";
        this->Text = S"Month Calendar";
        this->ResumeLayout(false);
    }
private:
    System::Void monthCal_DateChanged(System::Object *  sender,
                 System::Windows::Forms::DateRangeEventArgs *  e)
    {
        // Update start and end range labels when date changes
        Start->Text = e->Start.Date.ToShortDateString();
        End->Text   = e->End.Date.ToShortDateString();
    }
};
}
```

The only thing unusual about the preceding code is that you need to remember that System::DateTime is a value type structure and thus you don't create it on the stack with the new statement. Also, when you use them in a statement, you use the operator . and not ->.

Figure 10-10 shows what MonthCalendar.exe looks like when you execute it.

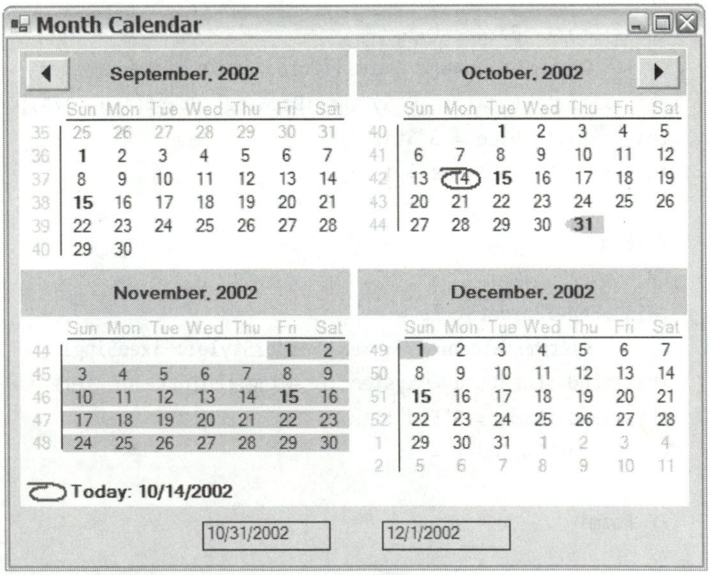

Figure 10-10. The MonthCalendar control

ErrorProvider

The ErrorProvider control is a nice piece of eye candy, especially when it comes to form validation, as you can use it to provide visual attention to data entry errors on the form. It has the additional bonus of being able to tell the user the reason for the data entry error. It provides this functionality by placing an icon next to the control in error and then providing a ToolTip-like pop-up displaying the reason for the error when the mouse pauses over the icon. Actually, it displays any text that you provide to it. In theory, this text should be the reason for the error.

Another interesting feature of the ErrorProvider control is that you need only one for your entire form. Yet, at the same time, it provides a specific error message for each control in error.

To implement the ErrorProvider control, drag and drop it to your design form from the Toolbox view. Then, when an error occurs in your validation process, place an error message along with a pointer to the control in error into the ErrorProvider.

To customize the look and feel of the ErrorProvider control, a few members are provided. These are the properties that you will most likely change:

- BlinkRate is an Int32 that represents the flash rate of the icon in milliseconds. The default is 250 milliseconds.

- BlinkStyle is an ErrorBlinkStyle enum that represents the style that the icon blinks. The possible values are AlwaysBlink, NeverBlink, and the default BlinkIfDifferentError.

- Icon is an Icon object that represents the icon to be displayed on error. The default is a red circle with a white exclamation point inside.

- SetError() is a method that sets the error for a specified control to display when the mouse pauses over the icon. When the message is an empty string, no icon or error is displayed.

- SetIconAlignment() is a method that sets the icon's location relative to a specified control. The default is MiddleRight.

- SetIconIconPadding() is a method that specifies the number of pixels of padding to add between an icon and a specified control. Because many controls have white space surrounding them, this control is not used too often.

Listing 10-9 shows the ErrorProvider control in action. The code is the start of a login form that validates that a name and password have been entered. When either of these fields is blank, the ErrorProvider control is added after the control on the form. Just for grins and giggles, I show how to place the icon on the left side of the control when validating on the Button control.

Listing 10-9. The ErrorProvider Control

```
namespace ErrProvider
{
    using namespace System;
    using namespace System::ComponentModel;
    using namespace System::Collections;
    using namespace System::Windows::Forms;
    using namespace System::Data;
    using namespace System::Drawing;


    public __gc class Form1 : public System::Windows::Forms::Form
    {
    public:
        Form1(void)
        //...
    protected:
        void Dispose(Boolean disposing)
        //...
    private: System::Windows::Forms::ErrorProvider *  eProvider;
    private: System::Windows::Forms::TextBox *  tbName;
    private: System::Windows::Forms::TextBox *  tbPword;
    private: System::Windows::Forms::Button *  bnLogin;
    private: System::Windows::Forms::Label *  lbName;
    private: System::Windows::Forms::Label *  lbPword;
    private: System::ComponentModel::Container * components;

        void InitializeComponent(void)
        {
            this->eProvider = new System::Windows::Forms::ErrorProvider();
            this->tbName = new System::Windows::Forms::TextBox();
            this->tbPword = new System::Windows::Forms::TextBox();
            this->bnLogin = new System::Windows::Forms::Button();
            this->lbName = new System::Windows::Forms::Label();
            this->lbPword = new System::Windows::Forms::Label();
            this->SuspendLayout();
            //
```

```
        // errorProvider1
        //
        this->eProvider->ContainerControl = this;
        //
        // tbName
        //
        this->tbName->Location = System::Drawing::Point(112, 32);
        this->tbName->Name = S"tbName";
        this->tbName->TabIndex = 0;
        this->tbName->Text = S"";
        this->tbName->Validating +=
new System::ComponentModel::CancelEventHandler(this, textBox_Validating);
        //
        // tbPword
        //
        this->tbPword->Location = System::Drawing::Point(112, 80);
        this->tbPword->Name = S"tbPword";
        this->tbPword->PasswordChar = '*';
        this->tbPword->TabIndex = 1;
        this->tbPword->Text = S"";
        this->tbPword->Validating +=
            new System::ComponentModel::CancelEventHandler(this,
                            textBox_Validating);
        //
        // button1
        //
        this->bnLogin->Location = System::Drawing::Point(80, 128);
        this->bnLogin->Name = S"bnLogin";
        this->bnLogin->TabIndex = 2;
        this->bnLogin->Text = S"&Login";
        this->bnLogin->Click +=
            new System::EventHandler(this, bnLogin_Click);
        //
        // lbName
        //
        this->lbName->Location = System::Drawing::Point(32, 40);
        this->lbName->Name = S"lbName";
        this->lbName->Size = System::Drawing::Size(64, 16);
        this->lbName->TabIndex = 0;
        this->lbName->Text = S"&Name";
        //
        // lbPword
        //
```

```
                    this->lbPword->Location = System::Drawing::Point(32, 88);
                    this->lbPword->Name = S"lbPword";
                    this->lbPword->Size = System::Drawing::Size(64, 16);
                    this->lbPword->TabIndex = 1;
                    this->lbPword->Text = S"&Password";
                    //
                    // Form1
                    //
                    this->AutoScaleBaseSize = System::Drawing::Size(6, 15);
                    this->ClientSize = System::Drawing::Size(256, 178);
                    this->Controls->Add(this->lbPword);
                    this->Controls->Add(this->lbName);
                    this->Controls->Add(this->bnLogin);
                    this->Controls->Add(this->tbPword);
                    this->Controls->Add(this->tbName);
                    this->Name = S"Form1";
                    this->Text = S"System Login";
                    this->ResumeLayout(false);
                }
            private:
                System::Void textBox_Validating(System::Object * sender,
                                        System::ComponentModel::CancelEventArgs * e)
                {
                    try
                    {
                        TextBox *tb = dynamic_cast<TextBox*>(sender);

                        if (tb->Text->Equals(""))
                            eProvider->SetError(tb, "**Error** Missing Entry!");
                        else
                            eProvider->SetError(tb, "");
                    }
                    catch (...)
                    {
                        // Not TextBox
                    }
                }
            private:
                System::Void bnLogin_Click(System::Object *sender, System::EventArgs *e)
                {
                        if (tbName->Text->Equals(""))
                            eProvider->SetError(tbName, "**Error** Missing Entry!");
```

```
        else
            eProvider->SetError(tbName, "");

        if (tbPword->Text->Equals(""))
        {
            // Place the icon on left side of control
            eProvider->SetIconAlignment(tbPword,

ErrorIconAlignment::MiddleLeft);
            eProvider->SetError(tbPword, "**Error** Missing Entry!");
        }
        else
            eProvider->SetError(tbPword, "");
    }
};
}
```

What you'll want to notice about the preceding example is the Validating event, which is raised whenever the next control receives focus. The next control must also have the CausesValidation property set to true.

Figure 10-11 shows what ErrProvider.exe looks like when you execute it.

Figure 10-11. The ErrorProvider control

NotifyIcon

If you've tried to add an icon to the notification area in your past life, you know that it wasn't a simple task. Well, with the .NET Framework, it is. All it takes is a drag and drop of the NotifyIcon control from the Toolbox view to your design form.

The `NotifyIcon` control also provides four properties that you'll probably change:

- `Icon` is an `Icon` object that represents the icon to display on the notification area. The default is `null`, which causes no icon to be displayed. (Why someone would do this, I'm not sure.)

- `Text` is a `String` that represents the `ToolTip` text to be displayed when the mouse pauses over the icon in the notification area. The default is `null`, which causes no text to be displayed.

- `ContextMenu` is a `ContentMenu` object that represents a pop-up menu displayed when the icon is right-clicked. The default is `null`, which causes no menu to be displayed. (I cover `ContentMenus` later in this chapter.)

- `Visible` is a `Boolean` that represents whether the icon is displayed in the notification area. The default is `true`, which displays the icon.

Listing 10-10 shows the `NotifyIcon` control in action. To give the example some life, I added two buttons. The first toggles the icon in the notification area and the second toggles the program display in the taskbar. When you write your own program, you may want to display either in the notification area or in the taskbar, but not in both.

Listing 10-10. The NotifyIcon Control

```
namespace NotifyIconEx
{
    using namespace System;
    using namespace System::ComponentModel;
    using namespace System::Collections;
    using namespace System::Windows::Forms;
    using namespace System::Data;
    using namespace System::Drawing;

    public __gc class Form1 : public System::Windows::Forms::Form
    {
    public:
        Form1(void)
        //...
    protected:
        void Dispose(Boolean disposing)
        //...
```

```
private: System::Windows::Forms::NotifyIcon *  notifyIcon;
private: System::Windows::Forms::Button *  bnNotify;
private: System::Windows::Forms::Button *  bnTaskbar;
private: System::ComponentModel::IContainer *  components;

    void InitializeComponent(void)
    {
        this->components = new System::ComponentModel::Container();
        System::Resources::ResourceManager *  resources =
      new System::Resources::ResourceManager(__typeof(NotifyIconEx::Form1));
        this->notifyIcon =
            new System::Windows::Forms::NotifyIcon(this->components);
        this->bnNotify = new System::Windows::Forms::Button();
        this->bnTaskbar = new System::Windows::Forms::Button();
        this->SuspendLayout();
        //
        // notifyIcon
        //
        this->notifyIcon->Icon = (dynamic_cast<System::Drawing::Icon * >
                            (resources->GetObject(S"notifyIcon.Icon")));
        this->notifyIcon->Text = S"Notify Icon Example";
        this->notifyIcon->Visible = true;
        //
        // bnNotify
        //
        this->bnNotify->Location = System::Drawing::Point(48, 32);
        this->bnNotify->Name = S"bnNotify";
        this->bnNotify->Size = System::Drawing::Size(144, 23);
        this->bnNotify->Text = S"Toggle Notify Icon";
        this->bnNotify->Click +=
            new System::EventHandler(this, bnNotify_Click);
        //
        // bnTaskbar
        //
        this->bnTaskbar->Location = System::Drawing::Point(48, 72);
        this->bnTaskbar->Name = S"bnTaskbar";
        this->bnTaskbar->Size = System::Drawing::Size(144, 24);
        this->bnTaskbar->Text = S"Toggle TaskBar Icon";
        this->bnTaskbar->Click +=
            new System::EventHandler(this, bnTaskbar_Click);
        //
        // Form1
        //
```

```
                    this->AutoScaleBaseSize = System::Drawing::Size(6, 15);
                    this->ClientSize = System::Drawing::Size(240, 154);
                    this->Controls->Add(this->bnTaskbar);
                    this->Controls->Add(this->bnNotify);
                    this->Icon = (dynamic_cast<System::Drawing::Icon * >
                                 (resources->GetObject(S"$this.Icon")));
                    this->Name = S"Form1";
                    this->Text = S"Notify Icon";
                    this->ResumeLayout(false);
                }
        private:
            System::Void bnNotify_Click(System::Object *  sender,
                                        System::EventArgs *  e)
            {
                notifyIcon->Visible = !notifyIcon->Visible;
            }

        private:
            System::Void bnTaskbar_Click(System::Object *  sender,
                                         System::EventArgs *  e)
            {
                this->ShowInTaskbar = ! this->ShowInTaskbar;
            }
        };
}
```

There really isn't much to the preceding code, and building it is a snap (or a few drags and drops, to be more accurate). You simply drag the NotifyIcon and two buttons to the form and change a few properties. Then you add the events to toggle the icon and taskbar entry.

You change the program's icon and the NotifyIcon's icon in the exact same way. Just double-click the app.ico in the Resource folder of Solution Explorer. This brings up a paint editor on which you can draw your icon.

TIP *Within an icon file are multiple icons of different sizes. Remember to change all the different sizes or you will get mismatching icons when the system uses icons of different sizes. (To switch to an icon of a different size, right-click in the graphic design view, outside of your icon drawing area, and select the Current Icon Image Types menu item. Then select the submenu item for the icon size you want to edit.)*

Figure 10-12 shows what NotifyIconEx.exe looks like when you execute it.

Figure 10-12. The NotifyIcon control

The Menu

I finish the discussion of .NET Framework Form controls with the menu. Though it's not really a control, because it isn't derived from the Control class, you implement a menu in the exact same way. Like a control, the menu is inherited from the Component class, so it inherits all the Component's functionality. The menu (as just mentioned) doesn't inherit from the Control class—in its place is the abstract Menu class.

Menu Basics

The creation of menus requires two classes: MainMenu and MenuItem. The MainMenu class and its members handle all the functionality associated with the bar that runs across the top of the form. You will usually not use many of MainMenu's members, except maybe the following two:

- GetForm() is a method that returns a pointer to a Form object that contains the menu. It will return null if the menu is not contained within a Form.

- MenuItems is a MenuItemCollection object that represents all the MenuItem objects associated with the menu. The default is null or no menu items exist in the menu.

The MenuItem class, with its associated properties, handles all the entries that make up the menu. Here are some of the more common properties:

- Checked is a Boolean that represents whether a check mark appears next to the menu item. The default is false, which means it won't display the check mark.

- Enabled is a Boolean that represents whether the menu item is enabled. The default is true, which means it can be accessed.

- Index is a zero-based Int32 that represents the index of the current menu item within its parent menu.

- Parent is a Menu object that represents the parent menu of the current menu item.

- RadioCheck is a Boolean that represents whether to display a radio-style check mark or a standard check mark. Note that no logic is provided to handle radio-style check marks. This property simply changes the image. You need to code the radio logic yourself.

- Shortcut is a Shortcut enum that represents the shortcut keystroke associated with the menu item. The default is Shortcut::None, which associates no shortcut.

- ShowShortCut is a Boolean that represents whether the shortcut is displayed. The default is true.

- Text is a String that represents the text to display for the menu item.

The steps involved in creating a menu are not difficult, especially if you're creating a static menu with the GUI design tool. On the other hand, laying out and keeping track of all the MenuItems for a runtime built menu can be a royal pain in the...(hmmm, I'm not allowed to say that, am I?). You'll start learning how to create a menu by hand by taking a look at the simplest menu (that actually does something) that you can create (see Listing 10-11). It is a MainMenu with two MenuItems. In truth, you could create a menu with one MenuItem, but then it would be a button in a menu's cloak and not a menu.

Listing 10-11. The Simplest Menu

```
namespace SimpleMenu
{
    using namespace System;
    using namespace System::ComponentModel;
    using namespace System::Collections;
    using namespace System::Windows::Forms;
    using namespace System::Data;
    using namespace System::Drawing;
```

```cpp
public __gc class Form1 : public System::Windows::Forms::Form
{
public:
    Form1(void)
    {
        InitializeComponent();

        // Create MenuItem
        exitItem = new MenuItem();
        exitItem->Text   = S"E&xit";
        exitItem->Click += new EventHandler(this, menuItem_Click);

        // Create Root MenuItem and submenu items
        fileMenu = new MenuItem();
        fileMenu->Text  = S"&File";
        fileMenu->MenuItems->Add(exitItem);

        // Create MainMenu and add root menuitem
        mainMenu = new MainMenu();
        mainMenu->MenuItems->Add(fileMenu);

        // Add MainMenu to Form
        Menu = this->mainMenu;
    }
protected:
    void Dispose(Boolean disposing)
    //...
private: MainMenu *mainMenu;
private: MenuItem *fileMenu;
private: MenuItem *exitItem;
private: System::ComponentModel::Container * components;

    void InitializeComponent(void)
    {
        this->components = new System::ComponentModel::Container();
        this->Size = System::Drawing::Size(300,300);
        this->Text = S"A simple Menu";
    }
private:
    void menuItem_Click(Object *sender, EventArgs *e)
    {
        if (sender == exitItem)
        {
```

```
                    Application::Exit();
            }
        }
    };
}
```

As you can see from the preceding code, the process of creating a menu is simply to create and then add MenuItems to a root MenuItem:

```
// Create MenuItem
exitItem = new MenuItem();
exitItem->Text   = S"E&xit";
exitItem->Click += new EventHandler(this, menuItem_Click);

// Create Root MenuItem
fileMenu = new MenuItem();
fileMenu->Text  = S"&File";

// Add MenuItem to Root MenuItem
fileMenu->MenuItems->Add(exitItem);
```

Add the root MenuItem to the MainMenu:

```
mainMenu = new MainMenu();
mainMenu->MenuItems->Add(fileMenu);
```

Finally, add the MainMenu to the Form:

```
Menu = this->mainMenu;
```

All this is pretty straightforward. Figure 10-13 shows what SimpleMenu.exe looks like when you execute it.

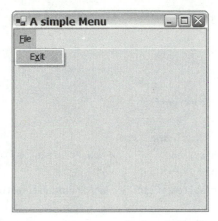

Figure 10-13. A simple menu

A menu handles events in a similar fashion as the button. The menu triggers click events for each MenuItem. You need to create an event handler to handle these events. You may have noticed in the example that you verify the MenuItem that generated the event. In the simple menu, as previously, this is a little redundant, but in larger menus you will probably have many MenuItems handled by the same handler. This checking of which MenuItem is how you go about processing each MenuItem uniquely. If this isn't clear, the next example expands on the concept a bit, which should make things clearer.

Oh, by the way, if you don't know, the Application::Exit() method stops execution of your program.

More Menu Features

Okay, you have the basics of the menu. Let's take a look at a menu (see Listing 10-12) that is more feature-rich, though still small in size. This example has two root menus, multiple sub-MenuItems, and nested sub-MenuItems.

Listing 10-12. A More Elaborate Menu

```
namespace ElaborateMenu
{
    using namespace System;
    using namespace System::ComponentModel;
    using namespace System::Collections;
    using namespace System::Windows::Forms;
    using namespace System::Data;
    using namespace System::Drawing;
```

```
public __gc class Form1 : public System::Windows::Forms::Form
{
public:
    Form1(void)
    {
        InitializeComponent();

        // Create "This" MenuItem
        file_do_this_Item          = new MenuItem();
        file_do_this_Item->Text    = S"Thi&s";
        file_do_this_Item->Click += new EventHandler(this, menuItem_Click);

        // Create "That" MenuItem
        file_do_that_Item          = new MenuItem();
        file_do_that_Item->Text    = S"Tha&t";
        file_do_that_Item->Click += new EventHandler(this, menuItem_Click);

        // Create "Other Thing" MenuItem
        file_do_other_Item         = new MenuItem();
        file_do_other_Item->Text   = S"Othe&r Thing";
        file_do_other_Item->Click += new EventHandler(this, menuItem_Click);

        // Create "DO" MenuItem
        file_do_Item        = new MenuItem();
        file_do_Item->Text  = S"&Do";

        // Add sub MenuItems
        file_do_Item->MenuItems->Add(file_do_this_Item);
        file_do_Item->MenuItems->Add(file_do_that_Item);
        file_do_Item->MenuItems->Add(file_do_other_Item);

        // Create "Exit" MenuItem
        file_exit_Item          = new MenuItem();
        file_exit_Item->Text    = S"E&xit";
        file_exit_Item->Click += new EventHandler(this, menuItem_Click);

        // Create "File" MenuItem
        file_Menu        = new MenuItem();
        file_Menu->Text  = S"&File";

        // Add Sub MenuItems
        file_Menu->MenuItems->Add(file_do_Item);
        file_Menu->MenuItems->Add(new MenuItem(S"-"));  // <- Separator
        file_Menu->MenuItems->Add(file_exit_Item);
```

```
        // Create "About" MenuItem
        help_about_Item           = new MenuItem();
        help_about_Item->Text    = S"&About";
        help_about_Item->Click += new EventHandler(this, menuItem_Click);

        // Create "Help" MenuItem
        help_Menu           = new MenuItem();
        help_Menu->Text   = S"&Help";

        // Add Sub MenuItems
        help_Menu->MenuItems->Add(help_about_Item);

        // Create MainMenu
        main_Menu = new MainMenu();

        // Add Sub MenuItems
        main_Menu->MenuItems->Add(file_Menu);
        main_Menu->MenuItems->Add(help_Menu);

        // Add MainMenu to Form
        Menu = this->main_Menu;
    }
protected:
    void Dispose(Boolean disposing)
    //...
private: MainMenu *main_Menu;
private: MenuItem *file_Menu;
private: MenuItem *file_do_Item;
private: MenuItem *file_do_this_Item;
private: MenuItem *file_do_that_Item;
private: MenuItem *file_do_other_Item;
private: MenuItem *file_exit_Item;
private: MenuItem *help_Menu;
private: MenuItem *help_about_Item;
private: System::ComponentModel::Container * components;

    void InitializeComponent(void)
    {
        this->components = new System::ComponentModel::Container();
        this->Size = System::Drawing::Size(300,300);
        this->Text = S"A Less Simple Menu";
    }
```

```
    private:
        void menuItem_Click(Object *sender, EventArgs *e)
        {
            if (sender == file_exit_Item)
            {
                Application::Exit();
            }
            else if (sender == help_about_Item)
            {
                MessageBox::Show(S"Main Menu v.1.0.0.0");
            }
            else
            {
                MessageBox::Show(S"Another MenuItem");
            }
        }
    };
}
```

Figure 10-14 shows what ElaborateMenu.exe looks like when you execute it.

Figure 10-14. A more elaborate menu

The first thing you may notice is that there's a lot of code there for such a small menu. Now think about your favorite applications and how big their menus are. Because there's so much code, you'll probably end up building most of your menus using the GUI design tool, even if it's just to template them out if you plan to ultimately build your menus at runtime.

First, creating a menu hierarchy is similar to the tree hierarchy you looked at earlier. MenuItems can be added to another MenuItem. (You already saw this, by the way, when you added MenuItems to the root MenuItem.) Adding a MenuItem to another MenuItem builds the hierarchy:

```
file_do_this_Item          = new MenuItem();
file_do_this_Item->Text    = S"Thi&s";
file_do_this_Item->Click += new EventHandler(this, menuItem_Click);
//...Other Sub MenuItems

file_do_Item          = new MenuItem();
file_do_Item->Text    = S"&Do";
file_do_Item->MenuItems->Add(file_do_this_Item);
file_do_Item->MenuItems->Add(file_do_that_Item);
file_do_Item->MenuItems->Add(file_do_other_Item);
```

Something you may want to notice is that there's no handling of the Click event on a MenuItem that adds other MenuItems. The event is not sent, so handling it does nothing.

To create a separator, simply create a MenuItem with a hyphen (-) as a parameter.

```
file_Menu->MenuItems->Add(new MenuItem(S"-"));   // <- Separator
```

Managed C++ garbage collection comes in handy in a little trick that I use with menu separators. Notice that I add them to the parent MenuItem without creating a variable to store it in. You can't do anything with a separator, so there's no reason to keep track of it. That's the garbage collector's job.

A Radio-Checked ContextMenu

Menus don't always appear from the top of the form. Sometimes they drop down from buttons or appear when you right-click items. This type of menu is called a *context menu*.

Implementing a context menu is not much different than implementing the standard main menu. The only real difference is that you replace the MainMenu class with the ContextMenu class. And you attach the menu to the ContentMenu property of the control or Form.

Check marks on the ContextMenu (or the MainMenu, for that matter) are not handled automatically. Instead, you have to do a little work of your own, and I stress *little*. Listing 10-13 shows the implementation of a ContextMenu attached to a form. It also shows how to implement a radio-checked menu.

Listing 10-13. A Radio-Checked Menu

```
namespace RadioMenu
{
    using namespace System;
    using namespace System::ComponentModel;
    using namespace System::Collections;
    using namespace System::Windows::Forms;
    using namespace System::Data;
    using namespace System::Drawing;


    public __gc class Form1 : public System::Windows::Forms::Form
    {
    public:
        Form1(void)
        {
            InitializeComponent();

            // Default first menu item as checked
            checkMenuItem = menuItem1;
            checkMenuItem->Checked = true;
        }


    protected:
        void Dispose(Boolean disposing)
        //...
    private: System::Windows::Forms::MenuItem *  menuItem1;
    private: System::Windows::Forms::MenuItem *  menuItem2;
    private: System::Windows::Forms::MenuItem *  menuItem3;
    private: System::Windows::Forms::ContextMenu *  contextMenu;
    private: System::ComponentModel::Container * components;
    private: MenuItem *checkMenuItem;  // The holder of the check mark  private:

        void InitializeComponent(void)
        {
            this->contextMenu = new System::Windows::Forms::ContextMenu();
            this->menuItem1 = new System::Windows::Forms::MenuItem();
            this->menuItem2 = new System::Windows::Forms::MenuItem();
            this->menuItem3 = new System::Windows::Forms::MenuItem();
            //
            // contextMenu
            //
            System::Windows::Forms::MenuItem* __mcTemp__1[] =
```

```
                        new System::Windows::Forms::MenuItem*[3];
        __mcTemp__1[0] = this->menuItem1;
        __mcTemp__1[1] = this->menuItem2;
        __mcTemp__1[2] = this->menuItem3;
        this->contextMenu->MenuItems->AddRange(__mcTemp__1);
        //
        // menuItem1
        //
        this->menuItem1->Index = 0;
        this->menuItem1->RadioCheck = true;
        this->menuItem1->Text = S"Item one";
        this->menuItem1->Click +=
                new System::EventHandler(this, menuItem_Click);
        //
        // menuItem2
        //
        this->menuItem2->Index = 1;
        this->menuItem2->RadioCheck = true;
        this->menuItem2->Text = S"Item Two";
        this->menuItem2->Click +=
                new System::EventHandler(this, menuItem_Click);
        //
        // menuItem3
        //
        this->menuItem3->Index = 2;
        this->menuItem3->RadioCheck = true;
        this->menuItem3->Text = S"Item Three";
        this->menuItem3->Click +=
                new System::EventHandler(this, menuItem_Click);
        //
        // Form1
        //
        this->AutoScaleBaseSize = System::Drawing::Size(6, 15);
        this->ClientSize = System::Drawing::Size(292, 270);
        this->ContextMenu = this->contextMenu;
        this->Name = S"Form1";
        this->Text = S"ContextMenu - Right Click Form";
    }
private:
    void menuItem_Click(Object *sender, System::EventArgs *e)
    {
        // Uncheck Original checked MenuItem
        checkMenuItem->Checked = false;
```

```
            // Set the check menu to the selected MenuItem
            checkMenuItem = dynamic_cast<MenuItem*>(sender);
            // Check the new MenuItem
            checkMenuItem->Checked = true;
        }
    };
}
```

Most of the preceding code was autogenerated by the design tool as I created this example using the Menu design tool. Using the Menu design tool is pretty self-explanatory. The only tricky thing (at least for me) is making sure you drag the correct menu control to the design form and that you select the correct menu when you are editing (especially if the menus are similar). If you are creating a main menu, then you need to drag the MainMenu control. If you are creating a context menu (as you are in the preceding code), then you need to drag the ContextMenu control. After that, the steps for building a menu are virtually the same for all menus. All you have to do is type in the menu item text in place and then add event handlers.

You don't need to add much code to handle the radio check mark. First, you need an extra MenuItem to hold a pointer to the currently checked menu item:

```
MenuItem *checkMenuItem;   // The holder of the check mark
```

Next, you assign to this menu item then actual MenuItem that will start off with the check. Then, check the MenuItem:

```
checkMenuItem = menuItemOne;
checkMenuItem->Checked = true;
```

Finally, in the Click event of the menu, uncheck checkMenuItem, assign the checkMenuItem with the currently selected MenuItem, and then check the checkMenuItem:

```
checkMenuItem->Checked = false;
checkMenuItem = dynamic_cast<MenuItem*>(sender);
checkMenuItem->Checked = true;
```

I did warn you that there wasn't much to it. Figure 10-15 shows what the preceding example code looks like when you execute it.

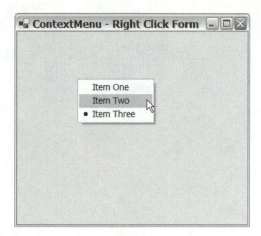

Figure 10-15. A radio-checked menu

Dialog Boxes

First things first: Dialog boxes are just Forms that are called or started differently and can, if you want, pass and/or return data and return a DialogResult. That's it! Forget what you once knew about dialog boxes (if you were a classic Visual C++ MFC programmer)—things have gotten a lot easier.

Everything that you've learned so far in this chapter works the same for dialog boxes. All you need to do is learn a couple of optional features and how to call the dialog box itself, and then you'll know all you need to develop dialog boxes.

Custom Dialog Boxes

Building a custom dialog box is almost exactly the same as creating the main Win Form, except it requires two additional steps. Here are the steps you follow to create a custom dialog box:

1. Right-click the project folder within Solution Explorer.

2. Select Add New Item from the drop-down menu item Add. A dialog box similar to the one in Figure 10-16 appears.

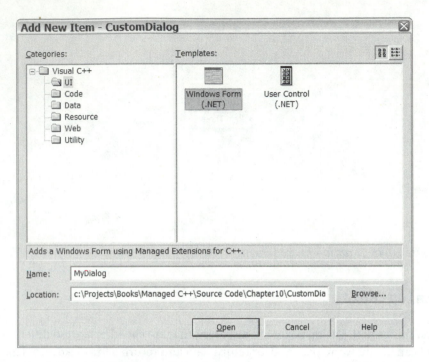

Figure 10-16. The Add New Item dialog box

3. Select the Windows Form (.NET) icon from the Templates panel and give the dialog box a name. I used **MyDialog**.

4. Click Open. This will provide you with an empty form in the design window.

5. Build the form exactly as you do the main form.

You can now work with this form in exactly the same way as you do with the application's main form, except for a couple of minor things.

The first minor difference is that if you want to pass information to the dialog box or get information back from the dialog box, you need to add properties to your form to get and set the information:

```
public:
__property void set_PassedValue(String *value)  // PassedValue property
{
    tbPassedValue->Text = value;
}
__property String *get_PassedValue()
{
    return tbPassedValue->Text;
}
```

Another method of doing this would be to change the constructor to send data to the dialog box, but I prefer properties. Plus, if you use the constructor to pass data to the dialog box, you still need to create properties or methods to send data back, so why not bite the bullet and use properties in both cases? This method is clean and safe (because you can verify the validity of the passed data) and it's easy to use.

The second change that you can make, which is totally optional, is to change the style of the dialog box to look more like a dialog box and less like a form:

```
this->FormBorderStyle =
        System::Windows::Forms::FormBorderStyle::FixedToolWindow;
// Or
this->FormBorderStyle =
        System::Windows::Forms::FormBorderStyle::SizableToolWindow;
```

The third difference is that you want to have any buttons that close your dialog box return a DialogResult. The .NET Framework class library provides a number of possible DialogResults (see Table 10-2).

Table 10-2. DialogResults

TYPE	DESCRIPTION
Abort	Return the value Abort. Usually you will have a button labeled Abort to handle this.
Cancel	Return the value Cancel. This is the value returned when the Esc key is pressed (if enabled) or the close dialog box button is clicked. Also, you will have a button on the form labeled Cancel.
Ignore	Return the value Ignore. Usually you will have a button labeled Ignore to handle this.
No	Return the value No. Usually you will have a button labeled No to handle this.
None	Nothing is returned. You will use this with a modal dialog box, which is discussed later.
OK	Return the value OK. This is the value returned when the Enter key is pressed (if enabled). Also, you will have a button on the form labeled OK.
Retry	Return the value Retry. Usually you will have a button labeled Retry to handle this.
Yes	Return the value Yes. Usually you will have a button labeled Yes to handle this.

To return a DialogResult value to the calling form, you need to assign, to the button that will end the dialog, the desired DialogResult value:

```
bnOK->DialogResult = DialogResult::OK;
```

When the button is clicked, it will automatically return the DialogResult it was set to (DialogResult::OK is set in the preceding code). By the way, you can still handle the Click event, if you need to, for the button. (You can even change its DialogResult in the handler if you really want to. For example, you could turn DialogResult::OK into DialogResult::Cancel if no text is entered in the dialog box.)

The final change you are probably going to want to make is to assign default buttons to respond to the Accept and Cancel conditions. You do this by assigning a button to the form's AcceptButton and CancelButton properties:

```
AcceptButton = bnOK;
CancelButton = bnCancel;
```

Once you have performed the preceding additional steps, you have a complete custom dialog box. Listing 10-14 shows the code of a custom dialog box that takes in some text, places it in a text box, allows it to be updated, and then returns the text back updated to the calling form. The dialog box also allows the user to abort or cancel the dialog box.

Listing 10-14. The MyDialog Class File

```
#pragma once

using namespace System;
using namespace System::ComponentModel;
using namespace System::Collections;
using namespace System::Windows::Forms;
using namespace System::Data;
using namespace System::Drawing;


namespace CustomDialog
{
    public __gc class MyDialog : public System::Windows::Forms::Form
    {
    public:
        MyDialog(void)
        {
            InitializeComponent();
        }

    public:
        __property void set_PassedValue(String *value)  // PassedValue property
        {
            tbPassedValue->Text = value;
        }
        __property String *get_PassedValue()
        {
            return tbPassedValue->Text;
        }

    protected:
        void Dispose(Boolean disposing)
        {
            if (disposing && components)
            {
                components->Dispose();
```

```
        }
        __super::Dispose(disposing);
    }

private: System::Windows::Forms::Button *  bnOK;
private: System::Windows::Forms::Button *  bnAbort;
private: System::Windows::Forms::Button *  bnCancel;
private: System::Windows::Forms::TextBox *  tbPassedValue;
private: System::ComponentModel::Container * components;

    void InitializeComponent(void)
    {
        this->tbPassedValue = new System::Windows::Forms::TextBox();
        this->bnOK = new System::Windows::Forms::Button();
        this->bnAbort = new System::Windows::Forms::Button();
        this->bnCancel = new System::Windows::Forms::Button();
        this->SuspendLayout();
        //
        // tbPassedValue
        //
        this->tbPassedValue->Location = System::Drawing::Point(15, 25);
        this->tbPassedValue->Name = S"tbPassedValue";
        this->tbPassedValue->Size = System::Drawing::Size(250, 22);
        this->tbPassedValue->TabIndex = 0;
        this->tbPassedValue->Text = S"";
        //
        // bnOK
        //
        this->bnOK->DialogResult =
                System::Windows::Forms::DialogResult::OK;
        this->bnOK->Location = System::Drawing::Point(15, 72);
        this->bnOK->Name = S"bnOK";
        this->bnOK->TabIndex = 1;
        this->bnOK->Text = S"OK";
        //
        // bnAbort
        //
        this->bnAbort->DialogResult =
                System::Windows::Forms::DialogResult::Abort;
        this->bnAbort->Location = System::Drawing::Point(104, 72);
        this->bnAbort->Name = S"bnAbort";
        this->bnAbort->TabIndex = 2;
```

```
            this->bnAbort->Text = S"Abort";
            //
            // bnCancel
            //
            this->bnCancel->DialogResult =
                    System::Windows::Forms::DialogResult::Cancel;
            this->bnCancel->Location = System::Drawing::Point(192, 72);
            this->bnCancel->Name = S"bnCancel";
            this->bnCancel->TabIndex = 3;
            this->bnCancel->Text = S"Cancel";
            //
            // MyDialog
            //
            this->AcceptButton = this->bnOK;
            this->AutoScaleBaseSize = System::Drawing::Size(6, 15);
            this->CancelButton = this->bnCancel;
            this->ClientSize = System::Drawing::Size(300, 120);
            this->Controls->Add(this->bnCancel);
            this->Controls->Add(this->bnAbort);
            this->Controls->Add(this->bnOK);
            this->Controls->Add(this->tbPassedValue);
            this->FormBorderStyle =
                    System::Windows::Forms::FormBorderStyle::FixedToolWindow;
            this->Name = S"MyDialog";
            this->Text = S"My Custom Dialog";
            this->ResumeLayout(false);
        }
    };
}
```

Figure 10-17 shows what the preceding example looks like when you execute it.

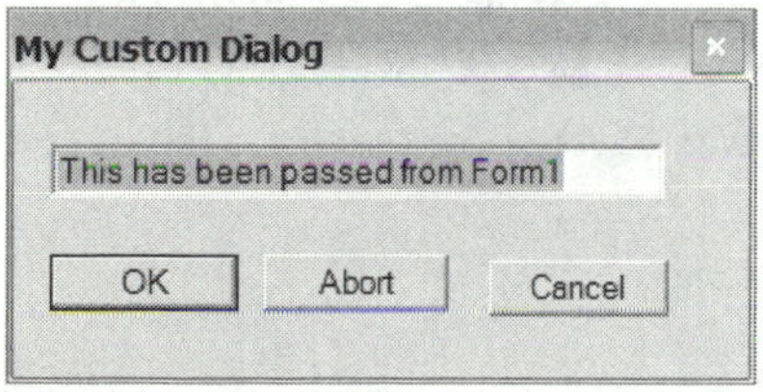

Figure 10-17. A custom dialog box

Now let's take a look at the code to implement a custom dialog box (see Listing 10-15). The example calls the dialog box by clicking anywhere in the form.

Listing 10-15. Implementing a Custom Dialog Box

```
namespace CustomDialog
{
    using namespace System;
    using namespace System::ComponentModel;
    using namespace System::Collections;
    using namespace System::Windows::Forms;
    using namespace System::Data;
    using namespace System::Drawing;

    public __gc class Form1 : public System::Windows::Forms::Form
    {
    public:
        Form1(void)
        //...
    protected:
        void Dispose(Boolean disposing)
        //...
    private: System::Windows::Forms::Label *  lbRetVal;
    private: System::Windows::Forms::Label *  lbRetString;
    private: System::ComponentModel::Container * components;

        void InitializeComponent(void)
        {
            this->lbRetVal = new System::Windows::Forms::Label();
            this->lbRetString = new System::Windows::Forms::Label();
            this->SuspendLayout();
            //
            // lbRetVal
            //
            this->lbRetVal->Location = System::Drawing::Point(32, 40);
            this->lbRetVal->Name = S"lbRetVal";
            this->lbRetVal->Size = System::Drawing::Size(224, 23);
            //
            // lbRetString
            //
            this->lbRetString->Location = System::Drawing::Point(32, 88);
            this->lbRetString->Name = S"lbRetString";
            this->lbRetString->Size = System::Drawing::Size(224, 23);
```

```
        //
        // Form1
        //
        this->AutoScaleBaseSize = System::Drawing::Size(6, 15);
        this->ClientSize = System::Drawing::Size(292, 270);
        this->Controls->Add(this->lbRetString);
        this->Controls->Add(this->lbRetVal);
        this->Name = S"Form1";
        this->Text = S"Click Form to get dialog";
        this->Click += new System::EventHandler(this, Form1_Click);
        this->ResumeLayout(false);
    }
private:
    System::Void Form1_Click(System::Object * sender, System::EventArgs * e)
    {
        MyDialog *mydialog = new MyDialog();
        mydialog->PassedValue = S"This has been passed from Form1";

        if (mydialog->ShowDialog() == DialogResult::OK)
            lbRetVal->Text = S"OK";
        else if (mydialog->DialogResult == DialogResult::Abort)
            lbRetVal->Text = S"Abort";
        else
            lbRetVal->Text = S"Cancel";

        lbRetString->Text = mydialog->PassedValue;
    }
};
}
```

Figure 10-18 shows what the preceding example looks like when you execute it.

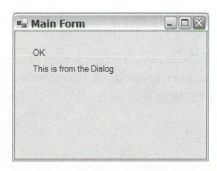

Figure 10-18. Calling a custom dialog box

Not much of a change, is there? First, you create an instance of the dialog box:

```
MyDialog *mydialog = new MyDialog();
```

Optionally, you can pass all the data you want to the dialog box:

```
mydialog->PassedValue = S"This has been passed from Form1";
```

Then you call the dialog box in one of two ways:

- ShowDialog()

- Show()

The first mode, ShowDialog(), is modal. In this mode, you wait for the dialog box to finish before you continue processing. Normally, you would check the DialogResult upon exit, as you do in the example, but that is not necessary:

```
if (mydialog->ShowDialog() == DialogResult::OK)
    lbRetVal->Text = S"OK";
else if (mydialog->DialogResult == DialogResult::Abort)
    lbRetVal->Text = S"Abort";
else
    lbRetVal->Text = S"Cancel";
```

The second mode, Show(), is modeless. In this mode, the dialog box opens and then returns control immediately back to its caller. You now have two threads of execution running. I cover threads in Chapter 16. I discuss modeless dialog boxes more then, but here is the code to start a modeless dialog box:

```
mydialog->Show();
```

The final thing you might do (again, this is optional) is grab the changed data out of the dialog box:

```
lbRetString->Text = mydialog->PassedValue;
```

By the way, I have been using Strings to pass data back and forth between the dialog box and the main application. This is not a restriction, though—you can use any data type you want.

Common Dialog Boxes

When you've worked with Windows for any length of time, you soon come to recognize some common dialog boxes that many applications use. The .NET Framework class library provides you easy access to using these same dialog boxes in your programs. Table 10-3 shows a list of the available common dialog boxes.

Table 10-3. The Common Dialog Boxes

DIALOG BOX	DESCRIPTION
ColorDialog	A dialog box to select a color
FontDialog	A dialog box to select a font
OpenFileDialog	A common Open File dialog box
PageSetupDialog	A dialog box that manipulates page settings, such as margins
PrintDialog	A dialog box to select a printer and the portion of the document you want to print
SaveFileDialog	A common File Save dialog box

You call the common dialog boxes in the same way you do the custom dialog box you just built. Listing 10-16 shows just how simple it is to call the ColorDialog. Calling all the other custom dialog boxes is done the same way.

Listing 10-16. Calling a Common ColorDialog

```
namespace ColorDlg
{
    using namespace System;
    using namespace System::ComponentModel;
    using namespace System::Collections;
    using namespace System::Windows::Forms;
    using namespace System::Data;
    using namespace System::Drawing;

    public __gc class Form1 : public System::Windows::Forms::Form
    {
    public:
        Form1(void)
        //...
    protected:
```

```
        void Dispose(Boolean disposing)
        //...
    private: System::ComponentModel::Container * components;

        void InitializeComponent(void)
        {
            this->AutoScaleBaseSize = System::Drawing::Size(6, 15);
            this->ClientSize = System::Drawing::Size(292, 270);
            this->Name = S"Form1";
            this->Text = S"Common Color Dialog - Click Form";
            this->Click += new System::EventHandler(this, Form1_Click);

        }
    private:
        System::Void Form1_Click(System::Object * sender, System::EventArgs * e)
        {
            ColorDialog *colordialog = new ColorDialog();

            if (colordialog->ShowDialog() == DialogResult::OK)
            {
                BackColor = colordialog->Color;
            }
        }
    };
}
```

There is nothing new or special here. First, check to make sure that the dialog box exited with the DialogResult of OK, and then set the color of the object you want changed with the value in the Color property of the ColorDialog.

Figure 10-19 shows what the example looks like when you execute it.

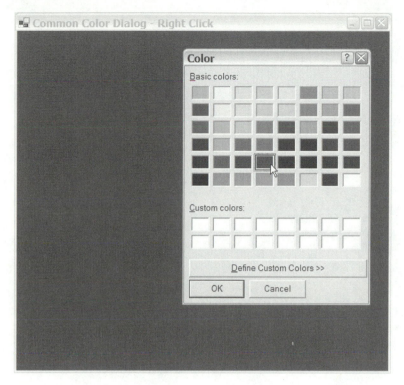

Figure 10-19. Calling a common ColorDialog

Summary

In this chapter you've covered many of the more powerful controls available to the Win Forms developer. You started off with a couple of views and then moved on to container controls. Next, you looked at the `ToolBar` and `StatusBar` controls. Then, to finish off the coverage of controls, you took a look at some of the more fun controls available. After your whirlwind tour of controls, you continued Win Form development with menus and then examined dialog boxes.

You should now be able to build a commercial-grade GUI interface that will impress all of your peers.

In the next chapter, you'll continue to examine the GUI interface provided by the .NET Framework class library, but this time you'll look at working with things such as fonts and prebuilt images, and drawing your own images from scratch.

Graphics Using GDI+

Using the .NET Framework class library's Win Form controls is not the only way to graphically present data to the user. Win Form controls are powerful, there is no doubt about it, but there are still going to be times when you will want more control over what exactly is displayed by the computer than Win Form controls can provide. This chapter covers another major method of displaying data to Windows applications: GDI+.

Unlike in a Win Forms application, when you write GDI+ code, you do it from scratch. There are no GUI drag-and-drop tools available to ease development, though you still lay out the form on which you plan to use GDI+ with the GUI design tool. The entire form does not need to be the target of the GDI+ images. Instead, GDI+ images can be painted on any control. Thus, you can develop a complex form and designate only a small portion of the form to working with GDI+.

In this chapter you will see just how easy it is to develop applications using GDI+. You will start with a high-level overview of GDI+ by looking at what it is and what it consists of. You will then look in detail at some of its functionality, such as fonts, pens, colors, and lines. Once you have covered the basics of GDI+, you will then look at more advanced topics, such as scrolling, optimization, and double buffering. Finally, to round off the discussion, you will discover that GDI+ is not just for displaying data to your monitor—you can also use it on printers.

At first glance, you might think this chapter is solely for the graphics guru. This is somewhat true, but many of the topics presented in this chapter are used by other areas of the .NET Framework class library such as Win Forms and Web Forms. For example, the Font class and the Color, Size, and Position structures are used frequently in Win Forms and Web Forms. Graphics gurus will want to read this chapter, and the average Win Forms or Web Forms developer should probably skim this chapter as well.

What Is GDI+?

In the simplest terms, *GDI+* is a set of namespaces that provides for the rendering of 2D graphics. For example, GDI+ provides support for colors, pens, fonts, image transformations, and antialiasing. GDI+ contains none of the advanced animation and 3D rendering features found in DirectX.

Notice that I didn't include the phrase "render to the video adaptor" in the preceding paragraph, because the device GDI+ renders to is immaterial. Well, almost immaterial—there are some differences that have to be accounted for between some devices. For example, video adaptors don't have to worry about form feeds, whereas printers obviously do. GDI+ is designed to support almost any graphical display device.

GDI+ originated from the Windows Graphical Device Interface (GDI), which has been around since Microsoft Windows 3.0. GDI+ shares many of the features of its predecessor, but with the .NET Framework class library there have been several improvements, thus the new name of GDI+.

A Quick Look at the GDI+ Namespaces

You can find the core functionality of GDI+ in the .NET Framework class library namespaces listed in Table 11-1.

Table 11-1. GDI+ Core Namespaces

NAMESPACE	DESCRIPTION
System::Drawing	This namespace is the core of GDI+. It consists of numerous classes to handle basic 2D rendering. It is also the location of the Graphics class from which all GDI+ functionality springs.
System::Drawing::Drawing2D	This namespace extends the 2D rendering capabilities of GDI+ by providing more advanced 2D rendering and vector graphics.
System::Drawing::Images	This namespace provides classes that allow direct manipulation of graphical images.
System::Drawing::Printing	This namespace provides classes that allow printing to a printer. It also provides classes to interact with the printer.
System::Drawing::Text	This namespace provides advanced font and font family functionality.

Primarily, most of the functionality that you'll be working with is found in the classes and structures in the System::Drawing namespace (see Table 11-2).

Table 11-2. Key System::Drawing Namespace Classes and Structures

CLASS/STRUCTURE	DESCRIPTION
Bitmap	A class that represents and provides limited manipulation capabilities for an image file with formats such as .bmp, .gif, and .jpg
Brush	A class used to specify the color and pattern to fill the interior of a shape such as a rectangle, ellipsis, or polygon
Brushes	A class made up of several static properties of predefined brushes
Color	A structure that represents a color
Font	A class that represents a font
FontFamily	A class that defines a group of fonts with the same basic design
Graphics	The core class of GDI+ that represents a drawing surface where you will place your text, shapes, and images
Icon	A class that represents a Windows icon
Image	An abstract base class used in all image type classes such as bitmaps and icons
Pen	A class used to specify the color, thickness, and pattern used to outline shapes
Pens	A class made up of several static properties of predefined pens
Point, PointF	A structure that represents an *x,y* coordinate as either a pair of Int32s or Singles
Rectangle, RectangleF	A structure that represents the size and location of a rectangle using either Int32 or Single values
Region	A sealed class that describes a geometric shape using rectangles
Size, SizeF	A structure that represents a size as either a pair of Int32s or Singles
SolidBrushes	A class that defines a Brush that fills a shape with a solid color

(continued)

Table 11-2. Key System::Drawing Namespace Classes and Structures (continued)

CLASS/STRUCTURE	DESCRIPTION
StringFormat	A sealed class that specifies the layout information such as alignment, formatting, and line spacing for a set of text
SystemBrushes	A class made up of several static properties of SolidBrushes using system colors
SystemColors	A class made up of several static properties of system colors
SystemIcons	A class made up of several static properties of Windows system icons
SystemPens	A class made up of several static properties of Pens using system colors
TextureBrush	A class that represents a Brush that uses an image to fill a shape interior

All of the functionality of GDI+ is located within the System.Drawing.dll assembly. Thus, you need to reference it at the top of your source code with the following #using statement:

```
#using <System.Drawing.dll>
```

"Hello, World!" GDI+ Style

Why break a trend I've set in the book? Here's "Hello, World!" again (see Listing 11-1). This time it's using GDI+ to render the "Hello World" text.

Listing 11-1. "Hello, World!" GDI+ Style

```
namespace HelloGDI
{
    using namespace System;
    using namespace System::ComponentModel;
    using namespace System::Collections;
    using namespace System::Windows::Forms;
    using namespace System::Data;
    using namespace System::Drawing;
```

```
public __gc class Form1 : public System::Windows::Forms::Form
{
public:
    Form1(void)
    {
        InitializeComponent();
    }


protected:
    void Dispose(Boolean disposing)
    {
        if (disposing && components)
        {
            components->Dispose();
        }
        __super::Dispose(disposing);
    }

private: System::ComponentModel::Container * components;

    void InitializeComponent(void)
    {
        this->ClientSize = System::Drawing::Size(300, 300);
        this->Name = S"Form1";
        this->Text = S"Hello GDI+";
        this->Paint +=
            new System::Windows::Forms::PaintEventHandler(this, Form1_Paint);
    }
private:
    System::Void Form1_Paint(System::Object * sender,
                             System::Windows::Forms::PaintEventArgs *  e)
    {
        Graphics *g = e->Graphics;
        g->DrawString(S"Hello World!",
        new Drawing::Font(S"Arial", 16), Brushes::Black, 75.0, 110.0);
    }
};
}
```

Figure 11-1 shows the results of the program HelloGDI.exe.

Figure 11-1. Results of "Hello, World!" GDI+ style

As you can see, there is not much new here. The big differences are the addition of the `PaintEventHandler` event handler and the implementation of the `Graphics` class. The rest of the code is identical to that of any program you looked at in the previous two chapters.

All controls generate a `Paint` event when they determine that it needs to be updated. The `Form` class happens to also be a child of the `Control` class. A `Paint` event is triggered whenever the control is created, resized, or restored, or when another control that had overlaid it is moved, re-exposing a portion or all of the overlaid control. An exception to the last condition to triggering the `Paint` event is when `MenuItems` overlay a control. This does not create a `Paint` event. In truth, if you recall, this is not really an exception because a `MenuItem` is not a control, as it does not have the `Control` class as a parent. Instead, a `MenuItem` handles its own overlaying.

As was pointed out previously, this "Hello, World!" example differs from the previous two chapters in that it implements an event handler, `PaintEventHandler`, and uses a `Graphics` class. `PaintEventHandler` takes a template that has two parameters. The first parameter is the sender of the `Paint` event. In this case, it is the form, but it can be almost any control. The second parameter is a pointer to the `PaintEventArgs` class. It is from the `PaintEventArgs` class that you will get two important pieces of information: the `Graphics` class and the `ClipRectangle` or the area that needs to be updated on the form. You will learn about the `ClipRectangle` later in the chapter when you look at optimi-zation.

The `Graphics` class is the key to GDI+, but I delay exploration of the class until its own section a little later in the chapter. For the example, all you need to know is that the `Graphics` class has a member method, `DrawString()`, that you will use to draw the string to the display device. To get access to the `Graphics` class, you usually extract its pointer from the `PaintEventHandler` parameter:

```
System::Void Form1_Paint(System::Object * sender,
                            System::Windows::Forms::PaintEventArgs *  e)
{
    Graphics *g = e->Graphics;
```

The final piece of this "Hello, World!" program is to actually render the "Hello World" string to the display device. The `DrawString` method takes a few parameters. This example shows rendering on the drawing surface, at location *x* equals 75 and *y* equals 100, in black, 16-point Arial font:

```
g->DrawString(S"Hello World!",
                new Drawing::Font(new FontFamily(S"Arial"), 16),
                Brushes::Black, 75.0, 110.0);
```

Something to note about rendering with GDI+ is that the location coordinates are based on the client area of the form or, more accurately, the control. Rendering to a location outside of the control will be clipped and won't be visible. Don't panic, you'll see how to add a scroll bar so you can scroll over and make hidden renderings visible.

OnPaint vs. PaintEventHandler

There's a second way of processing `Paint` events: the protected virtual `OnPaint()` method. Unlike what you've seen before, you don't call the `OnPaint()` method. Instead, you need to override it and then let the system handle it when it's called. Listing 11-2 shows the "Hello, World!" program again, this time using the virtual `OnPaint()` method.

Listing 11-2. "Hello, World!" Using OnPaint()

```
namespace HelloGDI_OnPaint
{
    using namespace System;
    using namespace System::ComponentModel;
    using namespace System::Collections;
    using namespace System::Windows::Forms;
    using namespace System::Data;
    using namespace System::Drawing;

    public __gc class Form1 : public System::Windows::Forms::Form
    {
    public:
        Form1(void)
```

```
        //...
    protected:
        void Dispose(Boolean disposing)
        //...
    private: System::ComponentModel::Container * components;

        void InitializeComponent(void)
        {
            this->ClientSize = System::Drawing::Size(300, 300);
            this->Name = S"Form1";
            this->Text = S"Hello GDI+";
        }


    protected:
        virtual void OnPaint(System::Windows::Forms::PaintEventArgs *e)
        {
            Form::OnPaint(e);

            Graphics *g = e->Graphics;
            g->DrawString(S"Hello World!",
                new Drawing::Font(new FontFamily(S"Arial"), 16),
                Brushes::Black, 75.0, 110.0);
        }
    };
}
```

The results of HelloGDI_OnPaint.exe when run are identical to the
PaintEventHandler version. Most of the code is the same as well. The first difference is that there's no handling of the Paint event within the
InitializeComponent() method. It isn't needed because the OnPaint() method
will handle the Paint events for you. That isn't to say that you can't have the handler. I see a possibility where a static set of graphic rendering activities are placed
within the OnPaint() method and then a set of other graphic rendering activities
are placed in multiple Paint event handlers and, based on conditions, dynamically delegated to the appropriate handler. However, you could do the same thing
using an OnPaint() or a Paint event handler alone.

So what's the difference (if any) between the OnPaint() method and the handler PaintEventHandler? Isn't the OnPaint() method just a prepackaged
PaintEventHandler? I thought so, like many other people (I assume), but I was
wrong. The fact is that the Control class's OnPaint() method is actually in charge
of the executing of all the delegated Paint event handlers. This means the only
way you can be assured that a Paint event happens is by overriding the OnPaint()
method, because it's possible to disable the Paint event handlers from actually

firing within the OnPaint() method. It's a very simple thing to do—you just have to not call the base class Form::OnPaint() within the OnPaint() method.

As you can see, the first statement within the OnPaint() method is to call the base class version of itself:

```
virtual void OnPaint(System::Windows::Forms::PaintEventArgs *e)
{
    Form::OnPaint(e);
    //...Do stuff
}
```

Placing the OnPaint() method first was a conscious decision on my part, as where the base method call is placed within the implementation of the method can make a difference. Placing it first, as shown in the preceding code, indicates that you must handle all the other delegated Paint events first or, in other words, do the rendering specified within this OnPaint() method last. Now if you place the base method call after doing the rendering of the method:

```
virtual void OnPaint(System::Windows::Forms::PaintEventArgs *e)
{
    //...Do stuff
    Form::OnPaint(e);
}
```

this indicates render first what is in this method, and then handle all other delegated Paint events. Both might be legitimate depending on what you want to do. Try the code in Listing 11-3 first by placing Form::OnPaint() as the first line in the overloaded method and then as the last.

Listing 11-3. Placing the OnPaint Base Class Method

```
namespace OnPaintWhere
{
    using namespace System;
    using namespace System::ComponentModel;
    using namespace System::Collections;
    using namespace System::Windows::Forms;
    using namespace System::Data;
    using namespace System::Drawing;

    public __gc class Form1 : public System::Windows::Forms::Form
    {
    public:
```

```
      Form1(void)
      //...
protected:
      void Dispose(Boolean disposing)
      //...
private: System::ComponentModel::Container * components;

      void InitializeComponent(void)
      {
          this->AutoScaleBaseSize = System::Drawing::Size(6, 15);
          this->ClientSize = System::Drawing::Size(292, 265);
          this->Name = S"Form1";
          this->Text = S"Hello GDI+";
          this->Paint +=
              new System::Windows::Forms::PaintEventHandler(this,Form1_Paint);
      }
protected:
      virtual void OnPaint(System::Windows::Forms::PaintEventArgs *e)
      {
//        Form::OnPaint(e);

          Graphics *g = e->Graphics;
          g->DrawString(S"Hello GDI+",
              new Drawing::Font(new FontFamily(S"Arial"), 16),
              Brushes::Black, 75.0, 110.0);

          Form::OnPaint(e);
      }
private:
      System::Void Form1_Paint(System::Object *  sender,
                                  System::Windows::Forms::PaintEventArgs * e)
      {
          Graphics *g = e->Graphics;

          g->DrawString(S"Hello GDI+",
              new Drawing::Font(new FontFamily(S"Arial"), 16),
              Brushes::Red, 75.0, 110.0);
      }
};
}
```

Figure 11-2 shows OnPaintWhere.exe in action where the text "Hello GDI+" is in red in this black-and-white image. Guess you'll have to take my word on it.

Figure 11-2. The rendering results if the base OnPaint is placed last in the method

When `Form::OnPaint()` is placed on the first line, the text turns out black, as the `OnPaint()` method's version of the `DrawString()` method is handled last. When `Form::OnPaint()` is placed at the end, on the other hand, the text is red because the `PaintEventHandler` version of `DrawString()` method is handled last. By the way, if you remove all the logic within the `OnPaint()` method, no text is displayed, because the `PaintEventHandler` is never triggered as `Form::OnPaint()` was not called to execute the delegated `Paint` events.

Now after saying all this, does it really matter if your `OnPaint()` method calls its base class version? The usual answer to this is "Not really." If you don't plan on using the `Paint` event handler yourself and the form that you created is never inherited (both normally being the case), then calling `OnPaint()` makes no difference. In fact, it might speed things up minutely if you don't call it because it isn't doing any unneeded method calls. (This is my take on it, though. The .NET Framework documentation says you should always call the base class method, so maybe you should take Microsoft's word, as there might be some hidden reason that I'm unaware of. That said, so far I haven't come across any problems.)

Which should you use: the `OnPaint()` method or the `Paint` event handler? I think the `OnPaint()` method, as it doesn't have the event delegate implementation overhead. But because it's easier to use than the `Paint` event (you only have to double-click the event handler in the Properties dialog box to add it) and the cost of the overhead is so minute, I use the `Paint` handler from here on in.

The Graphics Class

So what is this magical `Graphics` class? It's the heart of all rendering activity of GDI+. It's a device-independent representation of the drawing surface that you plan to render graphics on. It can represent a monochrome display device like many PDAs or cellular phones, a true-color display device like those supported on a good number of computers used today, or anything in between. It can also be used for printers, from plotter to dot matrix to color laser.

Graphics Class Members

The Graphics class works by providing a large number of rendering methods (see Table 11-3) to developers that they will ultimately use to render their images. The rendering methods of the Graphics class can be divided into two groups: lines/outlines (draws) and fills. (The Clear() method is technically a fill.) Draws are used to outline open-ended and closed shapes or, in other words, they draw lines and outline shapes. Fills . . . well, they fill shapes.

Table 11-3. Common Graphics Class Rendering Methods

METHOD	DESCRIPTION
Clear()	Clears the entire client area to the background color
DrawArc()	Draws a part of an ellipse
DrawClosedCurve()	Draws a closed curve defined by an array of points
DrawCurve()	Draws an open curve defined by an array of points
DrawEllipse()	Draws an ellipse
DrawIcon()	Draws an icon
DrawImage()	Draws an image
DrawImageUnscaled()	Draws an image without scaling
DrawLine()	Draws a line
DrawLines()	Draws a series of connected lines
DrawPie()	Draws a pie segment
DrawPolygon()	Draws a polygon defined by an array of points
DrawRectangle()	Draws a rectangle
DrawRectangles()	Draws a series of rectangles
DrawString()	Draws a text string
FillClosedCurve()	Fills a closed curve defined by an array of points
FillEllipse()	Fills an ellipse
FillPie()	Fills a pie segment

(continued)

Table 11-3. Common Graphics Class Rendering Methods (continued)

METHOD	DESCRIPTION
FillPolygon()	Fills a polygon defined by an array of points
FillRectangle()	Fills a rectangle
FillRectangles()	Fills a series of rectangles

Something that might disturb you a little bit is that there is no Graphics constructor. The main way of getting an instance of a Graphics class is by grabbing from

- A PaintEventArgs's Graphics property

- A control using its CreateGraphics() method

- An image using the Graphics static FromImage() method

- A handle to a window using the Graphics static FromHwnd() method

Usually you will only use PaintEventArgs's Graphics property or, as you will see in the "Double Buffering" section, the FromImage() method.

The Dispose Method

The Graphics object uses a lot of system resources. Some examples of Graphics objects are System::Drawing::Graphics, System::Drawing::Brush, and System::Drawing::Pen. It's important that if you create a graphics resource, you release it as soon as you're finished with it. You do this by using the Dispose() method. Basically, if you create an object that implements the IDisposable interface, you should call its Dispose() method as soon as you're done with it. This allows these resources to be reallocated for other purposes.

You're probably thinking, "Won't the garbage collector handle all this?" Yes, it will, but because you have no control over when the garbage collector will run on the object and because graphics resources are precious, it's better to call the destructor yourself. Be careful you only call the Dispose() method on objects you create. This way, you don't call it for the Graphics object you extracted from PaintEventArg, as you're just accessing an existing object and not creating your own. Listing 11-4 presents an example where you need to call the Dispose() method for a Graphics object.

Rendering Outside of the Paint Event

Now you'll examine `CreateGraphics()` in an example (see Listing 11-4) and see what happens when you minimize and then restore the window after clicking a few coordinates onto the form.

Listing 11-4. The Problem with Using CreateGraphics

```
namespace DisappearingCoords
{
    using namespace System;
    using namespace System::ComponentModel;
    using namespace System::Collections;
    using namespace System::Windows::Forms;
    using namespace System::Data;
    using namespace System::Drawing;

    public __gc class Form1 : public System::Windows::Forms::Form
    {
    public:
        Form1(void)
        //...
    protected:
        void Dispose(Boolean disposing)
        //...
    private: System::ComponentModel::Container * components;

        void InitializeComponent(void)
        {
            this->AutoScaleBaseSize = System::Drawing::Size(6, 15);
            this->ClientSize = System::Drawing::Size(292, 265);
            this->Name = S"Form1";
            this->Text = S"Click and see coords";
            this->MouseDown +=
            new System::Windows::Forms::MouseEventHandler(this,Form1_MouseDown);
        }
    private:
        System::Void Form1_MouseDown(System::Object * sender,
                        System::Windows::Forms::MouseEventArgs * e)
        {
            Graphics *g = this->CreateGraphics();
            g->DrawString(String::Format(S"({0},{1})",__box(e->X),__box(e->Y)),
                new Drawing::Font(new FontFamily(S"Courier New"), 8),
```

```
        Brushes::Black, (Single)e->X, (Single)e->Y);

    g->Dispose();  // we dispose of the Graphics object because we
                   // created it with the CreateGraphics() method.
  }
};
}
```

Figure 11-3 shows the program DisappearingCoords.exe with the coordinate strings clipped after resizing the form.

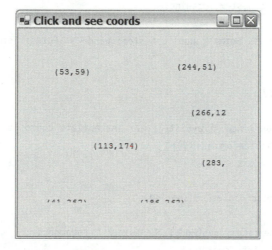

Figure 11-3. Clipped rendered coordinate strings

The coordinates disappear! What's happening here? When you minimize a window or overlay it with another window, its graphics device memory is released back to the system resource pool. Thus, everything that was displayed on the graphics device is lost, along with all the coordinates that you clicked onto the drawing surface.

With the preceding logic, the only time that a coordinate string is drawn to the graphics device is during a mouse click. Because this is the case, there is no way of restoring the coordinates without at least one mouse click occurring. This is why you want to use the Paint event; it is automatically triggered whenever more of the drawing surface area is exposed, either because it was restored, resized, or something that was obscuring it was removed.

Added to this, because none of the information about what was displayed on the drawing surface is stored anywhere when the surface area is reduced, you need to store the coordinates that you previously clicked so they can all be restored. Listing 11-5 shows how to fix the shortcomings of the previous example.

Listing 11-5. Corrected Clipping Problem

```
namespace CorrectingCoords
{
    using namespace System;
    using namespace System::ComponentModel;
    using namespace System::Collections;
    using namespace System::Windows::Forms;
    using namespace System::Data;
    using namespace System::Drawing;

    public __gc class Form1 : public System::Windows::Forms::Form
    {
    public:
        Form1(void)
        {
            coords = new ArrayList();  // Instantiate coords array
            InitializeComponent();
        }
    protected:
        void Dispose(Boolean disposing)
        //...
    private: System::ComponentModel::Container * components;
    private: ArrayList *coords;

        void InitializeComponent(void)
        {
            this->AutoScaleBaseSize = System::Drawing::Size(6, 15);
            this->ClientSize = System::Drawing::Size(292, 265);
            this->Name = S"Form1";
            this->Text = S"Click and see coords";
            this->MouseDown +=
            new System::Windows::Forms::MouseEventHandler(this,Form1_MouseDown);
            this->Paint +=
            new System::Windows::Forms::PaintEventHandler(this, Form1_Paint);
        }
    private:
        System::Void Form1_MouseDown(System::Object * sender,
                        System::Windows::Forms::MouseEventArgs * e)
        {
```

```
            coords->Add(__box(Point(e->X, e->Y)));
            Invalidate();
        }
    private:
        System::Void Form1_Paint(System::Object * sender,
                                    System::Windows::Forms::PaintEventArgs * e)
        {
            Graphics *g = e->Graphics;
            for (Int32 i = 0; i < coords->Count; i++)
            {
                Point *p = dynamic_cast<Point*>(coords->Item[i]);
                g->DrawString(String::Format(S"({0},{1})",__box(p->X),
                                                __box(p->Y)),
                    new Drawing::Font(new FontFamily(S"Courier New"), 8),
                    Brushes::Black, (Single)p->X, (Single)p->Y);
            }
        }
    };
}
```

Figure 11-4 shows CorrectingCoords.exe, though it's hard to tell after it has been minimized, resized, and overlaid. Notice the rendered string still appears as expected.

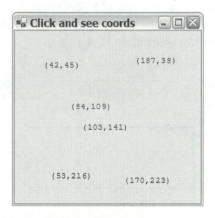

Figure 11-4. Correctly rendered coordinate strings

Now the MouseDown event handles the adding of the click coordinates to an array for safekeeping, and the responsibility of rendering the coordinates is back where it should be: in the Paint event handler (Form1_Paint()). Notice that every time the drawing surface is painted, every coordinate is rewritten, which is hardly efficient. You will look at optimizing this later.

How does the control know when to trigger a Paint event when the mouse clicks it on? That is the job of the Invalidate() method.

The Invalidate Method

What is this Invalidate() method and why was it called? The Invalidate() method is the manual way of triggering a Paint event. Thus, in the previous example, because you no longer draw the coordinate information to the screen in the MouseDown handler, you need to trigger the Paint event using the Invalidate() method.

Calling the Invalidate() method without any parameters, as shown in the preceding example, tells the form that its entire client area needs updating. The Invalidate() method also can take parameters. These parameters allow the Invalidate() method to specify that only a piece of the client area within the control needs to be updated. You will look at this type of the Invalidate() method in GDI+ optimization later in the chapter.

GDI+ Coordinate Systems

When you rendered the strings earlier, you placed them where they were supposed to be on the screen by specifying pixel distances from the top-left corner, increasing the X-axis when moving to the right and increasing the Y-axis when moving down to the bottom (see Figure 11-5).

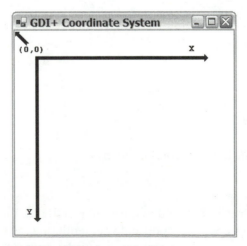

Figure 11-5. The default GDI coordinate system

A key aspect of GDI+ is that it is supposed to be device independent. How can that be, if everything is rendered based on a pixel standard? Pixels are only one of several coordinate systems supported by GDI+ (see Table 11-4). For example, instead of coordinate (100, 100), meaning 100 pixels to the right and 100 pixels down, the meaning could be 100 millimeters to the right and 100 millimeters down. To change the coordinate system to be based on a different unit of measure, you need to change the PageUnit property of the Graphics class to a different GraphicsUnit.

Table 11-4. GDI+-Supported GraphicsUnits

SYSTEM	DESCRIPTION
Display	Specifies 1/75 of an inch as a unit of measure
Document	Specifies 1/300 of an inch as a unit of measure
Inch	Specifies 1 inch as a unit of measure
Millimeter	Specifies 1 millimeter as a unit of measure
Pixel	Specifies 1 pixel as a unit of measure
Point	Specifies a printer's point or 1/72 of an inch as a unit of measure

It is also possible to move the origin (0, 0) away from the top-left corner to somewhere else the drawing surface. This requires you to translate the origin (0, 0) to where you want it located using the Graphics class's TranslateTransform() method.

The example in Listing 11-6 changes the unit of measure to millimeter and shifts the origin to (20, 20).

Listing 11-6. Changing the Unit of Measure and the Origin

```
namespace NewUnitsOrigin
{
    using namespace System;
    using namespace System::ComponentModel;
    using namespace System::Collections;
    using namespace System::Windows::Forms;
    using namespace System::Data;
    using namespace System::Drawing;

    public __gc class Form1 : public System::Windows::Forms::Form
    {
    public:
        Form1(void)
```

```
    //...
protected:
    void Dispose(Boolean disposing)
    //...
private: System::ComponentModel::Container * components;

    void InitializeComponent(void)
    {
        this->AutoScaleBaseSize = System::Drawing::Size(6, 15);
        this->ClientSize = System::Drawing::Size(442, 265);
        this->Name = S"Form1";
        this->Text = S"Millimeter Unit of measure Origin (20,20)";
        this->Paint +=
            new System::Windows::Forms::PaintEventHandler(this, Form1_Paint);
    }
private:
    System::Void Form1_Paint(System::Object * sender,
                                System::Windows::Forms::PaintEventArgs * e)
    {
        Graphics *g = e->Graphics;

        // Draw a rectangle before unit of measure and origin change
        g->DrawRectangle(Pens::Black, 5, 5, 50, 20);

        // Draw same rectangle after change
        g->PageUnit = GraphicsUnit::Millimeter;
        g->TranslateTransform(20,20);
        g->DrawRectangle(Pens::Black, 5, 5, 50, 20);
    }
};
}
```

As you can see in NewUnitsOrigin.exe, it is possible to use multiple types of units of measure and origins within the same Paint event handler. Figure 11-6 displays a small rectangle, which was generated by the default pixel unit of measure and origin. The larger and thicker lined rectangle is what was generated when the unit of measure was changed to millimeter and origin was moved to (20, 20).

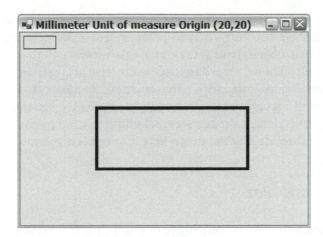

Figure 11-6. Changing the unit of measure and the origin

You should notice a couple of things in this example. First, the client size still uses pixel width and height. There is no PageUnit property for a form. Second, when you change the PageUnit of the Graphics class, all rendering from that point is changed to the new unit of measure. This is true even for the width of lines. Pens::Black creates lines 1 unit thick. When the unit is millimeters, Pens::Black will end up creating a line 1 millimeter thick.

Common Utility Structures

When you render your own text, shape, or image, you need to be able to tell the Graphics class where to place it and how big it is. It is not surprising that the .NET Framework class library provides a small assortment of structures and a class to do just that. Here they are in brief:

- Point/PointF is used to specify location.

- Size/SizeF is used to specify size.

- Rectangle/RectangleF is used to specify both location and size at the same time.

- Region is used to specify combinations of rectangles and regions.

All of these types use units of measure configured by the property PageUnit within the Graphics class. You need to take care that you always configure

PageUnit consistently, or you might find that even though the same values are placed in these structures, they in fact represent different locations and sizes.

All the structures have `Int32` and `Single` versions. Both provide the same functionality. The only real difference is the level of granularity that is supported in numeric values stored within the structures. In most cases, the `Int32` version will be good enough, but if you want finer granularity, you might want to choose the `Single` version. Just remember that ultimately, the resolution of the drawing surface will decide how the shape, image, or text is displayed.

Point and PointF

As the name of this structure suggests, `Point/PointF` is an (*x*, *y*) location in units. Remember that units do not necessarily mean pixels. Pixels are only the default. The `Point/PointF` structure provides a few members (see Table 11-5) to aid in their manipulation.

Table 11-5. Common Point/PointF Members

MEMBER	DESCRIPTION
+ operator	Translates a `Point/PointF` by a `Size/SizeF`.
- operator	Translate a `Point/PointF` by the negative of a `Size/SizeF`.
== operator	Compares the equality of two points. Both Xs and Ys must equal for the point to equal.
!= operator	Compares the inequality of two points. If either the Xs or Ys don't equal, then the points don't equal.
IsEmpty	Specifies if the point is empty.
Ceiling()	Static member that returns next higher integer `Point` from a `PointF`.
Offset()	Translates the point by the specified *x* and *y* amounts.
Round()	Static member that returns a rounded `Point` from a `PointF`.
Truncate()	Static member that returns a truncated `Point` from a `PointF`.
X	Specifies the *x* coordinate of the point.
Y	Specifies the *y* coordinate of the point.

To access the X or Y values within the `Point`/`PointF` structure, you simply need to access the X or Y property:

```
Drawing::Point a = Drawing::Point(10,15);
Int32 x = a.X;
Int32 y = a.Y;
```

Casting from `Point` to `PointF` is implicit, but to convert from `PointF`, you need to use one of two static methods: `Round()` or `Truncate()`. The `Round()` method rounds to the nearest integer, and the `Truncate()` method simply truncates the number to just its integer value.

```
Drawing::Point  a = Drawing::Point(10,15);
Drawing::PointF b = a;
Drawing::Point  c = Drawing::Point::Round(b);
Drawing::Point  d = Drawing::Point::Truncate(b);
```

The `Offset()` method is only found in `Point`, and it translates the point by the *x* and *y* coordinates passed to it.

```
a.Offset(2, -3);
```

The method is cumbersome as it returns void. I think it should return a `Point` type. I think it should also be a member of `PointF`.

Size and SizeF

Mathematically, `Size`/`SizeF` and `Point`/`PointF` are virtually the same. How they differ is really just conceptually. `Point`/`PointF` specifies where something is, whereas `Size`/`SizeF` specifies how big it is. `Point`/`PointF` and `Size`/`SizeF` even have many of the same members (see Table 11-6). The biggest difference is that sizes have widths and heights, whereas the points have *x* and *y* coordinates.

Table 11-6. Common Size/SizeF Members

MEMBER	DESCRIPTION
+ operator	Adds two sizes together.
- operator	Subtracts one size from another.
== operator	Compares the equality of two sizes. Both Widths and Heights must equal for the points to equal.
!= operator	Compares the inequality of two sizes. If either Widths or Heights don't equal, then the points don't equal.
IsEmpty	Specifies if the size is empty.
Ceiling()	Static member that returns the next higher integer Size from a SizeF.
Round()	Static member that returns a rounded Size from a SizeF.
Truncate()	Static member that returns a truncated Size from a SizeF.
Height	Specifies the height of the size.
Width	Specifies the width of the size.

It is possible to add or subtract two sizes and get a size in return. It is also possible to subtract a size from a point that returns another point. Adding or subtracting points generates a compiler error.

```
Drawing::Size sizeA = Drawing::Size(100, 100);
Drawing::Size sizeB = Drawing::Size(50, 50);
Drawing::Size sizeC = sizeA + sizeB;
Drawing::Size sizeD = sizeC - sizeB;

Drawing::Point pointA = Drawing::Point(10, 10) + sizeD;
Drawing::Point pointB = pointA - sizeC;
```

You can cast Point/PointF to Size/SizeF. What happens is the value of X becomes Width and the value of Y becomes Height and vice versa. The following code shows how to implement all the combinations. It also shows the Size to SizeF combinations:

```
size   = point;
point  = size;
sizeF  = pointF;
pointF = (Drawing::PointF)sizeF;
```

```
sizeF  = (Drawing::Size)point;
pointF = (Drawing::Point)size;
sizeF  = size;

size  = Drawing::Size::Round(pointF);
size  = Drawing::Size::Truncate(pointF);
point = Drawing::Point::Round((Drawing::PointF)sizeF);
point = Drawing::Point::Truncate((Drawing::PointF)sizeF);
size  = Drawing::Size::Round(sizeF);
size  = Drawing::Size::Truncate(sizeF);
```

Rectangle and RectangleF

As I'm sure you can guess, the Rectangle/RectangleF structure represents the information that makes up a rectangle. It's really nothing more than a combination of a Point structure and a Size structure. The Point specifies the starting upper-left corner and the Size specifies the size of the enclosed rectangular area starting at the point. There is, in fact, a Rectangle/RectangleF constructor that takes as its parameters a Point and a Size.

The Rectangle structure provides many properties and methods (see Table 11-7), a few of which are redundant. For example, there are properties called Top and Left that return the exact same thing as the properties X and Y.

Table 11-7. Common Rectangle/RectangleF Members

MEMBER	DESCRIPTION
==	Returns whether the rectangle has the same location and size
!=	Returns whether the rectangle has different location or size
Bottom	Returns the y coordinate of the bottom edge
Ceiling()	Static member that returns the next higher integer Rectangle from a RectangleF
Contains	Returns whether a point falls within the rectangle
Height	Specifies the height of the rectangle
Intersect()	Returns a Rectangle/RectangleF that represents the intersection of two rectangles
IsEmpty	Specifies whether all the numeric properties are zero
Left	Returns the x coordinate of the left edge

(continued)

Table 11-7. Common Rectangle/RectangleF Members (continued)

MEMBER	DESCRIPTION
Location	A Point structure that specifies the top-left corner
Offset()	Relocates a rectangle by a specified amount
Right	Returns the *x* coordinate of the right edge
Round()	Static member that returns a rounded Rectangle from a RectangleF
Size	A Size structure that specifies the size of the rectangle
Top	Returns the *y* coordinate of the top edge
Truncate()	Static member that returns a truncated Rectangle from a RectangleF
Union()	Returns a Rectangle/RectangleF that represents the smallest possible rectangle that can contain the two rectangles
Width	Specifies the width of the rectangle
X	Specifies the *x* coordinate of the top-left corner
Y	Specifies the *y* coordinate of the top-left corner

The rectangle provides three interesting methods. The first is the Intersection() method, which can take two rectangles and generate a third rectangle that represents the rectangle that the two others have in common. The second is the Union() method. This method does not really produce the union of two rectangles as the method's name suggests. Instead, it generates the smallest rectangle that can enclose the other two. The third interesting method is Contains(), which specifies if a point falls within a rectangle. This method could come in handy if you want to see if a mouse click fell inside a rectangle.

The example in Listing 11-7 uses these three methods. What this program does is check if a point falls within an intersection of the two rectangles or the union of two rectangles. (Obviously, if the point falls within the intersection, it also falls within the union.)

Listing 11-7. Intersection, Union, or Neither

```
namespace InterOrUnion
{
    using namespace System;
    using namespace System::ComponentModel;
    using namespace System::Collections;
```

```
using namespace System::Windows::Forms;
using namespace System::Data;
using namespace System::Drawing;

public __gc class Form1 : public System::Windows::Forms::Form
{
public:
    Form1(void)
    {
        // Build the rectangles from points and size
        Drawing::Point point1 = Drawing::Point(25,25);
        Drawing::Point point2 = Drawing::Point(100,100);
        Drawing::Size size    = Drawing::Size(200, 150);
        rect1 = Drawing::Rectangle(point1, size);
        rect2 = Drawing::Rectangle(point2, size);

        InitializeComponent();
    }
 protected:
    void Dispose(Boolean disposing)
    //...
private: System::ComponentModel::Container * components;

// intersecting and unions rectangles
private: Drawing::Rectangle rect1;
private: Drawing::Rectangle rect2;

    void InitializeComponent(void)
    {
        this->ClientSize = System::Drawing::Size(325, 275);
        this->Name = S"Form1";
        this->Text = S"Click in Window";
        this->MouseDown +=
        new System::Windows::Forms::MouseEventHandler(this,Form1_MouseDown);
        this->Paint +=
        new System::Windows::Forms::PaintEventHandler(this, Form1_Paint);
    }
private:
    System::Void Form1_Paint(System::Object *  sender,
                             System::Windows::Forms::PaintEventArgs * e)
    {
        // Grab Graphics from e
        Graphics *g = e->Graphics;
```

```
                // Draw a couple of rectangles
                g->DrawRectangle(Pens::Black, rect1);
                g->DrawRectangle(Pens::Black, rect2);
            }
        private:
            System::Void Form1_MouseDown(System::Object *  sender,
                            System::Windows::Forms::MouseEventArgs * e)
            {
                // build a point from x,y coords of mouse click
                Point p = Point(e->X, e->Y);

                // did we click in the intersection?
                if (Rectangle::Intersect(rect1, rect2).Contains(p))
                    Text = S"Intersection and Union";
                // did we click in the union?
                else if (Rectangle::Union(rect1, rect2).Contains(p))
                    Text = S"Union";
                // did we miss altogether?
                else
                    Text = S"Outside of Both";
            }
        };
    }
```

The first thing you need to do is declare and build two rectangles that you will make the mouse checks against.

```
Drawing::Rectangle rect1;
Drawing::Rectangle rect2;
//...
// Build the rectangles from points and size
Drawing::Point point1 = Drawing::Point(25,25);
Drawing::Point point2 = Drawing::Point(100,100);
Drawing::Size size    = Drawing::Size(200, 150);

rect1 = Drawing::Rectangle(point1, size);
rect2 = Drawing::Rectangle(point2, size);
```

You will learn about the DrawRectangle() method later, but as you can see in the code, it takes a Pen to draw with and then the Rectangle to draw.

```
g->DrawRectangle(Pens::Black, rect1);
```

Finally, in the `MouseDown` event, you check to see where the mouse was clicked and place the results in the title.

```
// build a point from x,y coords of mouse click
Point p = Point(e->X, e->Y);

// did we click in the intersection?
if (Rectangle::Intersect(rect1, rect2).Contains(p))
    Text = S"Intersection and Union";
// did we click in the union?
else if (Rectangle::Union(rect1, rect2).Contains(p))
    Text = S"Union";
// did we miss altogether?
else
    Text = S"Outside of Both";
```

Figure 11-7 shows the mouse being clicked in the intersection of the two rectangles in InterOrUnion.exe.

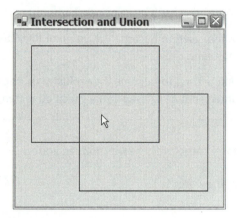

Figure 11-7. It's an intersection.

Region

The last of the utility types is the only class in the bunch. Region is a neat little class in that it alters itself with the help of other rectangles and regions into a more complex region. The alterations that the `Region` class does are things such as unions, intersections, exclusive or, and complements. A Region class has no properties of its own; instead, it is made up of a number of methods (see Table 11-8) that it uses to alter itself.

Table 11-8. Common Region Members

MEMBER	DESCRIPTION
Complement()	Alters itself to become the complement of itself. The region of the complement is restricted by a specified rectangle.
Exclude()	Alters itself to become the portion of region that does not intersect with the given rectangle or region.
GetBounds()	Specifies the smallest rectangle that the region can be contained within.
Intersect()	Alters itself to become the intersection of itself and a specified rectangle or region.
IsEmpty()	Specifies if the region is made up of an empty area.
IsInfinite()	Specifies if the region is infinite in size.
MakeEmpty()	Sets the region to empty.
MakeInfinite()	Sets the region to infinite.
Transform()	Transforms itself using a matrix.
Translate()	Translates itself by a specified amount.
Union()	Alters itself to become the union of itself and a specified rectangle or region.
Xor()	Alters itself to become the exclusive or (the union minus the intersection) of itself and a specified rectangle or region.

Listing 11-8 shows some of these methods in action.

Listing 11-8. Displaying a Region

```
namespace Region1
{
    using namespace System;
    using namespace System::ComponentModel;
    using namespace System::Collections;
    using namespace System::Windows::Forms;
    using namespace System::Data;
    using namespace System::Drawing;
```

```
public __gc class Form1 : public System::Windows::Forms::Form
{
public:
    Form1(void)
    {
        Drawing::Point point1 = Drawing::Point(25,25);
        Drawing::Point point2 = Drawing::Point(100,100);
        Drawing::Size size    = Drawing::Size(200, 150);
        Rectangle rect1       = Drawing::Rectangle(point1, size);
        Rectangle rect2       = Drawing::Rectangle(point2, size);

        region = new Drawing::Region(rect1);
        region->Xor(rect2);

        InitializeComponent();
    }
protected:
    void Dispose(Boolean disposing)
    //...
private: System::ComponentModel::Container * components;
private: Drawing::Region *region;

    void InitializeComponent(void)
    {
        this->ClientSize = System::Drawing::Size(325, 275);
        this->Name = S"Form1";
        this->Text = S"Filling A Region";
        this->Paint +=
            new System::Windows::Forms::PaintEventHandler(this,Form1_Paint);
    }
private:
    System::Void Form1_Paint(System::Object * sender,
                             System::Windows::Forms::PaintEventArgs * e)
    {
        Graphics *g = e->Graphics;
        g->FillRegion(Brushes::Blue, region);
    }

};
}
```

To save typing, I decided to cut and paste the code to build the rectangle from the previous example.

To build a Region class, you start with an empty Region and then add a rectangle or a Region to it:

```
Drawing::Region *region;
region = new Drawing::Region(rect1);
```

Now you can start to alter the Region. Notice that the Region methods return void. In other words, the Region actually gets changed with each method call to itself. To Xor it with another rectangle, call the Xor() method:

```
region->Xor(rect2);
```

You will cover filling regions later, but so that you know, the FillRegion() method takes a Brush to specify the color to fill it with and then the Region to fill.

Figure 11-8 shows the area that makes up the region that you built with Region.exe from two rectangles.

Figure 11-8. Displaying a region

Drawing Strings

Drawing strings almost doesn't require a section of its own. All it really is, is a single call to the DrawString() method found in the Graphics class. The more difficult part of drawing strings is setting up the font and color you want to print with. (I cover both topics later.)

Now you'll take a quick peek at the DrawString() method. If you were to look at the .NET Framework documentation, you'd find a plethora of overloads. When you examine them more closely, you'll discover that they all start with the parameters String, Font, and Brush. From there, it gets a little tricky because you have to decide if you just want to specify the starting upper-left corner of where you want the string displayed, using either (*x*, *y*) coordinates or a Point, or specify the entire rectangle that you want to restrict the string to.

```
g.DrawString(string, font, brush, xF, yF);
g.DrawString(string, font, brush, pointF);
g.DrawString(string, font, brush, rectangleF);
```

When you restrict the string to a rectangle, the text automatically word wraps, as Listing 11-9 shows. It unfortunately will also show half of a line of text if the vertical height is not enough.

Listing 11-9. Drawing a String to a Rectangle

```
namespace StringRect
{
    using namespace System;
    using namespace System::ComponentModel;
    using namespace System::Collections;
    using namespace System::Windows::Forms;
    using namespace System::Data;
    using namespace System::Drawing;

    public __gc class Form1 : public System::Windows::Forms::Form
    {
    public:
        Form1(void)
        //...
    protected:
        void Dispose(Boolean disposing)
        //...
    private: System::ComponentModel::Container * components;

        void InitializeComponent(void)
        {
            this->AutoScaleBaseSize = System::Drawing::Size(6, 15);
            this->ClientSize = System::Drawing::Size(292, 265);
            this->Name = S"Form1";
            this->Text = S"String in a Rectangle";
            this->Paint +=
                new System::Windows::Forms::PaintEventHandler(this, Form1_Paint);
```

```
          }
      private:
          System::Void Form1_Paint(System::Object * sender,
                                   System::Windows::Forms::PaintEventArgs * e)
          {
              Graphics *g = e->Graphics;

              // Draw the string
              g->DrawString(S"Let's draw string to a rectangle and go a little "
                            S"overboard on the size of the string that we place "
                            S"inside of it",
                      new Drawing::Font(new FontFamily(S"Arial"), 10),
                      Brushes::Black, Drawing::RectangleF(20.0, 40.0, 260.0, 50.0));
          }
      };
  }
```

Figure 11-9 shows that StringRect.exe draws a string to a rectangle that is too small.

Figure 11-9. A string restricted to a too-small rectangle

In reality, each of the overloads for the DrawString() method listed previously has one more parameter of type StringFormat, which has been defaulted to GenericDefault.

```
g.DrawString(string, font, brush, xF, yF, stringformat);
g.DrawString(string, font, brush, pointF, stringformat);
g.DrawString(string, font, brush, rectangleF, stringformat);
```

StringFormat is a class containing several properties (see Table 11-9) that allow the DrawString() method to do things such as draw the text vertically and left, right, or center align it.

Table 11-9. Common StringFormat Properties

PROPERTY	DESCRIPTION
Alignment	Specifies alignment of the text
FormatFlags	Specifies StringFormatFlags such as DirectionVertical and NoWrap
GenericDefault	A static method that gets the generic default StringFormat object
GenericTypographic	A static method that gets the generic typographic StringFormat object
LineAlignment	Specifies line alignment
Trimming	Specifies how to trim a string that doesn't fit completely within a display area

Listing 11-10 shows the same text as shown previously, but this time it is written in a downward direction and centered on each line.

Listing 11-10. Drawing Strings Downward in a Rectangle

```
namespace DownwardStringRect
{
    using namespace System;
    using namespace System::ComponentModel;
    using namespace System::Collections;
    using namespace System::Windows::Forms;
    using namespace System::Data;
    using namespace System::Drawing;

    public __gc class Form1 : public System::Windows::Forms::Form
    {
    public:
        Form1(void)
        //...
    protected:
        void Dispose(Boolean disposing)
        //...
    private: System::ComponentModel::Container * components;
```

```
        void InitializeComponent(void)
        {
            this->AutoScaleBaseSize = System::Drawing::Size(6, 15);
            this->ClientSize = System::Drawing::Size(292, 265);
            this->Name = S"Form1";
            this->Text = S"Downward String in a Rectangle";
            this->Paint +=
                new System::Windows::Forms::PaintEventHandler(this,Form1_Paint);
        }
    private:
        System::Void Form1_Paint(System::Object * sender,
                                    System::Windows::Forms::PaintEventArgs * e)
        {

        Graphics *g = e->Graphics;

        // create and configure the StringFormat object
        StringFormat *stringformat = new StringFormat();
        stringformat->FormatFlags  = StringFormatFlags::DirectionVertical;
        stringformat->Alignment     = StringAlignment::Center;

        // Draw the string
        g->DrawString(S"Let's draw a string to a rectangle and go a little "
                    S"overboard on the size of the string that we place "
                    S"inside of it",
            new Drawing::Font(new FontFamily(S"Arial"), 10),
            Brushes::Black, Drawing::RectangleF(20.0, 40.0, 242.0, 80.0),
            stringformat);
        }
    };
}
```

Figure 11-10 shows that DownwardStringRect.exe draws a string in a downward direction and centers it in a rectangle that is too small. This causes the string to be clipped on the final line.

Figure 11-10. A string drawn downward and restricted to a too-small rectangle

Fonts

It seems that many people seem overly concerned about the differences between GDI+'s Font class and FontFamily class. Here's my take on it: A Font class represents a single font and a FontFamily class represents a group of fonts that share many characteristics. You might think of a font family as "Arial" and a font as "Arial, 10-point, italic."

When you draw strings with GDI+, you don't have much of a choice. You have to build a Font class. You can't draw a string with a FontFamily class.

When you build a Font class, you have the choice of starting with a FontFamily class or a String containing the name of a font family. You'll probably use a String if you're planning on building a Font class from one of the standard fonts found on a computer (e.g., Arial, Courier, and Times New Roman). On the other hand, if your font is a little less common, you probably will search the computer for a list of font families currently loaded on your computer. If you find the FontFamily class in the list of font families, then it's a simple matter of using the FontFamily class instead of the String containing the font family's name. In general, I don't find the FontFamily class that useful as I tend to use the more common fonts in my programs, but you might have more exotic tastes. Basically, to use the FontFamily class, just replace the String in the first parameter of the Font constructor with the FontFamily class.

The process of building a font is quite easy. You do it using the Font constructors. You will use three constructors most often. They are really the same except that parameters are defaulted for two of them.

The first constructor defaults nothing and takes the name of the font family and the unit size, the font style, and the graphics unit:

```
Font *f = new Drawing::Font(S"Arial", 16, FontStyle::Bold, GraphicsUnit::Point);
```

In most cases, fonts default to a graphics unit of pixels. Therefore, Font provides a constructor with the graphics unit defaulted to pixels:

```
Font *f = new Drawing::Font(S"Arial", 16, FontStyle::Bold);
```

In addition, most of the time you are going to work with the font in the regular font style (not boldface, italic, or underline). So, again, Font provides a default for this:

```
Font *f = new Drawing::Font(S"Arial", 16);
```

Even though the Font class has several properties (see Table 11-10), they are all read-only. In other words, you can't change a font once you have constructed it.

Table 11-10. Common Font Properties

PROPERTY	DESCRIPTION
Bold	True if the font is boldface
FontFamily	Gets the font family
Height	Gets the height of the font in the current graphics unit
Italic	True if font is italicized
Name	Gets the name of the font
Size	Get the size of the font in the current graphics unit
SizeInPoints	Gets the size of the font in points (1/72 inch)
Strikeout	True if the font is struck out
Style	Gets the style information
Underline	True if the font is underlined
Unit	Gets the graphics unit

The code in Listing 11-11 creates ten random fonts and then displays them.

Listing 11-11. Generating Random Fonts

```
namespace FontsGalore
{
    using namespace System;
    using namespace System::ComponentModel;
    using namespace System::Collections;
    using namespace System::Windows::Forms;
    using namespace System::Data;
    using namespace System::Drawing::Text;
    using namespace System::Drawing;

    public __gc class Form1 : public System::Windows::Forms::Form
    {
    public:
        Form1(void)
        {
            fonts = new Drawing::Font*[10];
            fontstr = new String*[10];

            // Used to generate random fonts
            Single sizes[] = { 10.0, 12.5, 16.0 };
            FontStyle fontstyles[] = {
                FontStyle::Regular, FontStyle::Bold,
                FontStyle::Italic,
                (FontStyle)(FontStyle::Underline|FontStyle::Bold|FontStyle::Italic)
            };
            GraphicsUnit units[] = { GraphicsUnit::Point, GraphicsUnit::Pixel };

            // Get all fonts on computer
            InstalledFontCollection *availFonts = new InstalledFontCollection();
            FontFamily *fontfamilies[] = availFonts->Families;

            Random *rand = new Random();
            Int32 ff, s, fs, u;
            for (Int32 i = 0; i < fonts->Count; i++)
            {
                s  = rand->Next(0,3);
                fs = rand->Next(0,3);
                u  = rand->Next(0,2);
```

```
                        // Not all fonts support every style
                        do {
                            ff = rand->Next(0,fontfamilies->Count);
                        }
                        while (!fontfamilies[ff]->IsStyleAvailable(
                            (FontStyle)fontstyles[fs]));

                        // Display string of font
                        fontstr[i] = String::Format(S"{0} {1} {2}",
                            fontfamilies[ff]->Name,
                            __box(sizes[s])->ToString(),
                            String::Concat(__box(fontstyles[fs])->ToString(), S" ",
                                    __box(units[u])->ToString()));

                        // Create the font
                        fonts[i] = new Drawing::Font(fontfamilies[ff], sizes[s],
                                            (FontStyle)fontstyles[fs],
                                            (GraphicsUnit)units[u]);

                }
                InitializeComponent();
        }

protected:
        void Dispose(Boolean disposing)
        //...
private: System::ComponentModel::Container * components;
private: Drawing::Font *fonts[];
private: String *fontstr[];

        void InitializeComponent(void)
        {
            this->AutoScaleBaseSize = System::Drawing::Size(6, 15);
            this->ClientSize = System::Drawing::Size(292, 265);
            this->Name = S"Form1";
            this->Text = S"Many Fonts";
            this->Paint +=
                new System::Windows::Forms::PaintEventHandler(this, Form1_Paint);
```

```
        }
    private:
        System::Void Form1_Paint(System::Object *  sender,
                                  System::Windows::Forms::PaintEventArgs *  e)
        {
            Graphics *g = e->Graphics;

            Single lineloc = 0;
            for (Int32 i = 0; i < fonts->Count; i++)
            {
                // Display font
                g->DrawString(fontstr[i],fonts[i], Brushes::Black, 10, lineloc);

                // Calculate the top of the next line
                lineloc += fonts[i]->Height;
            }
        }
    };
}
```

Deep within the code is the routine to get a list of all the font families on your system:

```
InstalledFontCollection *availFonts = new InstalledFontCollection();
FontFamily *fontfamilies[] = availFonts->Families;
```

After these two lines are run, you have an array of all `FontFamilies` on your computer. It is pretty easy, no? The only hard part is remembering to add the namespace `System::Drawing::Text`, which you need to get access to the `InstalledFontCollection` class.

Something you might want to notice is how I figured out where to start the next line of `String`. I did this by adding the height of the font to the current line *y* coordinate after I finished drawing with it:

```
lineloc += fonts[i]->Height;
```

Figure 11-11 shows one instance of FontsGalore.exe running. I doubt you will ever see the same combination of fonts displayed twice.

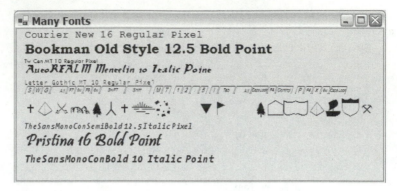

Figure 11-11. Displaying random fonts

Colors

Most current display device technology defines colors by breaking them up into their three basic components: red, green, and blue. Depending on the configuration of the display device, these components usually will have a value that ranges from 0 to 255. The principle is that by combining different amounts of red, green, and blue, you can generate any color. Thus, many of today's display devices can display up to 16,777,216 (256 cubed) unique colors.

But the story doesn't end there. Colors also provide an *alpha component*. This component represents how transparent the color is. If the alpha value is 0, then the color is completely transparent (a kind of useless color), and a value of 255 is completely opaque. In between these two points are varying degrees of transparency that will, when drawn to the screen, merge with any color already existing at that location. You see this effect used most often in computer games.

Many of the Graphics class's Drawing methods need a System::Drawing::Color structure containing one of the colors built from the values described previously before they can be used. The Color class has a number of members (see Table 11-11) available to get color information from. You can use only three common methods to place color information into a Color structure:

- FromArgb() returns a Color class based on the alpha, red, green, and blue values passed to it.

- FromKnownColor() returns a Color class based on a predefined color.

- FromName() returns a Color class based on the string color name passed.

You must use one of these three methods to create your color because there is no Color constructor.

Table 11-11. Common Color Members

MEMBER	DESCRIPTION
A	Gets the alpha component
B	Gets the blue component
G	Gets the green component
GetBrightness()	Gets the brightness of the color based on the hue-saturation-brightness (HSB) value of the color
GetHue()	Gets the hue of the color, based on the HSB value of the color
GetSaturation()	Gets the saturation of the color, based on the HSB value of the color
IsKnownColor()	True if it is a known color
IsNamedColor()	True if it is a named color
IsSystemColor()	True if it is a system color
Name	Gets the name of a "named" color
R	Gets the red component
ToArgb()	Gets the 32-bit ARGB value of the color
ToKnownColor()	Gets the KnownColor value of the color

There are two basic methods of defining a Color class: defining it using a combination of red, green, blue, and alpha component values or selecting the color from a list of predefined colors.

Custom Colors

To build your own custom color, you need to use the Color class's FromArgb() method. There are several overloads of the method, but you will most likely use two of them. The first method takes only the red, green, and blue components and defaults the alpha component to opaque (255). The second method allows you to specify the alpha component.

```
// Pure red
Color red1 = Color::FromArgb(255, 0, 0);
Color red2 = Color:: FromArgb(255, 255, 0, 0);
//Pure green
Color green1 = Color::FromArgb(0, 255, 0);
Color green2 = Color::FromArgb(255, 0, 255, 0);
//Pure blue
Color blue1 = Color::FromArgb(0, 0, 255);
Color blue2 = Color::FromArgb(255, 0, 0, 255);
```

You can make transparent or semitransparent colors by adjusting the alpha component passed to the FromArgb() method:

```
Color transparentgray = Color::FromArgb(127, 127, 127, 127);
```

Named Colors

The Color class provides a large number of predefined colors or *named* colors. There are two types of named colors. The first is a name that describes the color. These types of colors range (alphabetically) from AliceBlue to YellowGreen. The second type of color uses a name that describes its role in the Windows standard interface such as ControlText, ScrollBar, and Window.

The three ways of creating named colors are using the FromKnownColor() method, using the static named color method directly, or using the string name of the color.

```
Color c1 = Color::FromKnownColor(KnownColor::AliceBlue);
Color c2 = Color::AliceBlue;
Color c3 = Color::FromName(S"AliceBlue");
```

Pens and Brushes

When you render images to a drawing surface, you need an object to actually do the drawing. GDI+ provides two objects: the Pen and the Brush. (Makes sense, don't you think?) The Pen type is used to draw the outline of a shape, and the Brush type fills in an enclosed shape.

Pens

You've all worked with a pen, so the idea of what a pen does shouldn't be hard to visualize. Normally, you use a pen to draw the outline of the object. Most likely, you draw a solid line, but sometimes you might use a sequence of a bunch of dots and dashes. When you're drawing a line between two objects, you probably will put an arrow on one or both ends. If you like variety, you might even use a red or blue pen along with your black one.

The Pen type provided by GDI+ provides basically the same functionality.

Custom Pens

You use the Pen constructor to create a Pen object, and then you use its properties (see Table 11-12) to indicate how you want the Pen used. There are several constructors to create a Pen, but in most cases the simple color and width constructors do the trick.

```
Pen pen1 = new Pen(Color::Blue, 3.0);
```

Or if you want the Pen to be only 1 graphics unit thick, you could use the even easier:

```
Pen pen2 = new Pen(Color::Blue);
```

Notice I used the term "graphics unit." The Pen type's thickness is based on the graphics unit, not pixels, though the default is pixels.

Table 11-12. Common Pen Properties

PROPERTY	DESCRIPTION
Color	Specifies the color of the Pen
CompoundArray	Specifies the splitting of the width of a line into multiple parallel lines
CustomEndCap	Specifies a custom cap for the end of the line
CustomStartCap	Specifies a custom cap for the start of the line
DashCap	Specifies the dash-dot-space pattern used at the cap of a line
DashOffset	Specifies the distance from the start of the line to the beginning of the dash-dot-space pattern

(continued)

Table 11-12. Common Pen Properties (continued)

PROPERTY	DESCRIPTION
DashPattern	Specifies a predefined dash-dot-space pattern to be used for a line
DashStyle	Specifies the style of the dash lines
EndCap	Specifies a predefined cap to be used for the end of the line
LineJoin	Specifies the style of the join between two consecutive lines
PenType	Specifies the style of the line generated by the Pen
StartCap	Specifies a predefined cap to be used for the start of the line
Width	Specifies the width of the Pen

Named Pens

If you are creating a pen that is only 1 graphics unit thick and uses a named color, then you can use one of the pens found in the Pens class. The name of the pen is the same as the name of the named color it is using.

```
Pen *pen = Pens::AliceBlue;
```

System Pens

System pens are virtually the same as named pens, except that instead of a pen being named after a color, it is named after the role that the Pen would use on the Windows GUI interface. Also, you will find system pens in the SystemPens class and not in the Pens class.

```
Pen *pen = SystemPens::MenuText;
```

Listing 11-12 presents an example program that draws a few lines using the CompoundArray, DashStyle, StartCap, and EndCap properties.

Listing 11-12. Creating Some Random Lines

```
namespace DrawingLines
{
    using namespace System;
```

```cpp
using namespace System::ComponentModel;
using namespace System::Collections;
using namespace System::Windows::Forms;
using namespace System::Data;
using namespace System::Drawing;
using namespace System::Drawing::Drawing2D;

public __gc class Form1 : public System::Windows::Forms::Form
{
public:
    Form1(void)
    {
        pen = new Pen*[5];

        // a one unit width black pen
        pen[0] = Pens::Black;

        // a one unit with purple pen broken with dashes
        pen[1] = new Pen(Color::Purple);
        pen[1]->DashStyle = DashStyle::Dash;

        // a 4 unit width chocolate pen
        pen[2] = new Pen(Color::Chocolate, 4);

        // A 8 width royalblue pen made up of three lines narrow wide narrow
        pen[3] = new Pen(Color::RoyalBlue, 10);
        Single cArray[] = { 0.0f, 0.1f, 0.3f, 0.7f, 0.9f, 1.0f };
        pen[3]->CompoundArray = cArray;

        // a 5 width tomato pen with diamond start and round end anchors
        pen[4] = new Pen(Color::Tomato, 5);
        pen[4]->StartCap = LineCap::DiamondAnchor;
        pen[4]->EndCap = LineCap::RoundAnchor;

        InitializeComponent();
    }

protected:
    void Dispose(Boolean disposing)
    //...
private: System::ComponentModel::Container * components;
private: Pen *pen[];
```

```
        void InitializeComponent(void)
        {
            this->BackColor = System::Drawing::Color::White;
            this->ClientSize = System::Drawing::Size(300, 300);
            this->Name = S"Form1";
            this->Text = S"Drawing Some lines";
            this->Paint +=
                new System::Windows::Forms::PaintEventHandler(this,Form1_Paint);
        }
    private:
        System::Void Form1_Paint(System::Object * sender,
                                   System::Windows::Forms::PaintEventArgs * e)
        {
            Random *rand = new Random();
            Graphics *g = e->Graphics;
            for (Int32 i = 0; i < 10; i++)
            {
                g->DrawLine(pen[i%5], rand->Next(0,299),
                    rand->Next(0,299), rand->Next(0,299), rand->Next(0,299));
            }
        }
    };
}
```

Figure 11-12 shows one instance of DrawingLines.exe running. I doubt you will ever see the same combination of lines being displayed twice.

Figure 11-12. Displaying random lines

The preceding code is pretty self-explanatory, with the help of the embedded comments, except for two things. The first is that you need to add the `System::Drawing::Drawing2D` namespace. This namespace defines both the `DashStyle` and `LineCap` classes.

The second is the code that implements the `CompoundArray` property. This property splits a single line into multiple parallel lines. It does this by taking the width of a line and defining some portions as visible and other portions as not visible. The basic idea is, starting at 0 percent, find the first percent value that the line will be visible and write that into a `Single` area, and then find the percent where it becomes invisible again and write that value into the area. Repeat the process for all the parallel sublines that make up the full area, stopping at 100 percent.

If you want to define the entire line width as being visible (a waste of time, by the way), the array will look like this:

```
Single cArray[] = { 0.0f, 1.0f };
```

If you want to define the top half of the line as visible and the bottom as invisible (again, a waste of time), the array will look like this:

```
Single cArray[] = { 0.0f, 0.5f };
```

If you want the top 10 percent and the bottom 10 percent only to be visible, the array will look like this:

```
Single cArray[] = { 0.0f, 0.1f, 0.9f, 1.0f };
```

Notice that the compound array always has an even number of elements.

The preceding example breaks the line like this:

So the code ends up looking like this:

```
pen[3] = new Pen(Color::RoyalBlue, 10);
Single cArray[] = { 0.0f, 0.1f, 0.3f, 0.7f, 0.9f, 1.0f };
pen[3]->CompoundArray = cArray;
```

Brushes

You use brushes to fill in the objects that you drew with the pens you defined in the previous section. Unlike the Pen class, the Brush class is an abstract class. You don't create objects directly from the Brush class; instead, brushes are created from classes derived from the Brush class such as SolidBrush, HatchBrush, and TextureBrush.

You can also create named brushes and SystemBrushes. The Brushes class will fill a shape like the SolidBrush class. The only difference is that the brushes are predefined with names based on named colors.

```
Brush *brush = Brushes::AliceBlue;
```

SystemBrushes are like the Brushes class, but instead of colors, the SystemBrushes are named based on the Windows role they would represent.

```
Brush *brush = SystemBrushes:: ActiveBorder;
```

SolidBrush, HatchBrush, and TextureBrush are not the only brushes available, but I cover only them to give you some ideas on how to work with brushes.

Solid Brushes

The SolidBrush class is the easiest of the brushes. All it takes in its constructor is the color that you want to fill the shape with. Its only property with any relevance is the color you used in the constructor.

```
SolidBrush *brush = new SolidBrush(Color::Black);
```

Hatch Brushes

The HatchBrush class is a little more complicated than the SolidBrush class. First, you need to add the namespace System::Drawing::Drawing2D so that you can access the both the HatchBrush class and the HatchStyle enumeration. The HatchBrush uses the HatchStyle enumeration (see Table 11-13) to define the look of the brush. GDI+ provides numerous hatch styles.

Table 11-13. Ten of the Many HatchStyle Enumerations

ENUMERATION	DESCRIPTION
BackwardDiagonal	Specifies a pattern of diagonal lines from the upper right to lower left
Cross	Specifies a pattern of vertical and horizontal lines
DiagonalBrick	Specifies a pattern that looks like slanted bricks
Divots	Specifies a pattern that looks like divots (a golfer's nightmare)
Horizontal	Specifies a pattern of horizontal lines
Plaid	Specifies a pattern that looks like plaid
SmallConfetti	Specifies a pattern that looks like small confetti
Sphere	Specifies a pattern of spheres laid adjacent to each other
Vertical	Specifies a pattern of vertical lines
ZigZag	Specifies a pattern of horizontal lines that looks like zigzags

The constructor is a little more complicated too, as you need to pass the HatchStyle and two colors, the first being the foreground hatch color and the second being the background color.

```
using namespace System::Drawing::Drawing2D;
//...
HatchBrush *b = new HatchBrush(HatchStyle::Divots, Color::Brown, Color::Green);
```

Textured Brushes

A TextureBrush class allows you to place an image in the brush and then use it to fill in shapes. The best part of TextureBrush is how little code is needed to get it to work. The basic tasks behind the creation of a TextureBrush are loading the image and then placing it in the brush:

```
Image *brushimage = new Bitmap(S"MyImage.bmp");
TextureBrush *tbrush = new TextureBrush(brushimage);
```

Because I haven't covered images yet, I defer their explanation until later in the chapter. But as you can see in the preceding constructor, once you have an image available, it is a simple process to place it into a TextureBrush.

But that is not where the story ends. What happens if the brush is smaller than the shape it is trying to fill? The TextureBrush provides a WrapMode parameter (see Table 11-14) in the constructor (and also a property) to determine what to do—either clamp it or tile it. *Clamping* means that only one copy of the image is drawn, and *tiling* means that the image is repeatedly drawn until the area is filled.

Table 11-14. WrapModes Enumeration

ENUMERATION	DESCRIPTION
Clamp	Clamp the image to the object boundary
Tile	Tile the shape
TileFlipX	Tile the shape, flipping horizontally on each column
TileFlipXY	Tile the shape, flipping horizontally and vertically
TileFlipY	Tile the shape, flipping vertically on each row

There is one more piece of the puzzle. The first brush starts in the upper-left corner of the control you are drawing in. Thus, if you are filling a rectangle, for instance, and you want the brush to start in the upper-left corner of the rectangle, then you need to call the Brush class's TranslateTransform() method to translate the brush to start at that location:

```
// Translate brush to same start location as rectangle
tbrush->TranslateTransform(25,25);
// Fill rectangle with brush
g->FillRectangle(tbrush, 25, 25, 250, 250);
```

Listing 11-13 shows the tiling of the TextureBrush using WrapMode::TileFlipXY. It also shows how to translate the starting point of the tiling to the upper-left corner of the shape you are trying to fill.

Listing 11-13. Filling with a TextureBrush

```
namespace TextureBrush1
{
    using namespace System;
    using namespace System::ComponentModel;
    using namespace System::Collections;
    using namespace System::Windows::Forms;
    using namespace System::Data;
    using namespace System::Drawing;
    using namespace System::Drawing::Drawing2D;
```

```
public __gc class Form1 : public System::Windows::Forms::Form
{
public:
    Form1(void)
    //...
protected:
    void Dispose(Boolean disposing)
    //...
private: System::ComponentModel::Container * components;

    void InitializeComponent(void)
    {
        this->AutoScaleBaseSize = System::Drawing::Size(6, 15);
        this->ClientSize = System::Drawing::Size(292, 265);
        this->Name = S"Form1";
        this->Text = S"Texture Brush";
        this->Paint +=
            new System::Windows::Forms::PaintEventHandler(this,Form1_Paint);
    }
private:
    System::Void Form1_Paint(System::Object * sender,
                             System::Windows::Forms::PaintEventArgs * e)
    {
        Graphics *g = e->Graphics;

        // Load Image
        Image *bimage = new Bitmap(S"MCppCover.jpg");
        // Create brush
        TextureBrush *tbsh = new TextureBrush(bimage, WrapMode::TileFlipXY);

        // Translate brush to same start location as rectangle
        tbsh->TranslateTransform(25,25);
        // Fill rectangle with brush
        g->FillRectangle(tbsh, 25, 25, 250, 250);
    }
};
}
```

Figure 11-13 shows TextureBrush.exe in action. Remember to make sure that the bitmap file is in the current executable starting directory so the program can find it. If it is not in the current executable starting directory, the program will abort.

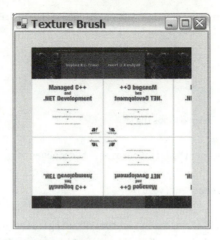

Figure 11-13. Displaying the tiled TextureBrush

Rendering Prebuilt Images

If you are implementing GDI+, you are probably planning to do one of two
things: Render an existing image or draw your own image. You will cover rendering an existing image first, as it is the easier of the two processes.

Here's the process in a nutshell. Load the image. Draw the image. That's it.
And it can be done in one line, too!

```
g->DrawImageUnscaled(Image::FromFile(S"MCppCover.jpg"), 0.0, 0.0);
```

Of course, if you want a little more control, there is another `DrawImage()`
method that you can work with. The `Image` class has a few members (see
Table 11-15) with which you can manipulate the image.

Table 11-15. Common Image Class Members

MEMBER	DESCRIPTION
FromFile()	Static method to load an image from a file
FromHbitmap()	Static method to load a bitmap from a Windows handle
FromStream()	Static method to load an image from a stream
GetBounds()	Returns a bounding rectangle for the image
Height	Specifies the height of the image
HorizontalResolution	Specifies the horizontal resolution of the image in pixels per inch
PhysicalDimensions	Specifies the size of the image

(continued)

Table 11-15. Common Image Class Members (continued)

MEMBER	DESCRIPTION
RotateFlip()	Rotates, flips, or rotates and flips the image
Save()	Saves the file to a stream
Size	Specifies the size of the image
VerticalResolution	Specifies the vertical resolution of the image in pixels per inch
Width	Specifies the width of the image

Before you can render an image, you need to load it from some source, either from a file as shown previously or a data stream (maybe the Internet?). Once the image is loaded, the Image class provides you the ability to flip and rotate the image.

NOTE   *The* Image *class doesn't use the* GraphicsUnit, *as you might expect. Instead, it uses pixels per inch.*

Once you have an image, you're ready to render it. You've seen the Graphics class's DrawImageUnscaled() method. That is about the extent of the functionality it provides. It can take an image and the location where you want to place it. A more flexible rendering method is DrawImage(). It takes myriad overloads (you can examine them at your leisure within the .NET Framework documentation), but the most useful overload takes the image and stretches it to the size you want (see Listing 11-14).

Listing 11-14. Stretching an Image

```
namespace DrawImage
{
    using namespace System;
    using namespace System::ComponentModel;
    using namespace System::Collections;
    using namespace System::Windows::Forms;
    using namespace System::Data;
    using namespace System::Drawing;

    public __gc class Form1 : public System::Windows::Forms::Form
    {
    public:
```

```
        Form1(void)
        //...
    protected:
        void Dispose(Boolean disposing)
        //...
    private: System::ComponentModel::Container * components;

        void InitializeComponent(void)
        {
            this->AutoScaleBaseSize = System::Drawing::Size(6, 15);
            this->ClientSize = System::Drawing::Size(292, 265);
            this->Name = S"Form1";
            this->Text = S"Draw Image";
            this->Paint +=
                new System::Windows::Forms::PaintEventHandler(this,Form1_Paint);
        }
    private:
        System::Void Form1_Paint(System::Object * sender,
                                    System::Windows::Forms::PaintEventArgs * e)
        {
        Graphics *g = e->Graphics;
        Image *img = Image::FromFile(S"MCppCover.jpg");
        g->DrawImage(img, 0, 0, img->Width*2, img->Height*2);
        }
    };
}
```

Figure 11-14 shows the end result of DrawImage.exe, which doubles the image with the DrawImage() method. It is a little blurry but not too bad.

Figure 11-14. Doubling an image's size

One last note about rendering images. So far you have only loaded images from files of type .jpg, but you can actually load .bmp, .gif, .png, and .tif image files without having to change a single line of code other than the name of the file.

Drawing Your Own Shapes and Lines

Now you can finally get to the fun part of GDI+: drawing your own images. You saw some of this in action earlier in the chapter. The steps involved are quite easy: Grab the `Graphics` class and then draw or fill the objects you want using the appropriate method. I listed all the methods you will likely use back in Table 11-3, so you might want to take a quick peek back there to refresh your memory.

Because all it really takes to draw an image is calling methods, let's create a simple piece of artwork with the example in Listing 11-15.

Listing 11-15. A Piece of Art

```
namespace HappyFace
{
    using namespace System;
    using namespace System::ComponentModel;
    using namespace System::Collections;
    using namespace System::Windows::Forms;
    using namespace System::Data;
    using namespace System::Drawing;

    public __gc class Form1 : public System::Windows::Forms::Form
    {
    public:
        Form1(void)
        //...
    protected:
        void Dispose(Boolean disposing)
        //...
    private: System::ComponentModel::Container * components;

        void InitializeComponent(void)
        {
            this->AutoScaleBaseSize = System::Drawing::Size(6, 15);
            this->ClientSize = System::Drawing::Size(300, 300);
            this->Name = S"Form1";
            this->Text = S"Happy Face";
            this->Paint +=
```

```
                       new System::Windows::Forms::PaintEventHandler(this,Form1_Paint);
                }
        private:
            System::Void Form1_Paint(System::Object * sender,
                                        System::Windows::Forms::PaintEventArgs * e)
            {
                Graphics *g = e->Graphics;
                Pen *b4pen = new Pen(Color::Black, 4);

                Rectangle rect = Drawing::Rectangle(25, 25, 250, 250);
                g->FillEllipse(Brushes::Yellow, rect);
                g->DrawEllipse(b4pen, rect);

                g->FillPie(Brushes::White, 100, 175, 100, 50, 0, 180);
                g->DrawPie(b4pen, 100, 175, 100, 50, 0, 180);

                rect = Drawing::Rectangle(100, 100, 25, 25);
                g->FillEllipse(Brushes::White, rect);
                g->DrawEllipse(b4pen, rect);

                rect = Drawing::Rectangle(175, 100, 25, 25);
                g->FillEllipse(Brushes::White, rect);
                g->DrawEllipse(b4pen, rect);
            }
        };
}
```

Figure 11-15 shows the results of HappyFace.exe, which is about the limit of my artistic abilities.

Figure 11-15. A happy face

Advanced GDI+

I kind of like the happy face I created in the last section, so I'll get a little more mileage out of it by using it to demonstrate a few more advanced GDI+ topics: scrollable windows, optimizing, and double buffering. By "advanced," I don't mean difficult—rather, I mean less obvious in how to implement. All three topics aren't that hard to implement.

Scrollable Windows

In the previous chapter on Win Forms, you didn't have to worry about a scrolling window as the Win Form handled it itself. With GDI+, on the other hand, it's up to you to add the necessary two lines in your code to get the scrollable window to work. Yep, you read correctly: *two lines of code.*

For those of you who aren't sure what a scrollable window is, it's a window that automatically attaches scroll bars to itself when the display information extends beyond its width. You use the scroll bar to shift the display area over so you can view this obscured displayed information.

To enable automatic scroll bars in a form, you need to update the AutoScrollMinSize property for the form:

```
this->AutoScrollMinSize = Drawing::Size(400, 400);
```

The size that you need to specify is the smallest area needed to display all the information. In my case, I was a little overzealous on the size so that you can see the scrolling better.

When you add the preceding line to your previous happy face example, you get scroll bars as shown in Figure 11-16, and everything seems hunky-dory.

Figure 11-16. A happy face in a scrollable window

Or is it? When you try to scroll the window, you get nothing but garbage, as you can see in Figure 11-17.

Figure 11-17. A not-so-happy happy face in a scrollable window

What's happening here? Believe it or not, the program is functioning perfectly—just not how you want it to. You can find the problem in the Paint event handler. The following steps show how the current program is working:

1. You click the scroll bar.

2. The window scrolls.

3. The Invalidate event is triggered for the clip area of the newly exposed window.

4. The Paint event handler executes.

5. The newly exposed window is replaced with any display data that belongs in it.

Sounds like it's working correctly to me, except for one minor detail. How does the program know what belongs in the newly exposed clip area? Notice that all the points in each of the drawing routines haven't been notified that the scroll took place. They're still drawing the same information at the same locations. Thus, the window is just repainting the newly exposed clip area with the original and wrong display information.

You have two (at least) ways of solving this problem. You might try adjusting each of the drawing routines by the amount of the scroll so that when they're called they render correctly. This solution isn't so bad when you're dealing with a handful of drawing and filling routines, but it's not good for a large number of routines.

An easier solution is to translate the origin of the Graphics class using the TranslateTransform() method (which I discussed earlier) to reflect the scroll. This solution has the same effect as the previous solution. The best part is that you have to add only one line of code, instead of changing every draw and fill routine. (Told you it would take two lines of code!)

```
g->TranslateTransform(AutoScrollPosition.X, AutoScrollPosition.Y);
```

It's also fortunate that the Form class provides a property, AutoScrollPosition, that indicates how much was scrolled.

Listing 11-16 shows the adjusted happy face program to handle scroll bars.

Listing 11-16. A Scrolling Happy Face

```
namespace ScrollingHappyFace
{
    using namespace System;
    using namespace System::ComponentModel;
    using namespace System::Collections;
    using namespace System::Windows::Forms;
    using namespace System::Data;
    using namespace System::Drawing;

    public __gc class Form1 : public System::Windows::Forms::Form
    {
    public:
        Form1(void)
        //...
    protected:
        void Dispose(Boolean disposing)
        //...
    private: System::ComponentModel::Container * components;

        void InitializeComponent(void)
        {
            this->AutoScrollMinSize = System::Drawing::Size(400, 400);
            this->AutoScaleBaseSize = System::Drawing::Size(6, 15);
```

```
        // Force scrolling
        // this should actually try to display as much as possible of the
        // image and not a small portion as this is doing
        this->ClientSize = System::Drawing::Size(250, 250);

        this->Name = S"Form1";
        this->Text = S"Scrolling Happy Face";
        this->Paint +=
            new System::Windows::Forms::PaintEventHandler(this,Form1_Paint);
    }
private:
    System::Void Form1_Paint(System::Object * sender,
                                System::Windows::Forms::PaintEventArgs * e)
    {
        Graphics *g = e->Graphics;
        g->TranslateTransform(AutoScrollPosition.X, AutoScrollPosition.Y);

        Pen *b4pen = new Pen(Color::Black, 4);

        Rectangle rect = Drawing::Rectangle(25, 25, 250, 250);
        g->FillEllipse(Brushes::Yellow, rect);
        g->DrawEllipse(b4pen, rect);

        g->FillPie(Brushes::White, 100, 175, 100, 50, 0, 180);
        g->DrawPie(b4pen, 100, 175, 100, 50, 0, 180);

        rect = Drawing::Rectangle(100, 100, 25, 25);
        g->FillEllipse(Brushes::White, rect);
        g->DrawEllipse(b4pen, rect);

        rect = Drawing::Rectangle(175, 100, 25, 25);
        g->FillEllipse(Brushes::White, rect);
        g->DrawEllipse(b4pen, rect);
    }
};
}
```

Figure 11-18 shows a happily scrolled happy face.

Figure 11-18. The left side of a happy face

Optimizing GDI+

You have many ways to optimize GDI+. This section describes the most obvious and easiest to implement methods.

Did you notice something about your `Paint` event handler method in the previous example? It executed every line in itself even if it was only replaying a small sliver of the graphic display. Wouldn't it be better and faster if only the parts of the `Paint` event handler method that need executing were executed? Let's see how you can do this.

The first thing you have to figure out is how to let a draw or fill method know that it needs to be executed.

What do all the draw and fill routines have in common in the preceding example? They all have a bounding rectangle. This rectangle indicates the area that it is supposed to update. Okay, so you know the area each draw or fill method needs to update.

```
Rectangle Head = Drawing::Rectangle(125, 25, 250, 250);
g->FillEllipse(Brushes::Yellow, Head);
```

Next, you need to know if this area is the same as what needs to be updated on the drawing surface. Remember way back near the beginning of the chapter where I wrote that the `PaintEventArgs` parameter provides two pieces of information: the `Graphics` and the `ClipRectangle`? This clip rectangle is the area that needs to be updated.

```
Drawing::Rectangle ClipRect = pea->ClipRectangle;
```

You now have two rectangles: one that specifies where it will update and another that specifies where it needs to be updated. So by intersecting these two rectangles, you can figure out if the draw routine needs to be executed, because when the intersection is not empty you know that the draw or fill needs to be executed.

```
if (!(Rectangle::Intersect(ClipRect, Head)).IsEmpty)
{
    //...Execute draw or fill method
}
```

The neat thing about this is that if you surround every draw and fill method with this comparison, when the `Paint` event handler is executed, only the draw or fill methods that need to be executed are.

There is one more wrinkle, though. The clip area is based on the client area and not the scroll area. This sounds familiar, doesn't it? So you have to adjust the clip area by the negative of `AutoScrollPosition`.

```
ClipRect.Offset(-AutoScrollPosition.X, -AutoScrollPosition.Y);
```

Why negative? You're doing the exact opposite of what you did in the previous example. This time you're moving the object on the drawing surface and keeping the drawing surface still. In the previous example, you kept the objects still and moved the drawing surface (well, it's not really doing this but it's easier to picture this way).

Listing 11-17 shows the scrollable happy face program with this optimization.

Listing 11-17. An Optimized Scrollable Happy Face

```
namespace OptimizedHappyFace
{
    using namespace System;
    using namespace System::ComponentModel;
    using namespace System::Collections;
    using namespace System::Windows::Forms;
    using namespace System::Data;
    using namespace System::Drawing;

    public __gc class Form1 : public System::Windows::Forms::Form
    {
    public:
        Form1(void)
```

```
        {
            Head  = Drawing::Rectangle(125, 25, 250, 250);
            Mouth = Drawing::Rectangle(200, 175, 100, 50);
            LEye  = Drawing::Rectangle(200, 100, 25, 25);
            REye  = Drawing::Rectangle(275, 100, 25, 25);
            b4pen = new Pen(Color::Black, 4);
            InitializeComponent();
        }
    protected:
        void Dispose(Boolean disposing)
        //...
    private: System::ComponentModel::Container * components;
    private: Drawing::Rectangle Head;
    private: Drawing::Rectangle Mouth;
    private: Drawing::Rectangle LEye;
    private: Drawing::Rectangle REye;
    private: Pen *b4pen;

        void InitializeComponent(void)
        {
            this->AutoScaleBaseSize = System::Drawing::Size(6, 15);
            this->AutoScroll = true;
            this->AutoScrollMinSize = System::Drawing::Size(400, 400);
            this->BackColor = System::Drawing::Color::Green;
            this->ClientSize = System::Drawing::Size(250, 250);
            this->Name = S"Form1";
            this->Text = S"Optimized Happy Face";
            this->Paint +=
                new System::Windows::Forms::PaintEventHandler(this,Form1_Paint);
        }
    private:
        System::Void Form1_Paint(System::Object * sender,
                                 System::Windows::Forms::PaintEventArgs * e)
        {
            Graphics *g = e->Graphics;

            Drawing::Rectangle ClipRect = e->ClipRectangle;
            ClipRect.Offset(-AutoScrollPosition.X, -AutoScrollPosition.Y);

            g->TranslateTransform(AutoScrollPosition.X, AutoScrollPosition.Y);

            if (!(Rectangle::Intersect(ClipRect, Head)).IsEmpty)
            {
```

```
            g->FillEllipse(Brushes::Yellow, Head);
            g->DrawEllipse(b4pen, Head);

            if (!(Rectangle::Intersect(ClipRect, Mouth)).IsEmpty)
            {
                g->FillPie(Brushes::White, Mouth, 0, 180);
                g->DrawPie(b4pen, Mouth, 0, 180);
            }
            if (!(Rectangle::Intersect(ClipRect, LEye)).IsEmpty)
            {
                g->FillEllipse(Brushes::White, LEye);
                g->DrawEllipse(b4pen, LEye);
            }
            if (!(Rectangle::Intersect(ClipRect, REye)).IsEmpty)
            {
                g->FillEllipse(Brushes::White, REye);
                g->DrawEllipse(b4pen, REye);
            }
        }
    }
};
}
```

Notice that in the code I threw in one more optimization in OptimizedHappyFace.exe. The Paint event handler method doesn't draw the mouth or eyes if the head doesn't need to be painted. I can do this because the mouth and eyes are completely enclosed within the head, so if the head doesn't need painting, there's no way that the mouth or eyes will either.

Double Buffering

Double buffering is the technique of using a secondary off-screen buffer to render your entire screen image. Then, in one quick blast, you move the completed secondary buffer onto your primary on-screen form or control.

Using double buffering speeds up the rendering process and makes image movement much smoother by reducing flickering. Let's give the happy face some life and let it slide repeatedly across the form.

Unbuffer Method

The first example in Listing 11-18 shows how you can implement this without double buffering. (There are other ways of doing this—some of them are probably more efficient.) There is nothing new in the code. You start by creating a `Timer` and telling it to invalidate the form each time it is triggered. Then you render the happy face repeatedly, shifting it over to the right and slowing it by changing the origin with the `TranslateTransform()` method. When the happy face reaches the end of the screen, you reset the happy face back to the left and start again.

Listing 11-18. Sliding the Happy Face the Ugly Way

```
namespace SingleBuffering
{
    using namespace System;
    using namespace System::ComponentModel;
    using namespace System::Collections;
    using namespace System::Windows::Forms;
    using namespace System::Data;
    using namespace System::Drawing;

    public __gc class Form1 : public System::Windows::Forms::Form
    {
    public:
        Form1(void)
        {
            X = -250;  // Preset to be just left of window
            InitializeComponent();
        }
    protected:
        void Dispose(Boolean disposing)
        //...
    private: System::ComponentModel::IContainer *  components;
    private: System::Windows::Forms::Timer *  timer1;
    private: Single X;          // Actual x coordinate of Happy face

        void InitializeComponent(void)
        {
            this->components = new System::ComponentModel::Container();
            this->timer1 = new System::Windows::Forms::Timer(this->components);
            //
            // timer1
            //
```

```
              this->timer1->Enabled = true;
              this->timer1->Interval = 10;
              this->timer1->Tick += new System::EventHandler(this, timer1_Tick);
              //
              // Form1
              //
              this->AutoScaleBaseSize = System::Drawing::Size(6, 15);
              this->ClientSize = System::Drawing::Size(500, 300);
              this->Name = S"Form1";
              this->Text = S"Sliding Happy Face";
              this->Paint +=
                    new System::Windows::Forms::PaintEventHandler(this,Form1_Paint);
        }
   private:
        System::Void Form1_Paint(System::Object * sender,
                                    System::Windows::Forms::PaintEventArgs * e)
        {
           Graphics *g = e->Graphics;

           // Move image at end of line start from beginning
           if (X < ClientRectangle.Width)
               X += 1.0;
           else
               X = -250.0;


           g->TranslateTransform(X, 25.0);

           // redraw images from scratch
           Pen *b4pen = new Pen(Color::Black, 4);

           Drawing::Rectangle Head  = Drawing::Rectangle(0, 0, 250, 250);
           g->FillEllipse(Brushes::Yellow, Head);
           g->DrawEllipse(b4pen, Head);

           Drawing::Rectangle Mouth = Drawing::Rectangle(75, 150, 100, 50);
           g->FillPie(Brushes::White, Mouth,0,180);
           g->DrawPie(b4pen, Mouth, 0, 180);

           Drawing::Rectangle LEye  = Drawing::Rectangle(75, 75, 25, 25);
           g->FillEllipse(Brushes::White, LEye);
           g->DrawEllipse(b4pen, LEye);
```

```
              Drawing::Rectangle REye  = Drawing::Rectangle(150, 75, 25, 25);
              g->FillEllipse(Brushes::White, REye);
              g->DrawEllipse(b4pen, REye);
          }
      private:
          System::Void timer1_Tick(System::Object * sender,
                                      System::EventArgs * e)
          {
              // Move the image
              Invalidate();
          }
      };
  }
```

When you run SingleBuffering.exe, you will see a rather ugly, flickering happy face sort of sliding across the screen. If you have a superpowered computer with a great graphics card, then the flickering may not be that bad, or it may be nonexistent. My computer is on the average side, and it still looks kind of pathetic.

Double Buffer Method

I change as little of the original code as possible in the double buffering example in Listing 11-19, which should enable you to focus on only what is needed to implement double buffering.

As the technique's name suggests, you need an extra buffer. Creating one is simple enough:

```
dbBitmap = new Bitmap(ClientRectangle.Width, ClientRectangle.Height);
```

You have not covered the Bitmap class. But for the purposes of double buffering, all you need to know is that you create a bitmap by specifying its width and height. If you want to know more about the Bitmap class, the .NET Framework documentation is quite thorough.

If you recall, though, you don't call draw and fill methods from a bitmap— you need a Graphics class. Fortunately, it's also easy to extract the Graphics class out of a bitmap:

```
dbGraphics = Graphics::FromImage(dbBitmap);
```

Now that you have a `Graphics` class, you can clear, draw, and fill it just like you would a form-originated `Graphics` class:

```
dbGraphics->FillEllipse(Brushes::Yellow, Head);
dbGraphics->DrawEllipse(b4pen, Head);
```

So how do you implement a double buffer? The process is pretty much the same as for a single buffer, except that instead of drawing to the display device directly, you draw to the buffer. Once the image is complete, you copy the completed image to the display device. Notice you copy the image or buffer and not the graphic.

```
e->Graphics->DrawImageUnscaled(dbBitmap, 0, 0);
```

The reason double buffering is faster than single buffering is because writing to memory is faster than writing to the display device. Flickering is not an issue because the image is placed in its complete state onto the screen. There is no momentary delay, as the image is being built in front of your eyes.

Listing 11-19 shows the changes needed to implement double buffering. I don't claim this is the best way to do it. The goal is to show you what you need to do using GDI+.

Listing 11-19. Sliding a Happy Face Double Buffer Style

```
namespace DoubleBuffering
{
    using namespace System;
    using namespace System::ComponentModel;
    using namespace System::Collections;
    using namespace System::Windows::Forms;
    using namespace System::Data;
    using namespace System::Drawing;

    public __gc class Form1 : public System::Windows::Forms::Form
    {
    public:
        Form1(void)
        {
            dbBitmap = 0;
            dbGraphics = 0;

            X = -250.0;   // Preset to be just left of window

            InitializeComponent();
```

```
            this->SetStyle(ControlStyles::Opaque, true);
    }


protected:
    void Dispose(Boolean disposing)
    //...
private: System::Windows::Forms::Timer *  timer1;
private: System::ComponentModel::IContainer *  components;
private: Bitmap    *dbBitmap;
private: Graphics *dbGraphics;
private: Single X;          // Actual x coordinate of Happy face


private:
    void InitializeComponent(void)
    {
        this->components = new System::ComponentModel::Container();
        this->timer1 = new System::Windows::Forms::Timer(this->components);
        //
        // timer1
        //
        this->timer1->Enabled = true;
        this->timer1->Interval = 10;
        this->timer1->Tick += new System::EventHandler(this, timer1_Tick);
        //
        // Form1
        //
        this->Resize += new System::EventHandler(this, Form1_Resize);
        this->Paint +=
            new System::Windows::Forms::PaintEventHandler(this,Form1_Paint);
        this->AutoScaleBaseSize = System::Drawing::Size(6, 15);
        this->ClientSize = System::Drawing::Size(500, 300);
        this->Name = S"Form1";
        this->Text = S"Sliding Happy Face";
    }
private:
    System::Void Form1_Paint(System::Object * sender,
                             System::Windows::Forms::PaintEventArgs * e)
    {
        // Move image at end of line start from beginning
        if (X < ClientRectangle.Width)
        {
            X += 1.0;
            dbGraphics->TranslateTransform(1.0, 0.0);
```

```
        }
        else
        {
            X = -250.0;
            dbGraphics->
                TranslateTransform(-(ClientRectangle.Width+250), 0.0);
        }
        // Clear background
        dbGraphics->Clear(Color::White);

        // redraw image from scratch
        Pen *b4pen = new Pen(Color::Black, 4);

        Drawing::Rectangle Head  = Drawing::Rectangle(0, 0, 250, 250);
        dbGraphics->FillEllipse(Brushes::Yellow, Head);
        dbGraphics->DrawEllipse(b4pen, Head);

        Drawing::Rectangle Mouth = Drawing::Rectangle(75, 150, 100, 50);
        dbGraphics->FillPie(Brushes::White, Mouth,0,180);
        dbGraphics->DrawPie(b4pen, Mouth, 0, 180);

        Drawing::Rectangle LEye  = Drawing::Rectangle(75, 75, 25, 25);
        dbGraphics->FillEllipse(Brushes::White, LEye);
        dbGraphics->DrawEllipse(b4pen, LEye);

        Drawing::Rectangle REye  = Drawing::Rectangle(150, 75, 25, 25);
        dbGraphics->FillEllipse(Brushes::White, REye);
        dbGraphics->DrawEllipse(b4pen, REye);

        // Make the buffer visible
        e->Graphics->DrawImageUnscaled(dbBitmap, 0, 0);
    }
private:
    System::Void Form1_Resize(System::Object * sender,
                              System::EventArgs * e)
    {
        // Get rid of old stuff
        if (dbGraphics != 0)
        {
            dbGraphics->Dispose();
            dbGraphics = 0;
```

```
        }
        if (dbBitmap != 0)
        {
            dbBitmap->Dispose();
            dbBitmap = 0;
        }
        if (ClientRectangle.Width > 0 && ClientRectangle.Height > 0)
        {
            // Create a bitmap
            dbBitmap =
                new Bitmap(ClientRectangle.Width,ClientRectangle.Height);

            // Grab its Graphics
            dbGraphics = Graphics::FromImage(dbBitmap);

            // Set up initial translation after resize (also at start)
            dbGraphics->TranslateTransform(X, 25.0);
        }
    }
}
private:
    System::Void timer1_Tick(System::Object * sender,
                             System::EventArgs * e)
    {
        // Move the image
        Invalidate();
    }
};
}
```

Let's take a look at some of the changes that were needed. I already mentioned the building of a bitmap, so I'll skip that.

The first difference is that you have to handle the resizing of the form. The reason you must do this is because the secondary off-screen buffer needs to have the same dimensions as the primary on-screen buffer. When a form is resized, the primary buffer changes size, therefore you need to change the secondary buffer.

Notice also that you dispose of the Graphics class and the Bitmap class. Both of these classes use a lot of resources between them, and disposing the old one before the new releases those resources. You need to check to make sure they have been initialized, because the first time this method is run they have not been initialized. Also, when the form is minimized you get rid of the buffer, so when the form is expanded you need to build the buffer again.

```
this->Resize += new EventHandler(this, Form_Resize);
//...
void Form_Resize(Object *sender, EventArgs *ea)
{
    // Get rid of old stuff
    if (dbGraphics != 0)
    {
        dbGraphics->Dispose();
        dbGraphics = 0;
    }
    if (dbBitmap != 0)
    {
        dbBitmap->Dispose();
        dbBitmap = 0;
    }
    if (ClientRectangle.Width > 0 && ClientRectangle.Height > 0)
    {
        // Create a bitmap
        dbBitmap = new Bitmap(ClientRectangle.Width,ClientRectangle.Height);
        // Grab its Graphics
        dbGraphics = Graphics::FromImage(dbBitmap);
        // Set up initial translation after resize (also at start)
        dbGraphics->TranslateTransform(X, 25.0);
    }
}
```

CAUTION   *You need to assign the* Resize *event handler before you set the size of the form. If you don't, the* Resize *event handler won't be called the first time to initialize* dbBitmap *and* dbGraphics.

The next difference is an important one. It is the setting of the style of the form to opaque. What this does is stop the form from clearing itself when it receives Invalidate().

```
SetStyle(ControlStyles::Opaque, true);
```

There is no need to clear the on-screen buffer because the off-screen buffer will overwrite everything on the on-screen buffer. All the clearing of the on-screen buffer does is momentarily leave the screen empty before the off-screen buffer writes to it, which produces a flicker.

CAUTION *If you forget to set the style to opaque, your image will flicker.*

The last difference that I haven't already discussed is the
TranslateTransform() changes. Notice that you translate by one each time and
not by "X". The reason for this is that the same Graphics class stays active the
entire time this program is running (unless the screen in resized). The same translation matrix is being used, so you only need to increment by one. When you reach
the end of the screen, you need to translate all the way back in one big jump.

```
if (X < ClientRectangle.Width)
{
    X += 1.0;
    dbGraphics->TranslateTransform(1.0, 0.0);
}
else
{
    X = -250.0;
    dbGraphics->TranslateTransform(-(ClientRectangle.Width+250), 0.0);
}
```

Figure 11-19 shows DoubleBuffering.exe sliding a happy face across the
form. Unfortunately, this still image doesn't show much of the sliding.

Figure 11-19. The sliding happy face

Printing

I'll finish off this discussion of GDI+ by showing that you aren't restricted to the display adapter when it comes to GDI+. As I've been suggesting throughout the chapter, GDI+ is device independent, so in theory you should be able to draw using GDI+ to the printer. You know what? You can.

The printer is not as closely linked to the computer as the display adaptor is, so to get GDI+ to work, you need to somehow provide for this link between your system and the printer. GDI+ does this through the `PrintDocument` class, which you can find in the `System::Drawing::Printer` namespace.

You can configure the `PrintDocument` class using its members (see Table 11-16), but letting the `PrintDialog` handle this is much easier.

Table 11-16. Common PrintDocument Members

MEMBER	DESCRIPTION
DefaultPageSettings	Specifies the default settings to be used on all pages printed
DocumentName	Specifies the name of the document being printed
Print()	A method to start the printing process of a `PrintDocument`
PrintController	Specifies the print controller that maintains the print process
PrinterSettings	Specifies the printer that prints the document

In the example in Listing 11-20, you'll print the happy face I'm so proud of. First, you'll bring up the happy face using the normal `Paint` event handler method. Then you'll right-click to bring up the `PrintDialog` to print the happy face to the printer of your choice.

Just to prove that the same GDI+ code works for both the screen and the printer, I separated the code that generates the happy face into a method of its own that both the screen and print processes access.

First, look at the code as a whole and then I'll walk you through the highlights.

Listing 11-20. Printing a Happy Face

```
namespace PrintHappyFace
{
    using namespace System;
    using namespace System::ComponentModel;
    using namespace System::Collections;
    using namespace System::Windows::Forms;
```

```
using namespace System::Data;
using namespace System::Drawing;
using namespace System::Drawing::Printing

public __gc class Form1 : public System::Windows::Forms::Form
{
public:
    Form1(void)
    //...
protected:
    void Dispose(Boolean disposing)
    //...
private: System::Windows::Forms::PrintDialog *  printDialog;
private: System::Drawing::Printing::PrintDocument *  printDocument;
private: System::ComponentModel::Container * components;

    void InitializeComponent(void)
    {
        this->printDialog = new System::Windows::Forms::PrintDialog();
        this->printDocument =
            new System::Drawing::Printing::PrintDocument();
        //
        // printDialog
        //
        this->printDialog->Document = this->printDocument;
        //
        // Form1
        //
        this->AutoScaleBaseSize = System::Drawing::Size(6, 15);
        this->ClientSize = System::Drawing::Size(300, 300);
        this->Name = S"Form1";
        this->Text = S"Click to Print";
        this->MouseDown +=
        new System::Windows::Forms::MouseEventHandler(this,Form1_MouseDown);
        this->Paint +=
            new System::Windows::Forms::PaintEventHandler(this,Form1_Paint);
    }
private:
    System::Void Form1_MouseDown(System::Object * sender,
                                    System::Windows::Forms::MouseEventArgs * e)
    {
        // Display Print dialog when mouse pressed
        if (printDialog->ShowDialog() == DialogResult::OK)
```

```
            {
                printDocument->PrintPage +=
                    new PrintPageEventHandler(this, PrintPage);
                printDocument->Print();
            }
        }
    private:
        void PrintPage(Object * sender, PrintPageEventArgs *e)
        {
            CreateHappyFace(e->Graphics); //Same call as Form1_Paint
            e->HasMorePages = false;
        }
    private:
        System::Void Form1_Paint(System::Object * sender,
                                    System::Windows::Forms::PaintEventArgs * e)
        {
            CreateHappyFace(e->Graphics); //Same call as printDocument_PrintPage
        }
    private:
        // Generic Happy Face Creator
        void CreateHappyFace(Graphics *g)
        {
            Pen *b4pen = new Pen(Color::Black, 4);

            Rectangle rect = Drawing::Rectangle(25, 25, 250, 250);
            g->FillEllipse(Brushes::Yellow, rect);
            g->DrawEllipse(b4pen, rect);

            g->FillPie(Brushes::White, 100, 175, 100, 50, 0, 180);
            g->DrawPie(b4pen, 100, 175, 100, 50, 0, 180);

            rect = Drawing::Rectangle(100, 100, 25, 25);
            g->FillEllipse(Brushes::White, rect);
            g->DrawEllipse(b4pen, rect);

            rect = Drawing::Rectangle(175, 100, 25, 25);
            g->FillEllipse(Brushes::White, rect);
            g->DrawEllipse(b4pen, rect);
        }
    };
}
```

The first thing I did when I created PrintHappyFace is dragged and dropped a PrintDocument and a PrintDialog control to the form and then set the Document property of the PrintDialog to the newly created PrintDocument. (It will show up in the Document property drop-down box.)

This autogenerates all the code needed to create a PrintDialog and a PrintDocument and then links them together. I need to link the PrintDialog to the PrintDocument so that any configuration changes made to the printers through the PrintDialog get reflected in the PrintDocument.

Next, I added an event handler for the MouseDown event that displays the PrintDialog (see Figure 11-20) and gathers the user's input on configuring the printer.

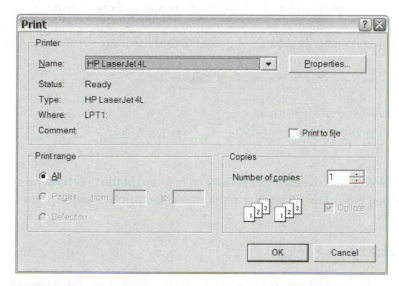

Figure 11-20. The printer dialog box

If the user is happy and wants to complete the print process, he or she will click the OK button, which will return DialogResult::OK. If the user doesn't want to complete the print process, he or she will click the Cancel button and DialogResult::Cancel will be returned. I ignore this result in the example, but you might want to acknowledge the cancel. Printers are frequently on the opposite end of the office (I don't know how this is possible, but it seems to be always true), and walking to the printer and waiting for something cancelled could be aggravating to users.

```
if (pdialog->ShowDialog() == DialogResult::OK)
```

When the `DialogResult::OK` is received, you then need to delegate a handler to the `PrintPage` event. It is through the `PrintPage` event that you will actually be processing your GDI+ statements.

```
printdoc->PrintPage += new PrintPageEventHandler(this, PrintPage);
```

Finally, you tell the `PrintDocument` to start printing. My guess is that it triggers a `PrintPage` event.

```
printdoc->Print();
```

The last thing to notice about the preceding example is the event handler. The `PrintPage` event handler handles the printing of only one page. If you want to print more than one page, you need to set the `HasMorePages` property of the `PrintPageEventArgs` parameter passed to the `PrintPage` event handler to true.

```
void PrintPage(Object *sender, PrintPageEventArgs *e)
{
    CreateHappyFace(e->Graphics);
    ppea->HasMorePages = false;    // false means only one page will be printed.
}
```

Notice that the exact same GDI+ code found in the `CreateHappyFace()` method is used for displaying to the screen and printing to the printer.

Summary

This has been another long chapter in which you covered a lot of ground. You started off with the basics of what GDI+ is. You created your third "Hello, World" program—this time with a GDI+ flavor. You then moved on and examined many of the GDI+ classes, the most important being the `Graphics` class, from which all GDI+ functionality derives. You played with strings, fonts, and predrawn images and ended up with the basics of drawing your own image. Next, you covered the advanced topics: scrollable windows, optimizing, and double buffering. You ended the chapter by demonstrating that you can also use GDI+ to print to printers.

You should now have all the information you need to display your own images and no longer be restricted to drawing with the controls provided by Win Forms.

In the next chapter, you get to play with databases using ADO.NET. Along the way, you will look at some of the tools Visual Studio .NET provides to work with databases.

CHAPTER 12

ADO.NET and Database Development

You've already looked at two of the four common methods of getting input into and out of your .NET Windows applications: streams and controls. ADO.NET, which you'll cover in detail in this chapter, is the third. In next chapter, you'll round it out with XML, the fourth and final common method. ADO.NET is a huge topic. In this chapter you'll learn about some of the more commonly used aspects of it.

When you're implementing with ADO.NET, you're dealing with data stores or, to use the better-known term, databases. Most developers are going to have to deal with the database. If that thought frightens you, it shouldn't, as ADO.NET has made the database an easy and, dare I say, fun thing to work with. The hard part now is no longer interfacing with the database, be it a 2-tier, 3-tier, or even n-tier architecture, but instead designing a good database. Hey—Visual Studio .NET even works with you there!

The language of relational databases is still SQL. That doesn't change with ADO.NET. If you don't know SQL, then you might need to read up on it a little bit. However, for those of you who don't know SQL, I made this chapter's SQL code rudimentary, to say the least. SQL is a very powerful language and most programmers should have at least some SQL knowledge. But don't fret if you don't, as the SQL you'll find in this chapter isn't important in your understanding of ADO.NET. What I'm basically trying to say in a long, roundabout way is that this chapter is about ADO.NET and not SQL.

This chapter starts by covering the basic concepts of ADO.NET. You'll then move on to building, from scratch, a (very simple) database using Visual Studio .NET. Then, using this database, you'll examine in detail the two methods provided by ADO.NET to access a database: connected and disconnected.

Those of you who have read my book *Real World ASP.NET: Building a Content Management System* (Apress, 2002) might find some of the material similar as you're going to be using the database I developed in that book.

What Is ADO.NET?

Databases are made up of tables, views, relationships, constraints, and stored procedures. They're usually the domain of the database architects, designers, developers, and administrators. ADO.NET, on the other hand, is how application developers get their hands on these (meaning the tables, views, and so forth—not the architects and designers, though sometimes I'd like to get my hands on the designers. . . .) With ADO.NET, it's possible to keep these two diverse software developing worlds separate, letting the specialists in both fields focus on what they do best.

ADO.NET is a set of classes that encompasses all aspects of accessing data sources within the .NET architecture. It's designed to provide full support for either connected or disconnected data access, while using an Extensible Markup Language (XML) format for transmitting data when data transfer is required. Chapter 13 contains more details about XML, so don't worry about it for now. Just think of ADO.NET as a programmer's window into a data source, in this case the DVC_DB database.

The classes that make up ADO.NET are located primarily in two assemblies: System.Data.dll and System.Xml.dll. To reference these two assemblies, you need to add the following two lines to the top of your application source:

```
#using <System.Data.dll>
#using <System.Xml.dll>
```

The addition of the System.Xml.dll assembly is due to the heavy reliance on XML in the internals of ADO.NET and in particular the class XmlDataDocument.

Seven namespaces house all of ADO.NET's functionality. These namespaces are described at a high level in Table 12-1.

Table 12-1. ADO.NET Namespaces

NAMESPACE	DESCRIPTION
System::Data	Contains most of the classes that make up ADO.NET. The classes found within this namespace are designed to work independently of the type of data source used. The most important class in this namespace is the DataSet class, which is the cornerstone of disconnected data source access.
System::Data::Common	Contains the common interfaces used by each of the managed providers.

(continued)

Table 12-1. ADO.NET Namespaces (continued)

NAMESPACE	DESCRIPTION
System::Data::Odbc	Contains the classes that make up the ODBC managed provider, which allows access to ODBC-connected databases such as MySQL. The classes contained within this namespace are all prefixed with Odbc.
System::Data::OleDb	Contains the classes that make up the OLE DB managed provider, which allows access to databases such as Sybase, Microsoft Access, and Microsoft SQL Server 6.5. The classes contained within this namespace are all prefixed with OleDb.
System::Data::Oracle	Contains the classes that make up the Oracle managed provider, which allows access to Oracle8*i* and later databases. The classes contained within this namespace are all prefixed with Oracle.
System::Data::SqlClient	Contains the classes that make up the SQL Server managed provider, which allows access to Microsoft SQL Server 7.0 and later databases. The classes contained within this namespace are all prefixed with Sql.
System::Data::SqlTypes	Contains classes for native data types associated with SQL Server.

Now that you have a basic understanding of what ADO.NET is, let's take a small sidetrack from Managed C++ and see how to build a database using Visual Studio .NET.

Building a Database with Visual Studio .NET

Visual Studio .NET is well equipped when it comes to the design and development of Microsoft SQL Server databases. It provides the functionality to create databases, tables, views, stored procedures, and many other features.

The starting point of all database utilities is Server Explorer. Select Server Explorer from the View menu to open it (see Figure 12-1). You will find your database in one of two places. If the database is a Microsoft SQL Server 7.0 or higher database, it will be located in the SQL Servers database folder inside your Servers folder. Otherwise, it will be located in the Data Connections folder just above the Servers folder.

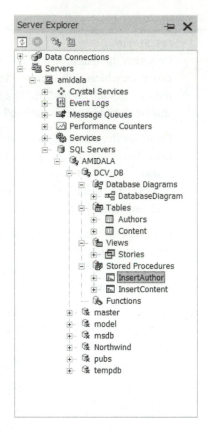

Figure 12-1. Server Explorer

Visual Studio .NET provides Microsoft SQL Server databases with much of the functionality that comes with SQL Enterprise Manager. On the other hand, all the other databases types are mostly restricted to viewing and editing records. This book focuses on Microsoft SQL Server and covers the functionality provided by Visual Studio .NET. If you are developing using any other database, much of the first part of this chapter will not help you because you will have to use the database maintenance tools provided by your database.

TIP *If you don't currently have a database installed on your system, I recommend that you install the MSDE 2000 database server provided with the .NET Framework samples. This database is a stripped-down version of Microsoft SQL Server, and with it you'll get a good feel for the functionality provided by Visual Studio .NET. Plus, you can always uninstall it later and use the database of your choice.*

There is nothing stopping you from building your Microsoft SQL Server databases outside of Visual Studio .NET, using the SQL Enterprise Manager, for example, and then adding the database to Server Explorer. Doing this is beyond the scope of this book, however.

Now you'll build your own simple content management database so that you can explore ADO.NET with intimate knowledge of its architecture, instead of as a black box as you would if you were using one of the preinstalled databases provided with MSDE 2000 or Microsoft SQL Server.

Creating a New Database

The first step in database development isn't creating one. Obviously, creating the data model, designing the logical database, and designing the physical database should come first. But hey, I'm a programmer. I'll code first and then go ask questions. (I'm joking—really!)

Visual Studio .NET makes creating databases so easy that it's almost not worth explaining how to do it.

 CAUTION *Be sure you really want the database you're creating because it's tricky to delete it once it's created in Visual Studio .NET. I had to go to the Microsoft SQL Enterprise Manager to delete my test databases. It's also possible to execute the* DROP DATABASE *command to remove a database.*

The following steps create the database DCV_DB, which contains author information and their related stories. You will use this database throughout the chapter.

1. Select Server Explorer from the View menu.

2. Expand the SQL Servers database folder from within your Servers folder.

3. Right-click the database server folder that you want to create the database in.

4. Select the New Database menu item, which displays the Create Database dialog box shown in Figure 12-2.

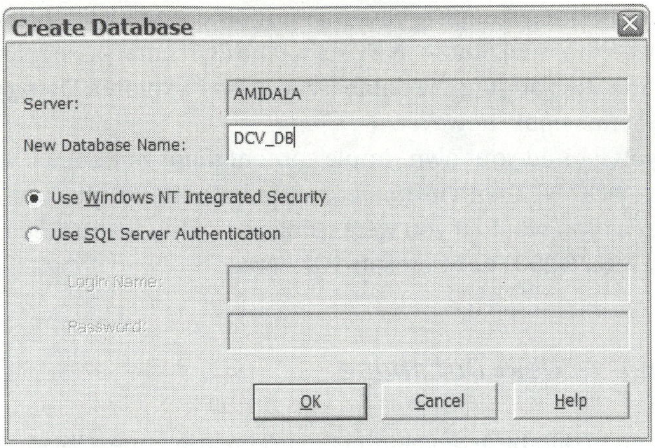

Create Database

Server: AMIDALA

New Database Name: DCV_DB

⦿ Use Windows NT Integrated Security

○ Use SQL Server Authentication

Login Name:

Password:

OK   Cancel   Help

Figure 12-2. The Create Database dialog box

5. Enter **DCV_DB** in the New Database Name field.

6. Select the Use SQL Server Authentication radio button.

7. Enter **sa** in the Login Name text box.

8. Click OK.

Microsoft SQL Server 2000 and MSDE 2000 support two types of security: Windows Integrated Security and SQL Server authentication (security). Covering these security systems is beyond the scope of this book. All you really need to know for now is that the connection strings will differ depending on which method you use. I cover these differences later in this chapter.

In the preceding database I use the most common (and probably least secure) security configuration. It uses the system administrator (sa) account with no password. You will find that many demonstration systems use this configuration.

NOTE   *If you selected Windows Integrated Security when you installed your Microsoft SQL Server 2000 or MSDE 2000 database, then you should select the Use Integrated NT Integrated Security radio button, because the security configuration described in this section causes a "Not associated with a trusted SQL Server connection" error.*

Now you should have a new database called DCV_DB in your database folder. You can expand it and see all the default folders built. If you click these folders, however, you will see that there is nothing in them. That's your next job.

Adding and Loading Tables and Views to a Database

An empty database is really quite useless, so now you'll add a couple of tables to the database to provide a place to store your content.

 NOTE *The tables and views you use in this chapter are purposely very simple (you might even call them minimal) and aren't the best schema around. I did this so that you don't get bogged down with the details of the database and so it doesn't take much effort or time for you to build these tables and views yourself.*

The first table is for storing authors and information about them, and the second table is for storing headlines and stories. The two databases are linked together by a common AuthorID key. Figure 12-3 shows a data diagram of the database.

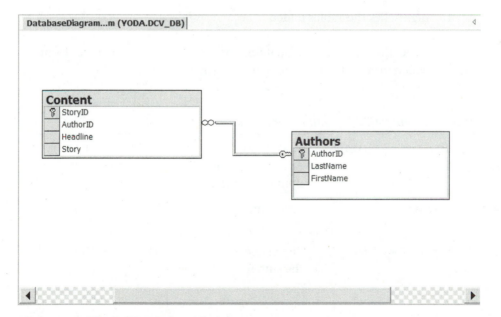

Figure 12-3. The DCV_DB data diagram

Having this separation means you have to store only one copy of the author information, even though the author may have written many stories. If you had created only one table to contain all the information, a lot of duplicated author information would have to be rekeyed each time a story is added to maintain the database. It also conveniently enables me to show you how to create a relationship between tables.

The process of building a new table is only slightly more difficult than creating a database. The hard part is figuring out what columns are needed and the format for each table in the database. It's nice to know you can spend most of your time designing the ultimate database schema instead of figuring out how to implement it.

Creating Tables

To create the first table, follow these steps:

1. Navigate down to the database server folder as you did in the "Creating a New Database" section.

2. Expand the database server folder.

3. Expand the DCV_DB folder.

4. Right-click the Tables folder.

5. Select the New Table menu item. You should now have an entry form in which to enter the database columns shown in Table 12-2.

Table 12-2. Authors Database Table Column Descriptions

COLUMN NAME	DATA TYPE	LENGTH	DESCRIPTION	IDENTITY	ALLOW NULLS
AuthorID	int	4	Autogenerated ID number for the author	Yes	No
LastName	varchar	50	Last name of the author	No	No
FirstName	varchar	50	First name of the author	No	No

6. Right-click the AuthorID row and select Set Primary Key from the drop-down menu.

7. Select Save Table1 from the File menu.

8. Enter **Authors** into the text field in the dialog box.

9. Click OK.

Go ahead and repeat these steps for the second table, but use the information in Table 12-3 and use StoryID as the primary key. Save the table as Content.

Table 12-3. Content Database Table Column Descriptions

COLUMN NAME	DATA TYPE	LENGTH	DESCRIPTION	IDENTITY	ALLOW NULLS
StoryID	int	4	Autogenerated ID number for the story	Yes	No
AuthorID	int	4	Foreign key to the Authors database	No	No
Headline	varchar	80	Headline for the content	No	No
Story	text	16	Story portion of the content	No	No

In this book I don't go into what all the data types mean, but if you're interested, many good books on Microsoft SQL Server and SQL cover this topic in great detail.

The Identity field, when set to Yes, will turn on autonumber generation for the column. Why the field is called "Identity" (instead of "Autonumber") is a mystery to me. I'm an application programmer, though, and not a database person. It's probably some special database term.

Okay, you now have your tables. The next step is to build a relationship between them. In this database, it is fairly obvious: AuthorID is the column that should link these two tables.

Creating a Relationship

To create a relationship between your tables, follow these steps:

1. Right-click the Content table in Server Explorer.

2. Select Design Table from the menu.

3. Right-click anywhere on the Table Designer.

4. Select Relationships from the menu. This will bring up a Relationships property page similar to the one shown in Figure 12-4.

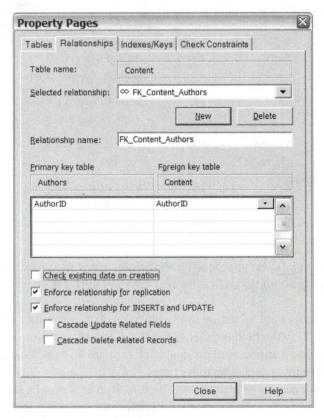

Figure 12-4. The Relationships property page

5. Click the New button.

6. Select Authors as the primary key side of the relationship from the Primary key table drop-down list.

7. Select AuthorID as the primary key in the grid beneath the Primary key table drop-down list.

8. Select Content as the foreign key side of the relationship from the Foreign key table drop-down list.

9. Select AuthorID as the foreign key in the grid beneath the Foreign key table drop-down list.

10. Click Close.

Now you have two tables and a relationship between them. Quite often, when you want to get data from a database, you need information from multiple tables. For example, in this case, you might want to get all stories with each author's first and last name. As mentioned previously, you could have created the Content table that way, but then you would have a lot of duplicate data floating around. There is nothing stopping you from executing a SQL statement, also known as a *query,* that gets this information, as shown in Listing 12-1.

Listing 12-1. Getting Data from Two Tables

```
SELECT      FirstName,
            LastName,
            Headline,
            Story
FROM        Authors,
            Content
WHERE       Authors.AuthorID = Content.AuthorID
ORDER BY    StoryID ASC
```

Personally, I prefer to be able to write a query something like this instead:

```
SELECT FirstName, LastName, Headline, Story FROM Stories
```
This is exactly what you can do with database views. Basically, you might think of a view as a virtual table without any data of its own, based on a predefined query. If you know you are going to use the same set of data based on a query, you might consider using the view instead of coding.

NOTE *Those of you who are knowledgeable about SQL and views might have noticed the* ORDER BY *clause. Microsoft SQL Server supports the* ORDER BY *clause in its views, unlike some older database systems.*

Creating a View

Follow these steps to create a view:

1. Right-click the Views table from within the DCV_DB folder in Server Explorer.

2. Select New View from the menu. This will bring up an Add Table dialog box similar to the one shown in Figure 12-5.

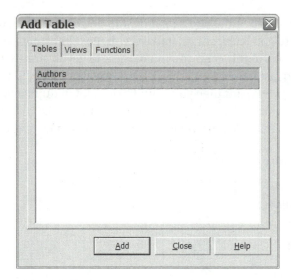

Figure 12-5. The Add Table dialog box

3. Select both Authors and Content.

4. Click the Add button. This generates a window similar to the one shown in Figure 12-6.

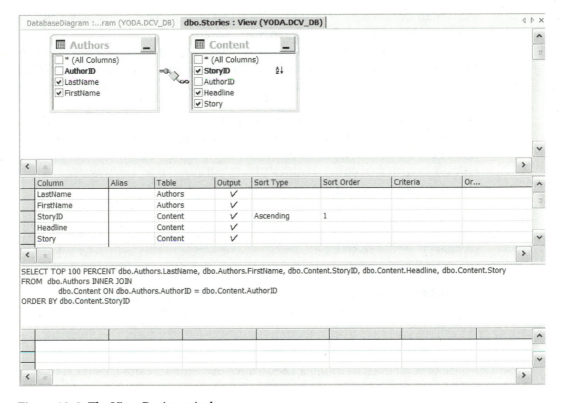

Figure 12-6. The View Design window

5. Click the Close button.

6. Click the check boxes for FirstName and LastName in the Authors table.

7. Click the check boxes for StoryID, Headline, and Story in the Content table.

8. Right-click StoryID and select Sort Ascending from the menu.

9. Select Save View1 from the File menu.

10. Enter **Stories** into text field.

11. Click OK.

Pretty painless, don't you think? You have the option of testing your view right there, too. Click the Run Query button on the main toolbar. (It's the button with an exclamation point on it.) The View Design window is pretty powerful. If you play with it for a while, you'll see what I mean.

Did you click the Run Query button and get nothing? Oops . . . I forgot to tell you to load some data into the database. You can do this with Visual Studio .NET as well. Simply double-click either of the tables you created, and an editable table will appear.

First enter the data for the authors. If you don't, you won't have an author ID to enter into the AuthorID column in the Content view. Enter the data from Table 12-4. Notice that there are no author IDs to enter—this field is automatically created. In fact, Visual Studio .NET will yell at you if you try to enter something in the AuthorID column.

Table 12-4. Author Data

LASTNAME	FIRSTNAME
Doors	Bill
Ellidaughter	Larry
Fraser	Stephen

Now enter the data in Table 12-5. Notice that StoryID cannot be entered. It, too, is an autogenerated number. You do have to enter AuthorID, though, because it is not automatically generated in this table.

Table 12-5. Content Data

AUTHORID	HEADLINE	STORY
1	.NET is the Best	According to my research. The .NET product has no competition, though I am a little biased.
2	Oracle is #1	Research suggests that it is the best database on the market, not that I have any biases in that conclusion.
3	Content Management is Expensive	Not anymore. It now costs the price of a book and a little work.
4	SQL Server Will Be #1	This database has no real competition. But then again, I am a little biased.

Building Stored Procedures

You don't have to use stored procedures, because anything you can run using stored procedures you can run using standard SQL. So, why cover this utility at all?

There are two main reasons. First, stored procedures let a software developer call database code using function calls with arguments. Second, and more important, the utility is compiled before it gets loaded. This makes the calls to the database faster and more efficient because it has already been optimized.

Because you haven't covered ADO.NET code yet, you won't be able to do much with the stored procedure you'll create. Fortunately, Visual Studio .NET provides an option so that it can be tested.

Unlike the previous utilities, you have to actually code stored procedures. If you don't know SQL, don't worry because the coding is short and, I think, pretty self-explanatory. As always, there are many good books you can read to get a better understanding of it.

You will create a stored procedure to insert data into the Authors table. You already did this process manually, so you should have a good idea of what the stored procedure needs to do.

To create a stored procedure, follow these steps:

1. Right-click the Stored Procedures table from within the DCV_DB folder in Server Explorer.

2. Select New Stored Procedure from the menu. This will bring up an editing session with the default code shown in Listing 12-2.

Listing 12-2. Default Stored Procedure Code

```
CREATE PROCEDURE dbo.StoredProcedure1
/*
    (
        @parameter1 datatype = default value,
        @parameter2 datatype OUTPUT
    )
*/
AS
    /* SET NOCOUNT ON */
    RETURN
```

First you have to set up the parameters that will be passed from the program. Obviously, you need to receive all the mandatory columns that make up the row. In the Authors table's case, that's the entire row except AuthorID, which is autogenerated. Listing 12-3 shows the changes that need to be made to the default code provided in order to add parameters. Note that the comments /*...*/ are removed.

Listing 12-3. Setting the Parameters

```
CREATE PROCEDURE dbo.StoredProcedure1
    (
        @LastName NVARCHAR(32) = NULL,
        @FirstName NVARCHAR(32) = NULL,
    )
AS
```

The SET NOCOUNT ON option prevents the number of rows affected by the stored procedure from being returned to the calling program every time it is called. If you need a count on the number of records affected, you can leave the SET NOCOUNT ON option commented out or you can delete the option altogether. Because I will use the count in a later example I left the option commented out.

Finally, you code the actual insert command. The key to this stored procedure is that instead of hard-coding the values to be inserted, you use the parameters you previously declared. Listing 12-4 is the final version of the stored procedure. Note that you rename the stored procedure to dbo.InsertAuthor.

Listing 12-4. InsertAuthor Stored Procedure

```
CREATE PROCEDURE dbo.InsertAuthor
    (
        @LastName NVARCHAR(32) = NULL,
        @FirstName NVARCHAR(32) = NULL,
    )
AS
    /* SET NOCOUNT ON */

    INSERT INTO    Authors ( LastName,  FirstName)
    VALUES                 (@LastName, @FirstName)

    RETURN
```

All that's left is to save the stored procedure. Saving the file will create a stored procedure with the name on the CREATE PROCEDURE line. If you made a mistake while coding, the save will fail and an error message will tell you where the error is.

To run or debug the stored procedure, just right-click the newly created stored procedure and select Run Stored Procedure or Step Into Stored Procedure.

You now have a database to work with for the rest of the chapter. Let's continue on and start looking at ADO.NET and how to code it using Managed C++.

Managed Providers

Managed providers provide ADO.NET with the capability to connect to and access data sources. Their main purpose, as far as most developers are concerned, is to provide support for the DataAdapter class. This class is essentially for mapping between the data store and the DataSet.

Currently only four managed providers exist for ADO.NET:

- *SQL Server managed provider:* Connects to Microsoft SQL Server version 7.0 or higher databases

- *OLE DB managed provider:* Connects to several supported OLE DB data sources

- *ODBC managed provider:* Connects to ODBC-connected databases such as MySQL

- *Oracle managed provider:* Connects to the Oracle8*i* or higher databases

Determining which of these managed providers is actually used depends on the database that ADO.NET interfaces with. Currently, ADO.NET interfaces with four groups of database types: Microsoft SQL Server 7.0 and later, Oracle8*i* and later, databases that provide ODBC support, and databases that provide OLE DB support. Which database group you are using determines if you implement the System::Data::SqlClient, System::Data::Oracle, System::Data::Odbc, or System::Data::OleDb namespace.

In addition, the group of databases interfaced with determines which classes you will use. You will find that if you are using the System::Data::SqlClient namespace, then all of your classes will be prefixed with Sql, as in SqlCommand() and SqlDataAdapter(). If you are using the System::Data::Oracle namespace, then the classes will be prefixed with Oracle, as in OracleCommand() and OracleDataAdapter(). If you are using the System::Data::Odbc namespace, then the classes will be prefixed with Odbc, as in OdbcCommand() and OdbcDataAdapter(). And, if are using the System::Data::OleDb namespace, then the classes will be prefixed with OleDb, as in OleDbCommand() and OleDbDataAdapter().

Once you have learned one managed provider, you have pretty much learned all four because they are nearly the same, except for the Sql, OleDb, Odbc, and Oracle prefixes and a few other small differences.

Because this book uses Microsoft SQL Server 2000, I use the SQL Server managed provider and thus the namespace associated with it.

Connected ADO.NET

As I stated previously, you have two distinct ways of accessing a database using ADO.NET. I cover the one that's easier to visualize and code (at least for me) first: connected access.

With *connected access,* you are continually connected to the database during the entire time you work with it. Like file access, you open the database, work with it for a while, and then you close it. Also like file I/O, you have the option of buffering data written to the database. This buffered access to the database is better known as *transactional database access.* I discuss this access method after I cover nontransactional database access.

Using Simple Connected ADO.NET

You'll start with the easiest way of working with database, where the commands you execute happen immediately to the database.

Figure 12-7 shows the basic flow of nontransactional database access.

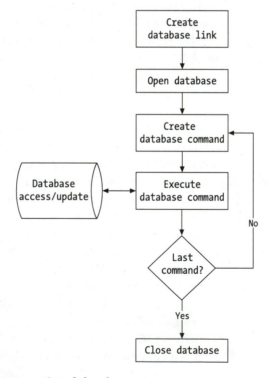

Figure 12-7. Nontransactional database access

1. Create a link to the database with a `SqlConnection`.

2. Open the database with the `Open()` method.

3. Create a database command with `SqlCommand`.

4. Execute the command by using one of the three methods within `SqlCommand` (see Table 12-6). The database is immediately updated.

Table 12-6. The Main SqlCommand SQL Statement Execution Methods

METHOD	DESCRIPTION
ExecuteNonQuery	Executes a statement that updates the database.
ExecuteReader	Executes a query to the database that could potentially return multiple rows from a database. This method returns a `SqlDataReader` object that provides forward-only read access to the retrieved data or result set.
ExecuteScalar	Executes a statement that returns a single value.

5. Repeat steps 3 and 4 until completed.

6. Close the database with the `Close()` method.

NOTE   *If you are using the SQL Server managed provider, use classes prefixed with* `Sql`. *On the other hand, when you are using the OLE DB managed provider, use classes starting with* `OleDb`; *when you are using the ODBC managed provider, use classes starting with* `Odbc`; *and when you are using the Oracle managed provider, use classes starting with* `Oracle`.

Connecting to, Opening, and Closing a Database

With connected nontransactional access to a database, you will always be connecting to, opening, and closing your database. To handle this, you need to work with one of the Connection classes: `SqlConnection`, `OleDbConnection`,

OdbcConnection, or OracleConnection. Which one of these you use depends on the managed provider you use.

This book uses Microsoft SQL Server, so you'll use the SQL Server managed provider. If you are using the OLE DB, ODBC, or Oracle managed provider, just remember to replace the prefix of every class starting with Sql with OleDb, Odbc, or Oracle and, of course, you will have to change the connection string, but I'll get to that shortly.

Listing 12-5 shows how to connect, open, and close a database in a nontransactional method.

Listing 12-5. Connecting, Opening, and Closing a Database

```
using namespace System;
using namespace System::Data;
using namespace System::Data::SqlClient;


Int32 main(void)
{
    SqlConnection *connection = new SqlConnection();

#ifdef SQLAuth
    //  SQL Server authentication
    connection->ConnectionString =
        S"User ID=sa; Password=;"
        S"Data Source=(local); Initial Catalog=DCV_DB;";
#else
    //  Windows Integrated Security
    connection->ConnectionString =
        S"Persist Security Info=False; Integrated Security=SSPI;"
        S"Data Source=(local); Initial Catalog=DCV_DB;";
#endif
    try
    {
        connection->Open();
        Console::WriteLine(S"We got a connection!");
    }
    catch (SqlException *e)
    {
        Console::WriteLine(S"No connection the following error occurred: {0}",
            e->Message);
    }
    __finally
    {
```

```
        connection->Close();
        Console::WriteLine(S"The connection to the database has been closed");
    }
    return 0;
}
```

The first thing you do (as with any other .NET application) is import the namespaces needed to access the ADO.NET basic functionality:

```
using namespace System;
using namespace System::Data;
using namespace System::Data::SqlClient;
```

For those of you using a database different than Microsoft SQL Server, use one of the following namespaces instead of System::Data::SqlClient: System::Data::OleDb, System::Data::Odbc, or System::Data::Oracle.

There is nothing special about creating an SqlConnection class. It is just a default constructor:

```
SqlConnection *connection = new SqlConnection();
```

The hardest part of this piece of coding is figuring out what the connection string is. For the SQL Server managed provider, this is fairly easy because it is usually made up of a combination of four out of six clauses:

- *The location of the server:* Data Source=(local);

- *The name of the database:* Initial Catalog=DCV_DB;

- *Whether security-sensitive information is returned as part of the connection:* Persist Security Info=False;

- *Whether Windows account credentials are used for authentication (this will be* False, *the default, for SQL Server authentication):* Integrated Security=SSPI;

- *The user ID (not recommended with Windows Integrated Security):* User ID=sa;

- *The user password (not recommended with Windows Integrated Security):* Password=; (notice that in this example the password is blank)

It will look like this in the code:

```
connection->ConnectionString =
    S"User ID=sa; Password=; Data Source=(local); "
    S"Initial Catalog=DCV_DB;";
```

or

```
connection->ConnectionString =
    S"Persist Security Info=False;Integrated Security=SSPI;"
    S"Data Source=(local); Initial Catalog=DCV_DB;";
```

The connection string for the Oracle managed provider is very similar to the SQL Server managed provider, whereas the OLE DB and ODBC managed providers always add an additional clause: for OLE DB, the Provider clause, and for ODBC, the Driver clause. For example:

```
connection->ConnectionString =
    S"Provider=SQLOLEDB; Data Source=(local); Initial Catalog=DCV_DB; "
    S"User ID=sa; Password=;";
```

and

```
connection->ConnectionString =
    S"Driver={SQL Server}; Data Source=(local); Initial Catalog=DCV_DB; "
    S"User ID=sa; Password=;";
```

 NOTE *In the preceding code I define two of the more common connection strings I use and use the compile-time directive #ifdef to allow me to choose the one I want. I do this to simplify things. In most cases, it would be better not to hard-code the connection string at all and instead retrieve it from a configuration file.*

You open and close the database in virtually the same way as you do a file, except the Open() method doesn't need any parameters:

```
connection->Open();
connection->Close();
```

You need to pay attention to the try statement. ADO.NET commands can abort almost anywhere, so it is always a good thing to enclose your ADO.NET logic within a try clause and capture any exceptions by catching SQLException (OleDbException, OdbcException, or OracleException).

It is also possible for ADO.NET to abort with the database still open. (Probably not in this example, but I felt having the correct code right from the beginning would make things clearer.) Therefore, it is a good idea to place your Close() method within a __finally clause so that it will always be executed.

Figure 12-8 shows the results of the preceding example program. Impressive, no?

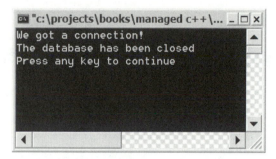

Figure 12-8. The database is successfully opened and closed.

Querying a Database

All queries made to a connected database are done using the SqlCommand, OleDbCommand, OdbcCommand, or OracleCommand class. As noted previously, the SqlCommand class provides three methods to send SQL commands to the database, with each depending on the type of command. To query the database, you need to use the ExecuteReader() method.

Before you run the ExecuteReader() method, you need to configure SqlCommand by placing the SQL command into it. There are two common ways of doing this. You can either place the SQL command, in text form, into the CommandText property or place the name of stored procedure containing the SQL command into the same property. The default method is the command in text form. If you plan to use a stored procedure, you need to change the CommandType property to CommandType::StoredProcedure.

Listing 12-6 shows both methods. The first command uses a text-formatted command and retrieves the contents of the Authors database for authors with a specified LastName, in this case hard-coded to "Doors". The second command, using a stored procedure, retrieves all Stories view records where LastName equals the value passed to the stored procedure, in this case also "Doors".

Both calls to the ExecuteReader() method after being configured return an instance of SqlDataReader, which is then iterated through to display the retrieved content.

Listing 12-6. The "Doors" Stories

```
using namespace System;
using namespace System::Data;
using namespace System::Data::SqlClient;


Int32 main(void)
{
    String *Name = S"Doors";

    SqlConnection *connection = new SqlConnection();

#ifdef SQLAuth
    //  SQL Server authentication
    connection->ConnectionString =
        S"User ID=sa; Password=;"
        S"Data Source=(local); Initial Catalog=DCV_DB;";
#else
    //  Windows Integrated Security
    connection->ConnectionString =
        S"Persist Security Info=False; Integrated Security=SSPI;"
        S"Data Source=(local); Initial Catalog=DCV_DB;";
#endif

    try
    {
        SqlCommand *cmd = new SqlCommand();
        cmd->Connection = connection;

        cmd->CommandType = CommandType::Text;
        cmd->CommandText =
            String::Format(S"SELECT FirstName, LastName FROM Authors "
                           S"WHERE LastName = '{0}'",
                           Name);

        connection->Open();

        SqlDataReader *reader = cmd->ExecuteReader();
```

```
    while(reader->Read())
    {
        Console::WriteLine(S"{0} {1}",
            reader->Item[S"FirstName"], reader->Item[S"LastName"]);
    }
    reader->Close();

    // CREATE PROCEDURE dbo.StoriesWhereLastName
    //   (
    //       @LastName NVARCHAR(32) = NULL
    //   )
    // AS
    //   /* SET NOCOUNT ON */

    //   SELECT StoryID, Headline, Story FROM Stories
    //   WHERE   LastName = @LastName
    //
    //   RETURN

    cmd->CommandType = CommandType::StoredProcedure;
    cmd->CommandText = S"StoriesWhereLastName";

    cmd->Parameters->Add(new SqlParameter(S"@LastName",SqlDbType::VarChar));
    cmd->Parameters->Item[S"@LastName"]->Value = Name;

    reader = cmd->ExecuteReader();

    Console::WriteLine(S"-----------------------");
    while(reader->Read())
    {
        Console::WriteLine(reader->Item[S"StoryID"]);
        Console::WriteLine(reader->Item[S"Headline"]);
        Console::WriteLine(reader->Item[S"Story"]);
        Console::WriteLine();
    }
    reader->Close();
}
catch (SqlException *e)
{
    Console::WriteLine(S"No connection the following error occurred: {0}",
        e->Message);
}
__finally
```

```
    {
        connection->Close();
    }
    return 0;
}
```

The code to query a database with a `CommandType` of `Text` is pretty easy (if you know SQL, that is). First, you set the `SqlCommand` class's `CommandType` property to `Text`:

```
cmd->CommandType = CommandType::Text;
```

Next, you place the SQL command you want to execute in the `CommandText` property. What makes this process easy is that you can use standard `String` formatting to build the command, as you see here:

```
cmd->CommandText =
    String::Format(S"SELECT * FROM Authors WHERE LastName='{0}'", Name);
```

Finally, you run the `SqlCommand` class's `ExecuteReader()` method. This method returns a `SqlDataReader` class from which you process the result set produced from the query:

```
SqlDataReader *reader = cmd->ExecuteReader();
```

The code to query a database with a `CommandType` of `StoredProcedure` is a little more difficult if passing parameters is required. (It is a little easier if no parameters are passed, as no SQL code has to be written by the application developer.) First, you set the `SqlCommand` class's `CommandType` property to `StoredProcedure`:

```
cmd->CommandType = CommandType::StoredProcedure;
```

Next, you place the name of the stored procedure you want to execute in the `CommandText` property:

```
cmd->CommandText = S"StoriesWhereLastName";
```

Now comes the tricky part. You need to build a collection of `SqlParameters`, within which you will place all the parameters that you want sent to the stored procedure. The `SqlCommand` class provides a property called `Parameters` to place your collection of `SqlParameters`.

The first step is to use the `Add()` method off of the `Parameters` property collection to add all the `SqlParameters` making up all the parameters that will be passed to the stored procedure. The constructor for the `SqlParameters` class takes two or three parameters depending on the data type of the parameter that will be passed to the stored procedure. If the data type has a predefined length like `Int` or a variable length like `VarChar`, then only two parameters are needed.

```
cmd->Parameters->Add(new SqlParameter(S"@LastName", SqlDbType::VarChar));
```

On the other hand, if the data type needs its length specified like `Char`, then the third parameter is used to specify the length.

```
cmd->Parameters->Add(new SqlParameter(S"@FixedSizeString",SqlDbType::Char,32));
```

When all the parameters are specified, you need to assign values to them so that the stored procedure can use them. You do this by assigning a value to the `Value` property of the indexed property `Item`, off of the `Parameters` property collection of the `SqlCommand` class. Clear as mud? The example should help:

```
cmd->Parameters->Item["@LastName"]->Value = Name;
```

Finally, when all the parameters are assigned values, you call the `SqlCommand` class's `ExecuteReader()` method just like you did for a `CommandType` of `Text`:

```
reader = cmd->ExecuteReader();
```

The processing of the result set within the `SqlDataReader` object is handled in a forward-only manner. The basic process is to advance to the next record of the result set using the `Read()` method. If the return value is `false`, you have reached the end of the result set and you should the call the `Close()` method to close the `SqlDataReader`. If the value is `true`, then you continue and process the next result set record.

```
while(reader->Read())
{
    Console::WriteLine(reader->Item[S"StoryID"]);
    Console::WriteLine(reader->Item[S"Headline"]);
    Console::WriteLine(reader->Item[S"Story"]);
    Console::WriteLine(S"");
}
reader->Close();
```

There are two different methods of processing the record set. You can, as I did, use the indexed `Item` property to get the value based on the column header.

You can also process the columns using an assortment of type-specific `Getxxx()` methods. The following code generates the same output as the preceding code:

```
while(reader->Read())
{
    Console::WriteLine(reader->GetInt32(0));
    Console::WriteLine(reader->GetString(1));
    Console::WriteLine(reader->GetString(2));
    Console::WriteLine(S"");
}
reader->Close();
```

Note the parameter passed in the position of the column starting at zero.

I personally find using column names easier, but the style you choose to use is up to you. Figure 12-9 shows the results of the preceding example program.

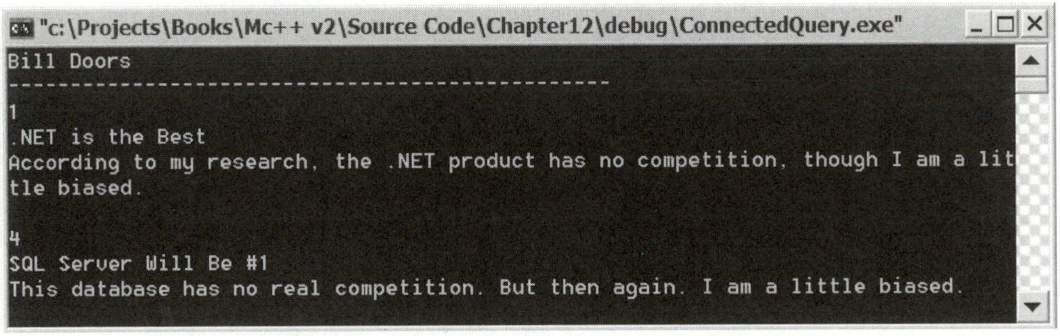

Figure 12-9. Retrieving Bill Doors's stories

Insert, Update, and Delete Commands

The code to modify the database (i.e., insert, update, and delete rows of the database) isn't much different from the code to query the database. Obviously, the SQL is different. The only other difference is that you call the `SqlCommand` class's `ExecuteNonQuery()` method instead of the `ExecuteReader()` method.

You can still use both `CommandType`s and you still need to set up the `SQLParameters` the same way for stored procedures.

In Listing 12-7 you insert a new record into the database, you change the `LastName` on the record, and then you delete the record. (A lot of work for nothing, don't you think?)

Listing 12-7. Modifying the Database

```cpp
using namespace System;
using namespace System::Data;
using namespace System::Data::SqlClient;

Int32 main(void)
{
    String *Name = S"Doors";

    SqlConnection *connection = new SqlConnection();

#ifdef SQLAuth
    //  SQL Server authentication
    connection->ConnectionString =
        S"User ID=sa; Password=;"
        S"Data Source=(local); Initial Catalog=DCV_DB;";
#else
    //  Windows Integrated Security
    connection->ConnectionString =
        S"Persist Security Info=False; Integrated Security=SSPI;"
        S"Data Source=(local); Initial Catalog=DCV_DB;";
#endif

    try
    {
        SqlCommand *cmd = new SqlCommand();
        cmd->Connection = connection;
        connection->Open();

        cmd->CommandType = CommandType::StoredProcedure;
        cmd->CommandText = S"InsertAuthor";

        cmd->Parameters->Add(new SqlParameter(S"@LastName", SqlDbType::VarChar));
        cmd->Parameters->Add(new SqlParameter(S"@FirstName",SqlDbType::VarChar));

        cmd->Parameters->Item[S"@LastName"]->Value  = S"Dope";
        cmd->Parameters->Item[S"@FirstName"]->Value = S"John";

        Int32 affected = cmd->ExecuteNonQuery();
        Console::WriteLine(S"Insert - {0} rows are affected", __box(affected));
```

```
            cmd->CommandType = CommandType::Text;
            cmd->CommandText = S"UPDATE Authors SET LastName = 'Doe'"
                                S"WHERE LastName = 'Dope'";

            affected = cmd->ExecuteNonQuery();
            Console::WriteLine(S"Update - {0} rows are affected", __box(affected));

            cmd->CommandType = CommandType::Text;
            cmd->CommandText = S"DELETE FROM Authors WHERE LastName = 'Doe'";

            affected = cmd->ExecuteNonQuery();
            Console::WriteLine(S"Delete - {0} rows are affected", __box(affected));
        }
        catch (SqlException *e)
        {
            Console::WriteLine(S"No connection the following error occurred: {0}",
                e->Message);
        }
        __finally
        {
            connection->Close();
        }
        return 0;
    }
```

As you can see, there is not much new going on here in the Managed C++ code, other than the call to ExecuteNonQuery(). This method returns the number of rows affected by the SQL command.

```
Int32 affected = cmd->ExecuteNonQuery();
```

Figure 12-10 shows the results of the preceding example program.

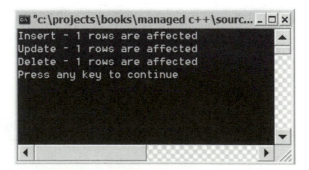

Figure 12-10. A lot of modifications to the database for no gain

Returning a Single Value from a Query

The final command executing method of the SqlCommand class is
ExecuteScalar(). This method is designed to return an Object pointer as the
result of the query. The returned Object points to a value like that produced by an
aggregated SQL function such as COUNT or SUM. Again, like the database modifying
command, there is not much changed between the source code needed to execute this type of method and that of a standard query.

Listing 12-8 shows how to count all the records in a database and also how
to sum a column. (The database does not have a column that you would want to
sum—I had to improvise.)

Listing 12-8. Counting and Summing

```
using namespace System;
using namespace System::Data;
using namespace System::Data::SqlClient;


Int32 main(void)
{
    SqlConnection *connection = new SqlConnection();

#ifdef SQLAuth
    //   SQL Server authentication
    connection->ConnectionString =
        S"User ID=sa; Password=;"
        S"Data Source=(local); Initial Catalog=DCV_DB;";
#else
    //   Windows Integrated Security
    connection->ConnectionString =
        S"Persist Security Info=False; Integrated Security=SSPI;"
        S"Data Source=(local); Initial Catalog=DCV_DB;";
#endif

    try
    {
        SqlCommand *cmd = new SqlCommand();
        cmd->Connection = connection;
        connection->Open();

        cmd->CommandType = CommandType::Text;
        cmd->CommandText = S"SELECT COUNT(*) FROM Authors";
```

```
            Object *NumAuthors = cmd->ExecuteScalar();
            Console::WriteLine(S"The number of Authors are {0}", NumAuthors);

            cmd->CommandType = CommandType::Text;
            cmd->CommandText = S"SELECT SUM(AuthorID) FROM Authors";

            Object *UselessNum = cmd->ExecuteScalar();
            Console::WriteLine(S"The Sum of AuthorIDs for fun is {0}", UselessNum);
        }
        catch (SqlException *e)
        {
            Console::WriteLine(S"No connection the following error occurred: {0}",
                e->Message);
        }
        __finally
        {
            connection->Close();
        }
        return 0;
    }
```

As you can see, other than the SQL code and the calling of the ExecuteScalar() method, there is not much new. The ExecuteScalar() method returns a pointer to an Object, which you can type cast to the type of the return value. In both cases, you could have type cast the return Object pointer to Int32, but the WriteLine() method can do it for you.

Figure 12-11 shows the results of the preceding example program.

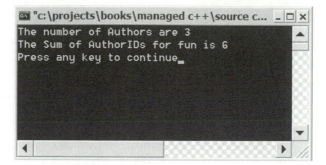

Figure 12-11. Counting rows and summing a column

Using Connected ADO.NET with Transactions

Think about this scenario. You buy a computer on your debit card, but while the purchase is being processed, the connection to the debit card company is lost. The response from the debit card reader is failure message. You try again and the debit card reader now responds that there is not enough money. You go home empty-handed, angry, and confused. Then a month later your bank statement says you bought a computer with your debit card.

It can't happen, right? Wrong. If you use the preceding immediate updating method, it's very possible, as each update to the database is stand-alone. One command can complete, for example, the withdrawal, while a second command may fail, for example, the sale.

This is where transactions come in handy. They make sure all database commands needed to complete a process are completed successfully before allowing the database to commit (or write) these commands. If one or more of the commands fail, the database can reject all of the commands and return to its original state before any of the commands where completed. This is known as *rolling back*.

Figure 12-12 shows the basic flow of transactional database access.

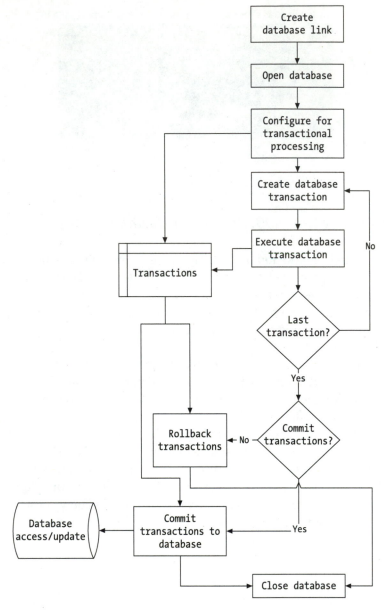

Figure 12-12. Transactional database access

1. Create a link to the database with a `SqlConnection`.

2. Open the database with the `Open()` method.

3. Configure for transactions.

4. Create a database transaction with the SqlCommand class.

5. Execute the transaction by using the ExecuteNonQuery() method of the SqlCommand class. The temporary copy of the database is updated.

6. Repeat steps 4 and 5 until completed.

7. When all transactions are complete, either commit the transactions to the database or roll them back.

8. Close the database with the Close() method.

Listing 12-9 shows how to convert the nontransactional example from Listing 12-7 into a transactional example.

Listing 12-9. Transactional Database Updates

```
using namespace System;
using namespace System::Data;
using namespace System::Data::SqlClient;

Int32 main(void)
{
    String *Name = S"Doors";

    SqlConnection   *connection = new SqlConnection();
    SqlTransaction *transaction;

#ifdef SQLAuth
    //  SQL Server authentication
    connection->ConnectionString =
        S"User ID=sa; Password=;"
        S"Data Source=(local); Initial Catalog=DCV_DB;";
#else
    //  Windows Integrated Security
    connection->ConnectionString =
        S"Persist Security Info=False; Integrated Security=SSPI;"
        S"Data Source=(local); Initial Catalog=DCV_DB;";
#endif

    try
    {
        connection->Open();
```

```
SqlCommand *cmd = new SqlCommand();

transaction = connection->BeginTransaction(
    IsolationLevel::Serializable, S"AuthorTransaction");

cmd->Connection  = connection;
cmd->Transaction = transaction;

cmd->CommandType = CommandType::StoredProcedure;
cmd->CommandText = S"InsertAuthor";

cmd->Parameters->Add(new SqlParameter(S"@LastName", SqlDbType::VarChar));
cmd->Parameters->Add(new SqlParameter(S"@FirstName",SqlDbType::VarChar));

cmd->Parameters->Item[S"@LastName"]->Value  = S"Dope";
cmd->Parameters->Item[S"@FirstName"]->Value = S"John";

Int32 affected = cmd->ExecuteNonQuery();
if (affected <= 0)
    throw new Exception(S"Insert Failed");
Console::WriteLine(S"Insert - {0} rows are affected", __box(affected));

cmd->CommandType = CommandType::Text;
cmd->CommandText = S"UPDATE Authors SET LastName = 'Doe'"
                   S"WHERE LastName = 'Dope'";

affected = cmd->ExecuteNonQuery();
if (affected <= 0)
    throw new Exception(S"Insert Failed");
Console::WriteLine(S"Update - {0} rows are affected", __box(affected));

// This transaction will return 0 affected rows
// because "Does" does not exist.
// Thus, the if condition throws an exception which causes all
// Transactions to be rolled back.
cmd->CommandType = CommandType::Text;
cmd->CommandText = S"DELETE FROM Authors WHERE LastName = 'Does'";

affected = cmd->ExecuteNonQuery();
if (affected <= 0)
    throw new Exception(S"Insert Failed");
Console::WriteLine(S"Delete - {0} rows are affected", __box(affected));
```

```
        transaction->Commit();
    }
    catch (Exception *e)
    {
        transaction->Rollback(S"AuthorTransaction");
        Console::WriteLine(S"Transaction Not completed");
        Console::WriteLine(S"SQL error occurred: {0}", e->Message);
    }
    __finally
    {
        connection->Close();
    }
    return 0;
}
```

As you can see there have not been many changes. First, you need to declare a SqlTransaction (OleDbTransaction, OdbcTransaction, or OracleTransaction) class:

```
SqlTransaction *transaction;
```

Next, you need to create a transaction set using the SqlConnection class's BeginTransaction() method. The BeginTransaction() method takes two parameters. The first parameter specifies the locking behavior of the transaction (see Table 12-7) and the second is the name of the transaction set:

```
transaction = connection->BeginTransaction(IsolationLevel::RepeatableRead,
                                    S"AuthorTransaction");
```

Table 12-7. Common Transaction IsolationLevels

LEVEL	DESCRIPTION
ReadCommitted	Specifies that locks are held while the data is read, but changes to the data can occur before the transaction is committed
ReadUncommitted	Specifies that changes can occur even while the data is being read
RepeatableRead	Specifies that locks are held on the data until the transaction is committed, but additional rows can be added or deleted
Serializable	Specifies that locks are held on the entire database until the transaction is committed

Now that you have a transaction set, you need to assign it to the `SqlCommand` class's property `Transaction`:

```
cmd->Transaction = transaction;
```

The last set of transactional database updates is to execute all the transactions. If everything completes successfully, then execute the `SqlTransaction` class's `Commit()` method:

```
transaction->Commit();
```

If, on the other hand, an error occurs, you would then execute the `SqlTransaction` class's `Rollback()` method:

```
transaction->Rollback(S"AuthorTransaction");
```

Figure 12-13 shows the results of the preceding example program failing because the name of the author was not found in the database.

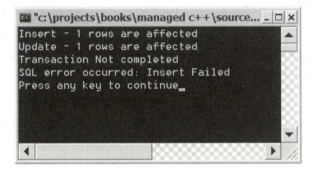

Figure 12-13. Transactional database update rollback

Disconnected ADO.NET

Let's switch gears and now look at disconnected ADO.NET. *Disconnected data access* is a key feature of ADO.NET. Basically, it means that most of the time when you're accessing a database, you aren't getting the data from the database at all. Instead, you're accessing a synchronized, in-memory copy of the data that was moved earlier to your client computer. Don't worry about all the technical issues surrounding this; just be glad that it works because it provides three major benefits:

- Less congestion on the database server because users are spending less time connected to it

- Faster access to the data because the data is already on the client

- Capability to work across disconnection networks such as the Internet

It also offers one benefit (associated with disconnected access) that is less obvious: Data doesn't have to be stored in a database-like format. Realizing this, Microsoft decided to implement ADO.NET using a strong typed XML format. The benefit is that having data in XML format enables data to be transmitted using standard HTTP. This causes a further benefit: Firewall problems disappear. An HTTP response with the body of XML flows freely through a firewall, unlike the pre-ADO.NET technology's system-level COM marshalling requests. If the previous bonus is Greek (or geek) to you, don't fret. In fact, be glad you have no idea what I was talking about.

The Core Classes

If you spend a lot of time working with ADO.NET, you may have an opportunity to work with almost all of ADO.NET's classes. For the purposes of this book, however, I've trimmed these classes down to the following:

- DataAdaptor

- DataSet

- DataTableCollection

- DataTable

- DataRow

- DataColumn

- DataRelationCollection

- DataRelation

- Constraint

All of these classes interact with each other in some way. Figure 12-14 shows the flow of the interaction. Essentially, the DataAdaptor connects the data store to the DataSet. The DataSet stores the data in a Tables property containing a DataTablesCollection made up of one or more DataTables. Each DataTable is made up of DataRows and DataColumns. All of the DataTables store their relationships in a Relations property containing a DataRelationCollection made up of DataRelations. Finally, each DataTable can be affected by Constraints. Simple, isn't it?

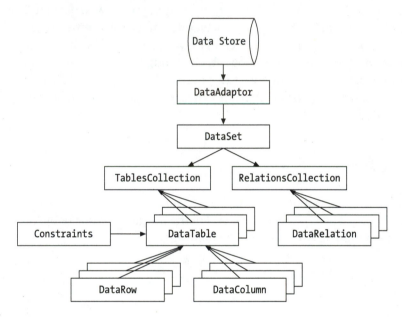

Figure 12-14. The disconnected ADO.NET class interaction

DataAdaptor

The `DataAdaptor` is the bridge between a data source (database) and the `DataSet`. Its purpose is to extract data out of the data source and place it in the `DataSet`. Then it updates, if required, the data source with the changes made in the `DataSet`.

It should be relatively easy to get comfortable with the `SqlDataAdaptor`, `OleDbDataAdaptor`, `OdbcDataAdaptor`, or `OracleDataAdaptor`, as they use (just like connected database access) a connection class to connect to the data source and a command class to add, update, and select data out of the data source.

The basic idea behind using the `DataAdaptor` is to provide SQL commands to the following four properties to handle sending and receiving data between the `DataSet` and the data store:

- `SelectCommand`

- `InsertCommand`

- `UpdateCommand`

- `DeleteCommand`

If you plan to only read data from the database, then only the `SelectCommand` property needs to be provided.

With these properties provided, it is a simple matter to call the `DataAdaptor` class's `Fill()` method to select data from the data store to the `DataSet` and to call the `Update()` method to insert, update, and/or delete data from the `DataSet` to the data store.

DataSet Class

The `DataSet` is the major controlling class for disconnected ADO.NET. A `DataSet` is a memory cache used to store all data retrieved from a data source, in most cases a database or XML file. The data source is connected to the `DataSet` using a `DataAdaptor`.

A `DataSet` consists of one or more data tables in a `DataTableCollection` class, which in turn is made up of data rows and data columns. Relationships between the tables are maintained via a `DataRelationsCollection` class. The `DataSet` also stores the format information about the data.

A `DataSet` is data source–independent. All it understands is XML. In fact, all data sent or received by the `DataSet` is in the form of an XML document. The

DataSet has methods for reading and writing XML, and these are covered in Chapter 13.

A DataSet also provides transactional access to its data. To commit all changes made to the DataSet from the time it was created or since the last time it was committed, call the DataSet class's AcceptChanges() method. If you want to roll back changes since the DataSet was corrected or since it was last committed, call the RejectChanges() method. What actually happens is a cascading effect where the AcceptChanges() and RejectChanges() methods execute their table's versions of the method, which in turn calls the table's rows' version. Thus, it is also possible to commit or roll back at the table and row levels.

DataTableCollection Class

A DataTableCollection is a standard collection class made up of one or more DataTables. Like any other collection class, it has functions such as Add, Remove, and Clear. Usually, you will not use any of this functionality. Instead, you will use it to get access to a DataTable stored in the collection.

The method of choice for doing this will probably be to access the DataTableCollection indexed property Item, using the name of the table that you want to access as the index:

```
DataTable *dt = dSet->Tables->Item["Authors"];
```

It is also possible to access the same table using the overloaded array property version of Item:

```
DataTable *dt = dSet->Tables->Item[0];
```

With this method, you need to know which index is associated with which table. When you use the indexed property, it is a little more obvious.

DataTable Class

Put simply, a DataTable is one table of data stored in memory. A DataTable also contains constraints, which help ensure the integrity of the data it is storing.

It should be noted that a DataTable can be made up of zero or more DataRows, because it is possible to have an empty table. Even if the table is empty, the Columns property will still contain a collection of the headers that make up the table.

Many properties and methods are available in the DataTable, but in most cases you will simply use it to get access to the rows of the table. Two of the most common methods are enumerating through the Rows collection:

```
IEnumerator *Enum = dt->Rows->GetEnumerator();
while(Enum->MoveNext())
{
    DataRow *row = dynamic_cast<DataRow*>(Enum->Current);
    //...Do stuff to row
}
```

and selecting an array of DataRows using the Select() method:

```
DataRow *row[] =
    dt->Select(String::Format(S"AuthorID={0}", __box(CurrentAuthorID)));
```

Another method that you will probably come across is NewRow(), which creates a new DataRow, which will later be added to the DataTable Rows collection:

```
DataRow *row = dt->NewRow();
//...Build row
dt->Rows->Add(row);
```

DataRow Class

The DataRow is where the data is actually stored. You will frequently access the data from the DataRow as indexed property Item, using the name of the column that you want to access as the index.

```
row->Item[S"LastName"] = tbLastName->Text;
```

It is also possible to access the same column using the overloaded array property version of Item:

```
row->Item[0] = tbLastName->Text;
```

With this method, you need to know which index is associated with which column. When you use the indexed property, it is a little more obvious.

DataColumn Class

You use the DataColumn class to define the columns in a DataTable. Each DataColumn has a data type that determines the kind of data it can hold. A DataColumn also has properties similar to a database, such as AllowNull and Unique. If the DataColumn autoincrements, then the AutoIncrement property is set. (Now, that makes more sense than Identity.)

DataRelationCollection Class

A DataRelationCollection is a standard collection class made up of one or more DataRelations. Like any other collection class, it has functions such as Add, Remove, and Clear. Usually, as with the DataTableCollection class, you will not use any of this functionality. Instead, you will simply use it to get access to the DataRelations it stores.

DataRelation Class

A DataRelation is used to relate two DataTables together. It does this by matching DataColumns between two tables. You can almost think of it as the ADO.NET equivalent of the foreign-key relationship in a relational database (like you previously set).

One important thing you have to keep in mind is that the DataColumns must be the same data type. Remember that ADO.NET has strong data types, and when comparing different data types, one data type must be converted to the other. This conversion is not done automatically.

Constraint Classes

The Constraint classes make it possible to add a set of constraints on a particular column in your DataTable. Two types of constraints are currently supported by ADO.NET:

- ForeignKeyConstraint disallows a row to be entered unless there is a matching row in another (parent) table.

- UniqueConstraint makes sure that a column is unique within a DataTable.

Creating a Table Manually in Code

Normally, database designers build the databases that you use, but the DataColumn, DataRelation, and Constraint classes allow you as a developer to build a DataTable dynamically. The following snippet of code shows how to create the Authors DataTable manually:

```
//Create an empty DataTable
DataTable *Authors = new DataTable(S"Authors2");

// Add all the columns
Authors->Columns->Add(new DataColumn(S"AuthorID",
                                    Type::GetType(S"System.Int32")));
Authors->Columns->Add(new DataColumn(S"LastName",
                                    Type::GetType(S"System.String")));
Authors->Columns->Add(new DataColumn(S"FirstName",
                                    Type::GetType(S"System.String")));

// Add autoincrement to AuthorID
Authors->Columns->Item[S"AuthorID"]->AutoIncrement = true;

// Make AuthorID unique
Authors->Constraints->Add(
    new UniqueConstraint(S"PK_AuthorID", Authors->Columns->Item[S"AuthorID"]));

// Make AuthorID the Primary key
DataColumn *key[] = new DataColumn*[1];
key[0] = Authors->Columns->Item[S"AuthorID"];
Authors->PrimaryKey = key;

// Create a relation between AuthorID in Authors and Content tables
dSet->Relations->Add(S"StoryLink",
        Authors2->Columns->Item["AuthorID"],
        dSet->Tables->Item[S"Content"]->Columns->Item["AuthorID"]);

// add table to DataSet
dSet->Tables->Add(Authors);
```

Developing with Disconnected ADO.NET

In the final example of this chapter, you're going to build a small Win Form application to maintain the Authors DataTable that you've been working with throughout the chapter. The example uses disconnected data source access with full select, insert, update, and delete capabilities that can be either committed or rolled back.

A good portion of the code (which you can find in the Downloads section of the Apress Web site, http://www.apress.com) is related to Win Forms and isn't included here. What you'll see in the example is the code that wasn't autogenerated by Visual Studio .NET. Figure 12-15 shows the final result of the example, from which you can build your own Win Form.

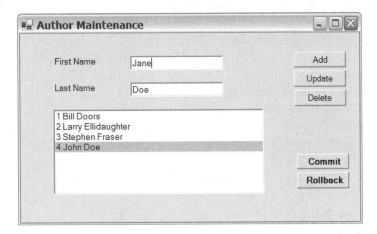

Figure 12-15. The Author Maintenance tool

Building the DataAdaptor

The first thing that you need to do is build the application's SqlDataAdaptor. Then you'll use the SqlDataAdaptor to place data in the DataSet. Eight major steps (three of which are optional) are involved in building a SqlDataAdaptor and populating and maintaining a DataSet:

1. Create a SqlConnection.

2. Create a SqlDataAdaptor.

3. Implement a SelectCommand property.

4.   Implement an `InsertCommand` property (optional).

5.   Implement an `UpdateCommand` property (optional).

6.   Implement a `DeleteCommand` property (optional).

7.   Create a `DataSet`.

8.   Populate (fill) the `DataSet`.

You build a `SqlConnection` for a disconnected database in the same way as you build a connected database:

```
SqlConnection *connect = new SqlConnection();

#ifdef SQLAuth
    //  SQL Server authentication
    connect->ConnectionString =
        S"User ID=sa; Password=;"
        S"Data Source=(local); Initial Catalog=DCV_DB;";
#else
    //  Windows Integrated Security
    connect->ConnectionString =
        S"Persist Security Info=False; Integrated Security=SSPI;"
        S"Data Source=(local); Initial Catalog=DCV_DB;";
#endif
```

Creating the `SqlDataAdapter` is a simple constructor call. You probably want to also add the primary key information. This ensures that incoming records that match existing records are updated instead of appended:

```
dAdapt = new SqlDataAdapter();
dAdapt->MissingSchemaAction = MissingSchemaAction::AddWithKey;
```

The `SelectCommand` is the SQL command that will be used to populate the DataSet. It can be as complex or as simple as you like. The implementation of the `SelectCommand` requires a standard `SqlCommand` like the one you created earlier with connected access. Notice that the constructor takes the SQL command and the data source connection:

```
dAdapt->SelectCommand =
    new SqlCommand(S"SELECT AuthorID, LastName, FirstName"
                   S"FROM Authors", connect);
```

The `InsertCommand` is the SQL command that will be executed to insert added `DataSet` rows back into the data source. The implementation of this property is a little tricky, as it requires parameters to be passed to the command. The `Add()` method to the `Parameters` property is similar to what you have seen previously, except it has one additional parameter and the size parameter is mandatory, even if it is obvious, as in the case of `Int`. The additional property is the name of the column that the data will be extracted from:

```
// Implement Insert command
dAdapt->InsertCommand =
    new SqlCommand(S"INSERT INTO Authors (LastName, FirstName) "
                    S"VALUES (@LastName, @FirstName)", connect);

// Add parameters
dAdapt->InsertCommand->Parameters->Add(S"@LastName", SqlDbType::VarChar, 50,
                                S"LastName");
dAdapt->InsertCommand->Parameters->Add(S"@FirstName", SqlDbType::VarChar, 50,
                                S"FirstName");
```

The `UpdateCommand` is the SQL command that will be executed to update rows in the data source that have been modified within the `DataSet`. The code does not contain anything new:

```
dAdapt->UpdateCommand =
    new SqlCommand(S"UPDATE Authors SET "
                    S"LastName = @LastName, FirstName = @FirstName, "
                    S"WHERE AuthorID = @AuthorID", connect);
dAdapt->UpdateCommand->Parameters->Add(S"@LastName", SqlDbType::VarChar, 50,
                                S"LastName");
dAdapt->UpdateCommand->Parameters->Add(S"@FirstName", SqlDbType::VarChar, 50,
                                S"FirstName");
dAdapt->UpdateCommand->Parameters->Add(S"@AuthorID", SqlDbType::Int, 4,
                                S"AuthorID");
```

In the preceding WHERE clause I use the key AuthorID, which is an autogenerated column that can't be changed, to find the row to update. This simplifies things because if the key used to find the row to update can be changed during the update process, then when it's changed the WHERE clause won't be able to find the right row due to the changed key not matching the original key in the database.

So, are you stuck with only being able to use unchangeable keys? Fortunately, the answer is no. When changed, `DataRows` store their original values so that they can be accessed for this exact reason (they can be used for rolling back changes as well). Let's pretend you can update AuthorID. Here is the code that needs to be changed:

```
dAdapt->UpdateCommand =
    new SqlCommand(S"UPDATE Authors SET "
                      S"LastName = @LastName, FirstName = @FirstName, "
                      S"AuthorID = @AuthorID "
                      S"WHERE AuthorID = @OldAuthorID", connect);
//...all the parameters plus
dAdapt->UpdateCommand->Parameters->Add(S"@OldAuthorID", SqlDbType::Int, 4,
          S"AuthorID")->SourceVersion = DataRowVersion::Original;
```

The DeleteCommand is the SQL command that will be executed when
a DataRow is removed from the DataSet, which needs to be deleted now from the
data source. Nothing new to explore here in the code:

```
dAdapt->DeleteCommand =
    new SqlCommand(S"DELETE FROM Authors "
                      S"WHERE AuthorID = @AuthorID", connect);
dAdapt->DeleteCommand->Parameters->Add(S"@AuthorID", SqlDbType::Int, 4,
                                  S"AuthorID");
```

You create a DataSet with a simple constructor. To fill the DataSet, you call
the SqlDataAdapter class's Fill() method. The Fill() method takes two parameters: a pointer to the DataSet and the name of the data source table that you will
be filling the DataSet with:

```
dSet = new DataSet();
dAdapt->Fill(dSet, S"Authors");
```

Selecting Rows

You have many ways of selecting records from the DataSet. A common way of
getting all the rows from a table is to use the DataRow collection found in the Rows
property of the table and then enumerate through the collection. You populate
the list box doing exactly that:

```
DataTable *dt = dSet->Tables->Item["Authors"];

if (dt == 0)
    throw new Exception(S"No Authors Table");

IEnumerator *Enum = dt->Rows->GetEnumerator();
while(Enum->MoveNext())
{
```

```
    DataRow *row = dynamic_cast<DataRow*>(Enum->Current);
    lbAuthors->Items->Add(ListBoxItem(row));
}
```

As you can see in the ListBoxItem() method, to grab the columns, you use the Item indexed property of the DataRow:

```
String *ListBoxItem(DataRow *row)
{
    return String::Format(S"{0} {1} {2}",
        row->Item[S"AuthorID"],
        row->Item[S"FirstName"],
        row->Item[S"LastName"]);
}
```

A way of getting a specific set of DataRows from a DataTable is by using the DataTable's Select() method. The method takes as a parameter a filter of the primary key:

```
DataRow *row[] =
    dt->Select(String::Format(S"AuthorID={0}", __box(CurrentAuthorID)));
```

You will see this code implemented later in updating and deleting rows.

Inserting Rows

Inserting a new row or, in this case, a new author is done by updating the text boxes with the information about the author and then clicking the Add button.

A good portion of the following code consists of validating, updating the list box, and cleaning up for text boxes. The actual ADO.NET-related code simply creates a new row, updates the columns with the information in the list boxes, and adds the row to the DataTable.

Notice that the actual insertion of the row into the data source with the Update() method is not found in this method. The reason for this is that I want to be able to commit or roll back all changes at one time using the Commit and Rollback buttons. Thus, the Update() method only occurs in the Commit button event. When the Update() method finally gets called, the UpdateCommand (which was coded previously) will get executed:

```
void bnAdd_Click(Object *sender, System::EventArgs *e)
{
    // Make sure the text boxes are populated
```

```
    if (tbFirstName->Text->Trim()->Length == 0 ||
        tbLastName->Text->Trim()->Length == 0)
        return;

    // Create a new row in the DataTable
    DataTable *dt = dSet->Tables->Item["Authors"];
    DataRow *row = dt->NewRow();

    // Update the columns with the new author information
    row->Item[S"FirstName"] = tbFirstName->Text;
    row->Item[S"LastName"]  = tbLastName->Text;

    // Add the row to the Rows collection
    dt->Rows->Add(row);

    // Add the new row to the list box
    lbAuthors->Items->Add(ListBoxItem(row));

    // blank out the text boxes
    tbFirstName->Text = S"";
    tbLastName->Text = S"";
}
```

Updating Rows

Updating an author row is handled when you select a row out of the list box,
update the text boxes, and finally click the Update button.

The ADO.NET-related code to update the author requires that you first select
the row to be updated using the DataTable class's Select() method. Once you
have the row, you update the author information in the row columns. Like when
you inserted a row, the Update() method does not get called until the Commit
button is clicked, but when the Update() method finally gets called, the
UpdateCommand ends up being executed:

```
void bnUpdate_Click(Object *sender, System::EventArgs *e)
{
    // make sure we have a selected author from the listbox
    if (CurrentAuthorID < 0)
        return;
```

```
// Select the author using its AuthorID
DataTable *dt = dSet->Tables->Item["Authors"];
DataRow *row[] =
    dt->Select(String::Format(S"AuthorID={0}", __box(CurrentAuthorID)));

// Since we know that AuthorID is unique only one row will be returned
// Update the row with the text box information
row[0]->Item[S"FirstName"] = tbFirstName->Text;
row[0]->Item[S"LastName"]  = tbLastName->Text;

// Update listbox
lbAuthors->Items->Insert(lbAuthors->SelectedIndex, ListBoxItem(row[0]));
lbAuthors->Items->RemoveAt(lbAuthors->SelectedIndex);
}
```

Deleting Rows

Deletion of an author DataRow happens when you click a row in the list box and then click the Delete button.

The code to handle deleting a row is a little tricky, as it requires the use of transactional access to the DataSet. First, you need to select the row. Then you call its Delete() method. Deleting a record in the DataSet does not actually occur until the change is accepted. At this point only, a flag is set in the DataRow.

Also, like inserting and updating, the actual updating of the database does not occur until the Update() method is called when the Commit button is clicked. Ultimately, when the Update() method is called, the DeleteCommand (built previously) will be executed:

```
void bnDelete_Click(Object *sender, System::EventArgs *e)
{
    // make sure we have a selected author from the listbox
    if (CurrentAuthorID < 0)
        return;

    // Select the author using its AuthorID
    DataTable *dt = dSet->Tables->Item["Authors"];
    DataRow *row[] =
        dt->Select(String::Format(S"AuthorID={0}", __box(CurrentAuthorID)));
```

```
// Since we know that AuthorID is unique only one row will be returned
// Delete the row
row[0]->Delete();

// all went well, delete the row from list box
lbAuthors->Items->RemoveAt(lbAuthors->SelectedIndex);
}
```

Committing and Rolling Back Changed Rows

You commit all author DataRows changed when you click the Commit button.

Because a DataSet is disconnected from the database, anything that you do to it will not get reflected in the actual database until you force an update using the Update() method. Because this is the case, it is really a simple matter to either commit or roll back any changes that you have made to the DataSet.

To commit the changes to the database, simply call the Update() method, which will walk through the DataSet and update any changed records in its corresponding database record. Depending on the type of change, the appropriate SQL command (insert, update, or delete) will be executed. To commit the changes to the DataSet, you need to call the AcceptChanges() method, which will cause the DataSet to accept all changes that were made to it:

```
dAdapt->Update(dSet, S"Authors");
dSet->AcceptChanges();
```

To roll back any changes, simply don't call the Update() method, and call the RejectChanges() method to delete all changes in the DataSet that you have made since you last committed:

```
dSet->RejectChanges();
```

Summary

In this chapter you covered a large portion of the .NET Framework's ADO.NET. You started out by covering the basics of ADO.NET. You then moved on to create a database to work with through the rest of the chapter using Visual Studio .NET. Next, you covered how connect, query, insert, update, delete, count, and sum rows of a database using connected access to the database. Finally, you learned how to do the same things with disconnected access, in the process building a simple Win Form author maintenance tool.

You have now learned the code you will need to implement ADO.NET in either a connected or disconnected manner. The world of databases should be now open to you when you create your applications.

In the next chapter you'll examine the mysterious world of XML, the last of the four common methods of getting input into and out of your .NET Windows applications.

CHAPTER 13

XML

THOUGH YOU'RE COVERING XML last of the four most common .NET Framework class library input/output (I/O) mechanisms, it's hardly the least important. In fact, much of the underlying architecture of .NET relies on XML, so much so that the .NET Framework class library provides a plethora of ways of working with XML. This chapter covers some of the more common classes.

A major goal of the .NET Framework class library is to simplify XML development. It has done this. But if you come from a background of implementing XML in the worlds of Microsoft XML Parser (MSXML) or Java, what you've already learned isn't lost. In fact, you'll find many similarities between these implementations and the one provided by the .NET Framework class library.

This chapter isn't intended to provide details about XML, though to provide a level playing field I do include some high-level coverage. Instead, the goal is to show you how to implement the many facets of XML development provided by the .NET Framework class library. In particular, you'll learn how to read, write, update, and navigate an XML file. After you've covered the common areas of XML that you'll more than likely develop code for, you'll move on and look at using XML with ADO.NET.

What Is XML?

First off, XML is not a computer language. Rather, it is a metalanguage for defining or specifying how to mark up a document in such a way as to identify its structure.

Say what?

How about this definition: XML is a method of arranging a document so that it's broken up into parts. For example, in this chapter you're going to create an XML document of role-playing monsters. The document will be broken up by monster name, hit dice, and weapon(s). (If you play Dungeons & Dragons [D&D], you know this is a very small subset of all the information available, but I didn't want or need to make the examples any more difficult.)

XML documents, in their simplest form, are made up of a hierarchy of two types of components: elements and attributes.

An *element* is made up of three parts:

- *Start element node,* often called the *start tag.* It is made up of an element text name enclosed in angle brackets: `<Element_Tag>`.

- *Content node(s)* made of a combination of zero or more *text nodes* (text enclosed between start and end element nodes) and child or nested elements (hence the hierarchical nature of XML).

- *End element node,* often called the *end tag.* It is made up of a backslash and text, which must exactly match the text name of the start element node, enclosed in angle brackets: `</Element_Tag>`.

An *attribute* is an extension to the start element node. It provides more information about the element. Attributes are one or more `name= "value"` pairs added after the element text name but before the closing angle bracket: `<Element_Tag name="value" >`.

Two additional components that you will encounter are the XML header declaration and the comment. The *header declaration* indicates that the file should be parsed as XML and in most cases will simply read

```
<?xml version="1.0" encoding="utf-8"?>
```

Comments provide the reader of the XML file additional information that will be ignored by the XML parser. The syntax of a comment is `<!-- comment_text -->`.

Listing 13-1 shows the XML document that you'll be using throughout the chapter.

Listing 13-1. An XML Monster File

```
<?xml version="1.0" encoding="utf-8"?>
<!-- Monster List -->
<MonsterList>
  <!-- Easy Monster -->
  <Monster>
    <Name>Goblin</Name>
    <HitDice Dice="1d8" Default="4"/>
    <Weapon Number="1" Damage="1d4">Dagger</Weapon>
  </Monster>
  <!-- Medium Monster -->
  <Monster>
    <Name>Succubus</Name>
    <HitDice Dice="6d8+6" Default="33"/>
    <Weapon Number="2" Damage="1d3+1">Claw</Weapon>
    <Weapon Number="1" Damage="1d4">Dagger</Weapon>
```

```
    </Monster>
    <!-- Tough Monster -->
    <Monster>
        <Name>Red Dragon</Name>
        <HitDice Dice="22d12+110" Default="253"/>
        <Weapon Number="1" Damage="2d8">Bite</Weapon>
        <Weapon Number="2" Damage="2d6">Claw</Weapon>
        <Weapon Number="2" Damage="1d8">Wing</Weapon>
    </Monster>
</MonsterList>
```

The .NET Framework XML Implementations

The .NET Framework class library provides two ways of processing XML data:

- Fast, noncached, forward-only stream

- Random access via an in-memory Document Object Model (DOM) tree

Both methods of processing XML data are equally valid. However, each has a definite time when it is better suited. At other times, both will work equally well, and the decision of which to use is up to the developer's taste.

The major deciding factors for choosing one method over the other are whether all data needs to be in memory at one time (large files take up large amounts of memory, which in many cases isn't a good thing) and whether random access to the data is needed. When either of these factors occurs, the DOM tree should probably be used because the process of repeatedly reading forward sequentially through a document to find the right place in the stream of XML to read, update, or write random data is time consuming.

On the other hand, if the data can be processed sequentially, a forward-only stream is probably the better choice because it is easier to develop and uses fewer resources more efficiently than a DOM tree. However, there is nothing stopping you from using a DOM tree in this scenario as well.

Implementing XML with the .NET Framework class library requires referencing the System.Xml.dll assembly. You would think that due to the heavy reliance on XML in the .NET Framework, it would be part of the mscorlib.dll assembly. Because it is not, your source code implementing XML requires the following code be placed at the top of your source code (this is done automatically for you by Visual Studio .NET for Windows Forms applications but not for console applications):

```
#using <system.xml.dll>
```

Five namespaces house all of the XML functionality within the .NET Framework class library. Table 13-1 describes these namespaces at a high level.

Table 13-1. XML Namespaces

NAMESPACE	DESCRIPTION
System::Xml	Provides the core of all XML functionality
System::Xml::Schema	Provides support for XML Schema definition language (XSD) schemas
System::Xml::Serialization	Provides support for serializing objects into XML formatted documents or streams
System::Xml::XPath	Provides support for the XPath parser and evaluation engine
System::Xml::Xsl	Provides support for Extensible Stylesheet Language Transformations (XSLT) transforms

Forward-Only Access

Forward-only access to XML is amazingly fast. If you can live with the restriction that you can process the XML data only in a forward-only method, then this is the way to go. The base abstract classes for implementing this method of access are named, intuitively enough, XmlReader and XmlWriter.

The .NET Framework class library's implementation of forward-only access, when you first look at it, seems a lot like the Simple API for XML (SAX), but actually they are fundamentally different. Whereas SAX uses a more complex push model, the class library uses a simple pull model. This means that a developer requests or pulls data one record at a time instead of having to capture the data using event handlers.

Coding using the .NET Framework class library's implementation of forward-only access seems, to me, more intuitive because you can handle the processing of an XML document as you would a simple file, using a good old-fashioned while loop. There is no need to learn about event handlers or SAX's complex state machine.

Reading from an XML File

To implement forward-only reading of an XML file, you need to use the XmlTextReader class. The XmlTextReader class inherits from the abstract XmlReader class and is made up of a number of properties and methods. Some of the more common XmlReader properties you will probably encounter are as follows:

- AttributeCount is an Int32 that specifies the number of attributes in the current Element, DocumentType, or XmlDeclaration node. Other node types don't have attributes.

- Depth is an Int32 that specifies the depth of the current node in the tree.

- EOF is a Boolean that's true if the reader is at the end of the file; otherwise, it's false.

- HasAttributes is a Boolean that's true if the current node has attributes; otherwise, it's false.

- HasValue is a Boolean that's true if the current node has a value; otherwise, it's false.

- IsEmptyElement is a Boolean that's true if the current node is an empty element, or in other words, the element ends in />.

- Item is the String value of an attribute specified by index or name within the current node.

- NodeType is an XmlNodeType enum that represents the node type (see Table 13-2) of the current node.

- Value is the String value for the current node.

Here are a few of the more common XmlTextReader methods:

- Close() changes the state of the reader to Closed.

- GetAttribute() gets the String value of the attribute.

- IsStartElement() returns the Boolean true if the current node is a start element tag.

- MoveToAttribute() moves to a specified attribute.

- MoveToContent() moves to the next node containing content.

- MoveToElement() moves to the element containing the current attribute.

- MoveToFirstAttribute() moves to the first attribute.

- MoveToNextAttribute() moves to the next attribute.

- Read() reads the next node.

- ReadAttributeValue() reads an attribute containing entities.

- ReadBase64() decodes Base64 and returns the binary bytes.

- ReadBinHex() decodes BaseHex and returns the binary bytes.

- ReadChars() reads character content into a buffer. It's designed to handle a large stream of embedded text.

- ReadElementString() is a helper method for reading simple text elements.

- ReadEndElement() verifies that the current node is an end element tag and then reads the next node.

- ReadStartElement() verifies that the current node is a start element tag and then reads the next node.

- ReadString() reads the contents of an element or text node as a String.

- Skip() skips the children of the current node.

The XmlTextReader class processes an XML document by tokenizing a text stream of XML data. Each token (or *node*, as it is known in XML) is then made available by the Read() method and can be handled as the application sees fit. A number of different nodes are available, as you can see in Table 13-2.

Table 13-2. Common XML Node Types

NODE TYPE	DESCRIPTION
Attribute	An element attribute
Comment	A comment
Document	The root of a document tree providing access to the entire XML document
DocumentFragment	A subtree of a document
DocumentType	A document type declaration
Element	A start element tag
EndElement	An end element tag
EndEntity	The end of an entity declaration
Entity	The start of an entity declaration
EntityReference	A reference to an entity
None	The value placed in NodeType before any Read() method is called
SignificantWhitespace	White space between markups in a mixed content model or white space within the xml:space="preserve" scope
Text	The text content
Whitespace	White space between markups
XmlDeclaration	An XML declaration

The basic logic of implementing the XmlTextReader class is very similar to that of a file:

1. Open the XML document.

2. Read the XML element.

3. Process the element.

4. Repeat steps 2 and 3 until the end of file (EOF) is reached.

5. Close the XML document.

The example in Listing 13-2 shows how to process the previous XML monster file. The output is a list box containing a breakdown of the nodes that make up the XML file. It is assumed that you know how to build the list box on your own. The code displays only the code relevant to the XML processing of the XML monster file. If you need a refresher on how to add a list box to a Windows Form, you might want to review Chapter 9.

Listing 13-2. Splitting the XML Monster File into Nodes

```
void BuildListBox()
{
    XmlTextReader *reader;
    try
    {
        reader = new XmlTextReader(S"Monsters.xml");
        while (reader->Read())
        {
            switch (reader->NodeType)
            {
                case XmlNodeType::Comment:
                    Output->Items->Add(
                        String::Format(S"{0}Comment node: Value='{1}'",
                        indent(reader->Depth), reader->Value));
                    break;
                case XmlNodeType::Element:
                    Output->Items->Add(
                        String::Format(S"{0}Element node: Name='{1}'",
                        indent(reader->Depth), reader->Name));
                    if (reader->HasAttributes)
                    {
                        while (reader->MoveToNextAttribute())
                        {
                            Output->Items->Add(String::Format(
                            S"{0}Attribute node: Name='{1}' Value='{2}'",
                            indent(reader->Depth),reader->Name,reader->Value));
                        }
                        reader->MoveToElement();
                    }
                    if (reader->IsEmptyElement)
                    {
                        Output->Items->Add(
                        String::Format(S"{0}End Element node: Name='{1}'",
                        indent(reader->Depth), reader->Name));
```

```
                    }
                    break;
            case XmlNodeType::EndElement:
                    Output->Items->Add(
                    String::Format(S"{0}End Element node: Name='{1}'",
                    indent(reader->Depth), reader->Name));
                    break;
            case XmlNodeType::Text:
                    Output->Items->Add(
                    String::Format(S"{0}Text node: Value='{1}'",
                    indent(reader->Depth), reader->Value));
                    break;
            case XmlNodeType::XmlDeclaration:
                    Output->Items->Add(
                    String::Format(S"Xml Declaration node: Name='{1}'",
                    indent(reader->Depth), reader->Name));
                    if (reader->HasAttributes)
                    {
                        while (reader->MoveToNextAttribute())
                        {
                            Output->Items->Add(String::Format(
                            S"{0}Attribute node: Name='{1}' Value='{2}'",
                            indent(reader->Depth),reader->Name,reader->Value));
                        }
                    }
                    reader->MoveToElement();
                    Output->Items->Add(
                    String::Format(S"End Xml Declaration node: Name='{1}'",
                    indent(reader->Depth), reader->Name));
                    break;
            case XmlNodeType::Whitespace:
                    // Ignore white space
                    break;
            default:
                    Output->Items->Add(
                    String::Format(S"***UKNOWN*** node: Name='{1}' Value='{2}'",
                    indent(reader->Depth), reader->Name, reader->Value));
            }
        }
    }
    catch (Exception *e)
    {
        MessageBox::Show(e->Message, S"Building ListBox Aborted");
```

```
    }
    __finally
    {
        if (reader->ReadState != ReadState::Closed)
        {
            reader->Close();
        }
    }
}


String *indent(Int32 depth)
{
    String *ind = "";
    return ind->PadLeft(depth*3, ' ');
}
```

The preceding code, though longwinded, is repetitively straightforward and, as pointed out, resembles the processing of a file in many ways.

You process all XML within an exception try block because every XML method in the .NET Framework class library can throw an exception.

You start by opening the XML file. Then you read the file, and finally you close the file. You place the Close() method in a __finally clause to ensure that the file gets closed even on an exception. Before you close the file, you verify that the file had in fact been opened in the first place. It is possible for the constructor of the XmlTextReader class to throw an exception and never open the XML file:

```
    XmlTextReader *reader;
    try
    {
        reader = new XmlTextReader(S"Monsters.xml");
        while (reader->Read())
        {
            //...Process each node.
        }
    }
    catch (Exception *e)
    {
        MessageBox::Show(e->Message, S"Building ListBox Aborted");
    }
    __finally
    {
        if (reader->ReadState != ReadState::Closed)
```

```
        {
            reader->Close();
        }
    }
```

The processing of each of the nodes is done using a simple `case` statement on the node type of the current node:

```
switch (reader->NodeType)
{
    case XmlNodeType::Comment:
        //...Process a comment
        break;
    case XmlNodeType::Element:
        //...Process an element
        break;
    //...etc.
}
```

The processing of most of the node types in the preceding example involves simply adding either the name or the value to the `ListBox`. One exception is the `Element` tag. It starts off like the other node types by adding its name to the `ListBox`, but then it continues on to check if it has attributes. If it does, it moves through each of the attributes and adds them to the `ListBox` as well. When it has finished processing the attributes, it moves the element back as the current node using the `MoveToElement()` method. You might think you have just broken the forward-only property, but in reality, attributes are only part of an element, so therefore the element is still the current node.

It is possible for an element to be empty using the syntax `<tag/>`, so you have to then check to see if the element is empty. If it is, you add the element's end tag to the `ListBox`:

```
case XmlNodeType::Element:
    Output->Items->Add(String::Format(S"{0}Element node: Name='{1}'",
                                      indent(reader->Depth), reader->Name));
    if (reader->HasAttributes)
    {
        while (reader->MoveToNextAttribute())
        {
            Output->Items->Add(String::Format(
                        S"{0}Attribute node: Name='{1}' Value='{2}'",
                        indent(reader->Depth),reader->Name,reader->Value));
        }
```

```
        reader->MoveToElement();
    }
    if (reader->IsEmptyElement)
    {
        Output->Items->Add(String::Format(S"{0}End Element node: Name='{1}'",
                        indent(reader->Depth), reader->Name));
    }
    break;
```

Figure 13-1 shows the results of ReadXML.exe. It's hard to believe so much information is contained within such a small XML file.

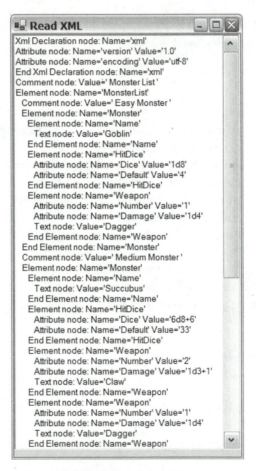

Figure 13-1. A list box dump of the XML monster file

Validating an XML File

The `XmlTextReader` class verifies that an XML file is *well-formed*—in other words, that it follows all the syntax rules of an XML file. The class doesn't verify, though, that the XML file is valid.

A valid XML file needs the nodes to be in a specific order, number, and type. You can use the following three standards for checking validity:

- Document type definition (DTD)

- Microsoft XML-Data Reduced (XDR) schema

- World Wide Web Consortium (W3C) schema

Validating an XML file requires a DTD or one of the schema files. Monsters.dtd (see Listing 13-3) is an example of a DTD for the Monsters.xml file. DTD is the easiest of the three file types to work with, so you will use it.

Listing 13-3. The Monsters.dtd File

```
<!ELEMENT MonsterList (Monster)+ >
<!ELEMENT Monster (Name, HitDice, Weapon+) >
<!ELEMENT Name (#PCDATA) >
<!ELEMENT HitDice EMPTY >
<!ATTLIST HitDice Dice CDATA #IMPLIED Default CDATA #IMPLIED >
<!ELEMENT Weapon (#PCDATA) >
<!ATTLIST Weapon Number CDATA #IMPLIED Damage CDATA #IMPLIED >
```

You will also need to make this minor change to the XML file so that it knows where to find the DTD file:

```
<?xml version="1.0" encoding="utf-8"?>
<!DOCTYPE MonsterList SYSTEM "Monsters.dtd">
<!-- Monster List -->
```

The two schema definitions, Microsoft XDR and W3C, are very different from the DTD. They are also much longer and, I think, a little less easy to read. They are, however, far more powerful. On the other hand, the application code is virtually the same for all three standards, so you won't go into the details of the schema definitions. But just to give you an idea of what a schema definition looks like, Listing 13-4 is the Microsoft XDR equivalent to Listing 13-3, which incidentally was autogenerated by right-clicking in the XML file while in Visual Studio .NET and selecting the Create Schema menu item.

Listing 13-4. The Monsters.xsd File

```xml
<?xml version="1.0"?>
<xs:schema id="MonsterList" targetNamespace="http://tempuri.org/Monsters.xsd"
  xmlns:mstns="http://tempuri.org/Monsters.xsd"
  xmlns="http://tempuri.org/Monsters.xsd"
  xmlns:xs="http://www.w3.org/2001/XMLSchema"
  xmlns:msdata="urn:schemas-microsoft-com:xml-msdata"
    attributeFormDefault="qualified" elementFormDefault="qualified">
  <xs:element name="MonsterList" msdata:IsDataSet="true"
    msdata:EnforceConstraints="False">
    <xs:complexType>
      <xs:choice maxOccurs="unbounded">
        <xs:element name="Monster">
          <xs:complexType>
            <xs:sequence>
              <xs:element name="Name" type="xs:string" minOccurs="0" />
              <xs:element name="Weapon" nillable="true" minOccurs="0"
                          maxOccurs="unbounded">
                <xs:complexType>
                  <xs:simpleContent msdata:ColumnName="Weapon_Text"
                                    msdata:Ordinal="2">
                    <xs:extension base="xs:string">
                      <xs:attribute name="Number" form="unqualified"
                                    type="xs:string" />
                      <xs:attribute name="Damage" form="unqualified"
                                    type="xs:string" />
                    </xs:extension>
                  </xs:simpleContent>
                </xs:complexType>
              </xs:element>
              <xs:element name="HitDice" minOccurs="0" maxOccurs="unbounded">
                <xs:complexType>
                  <xs:attribute name="Dice" form="unqualified"
                                type="xs:string" />
                  <xs:attribute name="Default" form="unqualified"
                                type="xs:string" />
                </xs:complexType>
              </xs:element>
            </xs:sequence>
          </xs:complexType>
        </xs:element>
      </xs:choice>
```

```
      </xs:complexType>
    </xs:element>
</xs:schema>
```

To verify an XML file, you need to implement the XmlValidatingReader class instead of the XmlTextReader class. There really isn't much difference between the two classes. The XmlValidatingReader class basically extends the functionality of the XmlTextReader class by adding verification logic.

The XmlValidatingReader class provides a few additional properties and methods beyond what is provided by XmlTextReader class to support validation:

- Reader is the XmlReader used to create the XmlValidatingReader.

- ReadTypedValue() is a method that returns an Object representing the CLR type for the specified XSD type.

- Schemas is an XmlSchemaCollection containing the collection of schemas used for validation. This enables you to validate without having to reload schemas every time.

- SchemaType is an Object that represents the schema type of the current node. The Object will be XmlSchemaDataType, XmlSchemaSimpleType, or XmlSchemaComplexType.

- ValidationType is a ValidationType enum that represents the validation type to perform on the XML file.

Listing 13-5 shows in a minimal fashion how to validate an XML file.

Listing 13-5. Validating the Monsters.xml File

```
using namespace System;
using namespace System::Xml;
using namespace System::Xml::Schema;

__gc class ValidateXML
{
public:
   ValidateXML(String *filename)
   {
      XmlValidatingReader *vreader;
      try
      {
         vreader = new XmlValidatingReader(new XmlTextReader(filename));
```

```
                vreader->ValidationType = ValidationType::DTD;
                while(vreader->Read())
                {
                    //...Process nodes just like XmlTextReader()
                }
                Console::WriteLine(S"Finished Processing");
            }
            catch (Exception *e)
            {
                Console::WriteLine(e->Message);
            }
            __finally
            {
                if (vreader->ReadState != ReadState::Closed)
                {
                    vreader->Close();
                }
            }
        }
    }
};

Int32 main(void)
{
    new ValidateXML(S"Monsters.xml");
    return 0;
}
```

As you can see, there isn't much difference between implementing XmlTextReader and XmlValidatingReader. In fact, the only difference is that the XmlValidatingReader class is being used and you are setting the ValidateType property to DTD.

When you run this on the Monsters.xml file listed previously, "Finished Processing" displays on the console. To test that validation is happening, change the Easy Monster to have its HitDice element placed after the Weapons, as shown in Listing 13-6.

Listing 13-6. Invalid Monsters.xml File

```
<?xml version="1.0" encoding="utf-8"?>
<!DOCTYPE MonsterList SYSTEM "Monsters.dtd">
<!-- Monster List -->
<MonsterList>
    <!-- Easy Monster -->
    <Monster>
```

```
        <Name>Goblin</Name>
        <Weapon Number="1" Damage="1d4">Dagger</Weapon>
        <HitDice Dice="1d8" Default="4" />
    </Monster>
    <!-- The rest of the document -->
</MonsterList>
```

Now the program ValidateXML.exe will abort as shown in Figure 13-2.

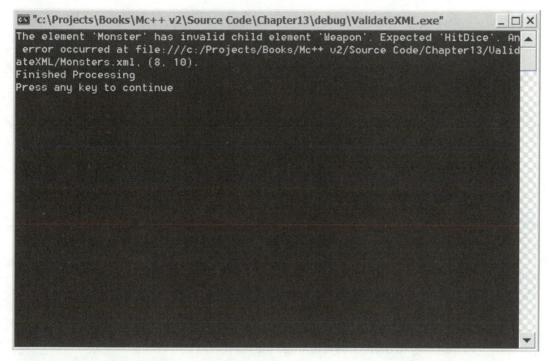

Figure 13-2. Aborting the Monsters.xml file

What happens if you want to handle the problems in the invalid XML file yourself, instead of just throwing the exception? You can override this exception being thrown by providing a handler to ValidationEventHandler. Within this handler, you can do whatever processing is necessary for the validation error.

ValidationEventHandler is triggered whenever a validation error occurs. The code for the handler is similar to all the other event handlers you've seen previously in the book. It takes two parameters, a pointer to an Object (which in this case you ignore), and a pointer to ValidationEventArgs. ValidationEventArgs provides in its properties information to tell you what caused the validation event to trigger.

Notice that you also need to import the `System::Xml::Schema` namespace:

```
using namespace System::Xml::Schema;
__gc class ValidateXML
{
public:
    void ValidationHandler (Object *sender, ValidationEventArgs *vea)
    {
        Console::WriteLine(vea->Message);
    }
    //...the rest of class
};
```

Delegating the event handler follows the same process you've seen before:

```
vreader = new XmlValidatingReader(new XmlTextReader(S"Monsters.xml"));
vreader->ValidationType = ValidationType::DTD;
vreader->ValidationEventHandler +=
    new ValidationEventHandler(this, ValidationHandler);
```

Now when you execute the application, you get the same message displayed to the console, as that is the logic I placed in the handler, but the program continues on to the end of the file without an exception being thrown.

Writing a New XML Stream

There will come a time when you'll need to generate some XML to be sent to some other application or stored off for later use by the current application. The easiest way of doing this is through the `XmlTextWriter` class.

The `XmlTextWriter` class is implemented as a forward-only XML stream writer and it inherits from the abstract `XmlWriter` class. There aren't many commonly used properties when it comes to the `XmlTextWriter` class:

- `BaseStream` is a `Stream` to which the class is writing.

- `Formatting` is a `Formatting` enum that represents whether the XML written out is Indented or not. The default is None or no indenting.

- `Indentation` is an `Int32` that represents the number of characters to indent per depth level. The default is 2.

- IndentChar is a Char that represents the character to use for indenting. The default is a space, but for an XML document to be valid, the character must be one of the following: 0x9, 0x10, 0x13, or 0x20.

Instead of properties, the XmlTextWriter class depends on a number of methods. Some of the more common methods are as follows:

- Close() closes the streams associated with the XML writer.

- Flush() flushes the write buffers.

- WriteAttributes() writes all attributes at the current location.

- WriteAttributeString() writes an attribute.

- WriteBase64() encodes the specified binary bytes as Base64 and then writes them out.

- WriteBinHex() encodes the specified binary bytes as BinHex and then writes them out.

- WriteCharEntity() writes out a char entity for the specified Unicode character. For example, a © symbol would generate a char entity of ©.

- WriteChars() writes out a text buffer at a time.

- WriteComment() writes out a comment.

- WriteDocType() writes out a DOCTYPE declaration.

- WriteElementString() writes out an element.

- WriteEndAttribute() writes out an end attribute, closing the previous WriteStartAttribute.

- WriteEndDocument() writes out end attributes and elements for those that remain open and then closes the document.

- WriteEndElement() writes out an empty element (if empty) or a full end element.

- WriteEntityRef() writes out an entity reference.

- WriteFullEndElement() writes out a full end element.

- WriteName() writes out a valid XML name.

- WriteNode() writes out everything out from the XmlReader to the XmlWriter and advances the XmlReader to the next sibling.

- WriteStartAttribute() writes out the start of an attribute.

- WriteStartDocument() writes out the start of a document.

- WriteStartElement() writes out the start tag of an element.

- WriteString() writes out the specified string.

- WriteWhitespace() writes out specified white space.

As you can see from the preceding lists, there is a write method for every type of node that you want to add to your output file. Therefore, the basic idea of writing an XML file using the XmlTextWriter class is to open the file, write out all the nodes of your file, and then close the file.

The example in Listing 13-7 shows how to create an XML monster file containing only a Goblin.

Listing 13-7. Programmatically Creating a Goblin

```
using namespace System;
using namespace System::Xml;

Int32 main(void)
{
    XmlTextWriter *writer;
    try
    {
        writer = new XmlTextWriter(S"Goblin.xml", 0);

        writer->Formatting = Formatting::Indented;
        writer->Indentation = 3;

        writer->WriteStartDocument();

        writer->WriteStartElement(S"MonsterList");
```

```
    writer->WriteComment(S"Program Generated Easy Monster");
    writer->WriteStartElement(S"Monster");

    writer->WriteStartElement(S"Name");
    writer->WriteString(S"Goblin");
    writer->WriteEndElement();

    writer->WriteStartElement(S"HitDice");
    writer->WriteAttributeString(S"Dice", S"1d8");
    writer->WriteAttributeString(S"Default", S"4");
    writer->WriteEndElement();

    writer->WriteStartElement(S"Weapon");
    writer->WriteAttributeString(S"Number", S"1");
    writer->WriteAttributeString(S"Damage", S"1d4");
    writer->WriteString(S"Dagger");
    writer->WriteEndElement();

    // The following not needed with WriteEndDocument
    // writer->WriteEndElement();
    // writer->WriteEndElement();

    writer->WriteEndDocument();

    writer->Flush();
}
catch (Exception *e)
{
    Console::WriteLine(S"XML Writer Aborted — {0}", e->Message);
}
__finally
{
    if (writer->WriteState != WriteState::Closed)
    {
        writer->Close();
    }
}
return 0;
}
```

This may seem like a lot of work to create just one monster in an XML file, but remember that all monsters have basically the same structure; therefore, you could create almost any number of monsters by removing the hard-coding and placing Weapons in a loop, as opposed to the expanded version shown in the preceding code. You, of course, also need some way of getting the monsters placed in the XML file. (A random generator would be cool—tough to code, but cool.)

The `XmlTextWriter` class takes as a constructor a `TextWriter`, a stream, or a filename. I showed the constructor using a filename previously. When using the filename, the constructor will automatically create the file or, if the filename exists, the constructor truncates it. In either case, you are writing to an empty file.

```
XmlTextWriter *writer = new XmlTextWriter(S"Goblin.xml", 0);
```

If you plan on allowing someone to read the generated XML, you might want to consider setting the `Formatting` property to `Indented`. If not, the output is one long continuous stream of XML text. When `Indented` is set, `XmlTextWriter` defaults to two spaces per element depth, but you can change this by setting the `Indentation` property:

```
writer->Formatting = Formatting::Indented;
writer->Indentation = 3;
```

Okay, now to actually write the XML, the first thing you need to do is start the document using the `WriteStartDocument()` method. This method adds the following standard XML header to the XML document:

```
<?xml version="1.0" encoding="utf-8"?>
```

Next, you simply write the XML document. You use the `WriteStartElement()`, `WriteString()`, and `WriteEndElement()` methods to add elements, and for attributes you use the `WriteAttributeString()` method. If you want to include comments, then you use the `WriteComment()` method. Once you've finished adding the XML document, you finish off with a `WriteEndDocument()` method. You might notice that the `WriteEndDocument()` method automatically ends any open elements.

```
writer->WriteComment(S"Add a weapon element");
writer->WriteStartElement(S"Weapon");
writer->WriteAttributeString(S"Number", S"1");
writer->WriteAttributeString(S"Damage", S"1d4");
writer->WriteString(S"Dagger");
writer->WriteEndElement();
```

Now that you have a new XML document, you must flush out any buffers and finally close the file so that some other process can access it. As you saw with the

`XmlTextReader` class, you check the status of the file to make sure it even needs to be closed:

```
writer->Flush();
if (writer->WriteState != WriteState::Closed)
{
    writer->Close();
}
```

Figure 13-3 shows Goblin.xml, the output of WriteXML.exe, dumped to the Visual Studio .NET editor.

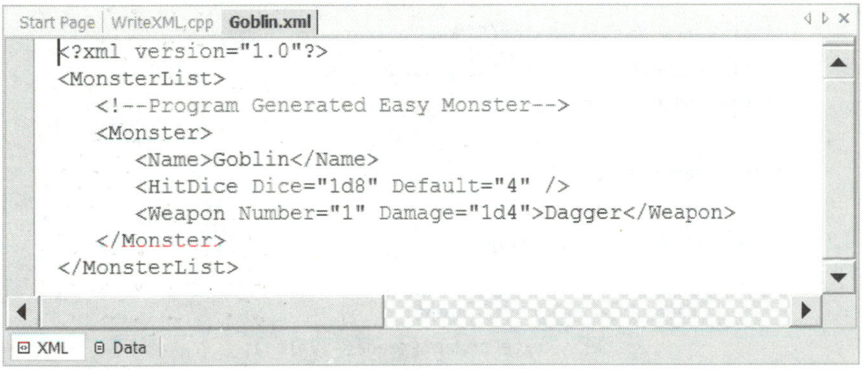

Figure 13-3. The generated Goblin.xml file

Updating an Existing XML File

You have many ways to update an XML file. Using a standard editor comes to mind. Another option, especially if you are working with a repetitive operation, is to read in the XML file using the `XmlTextReader` class, make your changes, and then write out the edited XML with `XmlTextWriter`.

A catch of using this method is that there is no backtracking with either the reader or the writer. Therefore, you must make all changes as the element or attribute becomes available or store them off temporarily.

There isn't anything new with this code. It simply isn't obvious how it's done. So here's an example of how to update an XML file in a forward-only manner. In Listing 13-8, you're adding the element `<Encountered>False</Encountered>` after the name of every monster.

Listing 13-8. Updating the XML Monster File

```
using namespace System;
using namespace System::Xml;

Int32 main(void)
{

    XmlTextReader *reader;
    XmlTextWriter *writer;
    try
    {
        reader = new XmlTextReader(S"Monsters.xml");

        writer = new XmlTextWriter(S"New_Monsters.xml", 0);
        writer->Formatting = Formatting::Indented;
        writer->Indentation = 3;

        while (reader->Read())
        {
            switch (reader->NodeType)
            {
                case XmlNodeType::Comment:
                    writer->WriteComment(reader->Value);
                    break;
                case XmlNodeType::Element:
                    writer->WriteStartElement(reader->Name);
                    writer->WriteAttributes(reader, false);
                    if (reader->IsEmptyElement)
                        writer->WriteEndElement();
                    break;
                case XmlNodeType::EndElement:
                    writer->WriteEndElement();

                    // *** Add new Monster Element
                    if (reader->Name->Equals(S"Name"))
                    {
                        writer->WriteStartElement(S"Encountered");
                        writer->WriteString(S"False");
                        writer->WriteEndElement();
                    }
                    break;
                case XmlNodeType::Text:
                    writer->WriteString(reader->Value);
```

```
                        break;
                case XmlNodeType::XmlDeclaration:
                    writer->WriteStartDocument();
                    break;
            }
        }
        writer->Flush();

        Console::WriteLine(S"Done");
    }
    catch (Exception *e)
    {
        Console::WriteLine(S"XML Update Aborted — {0}", e->Message);
    }
    __finally
    {
        if (writer->WriteState != WriteState::Closed)
        {
            writer->Close();
        }
        if (reader->ReadState != ReadState::Closed)
        {
            reader->Close();
        }
    }
    return 0;
}
```

Notice that there is no "open for update" mode for either the reader or the writer, so you need to open up an input and an output file:

```
XmlTextReader *reader = new XmlTextReader(S"Monsters.xml");
XmlTextWriter *writer = new XmlTextWriter(S"New_Monsters.xml", 0);
```

After that, the code is standard XmlTextReader and XmlTextWriter logic. Basically, you read in each element, attribute, comment, and so on and then write them out again. When the end element of "Name" shows up, write it out and then dump out the new element:

```
while (reader->Read())
{
    switch (reader->NodeType)
    {
        //...Other cases.
```

```
        case XmlNodeType::EndElement:
            writer->WriteEndElement();
            if (reader->Name->Equals(S"Name"))
            {
                writer->WriteStartElement(S"Encountered");
                writer->WriteString(S"False");
                writer->WriteEndElement();
            }
            break;
    //...The remaining cases.
```

Figure 13-4 shows New_Monster.xml, the output of UpdateXML.exe, dumped to the Visual Studio .NET editor.

Figure 13-4. The generated New_Monster.xml file

Working with DOM Trees

The DOM is a specification for how to store and manipulate XML documents in memory. This differs significantly from the forward-only access just discussed, because for that method only a single node of the XML document is in memory at any one time. Having the entire document in memory has some major advantages and a couple of significant disadvantages compared to forward-only access.

The most important advantage is that because the entire XML document is in memory, you have the ability to access any portion of the XML document at any time. This means you can read, search, write, change, and delete anywhere at any time in the document. Best of all, once you are through, you can dump the XML document back to disk with a single command.

The major disadvantages are that the DOM tree uses up a lot more memory than forward-only access and that there is a slight delay as the DOM tree is loaded. Are these disadvantages significant? In most cases the answer is not really. Most computers have more than enough memory to handle all but the very largest XML documents (and when a document gets that large, the data should probably be in a database anyway). The slight delay is usually masked in the start-up of the application, and for the delay to be noticeable at all, the XML document needs to be quite sizable. (Again, when an XML document gets that large, it should probably be placed in a database.)

The core underlying class of the DOM tree is the abstract class XmlNode. You should be able to get comfortable quickly with XmlNode, as the classes derived from XmlNode have a close resemblance to the node types you worked with in the previous section. As you can see in Table 13-3, every type of node that is part of an XML document inherits from XmlNode. In fact, even the XmlDocument class is inherited from XmlNode.

Table 13-3. Classes Derived from XmlNode

CLASS	DESCRIPTION
XmlAttribute	Represents an attribute
XmlCDataSection	Represents a CDATA section
XmlCharacterData	Provides text manipulation methods that are used by several inherited classes
XmlComment	Represents an XML comment
XmlDataDocument	Provides the ability to store, retrieve, and manipulate data through a relational DataSet
XmlDeclaration	Represents the XML declaration node
XmlDocument	Represents an XML document

(continued)

Table 13-3. Classes Derived from XmlNode (continued)

CLASS	DESCRIPTION
XmlDocumentFragment	Represents a fragment or hierarchical branch of the XML document tree
XmlDocumentType	Represents the DTD
XmlElement	Represents an element
XmlEntity	Represents an entity declaration
XmlEntityReference	Represents an entity reference node
XmlLinkedNode	Provides the ability to get the node before and after the current node
XmlNotation	Represents a notation declaration
XmlProcessingInstruction	Represents a processing instruction
XmlSignificantWhitespace	Represents white space between markup in a mixed content mode or white space within an xml:space= 'preserve' scope
XmlText	Represents the text content of an element or attribute
XmlWhitespace	Represents white space in element content

Because it's easier to visualize the XmlNode hierarchy than describe it in text, I've included the following illustration:

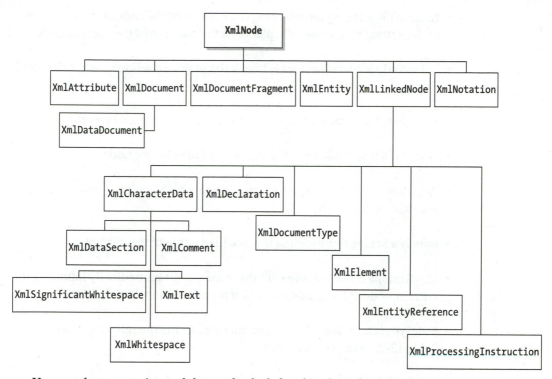

You use the properties and the methods defined in the XmlNode class to navigate, manipulate, and remove the nodes of DOM tree. Here are some of the more common XmlNode properties:

- Attributes is an XmlAttributeCollection containing the attributes of the current node.

- ChildNodes is an XmlNodeList containing all the child nodes of the current node.

- FirstChild is an XmlNode of the first child of the current node, probably the XML declaration. If there is no first child node, then the value is null.

- HasChildNodes is a Boolean that is true if the node has any children; otherwise, it is false.

- InnerText is a String concatenation of the value of the current node and all of its children.

- InnerXml is a String representing the markup of the children of the current node. Setting this property replaces all the children of the current node.

- IsReadOnly is a Boolean that is true if the node is read-only; otherwise, it is false.

- Item is an XmlElement child of the current node specified by name.

- LastChild is an XmlNode of the last child of the current node.

- LocalName is a String representing the name of the current node without the namespace prefix.

- Name is a String representing the qualified name of the current node.

- NextSibling is the XmlNode with the same parent immediately following the current node. It has a value of null if no subsequent sibling exists.

- NodeType is an XmlNodeType enum that represents the node type (see Table 13-2) of the current node.

- OuterXml is a String representing the markup of the current node and of the children of the current node.

- OwnerDocument is the XmlDocument of which the current node belongs.

- ParentNode is the XmlNode of the parent of the current node.

- PreviousSibling is the XmlNode with the same parent immediately before the current node. It has a value of null if no prior sibling exists.

- Value is a String representing the value of the current node.

As mentioned previously, XmlNode has methods. Here are some of the more common ones:

- AppendChild() adds a child to the end of the list of children for the current node.

- CloneNode() creates a duplicate of the current node.

- `CreateAttribute()` creates an `XmlAttribute`.

- `CreateNavigator()` creates an `XPathNavigator`.

- `CreateNode()` creates an `XmlNode`.

- `InsertAfter()` inserts a node immediately after the current node.

- `InsertBefore()` inserts a node immediately before the current node.

- `PrependChild()` adds a child at the beginning of the list of children for the current node.

- `RemoveAll()` removes all children and/or attributes for the current node.

- `RemoveChild()` removes the specified child node.

- `ReplaceChild()` replaces the specified child node.

- `SelectNodes()` selects a list of nodes that matches a specified XPath expression.

- `SelectSingleNode()` selects the first node that matches a specified XPath expression.

- `WriteContentTo()` saves all the children of the `XmlDocument` to an `XmlWriter`.

- `WriteTo()` saves the `XmlDocument` to an `XmlWriter`.

`XmlNodes` are placed in an `XmlNodeList`. This list is ordered and supports indexed as well as enumerated access. Any changes that you make to the `XmlNodes` in the DOM tree are immediately reflected in the `XmlNodeList` in which the `XmlNodes` reside. You can find the root of all `XmlNodeLists` in the `DocumentElement` property of the `XmlDocument` class.

The starting point of working with DOM trees is the `XmlDocument` class. Not only do you use this class to load and save the XML document to and from disk, but you also use it to query the DOM tree and create nodes to be added to the tree. As you might have noticed in Table 13-3, `XmlDocument` inherits from `XmlNode`, so the `XmlDocument` class has all the `XmlNode` class's properties and methods. Here are some of the more common properties unique to `XmlDocument`:

- DocumentElement is an XmlElement representing the root element of the document.

- DocumentType is an XmlDocumentType containing the DocumentType or DOC-TYPE declaration if the document has one.

- PreserveWhitespace is a Boolean that is true if white space is to be preserved; otherwise, it is false.

As you can see, the XmlDocument class provides quite a bit of additional functionality over the XmlNode class. The following are some of the XmlDocument class's unique methods:

- CreateCDataSection() creates an XmlCDataSection.

- CreateComment() creates an XmlComment.

- CreateDocumentFragment() creates an XmlDocumentFragment.

- CreateDocumentType() creates an XmlDocumentType.

- CreateElement() creates an XmlElement.

- CreateEntityReference() creates an XmlEntityReference.

- CreateTextNode() creates an XmlText.

- CreateXmlDeclaration() creates an XmlDeclaration.

- GetElementById() gets an element based on a specified ID.

- GetElementsByTagName() gets an XmlNodeList of all elements that match the specified tag.

- ImportNode() imports a node for another XmlDocument.

- Load() loads into the XmlDocument a File, Stream, TextReader, or XmlReader.

- LoadXml() loads into the XmlDocument a String.

- ReadNode() creates an XmlNode based on the current position of an XmlReader.

- Save() saves the XmlDocument to a specified filename, Stream, TextWriter, or XmlWriter.

Reading a DOM Tree

You have many different ways of navigating through a DOM tree. You'll start out by using only the basic methods found in XmlDocument, XmlNode, and XmlNodeList. Later you'll look at an easier way of navigating using XPaths.

Because the DOM is stored in a tree in memory, it's a good candidate for navigating via recursion. The example in Listing 13-9 demonstrates an implementation of recursively following the tree branch and dumping the node information it passed along the way. You dump the tree to a ListBox. (The code for the ListBox isn't included. Chapter 9 covers the ListBox.)

Listing 13-9. Reading a DOM Tree Recursively

```
void BuildListBox()
{
    XmlDocument *doc = new XmlDocument();
    try
    {
        XmlTextReader *reader = new XmlTextReader(S"Monsters.xml");
        doc->Load(reader);
        reader->Close();

        XmlNode *node = doc->FirstChild;   // I want the Xml Declaration

        // Recursive navigation of the DOM tree
        Navigate(node, 0);
    }
    catch (Exception *e)
    {
        MessageBox::Show(e->Message, S"Navigate Aborted");
    }
}
```

```
void Navigate(XmlNode *node, Int32 depth)
{
    if (node == 0)
        return;
    Output->Items->Add(String::Format(S"{0}: Name='{1}' Value='{2}'",
        String::Concat(indent(depth), __box(node->NodeType)->ToString()),
        node->Name, node->Value));

    if (node->Attributes != 0)
    {
        for (Int32 i = 0; i < node->Attributes->Count; i++)
        {
            Output->Items->Add(String::Format(
                S"{0}Attribute: Name='{1}' Value='{2}'",
                indent(depth+1),
                node->Attributes->ItemOf[i]->Name,
                node->Attributes->ItemOf[i]->Value));
        }
    }
    Navigate(node->FirstChild, depth+1);
    Navigate(node->NextSibling, depth);
}
```

As I stated before, you process all XML documents within an exception try block because every XML method in the .NET Framework class library can throw an exception.

Before you start reading the DOM tree, you need to load it. First, you create an XmlDocument to hold the tree. You do this using a standard constructor:

```
XmlDocument *doc = new XmlDocument();
```

Then you load the XML document into the XmlDocument. It is possible to pass the name of the XML file directly into the Load() method, which I think is a little easier. But, if you do it the following way, make sure you close the file after the load is complete, because the file resource remains open longer than it needs to be. Plus, if you try to write to the file, it will throw an exception because the file is already open.

```
XmlTextReader *reader = new XmlTextReader(S"Monsters.xml");
doc->Load(reader);
reader->Close();
```

In the previous example, I call the XmlDocument class's FirstChild() method instead of the DocumentElement() method because I want to start reading the XML document at the XML declaration and not the first element of the document.

```
XmlNode *node = doc->FirstChild;  // I want the Xml Declaration
```

Finally, you call a simple recursive method to navigate the tree. The first thing this method does is check to make sure that you have not already reached the end of the current branch of the tree:

```
if (node == 0)
    return;
```

Then it dumps to the ListBox the current node's type, name, and value. Notice that I use the little trick I mentioned in Chapter 3 to display the enum's (in this case, the NodeType's) String name:

```
Output->Items->Add(String::Format(S"{0}: Name='{1}' Value='{2}'",
    String::Concat(indent(depth), __box(node->NodeType)->ToString()),
    node->Name, node->Value));
```

The method then checks to see if the element has any attributes. If it does, it then iterates through them, dumping each to the ListBox as it goes:

```
if (node->Attributes != 0)
{
    for (Int32 i = 0; i < node->Attributes->Count; i++)
    {
        Output->Items->Add(String::Format(
            S"{0}Attribute: Name='{1}' Value='{2}'",
            indent(depth+1),
            node->Attributes->ItemOf[i]->Name,
            node->Attributes->ItemOf[i]->Value));
    }
}
```

The last thing the method does is call itself to navigate down through its children, and then it calls itself to navigate through its siblings:

```
Navigate(node->FirstChild, depth+1);
Navigate(node->NextSibling, depth);
```

Figure 13-5 shows the resulting `ListBox` dump for ReadXMLDOM.exe of all the nodes and attributes that make up the monster DOM tree.

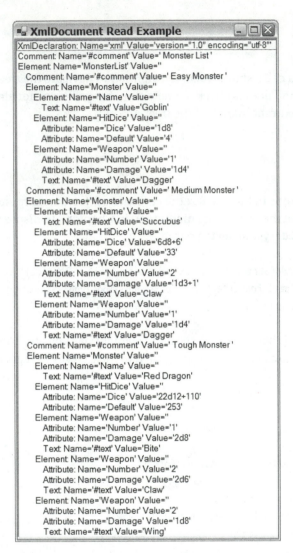

Figure 13-5. The ListBox dump of the monster DOM tree

Updating a DOM Tree

The process of updating a DOM tree is as simple as finding the correct node and changing the appropriate values. Finally, after all of the changes are made, save the changes.

In Listing 13-10, you continue to recursively navigate the DOM tree of Listing 13-1, but this time you're looking for a Goblin node that was mistakenly given a Dagger. The Goblin was supposed to have a Saber. The trick is that you can just globally change all Daggers to Sabers because the Succubus node also has a Dagger, so you have to verify that it is the Goblin node's Dagger. There are many ways of doing this, and I can think of a couple (better ones) using flags, but the method in Listing 13-10 shows the implementation of the largest number of different methods to find a node (without being redundant).

Listing 13-10. Updating the Monster DOM Tree

```
using namespace System;
using namespace System::Xml;

void Navigate(XmlNode *node)
{
    if (node == 0)
        return;

    if (node->Value != 0 && node->Value->Equals(S"Dagger"))
    {
        if (node->ParentNode->ParentNode->Item[S"Name"]->FirstChild->Value->
            Equals(S"Goblin"))
        {
            node->Value = S"Saber";
            node->ParentNode->Attributes->ItemOf[S"Damage"]->Value = S"1d8";
        }
    }

    Navigate(node->FirstChild);
    Navigate(node->NextSibling);
}

Int32 main(void)
{
    XmlDocument *doc = new XmlDocument();
    try
    {
        doc->Load(S"Monsters.xml");
        XmlNode *root = doc->DocumentElement;

        // Recursive navigation of the DOM tree
        Navigate(root);
```

```
        doc->Save(S"New_Monsters.xml");
    }
    catch (Exception *e)
    {
        Console::WriteLine(S"Navigate Aborted: {0}", e->Message );
    }
}
```

The main method looks familiar enough. The main difference is that you will write out the DOM tree when you are done to make sure the change actually occurred:

```
doc->Save(S"New_Monsters.xml");
```

The recursive function is pretty similar. Let's look closely at the `if` statement that does the update. First, you make sure the node has a value, as not all nodes have one. Calling the `Equals()` method on a node that doesn't have a value will cause an exception to be thrown:

```
if (node->Value != 0 && node->Value->Equals(S"Dagger"))
```

So you now know that you have a node with a value of Dagger. How do you check to make sure it belongs to a Goblin? You do this by checking the current node's grandparent's `Name` element for the value of Goblin:

```
if (node->ParentNode->ParentNode->Item[S"Name"]->FirstChild->Value->
Equals(S"Goblin"))
```

What I really want you to focus on in the preceding statement is `Item[S"Name"]`. The Item property of an `XmlNode` contains a collection of its child elements. This collection can be either an indexed property (as previously) or an array property where it is passed the numeric index of the child: `Item[0]`.

To change the value of a node, you simply assign it a new value:

```
node->Value = S"Saber";
```

The damage done by a Saber differs from a Dagger, so you need to change the Damage attribute of the Weapon node. Notice that it is the Weapon node, not the Saber node. The Saber node is an `XmlText` node. You need to navigate to the Saber node's parent first and then to its attributes. Notice that the attribute has a similar property to `XmlNode`, but it is called `ItemOf` and not `Item`.

```
node->ParentNode->Attributes->ItemOf[S"Damage"]->Value = S"1d8";
```

Figure 13-6 shows the new copy of the XML monster file created by UpdateXMLDOM.exe in the Visual Studio .NET editor.

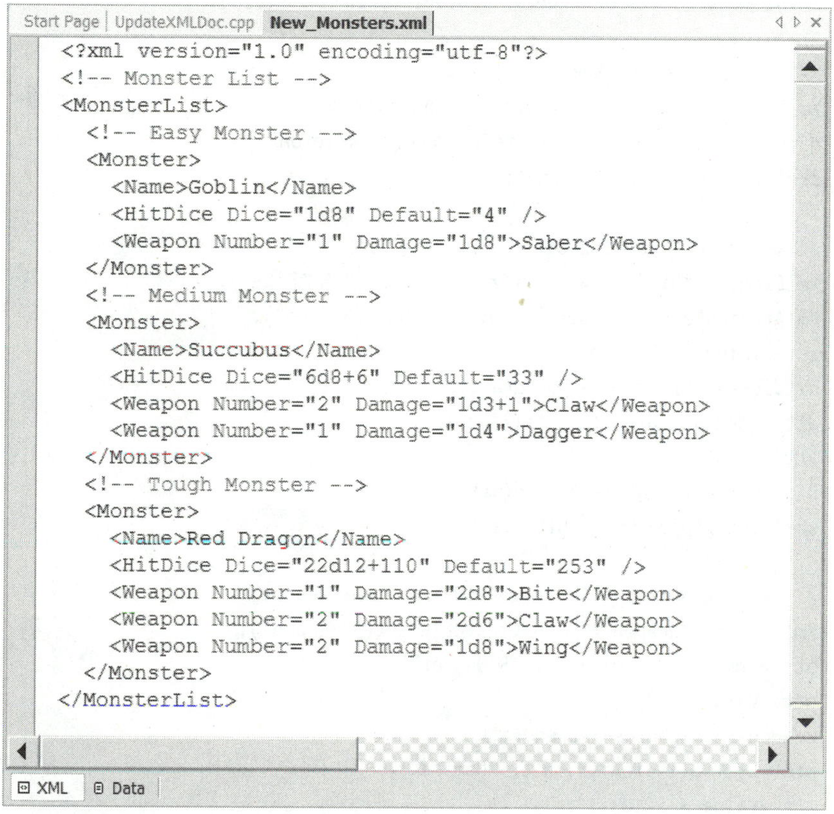

```
Start Page | UpdateXMLDoc.cpp | New_Monsters.xml                    ◁ ▷ ×
  <?xml version="1.0" encoding="utf-8"?>
  <!-- Monster List -->
  <MonsterList>
    <!-- Easy Monster -->
    <Monster>
      <Name>Goblin</Name>
      <HitDice Dice="1d8" Default="4" />
      <Weapon Number="1" Damage="1d8">Saber</Weapon>
    </Monster>
    <!-- Medium Monster -->
    <Monster>
      <Name>Succubus</Name>
      <HitDice Dice="6d8+6" Default="33" />
      <Weapon Number="2" Damage="1d3+1">Claw</Weapon>
      <Weapon Number="1" Damage="1d4">Dagger</Weapon>
    </Monster>
    <!-- Tough Monster -->
    <Monster>
      <Name>Red Dragon</Name>
      <HitDice Dice="22d12+110" Default="253" />
      <Weapon Number="1" Damage="2d8">Bite</Weapon>
      <Weapon Number="2" Damage="2d6">Claw</Weapon>
      <Weapon Number="2" Damage="1d8">Wing</Weapon>
    </Monster>
  </MonsterList>
⊞ XML   ⊟ Data
```

Figure 13-6. The updated XML monster file

Writing XmlNodes in a DOM Tree

You can truly get a good understanding of how a DOM tree is stored in memory by building a few XmlNodes manually. The basic process is to create a node and then append all its children on it. Then for each of the children, append all their children, and so on.

The last example (see Listing 13-11) before you get to XPaths shows how to add a new monster (a Skeleton) after the Goblin.

Listing 13-11. Adding a New Monster to the DOM Tree

```
using namespace System;
using namespace System::Xml;

XmlElement *CreateMonster(XmlDocument *doc)
{
    XmlElement *skeleton = doc->CreateElement(S"Monster");

    // <Name>Skeleton</Name>
    XmlElement *name = doc->CreateElement(S"Name");
    name->AppendChild(doc->CreateTextNode(S"Skeleton"));
    skeleton->AppendChild(name);

    // <HitDice Dice="1/2 d12" Default="3" />
    XmlElement *hitdice = doc->CreateElement(S"HitDice");
    XmlAttribute *att = doc->CreateAttribute(S"Dice");
    att->Value = S"1/2 d12";
    hitdice->Attributes->Append(att);
    att = doc->CreateAttribute(S"Default");
    att->Value = S"3";
    hitdice->Attributes->Append(att);
    skeleton->AppendChild(hitdice);

    // <Weapon Number="2" Damage="1d3-1">Claw</Weapon>
    XmlElement *weapon = doc->CreateElement(S"Weapon");
    att = doc->CreateAttribute(S"Number");
    att->Value = S"2";
    weapon->Attributes->Append(att);
    att = doc->CreateAttribute(S"Damage");
    att->Value = S"1d3-1";
    weapon->Attributes->Append(att);
    weapon->AppendChild(doc->CreateTextNode(S"Claw"));
    skeleton->AppendChild(weapon);

    return skeleton;
}

Int32 main(void)
{
    XmlDocument *doc = new XmlDocument();
```

```
    try
    {
        doc->Load(S"Monsters.xml");
        XmlNode *root = doc->DocumentElement;

        // Skip comment and goblin
        XmlNode *child = root->FirstChild->NextSibling;

        // Insert new monster
        root->InsertAfter(CreateMonster(doc), child);

        doc->Save(S"New_Monsters.xml");
    }
    catch (Exception *e)
    {
        Console::WriteLine(S"Navigate Aborted: {0}", e->Message );
    }
}
```

The method of inserting XmlNodes, though not difficult, needs a quick explanation. I first wondered why you needed to pass a pointer to the XmlNode that you are going to place on the new XmlNode before or after. Why not just call the Insert method for this node instead, like this:

```
childNode->InsertBefore(newNode);   // wrong
childNode->InsertAfter(newNode);    // wrong
```

Then I realized that I am not actually inserting after the child node. Instead I am inserting into the parent node after or before the child node. Thus the correct syntax:

```
parentNode->InsertBefore(newNode, childNode);
parentNode->InsertAfter(newNode, childNode);
```

Or as in the previous code:

```
root->InsertAfter(CreateMonster(doc), child);
```

Like the writing methods of forward-only only access, it seems there is a lot of effort needed to create such a simple XmlElement. You need to remember that the correct way to do this is without hard-coding, thus making it reusable.

The first issue with creating nodes dynamically is that you need access to the XmlDocument, as all the XmlNode creation methods are found in it. You have two choices: pass XmlDocument as a parameter as was done in this example or make XmlDocument a private member variable that all classes can access.

Now that you have access to the creation methods, it is a simple matter to create the element:

```
XmlElement *skeleton = doc->CreateElement(S"Monster");
```

Then you create and append any of its child elements:

```
XmlElement *weapon = doc->CreateElement(S"Weapon");
skeleton->AppendChild(weapon);
```

Of course, to create these child elements, you need to create and append the child elements attribute(s) and body text (which might need to create grandchildren nodes and so on):

```
XmlAttribute *att = doc->CreateAttribute(S"Number");
att->Value = S"2";
weapon->Attributes->Append(att);

att = doc->CreateAttribute(S"Damage");
att->Value = S"1d3-1";
weapon->Attributes->Append(att);

weapon->AppendChild(doc->CreateTextNode(S"Claw"));
```

Figure 13-7 shows the resulting new copy of the XML monster file from WriteXMLDOM.exe with the new inserted monster in the Visual Studio .NET editor.

```
Start Page | WriteXMLDoc.cpp | New_Monsters.xml |                    ◄ ▷ ×

<?xml version="1.0" encoding="utf-8"?>
<!-- Monster List -->
<MonsterList>
  <!-- Easy Monster -->
  <Monster>
    <Name>Goblin</Name>
    <HitDice Dice="1d8" Default="4" />
    <Weapon Number="1" Damage="1d4">Dagger</Weapon>
  </Monster>
  <Monster>
    <Name>Skeleton</Name>
    <HitDice Dice="1/2 d12" Default="3" />
    <Weapon Number="2" Damage="1d3-1">Claw</Weapon>
  </Monster>
  <!-- Medium Monster -->
  <Monster>
    <Name>Succubus</Name>
    <HitDice Dice="6d8+6" Default="33" />
    <Weapon Number="2" Damage="1d3+1">Claw</Weapon>
    <Weapon Number="1" Damage="1d4">Dagger</Weapon>
  </Monster>
  <!-- Tough Monster -->
  <Monster>
    <Name>Red Dragon</Name>
    <HitDice Dice="22d12+110" Default="253" />
    <Weapon Number="1" Damage="2d8">Bite</Weapon>
    <Weapon Number="2" Damage="2d6">Claw</Weapon>
    <Weapon Number="2" Damage="1d8">Wing</Weapon>
  </Monster>
</MonsterList>

⊞ XML   ⊟ Data
```

Figure 13-7. The XML monster file with a new monster

Navigating with XPathNavigator

Wouldn't it be nice to have easy sequential access through an XML file and the concept of a current location like you have with XmlTextReader discussed previously, but without the restriction of forward-only access? You do. It's called the XPathNavigator class.

If you were comfortable with the XmlTextReader class, then you should have no trouble adapting to the XPathNavigator class, as many of its properties and methods are very similar. Also, if you were comfortable with XmlDocument, you should have few problems with XPathNavigator because you will find a lot of overlap between them. The following are some of the more common XPathNavigator properties:

- HasAttributes is a Boolean that is true if the current node has attributes; otherwise, it is false.

- HasChildren is a Boolean that is true if the current node has children; otherwise, it is false.

- IsEmptyElement is a Boolean that is true if the current node is an empty element or, in other words, the element ends in />.

- LocalName is a String representing the name of the current node without the namespace prefix.

- Name is a String representing the qualified name of the current node.

- NodeType is an XmlNodeType enum that represents the node type (see Table 13-2) of the current node.

- Value is a String representing the value of the current node.

Here are some of the more commonly used XPathNavigator class methods:

- ComparePosition() compares the position of the current navigator with another specified navigator.

- Compile() compiles an XPath String into an XPathExpression.

- Evaluate() evaluates an XPath expression.

- GetAttribute() gets the attribute with the specified LocalName.

- IsDescendant() determines if the specified XPathNavigator is a descendant of the current XPathNavigator.

- IsSamePosition() determines if the current and a specified XPathNavigator share the same position.

- Matches() determines if the current node matches a specified expression.

- MoveTo() moves to the position of a specified XPathNavigator.

- MoveToAttribute() moves to the attribute that matches a specified LocalName.

- MoveToFirst() moves to the first sibling of the current node.

- MoveToFirstAttribute() moves to the first attribute of the current node.

- MoveToFirstChild() moves to the first child of the current node.

- MoveToId() moves to the node that has a specified String ID attribute.

- MoveToNext() moves to the next sibling of the current node.

- MoveToNextAttribute() moves to the next attribute of the current node.

- MoveToParent() moves to the parent of the current node.

- MoveToPrevious() moves to the previous sibling of the current node.

- MoveToRoot() moves to the root node of the current node.

- Select() selects a collection of nodes that match an XPath expression.

- SelectAncestor() selects a collection of ancestor nodes that match an XPath expression.

- SelectChildren() selects a collection of children nodes that match an XPath expression.

- SelectDescendants() selects a collection of descendant nodes that match an XPath expression.

As you can see by the list of methods made available by the XPathNavigator, it does what its name suggests: navigates. The majority of the methods are for navigating forward, backward, and, as you will see when you add XPath expressions, randomly through the DOM tree.

Basic XPathNavigator

Let's first look at the XPathNavigator class without the XPath functionality or simply its capability to move around a DOM tree. The example in Listing 13-12 is your third and final read through the monster XML file. This time you are going to use the XPathNavigator.

Listing 13-12. Navigating a DOM Tree Using XPathNavigator

```
using namespace System::Xml;
using namespace System::Xml::XPath;

String *indent(Int32 depth)
{
    String *ind = "";
    return ind->PadLeft(depth*4, ' ');
}

void BuildListBox()
{
    XmlDocument *doc = new XmlDocument();
    try
    {
        doc->Load(S"Monsters.xml");
        XPathNavigator *nav = doc->CreateNavigator();
        nav->MoveToRoot();
        Navigate(nav, 0);
    }
    catch (Exception *e)
    {
        MessageBox::Show(e->Message, S"Navigate Aborted");
    }
}

void Navigate(XPathNavigator *nav, Int32 depth)
{
    Output->Items->Add(String::Format(
        S"{0}: Name='{1}' Value='{2}'",
        String::Concat(indent(depth),__box(nav->NodeType)->ToString()),
        nav->Name, nav->Value));

    if (nav->HasAttributes)
    {
        nav->MoveToFirstAttribute();
        do {
            Output->Items->Add(String::Format(
                S"{0}Attribute: Name='{1}' Value='{2}'",
                indent(depth+1),nav->Name, nav->Value));
        }
        while(nav->MoveToNextAttribute());
```

```
        nav->MoveToParent();
    }

    if (nav->MoveToFirstChild())
    {
        Navigate(nav, depth+1);
        nav->MoveToParent();
    }
    if (nav->MoveToNext())
        Navigate(nav, depth);
}
```

The first thing you have to remember when working with the XPathNavigator class is that you need to import the namespace System::Xml::XPath using the following command:

```
using namespace System::Xml::XPath;
```

I personally think of the XPathNavigator as a token that I move around that shows where I currently am in the DOM tree. In the preceding program I use only one XPathNavigator object pointer that gets passed around. This pointer eventually passes by every node of the DOM tree.

You create an XPathNavigator from any class that inherits from the XmlNode class using the CreateNavigator() method:

```
XPathNavigator *nav = doc->CreateNavigator();
```

At this point, your navigator is pointing to the location of the node that you created it from. To set it at the first element of the DOM tree, you need to call the navigator's MoveToRoot() method:

```
nav->MoveToRoot();
```

Using recursion still holds true for XPathNavigator navigation as it does for standard XmlDocument navigation. You will probably notice that it has many similarities to the XmlDocument reader example. The biggest difference, though, is that with an XPathNavigator you need to navigate back out of a child branch before you can enter a new branch. Therefore, you see the use of the MoveToParent() method used much more frequently.

Something that you have to get used to if you have been using XmlDocument and XmlNode navigation is that the move methods return Boolean success values. What this means is that to find out if you successfully moved to the next node, you need to check to see if the move method returned true. If the move method can't successfully move to the next node, then it returns `false`. The move ends up changing an internal pointer in the `XPathNavigator`. This is considerably different than navigating with `XmlNodes`, where the nodes return the value of the next node or `null` if they can't navigate as requested.

One other thing you'll probably notice is that the `Value` property returns a concatenation of all its child node `Value` properties, and not just its own `Value`. You might not think it helpful, but I'll show how you can use this feature as a shortcut in the next example.

Figure 13-8 shows the `ListBox` dump, created by ReadXPathNav.exe, of all the nodes and attributes that make up the monster DOM tree.

Figure 13-8. A ListBox of all nodes of the XML monster file

XPathNavigator Using XPath Expressions

Using any of the methods in the previous section to navigate an XML file or DOM tree is hardly trivial. If you're trying to get specific pieces of information out of your XML files, going through the trouble of writing all that code seems hardly worth the effort. If there wasn't a better way, I'm sure XML would lose its popularity. The better way is the XPath expression.

With XPath expressions, you can quickly grab one particular piece of information out of the DOM tree or a list of information. The two most common ways of implementing XPath expressions are via the XPathNavigator class's Select() method and the XmlNode class's SelectNodes() method.

The XPath expression syntax is quite large and beyond the scope of this book. If you want to look into the details of the XPath language, then I recommend you start with the documentation on XPath provided by the .NET Framework.

For now, let's make do with some simple examples that show the power of the XPath (almost wrote "Force" there—hmmm . . . I must have just seen *Star Wars*).

The first example is the most basic form of XPath. It looks very similar to how you would specify a path or a file. It is simply a list of nodes separated by the forward slash (/), which you want to match within the document. For example,

```
/MonsterList/Monster/Name
```

specifies that you want to get a list of all "Name" nodes that have a parent node of Monster and MonsterList. The starting forward slash specifies that MonsterList be at the root. Here is a method that will execute the preceding XPath expression:

```
void GetMonsters(XPathNavigator *nav)
{
    XPathNodeIterator *list =
        nav->Select(S"/MonsterList/Monster/Name");

    Console::WriteLine(S"Monsters\n-----");
    while (list->MoveNext())
    {
        XPathNavigator *n = list->Current;
        Console::WriteLine(n->Value);
    }

//  The required code to do the same as above if no
//  XPathNavigator concatenation occurred.
/*
    list = nav->Select(S"/MonsterList/Monster/Name");
```

```
        Console::WriteLine(S"Monsters\n----");
        while (list->MoveNext())
        {
            XPathNavigator *n = list->Current;
            n->MoveToFirstChild();
            Console::WriteLine(n->Value);
        }
    */
}
```

Figure 13-9 presents the output of the snippet.

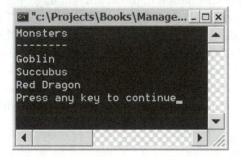

Figure 13-9. Output for the XPath expression MonsterList/Monster/Name

As promised earlier, this example shows how the concatenation of child values by the XPathNavigator can come in handy. Remember that the XmlText node is a child of the XmlElement node, so without the concatenation of the XPathNavigator class, the dumping of the values of the "Name" nodes will produce empty strings, because XmlElement nodes have no values.

That was simple enough. Let's look at something a little more complex. It is possible to specify that you don't care what the parents are by prefixing with a double forward slash (//). For example,

```
//Name
```

would get you all "Name" nodes in the document. Be careful, though: If you use the "Name" element start tag in different places, you will get them all.

Along the same lines, if you don't actually care what the parent is but you want only a node at specific depth, you would use the asterisk (*) to match any element. For example,

```
/MonsterList/*/Name
```

would get all the names with a grandparent of MonsterList, but it would matter who the parent was.

Conditional expressions are possible. You enclose conditionals in square brackets ([ ]). For example,

```
//Monster[Name]
```

would result in all monsters that have "Name" node (which would be all of them, as Name is a mandatory element—but that is another story). It is possible to specify an exact value for the conditional node or specify what values it cannot be. For example,

```
//Monster[Name = ''Goblin'']
//Monster[Name != ''Succubus'']
```

would result in the first expression grabbing the Monster node Goblin and the second expression grabbing every monster but the Succubus.

Here is a method that will execute a combination of the expressions you covered previously. Also notice that just to be different, the example uses the XmlNode class's SelectNodes() method. Because XmlNodes don't concatenate child values, you need to navigate to the child to get the desired value:

```
void GetDragonsWeapons(XmlNode *node)
{
    XmlNodeList *list =
        node->SelectNodes(S"//Monster[Name='Red Dragon']/Weapon");

    Console::WriteLine(S"\nDragon's Weapons\n-------");

    IEnumerator *en = list->GetEnumerator();
    while (en->MoveNext())
    {
        XmlNode *n = dynamic_cast<XmlNode*>(en->Current);
        Console::WriteLine(n->FirstChild->Value);
    }
}
```

Figure 13-10 shows the output of the snippet.

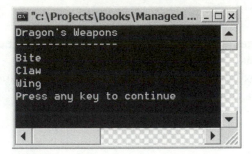

Figure 13-10. Output for the XPath expression //Monster[Name='Red Dragon']/Weapon

Let's expand on this expression just a little more. It is also possible to have conditionals with logical operators such as and, or, and not().

The following method shows the logical operator in practice. It also shows how to grab an attribute value out of the navigator:

```
void GetGoblinSuccubusHitDice(XPathNavigator *nav)
{
    XPathNodeIterator *list =
        nav->Select(S"//Monster[Name='Goblin' or Name='Succubus']/HitDice");

    Console::WriteLine(S"\nGoblin & Succubus HD\n-----------");
    while (list->MoveNext())
    {
        XPathNavigator *n = list->Current;
        n->MoveToFirstAttribute();
        Console::WriteLine(n->Value);
    }
}
```

Figure 13-11 shows the output of the snippet.

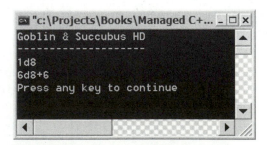

Figure 13-11. Output for the XPath expression //Monster[Name='Goblin' or Name='Succubus']/HitDice

To match attributes in an XPath expression, use the "at" sign (@) in front of the attribute's name. For example,

```
void GetGoblinSuccubusHitDice(XPathNavigator *nav)
{
    XPathNodeIterator *list =
        nav->Select(S"//Monster[Name='Goblin' or Name='Succubus']/HitDice/@Dice");

    Console::WriteLine(S"\nGoblin & Succubus HD\n----------");
    while (list->MoveNext())
    {
        XPathNavigator *n = list->Current;
        Console::WriteLine(n->Value);
    }
}
```

results in the same output as the previous example. Notice that you no longer have to move to the attribute before displaying it.

As a final example, the following snippet shows that you can make numeric comparisons. In this example, I grab all Weapon elements with a Number attribute of less than or equal to 1:

```
void GetSingleAttackWeapons(XPathNavigator *nav)
{
    XPathNodeIterator *list =
        nav->Select(S"//Weapon[@Number <= 1]");

    Console::WriteLine(S"\nSingle Attack Weapons\n----------");
    while (list->MoveNext())
    {
        XPathNavigator *n = list->Current;
        Console::WriteLine(n->Value);
    }
}
```

Figure 13-12 shows the output of the snippet.

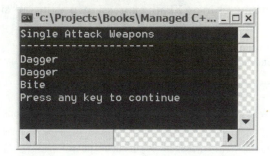

Figure 13-12. Output for the XPath expression //Weapon[@Number <= 1]

XML and ADO.NET

This topic almost doesn't merit a section of its own, as only one class, XmlDataDocument, needs to be examined, and XmlDataDocument inherits from XmlDocument. What am I trying to get at? To use ADO.NET and XML together, you need to create a DataSet (see Chapter 12) and create an XmlDataDocument with it. Then you can manipulate the database data just as you did with XmlDocument.

The XmlDataDocument class adds properties and members to streamline some activities and to make them more "relational database"–like, but other than that you have already learned what you need to work with XML originating from an ADO.NET database:

- DataSet is the DataSet used to create the XmlDataDocument.

- CreateEntityReference() is a method that is not supported and throws an exception.

- GetElementById() is a method that is not supported and throws an exception.

- GetElementFromRow() gets an XmlElement associated with a specified DataRow.

- GetRowFromElement() gets a DataRow associated with a specified XmlElement.

- Load() loads into the XmlDocument using a filename, Stream, TextReader, or XmlReader, and then synchronizes with the DataSet.

The example in Listing 13-13 is an exact duplicate of Listing 13-8, except that the source of the XML data is the DCV_DB database created in Chapter 12.

Listing 13-13. Dumping the DCV_DB Database to a ListBox Using XML

```
void BuildListBox()
{
    try
    {
        SqlConnection *connect = new SqlConnection();
#ifdef SQLAuth
        //  SQL Server authentication
        connect->ConnectionString =
            S"User ID=sa; Password=;"
            S"Data Source=(local); Initial Catalog=DCV_DB;";
#else
        //  Windows Integrated Security
        connect->ConnectionString =
            S"Persist Security Info=False; Integrated Security=SSPI;"
            S"Data Source=(local); Initial Catalog=DCV_DB;";
#endif
        SqlDataAdapter *dAdapt = new SqlDataAdapter();
        DataSet *dSet          = new DataSet();
        dAdapt->SelectCommand  =
            new SqlCommand(S"SELECT * FROM Authors", connect);
        dAdapt->Fill(dSet, S"Authors");

        XmlDataDocument *doc = new XmlDataDocument(dSet);
        Navigate(doc->DocumentElement, 0);
    }
    catch (Exception *e)
    {
        MessageBox::Show(e->Message, S"Navigate Aborted");
    }
}

void Navigate(XmlNode *node, Int32 depth)
{
    if (node == 0)
        return;

    Output->Items->Add(String::Format(
        S"{0}: Name='{1}' Value='{2}'",
        String::Concat(indent(depth),__box(node->NodeType)->ToString()),
        node->Name, node->Value));
```

```
    if (node->Attributes != 0)
    {
        for (Int32 i = 0; i < node->Attributes->Count; i++)
        {
            Output->Items->Add(String::Format(
                S"{0}Attribute: Name='{1}' Value='{2}'",
                indent(depth+1),node->Attributes->ItemOf[i]->Name,
                node->Attributes->ItemOf[i]->Value));
        }
    }
    Navigate(node->FirstChild, depth+1);
    Navigate(node->NextSibling, depth);
}
```

As you can see, the only code that is different from the original (Listing 13-9) is the standard code to create a DataSet and then the placing of the DataSet within an XmlDataDocument. If you need a refresher on creating a DataSet, please review Chapter 12.

```
SqlConnection *connect = new SqlConnection();
#ifdef SQLAuth
//  SQL Server authentication
connect->ConnectionString =
    S"User ID=sa; Password=;"
    S"Data Source=(local); Initial Catalog=DCV_DB;";
#else
//  Windows Integrated Security
connect->ConnectionString =
    S"Persist Security Info=False; Integrated Security=SSPI;"
    S"Data Source=(local); Initial Catalog=DCV_DB;";
#endif
SqlDataAdapter *dAdapt = new SqlDataAdapter();
DataSet *dSet          = new DataSet();
dAdapt->SelectCommand  = new SqlCommand(S"SELECT * FROM Authors", connect);
dAdapt->Fill(dSet, S"Authors");

XmlDataDocument *doc = new XmlDataDocument(dSet);
```

Figure 13-13 shows the resulting ListBox dump by ADONET.exe of all the nodes and attributes that make up the DCV_DB database DOM tree.

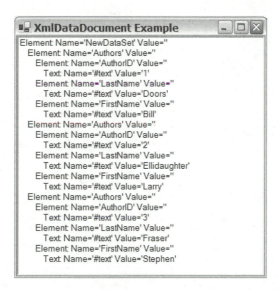

Figure 13-13. The ListBox dump of the DCV_DB database DOM tree

Summary

In this chapter you covered the last of the .NET Framework class library's standard I/O mechanisms. You started with a quick refresher on XML. You then examined how to read, validate, write, and update XML documents using forward-only access. Then you took a look at DOM trees and how to go about reading from, updating, and writing to them. Next, you took a brief look at the powerful XPath. You finished off by learning how simple it is to manipulate ADO.NET databases using XML.

Now with all four I/O systems covered, you should have no problems getting the information needed by your system into it.

In the next chapter, you move on to the world of the Internet and how to build ASP.NET applications using Managed C++.

Web Applications

You've looked at the console—nice, but not the most user-friendly environment for your application's users to work in. You've also looked at the Windows application. This, on the other hand, is a great environment for your users to work in. But these are only two of the three worlds in which to develop .NET applications. In fact, you haven't even covered the areas that make .NET special: the Internet and ASP.NET. In this chapter, you'll cover the first of the two pieces that make up ASP.NET: the *Web application* or, as it's more commonly known, the *Web Form*. In the next chapter, you'll cover Web services.

You may have heard that Managed C++ isn't the environment in which to develop Web applications or Web Forms. You may have even heard, as I did, that you can't create Web applications. If you believe these statements, you would be wrong on both accounts. It's possible and, in fact, quite easy to build Web Forms once you complete the initial manual configurations.

Visual Studio .NET doesn't have a "fully functioning" drag-and-drop GUI tool to directly build Managed C++–controlled Web Forms. (The design tool supports dragging and dropping controls to the Web Form, but there's no linking of these controls to the codebehind.) Even so, it's extremely easy to create Web Forms manually. The only hard part is that you have to know HTML/XML as well as Managed C++. In this chapter, I show you just how easy it is by manually implementing a few ASP.NET pages. I also show you how easy it is to create user controls. This book by no means covers all aspects of ASP.NET—this chapter, in fact, assumes prior knowledge of ASP.NET. Rather, this book focuses on how to implement ASP.NET with Managed C++ codebehind.

But before you get to that you need a little background information. Then you'll have to set up Visual Studio .NET so that you can develop your ASP.NET code.

Managed C++ Restriction for ASP.NET Support

A very powerful feature of ASP.NET, and one of the few restrictions of using Managed C++ with ASP.NET, is the codebehind feature. This feature allows for the complete separation of HTML and logic code into different files, thus letting HTML experts and software developers specialize in what they do best. It's also possible (though I personally don't recommend it) to embed your code logic directly within the ASP.NET source with other languages such as C#, Visual Basic .NET, and JScript .NET, just as you would with earlier ASP.

I mention that codebehind is a restriction, because it's the only way to develop ASP.NET code with Managed C++. In other words, you must place the code logic in a codebehind file and precompile it into an assembly before you make the Web page accessible to the Internet. The languages C#, Visual Basic .NET, and JScript .NET don't have this restriction. With these languages, you can embed logic, as I mentioned previously, and you can also leave the embedded code to be compiled the first time the page is accessed. These features are nice, though potentially dangerous (it's possible to make coding mistakes that aren't caught until a user executes the code) and not really that essential to ASP.NET development.

Configuring Visual Studio .NET for ASP.NET

It is possible to code ASP.NET with Managed C++ codebehind, but I find it easier to develop using Visual Studio .NET. Even if you are not using Visual Studio .NET, this section should still give you insight into how to configure your favorite development environment.

The first step in configuring Managed C++ for ASP.NET development is to make sure that ASP.NET is set up properly on your computer. The common problem you may run into is installing IIS after installing .NET. Unfortunately, this does not work. If you did this by mistake, your ASP.NET pages will not be processed properly by IIS. You will know you have made this mistake because after running an ASP.NET Web page, you will find within the source code of the HTML generated the original ASP.NET Web controls and not HTML (as it should have). Basically IIS is not translating the .aspx file because ASP.NET is not registered correctly on your system. To fix the problem, try running aspnet_regiis.exe from the Visual Studio .NET command prompt:

```
aspnet_regiis.exe -lv
```

Once you have ASP.NET configured properly, the next step is to create a class library by selecting the Class Library (.NET) template in the Add New Project dialog box (see Figure 14-1). You create a library because, in actuality, a codebehind is just an assembly with a few specific coding requirements.

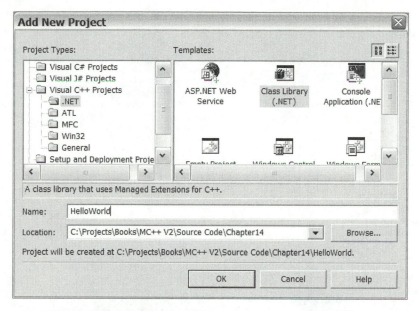

Figure 14-1. The Add New Project dialog box

In this chapter, I use a project called "HelloWorld". Use whatever name you want, just remember that it will be the name of the assembly that will be built, unless you change it in the configuration.

The next few configurations are optional. First, I rename (in Solution Explorer) the Header Files folder to **Class Files**. This is just my preference. I feel that because that is what I am going to place in this folder, it only makes sense to rename it. But for those of you who insist on the "same old, same old," these files do end in .h and are included so they are also header files.

Next, you can delete from the solution (and physically from the development directory) the generated .h file, in this case HelloWorld.h, as it is not needed. You can also delete the ReadMe.txt file and the Resource Files folder for the same reason.

I personally don't see the need for precompiled headers in the case of ASP.NET, so you can also delete stdafx.h and stdafx.cpp. If you do this, you need to change the properties of the project's configuration to not use precompiled headers (see Figure 14-2).

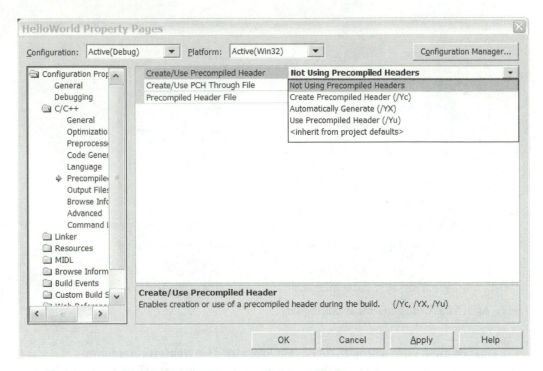

Figure 14-2. Precompiled headers Property Pages dialog box

The next step is optional, though I highly recommend it because it will keep your Solution Explorer much cleaner: Add a folder within Solution Explorer called **Web Forms** and provide it with a filter of **aspx;asax;ascx;config**. If you plan on making many Web Forms, you might consider changing the Web Forms folder into a complete hierarchy of folders but, because this is a simple example, this single folder will do.

The next two configuration steps are required. If you do not execute them, your Web Forms will not work. First, you need to make the directory where you created the project Web-shared and make it a virtual directory. You have several ways of doing this, but the easiest by far is using Windows Explorer (see Figure 14-3).

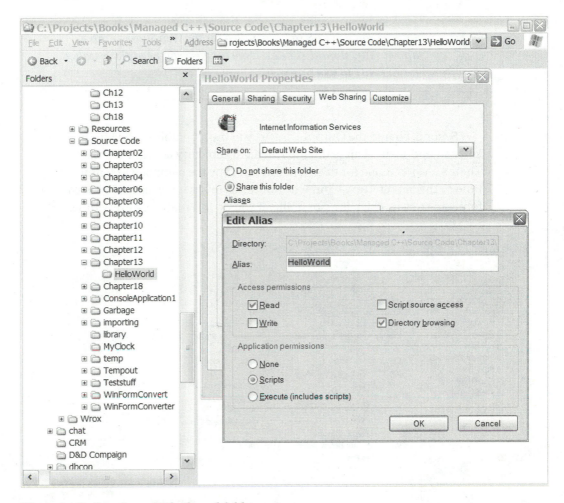

Figure 14-3. Creating a Web-shared folder

1. Navigate to the source code directory.

2. Right-click the directory folder to get the Properties dialog box.

3. Select the Web Sharing tab.

4. Select the Share this folder radio button to bring up the Edit Alias dialog box.

5. Enter the alias you want. I just take the default in this case.

6. Click the OK button twice to close both dialog boxes.

NOTE   *You need IIS to be installed for the Web Sharing tab to appear. This shouldn't be an issue because you need IIS installed for ASP.NET to work as well.*

Second, change the Output Directory of the assembly to the **bin** directory. You can optionally change the Intermediate Directory to **build** (see Figure 14-4). There's a workaround for this step. You can copy the compiled assembly every time to the bin directory—but why bother, as this is much easier? Plus you can't forget to copy it, which is a possibility if you do this manually every time.

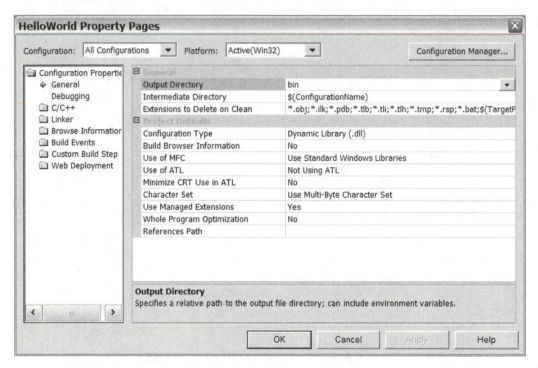

Figure 14-4. Changing the Output Directory in the Configuration Properties

At this point, you're ready to create ASP.NET Web Forms, but you'll first add three more files that might come in handy later.

The first file you should add is the Web.config file. This file defines configuration settings that are used at the time your Web application is first deployed. You can add or revise these configuration settings at any time with minimal impact to your Web application. If the file does not exist in the root directory of your application, then the system default is used.

Listing 14-1 is close to the same as that of either of the autogenerated Web.config files of C# or Visual Basic .NET, except that the `defaultLanguage` attribute of the `compilation` element has been removed, as well as comments. (I removed the comments to save space in the book.)

Listing 14-1. The Default Managed C++ Web.config File

```
<?xml version="1.0" encoding="utf-8" ?>
<configuration>
  <system.web>
    <compilation debug="true" />
    <customErrors mode="RemoteOnly" />
    <authentication mode="Windows" />
    <trace
      enabled="false"
      requestLimit="10"
      pageOutput="false"
      traceMode="SortByTime"
      localOnly="true"
    />
    <sessionState
      mode="InProc"
      stateConnectionString="tcpip=127.0.0.1:42424"
      sqlConnectionString="data source=127.0.0.1;user id=sa;password="
      cookieless="false"
      timeout="20"
    />
    <globalization requestEncoding="utf-8" responseEncoding="utf-8" />
  </system.web>
</configuration>
```

The second and third files you should add are the Global.asax file (Listing 14-2) and its codebehind (Listing 14-3). The Global.asax file is an optional file that contains code for responding to application-level events raised by ASP.NET. The following two listings were created using my wfconvert.exe tool on a C# version of the Global.asax file. (I again removed the comments to save space.)

Listing 14-2. The Default Global.asax File

```
<%@ Assembly Name="HelloWorld" %>
<%@ Application Inherits="HelloWorld.Global" %>
```

Listing 14-3. The Default Global.asax.h (Codebehind) File

```cpp
using namespace System;
using namespace System::Collections;
using namespace System::ComponentModel;
using namespace System::Web;
using namespace System::Web::SessionState;

namespace HelloWorld
{
    public __gc class Global : public System::Web::HttpApplication
    {
    public:
        Global()
        {
            InitializeComponent();
        }

    protected:
        void Application_Start(Object *sender, EventArgs *e)
        {
        }

    protected:
        void Session_Start(Object *sender, EventArgs *e)
        {
        }

    protected:
        void Application_BeginRequest(Object *sender, EventArgs *e)
        {
        }

    protected:
        void Application_EndRequest(Object *sender, EventArgs *e)
        {
        }

    protected:
        void Application_AuthenticateRequest(Object *sender, EventArgs *e)
        {
        }
```

```
    protected:
        void Application_Error(Object *sender, EventArgs *e)
        {
        }

    protected:
        void Session_End(Object *sender, EventArgs *e)
        {
        }

    protected:
        void Application_End(Object *sender, EventArgs *e)
        {
        }

    private:
        void InitializeComponent()
        {
        }
    };
}
```

Now you are ready to create your first Managed C++ Web Form. Just to make sure you got everything, take a look at Figure 14-5, which shows what Solution Explorer should now look like.

Figure 14-5. Solution Explorer is ready for ASP.NET.

"Hello, World" Web Form Style

Far be it from me to break the tradition established in this book, so let's create the first Web application as a "Hello, World" application. Actually, it is a "Hello <name>" application, but let's not be picky.

Managed C++ ASP.NET Web pages will always be made up of at least two files: the HTML/XML .aspx file and the Managed C++ codebehind file. In general, the .aspx file's purpose is to provide a definition of the Web interface of the application, and the codebehind provides code logic to support that interface.

In the case of HelloWorld, the .aspx file (see Listing 14-4) contains a simple interface that allows a user to enter his or her name and then, after clicking a button, have the name regurgitated back to him or her prefixed with "Hello". You should put HelloWorld.aspx in the Web Forms folder.

Listing 14-4. HelloWorld ASP.NET Style

```
<%@ Assembly Name="HelloWorld" %>
<%@ Page Inherits="HelloWorld.HelloForm" %>
<html>
  <head>
    <title>Hello World!</title>
  </head>
  <body>
    <form id="Form" method="post" runat="server">
      <P>
        <asp:Label id="Label" runat="server">Enter Your Name:</asp:Label>
         
        <asp:TextBox id="Input" runat="server"/>
      </P>
      <P>
        <asp:Button id="ClickMe" runat="server" Text="Click Me!"/>
      </P>
      <P>
        <asp:Label id="Output" runat="server"/>
      </P>
    </form>
  </body>
</html>
```

NOTE *For those of you who aren't familiar with the server controls (i.e., the tags starting with* `<asp:xxx>`*), you might want to consider reading up on ASP.NET before continuing with this chapter. I'm not including an explanation here simply because the size of the topic is just too big for (and really not relevant to) this book.*

TIP *It's possible to drag and drop the controls to the Web Form and update the controls' properties in the Properties view. Just make sure that you manually place all the code outside of the* `<form></form>` *tags in your .aspx file before you drag and drop controls into it.*

The code is pretty standard ASP.NET code. The only things of note are the @ `Assembly` and @ `Page` directives:

```
<%@ Assembly Name="HelloWorld" %
<%@ Page Inherits="HelloWorld.HelloForm" %>
```

The @ `Assembly` directive `Name` attribute associates a precompiled assembly with this page. IIS will expect to find this assembly in the bin directory off of the Web application's root virtual directory. Note that even though the assembly ends in .dll, you can't include it in the `Name` attribute, as it will cause an exception to be thrown when the Web page is accessed.

The @ `Page` directive has many attributes. Normally, it is here that you would find the attribute for the default language to be used. Because Managed C++ is not one of the supported embedded languages, you do not include the default language attribute. The minimal @ `Page` directive includes only the `Inherits` attribute, which associates a specific class out of the assembly with this page. Notice that if you use namespaces within the assembly, you also need to add them to the `Inherits` attribute.

The basic operation of the Web Form when requested by the user browser is that the ASP.NET runtime creates a `Page` class inherited from the precompiled assembly/class specified by the @ `Assembly` and @ `Page` directives. This `Page` class, along with the visual elements of the .aspx file, is compiled and executed. Upon executing, HTML is generated and sent back to the requesting user's browser.

The key to the capability for ASP.NET to work with Managed C++ is that the Page class generated by the ASP.NET runtime inherits from standard .NET assemblies, which Managed C++ creates.

Let's continue the example (see Listing 14-5) by examining the Managed C++ codebehind. By convention, it's named the same as the .aspx file suffixed by .h. But in reality, you can name it just about anything you want, as long as it's included in the linker (.cpp) file (which you'll cover later), so that it can be compiled into a library assembly. You should put HelloWorld.aspx.h in Class Files folder.

Listing 14-5. The HelloWorld Managed C++ Codebehind

```
using namespace System;
using namespace System::Web::UI;
using namespace System::Web::UI::WebControls;

namespace HelloWorld
{
    public __gc class HelloForm : public Page
    {
    protected:
        TextBox *Input;
        Button  *ClickMe;
        Label   *Output;

        void OnInit(EventArgs *e)
        {
            ClickMe->Click += new EventHandler(this, ClickMe_Click);
            Page::OnInit(e);
        }

    private:
        void ClickMe_Click(Object *sender, EventArgs *e)
        {
            Output->Text = String::Format(S"Hello {0}", Input->Text);
        }
    };
}
```

Just like the preceding ASP.NET code, this is pretty standard Managed C++. For those of you who have coded ASP.NET in C#, this code will look quite familiar. Except for the asterisks and a few double colons, this code is, in fact, virtually the same as that of a C# codebehind.

The preceding code is about the minimum you can get away with when it comes to this Web page. To get the Web Form to compile, you need references to the following assemblies:

- Mscorlib.dll

- System.dll

- System.Web.dll

Unexpectedly (at least to me), these references automatically get added when you add HelloWorld.aspx, along with a few others. Is ASP.NET going to support Managed C++ in a future release? Having these references automatically show up suggests that to me. Guess I'll just have to wait and see.

The only new reference is System.Web.dll, which is needed to provide browser-to-server communications. This assembly is needed for all Web applications.

Next, you import the namespaces used by the codebehind:

```
using namespace System;
using namespace System::Web::UI;
using namespace System::Web::UI::WebControls;
```

The namespace System::Web::UI contains classes and interfaces that allow the creation of ASP.NET server controls and pages. These server controls and pages will appear in your Web applications as user interface elements.

There are two types of controls available to you when you're developing ASP.NET pages: HTML server controls and ASP.NET Web Form controls. I personally use Web Form controls because I find them more consistent and easier to work with than HTML server controls. If you come from the HTML server control school, you'll need to change the preceding code to use your types of controls, but the basic logic will remain the same. Table 14-1 shows the ASP.NET Web Form control and its equivalent HTML server control.

Table 14-1. ASP.NET Web Form Control and HTML Server Control Comparison

ASP.NET WEB FORM CONTROL	HTML SERVER CONTROL
`<asp:Button>`	`<input type="button">` or `<input type="submit">`
`<asp:CheckBox>`	`<input type="checkbox">`
`<asp:DropDownList>`	`<select><option selected>`
`<asp:Hyperlink>`	`<a>`
`<asp:Image>`	`<img>`
`<asp:ImageButton>`	`<input type="image">`
`<asp:Label>`	`<span>`
`<asp:LinkButton>`	`<a><img/></a>`
`<asp:ListBox>`	`<select>`
`<asp:ListItem>`	`<option>`
`<asp:Panel>`	`<div>`
`<asp:RadioButton>`	`<input type="radio">`
`<asp:Table>`	`<table>`
`<asp:TableCell>`	`<td>`
`<asp:TableRow>`	`<tr>`
`<asp:TextBox>`	`<input type="text">` or `<input type="password">` or `<textarea>`

Because the example uses ASP.NET Web Form controls, it imports the namespace `System::Web::UI::WebControls`. If it were to use HTML server controls, it would need to import the namespace `System::Web::UI::HtmlControls`. It is also possible to use both control types within the same Web page. I personally think that, in most cases, combining the two control types could make things a little more confusing than necessary.

Once you have all the references and namespaces straightened away, you finally create the Page-derived Managed (__gc) class, which the Web page will inherit from:

```
public __gc class HelloForm : public Page
```

To access the controls in the Web Form, you need to create definitions of the controls. Notice that the `id` attribute matches the name of the control definition.

Each of these controls will have instances created for them by the Web page–
created class. Once instantiated, you have complete access to these controls'
properties and methods using these variables' definitions:

```
TextBox *Input;
Button  *ClickMe;
Label   *Output;
```

The processing of Web pages (see Table 14-2) and controls is by events. You
get access to these events using event handler delegation. You can reference
Chapter 4 for a refresher or Chapter 9, as Windows Forms use a very similar
method.

Table 14-2. Common Page Events

EVENT	DESCRIPTION
Error	Triggered when an unhandled exception is thrown
Init	Triggered when the controls are first initialized
Load	Triggered when the controls are loaded onto the page
Unload	Triggered when the controls are unloaded from the page

The Page class provides a handy virtual member called OnInit(), which triggers the Init event. To enable the codebehind to delegate its own event handlers,
you need to override this method:

```
void OnInit(EventArgs *e)
{
    ClickMe->Click += new EventHandler(this, ClickMe_Click);
    Page::OnInit(e);
}
```

CAUTION   *Be very careful to remember to call the* Page *base class
version of this method so that any functionality in the* Page *class's*
OnInit() *method will also be executed.*

In this example, the codebehind delegates an event handler to the `Button` control's `Click` event.

The final method found in the `HelloWorld` class is the event handler for the clicking of the Click Me! button. The logic simply copies the `Input` text control's `Text` property, prefixed with "Hello," to the `Text` property of the `Output Label` control.

```
void ClickMe_Click(Object *sender, EventArgs *e)
{
    Output->Text = String::Format(S"Hello {0}", Input->Text);
}
```

Anyone who has worked with Win Forms should see a strong similarity between the handling of events in Web Forms and in Win Forms. There are some major differences. The biggest is that not all controls immediately trigger an event that will be handled by the Web application. The round-trip from the client machine to the server can be expensive time-wise; thus some events are cached and then sent as a bundle to the server to be handled. For example, much of the default event handling of list box selection for the list box and the drop-down list box is done on the client machine. It should be noted, though, that it is possible to change this default behavior by setting the attribute `AutoPostBack` to `true`, which will then cause the item select events to be sent to the Web application.

Now that you have all the pieces needed to create a Web Form, you have to be able to precompile the codebehind so that it can be run by the Web server. You do this simply by adding the codebehind to the linker file HelloWorld.cpp (see Listing 14-6), which was autogenerated with the creation of the project.

Listing 14-6. The Linker File HelloWorld.cpp

```
#include "Global.asax.h"
#include "HelloWorld.aspx.h"
```

Though it's not really needed because you aren't handling any application-level events, I have included a link to Global.asax.h as well as HelloWorld.aspx.h. Now all you need to do to precompile the assembly is to . . . ah, precompile it.

Let's see if your handiwork was successful. Press Ctrl-F5, which compiles the HelloWorld assembly into the bin directory and then starts the Web page. In the dialog box that appears, enter **http://localhost/HelloWorld/HelloWorld.aspx** in the edit box "URL where the project can be accessed" (see Figure 14-6).

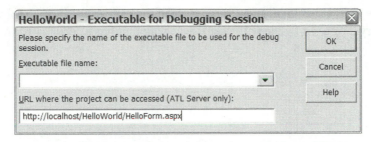

Figure 14-6. HelloWorld - Executable for Debugging Session dialog box

Now, if all went well, you should see something similar to Figure 14-7 in your browser. If you don't see this, try debugging the Web page.

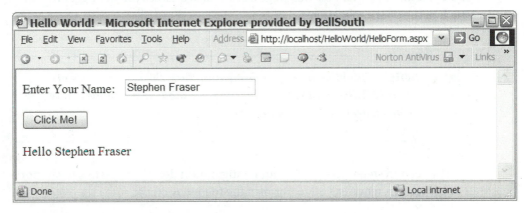

Figure 14-7. The HelloWorld Web page

Debugging ASP.NET

There is nothing special about the process of debugging Web applications. You do things such as set breakpoints, step through the code, examine variables, and so on. The tricky part is configuring Visual Studio .NET so that you can actually run the debugger. This requires two steps to be completed.

The first step is to make sure you have in the Web application's root virtual directory a Web.config file with `compilation` tag that has a `debug` attribute set to `true`:

```
<compilation debug="true" />
```

 CAUTION *The preceding code is case sensitive. You must enter the attribute exactly as shown previously or debug mode will not be set.*

With debug mode set, the ASP.NET runtime will generate debugging symbols for a dynamically generated Web page class. It also enables the debugger to attach to the Web application.

 NOTE *Enabling debug mode greatly affects the performance of your ASP.NET application. You should disable debug mode before you deploy your Web application.*

The second step is to update your configuration debug properties to support debugging. This requires you to perform the following steps:

1. Open up the Properties of the Web application.

2. Select the Debugging folder (see Figure 14-8).

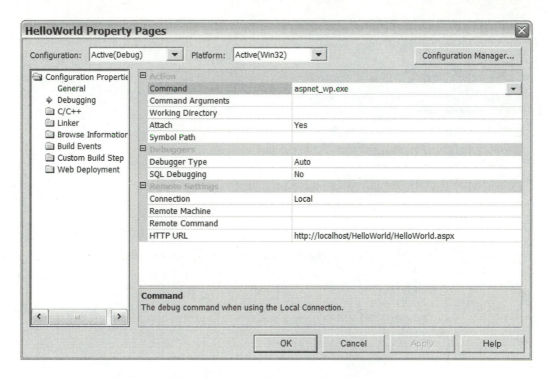

Figure 14-8. The HelloWorld Configuration Properties Debugging folder

3. Set the Command to **aspnet_wp.exe**. It might be required that you set the entire path to aspnet_wp.exe if the aspnet_wp.exe executable is not on the executables path.

4. Set Attach to **yes**.

Notice that the HTTP URL is already set correctly because you entered it when you executed the Web page earlier.

After you close the configuration dialog box, you press the F5 key to start debugging your Web Form or select Start from the Debug main menu. Figure 14-9 shows HelloWorld stopped at a breakpoint.

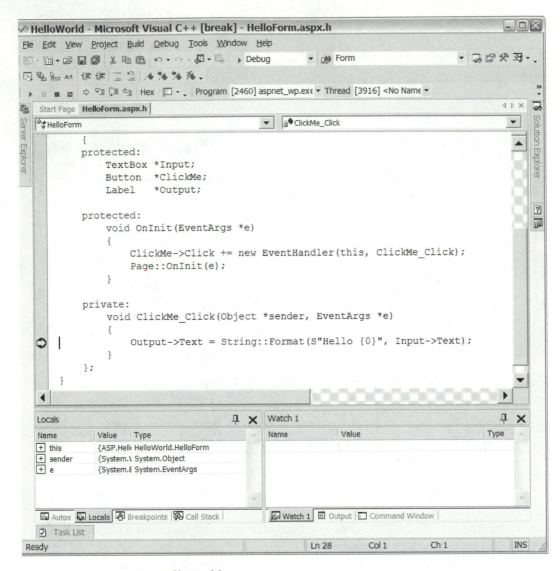

Figure 14-9. Debugging HelloWorld

TIP *If you get a dialog box that displays the message "Unable to start debugging on the Web server" instead of your Web application, when you start your debugging session, try specifying your machine name instead of "localhost" in the HTTP URL edit box. For example, on my system I would enter **http://Amidala/HelloWorld/HelloWorld.aspx**.*

Web Form Controls

You have covered the basics of Web applications and Web Forms, how to build a Web application within Visual Studio .NET for a Managed C++ codebehind, and how to set it up for debugging. Now you'll go ahead and make a few Web Forms that actually do something. To do this you need to add, as discussed briefly previously, what ASP.NET calls *Web Form controls*.

Web Form controls provide you the ability to build a Web interface in a modular fashion. Each Web Form control provides a specific type of input and/or output functionality to your Web Form. For example, there are Web Form controls to place a label or image on the screen, click a button, display and input text data, and select a data item from a list.

All Web Form controls inherit from the `WebControl` class, which provides a number of standard methods and properties. Each Web Form control has a few methods and properties of its own that make it unique. Also, all Web Form controls have events for which you can create handlers. You can find all controls provided by ASP.NET within the `System::Web::UI::WebControls` namespace.

Let's take a look at several of the Web Form controls provided by ASP.NET, starting with one of the easiest: `Label`.

NOTE *The following descriptions of the common properties used for each control assume that the Web control will be sent to a Cascading Style Sheets, level 1 (CSS1)–compliant browser. If ASP.NET determines that the browser is not CSS1 compliant, it will send HTML that best approximates these properties' functionality.*

NOTE *All properties that update the CSS1 style for a control can be overruled by the* `!IMPORTANT` *CSS1 property.*

Label

This useful, yet extremely simple, control allows you to display text at a set location on the page. Unlike static text, which you simply code directly in the .aspx file, you can dynamically change the text that is displayed using the Text property. A neat feature of the Label is that you can embed HTML tags within the text that you add. This makes the Label control extremely flexible.

The properties that you will most likely use with the Label control are as follows:

- BackColor is a System::Drawing::Color that represents the background color of the control and defaults to Color::Empty. This property gets or sets the CSS1 Style property background-color. You should note that this property will override any previous background-color CSS1 Style properties.

- Font is a property that gets the FontInfo object associated with the control. You will use the FontInfo object's properties to set the CSS1 Style font-family, font-size, and font-style properties for the control.

- ForeColor is a System::Drawing::Color that represents the foreground color of the control and defaults to Color::Empty. This property gets or sets the CSS1 Style property foreground-color. Just like BackColor, this property will override any previous foreground-color CSS1 Style properties.

- Text is a property that gets the text associated with the control. Note that if this property is empty, an empty <span></span> tag is still sent to the browser. The text may contain other HTML tags.

Color.aspx (see Listing 14-7) and Color.aspx.h (see Listing 14-8) are the GUI design and codebehind showing the Label control in action. The Web Form displays an italicized string with a random foreground and background color. To make things more interesting, I added the <meta http-equiv="Refresh" content="1"> tag to cause the form to update with random colors every second. Also, just to show that it can be done, I boldfaced a portion of the displayed string.

Listing 14-7. The ASP.NET GUI Design File Color.aspx

```
<%@ Assembly Name="WebForms" %>
<%@ Page Inherits="WebForms.ColorfulForm" %>
<html>
    <head>
        <title>Changing Colors</title>
        <meta http-equiv="Refresh" content="1">
    </head>
    <body>
        <form id="Form" method="post" runat="server">
            <asp:Label id="Label" runat="server"></asp:Label>
        </form>
```

```
    </body>
</html>
```

As you can see, the .aspx file is very simple—it's just an empty `<asp:Label>` control. The real work of the Web Form happens in the codebehind (see Listing 14-8).

Listing 14-8. The Codebehind Color.aspx.h

```cpp
using namespace System;
using namespace System::Drawing;
using namespace System::Web::UI;
using namespace System::Web::UI::WebControls;

namespace WebForms
{
    public __gc class ColorfulForm : public Page
    {
    protected:
        Label *Label;
    protected:
        void OnLoad(EventArgs *e)
        {
            Random *r = new Random();
            Label->ForeColor =
                Color::FromArgb(r->Next(255),r->Next(255),r->Next(255));
            Label->BackColor =
                Color::FromArgb(r->Next(255),r->Next(255),r->Next(255));
            Label->Text =
                S"Let's randomly change <b>colors</b> until you get sick "
                S"of watching it";
            Label->Font->Italic = true;

            Page::OnLoad(e);
        }
    };
}
```

In this example, you don't have any event to delegate, so you can safely omit the overriding of `OnInit()` method. The important overridable method in this example is the `OnLoad()` method. This method gets executed every time `Load` event is triggered. Another way of looking at it is that the `OnLoad()` method will be executed whenever the client browser page is about to be loaded.

Something you should note is that the OnLoad() method is executed before any other Web control events. For example, when you click a button on a control, the OnLoad() method is executed and then the button event. Because this is the case, you need to make sure to code only what you want executed every time the Web Form is loaded within the OnLoad() method.

There is one exception to this. The Page class provides an IsPostBack property that can be checked to see if this is the first time the OnLoad() method has been called for the Web Form for this session. You will look at IsPostBack in more detail later in the chapter.

In the preceding example, you want the same code executed on every Load event, so the OnLoad() method doesn't need to use the IsPostBack property. In this case, the OnLoad() method simply creates a random number generator class and then populates the ForeColor and BackColor properties using the Color class's static FromArgb() method. (You examine this method in detail in Chapter 11.) Next, you set the Italic property within the Font property to true. Finally, you call the base class's version of the OnLoad() method to make sure that any code in the base class's version of the OnLoad() method is also executed.

Figure 14-10 shows a "colorful" black-and-white still image of the Colorful Web Form.

Figure 14-10. The Colorful Web Form

Image

Sooner or later you are going to want to add something other than text to your Web Form. The Image control allows you to display images on the page. Unlike the static <img> tag, you can dynamically change the image that is being displayed by changing the ImageUrl property. In addition, it is possible to do things such as resize the image and change its Web Form alignment.

The properties that you will most likely use with the Image control are as follows:

- AlternateText gets or sets text that will be shown if the image is unavailable for display. For a browser that supports the ToolTip feature, this text is displayed.

- BorderColor gets or sets a System::Drawing::Color that represents the color of the control's border. It defaults to Color::Empty, which signifies that the property is not set. This property gets or sets the CSS1 Style property border-color.

- Height gets or sets a Unit object that represents the height of the control. It defaults to Unit::Empty, which signifies that the image should be displayed using its own default height. This property gets or sets the CSS1 Style property height.

- ImageAlign gets or sets an ImageAlign enum that represents the image's alignment in relationship to other elements on the Web Form. Common image alignments are Left, Right, Baseline, Top, Middle, and Bottom. The default is NotSet, which signifies that the property is not set. This property gets or sets the <img> tag Align attribute.

- ImageUrl gets or sets the relative or absolute URL of the image to be displayed. This property gets or sets the <img> tag Src attribute.

- Width gets or sets a Unit object that represents the width of the control. It defaults to Unit::Empty, which signifies that the image should be displayed using its own default width. This property gets or sets the CSS1 Style property width.

Happy.aspx (see Listing 14-9) and Happy.aspx.h (see Listing 14-10) are the GUI design and codebehind showing the Image control in action. The Web Form displays a happy face image expanding or contracting 10 pixels at every Web Form submit.

Listing 14-9. The ASP.NET GUI Design File Happy.aspx

```
<%@ Assembly Name="WebForms" %>
<%@ Page Inherits="WebForms.Happy" %>
<HTML>
  <HEAD>
    <title>Happy Face</title>
  </HEAD>
  <body>
    <form id="Happy" method="post" runat="server">
```

```
        <P>
          <asp:image id="imgHappy" runat="server"
                    ImageUrl="images/Happy.GIF" ImageAlign="Left">
          </asp:image>
        </P>
      </form>
    </body>
</HTML>
<script language="JavaScript">
    Happy.submit();
</script>
```

This .aspx file demonstrates a simple little trick that you can do using JavaScript. When JavaScript commands are found outside of a function within HTML code, they get executed immediately when encountered by the browser's interpreter. In the preceding example, you applied this trick by adding the following script after all the HTML code:

```
<script language="JavaScript">
    Happy.submit();
</script>
```

What this does is force the Web Form to be immediately submitted after the image is rendered to the client browser. You will see a more usable example of this trick in the "Tables" section later in this chapter when I show you how to update the browser status bar.

Listing 14-10. The Codebehind Color.aspx.h

```
using namespace System;
using namespace System::Web::UI;
using namespace System::Web::UI::WebControls;

namespace WebForms
{
    public __gc class Happy : public Page
    {
    protected:
        WebControls::Image *imgHappy;

        void OnLoad(EventArgs *e)
        {
            if (!IsPostBack)
            {
```

```
            //  Create a session object the first time Web Form is loaded
            Session->Item[S"cSize"] = __box(32);
        }

        // Copy the session object to local variable for easy access
        Int32 cSize = *dynamic_cast<Int32*>(Session->Item[S"cSize"]);

        if (cSize % 2 == 1)
        {
            cSize -= 10;
            if (cSize < 32)
                cSize = 32;
        }
        else
        {
            cSize += 10;
            if (cSize > 400)
                cSize -= 1;
        }
        imgHappy->Width = Unit::Pixel(cSize);
        imgHappy->Height = Unit::Pixel(cSize);

        // Update the session object for next post back
        Session->Item[S"cSize"] = __box(cSize);

        Page::OnLoad(e);
    }
};
}
```

Like the previous example, all the code logic of the codebehind falls within the OnLoad( ) method. The main thing to note about this example is the use of a Session object:

```
if (!IsPostBack)
{
    //  Create a session object the first time Web Form is loaded
    Session->Item[S"cSize"] = __box(32);
}
// Copy the session object to local variable for easy access
Int32 cSize = *dynamic_cast<Int32*>(Session->Item[S"cSize"]);
//...Use the session object
// Update the session object for next post back
Session->Item[S"cSize"] = __box(cSize);
```

A Session object is extremely handy and allows you to store data between one page load and another within a single session. It is implemented using a Hashtable collection of key/value pairs. The basic syntax to create and update a Session object is this:

```
Session->Item[S"String key"] = (Object*) value;
```

To get access to the Session object, you use the following syntax:

```
Object *value = dynamic_cast<Object*>(Session->Item[S"String key"]);
```

The codebehind, once you get past the Session object logic, is fairly straight-forward. First, the OnLoad() method uses the IsPostBack variable to see if this is the first page load and if it loads the Session object. Next, it loads a local version of the Session object for faster and easier access to its value. From there, it goes into the main logic of the codebehind, checking to see if the cSize is even or odd. If it is even, the happy face is expanding. If it is odd, the happy face is contracting. Two checks are made to see if you have reached either the minimum or maximum size of the happy face and, if so, the expansion/contraction process is reversed. The width and height of the happy face image are then updated. Finally, the cSize is placed back into the Session object for the next time the OnLoad() method for this particular session is called.

Figure 14-11 shows the happy face image as it starts to contract within the Happy Web Form.

Figure 14-11. The Happy Web Form

TextBox

I can almost guarantee that you will need to get some form of textual information from the users of your Web site. The TextBox control is the only Web Form control provided by ASP.NET that lets a user enter text.

Most of the properties that you will use with the TextBox will only be implemented at design time. For example, the TextMode property determines if the text box is SingleLine (the default), MultiLine, or Password. The width of the TextBox is specified by its Columns property. If the TextMode of the TextBox is set to MultiLine, then its height is specified by the Rows property. Under normal conditions, none of these properties would be changed at runtime. (Not that this isn't possible.)

An important property that you will normally leave alone but that occasionally comes in handy is the `EnableViewState` property. This `Boolean` property specifies if the state of the text is retained or, in other words, it specifies whether the text within the control remains after a trip from the client to the server and back.

The properties that you will most likely use with the `TextBox` control are as follows:

- `BackColor` is a `System::Drawing::Color` that represents the background color of the control and defaults to `Color::Empty`. This property gets or sets the CSS1 Style property `background-color`.

- `BorderColor` is a property that gets or sets a `System::Drawing::Color` that represents the color of the control's border. It defaults to `Color::Empty`, which signifies that the property is not set. This property gets or sets the CSS1 Style property `border-color`.

- `Enabled` is a property that gets or sets a `Boolean` value that specifies if the control is enabled. The default is `true`.

- `ForeColor` is a `System::Drawing::Color` that represents the foreground color of the control and defaults to `Color::Empty`. This property gets or sets the CSS1 Style property `foreground-color`.

- `Text` is a property that gets or sets a `String` value that represents the contents of the control. The default is `String::Empty`.

ChangeColor.aspx (see Listing 14-11) and ChangeColor.aspx.h (see Listing 14-12) are the GUI design and codebehind showing the `TextBox` control in action. The Web Form displays a `TextBox`, which requests the user to enter two colors separated by a comma. The first color is the foreground or text color and the second color is the background color of the `TextBox`. If you enter an invalid color, then the default color is displayed.

Listing 14-11. The ASP.NET GUI Design File ChangeColor.aspx

```
<%@ Assembly Name="WebForms" %>
<%@ Page Inherits="WebForms.ChangeColor" %>
<HTML>
  <HEAD>
    <title>Change Color</title>
  </HEAD>
  <body>
```

```
<form id="ChangeColor" method="post" runat="server">
    Enter "foreground color", "background color" then press return:
    <asp:TextBox id="tbChanger" runat="server" Columns="30"
                 AutoPostBack="True">
    </asp:TextBox>
  </form>
</body>
</HTML>
```

There is not much here of interest, except for the use of the AutoPostBack property within the TextBox. This property causes a post back whenever changes are made to the control. Normally, this post back is triggered when you leave the control by pressing the Tab key or by clicking another control but, because this is the only control on the Web Form, pressing the Enter key also works.

Listing 14-12. The Codebehind ChangeColor.aspx.h

```
using namespace System;
using namespace System::Drawing;
using namespace System::Web::UI;
using namespace System::Web::UI::WebControls;

namespace WebForms
{
    public __gc class ChangeColor : public Page
    {
    protected:
        TextBox *tbChanger;
    protected:
        void OnInit(EventArgs *e)
        {
            tbChanger->TextChanged +=
                new EventHandler(this, tbChanger_TextChanged);
            Page::OnInit(e);
        }
    private:
        void tbChanger_TextChanged(Object *sender, EventArgs *e)
        {
            Char AComma[] = {','};
            String *incolors[];

            // parse out the colors
            incolors = tbChanger->Text->Split(AComma);
```

```
        // change the foreground and background
        tbChanger->ForeColor = Color::FromName(incolors[0]);
        if (incolors->Length > 1)
            tbChanger->BackColor = Color::FromName(incolors[1]);
    }
};
}
```

Because the preceding example was only one control, you could have written the codebehind using an `OnLoad()` method like you did in the previous example. It would even have taken less code. This method makes more sense as you are capturing the change of the text in the `TextBox`, so why not use the correct event?

By the way, the `if` statement checking the number of colors entered into the `TextBox` avoids an exception being thrown. I found this out the hard way.

Figure 14-12 shows in black-and-white the `TextBox` with a blue background and yellow text. (Guess you will have to take my word on it.)

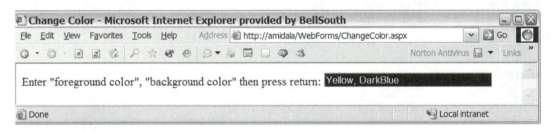

Figure 14-12. The ChangeColor form

Buttons and Hyperlinks

Entering text definitely has its place, but a mouse-click response is a much preferred way of providing input from the user's perspective. It's quick, simple, and the user's hands don't have to leave the mouse. Of course, you can't provide mouse-click responses for everything but, when you do, ASP.NET provides four buttons, a hyperlink, and a button that looks like a hyperlink from which you can choose:

- `Button` displays a push button to the user. This Web control is highly configurable to the point where you can change it to look like just a simple label on the Web Form.

- CheckBox displays a single check box that allows the user to select either a `true` or `false` condition. Note that this differs from a Win Form's `CheckBox` in that there is no `Indeterminate` state option. Like the `TextBox`, the `CheckBox`'s state is retained throughout the Web Form's session, unless the `EnableViewState` property is set to `false` (something very seldom done).

- ImageButton displays a push button to the user but, instead of text, the button displays an image.

- RadioButton displays a single radio button that the user can then select. If the buttons are grouped logically by sharing the same `GroupName`, then the user can select one radio button within the group and have all the others clear automatically.

- HyperLink displays a control that provides a link to another location in the current page or to a different Web page. Normally, you display the `HyperLink` as text by specifying the `Text` property. You can also display it as an image by specifying the `ImageUrl` property. If you specify both the `Text` and `ImageUrl` properties, then `ImageUrl` takes precedence.

- LinkButton displays a control that has the look and feel of a hyperlink but acts like a standard button. Personally, I would use this button to submit the current form and then transfer control to another Web Form, but there are no rules anywhere that say you can't use this button as an ordinary button (or an overkill hyperlink, for that matter, as shown in the following example).

Other than the `Enable` and `Visible` properties, in most cases, you will not be dealing with the properties of a button in the codebehind. Instead, you will configure the button in the design code and then simply handle the `Click` event of the button.

As you can probably guess, the `Enable` property specifies whether the button is or is not accessible to the user but is still displayed on the client browser. The `Visible` property makes the button disappear. In fact, if a button is invisible, the button does not even get sent to the client browser.

The `CheckBox` and `RadioButton` are a little different from the other buttons in that you will also need to work with the `Checked` property. The `Checked` property specifies whether the control has been selected or not.

Buttons.aspx (see Listing 14-13) and Buttons.aspx.h (see Listing 14-14) are the GUI design and codebehind showing buttons and hyperlinks in action. The Web Form looks a lot more complex than it is. It is just a four-cell table grouped by the button type. Each cell provides three buttons to select the three Web Forms created previously in the chapter.

Listing 14-13. The ASP.NET GUI Design File Buttons.aspx

```
<%@ Assembly Name="WebForms" %>
<%@ Page Inherits="WebForms.Buttons" %>
<HTML>
  <HEAD>
    <title>Buttons</title>
  </HEAD>
  <body>
    <form id="Buttons" method="post" runat="server">
      <TABLE cellSpacing="4" cellPadding="4" border="2">
        <TR>
          <TD>
            <asp:radiobutton id="rbColorful" runat="server" AutoPostBack="True"
                           Text="Colorful" GroupName="PageGroup">
            </asp:radiobutton>
            <P>
            <asp:radiobutton id="rbHappy" runat="server" AutoPostBack="True"
                           Text="Happy Face" GroupName="PageGroup">
            </asp:radiobutton>
            <P>
            <asp:radiobutton id="rbChange" runat="server" AutoPostBack="True"
                           Text="TextBox Color" GroupName="PageGroup">
            </asp:radiobutton>
          </TD>
          <TD>
            <asp:checkbox id="cbColorful" runat="server" Text="Colorful">
            </asp:checkbox>
            <P>
            <asp:checkbox id="cbHappy" runat="server" Text="Happy Face">
            </asp:checkbox>
            <P>
            <asp:checkbox id="cbChange" runat="server" Text="TextBox Color">
            </asp:checkbox>
            <P>
            <asp:button id="bnCheckBoxes" runat="server"
                        Text="Go to first checked box">
            </asp:button>
          </TD>
        </TR>
        <TR>
          <TD>
            <asp:button id="bnColorful" runat="server" Text="Colorful"
```

```
                        ForeColor="Navy" BorderColor="Purple"
                        BackColor="PaleGreen">
        </asp:button>
        <P>
        <asp:imagebutton id="ibnHappy" runat="server" BorderStyle="Outset"
                        ImageUrl="images/Happy.GIF">
        </asp:imagebutton>
        <P>
        <asp:button id="bnChange" runat="server" Text="TextBox Color">
        </asp:button>
      </TD>
      <TD>
        <asp:hyperlink id="hlColorful" runat="server"
                        NavigateUrl="Color.aspx">
          Colorful
        </asp:hyperlink>
        <P>
        <asp:HyperLink id="hlHappy" runat="server" NavigateUrl="Happy.aspx"
                        ImageUrl="images/Happy.GIF">
          Happy Face
        </asp:HyperLink>
        <P>
        <asp:LinkButton id="lbnChange" runat="server">
          TextBox Color
        </asp:LinkButton>
      </TD>
    </TR>
  </TABLE>
</form>
</body>
</HTML>
```

There is no special coding in the preceding design code. You might want to notice the use of standard HTML table tags. Later in this chapter, you will see Table control, which is a lot different coding-wise but very similar functionality-wise.

Listing 14-14. The Codebehind Buttons.aspx.h

```
using namespace System;
using namespace System::Drawing;
using namespace System::Web::UI;
using namespace System::Web::UI::WebControls;
```

```cpp
namespace WebForms
{
    public __gc class Buttons : public Page
    {
    protected:
        // Row 1 Column 1 — Controls
        RadioButton *rbColorful;
        RadioButton *rbHappy;
        RadioButton *rbChange;

        // Row 1 Column 2 — Controls
        CheckBox    *cbColorful;
        CheckBox    *cbHappy;
        CheckBox    *cbChange;
        Button      *bnCheckBoxes;

        // Row 2 Column 1 — Controls
        Button      *bnColorful;
        ImageButton *ibnHappy;
        Button      *bnChange;

        // Row 2 Column 2 — Control
        LinkButton  *lbnChange;

        void OnInit(EventArgs *e)
        {
            // Row 1 Column 1 — Event Delegations
            rbColorful->CheckedChanged += new EventHandler(this, RB_ChkChanged);
            rbHappy->CheckedChanged    += new EventHandler(this, RB_ChkChanged);
            rbChange->CheckedChanged   += new EventHandler(this, RB_ChkChanged);

            // Row 1 Column 2 — Event Delegation
            bnCheckBoxes->Click += new EventHandler(this, bnCheckBoxes_Click);

            // Row 2 Column 1 — Event Delegations
            bnColorful->Click += new EventHandler(this, bnColorful_Click);
            ibnHappy->Click += new ImageClickEventHandler(this, ibnHappy_Click);
            bnChange->Click    += new EventHandler(this, bnChange_Click);

            // Row 2 Column 2 — Event Delegation
            lbnChange->Click += new EventHandler(this, lbnChange_Click);
```

```cpp
        Page::OnInit(e);
    }
private:
    // Row 1 Column 1 - Event Handler
    void RB_ChkChanged(Object *sender, EventArgs *e)
    {
        if (rbColorful->Checked)
            Response->Redirect(S"Color.aspx");
        else if (rbHappy->Checked)
            Response->Redirect(S"Happy.aspx");
        else if (rbChange->Checked)
            Response->Redirect(S"ChangeColor.aspx");
    }


    // Row 1 Column 2 - Event Handler
    void bnCheckBoxes_Click(Object *sender, EventArgs *e)
    {
        if (cbColorful->Checked)
            Response->Redirect(S"Color.aspx");
        else if (cbHappy->Checked)
            Response->Redirect(S"Happy.aspx");
        else if (cbChange->Checked)
            Response->Redirect(S"ChangeColor.aspx");
    }


    // Row 2 Column 1 - Event Handlers
    void bnColorful_Click(Object *sender, EventArgs *e)
    {
        Response->Redirect(S"Color.aspx");
    }


    void ibnHappy_Click(Object *sender, ImageClickEventArgs *e)
    {
        Response->Redirect(S"Happy.aspx");
    }


    void bnChange_Click(Object *sender, EventArgs *e)
    {
        Response->Redirect(S"ChangeColor.aspx");
    }


    // Row 2 Column 2 - Event Handler
    void lbnChange_Click(Object *sender, EventArgs *e)
```

```
            {
                Response->Redirect(S"ChangeColor.aspx");
            }
        };
}
```

The Buttons codebehind has a few things worth noting. The first is that you can have multiple events handled by the same event handler. In the preceding example, you see this done with the RadioButton control's CheckedChanged events (which, incidentally, you also set for AutoPostBack in each RadioButton):

```
rbColorful->CheckedChanged += new EventHandler(this,RadioButton_CheckedChanged);
rbHappy->CheckedChanged += new EventHandler(this, RadioButton_CheckedChanged);
rbChange->CheckedChanged += new EventHandler(this, RadioButton_CheckedChanged);
```

You might also note that only the handler for the control that actually gets clicked is triggered even though the name of the event seems to imply that both the radio button that was checked and the radio button that became unchecked should also be triggered (as it changed also). Because of this, it would also have been possible to code this example by checking which control sent the event and then processing for that event. This makes the checked property unneeded:

```
void RadioButton_CheckedChanged(Object *sender, EventArgs *e)
{
    if (sender == rbColorful)
        Response->Redirect(S"Colorful.aspx");
    else if (sender == rbHappy)
        Response->Redirect(S"Happy.aspx");
    else if (sender == rbChange)
        Response->Redirect(S"ChangeColor.aspx");
}
```

Another thing that might cause you a few minutes of research (although after reading this, this should not be the case) is that ImageButtons differ from all the other button Click events, in that they use a different event handler. They use ImageClickEventHandler instead of the more standard EventHandler:

```
ibnHappy->Click += new ImageClickEventHandler(this, ibnHappy_Click);
```

Probably the most important thing shown in the preceding example is how to programmatically jump to a new Web page using the Redirect() method within the Response property of the Page class:

```
Response->Redirect(S"Colorful.aspx");
```

The preceding example shows how to jump to a local Web Form. To jump to a Web Form on a different server, you need to use the full URL, starting with `http://`:

```
Response->Redirect(S"http://www.contentmgr.com/default.aspx");
```

Figure 14-13 shows an assortment of buttons from which you can select the previous examples.

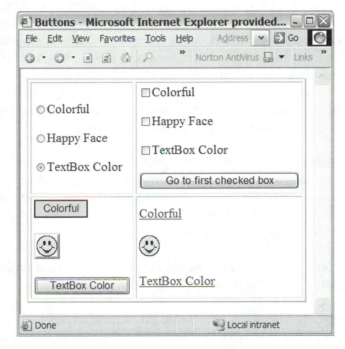

Figure 14-13. The Buttons form

Lists

A list control is really nothing more than a control that displays a list of items in the client browser. Many of the list controls provided by ASP.NET allow for user input, but that is not a requirement for it to be a list control. ASP.NET provides seven list controls to choose from:

- DataGrid displays the fields of a data source as columns in a table. Each row represents a record in the data source. The DataGrid not only supports the display of a list of items, but it also allows for selecting, editing, deleting, paging, and sorting.

- DataList displays a data bound list using a template. The DataList supports displaying, selecting, and editing of its items.

- DropDownList displays a single, select drop-down list control of ListItem objects. You can create the DropDownList using a data bound list as well.

- CheckBoxList displays a multiselect check box grouped list of ListItem objects. You can dynamically create the CheckBoxList using a data bound list. This control provides the same functionality as that of the standard CheckBox control, with the added benefit of data binding, but at the expense of fewer formatting choices.

- ListBox displays a single or multiselect list box control of ListItem objects. You can create the ListBox using a data bound list as well.

- RadioButtonList displays a single, select radio button grouped list of ListItem objects. You can dynamically create the RadioButtonList using a data bound list. This control provides the same functionality as that of the standard RadioButton control, with the added benefit of data binding, but at the expense of fewer formatting choices.

- Repeater displays a data bound list. The Repeater does not support format templating, selecting, or editing of its items.

In the preceding list, it was shown that list controls display bound data. Basically, bound data are collections that support the IEnumerable, ICollection, or IListSource interface. In other words, you can display the collections discussed in Chapter 7 and the DataView, DataSet, and DataReader objects discussed in Chapter 12 using list controls.

Two members that all list controls have in common are the DataSource property and the DataBind() method. To dynamically create a list requires you to use both members together. The DataSource property associates a bound data source with the list control. The DataBind() method then binds the data source to the control. A common mistake is to forget to call DataBind(). You will know when you have done this because you will get no data being displayed in the list control for which you have set the DataSource property.

To determine which item was selected, you will probably use the `SelectedItem` property. You can use the `SelectedIndex` property in conjunction with the `Items` property but, as you can see here, using `SelectedItem` is much easier:

```
String *val1 = listBox->SelectedItem->Value;
String *val2 = listBox->Items->Item[listBox->SelectedIndex]->Value;
```

To set an item in a list control as selected, you use the `SelectedIndex` property:

```
listBox->SelectedIndex = 3;    // remember items start at an index of 0
```

Remember, the `Repeater` control doesn't allow for item selection, therefore it doesn't define either the `SelectedItem` property or the `SelectedIndex` property.

Lists.aspx (see Listing 14-15) and Lists.aspx.h (see Listing 14-16) are the GUI design and codebehind showing a few list controls in action. You might want to pay attention to this example as it shows how to extract the tables out of an OLE DB database and place them in a table for selection. Once the table is selected, a `DataGrid` of the table displays all the content of the table. Personally, I think this example may come in handy in your future. I also threw in a drop-down control that changes the background color of the `DataGrid` control to show how to manually create a list control.

Listing 14-15. The ASP.NET GUI Design File Lists.aspx

```
<%@ Assembly Name="WebForms" %>
<%@ Page Inherits="WebForms.Lists" %>
<HTML>
  <HEAD>
    <title>Lists</title>
  </HEAD>
  <body>
    <form id="Lists" method="post" runat="server">
      <P>
        <asp:ListBox id="selListBox" runat="server" AutoPostBack="True">
        </asp:ListBox>
      </P>
      <P>
        <asp:DataGrid id="dataGrid" runat="server">
        </asp:DataGrid>
      </P>
      <P>
        <asp:DropDownList id="colorList" runat="server"
```

```
                              Enabled="False" AutoPostBack="True">
                <asp:ListItem Value="white">Select Background Color</asp:ListItem>
            </asp:DropDownList>
        </P>
    </form>
  </body>
</HTML>
```

There's nothing new in this design file other than it disables the drop-down list when the Web Form is first created. It doesn't make sense to have it enabled until there's a DataGrid for which to change the background.

Listing 14-16. The Codebehind Lists.aspx.h

```cpp
using namespace System;
using namespace System::Data;
using namespace System::Data::OleDb;
using namespace System::Drawing;
using namespace System::Web::UI;
using namespace System::Web::UI::WebControls;

namespace WebForms
{
    public __gc class Lists : public Page
    {
    protected:
        ListBox        *selListBox;
        DataGrid       *dataGrid;
        DropDownList *colorList;

        void OnLoad(EventArgs *e)
        {
            OleDbConnection *con;

            try
            {
#ifdef OLEDBAuth
                // SQL Server authentication
                String *conStr = S"Provider=SQLOLEDB.1;"
                    S"User ID=sa; Password=;"
                    S"Data Source=(local); Initial Catalog=DCV_DB;";
#else
                // Windows Integrated Security
                String *conStr = S"Provider=SQLOLEDB.1;"
```

```
                        S"Persist Security Info=False; Integrated Security=SSPI;"
                        S"Data Source=(local); Initial Catalog=DCV_DB;";
#endif
              con = new OleDbConnection(conStr);
              con->Open();

              if (!IsPostBack)
              {
                  // Set up database table list box
                  Object *restrict[] = {0, 0, 0, S"TABLE"};
                  DataTable *dt =
                      con->GetOleDbSchemaTable(OleDbSchemaGuid::Tables,
                                                    restrict);

                  selListBox->DataSource = dt->DefaultView;
                  selListBox->DataTextField = S"TABLE_NAME";
                  selListBox->DataBind();

                  // Set up Background color list box
                  colorList->Items->Add(S"Yellow");
                  colorList->Items->Add(new ListItem(S"Green",S"LightGreen"));
                  colorList->Items->Add(S"Red");
              }
              else
              {
                  // Build data grid from selected database table
                  String *selectedTable = selListBox->SelectedItem->Value;
                  String *Cmd =
                      String::Concat(S"SELECT * FROM ", selectedTable);
                  OleDbDataAdapter *dAdapt = new OleDbDataAdapter(Cmd, con);
                  DataSet *dSet = new DataSet();
                  dAdapt->Fill(dSet);

                  dataGrid->DataSource = dSet;
                  dataGrid->DataBind();
                  dataGrid->BackColor =
                      Color::FromName(colorList->SelectedItem->Value);

                  // enable background color list box
                  colorList->Enabled = true;
              }
          }
```

```
        catch(Exception *exp)
        {
            // Do Exception handling
            throw exp;
        }
        __finally
        {
            // Close down the database
            con->Close();
        }
    }
};
}
```

This codebehind could have been written so that processing was handled within `SelectedIndexChange` event handlers, but as I started coding, I realized that the same code was being executed no matter which control event was triggered. The only time this differed was on the initial Web Form generated. In other words, the same code was always run on every post back—only the initial post did something different. Because this was the case, it was possible to write all the logic within the `OnLoad()` method, as seen previously, because the `OnLoad()` method is called for every post back.

The first thing the `OnLoad()` method does is open up the database. Then if this is the first time the Web Form is loaded, it creates two list controls. The first is a `ListBox` of all the tables within the database. The second is a `DropDownList` of all the colors that the `DataGrid` background can be set to.

To get all the tables in a database, you need to use the `GetOleDbSchemaTable()` method. The first parameter you pass is an `OleDbSchemaGuid` value that specifies the schema table to return. The second parameter is an array of restriction values. To get the tables in the database, you need to first pass `OleDbSchemaGuid::Tables`, which specifies that you want the schema table of all the tables in the database. Then you restrict the fourth column to "TABLE". The valid restrictions for the fourth column are "ALIAS", "TABLE", "SYNONYM", "SYSTEM TABLE", "VIEW", "GLOBAL TEMPORARY", "LOCAL TEMPORARY", and "SYSTEM VIEW".

```
Object *restrict[] = {0, 0, 0, S"TABLE"};
DataTable *dt = con->GetOleDbSchemaTable(OleDbSchemaGuid::Tables, restrict);
```

When the `GetOleDbSchemaTable()` method returns, you have a `DataTable` containing information about the tables in the database. Now all you have to do is place the column in the `DataTable` containing the table name in the `ListBox`. You do this by first making the default view of the `DataTable` the data source of the

ListBox and then selecting the TABLE_NAME column to be used as the item to be displayed in the ListBox using the DataTextField property. Don't forget to call the DataBind() method:

```
selListBox->DataSource = dt->DefaultView;
selListBox->DataTextField = S"TABLE_NAME";
selListBox->DataBind();
```

To build a list control dynamically, you use the Add() method found within the Items property. Then you can either add a ListItem object, which allows you to specify different Text and Value properties to the list control, or add a String object, which sets the Text and Value to the same value (the passed String).

```
colorList->Items->Add(new ListItem(S"Green",S"LightGreen"));
colorList->Items->Add(S"Red");
```

By the way, it is also possible to Insert(), Remove(), and Clear() ListItems from a list control.

On a post back, the OnLoad() method does not need to load the Tables or Colors list control because the Web Form will retain the list control information and state between post backs. Instead, what needs to be built is the DataGrid of the contents of the selected Table. You do this by assigning the DataSet of the Table's contents to the DataGrid and then calling DataBind(). You saw how to create a DataSet in Chapter 12.

```
String *selectedTable = selListBox->SelectedItem->Value;
String *Cmd = String::Concat(S"SELECT * FROM ", selectedTable);
OleDbDataAdapter *dAdapt = new OleDbDataAdapter(Cmd, con);
DataSet *dSet = new DataSet();
dAdapt->Fill(dSet);

dataGrid->DataSource = dSet;
dataGrid->DataBind();
```

You grab the background color to display out of the color drop-down list. Notice that the first time this is called, the drop-down list is not enabled and its value is White, even though the text says "Select Background Color". Once you have created a DataGrid, you can then enable the color drop-down list.

```
dataGrid->BackColor = Color::FromName(colorList->SelectedItem->Value);
// enable background color list box
colorList->Enabled = true;
```

Figure 14-14 shows the content of the Content database table, with a green background. (I know it looks gray to you, but it really is green—honest.)

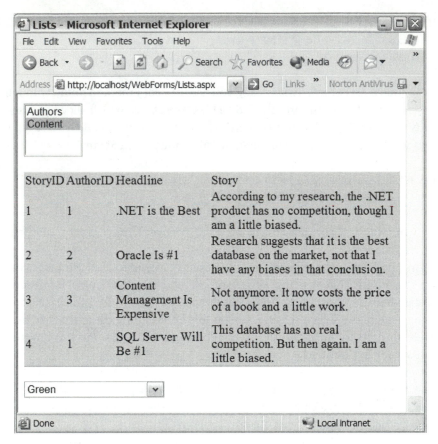

Figure 14-14. The list form

Tables

You are probably very familiar with the HTML table tag. You might be wondering why you would need another table in the form of a control. The answer is primarily its ability to be dynamically maintained within ASP.NET. With the Table control, you have much more flexibility and control when it comes to dynamically changing the look and feel of the content, layout, and so forth of your tables. Ultimately, though, the HTML generated will be standard HTML table tags.

When you work with the Table control, you will be working primarily with three classes:

- `Table` defines the properties and creates a table.

- `TableRow` represents a row of a `Table` control.

- `TableCell` represents a single cell or column in a row of a `Table` control.

Unlike some of the other controls described previously, the `Table` control is designed to be used programmatically. Thus, you will be frequently working with the members of the `Table` control in the codebehind, instead of setting them once within the GUI design file.

Some of the more common properties of the `Table` control are as follows:

- `BackColor` is a `System::Drawing::Color` that represents the background color of the control and defaults to `Color::Empty`. This property gets or sets the CSS1 Style property `background-color`.

- `BackImageUrl` is the URL of the background image to display behind the table. The image will be tiled if it is smaller than the table.

- `BorderColor` is a `System::Drawing::Color` that represents the color of the control's border. It defaults to `Color::Empty`, which signifies that the property is not set. This property gets or sets the CSS1 Style property `border-color`.

- `BorderWidth` is a `Unit` object that represents the width of the border of the control. It defaults to `Unit::Empty`, which signifies that the default width of 1 pixel is used. Note that if the `GridLines` property is not set, then this property is ignored.

- `CellPadding` is the distance in pixels (only) between the border and the contents of the table's cell.

- `CellSpacing` is the distance in pixels (only) between each table cell.

- `ForeColor` is a `System::Drawing::Color` that represents the foreground color of the control and defaults to `Color::Empty`. This property gets or sets the CSS1 Style property `foreground-color`.

- `GridLines` is a `GridLine` enum that represents whether the table displays grid lines and, if so, whether the lines are vertical, horizontal, or both. The default is no grid lines.

- HorizontalAlign is a HorizontalAlign enum that represents the horizontal alignment of the table within the Web Form.

- Rows is a TableRowCollection that represents the rows within the table. You use this control to add rows to the Table control.

Like the Table control, you will be working frequently with TableRow control's properties. Many of the properties of the TableRow are the same as those of the Table control. Where they are the same, the TableRow control property overrules the Table control's property. Here are some of the more common TableRow controls:

- BackColor is a System::Drawing::Color that represents the background color of the control and defaults to Color::Empty. This property gets or sets the CSS1 Style property background-color.

- Cells is a TableCellCollection that represents the cell within the row. You use this control to add TableCells to the TableRow control.

- ForeColor is a System::Drawing::Color that represents the foreground color of the control and defaults to Color::Empty. This property gets or sets the CSS1 Style property foreground-color.

- Height is a property that gets or sets a Unit object that represents the height of the control. It defaults to Unit::Empty, which signifies that the row should be determined based on the height of the tallest cell.

- Width is a property that gets or sets a Unit object that represents the width of the control. It defaults to Unit::Empty, which signifies that the row should be determined based on the smaller of the sum of the widths of the cells and the width of the browser client window.

Just like the other two table controls, you will be frequently using TableCell control properties—if you are creating tables, that is. There are also many common properties among all three table controls. The TableCell control property ultimately overrules all others. Here are some of the more common TableCell properties:

- `BackColor` is a `System::Drawing::Color` that represents the background color of the control and defaults to `Color::Empty`. This property gets or sets the CSS1 Style property `background-color`.

- `ColumnSpan` is an integer value that represents the number of columns the `TableCell` spans.

- `Controls` is a `ControlCollection` that represents the controls within the cell. You use this control to add controls to the `TableCell` control.

- `ForeColor` is a `System::Drawing::Color` that represents the foreground color of the control and defaults to `Color::Empty`. This property gets or sets the CSS1 Style property `foreground-color`.

- `Height` is a property that gets or sets a `Unit` object that represents the height of the control. It defaults to `Unit::Empty`, which signifies that the cell should be determined based on the height of its tallest control.

- `HorizontalAlign` is a `HorizontalAlign` enum that represents the horizontal alignment of the cell.

- `RowSpan` is an integer value that represents the number of rows the `TableCell` spans.

- `Text` is a `String` that represents the text contents of the `TableCell`. The property defaults to the value of `String::Empty`.

- `ToolTip` is a `String` that represents the text that is displayed when the mouse hovers over the `TableCell`. The property defaults to the value of `String::Empty`.

- `VerticalAlign` is a `VerticalAlign` enum that represents the vertical alignment of the cell.

- `Width` is a property that gets or sets a `Unit` object that represents the width of the control. It defaults to `Unit::Empty`, which signifies that the row should be determined based on the smaller of the sum of the widths of the cells and the width of the browser client window.

- `Wrap` is a `Boolean` value that specifies if the content of the `TableCell` wraps when the width of the cell is insufficient. The property defaults to `true`.

When you create tables using the Table control, you will be in essence coding the same steps every time. The basic steps to building a table using the Table control are as follows:

1. Create a Table control via the GUI design file.

2. Create a TableRow.

3. Create a TableCell.

4. Create a Web Form control.

5. Place the control in the TableCell.

6. Place the TableCell in the TableRow.

7. Repeat steps 3 through 6 for each TableCell in the TableRow.

8. Place the TableRow in the Table.

9. Repeat steps 2 through 8 for each TableRow in the Table.

 CAUTION   *Programmatic changes made to a* Table *control are not persistent across post backs. Therefore, any changes you make to* TableRows *and/or* TableCells *need to be reconstructed after each post back. If you expect substantial changes, then you should use the* DataList *or* DataGrid *controls instead.*

Tables.aspx (see Listing 14-17) and Tables.aspx.h (see Listing 14-18) are the GUI design and codebehind showing a table control in action. This Web Form displays all the files in the Web Form root directory along with a little information about each. Also, hidden in the code is how to update the status bar of the browser client.

Listing 14-17. The ASP.NET GUI Design File Tables.aspx

```
<%@ Assembly Name="WebForms" %>
<%@ Page Inherits="WebForms.Tables" %>
<HTML>
```

```
<HEAD>
  <title>Tables</title>
</HEAD>
<body>
  <form id="Tables" method="post" runat="server">
    <asp:Table id="FilesTable" runat="server" GridLines="Both">
      <asp:TableRow>
        <asp:TableCell Text="Name"></asp:TableCell>
        <asp:TableCell Text="Created"></asp:TableCell>
        <asp:TableCell Text="Length"></asp:TableCell>
        <asp:TableCell Text="Attributes"></asp:TableCell>
        <asp:TableCell Style="FONT-SIZE: XX-small" Text="Make Happy">
        </asp:TableCell>
      </asp:TableRow>
    </asp:Table>
  </form>
</body>
</HTML>
```

It would have been perfectly legitimate to have created the entire table in the codebehind, but because I know that the headings will always be the same, I thought it better to place them within the GUI design file. Notice that you can use CSS1 Style within the Table classes. I show only styles being done in the TableCell, but you can do it within the other controls as well.

Listing 14-18. The Codebehind Tables.aspx.h

```cpp
using namespace System;
using namespace System::IO;
using namespace System::Web::UI;
using namespace System::Web::UI::WebControls;

namespace WebForms
{
    public __gc class Tables : public System::Web::UI::Page
    {
    protected:
        // Create a Table control (Step 1)
        Table *FilesTable;

        void OnLoad(EventArgs *e)
        {
            LiteralControl *lit;
            TableCell      *cell;
```

```
String *files[] = Directory::GetFiles(Server->MapPath("."));

for (Int32 i = 0; i < files->Length; i++)
{
    FileInfo *finfo = new FileInfo(files[i]);

    if (!finfo->Exists)
        continue;

    // Create a TableRow (Step 2)
    TableRow *row = new TableRow();

    // Create a TableCell (Step 3)
    cell = new TableCell();

    // Create a Web Form control (Step 4)
    // Creating a hyperlink control
    HyperLink *link = new HyperLink();
    link->Text = finfo->Name;
    link->NavigateUrl = finfo->FullName;

    // Place the control in the TableCell (Step 5)
    cell->Controls->Add(link);

    // Place the TableCell in the TableRow (Step 6)
    row->Cells->Add(cell);

    // Repeat steps 3 through 6 (Step 7)
    // Creating a literal control
    lit = new LiteralControl(
        String::Concat(finfo->CreationTime.ToShortDateString(),
                       S" ",
                       finfo->CreationTime.ToLongTimeString()));
    cell = new TableCell();
    cell->Controls->Add(lit);
    row->Cells->Add(cell);

    lit = new LiteralControl(finfo->Length.ToString());
    cell = new TableCell();
    cell->Controls->Add(lit);
    row->Cells->Add(cell);
```

```
                    lit = new LiteralControl(__box(finfo->Attributes)->ToString());
                    cell = new TableCell();
                    cell->Controls->Add(lit);
                    row->Cells->Add(cell);

                    // Creating an image button control
                    ImageButton *ibn = new ImageButton();
                    ibn->Command += new CommandEventHandler(this, btnHappy);
                    ibn->ImageUrl = S"Images/Happy.gif";
                    ibn->CommandArgument = finfo->Name;
                    cell = new TableCell();
                    cell->HorizontalAlign = HorizontalAlign::Center;
                    cell->Controls->Add(ibn);
                    row->Cells->Add(cell);

                    // Place Row in Table (Step 8)
                    FilesTable->Rows->Add(row);

                // Repeat steps 2 through 8 (Step 9)
                }
            }

    private:
        void btnHappy(Object *sender, CommandEventArgs *e)
        {
            this->Controls->Add(new LiteralControl(String::Concat(
                S"<script language=javascript>"
                S"window.status='The file ", e->CommandArgument,
                S" is now happy'"
                S"</script>"
                )));
        }
    };
}
```

The preceding example shows how you can place a hyperlink, three literals, and an image button within TableCells of a Table control.

Two things worth noting are the use of the CommandEventHandler and the updating of the browser status bar. The CommandEventHandler allows you to delegate an event and pass it an argument of your choosing. This process is done in two steps. First, you delegate an event handler to the Command event. Second, you place the argument you want to pass on the CommandArgument property. In the preceding example, I pass the name of the file that I want to make happy on the CommandArgument property. Now, when the event is triggered as you click the image button, the handler is called along with the parameter passed. I use this parameter to specify which file is happy on the browser's status bar.

If you recall, earlier in the chapter I pointed out that JavaScript, when placed out of a function call, gets called immediately when encountered. I use that to my advantage in the preceding example. What is happening here is that I am placing a string literal in the HTML stream that gets sent to the client browser. This literal happens to also be JavaScript code. So, when the browser interpreter is parsing the HTML, it encounters the JavaScript, runs it, and then continues on. In this case, the JavaScript calls the window.status method, which updates the status bar with the string assigned to it. Pretty neat, don't you think?

Figure 14-15 shows all the files in the Web Form's root directory as well as a happy file. Look at the status bar.

Name	Created	Length	Attributes	Make Happy
AssemblyInfo.cpp	5/29/2002 1:07:30 AM	2332	Archive	☺
Buttons.aspx	6/25/2002 2:27:26 PM	2624	Archive	☺
Buttons.aspx.h	6/25/2002 2:27:26 PM	3357	Archive	☺
ChangeColor.aspx	6/24/2002 1:34:50 AM	440	Archive	☺
ChangeColor.aspx.h	6/24/2002 1:34:50 AM	1003	Archive	☺
Colorful.aspx	5/29/2002 1:18:55 AM	361	Archive	☺
Colorful.aspx.h	5/29/2002 1:18:55 AM	919	Archive	☺
Global.asax	5/29/2002 1:16:05 AM	78	Archive	☺
Global.asax.h	5/29/2002 1:09:47 AM	1814	Archive	☺
Happy.aspx	6/21/2002 2:47:35 AM	456	Archive	☺
Happy.aspx.h	6/21/2002 2:47:35 AM	1080	Archive	☺
Lists.aspx	7/2/2002 2:00:49 PM	698	Archive	☺
Lists.aspx.h	7/2/2002 2:00:49 PM	2931	Archive	☺
MyName.aspx	6/13/2002 7:35:52 PM	1688	Archive	☺
MyName.aspx.h	6/13/2002 7:35:52 PM	3429	Archive	☺

Figure 14-15. The Tables form

User Controls

User controls provide Web developers with a quick way to repeat the same little section of a Web Form on multiple Web Forms. You can create a user control once and then deploy it to as many Web Forms as you like. Something in the user control that gets changed immediately shows up in all Web Forms that use the user control. No longer do you have to wade through multiple Web Forms to make the same correction to all of them.

Here are five things that you need to know about user controls:

1. User controls are basically the same thing as a Web Form, except they don't have an <HTML>, <BODY>, or <FORM> tag. This is because a Web Form is only allowed one copy of each of these, and the main Web Form where you inserted the user control will already have them. It also has a @ Control directive instead of a @ Page directive, though the contents of the directive other than the directive name would be, in most cases, the same.

2. A user control has the suffix .ascx, which enables the compiler to differentiate between a Web Form and a user control. Also, it stops the compiler from generating an error for the missing aforementioned tags.

3. By convention, a user control codebehind has the suffix .ascx.h, though truthfully you can use just about anything.

4. The codebehind class is virtually the same as a Web Form's except that it is abstract and inherits from System::Web::UI::UserControl.

5. A user control can't execute on its own. It has to be inserted into a Web Form to run. Personally, I like to lay out the Web Form using a table tag or Table control and then insert the appropriate user control into each table cell. This isn't required, though. You can use a user control just like any HTML or intrinsic control. Therefore, you can place a user control however you like on a Web Form.

Other than that, there isn't much to user controls.

Creating a User Control

Probably one of the most common user controls you will come across when developing Web Forms is the Header user control. Virtually every page on a Web site will have a header. It only makes sense that you create a control to display it, if only for the reason that if you need to change your header, you will only need to do it once with a user control.

Header.ascx (see Listing 14-19) and Header.ascx.h (see Listing 14-20) are the GUI design and codebehind for the simple Header user control found on my Web site http://www.contentmgr.com. You might recognize the code if you read my book, *Real World ASP.NET: Building a Content Management System.*

Listing 14-19. The ASP.NET GUI Design File Header.ascx

```
<%@ Assembly Name="WebForms" %>
<%@ Control Inherits="WebForms.uc.Header" %>

<asp:Image id=imgHeader runat="server"></asp:Image>
<BR>
<HR width="100%" SIZE="1">
```

Not much to it, is there? The only thing you need to note is the GUI design code for the user control can't contain any <HTML>, <BODY>, or <FORM> tags, and you use the @ Control directive and not the @ Page directive. Other than that, user controls and Web Form GUI design code are exactly the same.

Listing 14-20. The Codebehind Header.ascx.h

```
using namespace System;
using namespace System::Web::UI;
using namespace System::Web::UI::WebControls;

namespace WebForms
{
    namespace uc
    {
        public __gc __abstract class Header : public UserControl
        {
        private:
            String *level;

        protected:
            WebControls::Image *imgHeader;
```

```cpp
    void OnLoad(EventArgs *e)
    {
        // Set the image based on passed header level
        imgHeader->ImageUrl =
            String::Concat(S"Images/", level, S".jpg");

        UserControl::OnLoad(e);
    }

public:
    // Create property to pass header level
    __property String *get_Level()
    {
        return level;
    }

    __property void set_Level(String *level)
    {
        this->level = level;
    }
};
}
}
```

Not much different from a Web Form, is it? First, I added another level to the namespace hierarchy, just to remind me that this is a user control. This is completely optional, but it helps me understand better where I am in the code.

The second and probably most important thing to notice is that the user control class inherits from `System::Web::UI::UserControl` and not `System::Web::UI::Page`. Because of this, you also have to call the `UserControl::OnLoad()` method and not the `Page::OnLoad()` method.

If you are observant, you may have noticed that you did not define the header's image URL within the design code. The reason is that you want to be able to change it based on which page it is currently heading. This dynamic functionality needs to be added to the codebehind.

The solution is elegant and very simple. Make anything you want passed to the user control a property. Then, if the user control is implemented statically within the GUI design file, pass the information as an attribute in the user control tag, or in the codebehind set the value using the property. On the other hand, if the user control is implemented dynamically, your only option is setting the property within the codebehind. You will see both of these methods later in the chapter. The code within the user control's codebehind to handle passed values is standard property logic.

Statically Implementing a User Control

As you can see in Listing 14-21, the static implementation of a user control is done entirely within the GUI design file. No changes are needed in the codebehind.

Listing 14-21. The ASP.NET GUI Design File Blank.aspx Implementing a User Control

```
<%@ Assembly Name="WebForms" %>
<%@ Page Inherits="WebForms.Blank" %>
<%@ Register TagPrefix="myUC" TagName="Header" Src="Header.ascx" %>
<HTML>
  <HEAD>
    <title>Blank</title>
  </HEAD>
  <body>
    <form id="Blank" method="post" runat="server">
      <myUC:Header id="pgHeader" Level="Home" runat="server"></myUC:Header>
    </form>
  </body>
</HTML>
```

The first step in implementing a user control is to register it with the @ Register directive.

TagPrefix is used to ensure that the user control tag is unique and can be anything you want, so long as it abides by standard C++ variable-naming rules. For example, it is possible that you may have two user controls that have the exact same name, especially if you use third-party user controls. So, by prefixing these identically named user controls with different TagPrefixes, you will make the user control names unique.

TagName is an alias to associate the user control with its class. It should match the name you gave the user control when you created it.

Src is the name of the user control's GUI design filename. Src may also include a path. Unfortunately, it must be relative to the root directory of the Web application and can't be a URI.

```
<%@ Register TagPrefix="myUC" TagName="Header" Src="Header.ascx" %>
```

The second (and last) step is to place the user control within the form tag of your Web Form. Optionally, as I show in the example, you can pass a value to the user control using an attribute. The name of the attribute must match exactly the name of the property that you placed within your user control's codebehind.

```
<myUC:Header id="pgHeader" Level="Home" runat="server"></myUC:Header>
```

What if you don't know the name of the image you want to place in the header at design time? Or what if you need to calculate it based on some set of values? To solve these problems, you need to set the Image property of the user control within the Web Form's codebehind.

Listing 14-22 shows how to call the user control without any user control–specific attributes. Notice that the only difference is that the Level attribute is not specified.

Listing 14-22. The ASP.NET GUI DESIGN FILE Blank2.aspx Implementing a User Control

```
<%@ Assembly Name="WebForms" %>
<%@ Page Inherits="WebForms.Blank2" %>
<%@ Register TagPrefix="myUC" TagName="Header" Src="Header.ascx" %>
<HTML>
  <HEAD>
    <title>Blank</title>
  </HEAD>
  <body>
    <form id="Blank" method="post" runat="server">
      <myUC:Header id="pgHeader" runat="server"></myUC:Header>
    </form>
  </body>
</HTML>
```

Listing 14-23 shows how to update the attributes within the codebehind.

Listing 14-23. The Codebehind Blank2.aspx.h

```
using namespace System;
using namespace System::Web::UI;
using namespace System::Web::UI::WebControls;

namespace WebForms
{
    public __gc class Blank2 : public Page
    {
    protected:
        WebForms::uc::Header *pgHeader;
```

```
void OnLoad(EventArgs *e)
{
    // set image to home in user control
    pgHeader->Level = S"Home";
}
};
}
```

As you can see, the code is hardly rocket science. The only thing worth noting is that you use a definition to the user control within this class. Therefore, you need to define the user control before you define this class. In other words, make sure you place user controls before Web Forms in the linker file.

Figure 14-16 shows the user control header at the top of a blank page.

Figure 14-16. The user control header

Dynamically Implementing a User Control

The process of creating user controls dynamically is not difficult. It is just not obvious how it needs to be done. You would think that you could simply create a new user class with the new operator and you are done:

```
Header *header = new Header();  // Invalid code
```

If you were to compile the preceding code, you would get an error. Remember, I said earlier that a user control's codebehind class is abstract. Abstract classes can't be instantiated directly. In other words, you can use the new operator with them.

So how do you create a user control? The answer is, you don't. Instead, you load the user control using the Page class's LoadControl() method. The basic syntax of the LoadControl() method is as follows:

```
Control* LoadControl(String *virtualPathToControl);
```

Because the LoadControl() method returns a control, you need to typecast it to the specific user control type you are loading. Notice that I also stated that it takes a virtual path as a parameter. This means that it can take only paths with a root of the Web application. This means that a URI to the user control's .ascx file is not allowed:

```
Header *header = dynamic_cast<Header*>(LoadControl("Header.ascx"));
```

ManyHeadings.aspx (see Listing 14-24) and ManyHeadings.aspx.h (see Listing 14-25) are the GUI design and codebehind showing how to dynamically create user controls. This Web Form simply places two headers at the top of an otherwise empty Web Form.

Listing 14-24. The ASP.NET GUI Design File ManyHeadings.aspx

```
<%@ Assembly Name="WebForms" %>
<%@ Page Inherits="WebForms.ManyHeadings" %>
<HTML>
  <HEAD>
    <title>ManyHeadings</title>
  </HEAD>
  <body>
    <form id="ManyHeadings" method="post" runat="server">
      <asp:Table id="Table1" runat="server" Width="100%">
        <asp:TableRow>
          <asp:TableCell ID="cell00"></asp:TableCell>
          <asp:TableCell ID="cell01"></asp:TableCell>
        </asp:TableRow>
      </asp:Table>
    </form>
  </body>
</HTML>
```

As you can see, there is no trace of the user controls in the GUI design file. However, I did create two cells to simplify the coding in the codebehind. Normally, you would probably create the cells programmatically within the codebehind as you saw earlier in the chapter.

Listing 14-25. The Codebehind ManyHeadings.aspx.h

```
using namespace System;
using namespace System::Web::UI;
using namespace System::Web::UI::WebControls;

using namespace WebForms::uc;

namespace WebForms
{
    public __gc class ManyHeadings : public Page
    {
    protected:
        TableCell *cell00;
        TableCell *cell01;

        void OnLoad(EventArgs *e)
        {
            Header *header;

            header = dynamic_cast<Header*>(LoadControl("Header.ascx"));
            header->Level = S"Home";
            cell00->Controls->Add(header);

            header = dynamic_cast<Header*>(LoadControl("Header.ascx"));
            header->Level = S"Domain";
            cell01->Controls->Add(header);
        }
    };
}
```

Now that you know how to load user controls, the preceding code shows how easy it is to create them dynamically.

Figure 14-17 shows two dynamically created user control headers at the top of a blank page.

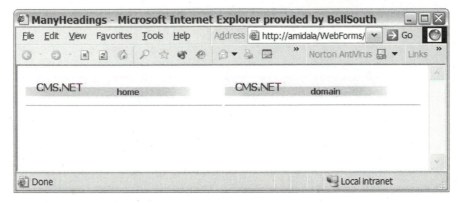

Figure 14-17. Two dynamic user control headers

Summary

This chapter was only the tip of the iceberg when it comes to covering ASP.NET and Managed C++. It started off by showing you how to configure Visual Studio .NET to support ASP.NET development or, more specifically, how to configure Web Forms development with Managed C++ codebehinds. You created yet another "Hello, World" program. After that, you learned how to configure Visual Studio .NET so that you can debug a Web Form application if you need to. Next, you covered in some detail many of the more common Web Form controls provided with ASP.NET. Finally, you learned about user controls and how to add them statically and dynamically to your Web Form.

Most of the material in this chapter was probably new to you, as this topic isn't normally covered. Even though you'll probably use C# or Visual Basic .NET to develop your Web Forms, I thought exposing you to this topic might help reinforce the idea that you don't have to learn a new language. Managed C++ is all you need.

In the next chapter, you'll continue your exploration of Managed C++'s support of ASP.NET by exploring the other major part of ASP.NET: Web services.

CHAPTER 15

Web Services

WEB SERVICES ARE THE CENTRAL HUB of everything that is .NET. The basic goal of Web services is to make distributed applications much easier to design and develop than ever before. They change the way Internet, intranet, extranet, or whichever-net-based applications are written. Basically, Web services put the "net" in .NET.

Web services aren't unique to Microsoft or .NET. In fact, all of the major industry players have a Web services offering. This chapter, however, focuses only on the Microsoft .NET Framework implementation of Web services.

The chapter starts by providing you with general understanding of Web services. You'll discover how to implement and consume a simple Web service using Managed C++. With the basics under your belt, you'll then be ready for a more elaborate implementation of a Web service, this time working with the ADO.NET skills you acquired back in Chapter 12.

What Are Web Services?

In simple terms, *Web services* are software components that can be accessed and executed remotely via a network by a client application using standard protocols such as Hypertext Transfer Protocol (HTTP) and Simple Object Access Protocol (SOAP), as shown in the following illustration.

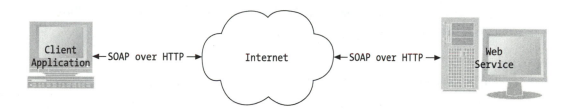

What does this mean in English? You can create a class, make it available on the Internet, and have someone on the other side of the world execute the methods on that class as if the methods were on their local machine. Likewise, Web services enable you to execute other developers' classes from anywhere around the world as long as they're hosted on the Internet. You can also place the class on a server within your LAN and execute it exactly the same way, but that simply isn't as exciting, so I'll stick to Web services' Internet capabilities in this chapter.

Another cool feature of Web services is that they aren't just a .NET thing. You can access Web services written in any computer language on any platform so long as they conform to a set of HTTP and SOAP standards to communicate. This feature allows for simple integration of diverse legacy systems and new .NET applications.

For those of you who have been coding for a few years, Web services are a much improved substitute for DCOM, COBRA, and the like.

Components of a Web Service

Web services are based on well-established networking protocols and a few newer technologies. In truth, you really don't have to know much about any of these technologies because .NET handles them, for the most part, in the background for you. In fact, the first few Web services I wrote were in complete blissful ignorance of these technologies. But, of course, true to my developer nature, I wanted to see what happens behind the curtain.

Basically, for a Web service to function, you need

- A communication protocol so that the service and its consuming client can communicate

- A description service so that the consuming client will be able to understand how to use the Web service

- A discovery service so that the consuming client can find the Web service

In the following sections you'll take a look at each requirement in a little more detail.

Communication Protocols

Communication between .NET Web services and client consumers is handled via generic HTTP using port 80. If you know something about Internet technology, you will recognize this as the same communication method used by standard Web browsers. Thus, if your system supports a Web browser, it can also support Web services. This is a key aspect of Web services, as other distributed application methods use their own specific communication protocols and ports.

Communication between a Web service and a consumer client is always initiated by the client. Clients communicate with the Web service over HTTP in two different ways:

- HTTP POST commands

- SOAP

If you have done any Web server programming, you should be quite comfortable with using HTTP POST commands. In fact, you used them with ASP.NET in the previous chapter but, just as you will see with Web services, this was hidden from you. Normally, you will not use this method when implementing Web services because it is limited to simple data types for passing between the client and the service.

 CAUTION *Make sure you are using HTTP POST and not HTTP GET. HTTP GET is supported by Web services, but you need to change your default machine.config file. (You must uncomment the line* `<add name="HttpGet"/>`*.) My guess is that Microsoft plans to phase this out, so I recommend that you don't use HTTP GET, and except for basic Web service testing, I don't really see any reason to use HTTP GET anyway.*

SOAP is a powerful XML-based protocol that packages up a method to be executed, along with any parameters it requires for implementing. This package is then sent using a standard HTTP request to the Web service. Upon the completion of the execution of a method, SOAP packages up any return values and sends them back to the client using a standard HTTP response.

The best part of SOAP, at least when it comes to .NET, is you get it for free, in almost all cases, as you have to know nothing about it so long as you code within the Common Language Specification (CLS) specified by .NET. As you will see later in this chapter when I show how to send a `DataSet` from a Web service to a client, it is possible to transmit fairly complex data objects using SOAP.

Description Service

It's all well and good that you send stuff back and forth between the client and the Web service. But before this communication can take place, the client needs some way to find out what it can request the Web service to do and what format the request needs to be in. (The format is also known as the *method signature*.)

You might think that you could use SOAP to handle the descriptive service, but SOAP was not designed to describe method signatures, only package them for transport.

The Web service provides this description of its interfaces using the relatively new standard called the *Web Services Description Language* (WSDL). Like SOAP, WSDL is XML based. But instead of packaging like SOAP, WSDL actually describes the method signatures. In fact, WSDL describes method signatures in such detail that Visual Studio .NET imports the WSDL's XML definitions and uses them to provide IntelliSense help.

Like all the previous technologies for Web services, WSDL is completely handled by Visual Studio .NET.

Discovery Service

Even if you can communicate between a client and a Web service and describe how this communication needs to take place, it's all still moot if the client doesn't know where to find the required Web service it needs to execute. This is the job of the *discovery service*. .NET provides two discovery services:

- Web Services Discovery tool (DISCO)

- Universal Description, Discovery, and Integration (UDDI)

DISCO is used to describe each Web service in any given virtual directory and any related subdirectories. Originally, .NET was going to use DISCO as its primary method of discovery, but with the advent of the superior UDDI, DISCO has become optional. It is still created automatically by Visual Studio .NET for those who want to stick with DISCO, but I think it will most probably disappear in the future.

UDDI's scope is more far-reaching than DISCO's. With UDDI, you register your Web service with a central agency. Once your Web service is registered, third parties can search the agency to locate your registered Web service.

The Web Services Namespaces

Five namespaces within the .NET Framework are directly related to Web services development:

- `System::Web::Services` is the primary namespace for Web services development. It consists of classes required for Web services creation.

- `System::Web::Services::Configuration` consists of classes that configure how Web services are created using ASP.NET.

- `System::Web::Services::Description` provides classes to programmatically interface with the WSDL.

- `System::Web::Services::Discovery` provides classes to programmatically discover Web services on a Web server.

- `System::Web::Services::Protocols` defines the protocols for transmitting data to and from the client and Web service over the network.

Most of the time when you develop Web services, you can be almost completely ignorant of the preceding namespaces. Normally, all you will need when implementing a Web service is two attributes, `WebServiceAttribute` and `WebMethodAttribute`, and an optional class, `WebService`. You use this class as a base class from which to inherit your Web service. You can find all three in the `System::Web::Services` namespace.

You use the `System::Web::Services::Protocols` namespace as well, but only indirectly within autogenerated code created when you add a Web reference.

A Simple Web Service

Enough theory, let's look at some code. In this example, you'll create an overly simplified Web service that finds a zip code based on city and state. It's so oversimplified that it finds the zip code only for two city and state combinations. In truth, it really doesn't matter what the internal workings of a Web service are, as they're just (in the case of this book) standard Managed C++ classes. What is special is the ability to access these classes over a network.

The process of creating a Web service is very easy. The first step is the same as that of any other project: Select the appropriate template (in this case, the ASP.NET Web Service template) to start building your Web service and give it a name. As you can see in Figure 15-1, I gave the project the name **FindZipCode**.

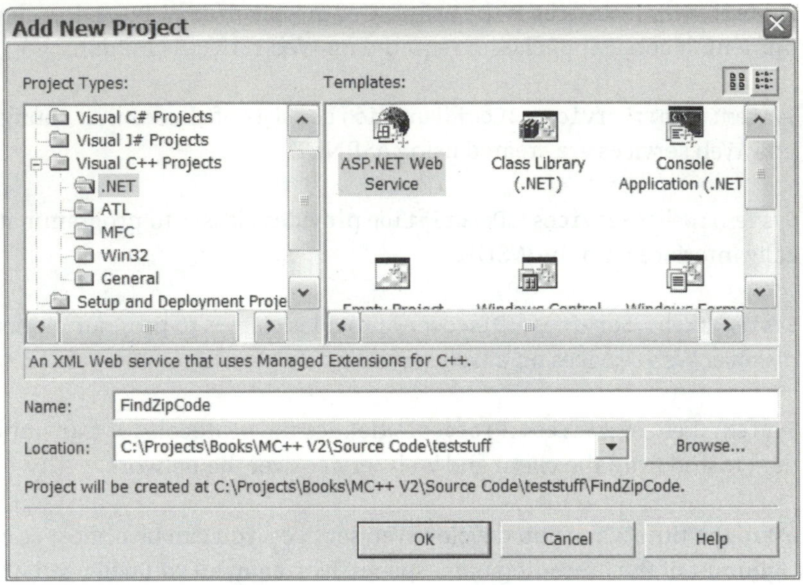

Figure 15-1. Selecting the ASP.NET Web Service template

Once the New Project Wizard finishes, you're left with (believe it or not) a fully functioning "Hello, World" Web service. Okay, let's modify the "Hello, World" service so that it provides zip code–finding functionality.

The first thing I usually do with the template is delete the generated Web service *.asmx, *.cpp, and *.h files. Then I add a new ASP.NET Web service with a more appropriate name. If you like the default name generated, then you can go ahead and use that one. In the case of this example, I actually like the default, FindZipCodeClass, so I won't go through the delete process.

As I discussed way back in Chapter 3, I like to use only one source file when I develop my classes. The code generated by the Web service wizard uses the old two-file format. I prefer to use *.h files to contain the source for my Managed C++ classes (this is also the standard used by Microsoft with Web Forms). Because of this, I open up FindZipCodeClass.cpp and delete all the pregenerated code except the #include directives. You can't simply delete FindZipCodeClass.cpp because, if you recall, only *.cpp gets compiled so I need to retain at least one *.cpp file to include all the relevant *.h files. Listing 15-1 shows the final contents of FindZipCodeClass.cpp.

Listing 15-1. FindZipCodeClass.cpp

```
#include "stdafx.h"
#include "FindZipCodeClass.h"
#include "Global.asax.h"
```

The next file you should look at is FindZipCodeClass.asmx. In almost all cases, you will not change the contents of this file. As you can see in Listing 15-2, the file contains a single WebService directive containing a Class attribute that specifies the name of the associated class with this .asmx file.

Listing 15-2. FindZipCodeClass.asmx

```
<%@ WebService Class=FindZipCode.FindZipCodeClass %>
```

Like with ASP.NET, Web services are not fully supported by Managed C++ and the only way to implement them is to precompile the source. In other languages, such as C# and Visual Basic .NET, there would be two additional attributes: the Language attribute, which specifies the language of the associated code, and the Codebehind attribute, which specifies the source file for the Web service. These other attributes allow the Web service to be compiled at runtime.

The last file of interest in this simple example is the FindZipCodeClass.h file, which I use to contain the actual logic of the Web service. When you first open the file, you will notice that it contains the default code used to support the GUI designer. Web services do not have a GUI front end, so it is safe to delete all this code. Listing 15-3 shows the final version of FindZipCodeClass.h.

Listing 15-3. FindZipCodeClass.h

```
#pragma once

using namespace System;
using namespace System::Web;
using namespace System::Web::Services;

namespace FindZipCode
{
    [WebService(Namespace=S"http://contentmgr.com",
                Description = S"Zip code retrieval service")]
    public __gc class FindZipCodeClass : public WebService
    {
    public:
        [WebMethod(Description = S"Get the zip code from city and state")]
        Int32 GetZip(String *city, String *state)
        {
            // Obviously very simplified
            if (city->Equals(S"Louisville") && state->Equals(S"KY"))
                return 40241;
            else if (city->Equals(S"Irvine") && state->Equals(S"CA"))
                return 92612;
```

```
            else
                throw new Exception(S"Zip Code not found");
        }
    };
}
```

As you can see, I removed the constructor, the `Dispose()` method, and the `InitializeComponent()` method along with the `components` variable because they are not needed. I also removed the redundant name qualifying because using namespace `System::Web::Services` does this for you.

The public method `GetZip()` is nothing particularly special, except that it throws an exception on an error. I could have just as easily returned a predetermined value to handle the not found condition, but I want to show you, when you build consuming clients later in the chapter, that exception handling works even over the Internet.

So far, nothing new has been done to this class to support Web services. You may have noticed that the class derives from `WebService`, but this is optional. The only reason that I can think of that you would need to add this is if you need to access the information found on the HTTP request or the session's state. In the previous example, the class inheritance can be safely deleted.

This only leaves the two attributes `WebService` and `WebMethod` to provide the magic of Web services.

As you might have noticed when you were entering the previous example, the first attribute `WebService` is not autogenerated. It too is optional. Though, in this case I recommend always adding it. The `WebService` attribute provides the Web service with two important features:

- A guaranteed unique namespace (if used properly)

- A description of the Web service for potential consumer clients to read and determine if it is the correct Web service to use

How do you guarantee a unique namespace? It is possible for some third-party developer to create a Web service with the exact same name and members as your Web service. So what a Web service does to stop this from happening is use your Web address as a root namespace, because a Web address is guaranteed to be unique for the Web server that hosts the Web service. Of course, it is still required that all Web services be unique on a single Web server.

Here is the code for the `WebService` attribute from the previous example:

```
[WebService(Namespace=S"http://contentmgr.com",
            Description = S"Zip code retrieval service")]
```

Notice that it uses a standard attribute syntax.

No Web service magic yet, so the magic must be (and is) this last `WebMethod` attribute. The `WebMethod` attribute is the only required element (other than the .asmx file) for a Web service. You must add it to any public methods that you want to be accessible within the Web service.

> **NOTE**   *Only public members with the* [WebMethod] *attribute are accessible within the Web service.*

Even if the member is public, it will not be accessible unless it has a `WebMethod` attribute. Just like the `WebService` attribute, you can include an optional `Description` of the `Method`.

```
[WebMethod(Description = S"Get the zip code from city and state")]
```

Okay, let's compile and run the Web service. You can do this the same way as any other application. I use Ctrl-F5, but you can use any method you are comfortable with. What you should get is a Web page that looks something like the one shown in Figure 15-2.

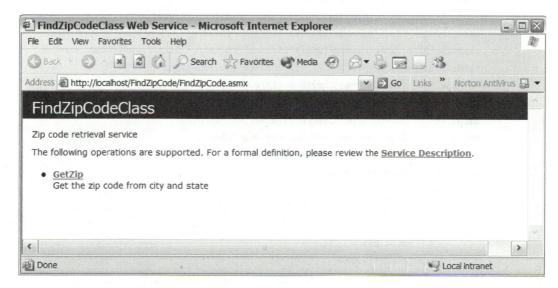

Figure 15-2. The FindZipCode Web service Web page

TIP *You might get the error "Resource can't be found." If you do, check the URL that Visual Studio .NET is trying to execute. Most likely it is using the solution's URL instead of the project's. To fix this, go to Debugging properties of the project and change the HTTP URL to point to the correct place.*

I don't remember coding this, do you? This Web page was automatically created when you compiled your Web service. This page is how a third-party developer will get information about your Web service. Note that I used the term "developer." The client application will get its information using WSDL. Because I wasn't very detailed in my descriptions on the `WebService` and `WebMethod` attributes, this page isn't very helpful. I personally recommend that you be as detailed in those attribute descriptions as possible. This will make it easier for a developer to use your Web service.

Go ahead and click the Service Description hyperlink to generate and display the WSDL for your Web service. As you can see in Listing 15-4, it's interesting, but I personally won't use it. I'll let the computer figure all this out for me.

Listing 15-4. FindZipCode's WSDL

```
<?xml version="1.0" encoding="utf-8"?>
<definitions xmlns:soap12="http://schemas.xmlsoap.org/wsdl/soap12/"
xmlns:soap="http://schemas.xmlsoap.org/wsdl/soap/"
xmlns:s="http://www.w3.org/2001/XMLSchema" xmlns:s0="http://contentmgr.com"
xmlns:soap12enc="http://www.w3.org/2002/06/soap-envelope"
xmlns:http="http://schemas.xmlsoap.org/wsdl/http/"
xmlns:soapenc="http://schemas.xmlsoap.org/soap/encoding/"
xmlns:tm="http://microsoft.com/wsdl/mime/textMatching/"
xmlns:mime="http://schemas.xmlsoap.org/wsdl/mime/"
targetNamespace="http://contentmgr.com"
xmlns="http://schemas.xmlsoap.org/wsdl/">
  <types>
    <s:schema elementFormDefault="qualified"
              targetNamespace="http://contentmgr.com">
      <s:element name="GetZip">
        <s:complexType>
          <s:sequence>
            <s:element minOccurs="0" maxOccurs="1" name="city"
                       type="s:string" />
```

```
            <s:element minOccurs="0" maxOccurs="1" name="state"
                          type="s:string" />
          </s:sequence>
        </s:complexType>
      </s:element>
      <s:element name="GetZipResponse">
        <s:complexType>
          <s:sequence>
            <s:element minOccurs="1" maxOccurs="1" name="GetZipResult"
                          type="s:int" />
          </s:sequence>
        </s:complexType>
      </s:element>
    </s:schema>
  </types>
<message name="GetZipSoapIn">
  <part name="parameters" element="s0:GetZip" />
</message>
<message name="GetZipSoapOut">
  <part name="parameters" element="s0:GetZipResponse" />
</message>
<portType name="FindZipCodeClassSoap">
  <operation name="GetZip">
    <documentation>Get the zip code from city and state</documentation>
    <input message="s0:GetZipSoapIn" />
    <output message="s0:GetZipSoapOut" />
  </operation>
</portType>
<binding name="FindZipCodeClassSoap" type="s0:FindZipCodeClassSoap">
  <soap:binding transport="http://schemas.xmlsoap.org/soap/http"
                  style="document" />
  <operation name="GetZip">
    <soap:operation soapAction="http://contentmgr.com/GetZip"
                      style="document" />
    <input>
      <soap:body use="literal" />
    </input>
    <output>
      <soap:body use="literal" />
    </output>
  </operation>
```

```
    </binding>
    <binding name="FindZipCodeClassSoap12" type="s0:FindZipCodeClassSoap">
      <soap12:binding transport="http://schemas.xmlsoap.org/soap/http"
                      style="document" />
      <operation name="GetZip">
        <soap12:operation soapAction="http://contentmgr.com/GetZip"
                          style="document" />
        <input>
          <soap12:body use="literal" />
        </input>
        <output>
          <soap12:body use="literal" />
        </output>
      </operation>
    </binding>
    <service name="FindZipCodeClass">
      <documentation>Zip code retrieval service</documentation>
      <port name="FindZipCodeClassSoap" binding="s0:FindZipCodeClassSoap">
        <soap:address location="http://localhost/FindZipCode/FindZipCode.asmx" />
      </port>
      <port name="FindZipCodeClassSoap12" binding="s0:FindZipCodeClassSoap12">
        <soap12:address location="http://localhost/FindZipCode/FindZipCode.asmx"/>
      </port>
    </service>
</definitions>
```

Now go back to the previous page and click the GetZip hyperlink. On this page, you get a simple dialog box to test your Web service. I'll show you the code to do this yourself a little later in this chapter.

Another interesting, but unnecessary, bit of information provided on this page are the HTTP request (see Listing 15-5) and response (see Listing 15-6) SOAP wrappers for your Web service. The reason that I think that they are provided (other than they look cool) is that other platforms are not as lucky as .NET and have to build and parse these SOAP wrappers themselves.

Listing 15-5. FindZipCode's Request SOAP Wrapper

```
POST /FindZipCode/FindZipCode.asmx HTTP/1.1
Host: localhost
Content-Type: text/xml; charset=utf-8
Content-Length: length
SOAPAction: "http://contentmgr.com/GetZip"
```

```
<?xml version="1.0" encoding="utf-8"?>
<soap:Envelope xmlns:xsi="http://www.w3.org/2001/XMLSchema-instance"
xmlns:xsd="http://www.w3.org/2001/XMLSchema"
xmlns:soap="http://schemas.xmlsoap.org/soap/envelope/">
  <soap:Body>
    <GetZip xmlns="http://contentmgr.com">
      <city>string</city>
      <state>string</state>
    </GetZip>
  </soap:Body>
</soap:Envelope>
```

Listing 15-6. FindZipCode's Response SOAP Wrapper

```
HTTP/1.1 200 OK
Content-Type: text/xml; charset=utf-8
Content-Length: length
<?xml version="1.0" encoding="utf-8"?>
<soap:Envelope xmlns:xsi="http://www.w3.org/2001/XMLSchema-instance"
xmlns:xsd="http://www.w3.org/2001/XMLSchema"
xmlns:soap="http://schemas.xmlsoap.org/soap/envelope/">
  <soap:Body>
    <GetZipResponse xmlns="http://contentmgr.com">
      <GetZipResult>int</GetZipResult>
    </GetZipResponse>
  </soap:Body>
</soap:Envelope>
```

The last things shown on this page are the request (see Listing 15-7) and response (see Listing 15-8) for an HTTP POST. You'll probably use this information only in the simplest of Web services and, even then, probably only during the debug phase of that Web service's development. Other platforms, on the other hand, may need to use this information because they don't have SOAP support.

Listing 15-7. FindZipCode's HTTP POST Request

```
POST /FindZipCode/FindZipCode.asmx/GetZip HTTP/1.1
Host: localhost
Content-Type: application/x-www-form-urlencoded
Content-Length: length

city=string&state=string
```

Listing 15-8. FindZipCode's HTTP POST Response

```
HTTP/1.1 200 OK
Content-Type: text/xml; charset=utf-8
Content-Length: length

<?xml version="1.0" encoding="utf-8"?>
<int xmlns="http://contentmgr.com">int</int>
```

Congratulations, you've made your first Managed C++ Web service! Now let's look at an assortment of ways to access your Web service.

Accessing a Web Service Using HTTP POST

Using HTTP POST commands is the easier of the two methods of consuming your Web service. All it requires is some simple HTML code and a Web browser. The problem with using HTTP POST is that the response back from the Web service is an XML document that you will need to parse yourself.

Listing 15-9 shows a sample of some HTML code you might use to consume the Web service. It is basically a stripped-down version of the code generated when you access FindZipCode.asmx.

Listing 15-9. HTML to Consume the FindZipCode Web Service

```
<HTML>
    <BODY>
        To execute click the 'Invoke' button.
        <form action='http://localhost/FindZipCode/FindZipCode.asmx/GetZip'
            method="POST">
            <table>
                <tr>
                    <td>Parameter</td>
                    <td>Value</td>
                </tr>
                <tr>
                    <td>city:</td>
                    <td><input type="text" name="city"></td>
                </tr>
                <tr>
                    <td>state:</td>
                    <td><input type="text" name="state"></td>
                </tr>
                <tr>
```

```
            <td colspan="2" align="center">
                <input type="submit" value="Invoke">
            </td>
        </tr>
    </table>
</form>
</BODY>
</HTML>
```

As you can see, there is not much to this HTML. The only tricky parts are as follows:

- Use a form action attribute that is made up of the Web service's name, including the .asmx suffix, followed by the name of the method you want to consume.

- Remember to use within your `<form>` tag a method attribute of POST and not the more common GET.

- Make sure the names of the input types match the Web service method parameters' names.

Figure 15-3 shows the data entry code getzip.html in action. Figure 15-4 shows what the response is after you click the Invoke button.

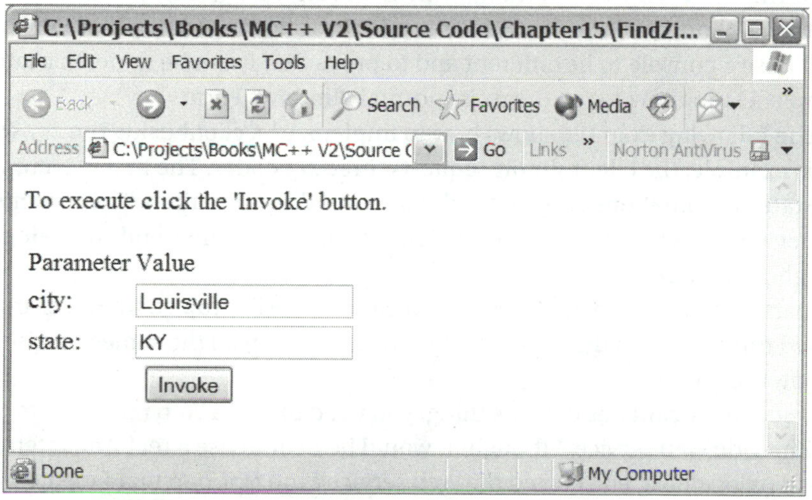

Figure 15-3. Consuming the FindZipCode Web service using getzip.html

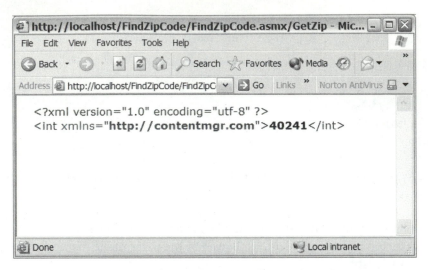

Figure 15-4. Response to getzip.html from the FindZipCode Web service

Accessing a Web Service Using SOAP

With .NET, the only real way to consume Web services is to use SOAP. As you saw previously, the SOAP wrapper is quite complex. Fortunately, if you're using Visual Studio .NET and Managed C++ (or any other .NET language, for that matter) you don't have to know squat about SOAP, because everything about SOAP is taken care of for you.

Normally, when you're working with distributed programs, the client would be either a Windows Form or a Web Form. In the following example, on the other hand, I use a console to be different and to prove that it can be done. In a later example, I show how to use the more normal Windows Form.

The following example shows how to implement a client using the console. In this example, the client simply requests three zip codes. The first two are valid city/state combinations and the third is an invalid combination. The response to all three requests is written to the console. The third response ends up being a caught exception.

Start by creating a new Console Application (.NET) project. (In the example, I added this project to the chapter solution just to keep all the same code for a chapter together.)

Once the wizard has done its thing, you need to add a Web reference to the FindZipCode Web service. I thought it would be neat to use a real Web reference instead of localhost, so I copied the Web service FindZipCode that I created previously to my Web site host server, Contentmgr.com. Unfortunately, Contentmgr.com does not support .NET Framework version 1.1, so I had to place a .NET Framework version 1.0 copy of the Web service there, but the result is ultimately the same.

TIP *For those of you who want to try out a remote copy of the Web service, I keep a copy of FindZipCode on Contentmgr.com. You can find the Web service at* http://contentmgr.com/FindZipCode.asmx.

To add a Web reference, you right-click the References folder of your client application and select Add Web Reference. This will cause the Add Web Reference dialog box to appear (see Figure 15-5).

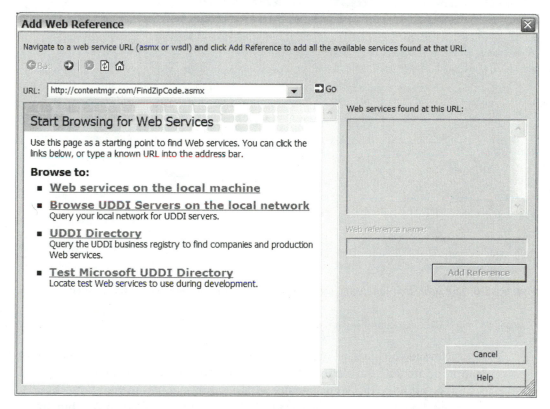

Figure 15-5. The Add Web Reference dialog box that appears before you select a Web service

From here, you can either click one of the links within the dialog box to search for the Web service or type the URL of the Web service in the supplied text box. In Figure 15-5 I typed in the URL of the Web service, but if you don't have access to a Web server or don't want to use my copy of the Web service, then select the "Web services on the local machine" link, which will find and make available the Web service you built previously. Once you select the Web service, you want the Add Web Reference dialog box changes to look like Figure 15-6.

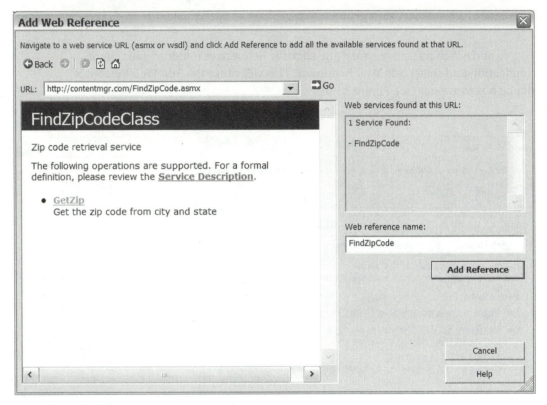

Figure 15-6. The Add Web Reference dialog box after you have selected a Web service

Now all you have to do is change the Web reference name to something more appropriate than the Web server's name, and then click the Add Reference button.

The addition of a Web reference adds a number of files to your project. Among them are a WSDL file and a DISCO file. Both are nice to look at but, in most cases, you will do nothing with them directly. The only file of real importance is the include file with the same name as the Web reference name you changed previously. All you need to do with this file is include it at the top of your client application. If you are curious, you can open this file to see some of the details of how the connection to the Web service is made.

Now you need to make the changes to your main .cpp file, as shown in Listing 15-10.

Listing 15-10. A Console Web Services Client Application

```
#include "stdafx.h"
#include "FindZipCode.h"

using namespace System;
using namespace FindZipCode;

void _tmain()
{
    FindZipCodeClass *fzc = new FindZipCodeClass();

    try
    {
        Console::WriteLine(fzc->GetZip("Louisville", "KY").ToString());
        Console::WriteLine(fzc->GetZip("Irvine", "CA").ToString());
        Console::WriteLine(fzc->GetZip("xx", "cc").ToString());
    }
    catch (Exception *e)
    {
        Console::WriteLine(e->Message);
    }
}
```

Believe it or not, that's all the coding you have to do. Notice that you instantiate a Web service class in the same way as you do any other class:

```
FindZipCodeClass *fzc = new FindZipCodeClass();
```

Also notice that you access methods in the same way:

```
fzc->GetZip("Louisville", "KY").ToString();
```

From the client programming perspective, there is no difference between using a local class and using a Web service class. If I were to give this code to a developer, he or she would have no way of knowing it uses Web services unless he or she opened the FindZipCode.h include file.

Go ahead and run the client. Figure 15-7 shows the result of the client application ZipCodeConsoleClient.exe. As is expected, two zip codes are printed to the console, and then the exception is captured and printed to the console (just as I predicted at the beginning of this example).

```
c:\Projects\Books\Mc++ v2\Source Code\Chapter15\debug\ZipCodeConsoleClient.exe  _ □ ×
40241
92612
System.Web.Services.Protocols.SoapException: Server was unable to process reques
t. ---> System.Exception: Zip Code not found
   at FindZipCode.FindZipCodeClass.GetZip(String city, String state)
   --- End of inner exception stack trace ---
Press any key to continue
```

Figure 15-7. The client consumer of Web service FindZipCode in action

Debugging a Web Service

Debugging a Web service on its own is really no different than debugging any other .NET application. Simply compile within the debug solution configuration and then set breakpoints where you want the execution to stop.

There is only one scenario that requires you to do anything special, and that is if you create your Web service within a solution that has a different name than the Web service. When you do this, starting the debugger causes the error shown in Figure 15-8.

Figure 15-8. The debugging Web service error

The wording of the error doesn't really explain what caused the error. But it's very easy to solve the problem. What has happened is that the URL to your Web service is incorrect. When you build a Web service from an existing solution, Visual Studio .NET creates a URL to your Web service using the solution's path instead of the Web service's. Thus, if you look in the Web service project properties under the Configuration Properties ➢ Debugging folder, you'll find that the HTTP URL has a value of http://localhost/solutiondir/webservicename.asmx when it should have the value http://localhost/webservicedir/webservicename.asmx. To fix the problem, simply type the correct HTTP URL in the text box.

Debugging a Web service when it is being consumed by a client is, on the other hand, not as simple and requires a little more effort to set up.

The first step is to set a breakpoint just before the first call to the Web service. Read that carefully: It says the first time the Web service is called, not the first time you want to call the Web service with the debugger.

Then, the only way you can get the debugger to work is to *step into* the Web service the first time the Web service is used in the client application. If you fail to *step into* the Web service the first time, you get the dreaded "breakpoint cannot be set" error (see Figure 15-9) whenever you try to break within the Web service.

Figure 15-9. The "breakpoint cannot be set" error

Basically, once this initial connection between client and Web service is established, by stepping into the Web service, you can then debug the Web service just like normal.

Passing Data Using a Web Service

I'm going to finish off this chapter with an elaborate example of a Web service. It will take the MaintAuthors detached database project example you created back in Chapter 12 and convert it to a Web service.

With this example, you will truly see a detached (figuratively speaking) database, where the client is on one system and the Web service (database) is located somewhere else on the Internet.

The Web service is made up of two methods: The first returns a DataSet of authors and the second takes in a DataSet of authors and updates the database based on the batched processes made by the client to the authors DataSet. You should note that this example takes no concurrency issues into consideration (i.e., what happens if multiple clients update the database via the multiple Web service instances at the same time?).

The Windows Form client application receives a DataSet of authors and then allows additions, updates, and deletions to the DataSet.

Returning a DataSet

The easier of the two Web service methods to implement relates to filling
a DataSet of all authors and then sending the DataSet from the Web service to
the consuming client (see Listing 15-11).

Listing 15-11. Building the Authors DataSet Web Service

```
using namespace System;
using namespace System::Data;
using namespace System::Data::SqlClient;
using namespace System::Web;
using namespace System::Web::Services;


namespace AuthorWS
{
    [WebService(Namespace = S"http://contentmgr.com",
    Description = S"A Web Service to handled the CRUD of the Authors Database")]
    public __gc class AuthorWSClass : public WebService
    {
    private:
        static String *connstring =
                        S"server=localhost;uid=sa;pwd=;database=DCV_DB";
    public:
        [WebMethod(
        Description = S"Method to retrieve All Authors from the database")]
        DataSet *GetAuthors()
        {
            SqlConnection *connect;
            SqlDataAdapter *dAdapt;
            DataSet *dSet;

            connect = new SqlConnection(connstring);
            dAdapt = new SqlDataAdapter();
            dAdapt->MissingSchemaAction = MissingSchemaAction::AddWithKey;

            dAdapt->SelectCommand = new SqlCommand(
                S"SELECT AuthorID, LastName, FirstName FROM Authors",
                connect);

            dSet = new DataSet();
            dAdapt->Fill(dSet, S"Authors");
```

```
        return dSet;
    }

    //...
};
}
```

As you can see, a Web service has no problems sending the complex DataSet object using SOAP. In fact, if it wasn't for the WebMethod attribute, this method would look like any other ADO.NET DataSet fill method.

One big difference, though, is that this method uses its own method scope version of the Connection, DataAdapter, and DataSet. The reason is that a Web service (unless otherwise specified using EnableSession property of the WebMethod attribute) is stateless. Basically, each time the Web service is called, it is from scratch. Thus, there is no need to have the Connection, DataAdapter, or DataSet stick around after the Web service method has finished. For this same reason, there is no reason to assign the InsertCommand, UpdateCommand, and DeleteCommand properties to the DataAdapter as they are not used in the method.

Inserting, Updating, and Deleting Rows in a DataSet

Inserting, updating, and deleting rows in a DataSet via a Web service is handled in virtually the same way as standard, nondistributed ADO.NET. The following UpdateAuthors() method (see Listing 15-11) is made up of code that is almost exactly the same as what you saw in Chapter 12.

Listing 15-11. Updating the Authors Database Web Service

```
using namespace System;
using namespace System::Data;
using namespace System::Data::SqlClient;
using namespace System::Web;
using namespace System::Web::Services;

namespace AuthorWS
{
    [WebService(Namespace = S"http://contentmgr.com",
    Description = S"A Web Service to handled the CRUD of the Authors Database")]
    public __gc class AuthorWSClass : public WebService
    {
        //...
```

```
[WebMethod(Description =
S"Method to Commit changed made on client with Server database")]
void UpdateAuthors(DataSet *dSet)
{
    SqlConnection *connect;
    SqlDataAdapter *dAdapt;

    connect = new SqlConnection(connstring);
    dAdapt = new SqlDataAdapter();
    dAdapt->MissingSchemaAction = MissingSchemaAction::AddWithKey;

    dAdapt->InsertCommand =
    new SqlCommand(S"INSERT INTO Authors (LastName, FirstName) "
                S"VALUES (@LastName, @FirstName)", connect);
    dAdapt->InsertCommand->Parameters->Add(
            S"@LastName", SqlDbType::VarChar, 50, S"LastName");
    dAdapt->InsertCommand->Parameters->Add(
            S"@FirstName", SqlDbType::VarChar, 50, S"FirstName");

    dAdapt->UpdateCommand = new SqlCommand(
            S"UPDATE Authors SET LastName = @LastName, "
            S"FirstName = @FirstName"
            S"WHERE AuthorID = @AuthorID", connect);
    dAdapt->UpdateCommand->Parameters->Add(
            S"@LastName", SqlDbType::VarChar, 50, S"LastName");
    dAdapt->UpdateCommand->Parameters->Add(
            S"@FirstName", SqlDbType::VarChar, 50, S"FirstName");
    dAdapt->UpdateCommand->Parameters->Add(
            S"@AuthorID", SqlDbType::Int, 4, S"AuthorID");

    dAdapt->DeleteCommand = new SqlCommand(
            S"DELETE FROM Authors WHERE AuthorID = @AuthorID", connect);
    dAdapt->DeleteCommand->Parameters->Add(
            S"@AuthorID", SqlDbType::Int, 4, S"AuthorID");

    dAdapt->Update(dSet, S"Authors");
    }
};
}
```

I'm sure you are seeing the pattern here. Distributed code using Web services is usually very close to, if not the same as, its nondistributed equivalent. The only real difference is that the class state is not maintained. Therefore, you have to be careful about global and class variables.

Unlike the plain ADO.NET version in Chapter 12, the Web service creates a new version of the `DataAdapter` each time a `DataSet` update is required. The reason, as I stated previously, is that the Web service is stateless, so on the call to the `AuthorUpdate()` method, no `DataAdapter` object exists. Having a new or different `DataAdapter` from the one when the `DataSet` was created is not an issue, because a `DataAdapter` is not strongly linked to the `DataSet` it is supporting. In fact, so long as the database schema is the same, `DataSets` are interchangeable as far as `DataAdapters` are concerned. As you will see later, the `DataSet` of the `Update` process can be a subset of the one sent by the `GetAuthors()` method, because only changed rows are contained within this `DataSet`.

What is neat about this method is that it can handle inserted, updated, and deleted records, all in a batch-like manner, instead of requiring a separate method for each of these process types.

 CAUTION   *To simplify this example, I didn't add any code to handle database concurrency.*

Authors DataSet Processing Web Service Client

In truth, there is little reason to include this section in the chapter other than to show that very little has changed in the Web service client application when you compare it to the ADO.NET example in Chapter 12. Listing 15-12 has been included so that you can compare it to the source code of the MaintAuthors example in Chapter 12.

Listing 15-12. Web Server Version of the MaintAuthors Application

```
#include "AuthorWS.h"

namespace MaintAuthors
{
    using namespace System;
    using namespace System::ComponentModel;
    using namespace System::Collections;
    using namespace System::Windows::Forms;
    using namespace System::Data;
    using namespace System::Data::SqlClient;
    using namespace System::Drawing;
```

```
using namespace AuthorWS;

public __gc class Form1 : public System::Windows::Forms::Form
{
public:
    Form1(void)
    {
        InitializeComponent();

        authors = new AuthorWSClass();
        dSet = authors->GetAuthors();

        DataTable *dt = dSet->Tables->Item["Authors"];

        if (dt == 0)
            throw new Exception(S"No Authors Table");

        IEnumerator *Enum = dt->Rows->GetEnumerator();
        while(Enum->MoveNext())
        {
            DataRow *row = dynamic_cast<DataRow*>(Enum->Current);
            lbAuthors->Items->Add(ListBoxItem(row));
        }
        CurrentAuthorID = -1;
    }

protected:
    void Dispose(Boolean disposing)
    //...

    DataSet *dSet;
    Int32 CurrentAuthorID;
    AuthorWSClass *authors;

    void InitializeComponent(void)
    //...Not shown to save space

private:
    String *ListBoxItem(DataRow *row)
    //...Same as Chapter 12
```

```
private:
    System::Void bnAdd_Click(System::Object * sender, System::EventArgs * e)
    {
        if (tbFirstName->Text->Trim()->Length == 0 ||
            tbLastName->Text->Trim()->Length == 0)
            return;

        DataTable *dt = dSet->Tables->Item["Authors"];

        DataRow *row = dt->NewRow();

        row->Item[S"FirstName"] = tbFirstName->Text;
        row->Item[S"LastName"]  = tbLastName->Text;

        dt->Rows->Add(row);

        lbAuthors->Items->Add(ListBoxItem(row));

        tbFirstName->Text = S"";
        tbLastName->Text = S"";
    }

private:
    System::Void bnUpdate_Click(Object * sender, System::EventArgs * e)
    {
        if (CurrentAuthorID < 0)
            return;

        DataTable *dt = dSet->Tables->Item["Authors"];
        DataRow *row[] =
        dt->Select(String::Format(S"AuthorID={0}", __box(CurrentAuthorID)));

        row[0]->Item[S"FirstName"] = tbFirstName->Text;
        row[0]->Item[S"LastName"]  = tbLastName->Text;

        lbAuthors->Items->Insert(lbAuthors->SelectedIndex,
                                    ListBoxItem(row[0]));
        lbAuthors->Items->RemoveAt(lbAuthors->SelectedIndex);
    }
```

```
        private:
            System::Void bnDelete_Click(Object * sender, System::EventArgs * e)
            {
                if (CurrentAuthorID < 0)
                    return;

                DataTable *dt = dSet->Tables->Item["Authors"];
                DataRow *row[] =
                dt->Select(String::Format(S"AuthorID={0}", __box(CurrentAuthorID)));

                row[0]->Delete();

                lbAuthors->Items->RemoveAt(lbAuthors->SelectedIndex);
            }


        private:
            System::Void lbAuthors_SelectedIndexChanged(System::Object * sender,
                                                         System::EventArgs * e)
            //...Same as Chapter 12


        private:
            System::Void bnCommit_Click(Object * sender, System::EventArgs * e)
            {
                authors->UpdateAuthors(dSet->GetChanges());
                dSet->AcceptChanges();

                lbAuthors->Items->Clear();

                DataTable *dt = dSet->Tables->Item["Authors"];

                IEnumerator *Enum = dt->Rows->GetEnumerator();
                while(Enum->MoveNext())
                {
                    DataRow *row = dynamic_cast<DataRow*>(Enum->Current);
                    lbAuthors->Items->Add(ListBoxItem(row));
                }
                CurrentAuthorID = -1;
            }
        private:
            System::Void bnRollback_Click(Object * sender, System::EventArgs * e)
            {
                dSet->RejectChanges();
```

```
        lbAuthors->Items->Clear();

        DataTable *dt = dSet->Tables->Item["Authors"];

        IEnumerator *Enum = dt->Rows->GetEnumerator();
        while(Enum->MoveNext())
        {
            DataRow *row = dynamic_cast<DataRow*>(Enum->Current);
            lbAuthors->Items->Add(ListBoxItem(row));
        }
        CurrentAuthorID = -1;
    }
  };
}
```

As you can see, the code is the same except that the ADO.NET DataAdapter and DataSet logic has been removed. In actuality, this logic should probably have been moved to its own class in the example in Chapter 12, but this was not done because it simplifies the code listing.

Figure 15-10 shows the Web service version of MaintAuthors.exe in action. Those of you looking for differences between this and the original version in Chapter 12 won't find any.

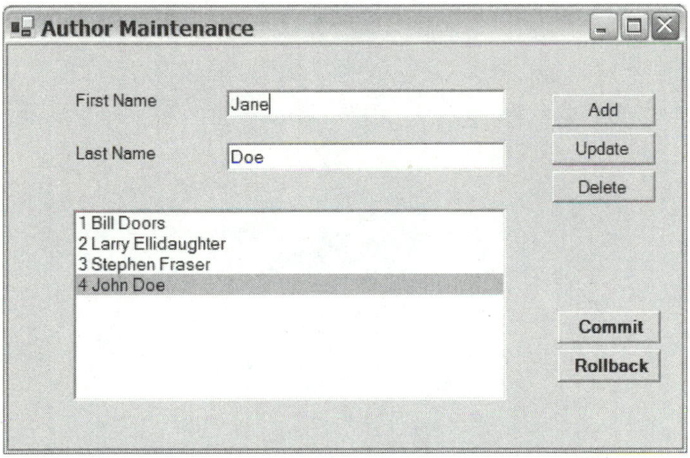

Figure 15-10. Web service version of MaintAuthors

Summary

In this chapter you examined the "net" in .NET: Web services. What you found out is that Web services are extremely easy to develop and code because you aren't doing anything different when coding Web services as compared to developing any other class. In general, any complexities associated with the distributed application nature of Web services are hidden from you. The only real difference of note is that Web services are generally coded in a stateless manner.

You started the chapter by covering the basics of Web services. Then you moved on to examine two different examples of Web services and multiple ways to write consumer clients. The second example was relatively complex, but the complex logic actually had very little to do with Web services and more to do with coding ADO.NET in a stateless manner.

In the next chapter, you'll look at the normally complex topic of multi-threaded programming.

Multithreaded Programming

NORMALLY, MULTITHREADED PROGRAMMING would be one of the more advanced topics, if not *the* most advanced topic, in a book, but due to the .NET Framework, it is no more advanced than any other topic in this book. Why, you might ask? Well, the answer is that the .NET Framework (as usual) has hidden most of the complexities of this habitually complex area of software development within its classes.

Having the complexities hidden doesn't mean it's any less powerful or flexible than you doing the entire complex coding yourself. In fact, true to the nature of the .NET Framework, if you want to get lost in the details, you can still do so. On the other hand, because this chapter is about developing multithreaded programs using Managed C++ and not about multithreaded programming in general, I try to stay away from these details and let the .NET Framework deal with them. However, for those of you who like to delve into the details, I try to point you in the right direction for future exploration.

This chapter starts off by covering multithreaded programming at a high level, so those of you who are new to multithreaded programming can get comfortable with the concept. Next, you'll explore the more commonly used and, fortunately, easy-to-understand multithreaded programming features provided by the .NET Framework. With the basics covered, you'll explore some of the more complex areas of multithreaded programming, including thread states, priorities, and the weighty topic of synchronization. Finally, you'll learn about a second way of handling multithreaded programming: thread pools.

What Is Multithreaded Programming?

Most developers are comfortable with the concept of *multitasking*, or the capability of computers to execute more than one application or process at the same time. However, *multithreading* may be a more alien term. Many programmers have not had any cause to program in a multithreaded fashion. In fact, for some programming languages (before .NET, that is), there was no way to do multithreaded programming without jumping through some very convoluted programming hoops.

So, what is multithreaded programming? You might want to think of it as multitasking at the program or process level. A program has two options for executing itself. The first option is to run itself in one thread of execution. In this method of execution, the program follows the logic of the program from start to end in a sequential fashion. You might want to think of this method of execution as *single threaded*. The second option is that the program can break itself into multiple threads of execution or, in other words, split the program into multiple segments (with beginning and end points) and run some of them concurrently (at the same time). This is what is better known as *multithreading*. It should be noted, though, that the end result of either a single-threaded or a multithreaded program will be the same.

Of course, if you have a single processor machine, true concurrency is not possible as only one command can be run at a time through the CPU. (With Intel Corporation's new Hyper-Threading Technology, you can execute more than one command at the same time on a single CPU, but that is a topic for another book altogether.) This is an important concept to grasp because many programmers mistakenly think that if they break a computational bound section of a program into two parts and run them in two threads of execution, then the program will take less time to run. The opposite is actually the case—it will take longer. The reason is that the same amount of code is being run for the program, plus additional time must be added to handle the swapping of the thread's context (the CPU's registers, stack, and so on).

So for what reason would you use multithreading for a single process computer if it takes longer than single threading? The reason is that, when used properly, multithreading can provide better I/O-related response time, as well as better use of the CPU.

Wait a second, didn't I just contradict myself? Well, actually, I didn't.

The key point about proper use of multithreading is the types of commands the threads are executing. Computational bound threads (i.e., threads that do a lot of calculations) gain very little when it comes to multithreading, as they are already working overtime trying to get themselves executed. Multithreading actually slows this type of thread down. I/O threads, on the other hand, gain a lot. This gain is most apparent in two areas: better response and CPU utilization.

I'm sure you've all come across a program that seemed to stop or lock up and then suddenly came back to life. The usual reason for this is that the program is executing a computation bound area of the code. And, because multithreading wasn't being done, there were no CPU cycles provided for user interaction with the computer. By adding multithreading, it's possible to have one thread running the computational bound area and another handling user interaction. Having an I/O thread allows the user to continue to work while the CPU blasts its way through the computational bound thread. True, the actual computational bound thread will take longer to run, but because the user can continue to work, this minute amount of time usually doesn't matter.

I/O threads are notorious for wasting CPU cycles. Humans, printers, hard drives, monitors, and so forth are very slow when compared to a CPU. I/O threads spend a large portion of their time simply waiting, doing nothing. Thus, multithreading allows the CPU to use this wasted time.

Basic .NET Framework Class Library Threading

There is only one namespace that you need to handle threading: System::Threading. What you plan to do while using the threads will determine which of the classes you will use. Many of the classes provide different ways to do the same thing, usually differing in the degree of control. Here is a list of some of the more common classes within the System::Threading namespace:

- AutoResetEvent notifies a waiting thread that an event has occurred. You use this class to allow communication between threads using signaling. Typically, you use this class for threads that need exclusive access.

- Interlocked allows for atomic operation on a variable that is shared between threads.

- ManualResetEvent notifies one or more threads that an event has occurred. You use this class to allow communication between threads using signaling. Typically, you use this class for scenarios where one thread must complete before other threads can proceed.

- Monitor provides a mechanism to synchronize access to objects by locking access to a block of code, commonly called a *critical section*. While a thread owns the lock for an object, no other thread can acquire that lock.

- Mutex provides a synchronization primitive that solves the problem of two or more threads needing access to a shared resource at the same time. It ensures that only one thread at a time uses the resource. This class is similar in functionality to Monitor, except Mutex allows for interprocess synchronization.

- ReaderWriterLock allows a single writer and multiple readers access to a resource. At any given time, it allows either concurrent read access for multiple threads or write access to a single thread.

- Thread is the core class to create a thread to execute a portion of the program code.

- ThreadPool provides access to a pool of system-maintained threads.

- WaitHandle allows for the taking or releasing of exclusive access to a shared system-specific resource.

From the preceding list of classes, you can see that the .NET Framework class library provides two ways to create threads:

- Thread

- ThreadPool

The difference between the two primarily depends on whether you want to maintain the Thread object or you want the system to handle it for you. In effect, nearly the same results can be achieved with either method. I cover Thread first, as it provides you with complete control of your threads. Later in this chapter, I cover ThreadPool, where the system maintains the process threads. Though, even with this reduction in control, you will see later in the chapter that ThreadPools can be used just as effectively as Threads. But, before you cover either method, you'll take a look at thread state and priority.

Thread State

The .NET Framework thread model is designed to model an execution thread. Many of the Threading namespace classes and members map directly to an execution state of a thread. Personally, I found knowing the execution states of a thread ultimately made it easier for me to understand threading, so using Figure 16-1 and Table 16-1, I'll walk you through the state and the action required to change states within the .NET Framework thread model.

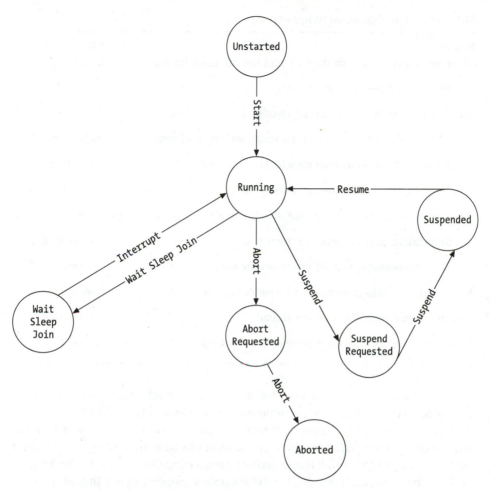

Figure 16-1. The execution states of a thread

You might want to note that the states in Table 16-1 map directly to the System::Threading::ThreadState enumeration. And, if you need to determine the current state, you would look in the ThreadState property in the Thread class.

Table 16-1. The Execution States of a Thread

ACTION	STATE
The thread is created with the CLR and has not been invoked.	Unstarted
The thread executes its start process.	Running
The thread continues to run until another action occurs.	Running
The running thread calls sleep for a specified length of time.	WaitSleepJoin
The running thread calls wait on a locked resource.	WaitSleepJoin
The running thread calls join on another thread.	WaitSleepJoin
Another thread calls interrupt on the WaitSleepJoin thread.	Running
Another thread calls suspend on the thread.	SuspendRequest
The SuspendRequested thread processes the suspend call.	Suspended
Another thread calls resume on a Suspended thread.	Running
Another thread calls abort on the thread.	AbortRequest
The AbortRequested thread processes the abort call.	Aborted

In addition to these states is a Background state, which means the thread is executing in the background (as opposed to in the foreground). The biggest difference between a background thread and a foreground thread is that a background thread ends when the main application thread ends. A foreground thread continues executing until it is aborted or finishes executing. You set a thread to be in the background by setting the IsBackground property of the Thread class.

Thread Priorities

Not all threads are created equal. Well, that's not really true, all threads are created equal. You just make them unequal later by updating the Priority property of the Thread class. With the .NET Framework, you have five levels of priorities available to place on a thread:

- Highest

- AboveNormal

- Normal

- BelowNormal

- Lowest

You can find each of the preceding priorities in the
`System::Threading:ThreadPriority` enumeration.

The basic idea behind priorities is that all threads are created at a `Normal` priority. When unaltered, each "running" thread gets an equal share of processor time. If, on the other hand, you change the priority of the thread to a higher level—`AboveNormal`, for example—then the documentation says it will be scheduled to execute prior to threads at a lower level. Well, this is sort of the case. If that were truly how the Framework did it, then lower level threads would never run (in other words, they would *starve*) until the higher level thread finished. This doesn't happen, so it appears that the .NET Framework has additional logic in it to allow lower level priority threads to have at least a little processor time.

Normally you don't want to mess with priorities, but for those rare occasions, the functionality, as you have come to expect with the .NET Framework, is provided.

Using Threads

Of the two methods available in the .NET Framework for creating threads, `Thread` and `ThreadPool`, the `System::Threading::Thread` class provides you with the most control and versatility. The cost is a minor amount of additional coding complexity.

Like all classes in the .NET Framework, the `Thread` class is made up of properties and methods. The ones you will most likely use are as follows:

- `Abort()` is a method that raises a `ThreadAbortException` in the thread on which it is invoked, which starts the process of terminating the thread. Calling this method normally results in the termination of the thread.

- `CurrentThread` is a static `Thread` property that represents the currently running thread.

- `Interrupt()` is a method that interrupts a thread that is currently in the `WaitSleepJoin` thread state, thus resulting in the thread returning to the `Running` thread state.

- `IsBackground` is a Boolean property that represents whether a thread is a background or a foreground thread. The default is `false`.

- `Join()` is a method that causes the calling thread to block until the called thread terminates.

- `Name` is a `String` property that represents the name of the thread. You can write the name only once to this property.

- `Priority` is a `ThreadPriority` enumerator property that represents the current priority of the thread. The default is `Normal`.

- `Resume()` is a method that resumes a suspended thread and makes its thread state `Running`.

- `Sleep()` is a method that blocks the current thread for a specified length of time and makes its thread state `WaitSleepJoin`.

- `Start()` is a method that causes the thread to start executing and changes its thread state to `Running`.

- `Suspend()` is a method that causes the thread to suspend. The thread state becomes `Suspended`.

- `ThreadState` is a `ThreadState` enumerator property that represents the current thread state of the thread.

The idea of running and keeping track of two or more things at the same time can get confusing. Fortunately, in many cases with multithreaded programming, you simply have to start a thread and let it run to completion without interference.

I start off by showing you that exact scenario first. Then I show you some of the other options available to you when it comes to thread control.

Starting Threads

The first thing that you need to do to get the multithreaded programming running is to create an instance of a `Thread`. You don't have much in the way of options, as there is only one constructor:

```
System::Threading::Thread ( System::Threading::ThreadStart *start );
```

The parameter `ThreadStart` is a delegate to the method that is the starting point of the thread. The signature of the delegate is a method with no parameters that returns void:

```
public __gc __delegate void ThreadStart();
```

One thing that may not be obvious when you first start working with threads is that creating an instance of the Thread object doesn't cause the thread to start. The thread state after creating an instance of the thread is, instead, Unstarted. To get the thread to start, you need to call the Thread class's Start() method. It kind of makes sense, don't you think?

I think it's about time to look at some code. Take a look at the example of a program that creates two threads in Listing 16-1. The first thread executes a static method of a class and the second thread executes a member class.

Listing 16-1. Starting Two Simple Threads

```
using namespace System;
using namespace System::Threading;

__gc class MyThread
{
public:
    static void StaticThread()
    {
        for (Int32 i = 0; i < 5000001; i++)
        {
            if (i % 1000000 == 0)
                Console::WriteLine(S"Static Thread {0}", i.ToString());
        }
    }

    void NonStaticThread()
    {
        for (Int32 i = 0; i < 5000001; i++)
        {
            if (i % 1000000 == 0)
                Console::WriteLine(S"Member Thread {0}", i.ToString());
        }
    }
};

Int32 main()
{
    Console::WriteLine(S"Main Program Starts");

    // Creating a thread start delegate for a static method
    ThreadStart *thrStart = new ThreadStart(0, &MyThread::StaticThread);
    // Use the ThreadStart object to create a Thread pointer Object
    Thread *tid1 = new Thread(thrStart);
```

```
MyThread *myThr = new MyThread();
// Creating a Thread reference object in one line from a member method
Thread &tid2 =
    *new Thread(new ThreadStart(myThr, &MyThread::NonStaticThread));

//    Uncomment for background vs foreground exploration
//    thr1->IsBackground = true;
//    thr2.IsBackground = true;

// Actually starting the pointer and reference threads
tid1->Start();
tid2.Start();

Console::WriteLine(S"Main Program Ends");
return 0;
}
```

There are some things you might want to notice about Listing 16-1. First, Threads can be pointers or references, as you should have expected, because they are classes like any other.

The second thing of note is the subtle difference between creating an instance of a delegate from a static method and creating an instance of a delegate from a member method:

```
new ThreadStart(0, MyThread::StaticThread)
new ThreadStart(myThr, &MyThread::MemberThread)
```

The first parameter is a pointer to the class that contains the delegate method. For a static method there is no class pointer, so the first parameter is set to null or 0. The second parameter is a pointer to the fully qualified method.

The third thing of note is that I had to use really big loops for this example to show the threading in process. For smaller loops, the first thread finished before second thread even started. (Wow, computers are fast!)

Okay, execute StartingThreads.exe by pressing Ctrl-F5. This will compile the program and start it without the debugger. If you have no error, you should get something like Figure 16-2.

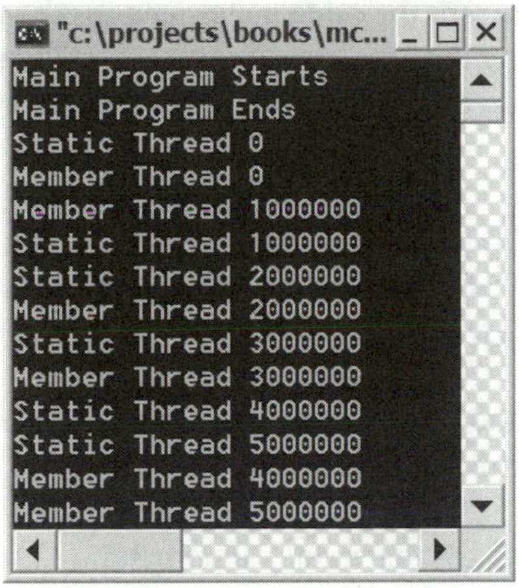

Figure 16-2. The StartingThreads program in action

Take a look at the top of your output. Your main program started and ended before the threads even executed their first loop. As you can see, foreground threads (which these are) continue to run even after the main thread ends.

If you were to uncomment these two lines, before the start method calls, with the lines

```
thr1->IsBackground = true;
thr2.IsBackground = true;
```

then you would find that the threads stop abruptly without completing when the main thread ends, just as you would expect. Something I didn't expect, though, was that if you set only one of the threads to the background, it doesn't end when the main thread ends but instead continues until the second "foreground" thread completes.

Getting a Thread to Sleep

When you develop your thread, you may find that you don't need it to continually run or you might want to delay the thread while some other thread runs. To handle this, you could place a delay loop like a "do nothing" for loop. However, doing this wastes CPU cycles. What you should do instead is temporarily stop the thread or put it to sleep.

Doing this couldn't be easier. Simply add the following static Thread method:

```
Thread::Sleep(timeToSleepInMilliseconds);
```

This line causes the current thread to go to sleep for the interval specified either in milliseconds or using the TimeSpan structure. The TimeSpan structure specifies a time interval and is created using multiple overloaded constructors:

```
TimeSpan(Int64 ticks);
TimeSpan(Int32 hours,Int32 minutes,Int32 seconds);
TimeSpan(Int32 days,Int32 hours,Int32 minutes,Int32 seconds);
TimeSpan(Int32 days,Int32 hours,Int32 minutes,Int32 seconds,Int32 milliseconds);
```

The Sleep() method also takes two special values: Infinite, which means sleep forever, and 0, which means give up the rest of the thread's current CPU time slice.

A neat thing to notice is that main() and WinMain() are also threads. This means you can use Thread::Sleep() to make any application sleep. In Listing 16-2, both worker threads and the main thread are all put to sleep temporarily.

Listing 16-2. Making a Thread Sleep

```
using namespace System;
using namespace System::Threading;

__gc class MyThread
{
public:
    static void ThreadFunc()
    {
        Thread *thr = Thread::CurrentThread;
        for (Int32 i = 0; i < 101; i++)
        {
            if (i % 10 == 0)
                Console::WriteLine(S"{0} {1}", thr->Name, i.ToString());
            Thread::Sleep(10);   // sleep 10 milliseconds
        }
    }
};

Int32 main()
{
    Console::WriteLine(S"Main Program Starts");

    MyThread *myThr1 = new MyThread();
```

```
Thread &thr1 = *new Thread(new ThreadStart(myThr1, &MyThread::ThreadFunc));
Thread &thr2 = *new Thread(new ThreadStart(myThr1, &MyThread::ThreadFunc));

thr1.Name = S"Thread1";
thr2.Name = S"Thread2";

thr1.Start();
thr2.Start();

Int32 iHour = 0;
Int32 iMin = 0;
Int32 iSec = 1;
Thread::Sleep(TimeSpan(iHour, iMin, iSec)); // sleep one second

Console::WriteLine(S"Main Program Ends");
return 0;
}
```

Listing 16-2 has a couple of additional bits of bonus logic. First, it shows how to get a pointer to the current thread using the Thread class's CurrentThread property:

```
Thread *thr = Thread::CurrentThread;
```

Second, it shows how to assign a name to a thread using the Thread class's Name property, which you can retrieve later within the thread:

```
// when creating thread add
thr1.Name = S"Thread1";
// then later in thread itself
String *threadName = Thread::CurrentThread->Name;
```

 TIP *Though it isn't the purpose of the thread's* Name *property, you could use the* Name *property to pass a parameter (in* String *format) to a thread, instead of (or as well as) the name of the thread.*

The results of SleepingThreads.exe are shown in Figure 16-3.

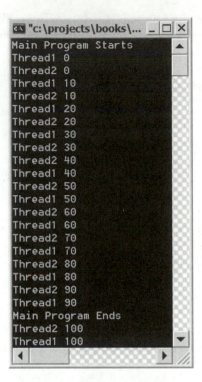

Figure 16-3. The SleepingThreads program in action

Notice that the main thread ends in the middle of the thread execution, instead of before it starts, like in the previous example. The reason being the main thread is put to sleep while the worker threads run and then it wakes up just before the other threads end.

Aborting Threads

You might, on occasion, require that a thread be terminated within another thread before it runs through to its normal end. In such a case, you would call the Abort() method. This method will, normally, permanently stop the execution of a specified thread.

Notice that I used the term "normally." What actually happens when a thread is requested to stop with the Abort() method is that a ThreadAbortException exception is thrown within the thread. This exception, like any other, can be caught but, unlike most other exceptions, ThreadAbortException is special as it gets rethrown at the end of the catch block unless the aborting thread's ResetAbort() method is called. Calling the ResetAbort() method cancels the abort, which in turn prevents ThreadAbortException from stopping the thread.

CAUTION *Something that you must be aware of is that an aborted thread can't be restarted. If you attempt to do so, a* ThreadStateException *exception is thrown instead.*

Listing 16-3 shows the Abort() method in action. First it creates two threads, and then it aborts them. Just for grins and giggles, I then try to restart an aborted thread, which promptly throws an exception.

Listing 16-3. Aborting a Thread

```
using namespace System;
using namespace System::Threading;

__gc class MyThread
{
public:
    static void ThreadFunc()
    {
        Thread *thr = Thread::CurrentThread;
        try
        {
            for (Int32 i = 0; i < 100; i++)
            {
                Console::WriteLine(S"{0} {1}", thr->Name, i.ToString());
                Thread::Sleep(1);
            }
        }
        catch (ThreadAbortException*)
        {
            Console::WriteLine(S"{0} Aborted", thr->Name);
            // Reset the abort so that the method will continue processing
            // thr->ResetAbort();
        }
    }
};


Int32 main()
{
    Console::WriteLine(S"Main Program Starts");
```

```
Thread &thr1 = *new Thread(new ThreadStart(0, &MyThread::ThreadFunc));
Thread &thr2 = *new Thread(new ThreadStart(0, &MyThread::ThreadFunc));

thr1.Name = S"Thread1";
thr2.Name = S"Thread2";

thr1.Start();
thr2.Start();

Thread::Sleep(6);
thr1.Abort();
Thread::Sleep(6);
thr2.Abort();

try
{
    thr1.Start();
}
catch (ThreadStateException *tse)
{
    Console::WriteLine(tse->ToString());
}

Console::WriteLine(S"Main Program Ends");
return 0;
}
```

In the exception of the Thread method, I've added (but commented out) the code required to reset the abort so that the thread continues instead of ending.

Figure 16-4 shows AbortingThreads.exe in action. As you can see, even though I catch the ThreadAbortException exception in the thread, the thread still aborts after leaving the catch block. As expected, when I try to restart a thread, a ThreadStateException exception is thrown.

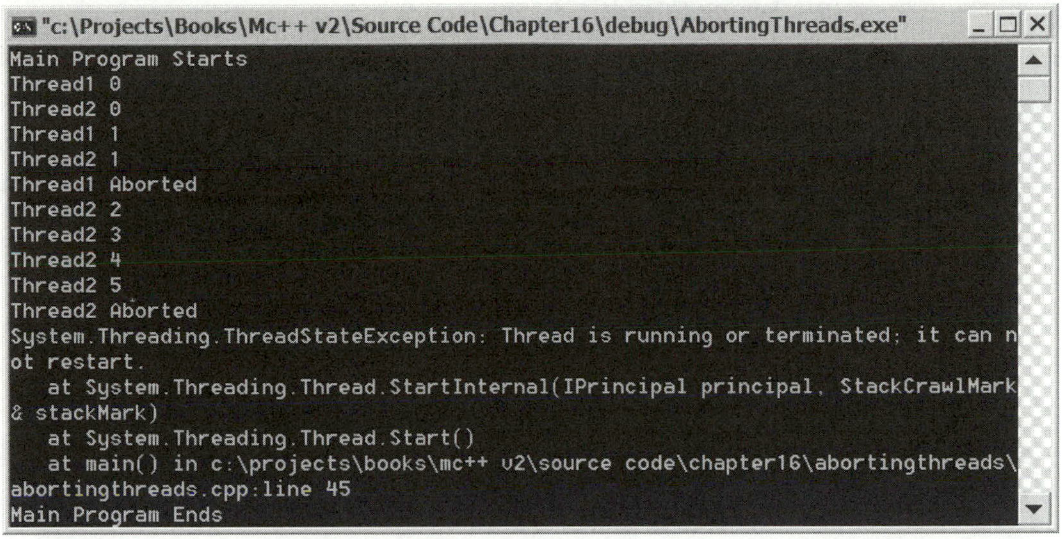

Figure 16-4. The AbortingThreads program in action

Joining Threads

Back in the first example in this chapter, you saw that after you created your threads and started them, the main program then proceeded to terminate. In the case of the first example this is fine, but what if you want to execute something after the threads finish? Or, more generally, how do you handle the scenario where one thread needs to wait for another thread to complete before continuing?

What you need to do is join the threads using the Thread class's Join() method. You can join threads in three different ways by using one of the three overloaded Join() methods. The first overloaded method takes no parameters and waits until the thread completes, and the second takes an int parameter and then waits the parameter's specified number of milliseconds or for the thread to terminate, whichever is shorter. The third overload takes a TimeSpan struct and functions the same as the previous overload.

The simple example in Listing 16-4 joins the main thread to the first worker thread and then waits for the worker thread to complete before starting the second worker thread.

Listing 16-4. Joining Threads

```
using namespace System;
using namespace System::Threading;

__gc class MyThread
{
public:
    static void ThreadFunc()
    {
        Thread *thr = Thread::CurrentThread;
        for (Int32 i = 0; i < 5; i++)
        {
            Console::WriteLine(S"{0} {1}", thr->Name, i.ToString());
            Thread::Sleep(1);
        }
    }
};

Int32 main()
{
    Console::WriteLine(S"Before starting thread");

    Thread &thr1 = *new Thread(new ThreadStart(0, &MyThread::ThreadFunc));
    Thread &thr2 = *new Thread(new ThreadStart(0, &MyThread::ThreadFunc));

    thr1.Name = S"Thread1";
    thr2.Name = S"Thread2";

    thr1.Start();
    thr1.Join();

    thr2.Start();

    Console::WriteLine("End of Main");
}
```

Figure 16-5 shows JoiningThreads.exe in action. Notice that the main thread terminates again after both threads are started, but this time the main thread waited for the first worker thread to end before starting the second thread.

Figure 16-5. The JoiningThreads program in action

Interrupting, Suspending, and Resuming Threads

It is completely possible to take a worker thread and place it in a tight loop, waiting for some event to occur. Doing this would be a big waste of CPU cycles. It would be better to let the worker thread sleep and then be woken up when the event occurs. You can do exactly that using a combination of `Sleep()` and `Interrupt()` methods, in conjunction with the `System::Threaded::ThreadInterruptedException` exception.

The basic idea is to put the worker thread to sleep using the static `Sleep()` method, and then interrupt (the sleep of) the worker thread when the required event occurs using the `Interrupt()` member method. Simple enough, I think, except that the `Interrupt()` method throws a `ThreadInterruptedException` exception instead of just terminating the `Sleep()` method. Thus, you need to place the `Sleep()` method in the `try` of a `try/catch` block, and then have the worker thread continue execution in the `catch`.

Here's the worker thread:

```
try
{
    // Wait for event to occur
    Thread::Sleep(Timeout::Infinite);
}
catch(ThreadInterruptedException*)
{
    /*continue processing*/
}
```

Here's some other thread:

```
WorkerThread->Interrupt();
```

The preceding scenario will work if the worker thread knows when to go to sleep. It may also be necessary to allow another thread to temporarily stop a different thread and then restart it again later.

For example, a worker thread could be doing some intense number crunching when along comes another thread that needs to put a large graphic up on the monitor as soon as possible (the user interface should almost always get priority).

You can resolve this scenario in at least three ways. First, you could do nothing special and let the multithreading engine slowly display the graphic. Second, you could raise the priority of the graphic display thread (or lower the priority of the worker thread), thus giving the graphic display more cycles. Or third, you could suspend the worker thread, then draw the graphic and, finally, resume the worker thread. Doing it this way requires two methods and would be done like this:

```
WorkerThread->Suspend();
// do stuff
WorkerThread->Resume();
```

CAUTION   *Choosing either the second or third methods mentioned previously can have some negative side effects. Changing priorities could lead to sluggish interface response time because the interface thread is now a lower priority. Suspending a thread could lead to thread starvation as the suspended thread might hold resources needed by other threads.*

Listing 16-5 shows how to implement both of the Thread class's sleep/interrupt and suspend/resume functionalities.

Listing 16-5. Sleeping/Interrupting and Suspending/Resuming a Thread

```
using namespace System;
using namespace System::Threading;

__gc class MyThread
{
public:
```

```
    static void ThreadFunc1()
    {
        Console::WriteLine(S"Before long sleep");
        try
        {
            Thread::Sleep(Timeout::Infinite);
        }
        catch(ThreadInterruptedException*){/*continue processing*/}
        Console::WriteLine(S"After long sleep");
    }
    static void ThreadFunc2()
    {
        for (Int32 i = 0; i < 5; i++)
        {
            Console::WriteLine(S"Thread {0}",i.ToString());
            Thread::Sleep(2);
        }
    }
};

Int32 main()
{
    Thread &thr1 = *new Thread(new ThreadStart(0, &MyThread::ThreadFunc1));
    Thread &thr2 = *new Thread(new ThreadStart(0, &MyThread::ThreadFunc2));

    Console::WriteLine(S"Sleep/interrupt thread");
    thr1.Start();

    Thread::Sleep(4);
    for (Int32 i = 0; i < 4; i++)
    {
        Console::WriteLine(S"**Main2 {0}", i.ToString());
        Thread::Sleep(2);
    }
    thr1.Interrupt();
    thr1.Join();

    Console::WriteLine(S"\nSuspend/resume thread");
    thr2.Start();

    Thread::Sleep(8);
    thr2.Suspend();
```

```
for (Int32 i = 0; i < 4; i++)
{
    Console::WriteLine(S"**Main1 {0}", i.ToString());
    Thread::Sleep(2);
}
thr2.Resume();

return 0;
}
```

You can see the results of ISRingThreads.exe in Figure 16-6.

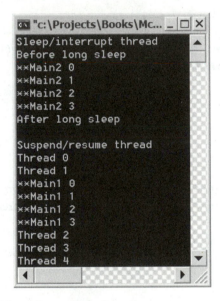

Figure 16-6. The ISRingThreads program in action

Notice how both provide a similar flow through their threads. The major difference between sleep/interrupt and suspend/resume is which thread initiates the temporary stopping of the worker thread.

Using ThreadPools

As the name of the class suggests, System::Threading::ThreadPool provides a system-managed pool of threads on which to run your application's threads. Being managed by the system, your multithreaded application loses control of how threads are created, managed, and cleaned up. But, in many cases, your application has no real need to manage threads, as aborting, joining, interrupting, suspending, and resuming a thread in an application is not always needed.

What you lose in control you get back in ease of use. Plus, it simplifies multi-threaded programming, especially if your application is made up of numerous threads. With thread pooling, you're able to focus on developing your business logic without getting bogged down with thread management.

For those of you who are interested, this is, at a high level, how a thread pool works. Basically, a thread pool is created the first time `ThreadPool` is called. Thread pools use a queuing system that places a work item (a thread request) on an available thread pool thread. If no thread pool thread is available, then a new one is created up to a default maximum of 25 threads per available processor. (You can change this maximum using `CorSetMaxThreads`, defined in the mscoree.h file.) If the maximum number of threads is reached, then the work item remains on a queue until a thread pool thread becomes available. There is no limit to the number of work items that can be queued. (Well, that's not quite true. You are restricted to available memory.)

Each thread pool thread runs at the default priority and can't be cancelled.

 NOTE *Thread pool threads are background threads. As such, you need the main program thread or some other foreground thread to remain alive the entire life of the application.*

You add a work item to the thread pool queue by calling the `ThreadPool` class's static `QueueUserWorkItem()` method. The `QueueUserWorkItem()` method takes a `WaitCallback` delegate as a parameter and an `Object` pointer parameter to allow you to pass information to the generated thread. (The method is over-loaded so that you don't have to pass an `Object` parameter if none is required.) The `WaitCallback` delegate has the following signature:

```
public __gc __delegate void WaitCallback(Object* state);
```

The `Object* state` parameter will contain the `Object` pointer that was passed as the second parameter to the `QueueUserWorkItem()` method. The `QueueUserWorkItem()` method returns `true` if the method successfully queues the work item; otherwise, it returns `false`.

The example in Listing 16-6 shows how simple it is to create two `ThreadPool` threads.

Listing 16-6. Using Thread Pools

```
using namespace System;
using namespace System::Threading;


__gc class MyThread
{
public:
    void ThreadFunc(Object* stateInfo)
    {
        for (Int32 i = 0; i < 10; i++)
        {
            Console::WriteLine(S"{0} {1}", stateInfo, i.ToString());
            Thread::Sleep(100);
        }
    }
};


Int32 main()
{
    Console::WriteLine(S"Main Program Starts");

    MyThread *myThr1 = new MyThread();

    ThreadPool::QueueUserWorkItem(
        new WaitCallback(myThr1, &MyThread::ThreadFunc), S"Thread1");
    ThreadPool::QueueUserWorkItem(
        new WaitCallback(myThr1, &MyThread::ThreadFunc), S"Thread2");

    Thread::Sleep(2000);
    Console::WriteLine(S"Main Program Ends");
    return 0;
}
```

There are only a couple of things of note in the preceding example. The first is the second parameter in the call to the QueueUserWorkItem() method. This parameter is actually extremely flexible, as you can pass it any managed data type supported by the .NET Framework. In the preceding example, I passed a String, but you could pass it an instance to an extremely large and complex class if you want.

The second thing of note is the Sleep() method used to keep the main thread alive. Once the main thread dies, so do all the threads in the ThreadPool, no matter what they are doing.

You can see the results of ThreadPooling.exe in Figure 16-7.

Figure 16-7. The ThreadPooling program in action

Synchronization

As threads become more complex, you will find that they more than likely start to share resources between themselves. The problem with shared resources is that only one thread can safely update them at any one time. Multiple threads that attempt to change a shared resource at the same time will eventually have subtle errors start to occur in themselves.

These errors revolve around the fact that Windows uses preemptive mode multithreading and that Managed C++ commands are not atomic or, in other words, require multiple commands to complete. This combination means that it is possible for a single Managed C++ operation to be interrupted partway through its execution. This, in turn, can lead to a problem if this interruption happens to occur when updating a shared resource.

For example, say two threads are sharing the responsibility of updating a collection of objects based on some shared integer index. As both threads update the collection using the shared index, most of the time everything will be fine, but every once in a while something strange will happen due to the bad timing of the preemptive switch between threads. What happens is that when thread 1 is in the process of incrementing the shared integer index and just as it is about to store the newly incremented index into the shared integer, thread 2 takes control. This thread then proceeds to increment the shared value itself and updates the collection object associated with the index. When thread 1 gets control back, it completes its increment command by storing its increment value in the stored index, overwriting the already incremented value (from thread 2) with the same value. This will cause thread 1 to update the same collection object that thread 2 has already completed. Depending on what updates are being done to the collection, this repeated update could be nasty. For example, maybe the collection was dispersing $1 million to each object in the collection and now that account in question has been dispersed $2 million.

The *ThreadStatic* Attribute

Sometimes your synchronizing problem is the result of the threads trying to synchronize in the first place. What I mean is you have static class scope variables that store values within a single threaded environment correctly but, when the static variables are migrated to a multithreaded environment, they go haywire.

The problem is that static variables are not only shared by the class, they are also shared between threads. This may be what you want, but there are times that you only want the static variables to be unique between threads.

To solve this, you need to use the `System::Threading::ThreadStaticAttribute` class. A static variable with an attribute of [ThreadStatic] is not shared between threads. Each thread has its own separate instance of the static variable, which is independently updated. This means that each thread will have a different value in the static variable.

CAUTION *You can't use the class's static constructor to initialize a* [ThreadStatic] *variable because the call to the constructor only initializes the main thread's instance of the variable. Remember, each thread has its own instance of the* [ThreadStatic] *variable and that includes the main thread.*

Listing 16-7 shows how to create a thread static class variable. It involves nothing more than placing the attribute [ThreadStatic] in front of the variable that you want to make thread static. I added a little wrinkle to this example by making the static variable a pointer to an integer. Because the variable is a pointer, you need to create an instance of it. Normally, you would do that in the static constructor, but for a thread static variable this doesn't work as then only the main thread's version of the variable has been allocated. To fix this, you need to allocate the static variable within the thread's execution.

Listing 16-7. Synchronizing Using the ThreadStatic Attribute

```cpp
using namespace System;
using namespace System::Threading;

__gc class MyThread
{
public:
    [ThreadStatic]
    static int *iVal;
public:
    static MyThread()
    {
        iVal = new int;
    }

    void ThreadFunc()
    {
        iVal = new int;
        *iVal = 7;

        SubThreadFunc();
    }

    void SubThreadFunc()
    {
        Int32 max = *iVal + 5;

        while (*iVal < max)
        {
            Thread *thr = Thread::CurrentThread;
            Console::WriteLine(S"{0} {1}", thr->Name, iVal->ToString());
            Thread::Sleep(1);
            (*iVal)++;
        }
    }
};
```

```
Int32 main()
{
    Console::WriteLine(S"Before starting thread");

    MyThread *myThr1 = new MyThread();

    Thread &thr1 = *new Thread(new ThreadStart(myThr1, &MyThread::ThreadFunc));
    Thread &thr2 = *new Thread(new ThreadStart(myThr1, &MyThread::ThreadFunc));

    Thread::CurrentThread->Name = S"Main";
    thr1.Name = S"Thread1";
    thr2.Name = S"Thread2";

    thr1.Start();
    thr2.Start();

    (*myThr1->iVal) = 5;
    myThr1->SubThreadFunc();

    return 0;
}
```

First off, when you comment out the [ThreadStatic] attribute and run the
ThreadStaticVars.exe program, you get the output shown in Figure 16-8. Notice
how the value is initialized three times and then gets incremented without regard
to the thread that is running. Maybe this is what you want, but normally it isn't.

Figure 16-8. The attribute commented-out ThreadStaticVars program in action

Okay, uncomment the [ThreadStatic] attribute and run ThreadStaticVars.exe
again. This time you'll get the output shown in Figure 16-9. Notice now that each
thread (including the main thread) has its own unique instance of the static
variable.

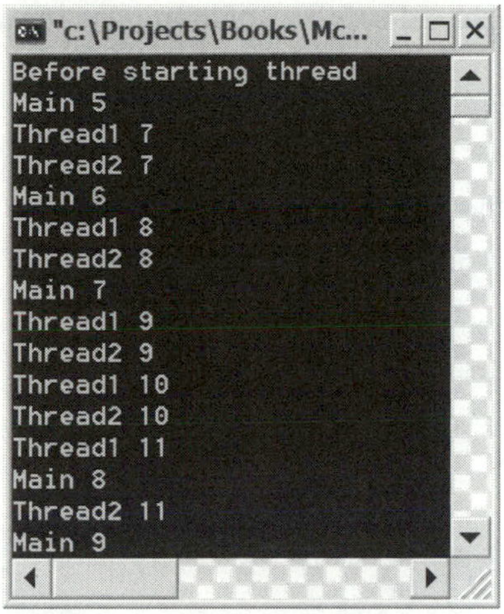

Figure 16-9. The ThreadStaticVars program in action

Notice that the static constructor works as expected for the main thread, whereas for worker threads you need to create an instance of the variable before you use it. To avoid having the main thread create a new instance of the static variable, the class separates the logic of initializing the variable from the main logic that the thread is to perform, thus allowing the main thread to call the application's logic without executing the static variable's new command.

The Interlocked Class

The opposite of the thread static variable is the interlocked variable. In this case, you want the static variable to be shared across the class and between threads. The Interlocked class provides you with a thread-safe way of sharing an integer type variable (probably used for an index of some sort) between threads.

For the sharing of an integer to be thread-safe, the operations to the integer must be atomic. In other words, operations such as incrementing, decrementing, and exchanging variables can't be preempted partway through the operation. Thus, the $2 million problem from earlier won't occur.

Using an interlocked variable is fairly straightforward. Instead of using the increment (++) or decrement (--) operator, all you need to do is use the corresponding static System::Threading::Interlocked class method. Notice in the following declarations that you pass a pointer to the variable you want interlocked and not the value:

```
static Int32 Interlocked::Increment(Int32 *ival);
static Int64 Interlocked::Decrement(Int64 *lval);
static Object* Exchange(Object **oval, Object **oval);
```

841

Listing 16-8 shows a thread-safe way of looping using an interlocked variable.

Listing 16-8. Using the Interlocked Class

```
using namespace System;
using namespace System::Threading;

__gc class MyThread
{
    static Int32 iVal;
public:
    static MyThread()
    {
        iVal = 5;
    }

    void ThreadFunc()
    {
        while (Interlocked::Increment(&iVal) < 15)
        {
            Thread *thr = Thread::CurrentThread;
            Console::WriteLine(S"{0} {1}", thr->Name, __box(iVal));
            Thread::Sleep(1);
        }
    }
};

Int32 main()
{
    MyThread *myThr1 = new MyThread();

    Thread &thr1 = *new Thread(new ThreadStart(myThr1, &MyThread::ThreadFunc));
    Thread &thr2 = *new Thread(new ThreadStart(myThr1, &MyThread::ThreadFunc));

    thr1.Name = S"Thread1";
    thr2.Name = S"Thread2";

    thr1.Start();
    thr2.Start();

    return 0;
}
```

Notice that unlike the thread static variable, the static constructor works exactly as it should as there is only one instance of the static variable being shared by all threads.

Figure 16-10 shows InterlockedVars.exe in action, a simple count from 6 to 14, though the count is incremented by different threads.

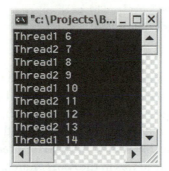

Figure 16-10. The InterlockedVars program in action

The Monitor Class

The `Monitor` class is useful if you want a block of code to be executed as single threaded, even if the code block is found in a thread that can be multithreaded. The basic idea is that you use the static methods found in the `System::Threading::Monitor` class to specify the start and end points of the code to be executed as a single task.

It is possible to have more than one monitor in an application. Therefore, a unique `Object` is needed for each monitor that you want the application to have. To create the `Object` to set the `Monitor` lock on, simply create a standard static `Object`:

```
static Object* MonitorObject = new Object();
```

You then use this `Object` along with one of the following two methods to specify the starting point that the `Monitor` will lock for single thread execution:

- `Enter()` method

- `TryEnter()` method

The `Enter()` method is the easier and safer of the two methods to use. It has the following syntax:

```
static void Enter(Object* MonitorObject);
```

Basically, the Enter() method allows a thread to continue executing if no other thread is within the code area specified by the Monitor. If another thread occupies the Monitor area, then this thread will sit and wait until the other thread leaves the Monitor area (known as *blocking*).

The TryEnter() method is a little more complex in that it has three overloads:

```
static bool TryEnter(Object* MonitorObject);
static bool TryEnter(Object* MonitorObject, int wait);
static bool TryEnter(Object* MonitorObject, TimeSpan wait);
```

The first parameter is the MonitorObject, just like the Enter() method. The second parameter that can be added is the amount of time to wait until you can bypass the block and continue. Yes, you read that right. The TryEnter() method will pass through even if some other thread is currently in the Monitor area. The TryEnter() method will set the start of the Monitor area only if it entered the Monitor when no other thread was in the Monitor area. When the TryEnter() method enters an unoccupied Monitor area, then it returns true; otherwise, it returns false.

This doesn't sound very safe, does it? If this method isn't used properly, it isn't safe. Why would you use this method if it's so unsafe? It's designed to allow the programmer the ability to do something other than sit at a blocked monitor and wait, possibly until the application is stopped or the machine reboots. The proper way to use the TryEnter() method is to check the Monitor area. If it's occupied, wait a specified time for the area to be vacated. If, after that time, it's still blocked, go do something other than enter the blocked area:

```
if (!Monitor::TryEnter(MonitorObject))
{
    Console::WriteLine(S"Not able to lock");
    return;
}
//...Got lock go ahead
```

Of course, as you continue into the block Monitor area, your code is no longer multithread-safe. Not a thing to do without a very good reason. If you code the TryEnter() method to continue into the Monitor area, even if the area is blocked, be prepared for the program to not work properly.

To set the end of the Monitor area, you use the static Exit() method, which has the following syntax:

```
static void Exit(Object* MonitorObject);
```

Not much to say about this method other than once it's executed, the Monitor area blocked by either the Entry() method or the TryEnter() method is opened up again for another thread to enter.

In most cases, using these three methods should be all you need. For those rare occasions, the Monitor provides three additional methods that allow another thread to enter a Monitor area even if it's currently occupied. The first method is the Wait() method, which releases the lock on a Monitor area and blocks the current thread until it reacquires the lock. To reacquire a lock, the block thread must wait for another thread to call a Pulse() or PulseAll() method from within the Monitor area. The main difference between the Pulse() and PulseAll() methods is that Pulse() notifies the next thread waiting that it's ready to release the Monitor area, whereas PulseAll() notifies all waiting threads.

Listing 16-9 shows how to code threads for a Monitor. The example is composed of three threads. The first two call synchronized Wait() and Pulse() methods, and the last thread calls a TryEnter() method, which it purposely blocks to show how to use the method correctly.

Listing 16-9. Synchronizing Using the Monitor Class

```cpp
using namespace System;
using namespace System::Threading;

__gc class MyThread
{
    static Object* MonitorObject = new Object();
public:
    void ThreadFuncOne()
    {
        Console::WriteLine(S"Func1 enters monitor");
        Monitor::Enter(MonitorObject);
        for (Int32 i = 0; i < 3; i++)
        {
            Console::WriteLine(S"Func1 Waits  {0}", i.ToString());
            Monitor::Wait(MonitorObject);
            Console::WriteLine(S"Func1 Pulses {0}", i.ToString());
            Monitor::Pulse(MonitorObject);
            Thread::Sleep(1);
        }
        Monitor::Exit(MonitorObject);
        Console::WriteLine(S"Func1 exits monitor");
    }
```

```
    void ThreadFunctwo()
    {
        Console::WriteLine(S"Func2 enters monitor");
        Monitor::Enter(MonitorObject);
        for (Int32 i = 0; i < 3; i++)
        {
            Console::WriteLine(S"Func2 Pulses {0}", i.ToString());
            Monitor::Pulse(MonitorObject);
            Thread::Sleep(1);
            Console::WriteLine(S"Func2 Waits  {0}", i.ToString());
            Monitor::Wait(MonitorObject);
        }
        Monitor::Exit(MonitorObject);
        Console::WriteLine(S"Func2 exits monitor");
    }

    void ThreadFuncthree()
    {
        if (!Monitor::TryEnter(MonitorObject))
        {
            Console::WriteLine(S"Func3 was not able to lock");
            return;
        }
        Console::WriteLine(S"Func3 got a lock");

        Monitor::Exit(MonitorObject);
        Console::WriteLine(S"Func3 exits monitor");
    }
};

Int32 main()
{
    MyThread *myThr1 = new MyThread();
    (new Thread(new ThreadStart(myThr1, &MyThread::ThreadFuncOne)))->Start();
    (new Thread(new ThreadStart(myThr1, &MyThread::ThreadFunctwo)))->Start();
    (new Thread(new ThreadStart(myThr1, &MyThread::ThreadFuncthree)))->Start();
    return 0;
}
```

Notice that a Monitor area need not be a single block of code but, instead, it can be multiple blocks spread out all over the process. In fact, it's not apparent due to the simplicity of the example, but the Monitor object can be in another class and the Monitor areas can spread across multiple classes so long as the

Monitor object is accessible to all `Monitor` area classes and the `Monitor` areas fall within the same process.

The `Wait()` and `Pulse()` methods can be tricky to synchronize and, if you fail to call a `Pulse()` method for a `Wait()` method, the `Wait()` method will block until the process is killed or the machine is rebooted. You can add timers to the `Wait()` method in the same fashion as you do the `TryEnter()` method, to avoid an infinite wait state. Personally, I think you should avoid using the `Wait()` and `Pulse()` methods unless you have no other choice.

Figure 16-11 shows SyncByMonitor.exe in action.

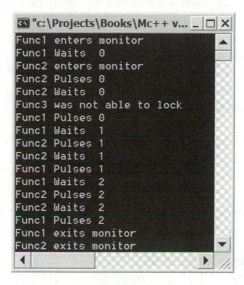

Figure 16-11. The SyncByMonitor program in action

The Mutex Class

The `Mutex` class is very similar to the `Monitor` class in the way it synchronizes between threads. You define regions of code that must be single threaded or MUTually EXclusive, and then, when a thread runs, it can only enter the region if no other thread is in the region. What makes the `Mutex` class special is that it can define regions across processes. In other words, a thread will be blocked in process 1 if some thread in process 2 is in the same name `Mutex` region.

Before I go into detail about `Mutex`, let's sidetrack a little and see how you can have the .NET Framework start one process within another. Creating a process inside another process is fairly easy to do, but within the .NET Framework it's far from intuitive because the methods to create a process are found within the `System::Diagnostic` namespace.

The process for creating a process is similar to that of a thread in that you create a process and then start it. The actual steps involved in creating a process, though, are a little more involved. To create a process, you simply create an instance using the default constructor:

```
Process* proc = new Process();
```

Next, you need to populate several properties found in the StartInfo property. These properties will tell the Framework where the process is, what parameters to pass, whether to start the process in its own shell, and whether to redirect standard input. There are several other properties as well but these are the most important:

```
proc->StartInfo->FileName = S"../debug/SyncByMutex.exe";
proc->StartInfo->Arguments = S"1";
proc->StartInfo->UseShellExecute = false;
proc->StartInfo->RedirectStandardInput = true;
```

Finally, once the process is defined, you start it:

```
proc->Start();
```

Listing 16-10 shows how to start two copies of the Mutex process that you will build next in this chapter.

Listing 16-10. Creating Subprocesses

```
using namespace System;
using namespace System::Diagnostics;
using namespace System::Threading;

Int32 main()
{
    Process* proc1 = new Process();
    proc1->StartInfo->FileName = S"../debug/SyncByMutex.exe";
    proc1->StartInfo->Arguments = S"1";
    proc1->StartInfo->UseShellExecute = false;
    proc1->StartInfo->RedirectStandardInput = true;
    proc1->Start();

    Thread::Sleep(20);
```

```
Process* proc2 = new Process();
proc2->StartInfo->FileName = S"../debug/SyncByMutex.exe";
proc2->StartInfo->Arguments = S"2";
proc2->StartInfo->UseShellExecute = false;
proc2->StartInfo->RedirectStandardInput = true;
proc2->Start();

Thread::Sleep(2000);  // added just to clean up console display
return 0;
}
```

You don't need to use MutexSpawn.exe to run the following Mutex example, but it makes things easier when you're trying to test multiple processes running at the same time.

Okay, let's move on to actually looking at the Mutex class. In general, you'll use only three methods on a regular basis within the Mutex class:

- The constructor

- WaitOne()

- ReleaseMutex()

Unlike the Monitor class, in which you use a static member, the Mutex class requires you to create an instance and then access its member methods. Like any other class, to create an instance of Mutex requires you call its constructor. The Mutex constructor provides four overloads:

```
Mutex();
Mutex(Boolean owner);
Mutex(Boolean owner, String* name);
Mutex(Boolean owner, String* name, Boolean * createdNew);
```

When you create the Mutex object, you specify whether you want it to have ownership of the Mutex or, in other words, block the other threads trying to enter the region. Be careful, though, that the constructor doesn't cause a thread to block. This requires the use of the WaitOne() method, which you'll see later in the chapter.

You can create either a named or unnamed instance of a Mutex object but, to share a Mutex across processes, you need to give it a name. When you provide a Mutex with a name, the Mutex constructor will look for another Mutex with the same name. If it does find one, then they will synchronize blocks of code together.

The last constructor adds an output parameter that will have a value of true if this call was the first constructor to build a Mutex of the specified name; otherwise, the name already exists and will have the value of false.

Once a `Mutex` object exists, you then must tell it to wait for the region to be unoccupied before entering. You do this using the `Mutex` class's `WaitOne()` member method:

```
bool WaitOne();
bool WaitOne(int milliseconds, bool /*not used in Mutex*/);
bool WaitOne(TimeSpan span, bool /*not used in Mutex*/);
```

The `WaitOne()` method is similar to a combination of the `Monitor` class's `Enter()` and `TryEnter()` methods, in that the `WaitOne()` method will wait indefinitely like the `Monitor::Enter()` method if you pass it no parameters. If you pass it parameters, though, it blocks for the specified time and then passes through like the `Monitor::TryEnter()` method. Just like the `TryEnter()` method, you should not, normally, let the thread execute the code within the `Mutex` region, as that will make the region not thread-safe.

To specify the end of the `Mutex` region, you use the `Mutex` class's `ReleaseMutex()` member method. Just like `Monitor`'s `Enter()` and `Exit()` method combination, you need to match `WaitOne()` calls with `ReleaseMutex()` calls.

Listing 16-11 shows how to code a multithreaded single process. There is nothing special about it. In fact, I would normally just use a `Monitor`. Where this example really shines is when it is used in conjunction with MutexSpawn.exe, as it shows the `Mutex` class's real power of handling mutually exclusive regions of code across processes.

Listing 16-11. Synchronizing Using the Mutex Class

```
using namespace System;
using namespace System::Threading;

__gc class MyThread
{
public:
    void ThreadFunc()
    {
        Thread *thr = Thread::CurrentThread;
        Mutex *m;
        for (Int32 i = 0; i < 4; i++)
        {
            m = new Mutex(true, "SyncByMutex");
            m->WaitOne();
            Console::WriteLine(S"{0} - {1}", thr->Name, __box(i));
            m->ReleaseMutex();
            Thread::Sleep(100);
```

```
        }
    }
};

Int32 main(Int32 argc, SByte __nogc *argv[])
{
    MyThread *myThr = new MyThread();

    Thread &thr1 = *new Thread(new ThreadStart(myThr, &MyThread::ThreadFunc));
    Thread &thr2 = *new Thread(new ThreadStart(myThr, &MyThread::ThreadFunc));

    thr1.Name = String::Format(S"Process {0} - Thread 1", new String(argv[1]));
    thr2.Name = String::Format(S"Process {0} - Thread 2", new String(argv[1]));

    thr1.Start();
    Thread::Sleep(500);
    thr2.Start();

    return 0;
}
```

Because you've already seen how to use the Monitor, the preceding example should be quite straightforward. The only real difference (other than the names of the methods being different, of course) is that the Mutex uses an instance object and member method calls, and the Monitor uses static method calls.

Figure 16-12 shows SyncByMutex.exe in action. Notice that threads in both processes are blocked and get access to the named Mutex region.

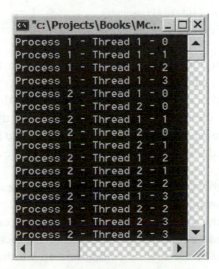

Figure 16-12. A pair of SyncByMutex programs in action

The ReaderWriterLock Class

The System::Threading::ReaderWriterLock class is a little different from the previous two types of synchronization in that it uses a multiple-reader/single-writer mechanism instead of the all-or-nothing approach. What this means is that the ReaderWriterLock class allows any number of threads to be in a block of synchronized code so long as they are only reading the shared resource within it. On the other hand, if a thread needs to change the shared resource, then all threads must vacate the region and give the updating thread exclusive access to it.

This type of synchronization makes sense because if a thread isn't changing anything, then it can't affect other threads. So, why not give the thread access to the shared resource?

The ReaderWriterLock class is very similar to both the Monitor class and the Mutex class. You specify a region to be synchronized and then have the threads block or pass into this area based on whether an update is happening in the region.

Like the Mutex class, you create an instance of the ReaderWriterLock class and work with its member method. To create an instance of the ReaderWriterLock object, you call its default constructor:

```
ReaderWriterLock();
```

Once you have a ReaderWriterLock object, you need to determine if the region of code you want to block will do only reading of the shared resource or if it will change the shared resource.

If the region will only read the shared resource, then use the following code to set the region as read-only:

```
void AcquireReaderLock(int milliseconds);
void AcquireReaderLock(TimeSpan span);
```

You pass both of these overloaded methods a parameter, so specify the length of time you're willing to wait before entering the region. Due to the nature of this synchronization method, you can be sure of one thing: If you're blocked by this method call, then some other thread is currently updating the shared resource within. The reason you know some other thread is writing to the region is because the thread doesn't block if other threads in the region are only reading the shared resource.

Because you know that some thread is writing in the region, you should make the time you wait longer than the time needed to complete the write process. Unlike any of the other synchronization methods you've seen in this chapter, when this method times out, it throws an ApplicationException exception. So if you specify anything other than an infinite wait, you should catch the exception. The reason these methods throw an exception is that the only reason the wait time should expire is due to a thread deadlock condition. *Deadlock* is when two threads wait forever for each other to complete.

To specify the end of a synchronized read-only region, you need to release the region:

```
void ReleaseReaderLock();
```

If the region will require updating of the shared resource within the region, then you need to acquire a different lock:

```
void AcquireWriterLock(int milliseconds);
void AcquireWriterLock(TimeSpan span);
```

Like the reader, these methods pass parameters to avoid the deadlock situation. Unlike the reader lock, though, these methods block no matter what type of thread falls within the region, because they allow only one thread to have access. If you were to use only writer locks, then you would, in effect, be coding a Monitor or a Mutex.

As you would expect, once you're finished with the writer region, you need to release it:

```
void ReleaseWriterLock();
```

Listing 16-12 shows how to implement a multithread application using ReaderWriterLock. Also, just for grins and giggles, I added an Interlocked::Decrement() method to show you how that works as well.

Listing 16-12. Synchronizing Using the ReaderWriterLock Class

```
using namespace System;
using namespace System::Threading;

__gc class MyThread
{
    static ReaderWriterLock *RWLock = new ReaderWriterLock();
    static Int32 iVal = 4;

public:
    static void ReaderThread()
    {
        String *thrName = Thread::CurrentThread->Name;
        while (true)
```

```
            {
                try
                {
                    RWLock->AcquireReaderLock(-1);  // Wait forever

                    Console::WriteLine(S"Reading in {0}. iVal is {1}",
                        thrName, __box(iVal));

                    RWLock->ReleaseReaderLock();
                    Thread::Sleep(4);
                }
                catch (ApplicationException*)
                {
                    Console::WriteLine(S"Reading in {0}. Timed out", thrName);
                }
            }
        }

        static void WriterThread()
        {
            while (iVal > 0)
            {
                RWLock->AcquireWriterLock(-1);  // wait forever

                Interlocked::Decrement(&iVal);
                Console::WriteLine(S"Writing iVal to {0}", __box(iVal));
                Thread::Sleep(20);

                RWLock->ReleaseWriterLock();
            }
        }
};

Int32 main()
{
    Thread &thr1 = *new Thread(new ThreadStart(0, &MyThread::ReaderThread));
    Thread &thr2 = *new Thread(new ThreadStart(0, &MyThread::ReaderThread));
    Thread &thr3 = *new Thread(new ThreadStart(0, &MyThread::WriterThread));

    thr1.Name = S"Thread1";
    thr2.Name = S"Thread2";
    thr1.IsBackground = true;
    thr2.IsBackground = true;
```

```
        thr1.Start();
        thr2.Start();
        thr3.Start();

        thr3.Join();
        Thread::Sleep(2);
        return 0;
}
```

In actuality, the preceding code shouldn't need to use `Interlock` because the region is already locked for synchronization. Notice that I created infinite loops for my reader threads. To get these threads to exit at the completion of the program, I made the background threads.

Figure 16-13 shows SyncByRWLock.exe in action. Notice that I purposely don't specify a long-enough wait for the writing process to complete so that the exception is thrown.

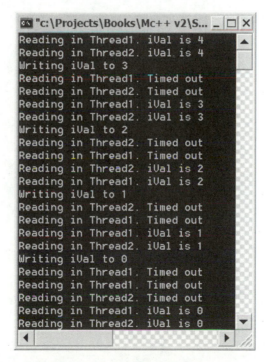

Figure 16-13. The SyncByRWLock program in action

Summary

In this chapter, you examined multithreaded programming within the .NET Framework. You started by learning the basics of multithreaded programming. Next, you moved on and explored the two ways of creating threads: Thread and ThreadPool. You finished off the chapter by covering the weighty topic of thread synchronization.

This is a rather complex topic, and I have barely scratched the surface of it. In fact, most of the text in this chapter relates to how to implement multithreaded programming using the .NET Framework and not the theory behind it. If you find this topic interesting, there are many books and articles available on the proper implementation of multithreaded programming.

In the next and final chapter of this book, you'll cover assembly programming and how you can augment your assemblies with resources, localization, attributes, and type reflection.

CHAPTER 17

Assembly Programming

BEFORE YOU ROLL YOUR EYES and mumble under your breath, "Not another chapter on assemblies," read the chapter title again. This chapter is about programming an assembly and not about the assembly. By now I'm assuming you know what an assembly is, its structure, how it eliminates DLL Hell, and so forth. Instead, this chapter focuses on programmatically playing with the assembly.

As I've pointed out a few times in this book, the assembly is the cornerstone of .NET Framework deployment. To paraphrase, all roads lead to the assembly. Because this is the case, it only makes sense that the .NET Framework provides the programmer many programmatic tools to interact directly with the assembly.

In this chapter you'll look at some of these programming tools. Most of these tools are for the more advanced Managed C++ programmer. In most cases, you won't have to use them for most of your programs. On the other hand, knowing these tools will provide you with a powerful weapon in your .NET software development arsenal and, inevitably, sometime in your coding career you'll need to use each of these tools.

The first tool, reflection, gives you the ability to look inside an assembly to see how it works. You've used system-defined attributes on several occasions in this book. In this chapter you'll have the opportunity to create some of your own attributes. Up until now, you've worked only with private assemblies, but it's also possible to share them. Most of the time, you'll take versioning (the second tool) for granted, but you can take a much more active role. Assemblies need not be just metadata and MSIL code. They can house almost any resource that your program needs to run. The last tool—but definitely not the least—is globalization and localization. Your culture may be central to your life, but there are many other cultures out there. Why not make your programs work with these cultures as well?

Reflection

Reflection is the ability to retrieve and examine at runtime the metadata that describes .NET Framework assemblies, modules, and types. You can then turn around and create dynamically, using the retrieved information, an instance of these types and then invoke its methods or access its properties or member variables.

The System::Reflection namespace, which the .NET Framework uses to support reflection, is made up of more than 40 classes. Most of these classes you will probably not use directly, if at all. Several of the more common classes you will use are listed in Table 17-1.

Table 17-1. Common System::Reflection Namespace Classes

CLASS NAME	DESCRIPTION
Assembly	Defines an assembly
AssemblyName	Provides access to all the parts of an assembly's name
ConstructorInfo	Provides access to the constructor's attributes and metadata
EventInfo	Provides access to the event's attributes and metadata
FieldInfo	Provides access to the field's attributes and metadata
MemberInfo	Provides access to the member's attributes and metadata
MethodInfo	Provides access to the method's attributes and metadata
Module	Defines a module
ParameterInfo	Provides access to the parameter's attributes and metadata
Pointer	Provides a wrapper class for a pointer
PropertyInfo	Provides access to the property's attributes and metadata
TypeDelegator	Provides a wrapper for an object and then delegates all methods to that object

Just to make things a little confusing, the key to .NET Framework reflection is the System::Type class which, as you can see, isn't even found within the Reflection namespace. My guess for its not being placed in the Reflection namespace is because it's used frequently and the designers of the Framework didn't want to force the import of the Reflection namespace.

Examining Objects

A key feature of reflection is the ability to examine metadata using the System::Type class. The basic idea is to get a Type reference of the class you want to examine and then use the Type class's members to get access to the metadata information about the type, such as the constructors, methods, fields, and properties.

Getting the Type Reference

In most cases, you will get the Type reference to the class by one of four methods:

- Using the __typeof() operator

- Calling the class's GetType() method

- Calling the Type class's static GetType() method, passing it the name of the class to be examined as a String

- Iterating through collection of all types within an assembly retrieved by the Assembly class's GetTypes() method

The first method is the easiest of the four ways to get a Type reference. With the __typeof() operator, you pass it the data type and it returns a Type reference to the class:

```
System::Type *myClassRef = __typeof(MyClass);
```

To use the second method you need to already have an instance of the managed object you want to examine, and with this instance you call its GetType() method. The key to the second method is the fact that all managed classes and value types inherit from the Object class and the Object class has a GetType() method. For example, here is how you would get the Type reference to the myClass class:

```
__gc class myClass
{
    // members
};
MyClass *myClass = new MyClass();
Type *myClassRef = myClass->GetType();
```

It is a little trickier if the type you are trying to get the Type reference from is a value type, because you have to __box the object before calling the GetType() method (a compile-time error points this out to you as well):

```
__value struct MyStruct
{
    // members
};
MyStruct myStruct;
Type *myStructRef = __box(myStruct)->GetType();
```

The third method is kind of cool in that you pass the string equivalent of the type you want to reference to the Type class's static GetType() method. You might want to note that Type is an abstract class, so you can't create an instance of it but, as you can see here, you can still call its static methods:

```
Type *myClassRef = Type::GetType(S"MyClass");
```

One thing all the preceding methods have in common is that you need to have something of the type you wanted to reference at runtime—either the data type and instance of the type, or the name of the type. The fourth method allows you to get a Type reference without any knowledge of the object beforehand. Instead, you retrieve it out of a collection of Types with an assembly:

```
Assembly* assembly = Assembly::LoadFrom(S"MyAssembly.dll");
Type *types[] = assembly->GetTypes();
for (Int32 i = 0; i < types->Length; i++)
{
    Type *myTypeRef = types[i];
}
```

Getting the Metadata

Getting the metadata out of a Type reference is the same no matter what method you use to attain the Type reference. The Type class contains numerous methods, many of which allow you to access metadata associated with the type. Table 17-2 lists of some of the more common methods available to you for retrieving metadata.

Table 17-2. Common Type Metadata Retrieval Methods

METHOD	DESCRIPTION
GetConstructor()	Gets a ConstructorInfo object for a specific constructor of the current Type
GetConstructors()	Gets a collection of ConstructorInfo objects for all the constructors for the current Type
GetEvent()	Gets an EventInfo object for a specific event declared or inherited from the current Type
GetEvents()	Gets a collection of EventInfo objects for all the events declared or inherited from the current Type
GetField()	Gets a FieldInfo object for a specific member variable from the current Type
GetFields()	Gets a collection of FieldInfo objects for all the member variables from the current Type
GetInterface()	Gets a Type object for a specific interface implemented or inherited from the current Type
GetInterfaces()	Gets a collection of Type objects for all the interfaces implemented or inherited from the current Type
GetMember()	Gets a MemberInfo object for a specific member from the current Type
GetMembers()	Gets a collection of MemberInfo objects for all the members from the current Type
GetMethod()	Gets a MethodInfo object for a specific member method from the current Type
GetMethods()	Gets a collection of MethodInfo objects for all the member methods from the current Type
GetProperty()	Gets a PropertyInfo object for a specific property from the current Type
GetProperties()	Gets a collection of PropertyInfo objects for all the properties from the current Type

Along with the "Get" methods, the Type class also has a number of "Is" properties (see Table 17-3), which you use to see if the current type "is" something.

Table 17-3. Common "Is" Properties

"IS" PROPERTY	DESCRIPTION
IsAbstract	Is a Boolean that represents whether the Type is abstract
IsArray	Is a Boolean that represents whether the Type is a managed array
IsClass	Is a Boolean that represents whether the Type is a managed (__gc) class
IsEnum	Is a Boolean that represents whether the Type is a __value enumeration
IsImport	Is a Boolean that represents whether the Type is an import
IsInterface	Is a Boolean that represents whether the Type is a .NET interface
IsNotPublic	Is a Boolean that represents whether the Type is not public
IsPointer	Is a Boolean that represents whether the Type is a pointer
IsPrimitive	Is a Boolean that represents whether the Type is a .NET primitive (Int32, Single, Char, and so on)
IsPublic	Is a Boolean that represents whether the Type is public
IsSealed	Is a Boolean that represents whether the Type is sealed
IsSerializable	Is a Boolean that represents whether the Type is serializable
IsValueType	Is a Boolean that represents whether the Type is a value type

Listing 17-1 shows a how to build a handy little tool that displays the member methods, properties, and variables of the classes found in the six most commonly referenced assemblies in the .NET Framework using reflection.

NOTE   *To save space and because it isn't directly relevant, all the code examples in this chapter don't include the autogenerated Windows Form GUI code. (See Chapters 9 and 10 for more information on Windows Form development.)*

Listing 17-1. Referencing the Class Members of the .NET Framework

```
namespace Reflecting
{
    //...Standard Usings
    using namespace System::Reflection;

    public __gc class Form1 : public System::Windows::Forms::Form
    {
        //...Auto generated GUI Interface code

    private: Type *types[];
    private: static String *assemblies[] = {
        S"System",
        S"System.Drawing",
        S"System.Xml",
        S"System.Windows.Forms",
        S"System.Data",
        S"mscorlib"
    };
    private:
        System::Void Form1_Load(System::Object *sender, System::EventArgs *e)
        {
            for (Int32 i = 0; i < assemblies->Length; i++)
            {
                cbAssemblies->Items->Add(Path::GetFileName(assemblies[i]));
            }
            cbAssemblies->SelectedIndex = 0;
        }
    private:
        System::Void cbAssemblies_SelectedIndexChanged(System::Object * sender,
                                                       System::EventArgs *  e)
        {
            Assembly* assembly = Assembly::LoadWithPartialName(
                                    assemblies[cbAssemblies->SelectedIndex]);

            types = assembly->GetTypes();

            cbDataTypes->Items->Clear();
            for (Int32 i = 0; i < types->Length; i++)
            {
                cbDataTypes->Items->Add(types[i]->ToString());
            }
```

```
                cbDataTypes->SelectedIndex = 0;
        }
    private:
        System::Void cbDataTypes_SelectedIndexChanged(System::Object * sender,
                                              System::EventArgs * e)
        {

            Type *type = types[cbDataTypes->SelectedIndex];

            MemberInfo *methods[] = type->GetMethods();
            lbMethods->Items->Clear();
            for (Int32 i = 0; i < methods->Length; i++)
            {
                lbMethods->Items->Add(methods[i]->ToString());
            }

            PropertiesInfo *properties[] = type->GetProperties();
            lbProperties->Items->Clear();
            for (Int32 i = 0; i < properties->Length; i++)
            {
                lbProperties->Items->Add(properties[i]->ToString());
            }

            MemberInfo *variables[] = type->GetFields();
            lbVariables->Items->Clear();
            for (Int32 i = 0; i < variables->Length; i++)
            {
                lbVariables->Items->Add(variables[i]->ToString());
            }
        }
    };
}
```

As you can see from the code in the preceding example, reflection can be fairly easy to work with. Simply "Get" the metadata needed and then loop through the metadata. Admittedly, the example is not the most elaborate, but it still shows the potential power it has in making the metadata information within an assembly available. It also helps point out why the header include file is no longer needed for library assemblies, as I explained in Chapter 4.

Most of the preceding code is simply to load the appropriate GUI controls, but one thing new in the preceding example that hasn't been covered before is the use of the `System::Reflection::Assembly` class. The `Assembly` class is a core building block of all .NET Framework applications, though normally, even as a .NET developer, you seldom have to know of its existence.

When it comes to reflection, the `Assembly` class contains the starting point for retrieving any public metadata information you want about the current active assembly or one that you load using one of the many different loading methods. The only reason I see that there are multiple load methods (each has multiple overload) is due to the duplicated method signature required to support the myriad ways available to load an assembly. Essentially, all load methods do the same thing—load the assembly—with the only differences relating to the amount of information known about the assembly being loaded and the source of the assembly.

The `LoadWithPartialName()` method requires the least amount of information—simply the name of an assembly. It does not care about version, culture, and so on. It is also the method that the .NET Framework frowns upon using for that exact reason. But in the case of this example it works just fine.

Figure 17-1 shows Reflecting.exe in action. As you can see, it's made up of two `ComboBoxes` and three `ListBoxes`. The first `ComboBox` provides a way of selecting the assembly, and the second allows you to select the type. The results of these two selections are the methods, properties, and variables displayed in the `ListBoxes`.

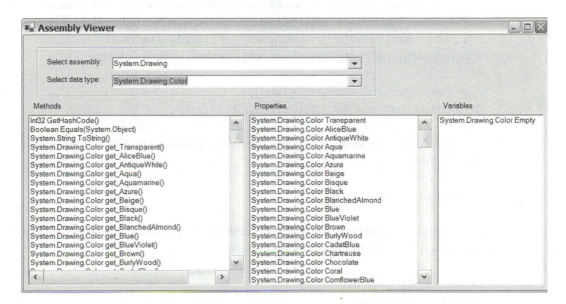

Figure 17-1. The Reflecting program in action

Dynamically Invoking or Late-Binding Objects

Reflection provides you with the rather powerful feature known as *late binding*. Late binding is the ability to determine which method is dynamically invoked at runtime as opposed to compile time.

A cool thing about reflection is that once you have a reference to the method you want to invoke (which I showed how to do previously), it is not a large step to execute that method in a dynamic fashion. In fact, all you have to do is invoke the method using the (you guessed it) MethodInfo::Invoke() method.

The trickiest part of invoking methods using reflection is realizing that there are two types of methods: static and instance. *Static* methods are the easiest to handle, as you don't need to create an instance of the method's class to invoke it. Simply find the Method reference type and then use the Invoke() method:

```
MethodInfo *method = type->GetMethod();
method->Invoke(0, 0);
```

Notice that in the preceding example the Invoke() method has two parameters. The first is the instance of the class for which you are invoking the method. The second is an array of parameters that will be passed to the method. As you can now tell, the preceding example is not only a static method. It also takes no parameters.

If the method you want to invoke is an *instance* method, it is not quite as easy because you need to create an instance of the type for that method. The .NET Framework provides you help in the way of the System::Activator class, which contains the static CreateInstance() method to create objects:

```
Type *type = assembly->GetType("MyType");
Object *typeInstance = Activator::CreateInstance(type);
```

Now that you have an instance of the method class, all you have to do is pass it as the first parameter:

```
method->Invoke(typeInstance, 0);
```

To pass parameters to the Invoke() method, simply create an array of them and assign the array to the second parameter:

```
Object *args[] = new Object*[2];
args[0] = parameterOne;
args[1] = parameterTwo;
```

That's really all there is to late binding.

Listing 17-2 shows how to execute both a static and an instance method using reflection. The first thing the example does is create an array using reflection of all the static color properties of the Color structure. It then displays the color as the background of a label by invoking the property's getter method. Next, the example dynamically invokes a method from one of two different classes to display the color name in the label. (There are much easier ways to do this without reflection, obviously.)

Listing 17-2. Using Reflection to Change the Properties of a Label

```
namespace Invoking
{
    //...Standard Usings
    using namespace System::Reflection;

    public __gc class Form1 : public System::Windows::Forms::Form
    {
        //...Auto generated GUI Interface code

    private: PropertyInfo *colors[];

    private:
        System::Void Form1_Load(System::Object * sender, System::EventArgs * e)
        {
            // Get the reference to the Color type
            Type* colorType = __typeof(Color);
            // Get all the Color type's properties
            colors = colorType->GetProperties();

            for (Int32 i = 0; i < colors->Length; i++)
            {
                // only display the static color properties
                if (colors[i]->ToString()->IndexOf(S"System.Drawing.Color") >=0)
                    cbColor->Items->Add(colors[i]->ToString());
            }
            cbColor->SelectedIndex = 0;
        }
    private:
        System::Void cbColor_SelectedIndexChanged(System::Object * sender,
                                                  System::EventArgs *  e)
        {
            static Boolean alternateWrite = true;
            PropertyInfo *property = colors[cbColor->SelectedIndex];
```

```
        // Get the property's getter method
        MethodInfo *PropMethod = property->GetGetMethod();
        // Invoke the static method
        lbColor->BackColor = *dynamic_cast<Color*>(PropMethod->Invoke(0,0));

        // Load the assembly Invoking.
        // You could also have used the currently executing assembly
        Assembly *assembly = Assembly::Load("Invoking");

        // get the type based on the Boolean status of alternateWrite
        Type *type;
        if (alternateWrite)
            type = assembly->GetType("Invoking.Writer1");
        else
            type = assembly->GetType("Invoking.Writre2");

        alternateWrite = !alternateWrite;

        // Get the aColor Method
        MethodInfo *ColorMethod = type->GetMethod("aColor");

        // Create an instance of the type
        Object *writerInst = Activator::CreateInstance(type);

        // Create the parameter - the color
        Object *args[] = new Object*[1];
        args[0] = PropMethod->Invoke(0,0);

        // Invoke the instance method
        lbColor->Text =
            dynamic_cast<String*>(ColorMethod->Invoke(writerInst, args));
    }
};

__gc class Writer1
{
public:
    String *aColor(Color *col)
    {
        return String::Format("[Writer 1] {0}", col->ToString());
    }
};
```

```
__gc class Writer2
{
public:
    String *aColor(Color *col)
    {
        return String::Format("[Writer 2] {0}", col->ToString());
    }
};
}
```

NOTE   *The* GetType() *method uses C# syntax when looking at the type within the assembly. Therefore, it uses a period (.) in place of a double colon (::).*

As you can see from the preceding example, there is quite a bit of overhead involved in reflection and late binding, so you should use these techniques sparingly.

Figure 17-2 shows Invoking.exe in action. Pay attention to the text that prefixes the color displayed in the label as it alternates from "[Writer 1]" to "[Writer 2]".

Figure 17-2. The Invoking program in action

Attributes

You have seen .NET Framework–defined attributes used a few times already in this book. For example:

- In Chapter 8 you used the Serializable attribute to enable serialization for a managed (__gc) class.

- In Chapter 15 you used the WebService and WebMethod attributes to enable a class and a method to be Web services.

- In Chapter 16 you used the ThreadStatic attribute to make a static variable unique in each thread.

The overriding theme in every .NET Framework attribute is that it changes the way the code normally functions. Basically, you can think of attributes as declarative tags that are written to an assembly at compile time to annotate or mark up a class and/or its members so that class and/or its members can be later extracted at runtime, possibly to change its normal behavior.

To add an attribute to a class or its members, you add code in front of the element you want to annotate with the following syntax:

```
[AttributeName(ConstructorArguments, optionalpropertyname=value)]
```

If you want to add more than one attribute, you simply add more than one attribute within the square brackets, delimited by commas:

```
[Attribute1(), Attribute2()]
```

An important feature to you (other than the changed behavior caused by the .NET Framework attributes) is that you can access attributes using reflection. A more important feature is that you can create your own custom attributes.

Creating a Custom Attribute

According to the Microsoft documentation, a *custom attribute* is just a class that is derived from the System::Attribute class with a few minor additional criteria. However, I found (by accident) that even if you don't derive from System::Attribute, it still seems to work. I recommend that you inherit from System::Attribute just to be safe, though.

The additional criteria are as follows:

- The custom attribute class needs to be public.

- By convention, the attribute name should end in "Attribute". A neat thing is that when you implement the attribute, you don't have to add the trailing "Attribute", as it's automatically added.

- There's an additional AttributeUsageAttribute that you can apply to your custom attribute.

- All properties that will be written to the metadata need to be public.

- The properties available to be written to the metadata are restricted to Integer type (Byte, Int32, and so on), floating point (Single or Double), Char, String, Boolean, or Enum. Note that this means the very common DateTime data type isn't supported. (I show you how to get around this limitation later in this chapter.)

Of all the additional criteria, the only one you need to look at in more detail is the AttributeUsageAttribute attribute. This attribute controls the manner in which the custom attribute is used. To be more accurate, it defines three behaviors: which data types the custom attribute is valid on, if the custom attribute is inherited, and whether more than one of the custom attributes can be applied to a single data type.

You can specify that the custom attribute can be applied to any assembly entity (see Table 17-4) by giving the AttributeUsageAttribute attribute an AttributeTargets::All value. On the other hand, if you want to restrict the custom attribute to a specific type or a combination of types, then you would specify one or a combination (by ORing) of the AttributeTargets enumerations in Table 17-4.

Table 17-4. AttributeTargets Enumeration

All	Assembly	Class	Constructor	Delegate
Enum	Event	Field	Interface	Method
Module	Parameter	Property	ReturnValue	Struct

The second parameter of the AttributeUsageAttribute attribute specifies whether any class that inherits from a class that implements the custom attribute inherits that custom attribute. The default is that a class does inherit the custom attribute.

The final parameter allows a custom attribute to be applied more than one time to a single type. The default is that only a single custom attribute can be applied.

There are three ways that you can have data passed into the attribute when implementing. The first is by the custom attribute's construction. The second is by a public property. The third is by a public member variable.

Listing 17-3 shows the creation of two custom documentation attributes. The first is the description of the element within the class, and the second is a change history. By nature you should be able to apply both of these attributes to any type within a class and you should also have the attributes inherited. These attributes mostly differ in that a description can be applied only once to an element in a class, whereas the change history will be used repeatedly.

Listing 17-3. Documentation Custom Attributes

```
using namespace System;
using namespace System::Text;
using namespace System::Reflection;

namespace Documentation
{
    [AttributeUsage(AttributeTargets::All, Inherited=true, AllowMultiple=false)]
    public __gc class DescriptionAttribute : public Attribute
    {
        String  *mAuthor;
        DateTime mCompileDate;
        String  *mDescription;

    public:
        DescriptionAttribute(String *Author, String *Description)
        {
            mAuthor = Author;
            mDescription = Description;
            mCompileDate = DateTime::Now;
        }

        __property String *get_Author()
        {
            return mAuthor;
        }

        __property String *get_CompileDate()
        {
            return mCompileDate.ToShortDateString();
        }

        __property String *get_Description()
        {
            return mDescription;
        }
    };
```

```
[AttributeUsage(AttributeTargets::All, Inherited=true, AllowMultiple=true)]
public __gc class HistoryAttribute : public Attribute
{
    String  *mAuthor;
    DateTime mModifyDate;
    String  *mDescription;

public:
    HistoryAttribute(String *Author, String *Description)
    {
        mAuthor = Author;
        mDescription = Description;
        mModifyDate = DateTime::Now;
    }

    __property String *get_Author()
    {
        return mAuthor;
    }

    __property String *get_ModifyDate()
    {
        return mModifyDate.ToShortDateString();
    }
    __property void set_ModifyDate(String *value)
    {
        mModifyDate = Convert::ToDateTime(value);
    }

    __property String *get_Description()
    {
        return mDescription;
    }
};
}
```

As you can see by the code, other than the [AttributeUsage] attribute (which is inherited from System::Attribute), there is nothing special about these classes. They are simply classes with a constructor and a few public properties and private member variables.

The only thing to note is the passing of dates in the form of a string, which are then converted to DateTime structure. Attributes are not allowed to pass the DateTime structure as pointed out previously, so this simple trick fixes this problem.

Implementing a Custom Attribute

As you can see in the following example (see Listing 17-4), you implement custom attributes in the same way as you do .NET Framework attributes. In this example, the DescriptionAttribute attribute you created earlier is applied to two classes, a constructor, a member method, and a property. Also, the HistoryAttribute attribute is applied twice to the first class and then later to the property.

Listing 17-4. Implementing the Description and History Attributes

```
using namespace System;
using namespace Documentation;

namespace DocTestLib
{
    [Description(S"Stephen Fraser",
        S"This is TestClass1 to test the documentation Attribute.")]
    [History(S"Stephen Fraser",
        S"Original Version.", ModifyDate=S"11/27/02")]
    [History(S"Stephen Fraser",
        S"Added DoesNothing Method to do nothing.")]
    public __gc class TestClass1
    {
        String *mVariable;
    public:
        [Description(S"Stephen Fraser",
            S"This is default constructor for TextClass1.")]
        TestClass1()
        {
        }

        [Description(S"Stephen Fraser",
            S"This is method does nothing for TestClass1.")]
        void DoesNothing()
        {
        }

        [Description(S"Stephen Fraser",
            S"Added Variable property.")]
        [History(S"Stephen Fraser",
            S"Removed extra CodeDoc Attribute")]
        __property String *get_Variable()
```

```
        {
            return mVariable;
        }
        __property void set_Variable(String *value)
        {
            mVariable = value;
        }
    };


    [Description(S"Stephen Fraser",
        S"This is TestClass2 to test the documentation Attribute.")]
    public __gc class TestClass2
    {
    };
}
```

Notice in Listing 17-4 that "Attribute" is stripped off the end of the attributes. This is optional and it is perfectly legal to keep "Attribute" on the attribute name.

Another thing that you might want to note is how to implement a named property to an attribute. This is done in the first use of the History attribute where I specify the date that the change was made:

```
[History(S"Stephen Fraser", S"Original Version.", ModifyDate=S"11/27/02")]
```

The modified date is also a string and not a DateTime as you would expect. This is because (as I pointed out previously) it is not legal to pass a DateTime to an attribute.

Using a Custom Attribute

You looked at how to use custom attributes when you learned about reflection. Custom attributes are just placed as metadata onto the assembly and, as you learned in reflection, it is possible to examine an assembly's metadata.

The only new thing about assembly reflection and custom attributes is that you need to call the GetCustomAttribute() method to get a specific custom attribute or the GetCustomAttributes() method to get all custom attributes for a specific type.

The tricky part with either of these two methods is that you have to typecast them to their appropriate type as both return an Object type. What makes this tricky is that you need to use the full name of the attribute or, in other words, unlike when you implemented it, you need the "Attribute" suffix added. If you created a custom attribute that doesn't end in "Attribute" (which is perfectly legal, I might add), then this won't be an issue.

Both of these methods have a few overloads, but they basically break down to one of three syntaxes. To get all custom attributes:

```
public: Object *GetCustomAttributes(Boolean useInhertiance);
// For example:
Object *CustAttr[] = info->GetCustomAttributes(true);
```

To get all of a specific type of custom attribute:

```
public: Object *GetCustomAttributes(Type *type, Boolean useInhertiance);
// For example:
Object *CustAttr[] = info->GetCustomAttributes(__typeof(HistoryAttribute),true);
```

Or to get a specific attribute for a specific type reference:

```
public: static Attribute* GetCustomAttribute(<ReflectionReference>*, Type*);
// For Example
Attribute *attribute =
    Attribute::GetCustomAttribute(methodInfo, __typeof(DescriptionAttribute));
```

 CAUTION   *If the type allows multiple custom attributes of a single type to be added to itself, then the* GetCustomAttribute() *method returns an* Array *and not an* Attribute.

Listing 17-5 is really nothing more than another example of assembly reflection, except this time it uses an additional GetCustomAttribute() and GetCustomAttributes() method. The example simply walks through an assembly that you passed to it and displays information about any class, constructor, method, or property that is found within it. Plus, it shows any custom Description or History attributes that you may have added.

Listing 17-5. Using Custom Attributes to Document Classes

```
using namespace System;
using namespace Reflection;
using namespace Documentation;
```

```
void DisplayDescription(Attribute *attr)
{
    if (attr != 0)
    {
        DescriptionAttribute *cd = dynamic_cast<DescriptionAttribute*>(attr);
        Console::WriteLine(S"  Author: {0}  -  Compiled: {1}",
            cd->Author, cd->CompileDate);
        Console::WriteLine(S"  Description: {0}", cd->Description);
        Console::WriteLine(S"    ---- Change History ----");
    }
    else
        Console::WriteLine(S"    No Documentation");
}

void DisplayHistory(Object *attr[])
{
    if (attr->Length > 0)
    {
        for (Int32 i = 0; i < attr->Length; i++)
        {
            HistoryAttribute *cd = dynamic_cast<HistoryAttribute*>(attr[i]);
            Console::WriteLine(S"    Author: {0}  -  Modified: {1}",
                cd->Author, cd->ModifyDate);
            Console::WriteLine(S"    Description: {0}", cd->Description);
        }
    }
    else
        Console::WriteLine(S"    No changes");
}

void DisplayAttributes(MemberInfo *info)
{
    DisplayDescription(Attribute::GetCustomAttribute(info,
                            __typeof(DescriptionAttribute)));
    DisplayHistory(info->GetCustomAttributes(__typeof(HistoryAttribute), true));
}

void PrintClassInfo(Type *type)
{
    Console::WriteLine(S"Class: {0}", type->ToString());
    DisplayAttributes(type);
```

```
        ConstructorInfo *constructors[] = type->GetConstructors();
        for (Int32 i = 0; i < constructors->Length; i++)
        {
            Console::WriteLine(S"Constructor: {0}", constructors[i]->ToString());
            DisplayAttributes(constructors[i]);
        }

        MethodInfo *methods[] = type->GetMethods(static_cast<BindingFlags>
          (BindingFlags::Public|BindingFlags::Instance|BindingFlags::DeclaredOnly));
        for (Int32 i = 0; i < methods->Length; i++)
        {
            Console::WriteLine(S"Method: {0}", methods[i]->ToString());
            DisplayAttributes(methods[i]);
        }

        PropertyInfo *properties[] = type->GetProperties(static_cast<BindingFlags>
          (BindingFlags::Public|BindingFlags::Instance|BindingFlags::DeclaredOnly));
        for (Int32 i = 0; i < properties->Length; i++)
        {
            Console::WriteLine(S"Property: {0}", properties[i]->ToString());
            DisplayAttributes(properties[i]);
        }
    }

Int32 main(Int32 argc, SByte __nogc *argv[])
{
    try
    {
        Assembly *assembly = Assembly::LoadFrom(new String(argv[1]));

        Type *types[] = assembly->GetTypes();

        for (Int32 i = 0; i < types->Length; i++)
        {
```

```
            PrintClassInfo(types[i]);
            Console::WriteLine();
        }
    }
    catch(System::IO::FileNotFoundException*)
    {
        Console::WriteLine(S"Can't find assembly: {0}\n", new String(argv[1]));
    }
    return 0;
}
```

One thing that this example has that the previous reflection example doesn't is the use of the BindingFlags enumeration. The BindingFlags enum specifies the way in which the search for members and types within an assembly is managed by reflection. In the preceding example I used the following flags:

```
BindingFlags::Public | BindingFlags::Instance | BindingFlags::DeclaredOnly
```

This combination of flags specified that only public instance members that have only been declared at the current level (in other words, not inherited) will be considered in the search.

Also notice that even though the DisplayAttributes() method is called with a parameter of type Type, ConstructorInfo, MethodInfo, or PropertyInfo, it is declared using a parameter of type MemberInfo. The reason this is possible is because all the previously mentioned classes inherit from the MemberInfo class.

Figure 17-3 shows DocumentationWriter.exe in action. The dates in Figure 17-3 are based on when I compiled the assembly and most likely will differ from your results.

```
c:\Projects\Books\Mc++ v2\Source Code\Chapter17\debug\DocumentationWriter.ex...  _ □ X
Class: DocTestLib.TestClass1
  Author: Stephen Fraser  --  Compiled: 11/29/2002
  Description: This is TestClass1 to test the documentation Attribute.
    ---- Change History ----
    Author: Stephen Fraser  --  Modified: 11/27/2002
    Description: Original Version.
    Author: Stephen Fraser  --  Modified: 11/29/2002
    Description: Added DoesNothing Method to do nothing.
Constructor: Void .ctor()
  Author: Stephen Fraser  --  Compiled: 11/29/2002
  Description: This is default constructor for TextClass1.
    ---- Change History ----
    No changes
Method: Void DoesNothing()
  Author: Stephen Fraser  --  Compiled: 11/29/2002
  Description: This is method does nothing for TestClass1.
    ---- Change History ----
    No changes
Method: System.String get_Variable()
    No Documentation
    No changes
Method: Void set_Variable(System.String)
    No Documentation
    No changes
Property: System.String Variable
  Author: Stephen Fraser  --  Compiled: 11/29/2002
  Description: Added Variable property.
    ---- Change History ----
    Author: Stephen Fraser  --  Modified: 11/29/2002
    Description: Removed extra CodeDoc Attribute

Class: DocTestLib.TestClass2
  Author: Stephen Fraser  --  Compiled: 11/29/2002
  Description: This is TestClass2 to test the documentation Attribute.
    ---- Change History ----
    No changes
Constructor: Void .ctor()
    No Documentation
    No changes
```

Figure 17-3. The DocumentationWriter program in action

Shared Assemblies

Up until now you have been developing only private assemblies. In other words, you have been developing assemblies that are local to the application and that can be accessed only by the application. In most cases, private assemblies will be all you really need to develop. But what happens if you have multiple applications that share a common assembly? You could make a copy of the assembly and copy it to each application's directory. Or you could use the second type of assembly, a *shared assembly*.

Shared assemblies are accessible to any program that is run on the same machine where the assembly resides. By the way, you work with shared assemblies whenever you use any of the classes or any other data type of the .NET Framework. This seems logical, as every .NET application shares these assemblies.

The Global Assembly Cache

Unlike private assemblies, shared assemblies are placed in a common directory structure known as the *global assembly cache* (GAC). If and when you go looking for the GAC, you will find it off of your <WINDIR> (Windows or Windows NT) directory, in a subdirectory aptly called assembly.

When you open the assembly directory in Windows Explorer, it has the appearance of being one big directory made up of many different assemblies (see Figure 17-4). In reality, the assembly directory has a complex directory structure that gets hidden (thankfully) by Windows Explorer.

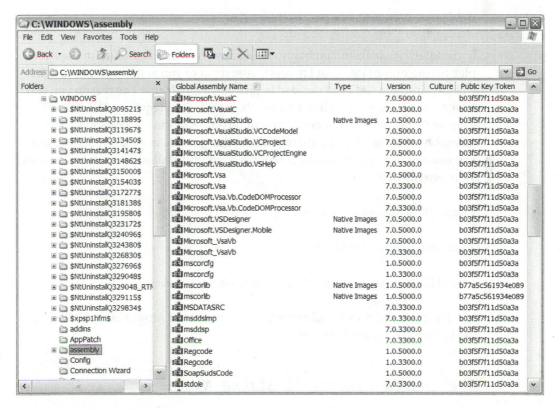

Figure 17-4. The GAC

In fact, the assembly directory itself only contains subdirectories. One subdirectory is called GAC, which in turn contains subdirectories for each assembly. Each of these subdirectories contains one or more subdirectories, one for each version of the assembly in the GAC. This directory finally contains the assembly's .dll file that your own assemblies reference.

Off of the <WINDIR>\assembly directory you will also find other subdirectories. You will find directories for each version of natively compiled code used by your system (i.e., any code that is precompiled in the machine language of the host machine). Normally, you work with MSIL code, but because this needs the additional step of compiling to machine code, the .NET Framework precompiles some of its more frequently used assemblies to save the time of performing this compile step. You will find that the native code directory structure is similar to that of the GAC.

There is also the possibility of finding another directory structure off of <WinDIR>\assembly. This one contains assemblies downloaded by ASP.NET, so that they can be used by Web Forms.

Adding Assemblies to the GAC

Fortunately, you can and probably should have remained ignorant of the complex nature of the GAC. (But I'm pretty sure most of you at one point or another will look into the GAC, so I decided to give you a heads up.) The reason you can be ignorant is because adding an assembly to the GAC requires you to simply drop and drag it from your development directory to the Windows Explorer assembly directory. If you want to perform this process in a batch routine, you can use a utility called gacutil.exe to install and uninstall your assembly. To install your assembly, use

```
> gacutil /i <assembly name>.dll
```

To uninstall the assembly, use

```
> gacutil /u <assembly name>.dll, Version=<version number>
```

It is even easier to install assemblies using a setup project because the copying to the GAC is handled for you.

The Shared Assembly's Strong Name

There is a catch to global assemblies. They require that they be signed by what is called a *strong name*. A strong name provides three necessary enhancements to assemblies:

- It makes the name of the assembly globally unique.

- It makes it so that no one else can steal and use the name (generally known as *spoofing*).

- It provides a means to verify that an assembly has not been tampered with.

The strong name provides these enhancements by adding three things to the assembly: a simple text name, a public key, and a digital signature. The combination of the first two items guarantees the name is unique, as the public key is unique to the party creating the assembly and it is assumed that the party will make the simple text assembly name unique within their own development environment.

The combination of the second and third items guarantees the second and third enhancements. It does this by adding public/private key encryption to the assembly.

NOTE *Public/private key encryption uses two keys as its name suggests. The private key is used to encrypt something, and the public key is used to decrypt it. What make this combination secure is that only a corresponding public key can be used to decrypt something encrypted by the private key.*

So how does public/private key encryption apply to global assemblies? Before you get all excited, you should know that an assembly is not encrypted. Instead, at compile time the compiler creates a hash signature based on the contents of the assembly and then uses the private key (of public/private encryption) to encrypt the hash signature into a digital signature. Finally, the digital signature is added to the assembly. Later, when the assembly is loaded by the CLR, the digital signature is decrypted using the public key back into the hash signature, and the hash signature is verified to make sure that the assembly is unchanged.

The reason this all works is that only the owner of the private key can create a valid digital signature that can be decrypted by the public key.

Like most things in .NET application development, what actually happens is a lot more complex than what you need to do to get it the happen. In this case, to add a strong name to an assembly requires two very simple steps. First, you create a strong name key file by typing the following statement at the command prompt:

```
> sn -k StrongNameFileName.snk
```

Then you update [AssemblyKeyFileAttribute] in the AssemblyInfo.cpp file, which incidentally is found in all projects:

```
[assembly:AssemblyKeyFileAttribute("StrongNameFileName.snk ")];
```

You can place the key in the project directory as the preceding example shows, or you can place it anywhere on your computer and provide a full path to the attribute.

Resigning an Assembly

If you are security conscious, you may have seen a big problem in the preceding strong name system. If you are developing software in a team environment, everyone who needs to update the assembly must have access to the private key so that the assembly can be accessed using the same public key. This means there are a lot of potential areas for security leaks.

To remedy this, the strong name utility sn.exe has an additional option. It provides the capability for an assembly to be re-signed. This allows privileged developers a chance to sign the assembly with the company's private key before releasing it to the public. The command you need to type at the command line is

```
> sn -R <assembly name> <strong key file name>
```

Notice this time instead of the –k option you use the –R option, stating you want to replace the key instead of create one. You also provide the utility a completed assembly and a previously created strong key file.

Signcoded Digital Signature

Nowhere in the preceding strong name process is the user of the assembly guaranteed that the creator of the strong key is a trusted source, only that it is unchanged from the time it was created.

To remedy this, you need to execute the signcode.exe wizard on your assembly to add an authentic digital certificate created by a third party. Once you have done this, the user of the assembly can find out who created the assembly and decide if he or she wants to trust it.

CAUTION *You need to compile the assembly with the "final" strong name before you signcode it. The signcode.exe wizard only works with strong named assemblies. Also, re-signing a signcoded assembly invalidates its authentic digital certificate.*

Versioning

Anyone who has worked with Windows for any length of time will probably be hit at least once with DLL Hell, the reason being that versioning was not very well supported in previous Windows developing environments. It was possible to swap different versions of .dlls in and out of the registry, which caused all sorts of compatibility issues. Well, with .NET this is no longer the case, as versioning is well supported.

That being said, a word of caution: The CLR ignores versioning in private assemblies. If you include a private assembly in your application's directory structure, the CLR assumes you know what you are doing and will use that version, even if the correct version, based on version number, is in the GAC.

The .NET Framework supports a four-part version: major, minor, build, and revision. You will most frequently see version numbers written out like this: 1.2.3.4. On occasion, however, you will see them like this: 1:2:3:4. By convention, a change in the major and minor numbers means that an incompatibility has been introduced, whereas a change in the build and revision numbers means compatibility has been retained. How you actually use version numbers, on the other hand, is up to you.

Here is how the .NET Framework handles versioning in a nutshell: Only the global assembly version that was referenced at compile time will work in the application. That is, all four version parts need to match. (Well, that is not quite true. You will see a way to overrule which version number to use later in this chapter.) This should not cause a problem even if there is more than one version of a shared assembly available, because multiple versions of a shared assembly can be placed without conflict into the GAC (see Figure 17-5). Okay, there might be a problem if the shared assembly with the corresponding version number is not in the GAC, as this throws a System::IO::FileNotFoundException exception.

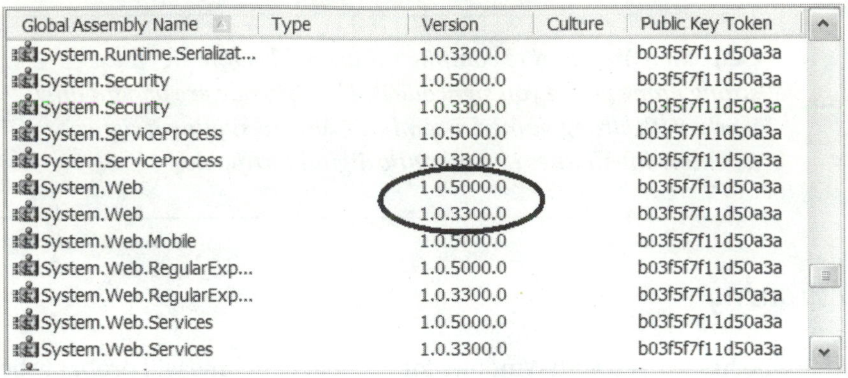

Figure 17-5. Multiple versions of an assembly in the GAC

Setting the Version Number

Version numbers are stored as metadata within the assembly, and to set the version number requires that you update the `AssemblyVersionAttribute` attribute. To make things easier for you, the Visual Studio .NET project template wizard automatically provides a default `AssemblyVersionAttribute` attribute within the AssemblyInfo.cpp file.

You set the version number by simply changing the dummy value

```
[assembly:AssemblyVersionAttribute("1.0.*")];
```

to a value that makes sense in your development environment, for example:

```
[assembly:AssemblyVersionAttribute("3.1.2.45")];
```

Notice the asterisk (*) in the default version number value provided by Visual Studio .NET. This asterisk signifies that the compiler will automatically create the build and revision numbers for you. When the compiler does this, it places the number of days since January 1, 2000, in the build and the number of seconds since midnight divided by two in the revision.

Personally, I think it's a mistake to use the autogenerated method, as the version numbers then provide no meaning. Plus, using autogenerated numbers forces you to recompile the application referencing the assembly every time you recompile the shared assembly. Autogenerated numbers aren't so bad if the application and the shared reference share into the same solution, but they aren't so good if the application and the shared reference share into different solutions, and even worse if different developers are developing the application and shared assembly.

Getting the Version Number

It took me a while to figure out how to get the version number out of the assembly (but that might just be me). As I found out, though, it's really easy to do, because it's just a property of the name of the assembly. I think the code is easier to understand than the explanation:

```
Assembly *assembly = Assembly::GetExecutingAssembly();
Version *version = assembly->GetName()->Version;
```

The only tricky part is getting the currently executing assembly, which isn't too tricky because the .NET Framework provides you with a static member to retrieve it for you.

No DLL Hell Example

Now that you've covered everything you need to create a shared assembly, you'll create one. Listing 17-6 shows the source code of a very simple class library assembly containing one class and one property. The property contains the version of the assembly.

Listing 17-6. A Shared Assembly That Knows Its Version

```
using namespace System;
using namespace System::Reflection;

namespace SharedAssembly
{
    public __gc class SharedClass
    {
    public:
        __property Version *get_Version()
        {
            Assembly *assembly = Assembly::GetExecutingAssembly();
            return assembly->GetName()->Version;
        }
    };
}
```

The code is short, sweet, and offers no surprises. Listing 17-7 contains a filled-in AssemblyInfo.cpp file. To save space, all the comments have been removed.

Listing 17-7. A standard AssemblyInfo.cpp File

```
using namespace System::Reflection;
using namespace System::Runtime::CompilerServices;

[assembly:AssemblyTitleAttribute(S"A Shared Assembly")];
[assembly:AssemblyDescriptionAttribute(S"An assembly that knows its version")];
[assembly:AssemblyConfigurationAttribute(S"Release Version")];
[assembly:AssemblyCompanyAttribute(S"FraserTraining")];
[assembly:AssemblyProductAttribute(S"Managed C++ Series")];
[assembly:AssemblyCopyrightAttribute(S"Copyright (C) by Stephen Fraser 2003")];
[assembly:AssemblyTrademarkAttribute(S"FraserTraining is a Trademark of blah")];
[assembly:AssemblyCultureAttribute(S"en-US")];


[assembly:AssemblyVersionAttribute("1.0.0.0")];


[assembly:AssemblyDelaySignAttribute(false)];
[assembly:AssemblyKeyFileAttribute("SharedAssembly.snk")];
[assembly:AssemblyKeyNameAttribute("")];
```

You saw most of the important code earlier in this chapter, so I won't go over this in detail. I also think that most of the rest of the code is self-explanatory. Only the AssemblyCultureAttribute attribute needs to be explained, and I do that a little later in this chapter.

Of all the attributes in the preceding source file, only two attributes need to be filled in to enable an assembly to be a shared one. The first attribute is AssemblyVersionAttribute. It already has a default value but I changed it to give it more meaning to me.

The second attribute is AssemblyKeyFileAttribute, in which you place the strong key. Remember, you can either pass a full path to the attribute or use a key in the project source directory. Because I'm using a strong key file in the project source, I have to copy my key file SharedAssembly.snk into the project's source directory.

Before you compile the project, change the project's output directory to be local to the project and not the solution. In other words, change the project's configuration properties' output directory to read only $(ConfigurationName) and not the default $(SolutionDir)$(ConfigurationName). The reason you want to do this is that you don't want a copy of SharedAssembly.dll in the same directory as the application assembly referencing it, because otherwise it will be used instead of the copy in the GAC.

Now, when you compile the project, an assembly called SharedAssembly.dll is generated in the project's Debug or Release directory, depending on which environment you're doing the build in. This file needs to be copied to the GAC either by dragging and dropping it there or via gacutil.exe. Figure 17-6 shows what the entry in the Windows Explorer GAC display looks like.

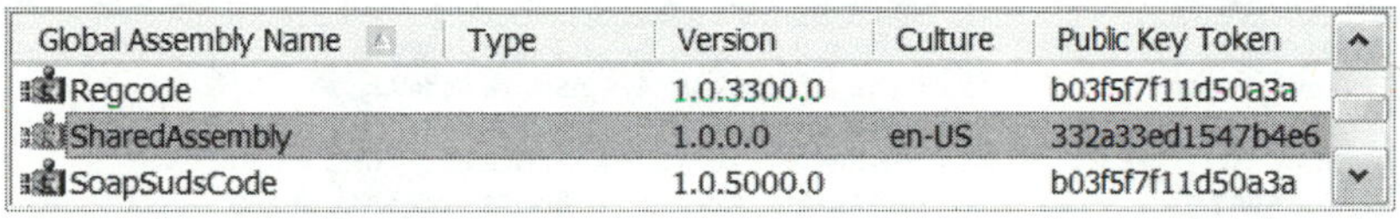

Global Assembly Name	Type	Version	Culture	Public Key Token	
Regcode		1.0.3300.0		b03f5f7f11d50a3a	
SharedAssembly		1.0.0.0	en-US	332a33ed1547b4e6	
SoapSudsCode		1.0.5000.0		b03f5f7f11d50a3a	

Figure 17-6. SharedAssembly in the GAC

Now you'll create an application assembly to reference the shared assembly (see Listing 17-8). All this application does is write out the version number of the shared assembly.

Listing 17-8. Referencing a Shared Assembly

```
using namespace System;
using namespace SharedAssembly;

Int32 main()
{
    SharedClass *sa = new SharedClass();
    Console::WriteLine(sa->Version);
    return 0;
}
```

The code is not new, but to get this to work you need to reference the assembly SharedAssembly.dll. It is important to understand that the assembly you reference during the compile does not need to be the same as the one that you actually execute at runtime. They just have to have the same name, version, and public key token. Therefore, even though you are going to use the assembly within the GAC, you reference the assembly within the solution to get the definition of the SharedClass class and the Version property.

To reference SharedAssembly.dll, you need to perform the following steps:

1. Right-click the References folder.

2. Select the Add Reference menu item. This will bring up the Add Reference dialog box (see Figure 17-7).

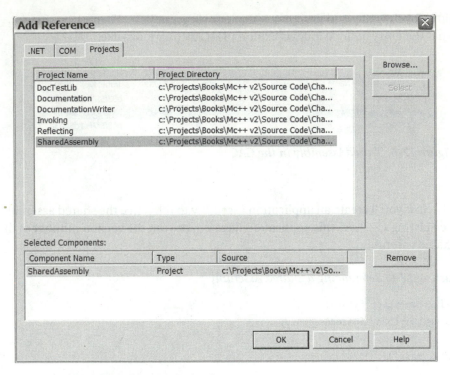

Figure 17-7. The Add Reference dialog box

3. Select the Projects tab.

4. Select the shared assembly from the list.

Or, if the shared assembly is in a different solution:

4. Click Browse, navigate to the location of the assembly, and then select the assembly.

5. Click OK.

Run ReferenceSharedAssembly.exe. You should get something similar to what is shown in Figure 17-8.

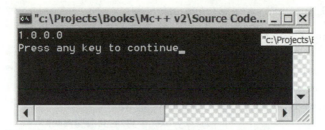

Figure 17-8. The result of executing ReferenceSharedAssembly

Now let's see what happens if you change your shared assembly and give it a new version number like this:

```
[assembly:AssemblyVersionAttribute("1.1.0.0")];
```

Recompile only the SharedAssembly project and then move the new assembly SharedAssembly.dll to the GAC. First off, notice that now there are two SharedAssembly entries in the GAC that differ by version number.

Run ReferenceSharedAssembly.exe again. (Important: *Do not* recompile when asked.) Nothing has changed, has it? You still get the same output. This is versioning in action. Why do you get the original version of the shared assembly? Because when you compiled the application program, you tightly bound it to version 1.0.0.0 of the shared assembly. Thus, when it executes, it can only load version 1.0.0.0.

Application Configuration Files

An alarm might be going off in your head right now. Does this mean that whenever you change a shared assembly, you have to keep the same version number or you have to recompile every application that uses shared assembly so that it can be accessed? How do you release a fix to a shared assembly?

The .NET Framework provides a solution to this problem by adding a configuration file to the application that specifies which assembly you want to load instead of the bound version. The application configuration file has the same name as the executable plus a suffix of .config. Therefore, for the preceding example, the application configuration file would be called ReferenceSharedAssembly.exe.config. Yes, the .exe is still in the name.

The application configuration file will look something like Listing 17-9.

Listing 17-9. An Application Configuration File

```
<configuration>
  <runtime>
    <assemblyBinding xmlns="urn:schemas-microsoft-com:asm.v1">
      <dependentAssembly>
        <assemblyIdentity name="SharedAssembly"
                          publicKeyToken="332a33ed1547b4e6"
                          culture="en-US" />
        <bindingRedirect  oldVersion="1.0.0.0"
                          newVersion="1.1.0.0" />
      </dependentAssembly>
    </assemblyBinding>
  </runtime>
</configuration>
```

The only two elements you have to worry about in the file are
`<assemblyIdentity>` and `<bindingRedirect>`. `<assemblyIndentity>` contains the
identity of the shared assembly that you want to use a different version with.
Notice that all the information you need to identify the shared assembly can be
found in the Windows Explorer GAC view.

Next is the key to assigning a different version to the `<bindingRedirect>` element. This element specifies the old version, or the version that the application
assembly currently references, and then the new version that you want it to
access instead. A cool feature is that the `oldVersion` tag can take a range:

```
<bindingRedirect oldVersion="1.0-1.1" newVersion="1.1.0.0" />
```

Now that you have the file created, place it in the same directory as the executable and run ReferenceSharedAssembly.exe again. (Important: *Do not*
recompile when asked.) This time you will get the output shown in Figure 17-9.

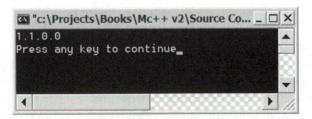

*Figure 17-9. The result of executing ReferenceSharedAssembly with an application
configuration file*

As a final note to application configuration files, you can also set the `newVersion` tag to a prior version of the assembly:

```
<bindingRedirect oldVersion="1.1.0.0" newVersion="1.0.0.0" />
```

This comes in handy when the new version is found to not be compatible and you need to fall back to a previous version.

Resources

When you finally get to the point of running your software, usually there are other things needed for it to run besides the executable. For example, you might find that you need images, icons, cursors or, if you are going to globalize the application, a culture's set of strings. You could fill your application directory full of a bunch of files containing these "resources." But if you did, you would run the risk of forgetting something when you deployed your application. I think a better solution is to group common resources into .resources files. Then, optionally, embed the .resources files into the assembly that uses the contents of the .resources files. My thought is that with fewer files floating around, fewer things can get lost.

You have three ways to work with grouped resources in the .NET Framework:

- You can place the grouped resources in .resources files and then work with them as separate entities. This allows you to switch and swap the .resources files as needed. It also allows you to work with the resources within the .resources files in a dynamic fashion.

- You can embed the resources directly into the assembly that uses them. This method has the least flexibility, but you can be secure in the knowledge that everything you need to run the assembly is available.

- You can combine the two previous methods and create what the .NET Framework calls *satellite assemblies*. These are assemblies containing only resources, but at the same time, they directly link to the assembly that uses the resources within them. You will see this use of resources when you look at globalization and localization later in this chapter.

Creating Resources

The .NET Framework provides you with two text formats for creating .resources files: a text file made up of name/value pairs and an XML-formatted file called a .resx file. Of the two, the name/value-formatted file is much easier to use, but it has the drawback of supporting only string resources. On the other hand, .resx files support almost any kind of resource, but unfortunately they are extremely hard to hand code. Most likely, because .resx files are so complex, you will choose a third way, which is to write a simple program to add nontext-formatted resources to a .resources file. I show you how to write the program later in this section.

Because .resx files are so complex, why are they included? They are what Visual Studio .NET uses to handle resources. In fact, you will use them quite extensively when you look at globalization and localization later in this chapter, but you will probably not even be aware that you are.

Building Text Name/Value Pair Resource Files

The simplest type of resource that you can create is the string table. You will probably want to create this type of resource using name/value pair files, as the format of the name/value pair file maps quite nicely to a string table. Basically, the name/value pair file is made up of many lines of name and value pairs separated by equal signs (=). Here is an example:

```
Name = Stephen Fraser
Email Address = srgfraser@frasertraining.com
Phone Number = (502) 555-1234
Favorite Equation = E=mc2
```

As you can see, spaces are allowed for both the name and the value. Also, the equal sign can be used in the value (but not the name), as the first equal sign is used to delimit the name and the value.

 CAUTION   *Don't try to line up the equal signs, because the spaces will become part of the name. As you'll see later in the chapter, doing this will make it harder to code the resource accessing method.*

ResGen

The text file you created previously is only an intermediate file. You might think of it as a source file just like a .cpp or .h file. You need to convert it to a .resources file so that your program will be able to process it as a resource. (By the way, you could process the file as a standard string file, but then you would lose many of the resources features provided by the .NET Framework.) To convert your text file, use the .NET Framework's ResGen.exe utility. There is not much to running the utility:

```
> ResGen filename.txt
```

When you run the preceding code, assuming that the text file consists of valid name/value pairs, you get an output file of filename.resources in the directory where you ran the utility. You can work with these files as separate entities or you can embed them into your assembly. You will see how to do that later in this chapter.

One more thing. If you are a glutton for punishment and write resource files using .resx files, then you would use the ResGen utility to convert them into .resources files as well.

ResourceWriter

As I stated previously, adding nontext resources is not possible using name/value pair files, and the .resx file is a bear to work with, so what are you to do if you simply need to create nontext resources (e.g., an image table)?

You can use the `System::Resources::ResourceWriter` class, because this class has the capability to place almost any type of data within a .resources file, so long as the total combined size of the file does not exceed 2GB. In fact, this class is what ResGen.exe uses to generate its .resources file. Why they didn't make ResGen.exe more robust and allow other types of data types escapes me.

Using the `ResourceWriter` class requires you to perform only three steps:

1. Open up a .resources file using the `ResourceWriter` class's constructor.

2. Add resources to the .resources file using the `AddResources()` method.

3. Close the .resources file using the `Close()` method.

Listing 17-10 presents all the code you need to add an image to a .resources file from a .jpg file.

Listing 17-10. Adding an Image to a .resources File

```
#using <System.Drawing.dll>   // Add the reference as it's not a default

using namespace System;
using namespace System::Resources;
using namespace System::Drawing;

Int32 main()
{
    ResourceWriter *rwriter = new ResourceWriter(S"filename.resources");
    rwriter->AddResource(S"ImageName", Images::FromFile(S"Imagefile.jpg"));
    rwriter->Close();

    return 0;
}
```

Embedding Resources

One way to make sure that everything that you need to execute an assembly is available is to put everything in the assembly itself. This way, executing an assembly is as easy as double-clicking the assembly's .exe file.

To embed resources from the command line, you use the assembly generation tool, al.exe, passing it the /embed option along with the name of the .resources file.

If you are using Visual Studio .NET, embedding resources is also fairly straightforward. In fact, if you are using .resx files as the source of your resources, you have to do nothing, because Visual Studio .NET will automatically handle everything for you. To embed resources using name/value pair files and prebuilt .resources files is not much more difficult.

I think the easiest way to explain how to embed resources is to actually walk through the process. In the following example, you will embed Animal.resx, Color.exe (name/value pair file), and Fruit.resources into an assembly called EmbeddingResources.exe.

The first step, as with any other .NET application project, is to use the project template wizard to build the basic structure of your project. In this case, you will build a standard Console Application (.NET) project and name it EmbeddingResources. To complete this project, perform the following steps:

1. Add a new item of type Assembly Resource File (.resx) and name it **Animal**. Then add some name/value pairs, as shown in Figure 17-10.

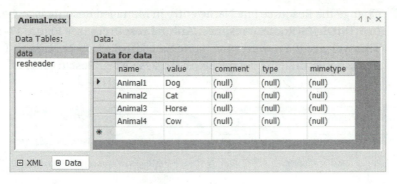

Figure 17-10. The Animal resource file

2. Add a new item of type Text File (.txt) and name it **Color**. Then add the following name/value pairs:

```
Color1 = Blue
Color2 = Red
Color3 = Yellow
Color4 = Green
```

3. Add an existing item called **Fruit.resources**. You will need to create this file at the command line using the ResGen tool on the name/value pair file containing the following entries:

```
Fruit1 = Apple
Fruit2 = Orange
Fruit3 = Grape
Fruit4 = Lemon
```

Now that you have all the resources ready, go ahead and embed them into the assembly. As I said previously, you don't have to do anything to embed a .resx file. Personally, though, I don't like the name that Visual Studio .NET gives the resource when it's embedded, so let's change it:

1. Right-click Animal.resx in Solution Explorer then select the Properties menu item.

2. Select All Configurations from the Configuration drop-down list.

3. Change the Resource File Name entry in Managed Resources ➤ General to **$(IntDir)/$(RootNamespace).Animal.resources** (see Figure 17-11). This will give the resource the name EmbeddingResources.Animal. I think this is better than the default EmbeddingResources.ResourceFiles.

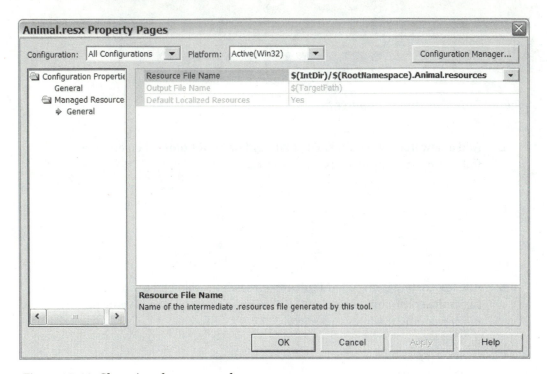

Figure 17-11. Changing the generated resource name

4. Click OK.

To embed the name/value pairs file Color.txt requires just one more step than Animal.resx: You have to change the build tool from Custom Build Tool to Managed Resource Compiler. You make this change also in the file's properties, but this time change the Tool entry in the Configuration Properties ➤ General page (see Figure 17-12). You might want to also go ahead and change the name of the generated resource file to **$(IntDir)/$(RootNamespace).Color.resources**.

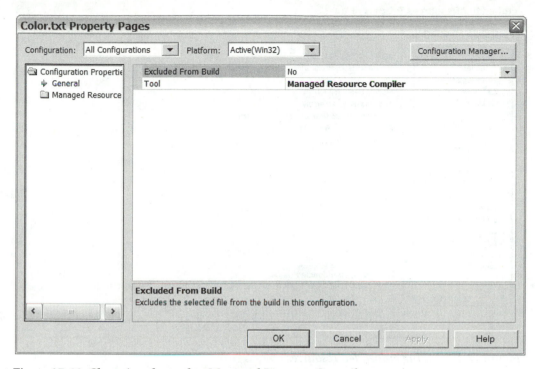

Figure 17-12. Changing the tool to Managed Resource Compiler

To embed an already-created .resources file requires that you add it as an input to the assembly linker. (By the way, you don't have to add it to Solution Explorer to get this to work—it just has to be in the project directory. I put it there so I remember that, in fact, I am embedding it.) The steps this time are a little different:

1. Right-click the EmbeddingResources project in Solution Explorer and select the Properties menu item. This will bring up a dialog box similar to Figure 17-13.

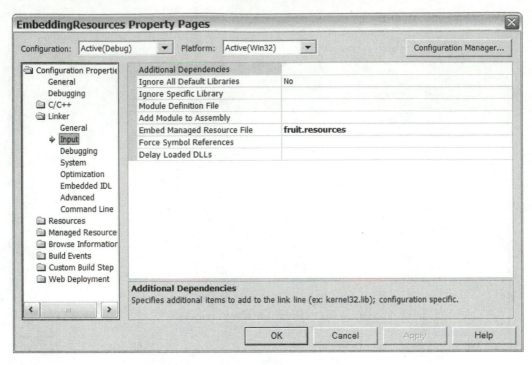

Figure 17-13. Adding embedded resources

2. In the Linker folder select Input.

3. Enter **Fruit.resources** in the Embed Managed Resource File text box.

4. Click OK.

When you compile the project, you will have three resources embedded into the application assembly. If you want proof, look in the assemblies manifest and you will find the following three entries:

```
.mresource public fruit.resources
{
}
.mresource public EmbeddingResources.Color.resources
{
}
.mresource public EmbeddingResources.Animal.resources
{
}
```

Accessing Resources

You've looked at creating resources and then embedding resources. Both are kind of neat but by themselves are quite useless unless you have some way of accessing these resources within your application. Obviously, the .NET Framework provides a class to get access to the resources. In fact, depending on where the resource is stored, it may provide two ways: the ResourceReader class and the ResourceManager class.

ResourceReader Class

The ResourceReader class is the counterpart of the ResourceWriter class. It enables you to iterate through a .resources file, treating it as though it were a simple file. Just like the ResourceWriter class, the ResourceReader class is very easy to implement:

1. Open the .resources file using the ResourceReader constructor.

2. Get IDictionaryEnumerator from the ResourceReader class's GetEnumerator() method.

3. Use the MoveNext() method to process all the entries in the .resources file.

4. Close the ResourceReader class with the Close() method.

Here is all the code you need to implement ResourceReader:

```
ResourceReader *rreader = new ResourceReader(S"filename.resources");
IDictionaryEnumerator *denum = rreader->GetEnumerator();
while (denum->MoveNext()) {
    Console::WriteLine(S"{0} = {1}", denum->Key, denum->Value );
}
rreader->Close();
```

 CAUTION *The order in which the key/value pairs are retrieved from the assembly may not match the order in which they were written.*

ResourceManager Class

Although the ResourceReader class is restricted to .resources files, the ResourceManager class gives you access to either .resources files or embedded resources. Another feature of the ResourceManager class that you will cover later in this chapter is that it can access the resources in a culture-specific manner.

To create an instance of a ResourceManager class, you need to pass the name of the resource and the assembly that the resource is embedded into:

```
ResourceManager rmgr = new ResourceManager(S"resourceName", assembly);
```

Along with embedded resources, it is also possible to open an instance of the ResourceManager from a .resources file using the CreateFileBasedResourceManager() static method. This method takes three parameters: the name of the .resources file without the .resources suffix, the path to the .resources file, and the culture to mask output with. I discuss cultures later in this chapter. The result of this method is a pointer to a ResourceManager:

```
ResourceManager rmgr =
    ResourceManager::CreateFileBasedResourceManager(S"resourceFilename", "", 0);
```

Once you have the instance of the ResourceManager, all you have to do is pass the name of the resource item you want either the GetString() or GetObject() method to return the value of:

```
String *Value = rmgr->GetString(S"Name");
Object *Value = rmgr->GetObject(S"Name");
```

Listing 17-11 expands on the previous section's project, EmbeddingResources. This example displays the Fruit.resources file using both the ResourceReader and ResourceManager and then continues on to display the embedded version of the Fruit resource using ResourceManager again.

Listing 17-11. EmbeddedResources Display Function

```
using namespace System;
using namespace System::Collections;
using namespace System::Reflection;
using namespace System::Resources;
```

```
Int32 main()
{
    Console::WriteLine(S"*** ResourceReader ***");
    ResourceReader *rreader = new ResourceReader(S"Fruit.resources");
    IDictionaryEnumerator *denum = rreader->GetEnumerator();
    while (denum->MoveNext())
    {
        Console::WriteLine(S"{0} = {1}", denum->Key, denum->Value);
    }
    rreader->Close();

    ResourceManager *rmgr;

    Console::WriteLine(S"\n*** ResourceManager From File ***");
    rmgr = ResourceManager::CreateFileBasedResourceManager(S"Fruit", "", 0);
    Console::WriteLine(rmgr->GetString(S"Fruit1"));
    Console::WriteLine(rmgr->GetString(S"Fruit2"));
    Console::WriteLine(rmgr->GetObject(S"Fruit3"));
    Console::WriteLine(rmgr->GetObject(S"Fruit4"));

    Console::WriteLine(S"\n*** ResourceManager From Assembly ***");
    Assembly *assembly = Assembly::GetExecutingAssembly();
    rmgr = new ResourceManager(S"Fruit", assembly);
    Console::WriteLine(rmgr->GetString(S"Fruit1"));
    Console::WriteLine(rmgr->GetString(S"Fruit2"));
    Console::WriteLine(rmgr->GetObject(S"Fruit3"));
    Console::WriteLine(rmgr->GetObject(S"Fruit4"));

    return 0;
}
```

Notice that you can use either GetString() or GetObject() to extract a String resource item. If, on the other hand, you were extracting an Image type resource item, you would need to use the GetObject() method and then typecast it back to an Image:

```
Image *img = dynamic_cast<Image*>(rmgr->GetObject(S"ImageName"));
```

Figure 17-14 shows EmbeddedResources.exe in action.

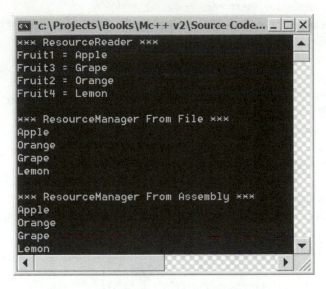

Figure 17-14. The result of executing the EmbeddedResources program

Globalization and Localization

The terms "globalization" and "localization" are frequently confused. Often people choose one of the terms to mean both when, in fact, each has a specific meaning:

- *Globalization* refers to designing and developing software that supports localized user interfaces and regional data for users of multiple cultures.

- *Localization* refers to the translation of the application's resources into localized versions for each culture supported by the application.

As you can see, you need both globalization and localization for an application to support multiple cultures. Basically, globalization is the underlying architecture and localization is the actual translation. This is why the .NET Framework provides a System::Globalization namespace and not a localization one.

To globalize an application, you need to be able to specify cultural differences in things such as numbers, dates, and calendars. For example, Table 17-5 shows some number formats based on culture.

Table 17-5. Number Formats Based on Culture

CULTURE	NUMBER FORMAT
France (French)	123 456 789,01
Germany (German)	123.456.789,01
Switzerland (German)	123'456'789.01
U.S. (English)	123,456,789.01

Notice in Table 17-5 that there are two different ways of displaying numbers in German cultures. The Swiss have what is known as a *subculture* (but don't tell the Swiss that!). This points out that to support globalization, an application must also support subcultures. Seems to me things are starting to get complex. Okay, let's throw Chinese and Japanese character sets into the mix—now you're talking complex!

Fortunately, the .NET Framework has a few things up its sleeve to help support all these complexities. Don't get me wrong: Writing globalization code isn't for the faint of heart. It's tough! This section will only show you where to begin in globalizing your application. Please consult the many books that have been written on the subject for further information.

The Globalization Tools

The first line of attack for handling globalization by the .NET Framework is that it uses Unicode to support the various cultural-specific encoding types you may use in your applications. Unicode allows you to support complex character sets such as Chinese and Japanese, as well as the generic ASCII character set.

The next thing the .NET Framework does is provide intelligence in its classes and structures to support multiple cultures. For example, the DateTime and String objects generate appropriate culture-specific information. To add this intelligence, the .NET Framework relies on the System::Globalization namespace (see Table 17-6) to provide support.

Table 17-6. Common System::Globalization Namespace Classes

CLASS NAME	DESCRIPTION
Calendar	Specifies how to divide time into pieces (e.g., weeks, months, and years)
CultureInfo	Provides specific information about a culture
DateTimeFormatInfo	Specifies how dates and times are formatted
NumberFormatInfo	Specifies how numbers are formatted
RegionInfo	Provides information about the country and region
TextInfo	Specifies the properties and behaviors of the writing system

The final thing that the .NET Framework does to help support globalization was hinted at previously when I covered resources. The .NET Framework supports culture-specific resources using the ResourceManager class.

Culture

A *culture* in computer terms is a set of display preferences based on the language, beliefs, social norms, and so on (i.e., culture) of the user. How a computer processes the actual program internally does not differ based on culture. Culture only changes how the information is finally displayed. For example, adding two Int32s together using the German culture will not differ from how it is done using the French culture—the difference lies in how the final outcome is displayed.

The .NET Framework uses culture names based on RFC1766. If that means nothing to you, don't worry. It just means the .NET Framework uses a two-letter language and a two-letter country/region code separated by a hyphen (-) to specify a culture. It's possible to only specify a two-letter language if the country/region isn't significant.

Table 17-7 lists some of the many cultures available to you.

Table 17-7. Computer Cultures

NAME	CODE
English	en
English (Canada)	en-ca
English (United Kingdom)	en-gb
English (United States)	en-us
French	fr
French (Canada)	fr-ca
French (France)	fr-fr
German	de
German (Germany)	de-de
German (Switzerland)	de-ch

You use the System::Globalization::CultureInfo class to convert one of the codes in Table 17-7 into something that the .NET Framework understands:

```
CultureInfo *cinfo = new CultureInfo(S"en-ca");
```

Setting the Culture

To get globalization to work within the CLR, you need to do one of two things:

- Use a special version of the ToString() method that takes the culture as a parameter.

- Set the culture you wish to use in the thread of execution.

The first method enables you to restrict globalization only to areas of your application that you specify. The second method of changing the CultureInfo in the CurrentThread changes the culture everywhere.

For example, if you want to display a date in multiple cultural styles, you could code it as shown in Listing 17-12.

Listing 17-12. Multicultural Dates

```
using namespace System;
using namespace System::Globalization;

Int32 main()
{
    DateTime dt = DateTime::Now;

    Console::WriteLine(S"en-us {0}",dt.ToString("D",new CultureInfo(S"en-us")));
    Console::WriteLine(S"en-gb {0}",dt.ToString("D",new CultureInfo(S"en-gb")));
    Console::WriteLine(S"fr-fr {0}",dt.ToString("D",new CultureInfo(S"fr-fr")));
    Console::WriteLine(S"de-de {0}",dt.ToString("D",new CultureInfo(S"de-de")));

    return 0;
}
```

Figure 17-15 shows MulticulturalDates.exe run on December 4, 2002.

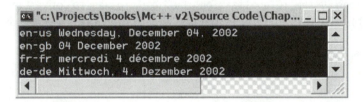

Figure 17-15. The result of executing the MulticulturalDates program

Now here comes a tricky part. There are two cultures you can set in the CurrentThread. The first is CurrentCulture, which is used by the Globalization namespace to handle culture-specific formatting. The second is CurrentUICulture, which is used by the ResourceManager to handle culture-specific resources. You may need to set one or both depending on what you are doing. Here is how you can set both to the French (France) culture:

```
Thread::CurrentThread->CurrentCulture = new CultureInfo(S"fr-fr");
Thread::CurrentThread->CurrentUICulture = Thread::CurrentThread->CurrentCulture;
```

The Localization Tools

Once you have an application designed and coded for multiple cultures, you then have to go through the long process of localizing it for each culture you want to support. Fortunately, Visual Studio .NET provides much of the functionality you need to localize your application if you happen to be building a Windows application. It also provides much of the localization functionality for a console application, providing you use a minor trick.

The way in which localization works is actually very elegant. First, you create a default version of all of your display elements, placing each in a resource file. Then for every other culture, you create a satellite resource file. Within that satellite resource file are replacement elements for the default view. Thus, when the culture is changed, the ResourceManager looks into the satellite resource of that culture first for display elements. If it finds the element it wants there, then it uses it. If it doesn't find the element it wants there, then it takes the default value.

Building a Multicultural Windows Application

The addition of localization to a Windows application is quite impressive. You really don't see how impressive it is until you try it yourself. Let's start off by creating a very simple Windows Form containing a single label that looks like Figure 17-16.

Figure 17-16. A very simple Windows Form

When you look at the autogenerated code in the InitializeComponent() method, you see pretty standard and unimpressive code (see Listing 17-13).

Listing 17-13. Very Simple Windows Form Code

```
void InitializeComponent(void)
{
    this->SuspendLayout();
    //
    // lbHello
    //
```

```
this->lbHello->Font =
    new System::Drawing::Font(S"Microsoft Sans Serif", 12,
                                    System::Drawing::FontStyle::Bold);
this->lbHello->ImeMode = System::Windows::Forms::ImeMode::NoControl;
this->lbHello->Location = System::Drawing::Point(24, 16);
this->lbHello->Name = S"label2";
this->lbHello->Size = System::Drawing::Size(424, 23);
this->lbHello->TabIndex = 6;
this->lbHello->Text = S"Hello, my name is Stephen";
//
// Form1
//

//...Standard Form stuff

this->ResumeLayout(false);
}
```

Okay, now let's take this same code and make it localizable. To do this, simply set the Form's Localizable property to true (see Figure 17-17).

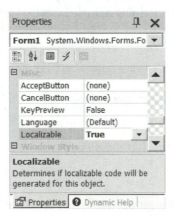

Figure 17-17. Setting the Localizable flag to true

Now take a look at the code in the InitializeComponent() method (see Listing 17-14).

Listing 17-14. Localizable Simple Application

```
void InitializeComponent(void)
{
    System::Resources::ResourceManager *resources =
```

```
        new System::Resources::ResourceManager(
            __typeof(MultiCulturalApp::Form1));
    this->SuspendLayout();
    //
    // lbHello
    //
    this->lbHello->AccessibleDescription =
        resources->GetString(S"lbHello.AccessibleDescription");
    this->lbHello->AccessibleName =
        resources->GetString(S"lbHello.AccessibleName");
    this->lbHello->Anchor = (*__try_cast<__box AnchorStyles*>
        (resources->GetObject(S"lbHello.Anchor")));
    this->lbHello->AutoSize = (*__try_cast<__box System::Boolean *>
        (resources->GetObject(S"lbHello.AutoSize")));
    this->lbHello->Dock = (*__try_cast<__box DockStyle *>
        (resources->GetObject(S"lbHello.Dock")));
    this->lbHello->Enabled = (*__try_cast<__box System::Boolean *>
        (resources->GetObject(S"lbHello.Enabled")));
    this->lbHello->Font = (__try_cast<System::Drawing::Font *>
        (resources->GetObject(S"lbHello.Font")));
    this->lbHello->Image = (__try_cast<System::Drawing::Image *>
        (resources->GetObject(S"lbHello.Image")));
    this->lbHello->ImageAlign = (*__try_cast<__box ContentAlignment*>
        (resources->GetObject(S"lbHello.ImageAlign")));
    this->lbHello->ImageIndex = (*__try_cast<__box System::Int32 *>
        (resources->GetObject(S"lbHello.ImageIndex")));
    this->lbHello->ImeMode = (*__try_cast<__box ImeMode *>
        (resources->GetObject(S"lbHello.ImeMode")));
    this->lbHello->Location = (*__try_cast<__box System::Drawing::Point *>
        (resources->GetObject(S"lbHello.Location")));
    this->lbHello->Name = S"lbHello";
    this->lbHello->RightToLeft = (*__try_cast<__box RightToLeft *>
        (resources->GetObject(S"lbHello.RightToLeft")));
    this->lbHello->Size = (*__try_cast<__box System::Drawing::Size *>
        (resources->GetObject(S"lbHello.Size")));
    this->lbHello->TabIndex = (*__try_cast<__box System::Int32 *>
        (resources->GetObject(S"lbHello.TabIndex")));
    this->lbHello->Text = resources->GetString(S"lbHello.Text");
    this->lbHello->TextAlign = (*__try_cast<__box ContentAlignment *>
        (resources->GetObject(S"lbHello.TextAlign")));
    this->lbHello->Visible = (*__try_cast<__box System::Boolean *>
        (resources->GetObject(S"lbHello.Visible")));
    //
```

```
// Form1
//

//...More resources stuff cut to save space

this->ResumeLayout(false);
}
```

Wow, we're not in Kansas anymore! Every aspect of the label has now become a resource. As such, it can take on any look and feel you want based on the values you place within the resource file that populates this label. At this point, all the information about the label (and the Form, incidentally) is stored in a resource file called Form1.resx. This resource file contains all the default information about the Windows Form, as I pointed out as the first part of localization.

Now you'll add a new culture, French (France), to the Form. To do this you set the Form's Language property to French (France). Scrolling up and down in the Language property's selection displays quite a few cultures, don't you think?

Notice any difference in the Windows Form design? Nope, me neither. Here's the fun part: Go wild and change any property of the label, but just don't delete it. Now toggle between the default language and the French (France) language. Notice that they retain the information specific to each culture. (Well, apparently you can't go too wild there, as it seems a few of the properties aren't stored in the resource file automatically. Border and background color are two that surprised me by not working.)

Anyway, now that you've created a French (France) culture, notice there's now a Form1.fr.resx file and a Form1.fr-fr.resx resource file added to your Solution Explorer. Both of these compile to satellite assemblies. You get both of these resource files because ResourceManager is designed to look at subculture, then culture, and finally the default for culture-related display changes. Because it checks both of these places, Visual Studio .NET is giving the culture for free when you create a subculture. If you look at the subculture resource file contents, you'll notice that it contain all the changes that you made to the default label and the culture resource is empty (unless you change the culture's display).

Now let's see what happens when you compile the Windows Form application. After you compile, go ahead and open Windows Explorer and navigate to the directory structure where the application runs. There are now two new directories, one for each culture using the culture's RFC1766 code as a name. Also, in each directory is a file called [ApplicationName].resources.dll, as shown in Figure 17-18. (My image has two additional directories because I also created a German culture.) These two new .dll files are your satellite assemblies.

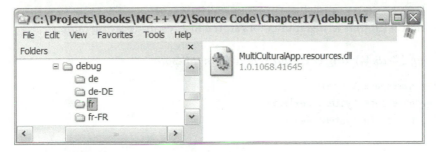

Figure 17-18. The Windows Explorer view of satellite assemblies

Run your new multicultured application. You see none of your French stuff, right? That is because your native culture is not French (France) so the ResourceManager took the default resource values and not the French one. (Oh, of course if you are reading this book in France and your machine is configured for French, then you would see the French. French readers might try some other culture for this example.)

As I stated previously, you need to change the CurrentThread class's CurrentUICulture to the satellite assembly's culture you want to access. Do this by adding the following lines before you call the InitializeComponent() method:

```
Thread::CurrentThread->CurrentCulture = new CultureInfo(S"fr-fr");
Thread::CurrentThread->CurrentUICulture = Thread::CurrentThread->CurrentCulture;
```

In the accompanying source code that you can download from the Downloads area of the Apress Web site (http://www.apress.com), I actually pop up a dialog box to select the culture, but the preceding code works just as well to demonstrate that the program works.

Figure 17-19 shows MultiCulturalApp.exe in action.

Figure 17-19. The result of executing the MultiCulturalApp program

Building a Multicultural Console Application

When you build an assembly that isn't a Windows application, things aren't quite as easy. But it doesn't take much to fool Visual Studio .NET into believing it's building Windows-like satellite assemblies.

Let's create a simple little program call `MulticulturalConsole` (see Listing 17-15) that writes four colors stored in a resource string table.

Listing 17-15. Writing Out Four Colors from a Resource

```
using namespace System;
using namespace System::Reflection;
using namespace System::Resources;

Int32 main()
{
    Assembly *assembly = Assembly::GetExecutingAssembly();
    ResourceManager *rmgr =
        new ResourceManager(S"MulticulturalConsole.Colors", assembly);

    Console::WriteLine(rmgr->GetObject(S"Color1"));
    Console::WriteLine(rmgr->GetObject(S"Color2"));
    Console::WriteLine(rmgr->GetObject(S"Color3"));
    Console::WriteLine(rmgr->GetObject(S"Color4"));

    return 0;
}
```

Add a new item of type Assembly Resource File (.resx) and name it **Colors**. Then add the string resources as shown in Figure 17-20. Finally, rename the generated resource file as **$(IntDir)/$(RootNamespace).Colors.resources**.

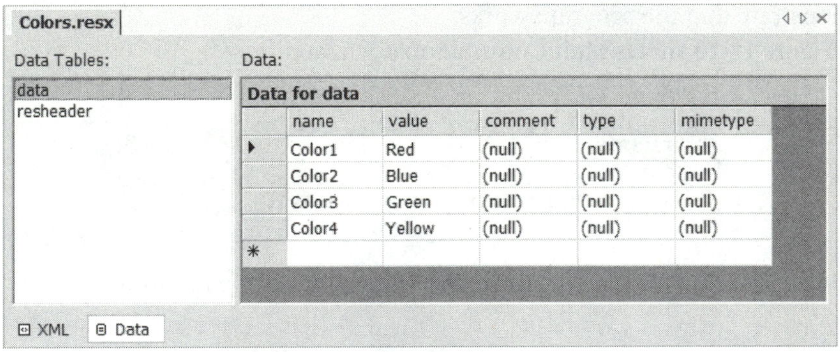

Figure 17-20. The Colors assembly resource file

When you run MulticulturalConsole.exe you should get something like Figure 17-21. There is nothing new so far.

Figure 17-21. The first result of MulticulturalConsole

Now let's make the program multicultural. The first step is to add the code to the application so that it will display based on another culture or, in other words, you globalize the application. You do this by setting the CurrentThread CurrentUICulture to something else. Let's change it to "fr-fr" or French (France), as shown in Listing 17-16.

Listing 17-16. Writing Out Four Colors from a Resource Multiculturally

```
using namespace System;
using namespace System::Reflection;
using namespace System::Resources;
using namespace System::Threading;
using namespace System::Globalization;

Int32 main()
{
    Assembly *assembly = Assembly::GetExecutingAssembly();
    ResourceManager *rmgr =
        new ResourceManager(S"MulticulturalConsole.Colors", assembly);

    Console::WriteLine(rmgr->GetObject(S"Color1"));
    Console::WriteLine(rmgr->GetObject(S"Color2"));
    Console::WriteLine(rmgr->GetObject(S"Color3"));
    Console::WriteLine(rmgr->GetObject(S"Color4"));

    Thread::CurrentThread->CurrentUICulture = new CultureInfo(S"fr-fr");

    Console::WriteLine(rmgr->GetObject(S"Color1"));
    Console::WriteLine(rmgr->GetObject(S"Color2"));
    Console::WriteLine(rmgr->GetObject(S"Color3"));
    Console::WriteLine(rmgr->GetObject(S"Color4"));

    return 0;
}
```

The only new thing you did was change the CurrentUICulture. I just cut and pasted the four lines that display the colors.

Now it's time to fool Visual Studio .NET. When Visual Studio .NET created its resource files (which later became satellite assemblies) for the multiculture example, it did so in a very specific manner. The fortunate thing is that if you create your resource files in the same way, even in a console application, you will also get correctly built satellite assemblies.

Basically, here is how you do it. Create an assembly resource file (.resx) named **WhatYouWant.resx** that contains all the resource items for the default language. Also rename the autogenerated resource file as **$(IntDir)/$(RootNamespace).WhatYouWant.resources**. Notice that this is the same procedure you followed earlier when you embedded the standard resource file.

Now here's the trick to add, let's say, a French culture. Create a new assembly resource file (.resx) and name it **WhatYouWant.fr-fr.resx**. Add all the replacement values that you want for that culture. Then rename the autogenerated resource file as **$(IntDir)/$(RootNamespace).WhatYouWant.fr-fr.resources**. That's it! Placing the culture just before the .resx and .resources files is enough to trick Visual Studio .NET into creating a culture-specific satellite assembly.

So for the previous MulticulturalConsole example, create an assembly resource file (.resx) named **Colors.fr-fr.resx**. Then add the string resources as shown in Figure 17-22.

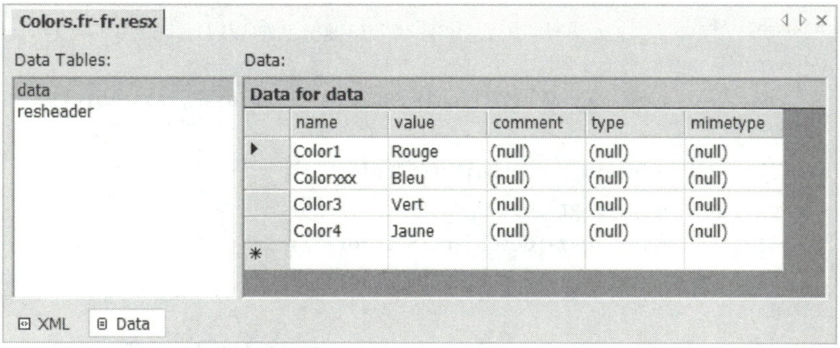

Figure 17-22. French Colors assembly resource file

Notice that it is important that the names of the name/value pairs match between the default and the French resource files. Finally, rename the generated resource file as **$(IntDir)/$(RootNamespace).fr-fr.Colors.resources**.

When you run the revised MulticulturalConsole.exe, you should get something like Figure 17-23. There is nothing new so far.

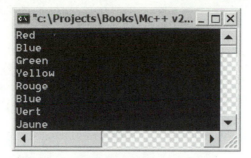

Figure 17-23. Revised result of MulticulturalConsole

As you can see, once you change the culture to French, the `ResourceManager` looks first in the French satellite assembly for the value. Because there is no Color2, the English (default) value is written.

Summary

In this chapter you looked at several ways to programmatically play with the .NET Framework assembly. You started by exploring reflection and then its counterpart, attributes. You moved on to look at shared assemblies. Next, you learned how to add more to assemblies than just code using resources. You finished off the chapter (and the book) by looking at globalization and localization.

Programming with assemblies, like many of the other topics covered in this book, is a weighty topic. I feel the only way to really learn how to program the assembly is to do so yourself. This chapter should have opened up many doors on how to do this.

Because there is no next chapter, I would like to instead thank you for reading my book. I hope you got as much out of reading this book as I did creating it.

Index

About Apress

Apress, located in Berkeley, CA, is a fast-growing, innovative publishing company devoted to meeting the needs of existing and potential programming professionals. Simply put, the "A" in Apress stands for *The Author's Press™*. Apress' unique approach to publishing grew out of conversations between its founders, Gary Cornell and Dan Appleman, authors of numerous best-selling, highly regarded books for programming professionals. In 1998 they set out to create a publishing company that emphasized quality above all else. Gary and Dan's vision has resulted in the publication of over 70 titles by leading software professionals, all of which have *The Expert's Voice™*.

Do You Have What It Takes to Write for Apress?

Apress is rapidly expanding its publishing program. If you can write and you refuse to compromise on the quality of your work, if you believe in doing more than rehashing existing documentation, and if you're looking for opportunities and rewards that go far beyond those offered by traditional publishing houses, we want to hear from you!

Consider these innovations that we offer all of our authors:

- **Top royalties with *no* hidden switch statements**
  Authors typically receive only half of their normal royalty rate on foreign sales. In contrast, Apress' royalty rate remains the same for both foreign and domestic sales.

- **Sharing the wealth**
  Most publishers keep authors on the same pay scale even after costs have been met. At Apress author royalties dramatically increase the more books are sold.

- **Serious treatment of the technical review process**
  Each Apress book is reviewed by a technical expert(s) whose remuneration depends in part on the success of the book since he or she too receives royalties.

Moreover, through a partnership with Springer-Verlag, New York, Inc., one of the world's major publishing houses, Apress has significant venture capital and distribution power behind it. Thus, we have the resources to produce the highest quality books *and* market them aggressively.

If you fit the model of the Apress author who can write a book that provides *What The Professional Needs To Know™*, then please contact us for more information:

editorial@apress.com